European Politics Today

THIRD EDITION

EDITORS

Gabriel A. Almond
Late, Stanford University

Russell J. Dalton
University of California, Irvine

G. Bingham Powell, Jr.
University of Rochester

Kaare Strøm
University of California, San Diego

PEARSON
Longman

New York   San Francisco   Boston
London   Toronto   Sydney   Tokyo   Singapore   Madrid
Mexico City   Munich   Paris   Cape Town   Hong Kong   Montreal

The editors and coauthors of the third edition of *European Politics Today* dedicate this book to the memory of Gabriel A. Almond, a giant in the field of comparative politics and a friend, colleague, and leader.

Executive Editor: Eric Stano
Senior Marketing Manager: Elizabeth Fogarty
Media and Supplements Editor: Kristi Olson
Production Manager: Eric Jorgensen
Project Coordination, Text Design, and Electronic Page Makeup: Shepherd, Inc.
Cover Designer/Manager: John Callahan
Cover Images: Courtesy of Getty Images, Inc.
Senior Manufacturing Buyer: Alfred C. Dorsey
Printer and Binder: Hamilton Press Co.
Cover Printer: The Lehigh Press

Library of Congress Cataloging-in-Publication Data

European politics today / editors Gabriel A. Almond . . . [et al.]—3rd ed.
   p.cm.
   Includes bibliographical references and index.
   ISBN 0-321-23652-1
    1. Europe, Western—Politics and government. 2. Europe—Politics and government—1989–
  3. Democracy—Europe. 4. Europe, Eastern—Politics and government—1989–
  5. Democratization—Europe. I. Almond, Gabriel A. (Gabriel Abraham), 1911–2002.
JN94.A58E89 2006
320.94—dc22

                                    2005044320

Visit us at http://www.ablongman.com

ISBN 0-321-23652-1

2 3 4 5 6 7 8 9 10—HT—08 07 06 05

Contributors

GABRIEL A. ALMOND
Late, Stanford University

RUSSELL J. DALTON
University of California, Irvine

G. BINGHAM POWELL, JR.
University of Rochester

KAARE STRØM
University of California, San Diego

KATHLEEN MONTGOMERY
Illinois Wesleyan University

THOMAS F. REMINGTON
Emory University

RICHARD ROSE
University of Strathclyde, Glasgow

ALBERTA SBRAGIA
University of Pittsburgh

MARTIN A. SCHAIN
New York University

DONALD SHARE
University of Puget Sound

RAY TARAS
Tulane University

Brief Contents

Detailed Contents

Preface

This new edition of *European Politics Today* updates our introduction to the politics of the new Europe in the twenty-first century. Unlike most European politics textbooks, it bridges the East/West divide, celebrating the extraordinary changes of the last decade. A continent historically torn by division and conflict now encompasses 39 nations that are almost all democratic in reality or aspiration and oriented toward market, rather than command economies. Many nations in new Europe, including some countries of the former Soviet orbit, have joined the European Union and the NATO military alliance. Where once Europe was divided at the Berlin Wall, now eight East European nations have joined the EU. This book recognizes the many implications of this unity, as well as the great diversity that still remains within Europe. The success of the first two editions in spanning this East/West divide has led to this new third edition.

Given its historical and cultural commonalities, Europe is a natural unit for an area studies approach to political science. Its nations have borrowed from each other and imitated each other, as well as competed against each other, for a very long time. Today, their economies and cultures are more closely interdependent than ever before. Europe's political cultures share many historical and political reference points. Its societies were all affected, in varying ways, by the Renaissance; by the Reformation and the subsequent religious wars; by the Enlightenment and the French Revolution; by the formation and later collapse of European-centered international empires; by the nineteenth-century industrial revolution (although most of Eastern and Southern Europe came to this later); by fascism and communism; by the terrible wars of the twentieth century, and the Holocaust; and by the Cold War. Learning about the general European setting helps us to understand the politics of each one of the particular European countries. Conversely, of course, the dynamic forces of the region cannot be understood independently of the politics of individual countries.

THE ORGANIZATION OF THIS BOOK

As a text studying a specific geographic region, this book can be used in various ways. The simplest, of course, is to follow the chapters in consecutive order. We begin with four chapters that consider the European experience as a whole. Chapter 1 describes the geography and history of the contemporary nations, as well as the two critical features differentiating them: the sharply varying levels of economic development and the patterns of ethnic and religious division. The chapter also introduces the student to the theme of Europe's special relationship with democracy and democratization. While providing a sophisticated overview, we try to keep technical political science terms to a minimum. We suggest that all courses begin with this introductory chapter.

Chapters 2 through 4 discuss the nature, bases, and variety of democracy across the European systems. Chapter 2 examines how Europeans think and act in politics, focusing especially on the mutual expectations of citizens and policymakers in democracies. Chapter 3 examines political organizations—interest groups and parties—and their roles within the democratic process. Chapter 4 offers an overview of the main constitutional arrangements and policymaking processes in European democracies. These chapters assume no specific background in political science or the politics of the individual countries. They provide concepts and generalizations that can help students understand the working of politics in specific countries. Thus, it may be helpful for students to read and discuss these chapters, their concepts and generalizations, before turning to the individual countries presented in the rest of the book.

Other instructors may prefer to have students read and discuss the politics of one or more specific countries and then return to Chapters 2 through 4 to see how the detailed play of the political culture and political process in a given country fits into the broader concepts and patterns.

The country authors introduce their materials with sufficient clarity and autonomy to make it possible for the students to read them after, before, or concurrently with Chapters 2 through 4. Chapters 5 and 6 introduce the politics of two well-established democracies (Britain and France), while Chapters 7 and 8 describe the political systems in two more recently consolidated ones (Germany and Spain). The last three country chapters (Russia, Poland, and Hungary) describe political systems that began transitions to democratic politics in the 1990s, and for which the issues of democratic consolidation are paramount.

Chapter 12 describes the political system of the European Union. We think it makes the most sense to conclude with an account of this new and very complex political system, which coordinates in a confederal system the politics and policies of 25 European countries, with potential future members in Eastern Europe. However, other instructors have chosen to begin with the EU to provide an overview of European politics.

Finally, the book contains an analytic appendix to help instructors coordinate the presentation of material in the introductory chapters and specific country chapters. The appendix outlines the framework of specific topics that are discussed in the introductory chapters and in each country study, indicating the pages where these topics are presented.

SPECIAL FEATURES OF THIS EDITION

- "Current policy challenges" sections at the beginning of each country chapter discuss the contemporary problems facing that nation. The issues sections help to interest students in the material and help them understand the problems facing the political system in each nation.
- **Example boxes** in each chapter provide students with current and topical examples that illustrate key concepts and theories in the text, increase student interest, and add visual appeal to the layout of the book.
- A "country bio" at the start of each chapter gives students a quick factual overview of the nation: its size, social composition, leadership, and so on.
- **Internet links** have been added to the end of each country chapter; the links enable students to locate government agencies, news media, and other online information sources.
- **Expanded theoretic framework** in Chapters 2 through 4 provides additional comparative information on political organization and institutions across Europe.

EUROPE AND THE STUDY OF POLITICS

This book responds to the dissolving barriers between Eastern and Western Europe by offering teacher and student the opportunity to apply political science analysis on a truly European scale. We can appreciate the commonalities and yet take advantages of the differences across Europe. We can apply the theories of modern political science in analysis of countries sharing the common European experience, but recently differentiated by history into quite different introductions to democratic politics and its concomitants.

In Western Europe, we examine how politics functions in established democracies. Our analyses show the richness and variety of the democratic experience, enabling the comparison of the politics of consensual and conflictual cultures, majoritarian and proportional institutional rules, two-party and multiparty electoral competition, and interventionist or market-dominated economic policies. We also examine how democracy has taken root in several Western European nations, such as Germany and Spain, within the last 50 years.

In Eastern Europe, a decade of experience since the collapse of Soviet domination provides remarkable opportunities to use modern political science techniques to observe the interaction between political culture and the formation of new political institutions. The new party systems of Eastern Europe provide natural experiments where we can examine processes of forming identities, organizations, and strategies. Furthermore, Eastern Europeans are experimenting with new forms of democratic institutions and new political-economic combinations. Of course, democracy itself faces severe challenges in some parts of Eastern Europe, with fundamental consequences for both democratic theory and world politics.

This book also builds upon the highly successful model of Almond, Powell, Strøm, and Dalton's introductory text, *Comparative Politics Today.*[1] We use the well-tested conceptual framework in describing the cultures and structures of the political system. Four of our country chapters (England, France, Germany, and Russia) are derived from that text, although completely revised for this new volume. However, it is not necessary to understand the formal theoretical framework of *Comparative Politics Today* in order to study the European experience in this volume.[2]

1. Gabriel A. Almond, G. Bingham Powell, Kaare Strøm, and Russell Dalton, eds. *Comparative Politics Today: A World View,* 8th ed. (New York: Addison Wesley Longman, 2004).
2. For those wanting to learn more about this general introductory framework, see Gabriel A. Almond, G. Bingham Powell, Kaare Strøm, and Russell Dalton, *Comparative Politics: A Theoretical Framework,* 4th ed. (New York: Addison Wesley Longman, 2004).

ACKNOWLEDGMENTS

This book began as a product of Gabriel A. Almond's comparative analysis of political science, first represented in *Comparative Politics Today* and then *European Politics Today.* Gabriel passed away in December 2002, and this is the first edition we completed without his participation and guidance. We retain Gabriel Almond as a coeditor to acknowledge his formative influence on this project, and the personal friendship and indebtedness all of the participants in the CPT and EPT volumes feel toward him.

The development of a book requires the support and advice of many people, and we want to acknowledge their contributions. Because this book builds on the success of *Comparative Politics Today,* we benefited from the contributors to this global introduction to comparative politics. We benefited indirectly from the experiences of our predecessor volume and directly by including four of its authors in this new book. As editors, we owe a special debt to the contributors to *European Politics Today.* They produced excellent accounts of politics in their nations of specialization, linked to the larger issues of comparative political studies. We want to acknowledge our debt to their written contribution and our admiration for their tolerance of our frequent editorial requests. It has been a pleasure working with each of them.

The support of the publisher is also essential to a book's success. Ed Costello has managed this book and *Comparative Politics Today* with admirable success. His wise advice and constant support is appreciated. We also thank Michael Jennings for preparing this manuscript for production with care and attention to detail.

We also profited from the advice of many colleagues. The following colleagues read all or portions of the manuscript and offered their advice: Michael Baun, Valdosta State; Larry Elowitz, George College and State University; Lyndelle Fairlie, San Diego State University; John G. Francis, University of Utah; Minton F. Goldman, Northeastern University; Thomas Lancaster, Emory University; Lynn M. Maurer, Southern Illinois University; Gunther Hega, Western Michigan University; Neil J. Mitchell, University of New Mexico; Patrick O'Neil, University of

Puget Sound; Pauletta Otis, University of Northern Colorado; Paul Pierson, Harvard University; Susan Scarrow, University of Houston; Mitchell P. Smith, University of Oklahoma; Lawrence Sullivan, Adelphi University; Bob Switky, University of Nebraska at Kearney; Rina V. Williams, University of Houston; and Oliver Woshinsky, University of Southern Maine.

Eleanor N. Powell and Julie J. Won provided valuable research assistance for the editors. Ivy Orr Hamerly created the index. The book is much improved because of all of these contributions.

SUPPLEMENTS

A new offering in this edition of *European Politics Today* is the integration of these country chapters with the *Comparative Politics Today* country chapters in a new online edition available through Pearson Custom Publishing. Instructors can now select from a menu of 16 country chapters to produce a custom version of the textbook for their courses. Additional material from the instructors can be included in this custom text to produce a volume uniquely suited to your teaching interests. Information on this new feature is available at:

    www.ablongman.com/custom/
      comparativepolitics

In addition, Longman has developed an interactive site to supplement the study of comparative politics. On this site students can try their hand at the interactive geography quizzes, find out just how much they know about the 24 countries featured on the site, and learn how to use the narrative and statistical data in the country profiles. This feature is available at: www.ablongman.com/comparativepolitics

European Politics Today marks a new era in Europe's history: a continent comprised of free, democratic, and market-oriented societies. We also hope that this new edition will continue the progress toward a new era in the study of European politics, where a comprehensive study of the European political experience replaces a curriculum dividing Europe in half. *European Politics Today* will help students and scholars understand the new Europe and the contribution this region continues to make to the development of political science.

RUSSELL J. DALTON
G. BINGHAM POWELL, JR.
KAARE STRØM

Chapter 1

The European Context

For centuries Europeans have dreamed of a prosperous continent leading the world in the pursuit of peace. One of the most fateful expressions of this feeling came from Mikhail Gorbachev, the last General Secretary of the Soviet Union, in his book *Perestroika (Opening)* from 1987. Addressing a then divided and unbelieving world, Gorbachev foresaw an end to the "Cold War" that had divided Europe into two nuclear armed camps for the better part of half a century. "Europe from the Atlantic to the Urals is a cultural-historical entity united by the common heritage of the Renaissance and Enlightenment. . . . Europe's historic chance and its future lie in peaceful cooperation between the states of that continent."[1] Just a few years later the Cold War did end, not in the way that Gorbachev preferred, but creating nonetheless a unique opportunity for European peace and integration.

One reason that Gorbachev's image of a cooperative and peaceful Europe seemed so unrealistic was that it contrasted sharply with the continent's past. Over the past century, Europe experienced not only the tensions and conflicts of the Cold War, but also the horrors of two world wars and the barbarisms, holocausts, and mass oppression of the totalitarian governments of the twentieth century. And previous centuries witnessed unremitting smaller wars and often brutal imperial conquests.

Yet, historic Europe has been an ambivalent force—destructive and creative at the same time. On the creative side, the dominant forms of political and economic organization in the world today—the effective service-producing state, representative democracy, the industrial market economy, and the ideas of universal human rights and freedoms—had their origins in Europe. They were created in a tempestuous period during which Europe changed from a comparative backwater to the most powerful and prosperous region in the world. A series of costly wars stretching from the seventeenth century to the twentieth shaped the modern state. The industrial *market economy* emerged in Protestant Europe and America. It has transformed these and other societies, with their class structures and patterns of social interaction, and sown the seeds of the democratic impulses of the nineteenth and twentieth centuries. The *industrial revolution*, which originated in Britain around 1770, has vastly changed the working lives and improved the standards of living of billions of people around the world. Representative democracy traces its modern origins to

1

the British struggle starting in the seventeenth century to democratize parliament and contain the arbitrary power of the king, and to the American and French Revolutions of 1776 and 1789. The first wave of democratization in the modern world was confined to Europe and a few of Europe's former colonies, but subsequent waves have affected more and more countries around the world.

Europe is a relatively small continent. Its influence on the contemporary world has been far out of proportion to its size and its earlier history. In the Middle Ages and early Renaissance, Europe was relatively backward and defensive, divided into a number of kingdoms, principalities, dukedoms, baronies, and independent cities. Much of Europe was in the thrall of a hierarchical and often corrupt Roman Catholic Church establishment.

Yet, in three fateful centuries the Renaissance, the Protestant Reformation, the Enlightenment, and the Industrial Revolution transformed Europe in fundamental ways—in its aspirations and ideas, its technology, its social structure, and in its political organization. Europe became concentrated into a small number of expansive, bureaucratically centralized states. These states drew upon a growing industry and commercial agriculture, and possessed professional and technologically sophisticated armies and navies. Between the sixteenth and the nineteenth centuries, Europe became the proactive continent, with the rest of the world increasingly reactive. Yet, while Europe was outwardly expansive, it was inwardly divided between states that were almost constantly at war with one another. Only after the fall of Napoleon in 1814 and with the emergence of British dominance did Europe experience a long spell of relative peace ("Pax Britanica") and unprecedented economic and technological progress. In the twentieth century, however, Europe's divisions and rivalries culminated in the two world wars. Since the end of World War II, Europe has tamed its national rivalries and relaxed its imperial ambitions, but not without leaving its values and institutions implanted on the rest of the world, where they have combined and interacted with indigenous forms and practices.

THE PURPOSE AND ORGANIZATION OF THIS BOOK

This book celebrates a new Europe. The progress of European integration after World War II, the end of the Cold War, and the demise of totalitarian governments have, we hope, altered Europe's historic pattern of division and conflict. Democratic in reality or in aspiration, and committed to market exchange and freedoms, the 39 states of this new Europe are no longer divided ideologically or pitted against each other in unremitting war. Large parts of this new Europe, including many countries of the former Soviet orbit, have begun the process of merging sovereignties in a European Union.

European Politics Today is about Europe, not just about Western Europe or Eastern Europe. Our first goal is to introduce Europe as a cultural and political region. The nations of Europe have different histories, but they all have been shaped by common social, economic, and political experiences. They were all affected in differing degrees by the Renaissance, the Reformation, the *Enlightenment*, and the Industrial Revolution. They shared actively or passively in the rising nationalism of the nineteenth century, and in the Communism, Fascism, and the terrible wars of the twentieth century. The European experience is also relevant to Americans who live in a modern democracy that originated as a transplanted fragment of Europe. America has not been able to avoid involvement in Europe's politics and wars, and has hosted successive generations of European exiles and refugees.

Our second goal is to use the political experience of Europe to introduce important concepts and theories in political science. Modern political science was formed in the attempt to grasp and explain the workings of the political and economic structures that originated in Europe: the bureaucratic state, the industrial market economy, and representative democratic government. Thus the unique European experience is relevant to anyone trying to understand and utilize modern political science. We use the concepts and tools of political science to examine the rich and varied democratic experience, its values, institutions, and processes, in well-established as well as in new democracies.

European Politics Today contains four introductory chapters and eight chapters presenting individual European political systems. The four introductory chapters set the stage for understanding today's political Europe. This first chapter places the European nations geographically and historically by tracing the emergence of contemporary nations through centuries of conflict and consolidation. Relations between European nations are an important part of the politics of each nation, and the importance of these relations has been heightened by the rapid and radical changes in Eastern Europe and by the increasing integration of the European Union (EU). This chapter also discusses two critical features of each country's domestic environment that help create different problems and possibilities for its politics: national economic conditions and ethnic division or unity. In conclusion, the chapter introduces a continuing theme of this book: Europe's special relationship with democracy and democratization.

Concerns about the nature, bases, and varieties of democracy in Europe also help shape the subsequent chapters. Chapter 2 provides an overview of how Europeans think and act politically. It focuses especially on what democracy expects of its citizens and what citizens in old and new democracies expect of their governments. Chapter 3 offers a similar overview of the interest group and political parties that Europeans use to participate in political decision making. Finally, Chapter 4 presents the main features of European constitutions, government institutions, and policymaking processes.

Chapters 5 through 11 apply these general themes to specific European political systems, including some well-established democracies (England and France), some that have made the transition to democracy after World War II (Germany and Spain), and some that have only in the last 15 years grappled with the transition to democratic politics (Russia, Poland, and Hungary). The chapters on specific political systems conclude in Chapter 12 with an analysis of the European Union, which since 2004 comprises 25 of Europe's countries, including 8 from Eastern Europe. Of the countries covered in Chapters 5 through 11, only Russia is not a member of the EU. The European Union is an in-creasingly important, though sometimes complex and inscrutable, supranational political system. It influences political decisions in all European countries, including those states that are not members.

The Appendix outlines the framework of specific topics that are discussed in the introductory chapters and in each country study, indicating the pages where these topics are treated. This appendix makes it possible to compare general topics from the introductory chapters across the political systems examined in the book.

THE EMERGENCE OF TODAY'S EUROPE

Europe is a large peninsula extending out of the Eurasian landmass, with its eastern border in the Ural Mountains and its western border on the Atlantic. It ranges from the Arctic Ocean in the north, to the Mediterranean Sea on the south, almost touching Africa at the Straits of Gibraltar. It is the next to smallest of the seven continents, larger than Australia, but smaller than Antarctica—roughly 4 million square miles in extent, with some three-quarters of a billion inhabitants.

The major changes in the political map of Europe over the past several centuries and up until the most recent years, have been formalized in a series of treaties following major European wars. The *Peace of Westphalia* terminated the "Thirty Years War" of religion (1618–1648), triggered by the *Protestant Reformation*. The Treaty of Westphalia tried to solve these conflicts by dividing Europe into Catholic countries (mainly in the South) and Protestant ones (mainly in the North and West). This peace settlement also established the principle of national sovereignty, which meant that each country would have the right to determine internal affairs, including religion, as it saw fit. Figure 1.1 presents Europe as it was organized following the Peace of Westphalia (1648). The whole of southeastern Europe lived within the Ottoman Empire, the domain of the Turkish sultanate. Central Europe, in the form of Austria, Prussia, Switzerland, and Poland, was just beginning to take shape out of the mist of the Holy Roman Empire. Northern Europe was dominated by Sweden, which was at the peak of its power after its

FIGURE 1.1   Europe in 1648

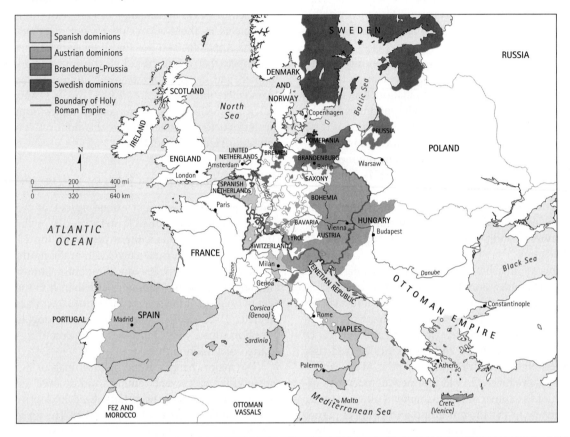

victories in the religious wars. But more than anything else, Europe's future was foreshadowed in a tier of countries bordering on the Atlantic Ocean with maritime access to the rest of the world—Spain, Portugal, England, the Netherlands, and France. This part of Europe evolved into a set of powerful states much earlier than other parts of Europe. In Italy and Germany, for example, control was split up between loose and ineffective empires and a patchwork of city-states and small principalities. Their size, seafaring capacity, and ability to mobilize resources enabled the Atlantic states to become the architects of world imperialism from the seventeenth to the nineteenth centuries. For two centuries after the Treaty of Westphalia, France and England became the leading European powers.

The next great European wars followed after France had gone through a political revolution and seen the rise to power of a brilliant general, Napoleon Bonaparte. However, Napolean's expansionist policies eventually led to military defeat. The *Treaty of Vienna* terminated the Napoleonic Wars that followed the French Revolution (1796–1815). The Europe that emerged after the Napoleonic Wars reflected the dissolution of the Holy Roman Empire and the retreat of the Ottoman Empire toward its roots in Asia Minor. Prussia was on its way to becoming a powerful state. Poland and Finland were gobbled up by Russia, as that enormous empire moved westward. Europe of the early nineteenth century was dominated by a "Holy Alliance" of conservative monarchs who sought to preserve their power and to prevent further social revolutions. Later in the nineteenth century, Europe became more concerned with an increasingly powerful and expansive Germany, which was unified in 1871 under Prussian leadership, and a united Italian state that emerged at about the same time. In the East, the Ottoman Empire gradually weakened and thus earned its reputation as the "sick man of Europe." It lost a part of Greece in the early nineteenth century, and Bulgaria in the early twentieth.

World War I (1914–1918) was the disastrous result of the great power rivalries of the late nineteenth and early twentieth centuries. The postwar *Treaty of Versailles* (1919) established the national right to self-determination. Each nation (a people with a common self-defined identity) sharing a common territory should have the right to determine whether they want to form their own state. The military results of World War I were hard on empires, and the Treaty of Versailles was not friendly to them, either. The defeated Ottoman Empire was driven back to its Turkish base, and the multiethnic Austro-Hungarian Empire was split into Austria, Hungary, Yugoslavia, and Czechoslovakia. The German Empire crumbled at the end of the war and was replaced by a fragile republic. The Russian Empire collapsed in 1917, and the ensuing revolution led to a radical, Bolshevik Russia, which became the Soviet Union. Devastated by war and treated with hostility by its neighbors, Russia gave up its control of Finland, Estonia, Latvia, Lithuania, and Poland. The map of Europe "between the wars" was much like contemporary Europe, except that Ukraine, Belarus, and Moldova were still parts of the Soviet Union. But the Treaty of Versailles failed to solve Europe's national tensions or to provide an umbrella of collective security.

World War II was brought on by the aggressions of the *Axis* powers (*Nazi [National Socialist]* Germany, Fascist Italy, and authoritarian Japan), which were countries that had largely been left behind in the age of imperial conquest. Within the first years of World War II, almost all of Western Europe, with the notable exception of the United Kingdom (Britain), was overpowered, brutalized, and "coordinated" by Nazi armies. Eventually the hold of Nazi Germany on Europe was broken by

1945, by the bloodied troops of the Soviet Union from the east, and the armed forces of the United States, Britain, and their allies from the west. World War II led to the formation of the United Nations in 1945 and to the proclamation of the Universal Declaration of Human Rights three years later.

Yet, the 1948 Communist coup in Czechoslovakia and the Soviet blockade of Berlin during the same year soon dashed hopes for a peaceful Europe of low tensions. The line separating the Soviet and the Anglo-American forces in the middle of Germany in 1945 became the *Iron Curtain* of the next generation. Figure 1.2 depicts the Europe of the *Cold War*—a sharply divided continent with its eastern part under Soviet political control and military occupation, and with a western part tightly drawn together under American leadership. Europe was frozen in what seemed like a permanent confrontation.

The most recent remaking of the European map resulted from the collapse of the Soviet Union and Yugoslavia. In 1989, communist governments all over Eastern Europe collapsed or were forced from power. The hated Berlin Wall, which for almost 30 years had separated East and West Germany, was torn down by ordinary people on both sides, while armed border guards stood by and watched. The Soviet Union acquiesced and withdrew from Eastern Europe and in 1991 split into 15 independent political entities, 7 of which are commonly counted as European. Four of these (Russia, Belarus, Ukraine, and Moldova) have retained close ties to one another, and the Soviet heritage has remained fairly strong and democratization uncertain. In contrast, the Baltic countries that had been independent between the two world wars—Estonia, Latvia, and Lithuania—quickly reasserted their independence and sought collaboration with Western Europe. Five countries emerged from the dissolution of Yugoslavia in 1991–1992: Slovenia, Croatia, Macedonia, Bosnia-Herzegovina, and Serbia and Montenegro. The latter contained a predominantly Albanian and deeply conflicted province of Kosovo. Except for Slovenia, all the former components of Yugoslavia have had a troubled and more or less violent history since the breakup of the larger country. Two nations emerged from the peaceful breakup of the former

FIGURE 1.2   Europe in the Cold War

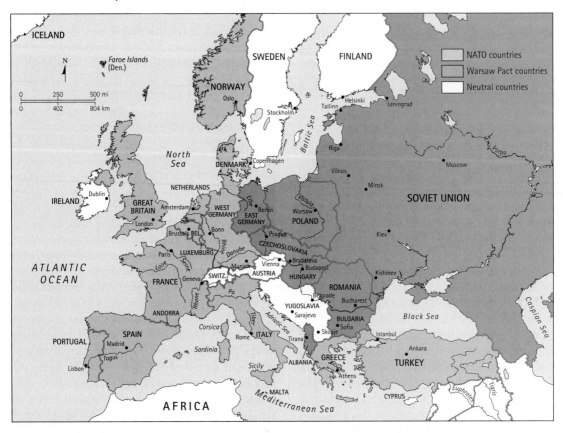

Czechoslovakia in 1993: the Czech Republic and Slovakia. Figure 1.3 presents a map of contemporary Europe after the end of the Cold War.

It is still common to think of Europe as divided into Western and Eastern parts, a view surviving from the Cold War. From this perspective, 19 of the 39 countries of contemporary Europe are the Eastern successors to the old Communist bloc: the 7 European successor states to the Soviet Union, the 5 components of the former Yugoslavia, plus Albania, Bulgaria, the Czech Republic, Hungary, Poland, Romania, and Slovakia. The remaining 20 countries that are considered Western include the 15 states that made up the European Union until its expansion in 2004: Austria,

Belgium, Denmark, Finland, France, Great Britain, Germany, Greece, Ireland, Italy, Luxembourg, the Netherlands, Portugal, Spain, and Sweden. In addition, there are two smaller Western countries, Cyprus and Malta, that only joined the EU in 2004, and three that have chosen to remain outside that organization: Iceland, Norway, and Switzerland. With patience, you should be able to count 39 countries in Figure 1.3.

When you consult that map, it is immediately obvious that Western Europe includes considerable parts that are not geographically "western." In longitudinal terms, for example, Greece is more "eastern" than Poland and the Czech Republic, and Cyprus even more so. Similarly, the northern Euro-

FIGURE 1.3   Europe Today

pean countries of Finland and Sweden are as far east as Hungary and Croatia. In this book, however, we most frequently refer to "Eastern" versus "Western" Europe, because of the important legacies of economic conditions, political histories, and international alliances.

EUROPEAN INTEGRATION

The history of state- and nation-building in Europe would not be complete without recent important trends toward integration. Since World War II, the industrialized countries of Western Europe found that the peaceful and free exchange of ideas, products, and persons across national boundaries greatly enhances productivity. Step by step since the 1950s,

Western Europeans have created a *common market economy* of ever-growing political integration.

The *European Economic Community (EEC)* was formed in 1957 and originally consisted of six countries: France, Germany, Italy, Belgium, the Netherlands, and Luxembourg.[2] The European Community expanded in the 1970s and 1980s to include Britain, Ireland, Denmark, Greece, Spain, and Portugal. The organization expanded again in 1995 to include Austria, Finland, and Sweden, and renamed itself the *European Union (EU)*.[3] In 2004 the European Union admitted ten new states. These included eight Eastern European countries: Estonia, Latvia, Lithuania, Poland, the Czech Republic, Slovakia, Hungary, and Slovenia. Also admitted were two smaller

Mediterranean island states: Cyprus and Malta. In the same year, EU leaders proposed a new "constitutional treaty," which each member states will have to ratify. The process of integration creates regional institutions with limited policymaking power and with resources to address common policy goals. The European Union might be called a "confederated state" in which the governing institutions have policymaking authority, but they must rely on the member governments for enforcement, implementation, and revenue. (See Chapter 12 for a more complete account of the European Union.)

Another change in the international structure involves security policy. The international security arrangements put in place during the Cold War no longer fit the contemporary geopolitical situation. The *North Atlantic Treaty Organization (NATO)* was formed early in the Cold War (1949) under American leadership in order to mobilize Western European countries against the communist threat. The Soviet bloc formed the *Warsaw Pact* (1955) to counter NATO; the *Council for Mutual Economic Assistance (COMECON)*, formed in 1959, coordinated the Eastern economies in response to the European Union. Both the Warsaw Pact and COMECON dissolved with the end of the Cold War.

The EU and NATO are still in operation and expanding in membership, but they are also searching for new equilibria in scope and function. The European Union in 2004 admitted eight Eastern European countries as members. Likewise, NATO has added ten Eastern European nations. Yet, while NATO has continued to expand, its role in the new Europe is uneasy. Russia opposes NATO expansion to the east, viewing it as a threat to isolate Russia internationally. And while NATO is still playing an important role in the former Yugoslavia, some of its functions in that area are being taken over by the EU. Thus, NATO's security functions in the new Europe are unclear. The close Cold War security relationship between the United States and Europe is no longer justified by a Soviet threat, even though some of the Eastern European countries still worry about their Russian neighbor. Thus, while substantial parts of the former East are now peacefully incorporated into a greater Europe of democracy and relative prosperity, there are still areas of internal and international instability.

DESCRIBING EUROPE: LARGE AND SMALL COUNTRIES

The variation in the size of European countries is enormous. Table 1.1 describes the differences in population for the Western and Eastern European countries in this book. Russia with over 140 million inhabitants is the European giant. Some 30 million Russians live east of the Urals, in the Asian part of the country. Even if we deduct these eastern residents, European Russia still dominates Europe with a population almost 50 percent larger than that of Germany, the second most populous European country. The population of European Russia is almost 400 times that of Iceland, which has fewer than 300,000 inhabitants. France is third in population size with close to 60 million residents. The United Kingdom is very close behind; Spain and Poland are next among the countries covered in this book, although Ukraine is larger than either. Hungary is a relatively small nation, with around 10 million inhabitants.

Grouping all 39 European countries according to population, we have 9 large European countries with populations of 20 million or more. Six of them are covered in this book; the remaining ones are Ukraine, Italy, and Romania. There are 15 medium-sized countries ranging from 5 million to about 15 million, 9 of these in Western Europe and the remaining 6 in Eastern Europe. The 15 smallest European countries have populations that range from fewer than 5 million inhabitants to under 1 million each for Cyprus, Luxembourg, Malta, and Iceland.[4]

When we compare European countries according to their geographic area (the second column in Table 1.1), we get a somewhat different pattern. European Russia comes out on top even more dramatically in geographic size; the ratio of its area to the second largest country is even greater than that of its population. Although European Russia is only half again as populous as Germany, it has seven times the area of Ukraine, the next largest European state, and eight times that of France, which is the largest country in Western Europe. The other West-

TABLE 1.1   Aspects of Economic Development for Selected European Countries

	Population (millions)	Average Inflation (%) 1998–2002	Per Capita GNP 2003	P.C. GDP Growth (%) 1998–2002	Per Capita PPP 2003	Percent of Labor Force in Agriculture (%)
Germany	82.6	1.4	$25,250	1.4	$27,460	3
France	59.7	1.3	24,770	2.3	27,460	2
United Kingdom	59.3	2.3	28,350	2.2	27,650	1
Spain	41.1	2.8	16,990	2.9	22,020	6
Russia	143.4	34.3	2,610	4.5	8,920	12
Hungary	10.1	9.7	6,330	4.3	13,780	6
Poland	38.2	7.3	5,270	3.1	11,450	19

Source: World Bank, *World Development Indicators 2004,* retrieved August 10, 2004 from https://publications.worldbank.org/subscriptions/WDI/. The inflation measure is the change in the consumer price index (CPI). World Bank, *Quick Reference Tables,* retrieved December 1, 2004 from http://www.worldbank.org/data/databytopic/GNIPC.pdf.

ern European countries with areas exceeding 100,000 square miles (about the size of Oregon) include Spain, Sweden, Norway, Germany, Finland, and Italy. The United Kingdom is slightly under the hundred thousand mark. The Eastern giants include Russia, Ukraine, and Poland, whereas Romania is just below the hundred thousand mark.

Magnitudes of population and area do not in themselves explain the politics of European states. The biggest ones in territory or population are not necessarily the richest or most powerful ones. Thus, the small country of Switzerland has been an independent, free, and prosperous country for centuries, whereas Ukraine is large but comparatively poor and has only recently gained its independence. Size, of course, does make a difference in warfare, as Napoleon and Hitler discovered on the wintry steppes of Russia. It also makes a difference in the availability of resources, in problems of governmental centralization, and the like. Similarly, the relation between area and population is important. America had a frontier for growth and expansion. Asian Russia (Siberia) has been a frontier for that country. The Netherlands and other densely populated European countries have very different and powerful geographic constraints on their economic development.

One of the most important population questions is the rate of increase, a fact that has important implications for economic growth. Recently, Europe

has had the smallest population growth rate of all the world regions. Between 1965 and 1998, Europe had only a 0.4 percent average annual increase, in comparison with the Middle East and North Africa (2.8), Sub-Saharan Africa (2.7), South Asia (2.2), and Latin America and the Caribbean (2.1).[5] This means that Europe does not have to worry about some of the issues that plague many developing countries with rapidly growing populations. However, the low European birthrates are raising serious concerns about the sustainability of that continent's welfare states, as their populations will age dramatically over the next few decades.

The sheer magnitude of a country's economy is also important. Thus we can think of large and small countries in terms of economic as well as population size. Germany is at the top among the European countries with close to a $2,000 billion economy as of 2001, contrasted with an Albanian economy of around $4.2 billion. The economic output of Germany is thus close to 500 times that of Albania. The other large Western European economies—France, the United Kingdom, and Italy—generate well over $1,000 billion each year, while the larger Eastern European economies range from the $250 billion mark for Russia, $163 billion for Poland, to around $50 billion for Hungary. By this measure the German economy in 2001 was about eight times the size of the Russian one, with only a little more than half the population.

DESCRIBING EUROPE: RICH AND POOR COUNTRIES

The economic measures most vital to internal politics are expressed in relationship to population size: what occupations divide the citizens in the labor force; how productive are their efforts; how is their collective income to be divided? Table 1.1 presents a comparison of the economic performance of those Western and Eastern European countries that are treated in depth in this book.

As a starting point, the last column in the table underscores the fact that the economies of Eastern Europe still have substantial agricultural sectors in comparison with the heavily industrialized and urbanized societies of Western Europe. In Germany, France, and the United Kingdom, the agricultural percentage of the labor force is well below 5 percent. Even in Spain only about 6 percent of the labor force is now employed in agriculture, a figure matched only by the most developed Eastern European economies, such as Hungary. In contrast, close to a fifth of Poland's labor force works in agriculture. The relative size of the agricultural labor force is significant for two reasons. For one thing, a large agricultural labor force usually indicates low economic development and productivity. Highly productive modern economies manage their agricultural needs with small farm populations, even if the nature of their land and skills make this sector valuable. Secondly, a large agricultural sector usually means strong interest groups that promote the farm sector, and these interests often resist economic modernization policies and international integration.

There are two measures of income and productivity in Table 1.1: per capita *Gross National Product (GNP)* based on prevailing currency exchange rates (columns 3 and 4) and *Purchasing Power Parities (PPP)* (column 5). Both of these measures take statistics in national currencies and recalculate them to allow for international comparisons. The first measure converts per capita GNP based on the exchange rates that are used in the international financial markets. This is the simplest and most common way to compare eco-

nomic output across countries, but it has two important problems. First, exchange rates sometimes fluctuate quite strongly. For example, as some of you may have noticed to your dismay, between 2001 and 2004 the U.S. dollar lost about one-third of its value against most Western European currencies. In comparative economic statistics, it may thus appear as if the U.S. economy shrunk dramatically compared to the European ones over that period, even though growth rates were generally higher in the United States than in most Western European countries.

Second, currency exchange rates are not necessarily accurate representations of what a given currency can purchase in food, shelter, clothing, and other amenities. For example, any international tourist who has visited both Bolivia and Switzerland will know that while both countries have spectacular mountains, one's money goes a lot further in the former country than in the latter. Purchasing power parities (PPP) are an attempt to measure the "true" values of different currencies, based on their respective capacities to purchase goods and services in the domestic market. These estimates can then be used to measure the comparative outputs of different economies. Most economists consider GNP per capita measures based on PPP equivalents to be a more appropriate estimate of personal income, although they are more difficult to measure.[6]

Table 1.1 clearly shows that the choice of measure can make a difference. If we use the exchange rate version of GNP to measure personal income, the ratio between Britain at the top and Russia at the bottom is more than 10 to 1. If we instead use the PPP indicator, the contrast between these two countries is less than 4 to 1. The PPP figure is closer to the reality of economic welfare in Europe today. The PPP statistics indicate that the economic contrasts between Eastern and Western Europe are striking, although less formidable than implied by the exchange rate-based statistics. The average PPP-based GNP per capita among the nations of Western Europe in 2003 was close to $30,000, while in Eastern Europe it was about $10,000. Hungary's average personal income is a little less than one-half that of Germany and France, and roughly two-thirds that of

Spain. Russia and Poland have economies yielding about one-third per capita of those of Britain, Germany, and France. These differences, while large, are within the range of what can be overcome in time through human effort, political organization and will, and constructive policies.

In terms of economic growth, the gap between Western and most Eastern European economies was growing, not diminishing, in the 1990s.[7] All the Western European countries had positive economic growth rates for the 1990s; the average country grew annually at about 2 percent. In contrast, most Eastern European countries struggled with the very difficult problems of transition from communist "command control" economies to market economies. The average Eastern country declined nearly 2.5 percent a year. By the late 1990s, however, this pattern changed and since 1998 the Eastern European countries have generally had stronger growth than those in the West.

The Eastern European average conceals great differences, moreover, in success in managing the economic transition. Poland and Hungary are among the most successful Eastern European economies, and their average gains of 3 to 5 percent per year are larger than those of most Western European countries. Russia, whose economy was greatly affected by the collapse of its military sector and the obsolescence of much of its heavy industry, experienced disastrous economic performance in the 1990s, as its economy lost an average of 7 percent a year. Fortunately, around 1998 the Russian economy began to turn around, and it has in recent years produced robust economic growth, even though drastic poverty persists.

Inflation was a major problem in Western Europe from the 1960s to about the 1980s. In recent years, however, the countries of the West have worried much less about this problem, as Table 1.1 indicates. But in Eastern Europe, inflation was a serious, and largely unfamiliar, phenomenon in the 1990s. For the period 1990–1998, Russia averaged an *annual* rate of inflation of 137 percent, Romania 118 percent, Poland about 30 percent, and Hungary 23 percent. The bulk of these price increases directly followed from the economic transitions of the late 1980s and early 1990s, and in many countries they have come down in recent years. But Eastern inflation rates are still troubling, as Russia and Romania continue to experience inflation rates of 30 to 40 percent. Governments confronted with inflation problems of this magnitude can easily encounter serious discontent, which can undermine support for democratic politics and market economies.

SOCIAL DEVELOPMENT AND WELFARE IN EUROPE

Gross economic statistics on economic production and inflation are far from the whole story on the economic and social realities facing Europeans today. Economic conditions and public policies jointly shape the welfare of citizens and, in turn, their satisfactions or frustrations with democratic politics. Table 1.2 presents four measures of social development and welfare in European countries: education, computer ownership, income distribution, and infant mortality. These measures reflect different aspects of wealth and resource abundance, but also the past performance of national governments. As shown in the first column of the table, most European countries, East and West, are successful in keeping their teenagers in school. There also seems to be gender equality in access to secondary education in both the West and the East. High levels of literacy are consistent with these education figures. The percentage of young people enrolled in colleges and universities, as shown in column 2, tells a similar story. All over Europe, and including most Eastern countries, about half of all young adults attend some level of college or university. In some countries, including Russia, the percentage is even higher. Even in the poorer European countries, college education is far more widespread than in many low-income countries in other parts of the world. Public expenditures on education are also relatively similar across these eight nations. In 1997 West Germany spent 4.8 percent of its GNP on education, the United Kingdom, 5.3 percent, compared with Russia's 3.5 percent and Poland's 7.5 percent. If, however, we consider that the GNP of the Western countries is several times larger than that of some Eastern countries, the effort converts

TABLE 1.2 Aspects of Social Development for Selected European Countries

	Percentage in School as Percentage of Age Group (secondary) (college)		Computers per 1000	Percentage of Income to Lower 20%	Percentage of Income to Upper 20%	Infant Mortality per 1000 Births
Germany	88	46	431	8.5	36.9	4
France	92	54	347	7.2	40.2	4
United Kingdom	95	59	406	6.1	44.0	5
Spain	93	57	196	7.5	40.3	5
Russia	na	68	89	4.9	51.3	18
Hungary	87	40	108	7.7	37.2	8
Poland	88	55	106	7.3	42.5	8

Source: World Bank, *World Development Indicators 2004,* retrieved August 10, 2004 from https://publications.worldbank.org/subscriptions/WDI/. Secondary school enrollment is percent net enrollment and Tertiary school enrollment is percent gross enrollment. The income share numbers for Spain date back to 1990 and for France to 1995. All other income share numbers are from 1999 and 2000.

into substantially larger Western European spending on such things as construction and maintenance of schools, teacher salaries, educational equipment, and the like.

Table 1.2 also shows computer ownership. In this respect, the richer Western European countries are significantly ahead of Spain as well as the Eastern European states. Yet, computer access is growing rapidly in all parts of Europe. As an indicator of public health, we include the infant mortality per thousand live births. Here again, the main difference runs not so much between East and West as between the poorest countries of the East and the rest. Thus, Russia has significantly higher infant death rates than any other country. Differences between the various Western European countries are almost nonexistent.

The distribution of income reported in Table 1.2 for Western and Eastern countries reflects an ironic situation: Only a few years after the introduction of a market economy, Russia, which for 75 years had a government ostensibly committed to social equality and the eradication of class differences, has the most unequal distribution of income among all the countries listed. More than half of Russia's total income goes to the top 20 percent of income recipients, and less than 5 percent goes to the bottom fifth. Although not as severe as the discrepancies in some South American countries and South Africa, it is among the world's least egalitarian distributions, which contributes to its political tensions (see Chapter 9). This situation is exacerbated by the fact that many recent fortunes have been gained quickly and often through shady deals involving the sell-off of former government assets. In contrast, Hungary and Poland are much more egalitarian, with around 40 percent of income going to the top fifth and 7 to 8 percent going to the bottom fifth. Distributions in most of Western Europe are fairly similar to these.

DEVELOPMENT, MODERNIZATION, AND DEMOCRACY

Statistical comparisons of Western and Eastern Europe thus yield substantial differences in economic levels and welfare provisions. If we take purchasing power parity as a measure of economic productivity, the Eastern European economies produce somewhat more than a third of the per capita level of the richer Western European economies. The Eastern countries have larger rural, agricultural sectors, and there are significant differences in the provision of higher education and health services. By these purely economic and social measures, most of our Eastern European countries fall into the World Bank classification of "middle income countries," ranging from "lower middle income" (e.g., Albania, Ukraine, Romania, and Russia) to "upper middle income" (e.g., Poland and Hungary).[8] Statistical measures also suggest that most Eastern Europeans are educated and literate people, exposed to the "world culture." They have the makings of "civil societies"; although long stultified by communist control, interest groups, voluntary associations, and competitive media of communication are growing (see Chapter 3).

On the troubling side, high rates of inflation and slow rates of growth in many Eastern states show that they are experiencing serious developmental difficulties. While some countries are making substantial progress, others continue to have great difficulty (see Table 1.1). They are involved in "dual transitions"—simultaneous efforts to replace collectivist with market economies, and to replace centralized, authoritarian regimes with pluralistic, democratic ones.[9]

Students of democratization have long debated the relationship between economic development and democratization. Indeed, the great ideological struggles of the nineteenth and twentieth centuries turned on these issues. Karl Marx anticipated that the development of the capitalist economy and the rise of the *"bourgeoisie"* would signal the decline of feudalism, and the introduction of bourgeois democracy, which would in turn be supplanted by socialist democracy after the working class ousts the bourgeoisie.

Modern political science replaced the Marxist view of the relationship between economics and politics with more limited observations and forecasts. Many leading political scientists drew attention to a strong statistical association between economic development, social and political mobilization, and democracy.[10] These "social mobilization" studies of the 1950s and 1960s pointed out that economic growth and industrialization were associated with urbanization, the spread of education and literacy, and exposure to the mass media of communication. They argued that these conditions would result in greater political awareness and activity ("mobilization"), the formation of voluntary associations and competitive political parties, and the attainment of what came to be called *civil society* (see Chapter 2). These elements of a

civil society would both demand and support more democratic political systems.

Contrary to early hopes, democracy proved fragile. All the Eastern European countries were forcefully assimilated into the Communist orbit at the onset of the postwar period. Efforts to break free in Hungary in 1956 (see Chapter 11) and Czechoslovakia in 1968 were repressed by Soviet troops. Spain and Portugal came through World War II as authoritarian regimes; Greece also fell under military control in the 1960s. It became evident that the road to economic development could be long and hard—and that at least in the short run, economic development could be politically destabilizing.[11]

However, development theory seemed to "kick in," so to speak, in the late 1970s and 1980s; rapid and sustained economic growth in authoritarian Spain (see Chapter 8), Portugal, Greece, and other nations around the world weakened the legitimacy of authoritarian regimes. The culmination of these events came with the dramatic collapse of the Soviet Union and the establishment of new democracies in the newly free countries of Eastern Europe. The dominant political ideas of the 1990s were democracy and the market economy.

In view of the experiences of the last decades, as well as the European historical experience, we have a better understanding of the complexity of the interaction of economic, social, and political institutions and forces.[12] There is no doubt that stable or "consolidated" democracy is strongly associated statistically with economic development. But the relationship occurs over the long run. It is shaped by the more dispersed resources for power and coercion in a complex economy, by the more participatory values, perceptions, and demands of an educated and organized citizenry, and by the presence of greater resources to meet human needs.[13] A whole set of connecting relationships—structural discontinuities, breakdowns and synergies, interventions of chance, and failures and triumphs of leaders—weaken or strengthen the connection between a growing economy and a democratic polity.

As we write of Europe in the early years of the third millennium, there is a division of realities and prospects. Western European countries—

economically developed, democratically consolidated, and largely organized in a confederation—have well-established democracies. A substantial group of Eastern European countries are approaching their economic level, and many of these have joined the European Union. A substantial set of Eastern European nations are far less economically productive, often plagued by inflation and economic stagnation, and struggling with democratic ways of coping with change and conflict. With such a short experience of political independence and such limited and fragile socioeconomic bases, we would expect substantial difficulty in sustaining stable democratic government in some parts of Eastern Europe.

Sadly enough, these forecasts seem to be accurate, with democratic freedoms under pressure in nearly half of Eastern Europe, especially in the countries with lower levels of economic development. Figure 1.4, depicts the relationship between economic development and political freedom for the nations of Europe. The *Freedom Scores* in the figure are taken from the 2003 report of Freedom House, a nonprofit organization that provides an-

nual ratings of political rights and civil liberties in each country. The economic development measure—expressed as purchasing power parity (PPP)—is taken from the World Bank's *World Development Report* for 2003.[14] Each circle or square dot in the figure represents a single country, with circles representing countries in Eastern Europe and squares countries in Western Europe.

Toward the top right of Figure 1.4, indicated by the small squares, we see the Western European countries. All have economic productivity levels higher than most of the Eastern European countries and all receive the top or next to top Freedom Score. The poorest Western European countries, Portugal and Malta, have PPP levels only slightly below the richest Eastern European country (Slovenia). Spain is somewhat better off than Slovenia and notably more economically developed than the Czech Republic and Hungary, the next most developed Eastern countries, with which it shares a similarly high Freedom Score.

Freedom House considers any country with a score of 10 or more to be "Free." All eight Eastern Eu-

FIGURE 1.4   Population of Selected European Countries in 2003

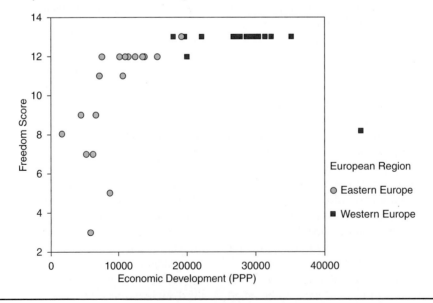

ropean countries with a PPP/capita over $10,500 achieve that designation (including Poland and Hungary). In the middle left of Figure 1.4 are five dually troubled Eastern European countries—Albania, Macedonia, Bosnia, Moldova, Russia, and Ukraine—which have PPP/capitas under $9,000 and all of which are rated only "Partly Free" by Freedom House. While each country has its own story, Freedom House's observers reported various pressures and constraints on the mass media, limited rights for minorities, and problems in establishing the rule of law as frequent themes. (See the discussion of the difficulties in establishing the rule of law generally in Chapter 4 and in Russia in particular in Chapter 9.) At the bottom left of the figure is Belarus, dominated by an increasingly powerful president, as the only European country scored as completely not free.

Another way of looking at Figure 1.4 is to observe that of the 15 Eastern European countries whose PPP per capita had been less than Hungary's $13,780, slightly less than half of them were fully free democracies on January 1, 2004. The rest were, at best, only "partly free." In a statistical sense, this suggests that some of these nations will succeed in sustaining democracy, but that others may falter or fail. In a human sense it means that good leadership may play a particularly critical role in these poorer nations. It also means that it is important that the lagging Eastern European countries begin to overcome the difficulties of economic transition and move toward growth and economic development, as Poland seems to have done (see Chapter 10).

Of course, in considering the prospects for democracy, economic development and modernization are not the only considerations. On the one hand, international norms and institutions may help support democracy as a political system. On the other, religious and ethnic cleavages create additional problems in many of the newly independent Eastern European countries. Democracy can arouse new expectations from suppressed minorities, and the absence of resources in the poorer nations can make accommodation of these particularly difficult. This consideration brings us to the troubling prospects of religious and ethnic conflict in Europe.

ETHNIC AND RELIGIOUS CONFLICT IN EUROPE

In the long course of European history, through the forces of population growth and decline, migration, warfare, famine, and disease, an ethno-religious distribution of great complexity has taken shape. There is evidence of a Celtic past, still surviving on the European periphery and in remote mountain valleys. Traces of a long Roman domination can still be seen. There is evidence of great migrations of Goths, Vandals, and Huns from the Asian steppes; Moors, Berbers, and Ottoman Turks from the Middle East; and Vikings and Norsemen from the North. These peoples brought their languages and religions with them. Over time these languages and beliefs combined and differentiated, partly through long-term processes of intermittent fighting, trading, and intermarrying, and partly through the deliberate actions of political and military elites seeking effective ways of extracting resources and recruiting military forces. Populations sharing the same beliefs and speaking in the same tongue could be mobilized and exploited more effectively.

Religion provided one central basis of differentiation. The great religions of the world offer coherent systems of values and standards of behavior beyond local customs and memories to their adherents. Periodically, they have swept across tribes and peoples to create, by force or example, more unified cultural systems. Before the Reformation, the Catholic Church had provided much of the cultural unity for the extremely fragmented political systems in Christian Europe. The birth of modern Europe in the *Renaissance* and the *Reformation* was associated with the shattering of religious unity. The religious wars of the sixteenth and seventeenth centuries created, at the cost of dreadful suffering, lines of religious cleavage that shaped the formation of the European nation-states and continue to influence their politics today.[15]

When the struggle between Catholicism and the forces of Protestant dissent stabilized, religious minorities within each state had largely been expelled or converted. This produced relatively homogeneous religious groupings in most countries. National governments dominated Protestant churches in northwest Europe, usually without much internal religious conflict. In much of Eastern Europe, too, secular governments established dominance over and collaboration with the Eastern Orthodox Church.

In southwestern Europe, the Catholic Church prevailed. The Counterreformation regained France and some German states from Protestantism, held Italy and the Austro-Hungarian empire (including Belgium and Spain), and reclaimed some ground from Islam to the East. The French Revolution of 1789 then unleashed a secular rebellion against the Catholic Church that left its mark on politics and party systems, as a "secular-clerical" divide, for two centuries. The emergence of democracy and the development of mass education resulted in intense internal conflict over the role of the Church in politics and public policy.

Along the fault line between North and South lay a series of states with both Catholic and Protestant populations—the Netherlands, Germany and Switzerland. In these states political conflict between Catholics and Protestants, as well as between clericalism and secularism, has been a fact of political life. This tension has endured through today, with a new focus on education, abortion, and the rights of women—areas in which religious identities and values have been particularly divisive. Apart from the religious issues as such, the followers of the faiths have been historically organized into separate communities with distinct social and political organizations.

A decline in church attendance and other religious practices throughout most of Western Europe since World War II has shifted the political balance in secular directions and decreased the sense of conflict associated with religious division. Nonetheless, at least until very recently a voter's frequency of church attendance was usually the best single predictor of his or her vote choice in most Western European nations with substantial Catholic populations.

Ethnicity may sometimes be associated with religion, but in the modern world it is additionally or even primarily associated with language, custom, and historical memories. Max Weber, in his (classic) introduction to sociological theory *Economy and Society*, defined ethnic groups as "those human groups that entertain a subjective belief in their common descent because of similarities of physical type or of customs or both, or because of memories of colonization and migration. . . . (I)t does not matter whether or not an objective blood relationship exists."[16]

Ethnicity can be a powerful force in politics. It provides an important basis for mobilization of common interests and deeply felt personal identities. It can be especially potent where allied with *nationalism*, a belief that a common ethnic group should be the basis of a geographically defined independent state. The formation of large nation-states between the sixteenth and the nineteenth centuries suppressed many of the lessor customs and dialects in favor of a few relatively dominant ones. The spread of printing and literacy replaced Latin as the international language of the educated and substituted national languages linked to larger independent states. The rise of mass education and mass media in the nineteenth and twentieth centuries obscured and devalued the surviving parochialisms. People identified themselves with some larger "nationality," and according to their social conditions and new ideological beliefs. They were the French, the Spaniards, the English, and the Germans; they were members of the working class or the bourgeoisie; they were conservatives, liberals, or socialists of one kind or another. Nation-states became both the foci of local political activity and, with enormous human costs, the actors in catastrophic international conflict. In the aftermath of World War II under the ideological pressure of the Cold War, ethnic particularisms within the nation-states were even further subordinated.

In Eastern Europe the implications of the withdrawal of Soviet control were, of course, very dramatic. As a matter of ideology, the political aspirations of ethnic minorities had been ruthlessly repressed. Yet, the bureaucratic and even party organizations in the Soviet Union, Czechoslovakia, and Yugoslavia were constructed to recognize and even encourage local ethnic cultures based on language and history, even while religion was generally suppressed. This duality in Soviet policy, dating back to Lenin's initial understanding of the problems created by ethnic nationalism, greatly facilitated the breakup of the Soviet Union, Yugoslavia, and later Czechoslo-

Box 1.1   Ethnicity Defined

The point that ethnicity is based on subjective belief in common descent, rather than a necessary physical reality, is stressed by Donald Horowitz, the leading contemporary authority on ethnicity and politics. Horowitz points out that the concept of ethnicity has to be elastic, since groups physically quite similar but differing in language, religion, customs, marriage patterns, and historical memories may consider themselves to be "ethnically" different. For example, the Serbs, Croats, and Muslim Bosnians (of the same physical stock) may believe themselves to be descended from different ancestors. Here, following Gurr and his associates, we use the term "ethnicity" even more generally to refer to all groups "whose core members share a distinctive and enduring collective identity based on cultural traits and lifeways that matter to them and to others with whom they interact."

Sources: Donald Horowitz, *Ethnic Groups in Conflict* (Berkeley: University of California Press, 1985), pp. 52–53. T. Robert Gurr, *Minorities at Risk: A Global View of Ethnopolitical Conflicts* (Washington: U.S. Institute of Peace Press, 1993), p. 3.

vakia, when central controls were removed. The overthrow of most of these authoritarian political systems and the introduction of free discussion and mass media, especially in the absence of well-entrenched democratic party systems, created political space for ethnic and religious particularisms to maneuver within the newly independent political systems.

Of all the countries in Europe, few are free of ethnic diversity, but in many countries there is little or no serious conflict. Table 1.3 provides a sense of the diversity, dangers, and promises of ethno-religious conflicts in Europe. There are several recent "hot spots," where conflict has taken the most violent form in recent years. Casualties in Bosnia, Cyprus, Chechnya, and Kosovo have numbered in the tens of thousands. While less deadly than all-out civil war, terrorism in Northern Ireland in the United Kingdom, in Basque Spain, and French Corsica has taken many lives and shattered the peace of these countries for many decades. These confrontations all involve efforts by one or more ethnic or religious groups to change the boundaries of existing states or to form new ones. Disputes over nation-state boundaries find no simple solution through democratic procedures. If the conflict comes to violence, the struggle can quickly degenerate into "ethnic cleansing," the forcible eviction or destruction of local minorities. Ethnic differences and historic grievances have this capacity to justify dehumanization of the "ethnically" different and cruelties of unimaginable proportions.

While ethnic conflict can inflict terrible costs, it need not. Table 1.3 also contains examples of ethno-religious conflicts that still retain sharp communal awareness, but there is now a stable and constitutionally protected status for group relations. Austria, Belgium (in its religious dispute), the Netherlands, and Switzerland are examples of this situation. A system of power-sharing offers security to communal groups at the cost of the efficiency and redistributive possibilities of majority rule. Austria, for example, used elaborate arrangements for sharing power between the Socialists and the Catholics in the 1950s and 1960s to prevent recurrence of the community conflicts that led to civil war in the early 1930s. The Netherlands and Belgium handled explosive religious conflicts in the same fashion.

While these more or less successful "solutions" to ethnic conflict indicate the possibilities for containing violence, they are each bought at substantial cost and require some tolerance from leaders and followers on all sides. Russia seems to have created a successful federal relationship with the Tatars. The Russian suspension of Chechnyan federal autonomy and the continuance of Chechnyan terrorism and guerrilla warfare illustrate failure, however. The more militant Chechnyans have been unwilling to lay down arms in a situation short of secession and the Russian central government has refused to allow this (see Chapter 9).

In addition to the current "hot spots" mentioned earlier, many of the successor countries in the territory of the former Soviet bloc have potential ethno-religious conflicts (even to the point of

TABLE 1.3   Examples of Ethno-Religious Conflict in Contemporary Europe

	Groups	Bases of Conflict
Austria	Catholics v. Socialists	Religion
Belarus	Belarussians v. Russians	Religion
Belgium	Flemings v. Walloons	Language
Bosnia	Serbs v. Muslims	Language, Religion
Bulgaria	Bulgarian v. Turks	Language, Religion
Croatia	Croats v. Serbs	Language, Religion
Cyprus	Greeks v. Turks	Language, Religion
Estonia	Estonians v. Russians	Language, Religion
France	French v. Corsicans	Language
Hungary	Hungarians v. Roma	Language, Religion
Latvia	Latvians v. Russians	Language, Religion
Macedonia	Macedonians v. Albanians	Language, Religion
Netherlands	Catholics v. Protestant v. Secular	Religion
Russia	Russians v. Muslims	Language, Religion
Serbia	Serbs v. Albanians	Language, Religion
Spain	Spanish v. Basque	Language
Switzerland	Germans v. French v. Italians	Language
	Catholics v. Protestants	Religion
Ukraine	Ukrainians v. Russians	Religion
United Kingdom	British v. Irish	Religion

violence). The breakup of the Soviet Union, Czechoslovakia, and Yugoslavia still left mixed ethnic populations in many states. Moreover, although religion was sharply suppressed under communist control, Eastern Europe is distinctive for the extent to which religion and language simultaneously divide many of the same groups. The substantial Russian populations left in most of the bordering countries after the breakup of the Soviet Union involve both domestic relationships with the host ethnic majority and an international relationship with Russia. For example, Russian minorities constitute around a third of the population of Estonia and Latvia, and a quarter in Ukraine. This situation has already created severe tensions, both domestic and "international," as was exemplified in the struggle over the Ukrainian "stolen election" in November–December 2004, which pitted the Russian-dominated east of the country (backed by Russia) against the Ukrainian-dominated west.

The states of the former Yugoslavia, with the exception of Slovenia, face a variety of complex ethnic pulls. Macedonia, for example, was on the verge of civil war in 2001–2002. Strife spilling over from the war in Kosovo pitted a guerrilla movement based in the Albanian minority against the central government. International intervention and NATO peacekeepers, as well as guarantees of minority rights, were needed to dampen the conflict.

Another source of ethnic conflict is the rapidly growing presence of recent immigrants and foreign workers, primarily in Western Europe. During previous periods of economic boom, a several Western European countries invited foreign workers to fill vacancies in the labor force. Many came, and their families often followed. Germany has almost 2 million Turks and Kurds; in Switzerland, nonresidents account for over 10 percent of the population. Although many do not have formal citizenship, these workers and their families have become long-term residents. The economic difficulties and political conflict in Eastern Europe since the breakdown of Soviet control, produced new waves of immigrants to Western European countries that would accept them. Moreover, Western European countries whose former colonial empires created special relationships with now independent nations in Africa, Asia, and the Caribbean have had substantial numbers of immigrants from those areas. For instance, 3 million Algerian Muslims now reside in France. Immigrants surged from 1 percent of the Spanish population in 1990 to a current 6 percent.

The presence of these groups, especially when coupled with high unemployment and other economic tensions, has stimulated expressions of ethnic nationalism by majority groups. Some members of ethnic majorities feel that their cultural and religious customs, as well as long-standing policies regulating church-state relations, are threatened. The minorities have been the target of rising, though still sporadic, ethnic violence in a number of countries. For example, there were numerous attacks and several foreigners were killed in Germany in the early 1990s. Although the situation has quieted as the economy has improved, German leaders have taken firmer antiviolence stands, and immigration has been curtailed. Immigrant groups have become a rallying point for disruptive nationalist parties calling for strong limits on immigration (adopted in many countries), the immediate expulsion of the groups, or worse (see Chapter 3).

In the euphoria of the 1989–1991 collapse of Communism and the Soviet Union, historian Francis Fukuyama forecasted that we would soon witness "the end of history" as secular democratic enlightenment and the market economy would come to dominate all over the world.[17] Since then, however, more pessimistic voices have also been heard. Samuel Huntington argues in "The Clash of Civilizations" that the political future will be dominated by clashing ethno-religious civilizations: the Judeo-Christian, the Eastern Orthodox Christian, the Islamic, the Chinese, the Japanese, the Hindu, and others.[18] He challenges the optimistic belief in the emergence of a unified, rational-secular *world culture*. Since the September 11, 2001 terrorist attacks in the United States, consciousness of international fundamentalist terrorism has increased. On March 11, 2004, the deadly terrorist attack on the Madrid train station brought the destructive dangers home to Europeans.

The EU has begun to move to strengthen anti-terrorism cooperation. These events have intensified European concerns about immigrants and given credence to Huntington's projection.

The starkly contrasting predictions of Fukuyama and Huntington capture the conflict between, on the one hand, an emerging democratic-market civilization, with its base in science, technology, secular education, mass communication, and the market, and on the other hand a world of persistent and intensely felt religious and ethnic identities that are often locally, nationally, or regionally based. Fukuyama may underestimate the perceived threats to the sense of identity and safety that many people derive from familiar beliefs, tongues, and historical experiences. However, Huntington may not properly recognize the powerful material and spiritual incentives of productivity, welfare, and participation that underlie the unifying trends. Only by considering both of these powerful messages can we begin to understand the future of political development, identity, and democracy.

FURTHER DEMOCRATIZATION?

Modern *democracy*, as Samuel Huntington points out, has emerged in *"three waves."*[19] The first began in the aftermath of the American and French revolutions and continued for more than a century through World War I, the "war to make the world safe for democracy." In this first wave successful democracy was largely a phenomenon of Europe and its colonial offspring, but it foundered on the Great Depression and then receded to form the "reverse wave" of *fascist* and *communist* authoritarianism in the 1930s. These disasters, above all the terrible replacement of Germany's democratic Weimar Republic by Hitler's brutal and aggressive Nazi dictatorship, are also a critical part of the European experience.

The second wave, which Huntington calls the "short wave," lasted from the defeat of Fascism in World War II and the breakup of the European colonial empires afterward, until approximately the mid-1960s. While a large number of countries in Europe, East Asia, Africa, and Latin America became formally democratic in these post–World War II years, most of them collapsed quickly into authoritarian regimes of one kind or another. The interwar democracies of Eastern Europe, like their authoritarian counterparts, were repressed by Soviet military force and replaced with Communist authoritarianism. The overthrow of democracy in Greece by military coup in 1967 represents Western Europe's contributions to the reversal of the second wave.

The third wave began in Southern Europe in the mid-1970s, with democratic transformations in Portugal, Spain (see Chapter 8), and Greece, and then quickly spread into Latin America, East Asia, and Africa. In the late 1980s, to the surprise of the rest of the world, it engulfed the Eastern European satellites of the Soviet Union. Then in the early 1990s the Soviet Union itself collapsed into its ethno-national components. Without warning from the worlds of scholarship and the media, democracy, now the formal regime in more than three-quarters of the independent countries in the world had become the "only game in town." It had no expansive, ideological rivals, with the possible exception of the theocratic Islamic regimes of the Middle East.

Given this history, Europe has been a primary laboratory of natural experiments with politics. The modern bureaucratic state, representative parliamentary institutions, various electoral systems, political parties and party systems, interest groups, specialized media of communication—the whole modern political apparatus—emerged first in Europe and its colonies. They emerged at different times, in different parts of the continent, in differing degrees and sequences, and as a consequence of different conditions and events. Most of the rest of the planet has now assimilated these institutions and practices and is in the process of combining them (sometimes more and sometimes less successfully) with indigenous cultures and institutions. Hence, when we study Europe we are observing the origins of modern politics and describing most of the political models for political institutions and theories in the rest of the world. We are also observing some of the greatest triumphs and greatest disasters of democratic politics.

Juan Linz and Alfred Stepan have cautioned that although we are currently in an era of democra-

tization, we should avoid the assumption that all countries of the world will move toward a stable *democratic consolidation.*[20] There are still totalitarian, and "post-totalitarian" regimes in the world, and several varieties and large numbers of authoritarian ones. Many formally democratic regimes in many parts of the world are teetering at the point of economic, social, and political breakdown.[21]

In addition, regimes that seem to be in *democratic transition* may not be moving ahead on some inevitable course toward "completing" the process, but may instead be pausing in "halfway houses." The last 25 years also have seen the growth of "electoral authoritarianism, in which a façade of democracy provides some space for political opposition, independent media, and social organizations that do not seriously criticize or challenge the regime."[22] There is serious concern that Russia (Chapter 9) and some other Eastern European regimes may follow that path and fail to complete or even backslide on the democratization process. Moreover, political corruption is an obstacle to democratic consolidation and performance that has proved to be very difficult to eradicate (see Chapter 4).

As the third wave of democracy seems to be reaching its peak and showing signs of reversal in some parts of the world, the 19 Eastern European countries are a crucial battleground in the long human struggle for freedom and welfare. Nothing would affect the balance of this struggle more than rapid economic growth and consolidated democratization in such countries as the Russian Federation, Ukraine, Belarus, and Romania. Moreover, the consolidated democracies of Western Europe can still go much further to achieve a more fully realized democratization that bases responsive public policies on a participating and confident citizenry.

These then are some of the major challenges of European political studies to which this book is an introduction. How can scholars draw effectively from the great fund of experience and knowledge, most richly based on Western European political and economic studies, in order to illuminate, interpret, and forecast the issues and prospects of a larger and unified democratic Europe?

Key Terms

Axis
bourgeoisie
bureaucratic state
civil society
Cold War
Council for Mutual
   Economic
   Assistance
   (COMECON)
democracy, three
   waves of
democratic transition

Enlightenment
ethnicity
European Economic
   Community (EEC)
European Union (EU)
fascist authoritarianism
Freedom Score
Gross National Product
   (GNP)/Gross
   Domestic Product
   (GDP)

industrial revolution
industrialization
Iron Curtain
market economy
nationalism
Nazism-National
   Socialism
North Atlantic Treaty
   Organization
   (NATO)
Peace of Westphalia

perestroika
Protestant Reformation
Purchasing Power
   Parity (PPP)
Reformation
Renaissance
Treaty of Versailles
Treaty of Vienna
Warsaw Pact
world culture

Suggested Readings

Budge, Ian, and Kenneth Newton, et al. *The Politics of the New Europe*. New York: Addison Wesley Longman, 1997.

Dahl, Robert A. *Democracy and Its Critics*. New Haven: Yale University Press, 1989.

———. *Polyarchy: Participation and Opposition*. New Haven: Yale University Press, 1971.

Diamond, Larry. *Developing Democracy: Toward Consolidation*. Baltimore: Johns Hopkins University Press, 1999.

Fukuyama, Francis. *The End of History and the Last Man*. New York: Avon Books, 1992.

Hall, Peter, and David Soskice. *Varieties of Capitalism: The Institutional Foundations of Comparative Advantage*. Oxford: Oxford University Press, 2001.

Horowitz, Donald. *Ethnic Groups in Conflict*. Berkeley: University of California Press, 1985.

Huntington, Samuel. *The Clash of Civilizations and the Remaking of the World Order*. New York: Simon and Schuster, 1996.

———. *The Third Wave: Democratization in the Late Twentieth Century*. Norman, OK: University of Oklahoma University Press, 1991.

Linz, Juan, and Alfred Stepan. *Problems of Democratic Transition and Consolidation*. Baltimore: Johns Hopkins University Press, 1996.

Sbragia, Alberta, ed. *Europolitics: Institutions, and Policymaking in the "New" European Community*. Washington: Brookings Institution, 1992.

Endnotes

1. Mikhail Gorbachev, *Perestroika: New Thinking for Our Country and the World* (New York: Harper and Row, 1987), pp. 190, 197.

2. See Chapter 12; also Leon Lindberg, *The Political Dynamics of European Economic Integration* (Stanford: Stanford University Press, 1963).

3. See Chapter 12; also Alberta Sbragia, *Europolitics: Institutions and Policymaking in the "New" European Community* (Washington: Brookings, 1992); Desmond Dian, *Ever Closer Union? An Introduction to the European Community* (Boulder: Lynne Rienner, 1994).

4. We excluded from our analysis the interesting "microstates" of Andorra, Liechtenstein, Monaco, San Marino, and Vatican City, all of them with populations of less than 50,000 permanent residents.

5. World Bank, *World Development Indicators 2000*; retrieved May 3, 2000 from http://www.worldbank.org/data/wdi2000/pdfs/tab1_4.pdf.

6. Goods generally cost less in agricultural societies than in urbanized, industrial societies; thus the PPP adjustments in Eastern Europe are greater because living costs are lower in these societies. At the same time, agricultural societies are also likely to generate lower living standards, as seen in Table 1.1.

7. Economic growth figures are based on Gross Domestic Product (GDP), which is similar to GNP, but (roughly speaking) excludes income sent home from nonresidents.

8. Moldova is clearly the poorest nation in Eastern Europe, falling into an international "lower income" category. Albania also seems to be substantially less economically developed than the rest of Eastern Europe.

9. Omar G. Encarnacion, "The Politics of Dual Transitions," *Comparative Politics* 28 (July 1996): 477–92.

10. Daniel Lerner, *The Passing of Traditional Society* (New York: Free Press, 1958); Karl Deutsch, "Social Mobilization and Political Development," *American Political Science Review* (September 1961): 493 ff.; Seymour Martin Lipset, "Some Social Requisites of Democracy," *American Political Science Review* (September 1959); James Coleman, "Conclusion: The Political Systems of the Developing Areas" in Almond and Coleman, *The Politics of the Developing Areas* (Princeton, NJ: the Princeton University Press, 1960), pp. 532–77.

11. A "dependency" school of political economy gained substantial headway among American, European, Latin American, African, and Asian intellectuals. The dependency movement argued that the idea of "developmentalism" was a sham that concealed the essential international exploitation by the leading capitalist powers. Dependency theorists saw the global political reality as control of the third world periphery by American and European "multinational" capitalist corporations, backed up by first-world military force, and also by the international capitalists' indigenous henchmen. These theorists believed that the authoritarian regimes instituted in many developing countries in the 1960s and 1970s were intended to enforce this systematic exploitation of "peripheral" economies. The dependency school gradually lost support among social scientists during the 1980s and has generated little scholarly research since then.

12. For a careful review and update of development theory, see Larry Diamond, "Economic Development and Democracy Reconsidered," in G. Marks and L. Diamond, eds., *Reexamining Democracy* (Newbury Park, CA: Sage, 1992); see also Seymour Martin Lipset, "Second Thoughts and Recent Findings," in Lipset, *Political Man*, rev. ed. (Baltimore: Johns Hopkins University Press, 1981).

13. On the theme of the dispersion of potential political resources in modernized societies, see especially Tatu Vanhanen, *Prospects of Democracy: A Study of 172 Countries* (New York: Routledge, 1997) and Robert E. Dahl, *Democracy and Its Critics* (New Haven: Yale University Press, 1989), pp. 251–54. Also, from a different but not unrelated point of view, see the "class" analyses of Dietrich Rueschemeyer, Evelyne Huber Stephens, and John D. Stephens, *Capitalist Development and Democracy* (Chicago: University of Chicago Press, 1992), pp. 75–78 ff. On the connections between modernization, citizen attitudes of trust and participation, and democracy, see especially Gabriel A. Almond and Sidney Verba, *The Civic Culture: Political Attitudes and Democracy in Five Nations* (Princeton: Princeton University Press, 1963) and Ronald Inglehart, and *Christian Welzel, Modernization, Cultural Change and Democracy* (New York: Cambridge University Press, 2005).

14. Freedom House ratings are taken from their website, http://www.freedomhouse.org/research/freeworld/2003/countries.htm, retrieved December 1, 2003. World Bank, Quick Reference Tables, retrieved December 1, 2004 from http://www.worldbank.org/data/databytopic/GNIPC.pdf. Comparative economic data were not available for Serbia and Montenegro (Yugoslavia) so it is not included in the figure.

15. Seymour Martin Lipset and Stein Rokkan, "Cleavage Structures, Party Systems and Voter Alignments: An Introduction," in Lipset and Rokkan, eds., *Party Systems and Voter Alignments* (New York: Free Press, 1967).

16. Max Weber, *Economy and Society: An Outline of Interpretive Sociology*, edited by Guenther Roth and Claus Wittich (Berkeley: University of California Press, 1978), p. 389.

17. Francis Fukuyama, *The End of History and the Last Man* (New York: Avon Books, 1992).

18. Samuel Huntington, *The Clash of Civilizations and the Remaking of the World Order* (New York: Simon and Schuster, 1996).

19. Samuel Huntington, *The Third Wave: Democratization in the Late Twentieth Century* (Norman, OK: University of Oklahoma Press, 1991).

20. Juan Linz and Alfred Stepan, *Problems of Democratic Transition and Consolidation: Southern Europe, South America, and Post-Communist Europe* (Baltimore: Johns Hopkins University Press, 1996).

21. Ibid. For a generally sober account of democratic prospects in the contemporary world, see Larry Diamond, *Is the Third Wave of Democratization Over?* (Baltimore: Johns Hopkins University Press, 1998). For accounts of earlier overthrows of democracies, see Juan Linz and Alfred Stepan, *The Breakdown of Democratic Regimes* (Baltimore: Johns Hopkins University Press, 1978).

22. Larry Diamond, "Thinking about Hybrid Regimes," *Journal of Democracy* 13 (2002): 26. In general see the articles by Diamond; Andreas Schedler; Steven Levitsky and Lucian Way; and Nicholas van de Valle, *Journal of Democracy* 13 (2002): pp. 21–80.

Chapter 2

Democratic Political Culture and Political Action

Virtually all the nations of today's Europe—east and west, north and south—have converged on a single political destiny: They are all democratic or claim to be. This is a radical change from Europe's modern history when world wars and political divisions wracked the continent. Now as the twenty-first century has begun, the nations of Western Europe and the 19 independent European nations carved out of the territories of the former Soviet Union all claim to follow the democratic model.

There is wide variation, however, in the institutions and practice of democracy (see Chapters 3 and 4). For instance, Britain has had organized and competitive political parties for well over a century and a half, while the Bulgarian party system is still developing. West Europeans are more likely to turn out to vote and to be engaged in other electoral activities. Western European nations have complex civil societies where individuals join organizations and participate in social and political affairs. These institutions and behaviors are just beginning to develop in the East.

Beyond institutional structures, political systems also differ because their citizens vary in how they think and act politically. People in the West have a long experience with democratic elections and autonomous social groups to represent their interests. These experiences have nurtured attachments to democratic values and an understanding of how the democratic process functions. Even within Western Europe, moreover, people emphasize different aspects of the democratic model. The French are more likely to engage in protest because of their revolutionary traditions; the British favor more conventional politics. Such variations in political norms shape the nature of a nation's politics.

The question of political norms has special relevance to the study of Eastern Europe. To what extent have democratic values and norms become consolidated in the new democracies of the East? Furthermore, East Europeans may have different expectations about the democratic process and their role within this new political system. What has been the legacy of their communist histories? Democracy requires that its citizens share its fundamental values, and the development of such values in the East remains one of the important questions in the study of European politics.

By examining citizen attitudes and behavior, this chapter should help us understand what democracy expects of its citizens, what citizens expect of their government, and the variations in how Europeans can participate in the political process.

THE CULTURAL FOUNDATIONS OF DEMOCRACY

As the democratization wave swept across Eastern Europe in the early 1990s, the key questions were whether, where, and how it might succeed. The answers not only determined the political fate of the East; they directly affected the peace and stability of Western Europe. Would the political values inherited from the prior communist regimes be congruent with the new democratic institutions they were building? Could the nations of Eastern Europe be successfully integrated into the democratic, capitalist system of the West? These questions repeated those that were posed by the earlier democratic transitions of Spain, Portugal, and Greece in the 1970s, and Germany and Italy in the 1950s.

Eastern Europe has made remarkable democratic progress over the past decade. Despite severe economic problems, struggles with new democratic procedures, and a host of social problems, most of these nations have maintained their democratic course. But beyond the institutional changes, there is a deeper question of whether East Europeans accept democratic principles and their rights and responsibilities under a democratic system. The futures of these new democracies partially depend on the values and beliefs of their citizens. If the people share the values of the political system, then it is more likely that they and the system can function more effectively. If the people reject the values of the system, it can lead to revolts like those that swept across Eastern Europe in the early 1990s,

when one communist regime after another fell in a series of revolutions.

These shared attitudes constitute the *political culture* of a nation.[1] The political culture includes what the people think and feel about politics, attitudes that have evolved from history and traditions. During times of regime change, the agreement between the public's political norms and the institutions and procedures of the new political system is especially important. For example, most scholars believe that the Weimar Republic collapsed in the 1930s because many Germans did not believe in democracy. Prior experiences had taught these Germans to accept authoritarian and ethnocentric values, attitudes that made them susceptible to Hitler's demagogic appeals. Thus post–World War II West Germany again faced the question of whether the new institutions of democracy could succeed if Germans lacked democratic values. Fortunately, military defeat and a postwar economic growth led to a transformation of the West German political culture (see Chapter 7). The Spanish transition to democracy generated similar questions, and fortunately a similarly positive answer (see Chapter 8).

Now we face the same question for Eastern Europe. What are the enduring historical, political, and cultural legacies of the communist regimes of Eastern Europe? Do Poles, Czechs, Russians, and the other nationalities of Eastern European hold political values that support the democratic process? Or, has prior communist rule created undemocratic and authoritarian values that may produce a fragile new political order?

These questions become all the more important as the nations of East Europe join the institutions of the West. The security net of the North Atlantic Treaty Organization now includes 10 nations from Eastern Europe. In addition, in 2004 18 new East European states joined the European Union. Will the incorporation of these new nations transform the institutions of Europe?

Political culture is not only important for predicting the viability of a new political system; it also influences the style of politics within a political system. The style of Italian politics, for example, differs from Dutch politics, although both are democracies with multiparty systems, parliamentary structures, and coalition governments. When Czechoslovakia divided in 1993 into the Czech and Slovak Republics, it was immediately apparent that citizen expectations varied in these two new nations despite their common political heritage. Institutional structures can explain a portion of these cross-national differences, but a substantial part of the explanation depends on how the public and the elites envision the political process.

The Congruence Principle

What does it take to become a democratic polity? The literature on democracy maintains that the political institutions of a nation must be congruent with the political culture of the public. A stable democracy thus requires a democratic social and political culture. Tocqueville, for instance, wrote that democracy should develop as a habit of the heart reflecting basic values and patterns of social relations: "The manners of the people may be considered as one of the great general causes to which the maintenance of a democratic republic in the United States is attributable."[2] The first president of Czechoslovakia, Tomas Masaryk, similarly argued that democracy is not only a form of government, it is not only what is written in constitutions; democracy is a view of life, rests on faith in man, in humanity, and in human nature.

Research on modern democracies shows that tolerance and patterns of cooperative social relationships are the wellsprings of the democratic process.[3] A society such as Norway, with its tolerance and social trust, provides a fertile ground for developing a democratic political culture and a democratic polity.[4] Other research suggests that social trust and cooperative social relations improve one's health, lower crime rates, improve child welfare, lessen social inequality, and generally improve the quality of life—a seeming panacea for societal needs.[5] Authoritarian political systems, such as Nazi Germany or Spain under Franco, often built upon (or fostered) societies in which interpersonal trust and cooperation were absent, and therefore democratic discourse was difficult to maintain.

This congruence theory about the cultural basis of democracy leads to speculation about the potential social base for democracy in Eastern Europe. On the one hand, the collectivism of communism sought to develop feelings of mutual solidarity among the public. Communist systems created parts of a civil society that might serve as a training ground for democratic social norms to develop. Worker collectives addressed employment-related problems, neighborhood collectives handled residential issues, and the state encouraged collective action. On the other hand, communist systems ultimately sustained themselves through force and coercion. The government told the public to be obedient to the state, and security police ensured conformity to the regime's directives. Collective action was allowed, but only under direction of the monopolistic Communist Party and the state. The type of spontaneous and autonomous social life that Tocqueville admired in America could not flourish in the East.

A recent survey illustrates the link between social relations and democratic politics. Researchers asked people in 37 European nations whether they trust their fellow citizens. Figure 2.1 illustrates how the levels of interpersonal trust vary across European nations (and the United States).[6] The nations with continuous democratic histories during this century display relatively high levels of interpersonal trust. In nations that experienced authoritarian disruption in mid-century, such as Germany, Italy, Spain, and Portugal, people are slightly less trustful.

Even a decade after the end of communism, levels of interpersonal trust are generally lower for Eastern Europe and the former states of the Soviet Union (Russia, Belarus, and the Baltic States). Communism did not create a trusting and tolerant citizenry and these patterns have carried over to the present. At the same time, the levels of social trust in Eastern Europe are not markedly different from the situation in the postwar transitional democracies in the West. But theory would suggest that social trust should develop if democracy is to grow deeper roots in these societies.

One may ask whether democracies create a trustful and tolerant society, or whether a trustful society leads to a democratic political system. Obviously, it works both ways. For example, West Germans became more trustful as the nation democratized following World War II. This may have been a

FIGURE 2.1   National Scores on Personal Trust and Democratic History

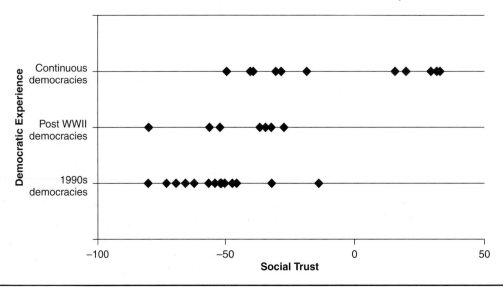

Source: Personal trust from the 1999–2000 European Values Survey and World Values Survey. The figure presents the difference between trustful and distrustful responses.

result of Westerners living in a democratic system as well as democracy encouraging this aspect of the culture. Trend data also suggest that East Germans are becoming more trustful since the democratic transition in 1990. The important conclusion is that there is a congruence between social and political life. It is difficult for democracy to endure when people lack trust and respect for each other. When these values exist, a democratic government must reinforce them; when they are lacking, an aspiring democracy must create them. The hope is that democratization will gradually change these norms among the publics of Eastern Europe.

The political culture begins with social relations, but it develops into more specific political attitudes. These elements of the political culture determine the viability of a democratic political system and the style of politics within the existing institutional structure.

THE LEVELS OF A POLITICAL CULTURE

Beyond social norms, the political culture embodies citizen orientations toward three areas: (1) the political system, (2) the political and policymaking

TABLE 2.1   The Aspects of Political Culture

Aspects of Political Culture	Examples
System	Pride in nation
	National identity
	Legitimacy of government
Process	Role of citizens
	Perceptions of political rights
	Norms of political process
Policy	Role of government
	Governmental policy priorities

process, and (3) policy outputs (Table 2.1). The *system* level involves public orientations toward the political community and the values and organizations that comprise the political system. Does the public identify with the nation and generally accept the political system?

The *process* level taps expectations of how politics should function and individuals' relationship to the political process. For instance, public attitudes toward the procedures of government and political institutions, such as the principles of pluralist democracy and support for parliamentary government, are important in defining how politics actually functions.

The *policy* level deals with what citizens expect from the government. What are the government's policy goals and how are they to be achieved?

The System Level

Attitudes toward the nation and the political system are an important component of a political culture. These sentiments are often acquired early in life, taught by parents and the educational system. Therefore, these are fairly stable beliefs that are relatively independent of attitudes on more specific political matters.

Public acceptance of the legitimacy of the political system provides a foundation for a successful, or at least enduring, polity. When citizens believe that they ought to obey the laws, then legitimacy is high. If they question the authority of the state, or if they comply only from fear, then legitimacy is low. A new political system often faces a challenge in convincing the people that the new government is legitimate, and thus its directives should be followed voluntarily.

A strong emotional tie to the nation also can provide a basis of support that reinforces acceptance of the polity and can maintain a political system through temporary periods of political stress. The deep sense of national pride and national destiny voiced by Winston Churchill during World War II struck a responsive chord with the British public, thus enabling Britain to endure in the midst of an intense military conflict. In contrast, most Germans did not identify with the democratic institutions of the Weimar Republic; and thus when they faced political and economic crisis, they shifted their loyalties to a new system.

A similar question now faces many of the nations of Eastern Europe. Some nations, such as Poland, have a strong national identity, but many others are relatively new political constructs that lack public identifications. Virtually all East European nations have new constitutions written during

FIGURE 2.2   Feelings of National Pride (percent "Very Proud" and "Proud")

West		East
Ireland United States	100	Poland
Denmark		Albania
Austria Britain/France/Spain Norway/Greece Sweden	90	Hungary Romania
Netherlands	80	Czech Republic
Germany	70	Russia Bosnia/Bugaria
	60	Ukraine Montenegro

Source: Selected nations from the 1999–2001 European Values Survey and World Values Survey. Figure presents the percent "very proud" and "proud"; missing data is not included in the calculation of percentages.

the 1990s, and most have existed as independent nations for barely a decade. There has also been considerable tumult and political debate in many Western European states in recent years. Thus, we might ask whether European publics—in West and East—have a strong sense of national identity.

Feelings of pride in one's nation are a revealing example of this aspect of the political culture, as shown in Figure 2.2. At the end of the 1990s, the worst upheavals of the political transition were past in most of Eastern Europe, and enduring national traits are more apparent. Most nations enjoy wide-spread feelings of pride among their citizens. Americans are noted for their expressions of national pride, but the Poles, the Irish, and other nationalities around the world, display equal enthusiasm. Strong feelings about the nation exist in both Western and Eastern Europe—the Danes express as much pride as the Albanians, for example. National pride is not a function of the longevity or past political form of the nation.

More problematic are the cases where the populace does not identify with the nation; this raises warning signals for the political system. For example, national pride was relatively low in Czechoslovakia in a 1990 survey—within three years, the nation had split in two. German political leaders have consciously avoided the nationalism of the past, and it shows. National pride is also relatively restrained in several Eastern nations that have struggled throughout the 1990s: Russia, Bulgaria, and the Ukraine. And in two regions trying to develop a national identity—Bosnia and Montenegro—these orientations are still in short supply.

Most Europeans, however, express pride in their nation virtually regardless of its historical traditions or national status. Like pride in a sports team, true fans are supportive regardless of what occurs on the field.

The Process Level

The second level of the political culture involves what the public expects of the political process. What do Hungarians think is expected of them as citizens, and what do they expect of their government? Are their views different from those of British or Spanish citizens?

Political theorists generally stress three norms as the basis of the Western democratic process. The first is the Lockean emphasis on popular sovereignty as the basis of governmental authority and the final arbiter of politics. Democracy must, above all, be based on the rule of the people. The second is a commitment to the equality of citizens based on the arguments of Jefferson, Bentham, and Paine. The third is the principle of majoritarian decision

making, with adequate protection of minority rights. These principles lead to specific procedures by which democratic processes are ensured, such as formulated in Robert Dahl's "conditions of polyarchy."[7] In short, the congruence principle also holds that democracies can survive only when the public endorses the values of a democratic regime.

Research on West European countries generally finds broad public support for *democratic values*.[8] Citizens and elites accept the principle of organizing political institutions based on popular control through regular elections, as well as party competition and the turnover of leadership through elections. Most Western Europeans recognize the legitimacy of conflict over political means and ends, while opposing violence as a political tool. Europeans also broadly endorse the right of individual participation and majority rule, paired with the protection of minority rights.

At the same time, we cannot become complacent about public support for democracy in the West. Often there is a gap between public support for these democratic principles and their application in specific cases. Many people say they support free speech, but they are less willing to actually grant this right to groups that challenge their values. Still, most citizens in the established democracies of the West accept the principles upon which their democratic system was founded and functions today.

Prior European transitions from authoritarianism to democracy show how a previous authoritarian state could leave a negative cultural heritage. Postwar Italy began with a cultural legacy of fascist attitudes that was not conducive to the workings of democracy. But the Italian culture was transformed and democratic values became the norm.[9] The postwar Germans held broadly undemocratic views, and the remaking of the political culture over the next generation was quite remarkable. Postwar Austria struggled to overcome a similar cultural inheritance from Fascism. The more recent democratic transitions in Spain and Portugal reflected this same pattern. The Francoist regime was an antidemocratic movement based on authoritarian norms. With Franco's failing health and Spain's efforts to integrate itself into Western Europe, the Spanish process of cultural transformation created a new political

Box 2.1   A Persistent Political Culture

Although Britain follows democratic procedures, it remains a constitutional monarchy and its traditions underscore the importance attached to the Crown. For example, the Queen of England presides over the opening of the new Parliament following the general elections. The Lords and Ladies assemble in the House of Lords, along with the Bishops of the Church, foreign ambassadors, members of the royal family, and other dignitaries. When the Queen arrives from the palace, the members of the House of Commons are summoned by Blackrod following a centuries old tradition. When both houses of parliament are assembled, the Queen delivers an address outlining the policies of "her" government during the next legislative session.

(The opening of Parliament, as well as weekly Question Hour in the House of Commons, are broadcast on C-SPAN by many U.S. cable television systems.)

culture that was more conducive to democracy (see Chapter 8).

In short, in several Western European nations the antidemocratic values of a prior right-wing authoritarian state created hostility toward pluralism and democratic procedures among the citizenry. The subsequent democratic regime inherited a public that was critical of its institutions and unsupportive of its norms. The new regime had to remold citizen beliefs into a culture compatible with democratic processes.

Communism raises a similar question of the cultural legacy of Eastern Europe. In the early 1990s, it was difficult to know whether these nations would face the same cultural problems as the previous authoritarian/democratic transitions in Western Europe. Democracy illustrated the internal contradictions of the communist system. Although the Soviet Union and other Eastern European states suppressed dissent and prohibited meaningful forms of representative democracy, the official rhetoric of these regimes often endorsed democratic principles. Elections were regularly held, and turnout routinely topped 90 percent of the eligible electorate. Many of these governments also mobilized people into an array of political organizations, ranging from labor unions to women's federations and state-sanctioned environmental groups. While some communist regimes were openly authoritarian, others displayed examples of a nascent form of democracy. Gorbachev's reforms of *perestroika* and *glasnost* built upon these tendencies, and some reform movements existed within Eastern Europe.[10]

Almost as soon as the Berlin Wall fell, survey researchers moved eastward, quickly assembling a wealth of findings on the attitudes of Russians and East Europeans toward democratic institutions and procedures. Researchers found surprisingly high levels of support for basic democratic principles in the former Soviet Union and other East European nations.[11] Figure 2.3 compares the opinions of Westerners and Easterners on two examples of democratic values: willingness to allow a revolutionary to publish a book and belief that elections make government responsive. Almost two-thirds of Western Europeans would allow even a revolutionary the opportunity to publish a book, and East Europeans average only a few percentage points lower. Similarly, most Westerners believe that elections make government pay attention to the people, and these opinions are only slightly lower in the East. Indeed, since the earliest surveys after the collapse of communism, East Europeans have displayed surprising support for democratic values. One should also note that democratic sentiments are among the lowest in Russia. This reflects the economic and social tumult that accompanied the transition toward democracy in Russia, as well as the deeper impact of a long authoritarian experience.

The support for democratic principles in Eastern Europe is somewhat surprising given the attempts of the prior regimes to instill communist values among the citizenry. To many Eastern Europeans, however, these democratic rights represent a new reality for which they had fought the old regime. The Solidarity demonstrations in Poland,

FIGURE 2.3 Democratic Values in Western and Eastern Europe, 1996

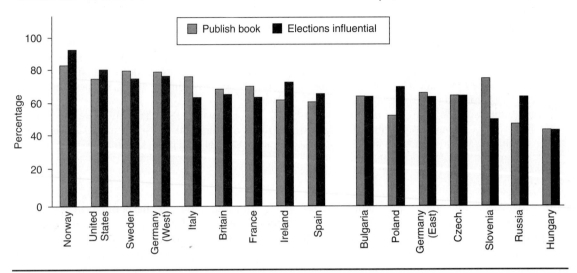

Note: Percentages indicate agreement with the statements "revolutionaries should be allowed to publish books expressing their views" and "elections are a good way of making governments pay attention to the important political issues facing our country." Missing data are excluded from the calculations of percentages.

Source: International Social Survey Program, 1996.

the protests in central Prague, the candlelight marches in Leipzig, and the public response to the August 1991 Russian coup demonstrate this commitment. Having newly won these freedoms, Eastern Europeans openly endorse them.

After half a century or more of communism, how did these publics come to express such support for democratic norms? There is no single answer, and researchers point to several factors. The limited empirical evidence suggests that support for the prior communist system eroded sharply during the 1980s. Eastern Europeans saw their living standards decline during the decade, and the government seemed unwilling or unable to respond. This eroded popular support for the communist system and its values. And, ironically, the old regimes had voiced support for democratic principles, even if the reality of the communist system was much different. These democratic sentiments were further encouraged by *perestroika* and *glasnost* reforms—albeit with different consequences than Gorbachev had

envisioned. The positive model of the West also appealed to many Easterners, as seen in the mass exodus from East Germany in 1989. Furthermore, the euphoria of the democratization wave in 1989–1991 undoubtedly boosted support for the new political creed. Even with these explanations, the broad support for democratic principles in Eastern Europe is still a surprising starting point for these democratic transitions.

Although democratic principles appear fairly similar in East and West, more striking differences often appear in how people evaluate the actual functioning of democracy in their nation. In some Eastern European nations there is a widening gap between the public's support for democratic principles and their views of the present political process. For instance, a recent poll found that three-fifths of the public in 10 Eastern European nations was dissatisfied with the way that democracy works in their nation.[12] People are frustrated by the inability of the new political institutions to deal with the economic and social problems existing in Eastern Europe, which may eventually carry over to public support for the democratic process itself.[13] Furthermore, events such as the Bosnian and Kosovo conflicts, the rise of an authoritarian government in Belarus, and the increasingly autocratic government in Russia constantly remind us that the prospects for democracy remain uncertain in many Eastern European states.

In the end, we should be cautious in reaching conclusions from Eastern European public opinion surveys as democracy is still developing in these nations. It is difficult to evaluate the depth of Easterners' feelings about democracy, whether these are enduring cultural norms or the temporary response to traumatic political events. Still, even if public expressions of democratic values cannot yet be described as an enduring political culture, the widespread expression of such values is a positive signal for democratic prospects in the East. The people in most post-communist states espouse strong support for democratic principles, which facilitates the democratization process. As two of the nations in this volume demonstrate, Poland and Hungary have made impressive progress in developing competitive elections, ensuring the rule of law, and protecting democratic liberties. Democratic development in Russia is less certain. Most Russians value democracy and freedom—although a significant minority still longs for a less democratic state. Rather than the apathy or hostility that greeted democracy after transitions from right-wing authoritarian states in Western Europe, the cultural legacy of communism in Eastern Europe appears to be more supportive of democratization.

By comparison, most Western Europeans broadly endorse democratic values and principles. However, dissatisfaction with the incumbents of office and the current governing parties is growing in the West.[14] For instance, the French political system recently has experienced a series of political scandals reaching up to the highest political officials. Criticisms of the political parties have become commonplace in many Western party systems, and public identification with political parties has generally eroded. Up to this point, the dissatisfaction with the holders of democratic office has not generalized into disaffection with the democratic process. Indeed, the goal of democratic politics is to give the public an institutionalized way to express their dissatisfaction by electing new public officials and changing the policies of government.

The Policy Expectations Level

A third level of the political culture is the public's expectations of what government should achieve. In part, these expectations involve specific policy demands. When Soviet mineworkers protest the government's privatization programs or British farmers lobby the European Union on agricultural policy, they are testing the democratic process. More broadly, public views about policy—the legitimate scope of government, the needs and wants that government should address, and the areas that should remain in the private sphere—define the parameters for government action.

The history of Western democracies records great conflict over just these questions. Industrialization raised issues about the government's role in providing the infrastructure for modern commerce. The labor and social democratic movements of the nineteenth century focused debate on the government's rightful role in the provision of basic social services and the management of the economy. The urbanization process created new demands on municipal governments, and new questions of urban development and redevelopment. More recently, the environmental movement is demanding that governments address the environmental costs of economic activity and ensure environmental quality. Other social interests press the government to be active in everything from training rock bands to preserving the nation's historic sites.

Indeed, nearly all Western European democracies have seen government activity grow during the latter half of the twentieth century (see Chapter 1). The various branches of government in the United States spend roughly a third of the GNP, but many European governments account for half (or more!) of the GNP. Governments are now responsible for a variety of social and personal conditions that were once outside the domain of government activity. Analysts attribute at least a portion of this growth to the expanding public expectations.[15] People demand more of their government and they are promised more by politicians; thus government has expanded to meet these expectations. As Anthony King has written: "Once upon a time, man looked to God to order the world. Then he looked to the market. Now he looks to government."[16]

These public expectations have several important implications for contemporary European politics. Although most Westerners expect more of their government, there are still sharp cross-national and domestic differences in exactly what is expected. Labor unions want government to expand the benefits given to workers; businesses want government to provide tax incentives and subsidies to spur economic growth. Environmentalists want the government to spend more on protecting the environment; commuters want the government to build more roads and expand public transportation. The essence of democratic politics is to find the balance between these competing interests.

As Western European governments grew over the past generation, some people began to complain against high taxation and the excess of government action. Some political analysts claim that excessive policy demands overload contemporary governments.[17] They argue that people are demanding more than what democratic government can provide in an effective and efficient way. Others maintain that government is usurping individual freedom and private initiative. Public opinion surveys show a renewed skepticism of government action as many Europeans began to question the government's appropriate role in society. Margaret Thatcher championed a neoconservative campaign in Britain in the 1980s that scaled back government by privatizing government-owned businesses and reducing the government's policy responsibilities. Conservative governments in the Netherlands, Scandinavia, Germany, and the United States have echoed these statements. Thus, in many Western European societies the debate about the appropriate role of government is continuing.

GOVERNMENT AND THE ECONOMY Just as Western Europeans began questioning the appropriate role of government in the 1980s, the political changes in Eastern Europe and the Soviet Union added a new theme to this discussion. State corporations and government agencies almost exclusively controlled the command economies of Eastern Europe. The government set both wages and prices as well as directing the economy. It was also responsible for providing for individual needs, ranging from guaranteed employment to the provision of housing and health care. "Cradle to grave socialism" was more than just a slogan in Eastern Europe.

The collapse of these systems created new questions. The lack of popular support for the communist political system weakened support for the socialist economic system. This clearly occurred in Eastern Europe, as non-communist governments and their citizens rushed to privatize their economies. This partially reflected the economic failures of the old regime. The Eastern European economies could provide the basic needs of their citizens, but they were uncompetitive in the world market and fell steadily behind the economic progress of the West. Thus, the democratization of Eastern European political systems was paralleled by a privatization of their economies.

To what extent do Eastern Europeans carry forward their expectations for government activities from the experiences of the prior regimes? Similarly, do Germans in the West and East have similar expectations about what services government should provide, or has unification created a public with sharply contrasting views of the government's appropriate role? The collapse of communism does not necessarily mean that Eastern Europeans reject the socialist principles of their former systems—principles that could often conflict with their new market economies.

We can describe the present policy norms of Europeans by comparing opinions in several areas. At the heart of the debate on the government's role is the question of government management of the economy. This separates both conservatives and liberals in the West, as well as forms a potential East-West divide. Comparative research shows that levels of economic development are one influence on these opinions; the citizens of less-affluent nations are generally more in favor of government action as a strategy for economic development.[18] In addition, we want to compare the nations with established market economies in the West with the new market economies in Eastern Europe.

Figure 2.4 shows how various groups of nations differ in their support for government control of wages and prices as examples of government management of the economy. The more-affluent countries of Northern Europe (for example, Germany, France, Britain, Sweden, and Denmark) are less likely to favor government management of the economy. Resistance to government management has grown over the past few decades, paralleling the privatization of government-owned businesses and the sell-off of government monopolies. The less-affluent nations of Western Europe (Ireland, Spain, and Italy) are more supportive of government management of the economy.

Equally interesting are the results for Eastern Europe. The dismantling of the socialist economies in the East was accompanied by popular endorse-

ment of a greater role for a market economy. But East Europeans still favor a greater role for government in the economy, especially in Russia. A full 90 percent of the Russian public feel the government should control prices—partially a reaction to the runaway inflation that plagued Russia in the 1990s—and 68 percent of Russians also believe the government should control wages. More generally, Russians remain relatively supportive of a socialist economy because the experience with capitalism has fallen far short of the experience in the West.[19]

It is illuminating to compare support for a government managed economy in the various social strata in Eastern Europe. The better-educated are the "carriers of the creed" in most societies.[20] These are the individuals who normally occupy positions of status and influence; they are the operators of the existing economic and political systems. In addition, accepting the regime norms was often required to gain access to higher education. One could not

FIGURE 2.4   Support for Government Management of the Economy

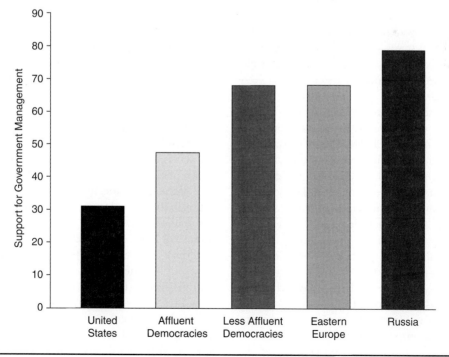

Source: International Social Survey Program, 1996. The figure averages support for government control of wages and control of prices.

attend the university without being a member in the correct communist youth groups, or without a good family record of regime support. Thus we would expect the better educated to espouse the values of the communist and socialist systems of pre-1989. In fact, just the opposite occurs. When the old regimes were just ending in the early 1990s, the better-educated Eastern Europeans showed little affection for socialism.[21] Instead of adhering to the values of the old regime, as is normally the case, the better educated advocated a privatized economy. In some ways this is not surprising; the intelligentsia of the communist society led the protests in East Berlin or Prague, and the faces of young university students were prominent in these crowds. Perhaps communism fell as rapidly as it did because it had lost the support of the managers and technicians of the old regime.

The communist regimes were better able to socialize the less educated into believing in government management of the economy. This pattern holds in most of the nations in Eastern Europe. Think of the irony: these regimes claimed to represent workers and peasants, and the less educated actually adhered to these socialist principles. The true beneficiaries of these regimes—the better educated and upper social status—doubted their value. Possibly the better educated were more aware of the superior productivity of the market systems of the West.

In contrast to the generally steady political progress that has been made over the past decade, Eastern Europeans have had a tumultuous economic experience (see Chapter 1). Living standards declined precipitously in many nations after the collapse of communism, and the economic shocks of capitalist market forces were unsettling to many. Yet, support for market principles still exists. A 1996 survey by the European Union found that market reforms received majority support among Eastern Europeans, although 65 percent of Russians said it was wrong for their nation.[22]

The 1998 *New Democracies Barometer* clearly illustrates the juxtaposition of economic and political images.[23] The survey asked residents in Central and Eastern Europe to judge the past, present, and future economic and political systems. Figure 2.5 shows that most Eastern Europeans, even in 1998,

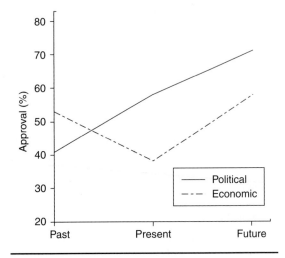

FIGURE 2.5   Public Approval of the Economic and Political Systems in Central and Eastern Europe, 1998

Source: Richard Rose and Christian Haerfer, *New Democracies Barometer V* (Strathclyde: Center for the Study of Public Policy, 1998): 17, 25; combined results from representative surveys in Bulgaria, the Czech Republic, Hungary, Poland, Romania, Slovakia, and Slovenia.

expressed greater approval for the pre-1989 socialist economy than for the contemporary economic system. Russian images show an even greater contrast: in 1996, 83 percent of Russians approved of the former economic system, versus only 18 percent for the present system.[24] This is a clear signal of the disaffection that has resulted from the drop in living standards and the economic insecurities that have accompanied the restructuring of these economies.

At the same time, there are several positive indicators in these opinion surveys. Approval of the present economic system has improved between 1991 and 1998. Furthermore, Eastern Europeans remain optimistic that the economic system in five years time will be much better. In addition, there is a significant juxtaposition of economic and political images. The citizens of Eastern Europe are more positive about their present political system than the pre-1989 system, and these impressions have improved since 1991. Political expectations for the future are optimistic, although most Eastern Europeans expect that it will require several more years to deal with the problems inherited from the communists.

The Government's Policy Responsibilities

Government management of the economy is one of the state's most basic policy activities. Governments are also involved in a great many other areas, from deterring crime to protecting the quality of the environment. Recent public opinion surveys show that many people believe the government is responsible for promoting individual well-being and guaranteeing the quality of life for its citizens—and both Westerners and Easterners share these expectations.

Table 2.2 displays the percentage of the public in several European nations (and the United States) who think the government is "definitely responsible" for dealing with specific social problems. East Europeans, who were conditioned by their former regimes to expect big government, have high expectations of their democratic governments. Most citizens in East Germany, Hungary, Poland, and Russia believe the government is definitely responsible for providing for health care, providing a decent standard of living for the elderly, protecting the environment, and lessening unemployment. Expectations of the state are especially high among Russians.

Many West Europeans share these high expectations of government. Thus support for government action to resolve social needs is a core element of the European political culture, even if there are significant cross-national differences in exactly what is expected.

In comparison to most Europeans, Americans are more reserved in accepting government action. Even in areas where the government is a primary actor, such as care of the elderly and unemployment, only a minority of Americans view these problems as definite government responsibilities. Analysts often explain the conservative socioeconomic attitudes of Americans by the individualist nature of American political culture and the absence of a socialist working-class party.

The public sentiments may partially explain why the scope of government has grown so large in Europe over the past generation. Other scholars claim that these opinions result from the growth of government activism, which conditions the public

to expect even more from government.[25] In either case, these expectations are another example of how political culture and political outcomes tend to converge. Governments can grow more easily when the public accepts (and expects) that they will grow. Governments are more likely to shrink when public support for government activism wanes. Thus it is more than a coincidence that the expansion of the welfare state in Scandinavian countries coincided with broad public support for social programs, while Margaret Thatcher's program of privatizing government-owned industries in Britain coincided with decreasing public support for nationalized industry.

Debates about the proper role of government will be a continuing feature of contemporary politics. However, it is clear that most Europeans expect their government to protect social welfare, help the economy, and guarantee the quality of life. The question is not whether government should act, but how it should manage the diverse demands the public makes upon it.

PARTICIPATION AND DEMOCRACY

Democracy empowers its citizens to affect the course of government and to influence policy. The history of modern democracies, however, is marked by the slow and often conflictual expansion of the public's participation in politics. The growth of democracy can be measured by the public's broadening access to politics and the government's responsiveness to public demands.

Modern democracy is *representative democracy*. It enshrines elections as the main institution of democracy and the primary vehicle for public participation and democratic governance. Through elections, the public controls the selection of political leaders, which determines the formation of government and the policies the government will likely implement.

Although *election turnout* is now a standard part of democratic participation, the expansion of the franchise in Europe occurred only during the past century. At the start of the twentieth century most European democracies severely restricted the franchise. Britain, for instance, limited election rolls

TABLE 2.2 Government Responsibility for Dealing with Social Issues (in %)

	United States	Britain	France	Spain	Italy	Sweden	Norway	West Germany	East Germany	Hungary	Poland	Russia
Provide health care for sick	39	82	53	81	81	71	87	51	66	71	69	82
Provide decent living standard for the elderly	38	73	51	80	76	69	86	48	64	63	68	87
Strict environmental laws	46	63	67	69	69	58	56	58	72	56	60	71
Give aid to needy college students	35	38	59	75	59	36	34	27	43	37	48	63
Keep prices under control	25	44	42	59	59	45	53	23	43	38	41	68
Provide job for everyone who wants one	14	29	40	61	41	35	48	28	57	47	58	71
Reduce income differences between rich and poor	17	36	49	57	41	43	41	25	48	41	48	49
Provide housing for those who need it	20	37	44	70	45	27	22	20	38	22	39	52
Provide a decent living standard for the unemployed	13	29	34	59	30	39	41	17	38	16	31	39
Provide industry with help	17	41	36	64	28	33	23	16	27	35	39	51
Average	26	47	48	68	53	46	49	31	50	43	50	63

Source: *1996 International Social Survey Program.* Table entries are the percentage who say that each area should definitely be the government's responsibility. Missing data were excluded in the calculation of percentages.

through residency and financial restrictions, and by allowing multiple votes for business owners and university graduates. In 1900 only 14 percent of the British adult population was eligible to vote. Similarly, Prussia used a weighted voting rule that gave a triple vote to the landed aristocracy and a single vote to laborers. Almost without exception, governments denied women the right to vote.

During the twentieth century, governments gradually extended suffrage rights to the adult population. Property restrictions were steadily rolled back. Most nations acknowledged the right of women to vote early in the century, but some countries delayed—most notably France until 1944 and Switzerland until 1970. During the 1970s, most nations also reduced the minimum voting age to 18. By the later half of this century, voting rights were essentially universal among the adult populations in Western Europe.

Even though the communist parties of Eastern Europe did not permit open competition, these nations also held regular elections, sometimes with multiple parties or a unified slate of candidates. Voting turnout routinely exceeded 90 percent of the eligible electorate; the last Soviet-era election of 1984 had an official turnout rate of 99.9 percent. Elections were not a method of popular influence, however; they were a means for the government to mobilize and indoctrinate the populace. Nonvoting signified opposition to the regime, which might jeopardize the nonvoter (and local officials who were responsible for ensuring a large turnout). Thus voting levels were consistently high even if some ballots had to be cast by election officials themselves. Nevertheless, elections were held and the public learned the mechanics of campaigns and the voting process.

Today, most eligible Europeans vote in national elections. Moreover, voting is a significant method of citizen influence because it selects political elites and determines the composition of the government. Elections also provide an opportunity for political activists to participate in the selection of party candidates and to try to influence the political views of others. In some countries as many as a tenth to a fifth of the electorate attend a campaign meeting, work for a party, or participate in other campaign activities. Elections are national civics lessons in which voters learn about the past and future programs of the parties, participate in the democratic process, and decide about the issues facing their nation.

Figure 2.6 displays the distribution of election turnout in Western and Eastern Europe in the most recent national election for which data are available. What is most striking is the large range in voting turnout across these nations. The lowest level of

FIGURE 2.6   Levels of Election Turnout in Western and Eastern Europe

West Europe		East Europe
Belgium	100	
Cyprus		
	90	
Denmark		
Luxembourg		
Italy/Austria		
Sweden/Netherlands	80	
Germany		
		Croatia
Greece/Norway		Hungary/Macedonia
		Latvia/Ukraine
	70	Slovakia/Slovenia
		Georgia
Spain		
Finland		Bulgaria
Ireland/Portugal		Romania
France	60	Russia/Belarus
Britain		Estonia/Lithuania
		Czech Republic
	50	
Switzerland		Poland

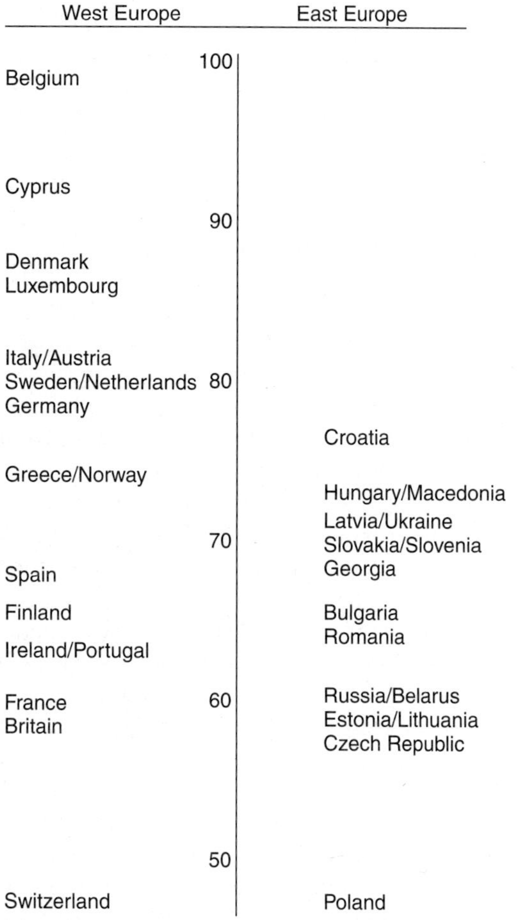

Source: Institute for Democracy and Electoral Systems (www.idea.int).
Figure plots percentage of registered voters who cast a ballot.
* Voting is compulsory in Belgium.

involvement is in a well-established democracy, Switzerland, where less than half of the eligible electorate (43 percent) actually voted in 1999. Voting rates are consistently higher in most other European nations; in two nations where voting is still compulsory, turnout tops 90 percent (Belgium and Cyprus). Turnout rates in Eastern Europe were often quite high in the first elections after the democratic transition. Now turnout in the East is a bit lower than the average levels of the established democracies in the West.

Cross-national research has identified a range of factors that affect levels of voting turnout.[26] Analysts find that laws and institutions, such as the type of electoral system or registration regulations, directly affect participation rates. In addition, political competition and the structure of party choices strongly influence turnout levels. For example, turnout in American elections is significantly below the norm for European democracies, and this can largely be explained by such uniquely American characteristics as complicated registration requirements and the frequency of elections.[27]

Voting is the most common form of political action and the basis of representative democracy. Thus it is somewhat worrisome that electoral participation has gradually declined in most of Western Europe over the last few decades.[28] Furthermore, participation in campaign activities beyond voting is also declining. Fewer citizens, even in established democracies, attend a campaign rally or display their partisan support during a campaign. Similarly, high turnout levels in the first democratic elections in Eastern Europe often were followed by a drop-off in later elections. If elections are the celebration of democratic politics, fewer individuals seem to be joining in these celebrations.

The decrease of electoral participation is even more surprising when compared with the socioeconomic development of Europe described in the previous chapter. Contemporary electorates are better educated, better informed, and more interested in politics than their predecessors. Europeans are also more democratic in their values than was the public a generation ago. Nevertheless, electoral participation has decreased. Richard Brody refers to this as "the puzzle of political participation."[29] Why is elec-

toral participation limited and decreasing, if the public's political skills and resources are increasing?

At the core of this question is a concern with the vitality of the democratic process. This view holds that higher levels of voting turnout are a positive feature for democracy. In general this is correct; democratic nations with high levels of turnout in elections are more successful in involving their citizens in the political process. Consequently, the decrease in turnout is often attributed to growing alienation from politics or a more general decline in civic life.[30]

Another explanation for reduced levels of electoral participation is the development of a new style of *participatory democracy* among Western European publics. Instead of indirect influence through elected officials, a growing share of the public now tries to influence politics directly. People seem more interested in contacting politicians or in participating in direct-action methods. Citizen-action groups and public interest groups are pressing for greater citizen input in policy formation and administration.[31]

The situation, of course, is different in Eastern Europe. These prior communist regimes involved the public in mass membership groups and state-sponsored political organizations.[32] In East Germany, for example, there were millions of members in the labor unions, the women's federation, and the German-Soviet Friendship Society. These were so-called "*civil society*" groups, except they were not autonomous and were controlled by the Communist Party and state agencies.

This situation changed with the democratic revolutions of the 1990s. The political demonstrations of Solidarity, the mass protests in Leipzig and East Berlin, and the public demonstrations in the streets of Prague toppled communist regimes across Eastern Europe. These were "people power" revolutions where public pressures brought down the old regimes and created democracies in their place. The Eastern Europeans very quickly became involved in democratic politics.

The extent of participatory democracy among Europeans can be estimated by the public's involvement in various non-electoral forms of participation. As Table 2.3 shows, many Europeans have signed a petition within the previous year, a mild form of participatory democracy. One can hardly

TABLE 2.3   Cross-National Levels of Non-Electoral Participation (in %)

Nation	Signed Petition	Lawful Demonstration	Contact Official	Boycott Product
Britain	40	4	18	26
Denmark	28	8	18	23
Germany	31	11	13	25
Finland	24	2	24	27
Greece	5	4	15	9
Ireland	27	7	22	13
Italy	19	11	12	8
Luxembourg	27	20	18	15
Netherlands	23	3	14	11
Norway	37	9	24	20
Portugal	7	4	11	3
Spain	22	16	12	23
Sweden	41	6	17	33
Switzerland	40	8	17	34
West Europe Average	**27**	**8**	**17**	**18**
Czech Republic	15	4	21	11
Hungary	4	4	15	5
Poland	7	1	10	4
Slovenia	12	3	12	5
East Europe Average	**10**	**3**	**15**	**6**

Source: 2002 *European Social Survey*. Respondents engaged in the activity during the previous 12 months.

enter a Marks & Spencer in Britain or a Kaufhof in Germany without being asked to sign a petition. For some people, this form of direct action is more common than voting in elections. Signing petitions is less common among Eastern Europeans, especially in the successor states of the Soviet Union (Russia, Ukraine, and Belarus).

Political protest is an even stronger measure of direct political action. The second column in Table 2.3 shows that participation in a demonstration is fairly common. Such unconventional action now often matches or exceeds normal involvement in campaign activities among Western Europeans.[33] Many West European publics are as likely to engage in protest activities as they are to participate in an election campaign beyond voting. Protest is now the extension of conventional politics used by the full range of societal interests (see Box 2.2). The level of protest activity is generally lower across Eastern Europe, and in most all of these nations

protest has declined as the tumultuous events of 1990–1991 have passed into history.

The third column of the table lists the percentage of the public who have directly contacted a politician or government official in the previous year. To an increasing degree, citizens are willing to be advocates for their own interests. And the expanded role of government more often brings them into contact with government. Again, participation levels are highest in the affluent advanced industrial democracies of Northern Europe, with lower participation levels in the South and East.

Perhaps the most interesting set of statistics come from the rightmost column in the table. This displays the percentage of people who say they have boycotted a product for a political or ethical reason. This form of economic participation is surprisingly common, especially in the established market economies of the West. Another question from the survey (not shown) indicates that Euro-

Box 2.2   Protest in Action

Coal miners in several Eastern European nations had been active in organizing protests against the communist regimes during the democratic transitions, and have become one of the more assertive participants under the new democratic system. In Russia, for example, miners organized a series of strikes in the mid-1990s to protest their unpaid back wages and government plans to close down several mines. The unions claimed that up to a fourth of their members went without a paycheck each week. In the spring of 1998, Siberian coal miners went on strike and blockaded the Trans-Siberian railway for more than a week. There were sporadic actions of violence, and some spouses went on a hunger strike. Hundreds of union members set up a camp outside of Moscow for the summer to continue their protests. The government eventually persuaded the miners to return to work by taking emergency measures to pay off wage arrears and promising to investigate the reasons that wages were chronically going unpaid. Coal miners had been the first group of workers to mobilize independently under the Soviet regime when they launched a massive strike under Gorbachev in 1989, and they continue to demonstrate their political influence in the post-communist period.

peans are even more likely to say they bought certain products for political or ethical reasons.

Thus, European political participation has changed in two significant ways over the last two decades. First, the public's involvement and interest in political matters is now widespread. Many Europeans turn out at the polls, others work on political campaigns, many individuals contact their representative directly, many people belong to local community organizations, and large numbers are members of public interest groups.[34] Therefore some analysts describe the last two decades as a *participatory revolution*, during which public involvement in the democratic process grew. Now, the expansion of democracy to Eastern Europe gives additional meaning to this term—although participation levels are generally lower in the East.

Second, the patterns of political participation have changed in qualitative terms. The methods of representative democracy—voting and campaign work—are important activities because they determine the control of government. However, these are relatively blunt democratic tools since the typical election involves many issues and candidates. And participation in elections and campaigns have decreased.

Participatory democracy produces a qualitatively different form of citizen input. Involvement in a citizen action group or direct contact with policymakers allows people to focus attention on a specific policy concern. The voice of the public is also louder when the citizens express their views themselves. Direct action gives citizens greater control over the timing and methods of participation, compared with the institutionalized framework of elections. Therefore the growing use of citizen-initiated participation increases popular control of political elites.

These developments may permanently change the style of political participation in advanced industrial democracies. *New social movements* have created an infrastructure for continued citizen involvement in the policy process. For instance, in Germany administrative law now gives the public more say in policy administration; in Italy new legislation gives the public legal standing in defending the environment in court, and the use of initiatives and referendums is generally increasing. Citizen groups such as these have legitimated direct-action methods of participation for other citizen groups. Today, Gray Panthers protest for senior citizen rights, consumers are active monitors of industry, and citizen groups of all kinds are proliferating.

Research finds that different kinds of people engage in these various forms of participation.[35] Because voting places the least demands upon its participants, it is the most common form of political action and involves a diverse mix of people. By comparison, direct-action methods require greater personal initiative and more sophisticated political skills. It is much more demanding to organize a letter-writing campaign or participate in a public interest group than to cast a ballot at the next election. Consequently, participation in direct forms of action often varies considerably by social status. While voting is spread across the electorate, direct action is now disproportionately used by the affluent and better educated. Similarly, only those with strong political beliefs are likely to become active in single-issue groups. This situation increases the participation gap between lower-status and higher-status individuals. As the better educated expand their political influence through direct-action methods, less-educated citizens might be unable to compete on the same terms. Ironically, overall increases in political involvement may mask growing inequalities in citizen participation and influence, which run counter to democratic ideals.

The strength of the democratic process is its ability to adapt, evolve, and become more democratic. In recent years the political systems in most Western European states have adopted forms of participatory democracy and given their citizenry new methods to participate in the decisions affecting their lives. The nations of Western Europe vary in their emphasis on representative and participatory democracy, but nearly all are now characterized by a mix of these styles.

As they are learning about democracy, many Eastern Europeans have ambivalent feelings toward both of these styles of democratic participation. They recognize elections and representative democracy as essential elements of the modern democratic process. At the same time, many Easterners are disillusioned by the competitive style of electoral politics as practiced in the West. Many people are drawn to the principles of participatory democracy, albeit with a plebiscitarian emphasis. The conditions of affluence and civil society that nurture participatory democracy in the West are underdeveloped in the East; therefore participation in citizen-action groups and direct-action methods is relatively low in Eastern Europe. Ray Taras's discussion of Polish participation patterns illustrates their ambivalence to both representative and participatory styles of action

(Chapter 10). Many Eastern Europeans still seem unsure about how best to participate in democratic politics, even if they support the principles of democracy.

The challenge for established and emerging democracies is to expand the opportunities for citizens to participate in the political process. To meet this challenge also means ensuring an equality of political rights and opportunities that will be even more difficult to guarantee with these new participation forms.

THE PUBLIC AND DEMOCRACY

In many ways, the citizenry defines the essence of democratic politics. In its practice, democracy is a German at the polls casting a vote for her preferred party, a French farmer driving his tractor to Paris to protest the government's agricultural policy, a Hungarian writing a letter to the Budapest *People's Freedom* to criticize government policy, or Russian mine workers protesting a cut in government benefits.

Public wants and needs set the priorities that democratic governments strive to address. Citizen expectations of the political process influence the ways in which that process works and the kinds of policies it produces. Citizen participation in the political process presses a democracy to match its lofty ideals.

This chapter's emphasis on the citizenry does not presume that political culture and citizen action determine policy outcomes. Other parts of the process—interest groups, political parties, and political leaders—act as intermediaries between the public and policy outcomes, and their direct impact is often greater in the short term. Similarly, if we want to predict the success of democracy in Eastern Europe, it is much more important in the short term to study the actions and values of elites and the role of institutions.

Thus, citizen politics does not primarily explain the daily outcomes of politics, but it determines the broad boundaries of the political system. One political scientist described public opinion as a set of dikes, channeling the course of democratic politics and defining its boundaries. The public's policy preferences influence policy outcomes in a democratic system—but this is through a complex and sometimes circuitous route.[36] In the same way, the public's expectations of politics and support for the political system determine the long-term functioning of the system. The immediate success of the new Eastern European democracies may depend on elite actions, but their long-term success depends on creating a democratic political culture among both the public and the elites. Democracy cannot endure in a nation without democrats.

There are nearly two dozen established democracies in the West and nearly an equal number of new democracies in the East. The citizens in these nations generally share a common democratic creed, and these political systems are built upon common principles. Most Europeans express support for their political system and a sense of national identity; expectations about an activist government are also common.

Where these publics differ is in their conceptions about *how* the democratic process should function. People in some nations display a more participatory style of democracy, with high levels of conventional and unconventional political action. The Dutch and the Danes, for example, are activist publics with institutional structures that encourage the representation of diverse political interests. Other Europeans, such as the British, accept a more representative style of democracy, placing greater reliance on elites and the role of elections as instruments of popular control. The French seem to follow a more conflictual style of politics, where protest and political strife are almost routine. Democracy follows a single set of principles, but it takes life in many forms.

The nations of Eastern Europe are now making choices about how to practice democracy as the new system becomes institutionalized and these nations join Western organizations such as the European Union and NATO. Communists ruled these nations for half a century, and these nations must surmount the legacy of this experience. Many Eastern European nations have suffered from violence and political corruption. Chapter 1 showed that several nations still merit poor scores for political rights and civil liberties. Some political experts argue that another form of authoritarian state lies in the future for some of these nations, and political progress in Russia remains uncertain.

We do not overlook these difficulties, but we also note that these democratic transitions generally began with a majority of the people and elites supporting democratic principles. Moreover, the international community is actively working to encourage freedom and political liberties in Eastern Europe. If democracy successfully takes root, Eastern Europeans will search for democratic forms that meet their particular histories and their expectations. Political debates over representative and participatory democracy, and over various institutional choices for democratic politics, are especially real in Eastern Europe as these systems are now taking shape. Thus the evolution of democracy continues with new trends among the consolidated democracies in the West and still unclear trends developing among the nations in Eastern Europe. How these two democratization processes develop will define the political fate of Europe in the next century.

Key Terms

civil society	new social movements	participatory revolution	representative
democratic values	participatory democracy	political culture	democracy
election turnout			

Internet Sources

The World Values Survey website has information on this global survey of values: www.worldvaluessurvey.org

The Eurobarometer website of the European Union has information on their latest citizen and elite surveys: europa.eu.int/comm/dg10/epo/

The Institute for Democracy and Electoral Assistance (IDEA) has data on election turnout around the globe: http://www.idea.int/

The International Social Survey Program (ISSP) website has additional information on these surveys: www.issp.org

 Suggested Readings

Almond, Gabriel, and Sidney Verba. *The Civic Culture.* Princeton: Princeton University Press, 1963.

———, eds. *The Civic Culture Revisited.* Boston: Little Brown, 1980.

Blais, Andre. *To Vote or Not? The Merits and Limits of Rational Choice Theory.* Pittsburgh: University of Pittsburgh Press, 2000.

Borre, Ole, and Elinor Scarbrough, eds. *The Scope of Government.* Oxford: Oxford University Press, 1995.

Dalton, Russell. *Citizen Politics: Public Opinion and Political Parties in Advanced Industrial Democracies.* 4th ed. Washington, DC: CQ Press, 2005.

———. *Democratic Challenges, Democratic Choices: The Erosion of Political Support in Western Democracies.* Oxford: Oxford University Press, 2004.

Eckstein, Harry, Frederic Fleron, Erik Hoffman, and William Reisinger, eds. *Can Democracy Take Root in Post-Soviet Russia? Explorations in State-Society Relations.* Latham, MD: Rowman & Littlefield, 1998.

Franklin, Mark. 2004. *Voter Turnout and the Dynamics of Electoral Competition in Established Democracies since 1945.* New York: Cambridge University Press.

Inglehart, Ronald. *Culture Shift in Advanced Industrial Society.* Princeton: Princeton University Press, 1990.

Inglehart, Ronald, and Christian Welzel. *The Human Development Model and Value Change.* New York: Cambridge University Press, 2005.

Jennings, M. Kent, and Jan van Deth, eds. *Continuities in Political Action.* Berlin: deGruyter, 1990.

Kaase, Max, and Ken Newton. *Beliefs in Government.* Oxford: Oxford University Press, 1995.

Klingemann, Hans-Dieter, and Dieter Fuchs, eds. *Citizens and the State.* Oxford: Oxford University Press, 1995.

Niemi, Richard, Lawrence LeDuc, and Pippa Norris, eds. *Comparing Democracies 2: New Challenges in the Study of Elections and Voting.* Newbury Park, CA: Sage, 2002.

Norris, Pippa. *Democratic Phoenix: Reinventing Political Activism.* New York: Cambridge University Press, 2002.

Petro, Nicholai. *The Rebirth of Russian Democracy: An Interpretation of Political Culture.* Cambridge: Harvard University Press, 1995.

Pharr, Susan, and Robert Putnam, eds. *Discontented Democracies: What's Troubling the Trilateral Countries?* Princeton, Princeton University Press, 2000.

Putnam, Robert. *Bowling Alone: The Collapse and Revival of American Community.* New York: Simon and Schuster, 2000.

Putnam, Robert, ed. *Democracies in Flux: The Evolution of Social Capital in Contemporary Society.* Oxford: Oxford University Press, 2002.

Rose, Richard, William Mishler, and Christian Haerpfer. *Democracy and Its Alternatives: Understanding Post-Communist Societies.* Johns Hopkins University Press, 1998.

Verba, Sidney, Kay Schlozman, and Henry Brady. 1995. *Voice and Equality: Civic Volunteerism in American Politics.* Cambridge: Harvard University Press.

White, Stephen, Richard Rose, and Ian McAllister. *How Russia Votes.* Chatham, NJ: Chatham House Publishers, 1996.

 Endnotes

1. Gabriel Almond and Sidney Verba, *The Civic Culture* (Princeton: Princeton University Press, 1963); Almond and Verba, eds., *The Civic Culture Revisited* (Boston: Little Brown, 1980).

2. Alexis de Tocqueville, *Democracy in America* (New York: Knopf, 1945), p. 299.

3. Almond and Verba, *The Civic Culture,* Ch. 10; Harry Eckstein, "Authority Relations and Government Performance," *Comparative Political Studies* 2 (1969): 269–325; Robert Putnam, *Making Democracy Work* (Cambridge: Harvard University Press, 1993).

4. Harry Eckstein, *Division and Cohesion in Democracy* (Princeton: Princeton University Press, 1966).

5. Robert Putnam, *Bowling Alone: The Collapse and Revival of American Community* (New York: Simon and Schuster, 2000).

6. For an interesting comparison, earlier editions of *European Politics Today* include the same figure based on 1990–1991 and then 1995–1998 survey data, and the same pattern is apparent. The survey asks: "Can most people be trusted, or can't you be too careful when dealing with people?" Also see Ronald Inglehart, *Culture Shift in Advanced Industrial Society* (Princeton: Princeton University Press, 1990), Ch. 1; Ronald Inglehart, *Modernism and Postmodernism* (Princeton: Princeton University Press, 1997).

7. Robert Dahl, *Polyarchy* (New Haven: Yale University Press, 1971).

8. Russell J. Dalton, *Democratic Challenges, Democratic Choices* (Oxford: Oxford University Press, 2004); Hans-Dieter Klingemann and Dieter Fuchs, eds., *Citizens and the State* (Oxford: Oxford University Press, 1995).

9. Giacamo Sani, "The Political Culture of Italy," in Almond and Verba, eds., *The Civic Culture Revisited.*

10. Nicholai Petro provocatively argues that there are strong currents of democracy and civil society that predate the communist era, in *The Rebirth of Russian Democracy: An Interpretation of Political Culture* (Cambridge: Harvard University Press, 1995); for a counterview see Harry Eckstein et al., *Can Democracy Take Root in Post-Soviet Russia?* (Lanham, MD: Rowman & Littlefield, 1998).

11. Richard Rose, William Mishler, and Christian Haerpfer, *Democracy and Its Alternatives: Understanding Post-Communist Societies* (Johns Hopkins University Press, 1998); William Reisinger, Arthur Miller, and Vicki Hesli, "Political Values in Russia, Ukraine, and Lithuania," *British Journal of Political Science* 24 (1994): 183–223; James Gibson et al., "Emerging Democratic Values in Soviet Political Culture," in A. Miller, W. Reisinger, and V. Hesli, eds., *Public Opinion and Regime Change* (Boulder, CO: Westview Press, 1993); Russell Dalton, "Communists and Democrats: Attitudes Toward Democracy in the Two Germanies," *British Journal of Political Science* 24 (1994): 469–93. Compare with Robert Rohrschneider, *Learning Democracy: Democratic and Economic Values in Unified Germany* (New York: Oxford University Press, 1999).

12. Richard Rose, "Advancing into Europe: Contrasting Goals of Post-Communist Countries," in *Nations in Transition 2002* (New York: Freedom House, 2002).

13. G. Evans and S. Whitefield, "The Politics and Economics of Democratic Commitment," *British Journal of Political Science* 25 (1995): 485–514; Arthur Miller, Vicki Hesli, and William Reisinger, "Reassessing Mass Support for Political and Economic Change in the Former USSR," *American Political Science Review* 88 (1994): 399–411; Stephen White, Richard Rose, and Ian McAllister, *How Russia Votes* (Chatham, NJ: Chatham House, 1996).

14. Dalton, *Democratic Challenges, Democratic Choices;* Susan Pharr and Robert Putnam, eds., *Discontented Democracies* (Princeton: Princeton University Press, 2000).

15. Ole Borre and Elinor Scarbrough, eds., *The Scope of Government* (Oxford: Oxford University Press, 1995).

16. Anthony King, "Overload: Problems of Governing in the 1970s," *Political Studies* 23 (1975): 166.

17. Richard Rose and Guy Peters, *Can Government Go Bankrupt?* (New York: Basic Books, 1978); Crozier, Huntington, and Watanuki, *The Crisis of Democracy;* Samuel Brittan, "The Economic Contradictions of Democracy," *British Journal of Political Science* 5 (1975): 129–59.

18. Inglehart, *Culture Shift*, Ch. 8; Ole Borre and Jose Manuel Viega, "Government Intervention in the Economy," in Borre and Scarborough, *The Scope of Government.*

19. See also Raymond Duch, "Tolerating Economic Reform," *American Political Science Review* 87 (1993): 590–608; Richard Rose, *New Democracies Barometer V: A Twelve Nation Survey* (Glasgow: University of Strathclyde, 1998).

20. For instance, the better educated are more likely to espouse democratic values if they live in a democratic system, and German public opinion surveys immediately after the collapse of the Third Reich found that the better educated were more likely to support the tenets of Fascism. This point is, however, debated for post-communist societies. See Ada Finifter, "Attitudes Toward Individual Responsibility and Political Reform in the Former Soviet Union," *American Political Science Review* 90 (1996): 138–52; Arthur Miller, William Reisinger, and Vicki Hesli, "Understanding Political Change in Post-Soviet Societies," *American Political Science Review* 90 (1996): 153–66.

21. See, for example, Figure 2.6 in the first edition of *European Politics Today*, p. 45.

22. Central and East European Eurobarometer 6.

23. Rose and Haerpfer, *New Democracies Barometer V;* more recent data suggest that East Europeans are still more positive about the present and the future than they are about the communist regimes. But images of the old regime had improved by 2001. See Rose, "Advancing into Europe."

24. Stephen White, Richard Rose, and Ian McAllister, *How Russia Votes* (Chatham, NJ: Chatham House, 1996), p.12.

25. Ole Borre, "Beliefs and the Scope of Government," in Borre and Scarbrough, *The Scope of Government.*

26. Mark Franklin, *Voter Turnout and the Dynamics of Electoral Competition in Established Democracies since 1945* (New York: Cambridge University Press, 2004); Andre Blais, *To Vote or Not to Vote? The Merits and Limits of Rational Choice Theory* (Pittsburgh: University of Pittsburgh Press, 2000).

27. G. Bingham Powell, "American Turnout in Comparative Perspective," *American Political Science Review* 80 (1986): 17–44; Ray Wolfinger and Steve Rosenstone, *Who Votes?* (New Haven: Yale University Press, 1980).

28. Mark Gray and Miki Caul, "The Decline of Election Turnout in Advanced Industrial Democracies," *Comparative Political Studies* 33 (2000); Andre Blais, *To Vote or Not?*

29. Richard Brody, "The Puzzle of Participation in America," in A. King, ed., *The New American Political System* (Washington: American Enterprise Institute, 1978).

30. Robert Putnam, ed., *Democracies in Flux: The Evolution of Social Capital in Contemporary Societies* (Oxford: Oxford University Press, 2002).

31. Pippa Norris, *The Democratic Phoenix* (New York: Cambridge University Press, 2000); Bruce Cain, Russell Dalton, and Susan Scarrow, eds., *Democracy Transformed? Expanding Citizen Access in Advanced Industrial Democracies* (Oxford: Oxford University Press, 2003).

32. Donald Schulz and Jan Adams, eds., *Political Participation in Communist Systems* (New York: Pergamon Press, 1981).

33. Dalton, *Citizen Politics*, Chs. 3, 4; Norris, *The Democratic Phoenix*, Ch. 2.

34. Klingemann and Fuchs, *Citizens and the State*, Chs. 2, 3; Norris, *The Democratic Phoenix*.

35. Sidney Verba, Norman Nie, and Jae-on Kim, *Participation and Political Equality* (Cambridge: Cambridge University Press, 1978); Dalton, *Citizen Politics*, Chs. 3, 4.

36. Benjamin Page and Robert Shapiro, *The Rational Public* (Chicago: University of Chicago Press, 1992); Christopher Wlezien, "Patterns of Representation: Dynamics of Public Preferences and Policy," *Journal of Politics* 66 (2004): 1–24.

Chapter 3

European Interest Groups and Parties

Citizens play a vital role in democratic politics. However, their impact on politics and policymaking is shaped and often overshadowed by the activities of political organizations. Politics in Western Europe has long been characterized by dense organizations of interest groups and political parties. The interest groups express the great variety of needs and demands in the society. The parties run candidates for office. Both have developed complex, intimate connections with the policymaking process, even serving on policymaking bodies.

As we discussed in Chapter 2, new citizen movements, parties, and tactics are challenging the traditional organizations and approaches. But the traditional groups retain great influence; we cannot understand Western European politics without taking account of them. In contrast, politics in Eastern Europe before 1989 was dominated by communist parties that not only monopolized elections, but controlled labor unions, professional associations, veterans' organizations, and all other organized groups. In these new democracies, organized groups and political parties have been struggling to emerge.

THE TYPES OF INTEREST GROUPS

Interest groups may take many forms. *Anomic interest groups* are generally spontaneous groups that form suddenly when many individuals respond to frustration, disappointment, or other strongly emotional events. They are flash affairs, rising and subsiding suddenly. Spontaneous student protests about tuition or an impromptu demonstration by frustrated soccer fans are examples of anomic groups. They normally act and then disperse. Like anomic groups, *nonassociational groups* rarely are well organized, and their activity is episodic. They differ from anomic groups because they are based on common interests of ethnicity, region, religion, occupation, or perhaps kinship. Because of these continuing economic or cultural ties, nonassociational groups have more continuity than anomic groups. *Institutional groups* have a formal structure and have other political or social functions besides interest articulation, such as business corporations, legislatures, armies, bureaucracies, and churches. Either as corporate bodies or as smaller groups within these bodies (legislative blocs, officer cliques, groups in the clergy, or ideological factions in bureaucracies), such groups express their own interests or represent the interest of other groups in the society. The influence of institutional interest groups is usually derived from the strength of their primary organizational base, for instance, the resources of their affiliated businesses or the access to policymaking of their bureaucrats.

Political scientists often focus on *associational groups*. These groups are organized explicitly to represent the interests of a particular group. This type of group includes trade unions, chambers of commerce and manufacturers' associations, ethnic associations, professional organizations, and environmental associations. These organizations have orderly procedures for formulating interests and demands, and they usually employ a full-time professional staff. Associational groups are often very active in representing the interests of their members in the policy process.

Thus, social interests can manifest themselves in many different ways. To highlight the different types of interest groups, we can describe various groups that involve members of the working class:

Anomic group: a spontaneous group of working class individuals living in the same neighborhood
Nonassociational group: the working class as a collective
Institutional group: the labor department within the government
Associational group: a labor union

One of the distinctive features of Western European democracies is the richness of the organizational life—all of these different types of groups exist. A recent study of 15 Western European countries showed that about a fifth of the citizens were members of sports or recreational groups; nearly as many belonged to religious groups or trade unions; about one-seventh belonged to cultural or educational groups.[1] In some countries these membership levels were much higher. Moreover, in recent decades there has been a flowering of new groups to protect the environment, ensure equal rights for women,

and advocate other public interests. Overall, about 60 percent of Western European citizens belong to some kind of organized group; nearly a quarter belong to three or more.[2]

Analysts often describe this organizational activity as comprising the *civil society* and maintain that a vibrant civil society is an essential base for a vibrant democracy.[3] Participation in associational and institutional groups socializes individuals into the types of political skills and cooperative relations that are part of a well-functioning society. Group activity also can help citizens to develop their own policy preferences, provide important information about politics, and articulate their interests to policymakers. In large groups citizens with common interests may be inhibited from acting on those interests by the high costs and low rewards for individual activity. But organizations can overcome these difficulties of collective action, drawing citizens into membership through individual benefits, often called "selective incentives," and coordinating their political activities.[4] (See Box 3.1.) Thus, an active public involved in a diversity of interest groups provides a fertile ground for democracy.

Many of the chapters on Eastern European countries in this book discuss the problems faced by these newly democratized nations in building a rich associational group life in societies where organized groups have long been suppressed or controlled.[5] The Communist Party and the government bureaucracy dominated these nations for over 40 years, and the government controlled associational life in order to pursue its own goals. The process of building new, independent associational groups to articulate special different citizen interests is proving difficult. In the recent European Values Survey average membership levels in sports, religious, educational, and environmental associations in 14 Eastern European countries were less than half of those in the Western European countries.[6] Only memberships in labor unions, a fundamental part of the communist regimes and still a conduit for many governmental benefits (see the discussion of Russia in Chapter 9), are more comparable between Western and Eastern Europe.

While Eastern Europe faces questions of how to develop a rich associational life, there are also

> ### Box 3.1 What Sustains Membership in Large Organizations: Selective Incentives in Swedish Unions
>
> One of the puzzles of organizational membership is what sustains citizen involvement in large organizations. In large organizations citizens may have little expectation that their individual involvement will make a difference. Why, then, should they take the trouble to join? One answer is that some organizations can provide "selective" incentives—benefits that come to all members and only to members. Such selective incentives can encourage citizens to join and keep them involved. In Sweden the many selective benefits that union members receive have probably helped keep membership high at a time when interest and memberships in unions are declining in many countries.
>
> "The idea of giving the unions control over the unemployment insurance scheme is a very good illustration of the relationship in Sweden between voluntary organizations and the state. On one hand, the unions get a very powerful selective incentive to help them recruit members. On the other hand, the
>
> unions also handle the very difficult question of deciding who is really to be considered unemployed, that is, what type of work one has to accept or risk losing the benefits. The government is thereby relieved of having to take responsibility for these very difficult decisions. . . .
>
> "It should be added that this is not the only type of selective incentives the Swedish unions have been granted by the government. A vast number of industrial laws and regulations give the local unions a say over working conditions, the implementation of work safety regulations and who has to go first when there is a shortage of jobs. In sum, this means that for many, if not most, employees, membership in the union is only formally a voluntary decision."
>
> *Source:* Bo Rothstein, "Sweden: Social Capital in the Social Democratic State," in Robert D. Putnam, ed., *Democracies in Flux* (New York: Oxford University Press, 2002), 310–11.

new questions about whether existing civil society is declining in the West. Memberships in labor unions and religious associations are down in most West European nations, as are memberships in some professional associations. Robert Putnam has found that Americans participate less in traditional group activities and has suggested that citizens in many countries may be disengaging themselves in groups all the way from bowling leagues to political parties.[7] Instead of getting together with others to solve community problems, as Tocqueville described the democratic ethos, Putnam claims that too many of us sit in front of our television screens and computer monitors experiencing a virtual reality. The evidence from Western Europe suggests that overall organizational involvement is increasing in some countries and declining in others, but that often new styles of engagement are replacing the declining membership in some traditional associational groups.[8] These changes may also affect the types of citizens who are drawn into the political process through organizations. This debate is still unresolved, but it underscores the importance at-

tached to organizational life as a foundation of democracy.

INTEREST GROUP SYSTEMS

In all modern societies associational groups play major roles in shaping public policy. However, research in comparative politics shows that democratic nations differ significantly in how interest groups are organized and how they are connected to government. The differences in organization and connections allow us to talk of different interest group systems in modern societies. Across the Western European democracies, interest group systems vary between two contrasting models: pluralist and democratic corporatist.[9]

Pluralist interest group systems are characterized by several features that involve both how interests are organized and how they participate in the political process:

- Multiple groups may represent a single societal interest.

- Membership in associational groups is non-compulsory and limited.
- Groups often have a loose, or decentralized organizational structure.
- Interest groups are clearly separated from the government.

For instance, not only are there different groups for each social sector, such as labor unions, business associations, and professional groups, but there may be many multiple labor unions or business associations within each sector. These groups compete among themselves for membership and influence, and all simultaneously press their demands on policymakers and the bureaucracies. The United States is the best-known example of a strongly pluralist interest group system. Britain (Chapter 5) is also usually characterized as pluralist, as is France (Chapter 6), because of the fragmentation of its interest organizations.

Corporatist interest group systems are more commonly found in the West European democracies. The corporatist systems are characterized by much more organized representation of interests:

- A single association normally represents each societal interest. (These are often called "peak" associations.)
- Membership in the peak association is often compulsory and nearly universal.
- The peak associations (also called umbrella groups) are centrally organized and direct the actions of their members.
- Groups are often systematically involved in making and implementing policy.

For instance, in a corporatist system there may be a single peak association that represents all the major business or industrial interests. The Federation of German Industry (BDI) is an example of a corporatist business association, which is matched by a corporatist labor organization: the German Federation of Trade Unions (DGB). This contrasts with the wide diversity of business groups and labor unions that act separately in a pluralist system.

In the corporatist systems national wage and benefit policies and related employment issues have often been set through "tri-partism," bargaining between the peak associations of labor and business

and the government. The direct involvement of large interest groups and the government in negotiating national policy and also in seeing that it is implemented (a process of joint responsibility sometimes called "concerted action" or "concertation") characterizes European corporatism in various policy areas.

The most thoroughly corporatist interest group and policy systems were developed in the Scandinavian nations, such as Norway and Sweden, and in Austria. Substantial democratic corporatist tendencies are also found in the Netherlands and Germany.

Because different sectors of a society may vary in their organized interest groups and in their government relations, we must be cautious about generalizing too much about interest group systems. However, Figure 3.1 shows the striking differences in organization of the labor movements and wage bargaining in some industrialized societies. The countries are arrayed along the horizontal axis in terms of the percentage of the total labor force that belongs to a labor union. The vertical axis displays the organizational level at which wages are negotiated. At the bottom level wages are negotiated at the level of individual industrial plants; at the middle levels, wages tend to cover specific industrial sectors, such as chemicals or food. At the top level in the figure are binding contracts covering the entire private sector of the society.

In Sweden, for example, nearly 90 percent of the nonagricultural workforce is organized into unions, and wages tend to be set through centralized, national bargaining. The United States, at the lower left of the figure, is the polar opposite of the Scandinavian pattern; only about a seventh of the labor force is unionized and negotiation is usually at the level of individual plants.

The patterns in Figure 3.1 illustrate the institutional diversity of the labor movement and the likely potential for influencing and participating in policymaking. The labor movement is larger and more influential in the countries at the upper right of the figure because of their size and bargaining coordination, and generally less effective in the nations at the lower left.

The best-studied consequences of democratic corporatist arrangements have been in the economic areas. Some studies indicate that countries

Figure 3.1   Interest Group Systems of Labor Unions

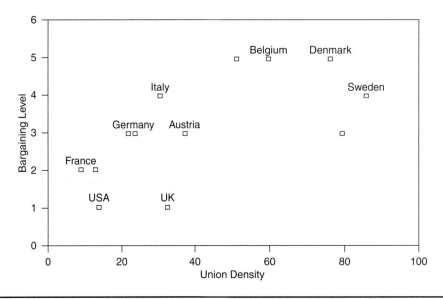

Source: Union members as a percent of the labor force and wage bargaining levels are both from Miriam Golden, Peter Lange, and Michael Wallerstein, "Union Centralization among Advanced Industrial Societies: An Empirical Study," 2002. Dataset available at http://www.shelley.polisci.ucla.edu/data. Version dated July 28, 2004. Union density is net (excludes self-employed and retired) except in Spain and UK, where only gross density was available. See text for explanation of bargaining level.

with corporatist economic systems had better records than more pluralist countries in sustaining employment and restraining inflation in the 1970s and 1980s.[10] This might have occurred because the large groups were able to negotiate with each other and the government and find common ground. Corporatist systems were also associated with increased social spending and greater income equality.

In the 1990s the environment, groups, and consequences of corporatism changed. Independent central banks and, increasingly, the European Union (Chapter 12), constrained national economic and social policymaking in many ways. Membership in labor unions declined quite sharply in some countries; some bargaining patterns became less centralized; problems of deadlock in corporatist negotiation became more prominent. Interestingly, the same countries that had relied on corporatism policymaking earlier tended to retain it, but in newly adapted forms with complex results.[11]

In Eastern Europe, communist parties (governments) penetrated and controlled virtually all organized groups until the collapse of Soviet control in 1989. Since then there has been an explosion of new groups and splintering and division of the ones previously dominated by the authoritarian governments. (See the discussions of interest groups in Russia, Poland, and Hungary in Chapters 9 through 11.) Yet, citizen memberships in these groups still lag far behind levels in Western Europe. One of the many problems of these societies has been to bring some order into this chaotic situation, while at the same time encouraging freedom in group formation and the representation of many varieties of interests. Although we do not have systematic studies that would allow us to place Eastern European countries in Figure 3.1, Poland provides an example. Poland has attempted to use corporatist involvement of labor, business, and government in negotiating labor policy, although fragmentation of the groups has made this difficult (see Chapter 10).

Another problem in Eastern Europe has been to prevent the remaining institutional groups of the old communist systems, especially in the government bureaucracy and the government-run industries and businesses—often now formally "privatized" but practically run by the same people—from dominating policymaking. (See especially Russia, Chapter 9.)

PARTIES AND PARTY COMPETITION

Political parties are organizations that run candidates for election. In liberal democracies political parties provide a critical link between citizens and policymakers. Before and during elections they mobilize voters and structure their choices; after the elections they organize governments and policymaking.

The party systems of Western Europe are highly developed. Party leaders and organizers have had many elections to build organizations, form alliances, and refine their strategies. Although each new election brings new challenges, new voters, and sometimes new parties, many lessons of the past are encoded in the surviving organizations as well as in the memories of voters, activists, and party leaders. The party system in a country—the number of parties, the partisan balance, the range and content of issues presented—tends to provide a fairly stable context from one election to the next.

In Eastern Europe, in contrast, until 15 years ago the Soviet-backed communist parties permitted no competition, and only selected allies, at most, were permitted to offer candidates. Moreover, the communist parties attempted to penetrate the entire society and pull all those interested in public life into their networks.

It has been very difficult to build new party organizations in the tumult-filled years since the democratic transitions in 1989–91. The sudden expansion of democratic opportunity initially overwhelmed the potential organizers of opposition parties, who had no experience with competitive politics. The absence of independent social and economic organizations, especially the trade unions and churches that were historically the focus of much initial party organization in Western Europe, has made building new party organizations far more difficult.[12] Democratic elections in Eastern Europe since 1989 have been typically characterized by many new parties, small parties, and independent candidates. Voter support for parties has been very volatile, shifting greatly between one election and the next.[13] After the elections, the assemblies have frequently experienced lack of coherence within parties and the break-offs of new party groups, as well as difficulties in forming governments based on stable coalitions between parties. Building strong new parties is an important challenge facing the new democracies of Eastern Europe.

The Social Base of Parties

Political sociologists Lipset and Rokkan observed that voter preferences based on social class and religion (called "cleavages") characterized most Western European party systems from the 1920s to the 1960s[14]. In the Catholic societies of Mediterranean Western Europe, for example, voters' frequency of church attendance was a strong predictor of their party attachments. In central Western Europe, religious affiliation as Protestant or Catholic often predicted party support, while in Northern Europe a voter's occupation most powerfully shaped his or her partisanship. These voter attachments were anchored by the alignments of social organizations (labor unions, churches, and voluntary associations) and party organizations. In some countries ethnicity and region were also important cleavages.

These historic cleavages continue to organize many Western European party systems today. But they have been diminished by the declines in church attendance and trade union strength, as well as by increased geographic mobility and the provision of welfare safety nets. New issues, such as immigration, and new values, are also beginning to obscure the traditional cleavages.[15]

Religious, ethnic, and economic cleavages may yet crystalize in Eastern Europe, too. Analyses of voting in Poland, for example, show some of the effects of church attendance that we might expect in a Catholic nation. But at present, the basis of voter support in Eastern Europe remains fluid with less connection to social groups than in the West. Voter volatility continues to be high.[16]

The Number of Parties

Political scientists have emphasized two major distinctions in analyzing the performance of Western European party systems: (1) number of parties and (2) extremist parties. The first distinguishes *multiparty systems* from two-party, or at least *majority-electing party systems*. Multiparty systems seem to offer a wider range of choices to voters, explicit representation of social and political groups, and more inclusiveness in policymaking. Majority-electing systems seem to offer clearer political responsibility, more stable governments, and the direct implementation of campaign promises.

Most Western European party systems fall clearly into the multiparty category (see Figure 3.2). In the average Western European election, six or seven parties win 1 percent of the vote or more,

with as many as twelve such parties in the Netherlands in the 1970s and Belgium in the 1980s. These numbers pale, however, when compared with the numbers of parties competing in the new electoral landscapes in Eastern Europe. In Russia in 1995, for example, 18 parties won over 1 percent of the vote. Such figures can be somewhat misleading if there are a few large parties together with many very small ones. It is more revealing to compare the relative numbers of parties through a weighting approach that calculates the "effective number" of parties in the election and in the legislature.[17]

If we take this approach, the average "effective" number of parties winning *votes* in Western Europe in the elections of the early 2000s was about four and a half. Austria, Britain, Greece, Malta, Portugal, and Spain were at the low end with effectively no more than about three parties, while Belgium was at the high end with about nine. The average in Eastern Europe was nearly a full party higher: about five and a half. Latvia, Slo-

FIGURE 3.2   Effective Number of Parties in the Legislature in Western and Eastern Europe in 2004

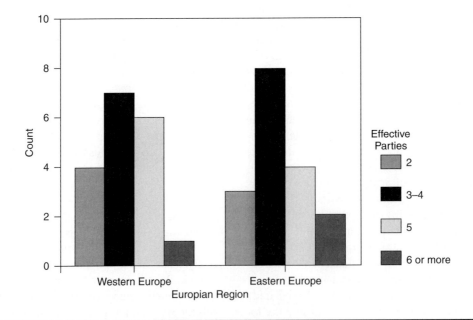

Source: See the discussion of the "Effective Number" of parties in this chapter and in Lijphart, 1999, Ch. 5.

vakia, and Ukraine had effectively over seven parties winning votes.

These numbers decline if we look at the legislature, because the election laws prevent many smaller parties from winning seats in parliament. The average number is a little under four effective parties in the legislatures in both East and West. Figure 3.2 groups countries by the effective number of parties in *legislatures*. The average reductions are greater in Eastern Europe because even low barriers shut out very small parties.

Figure 3.2 also displays quite wide variation across nations. In Western Europe, there are effectively two-party systems in the legislatures in Britain, France, Greece, Malta, and Spain.[18] We see that most countries have from three (Germany) to five (Denmark) effective parties in the legislature. At the more fragmented end, only Belgium has over six. In Eastern Europe there are several effective two-party systems (including Hungary and Russia) and quite a few with around three, but also a number with six or more.

The variety of party systems in Europe means that the context of party competition can be quite different in different countries. In the systems dominated by two large parties, each party must appeal to a sufficient range of voters to have a chance to win at least a large plurality. Each party faces pressures to reach out from its social or ideological "base" and seek centrist voters (as the British Labour Party did in 1997 and afterwards).[19] In this context, factions within the parties also know that if they split their party for the sake of offering another policy choice, they may bring an opposition majority power and doom themselves for years to the role of a weak voice of protest. Citizens who do not want to "waste" their votes must choose between the major alternatives, even if these seem less than ideal.

In contrast in multiparty contexts, a party's leaders can seek a smaller and more focused constituency. Party policies may reflect the preferences of specific groups, such as labor unions, business associations, or religious and ethnic groups. Historical issue commitments and ideological traditions also play a role.[20] As no party will win a majority, small parties can still hope to shape policy through negotiation and coalition with other parties. (See the discussion of government formation in Chapter 4.) Issue factions can also split to form new parties and still expect to play a role. Citizens will find a wide range of party choices to represent their interests. However, the parties will have to adjust their promises to the realities of building coalitions with other parties; citizens must anticipate this process.

Despite the general similarity in the distribution, Figure 3.2 overstates somewhat the comparability to Western Europe. Many of the larger Eastern European "parties" are really electoral coalitions of several parties and are less cohesive in their behavior in the legislature. Moreover, the greater volatility between elections in Eastern Europe makes it harder for voters to learn what parties stand for and to anticipate the implications of their voting choices for government policy. Figure 3.2, like the voting averages, should also remind Americans how unusual is their truly two-party system.

Extremist Parties

A second distinction in the literature on political parties focuses on "extremism" (or "polarization") in the party system. Many theorists suggest that the performance of democracy is threatened by *extremist parties*—parties espousing dramatically different policy packages (ideologies) or challenging the basic ground rules of the society.[21] Italian political scientist Giovanni Sartori argues that polarized systems enhance the ideological intensity of the policy debate, encouraging a pattern of irresponsible "outbidding" by extremist parties. Extremism also discourages turnovers of power that could keep incumbent parties responsible to citizens.[22]

Substantial research, based largely on Western Europe, suggests that support for extremist parties is associated with less durable governments, probably with mass turmoil as well, although not necessarily with instability of democracy itself.[23]

Data from the late 1970s and early 1980s showed parties that could be classified as "extremists"—in terms of either the extreme policy positions or the alienation of their supporters—had the support of over 20 percent of the electorate in Belgium, Denmark, Finland, France, and Italy,[24] but substantially less in the rest of Western Europe.

These percentages somewhat reduced by the early 1990s as the collapse of international communism moderated the position of some left parties. Moreover, before the 1990s Green parties were generally considered extremist parties, challenging environmental policies of other parties and attacking the political and economic establishment. But today they are a more accepted part of the political landscape, although this varies from country to country.

New, populist, rightist parties, often appealing to concerns about immigrants and/or relations with the European Union, as well as attacking the political establishment have been a new source of extremism in the last decade (see Box 3.2). Voters in Western Europe, as in the United States, are concerned about the impact of economic globalization on the outsourcing of jobs and the consequent rise in unemployment. Increases in levels of crime and drug-trafficking are also disturbing. Populist extremist parties have attacked the established parties as indifferent to all of these challenging issues. The

extreme right parties particularly blame these problems on the high levels of immigration encouraged by opening of borders and conflict in Eastern Europe, as well as by loosening of internal controls within the European Union. Immigration also threatens well-understood cultural communities. New differences of religion and custom raise a variety of new issues, such as the conflict over wearing religious symbols in schools in France, focusing on Moslem headscarves.

In some countries, such as Sweden and the Netherlands, support for extreme right parties surged suddenly behind a popular leader, then declined. In others, they have become a more permanent part of the political landscape. The National Front in France, for example, has won 10 to 15 percent in elections since 1986. The National Front's controversial leader Jean-Marie Le Pen has called for expulsion of illegal immigrants and all immigrants after a maximum stay of a year or two, a ban on even tourist visas for Africans and Arabs from North

 ## Box 3.2 List Pim Fortuyn and the 2002 Dutch Election: An Extreme Right Party

In a television interview on August 20, 2001, a political columnist and former professor named Pim Fortuyn announced his intention to run for the Dutch Parliament. He was not an ordinary member of the political establishment. He was "an outspoken homosexual with a flamboyant lifestyle—Ferrari, Bentley with chauffeur, butler, two lap dogs, portraits of John F. Kennedy in his lavishly decorated Rotterdam home which he referred to as Palazzo di Pietro." In short order he was chosen head of a small party, Livable Netherlands. His charismatic speeches and interviews attacked traditionally tolerant Dutch attitudes toward minority groups and brought his issues of foreigners, immigration policies, asylum-seekers and crime to the top of the political agenda. He put the traditional parties on the defensive. Then, on February 9, 2002, he published an interview that rocked Dutch politics, stating "that Islam was a backward culture, that no new asylum-seekers would be allowed, and that if necessary to protect Freedom of Speech, the first article of the Constitution should be repealed." (This article for-

bids discrimination.) His party immediately expelled him. But he formed his own party, List Pim Fortuyn, which immediately surged to second place in the public opinion polls. Pim Fortuyn himself became the center of the national election campaign. The country was shocked when he was assassinated 10 days before the election. However, his new party won 17 percent of the vote, becoming the second largest party in the fragmented Dutch parliament, and soon joined two other parties in forming the next (short-lived) parliamentary government. Public opinion polls showed that its success was built on Fortuyn's personal popularity, general cynicism about Dutch politics and the incumbent government, and issues of "sending back asylum-seekers" and that "foreigners should adapt" to Dutch culture and customs.

Source: Joop J. M. Van Holsteyn and Galen Irwin, "Never a Dull Moment: Pim Fortuyn and the Dutch Parliamentary Election of 2002," *West European Politics* 26 (April 2003): 41–66. Also see "Pim Fortuyn and the 'New' Far Right in the Netherlands," *Representation* 40 (2004): 131–45.

Africa, preferential treatment of French citizens in jobs and public housing, and very tight citizenship requirements.[25]

In recent elections right-wing populist parties won over 10 percent of the vote in Austria, Belgium, Denmark, France, Italy, and Norway.[26] Such extremist parties pose and reflect the familiar potential for unstable government and citizen turmoil. In the European Parliament elections in 2004 new parties opposing membership or extension of the EU won substantial support in a number of countries, including Britain.

In Western Europe, most of the new radical right-wing parties at least formally support political democracy, although they have less tolerance for minorities. In Eastern Europe voters in a number of countries have given substantial support to extremist parties that could well be considered antidemocratic. Zhirinovsky's (ill-named) Liberal Democratic Party in Russia, which promises personal dictatorship at home and wildly aggressive foreign policy abroad, would be a serious threat to democracy if its leader should come to power. The Greater Romanian Party is another extremist party whose commitment to basic democratic boundaries seems unclear.[27]

More typical of Eastern European politics than these extreme right-wing parties have been a variety of populist parties, campaigning against all the main parties and their governmental failures. Support for such parties often changes greatly from one election to the next; a fifth of the electorate or more has voted for such parties in several Eastern European nations.[28] The rejection of moderate centrist parties apparent in such voting reflects the hardships of the political and economic transitions, but also contributes to the difficulties of government.

A critical question in most of Eastern Europe concerns the parties that are direct descendants of the authoritarian communist parties that so long dominated the region. These parties generally call themselves "socialist" or "social democrat" (except in Russia) and claim to be democratic. (Many are required by the law or even the constitution to make this claim in order to compete in elections.) Some of them have undergone great changes in organization, people, and policies, while others are still largely unreconstructed in organization and

personnel from their communist predecessors. Some of them continue to adapt as circumstances change. The *formerly communist parties* and their potential "extremism" must be evaluated individually in each country. Compare, for example, the very different stances toward democracy and toward market economic policies of the communists in Russia, the Alliance of the Democratic Left (SLD) in Poland, and the Hungarian Socialist Party, as discussed in Chapters 9 through 11.[29]

The Content of Party Competition

People often discuss party competition in the multi-party systems of Western Europe by relating the parties to different positions on a *left-right continuum*.[30] The left-right language, which originated in the physical placement of the new members of the Assembly during the French Revolution 200 years ago, in time has become a shorthand summary of a number of the issues that are important to Western Europeans.

Economic or even "class" differences are a long term focus of party competition in Western Europe. Almost every party system has had one or more parties claiming to be on the "left" in the sense of representing the interests of the "working class." In most Western European countries socialist or *social democratic parties* are the predominant parties of the left with smaller communist or New Left challengers. Economic issues continue to define the main differences between "left" and "right" parties in Western Europe. However, the substance of difference has changed substantially in recent years, anticipating, but also encouraged by, the collapse of international communism.

Most "left" parties in Western Europe have now abandoned the idea of full government ownership of the economy, which was a major element of classic socialism. The combination of support for a large welfare system, redistribution of income from the better-off to the less fortunate through taxes and transfer payments, and a mixed (but predominately market) economy is often called a "social democratic" approach. It contrasts to varying degrees with a *"rightist" party* approach that stresses economic competition, less personal reliance on the government, and less government involvement of all kinds.

Figure 3.3 shows the parties on the "left-right" scale in the Western European democracies of Britain, France, Germany, and Spain, and the Eastern European democracy of Poland. The United States is shown for purposes of comparison. The position of the parties is based on the self-placement of citizens who voted for the party.[31] The height of the bars on the graph shows the voting support that each party received in the election year shown at the left of each line. Only parties getting about 4 percent of the vote or more are shown in the figure. The figure is best used as a guide to compare the distributions of party support within the countries, not comparing the centers of the party systems or the position of specific parties across countries. The average European voter places herself somewhat to the left of the average American voter, but we do not know that the voters have similar issues in mind.

The United States has only two parties, of course. Its uniqueness as the only purely two-party system is striking in Figure 3.3. In none of the other countries do the two largest parties get even 80 percent of the vote. The American parties have become somewhat more distinctive than they used to be, with the Democrats somewhat to the left and the Republicans similarly to the right of the average voter. The two main parties in Germany, in line 3 of the figure, are about as far apart as the American parties. In many democracies the two main parties are even further apart on the left-right scale, as we see in the distance between Labour and the Conservatives in Britain on line 2, and in the even larger distances in France and Spain.

As shown at the bottom of the figure, the "left-right" language also comfortably describes a wide party range in Poland, with the former communists (SLD) rather far to the left, several center parties, and a cluster of small (sometimes allied), parties to the right. Both religious and economic issues shape the left-right dialogue in Poland (see Chapter 10).

The figure also shows clearly the communist or formerly communist parties well on the left in France, Germany, Spain, and Poland, with more moderate social democratic or labor parties closer to the center. Britain and Germany have small centrist parties in the Liberal Democrats and FDP. Each country has one or more large parties of the moderate right. France stands out with 11 percent of the vote going to the right-extremist National Front Party.

Figure 3.3 also shows why in some multiparty systems, such as France, the number of parties and their dispersion across the left-right spectrum make this language helpful for voters. Without something like a single dimension to organize political discussion, it is difficult for voters in any democracy to compare their wishes with the promises and actions of policymakers.[32] With many smaller parties offering a variety of alternatives, voters find it especially helpful to characterize debate in terms of something like "left" and "right." In addition to economic issues the left-right language has begun to incorporate elements of the values distinction between welfare and security, on one hand, and quality of life issues, such as the environment, on the other.[33]

Economic issues have also been important in Eastern Europe, but they have often focused on the difficult transition from the old communist "command control" systems—in which the government owned the economy and directly decided wages, prices, investment, and so forth—to a system in which the market determines prices and government plays a lesser role.[34] While most contemporary parties favor the transition in general terms, they often disagree sharply on the pace and extent of this economic transition. For a variety of reasons, economic conditions have been difficult and quite painful to many groups in these societies. Not only did absolute living standards decline throughout Eastern Europe in the early 1990s, but groups accustomed to guaranteed jobs have had to face unemployment (real and potential), inflation that has made saving difficult, and increased income disparities. Naturally, some political parties have appeared to express the grievances and fears of the disadvantaged and call for moderation in the process or protection of the vulnerable. In the early days of the transition the issue of economic transformation was also entangled with the transition to political democracy.

Of course, other issues are also involved in party competition, in both West and East. Clashes between parties representing "new" and "traditional" values, including religious values, continue

Figure 3.3 Placement of Parties on the Left-Right Scale and Their Voter Support in Election

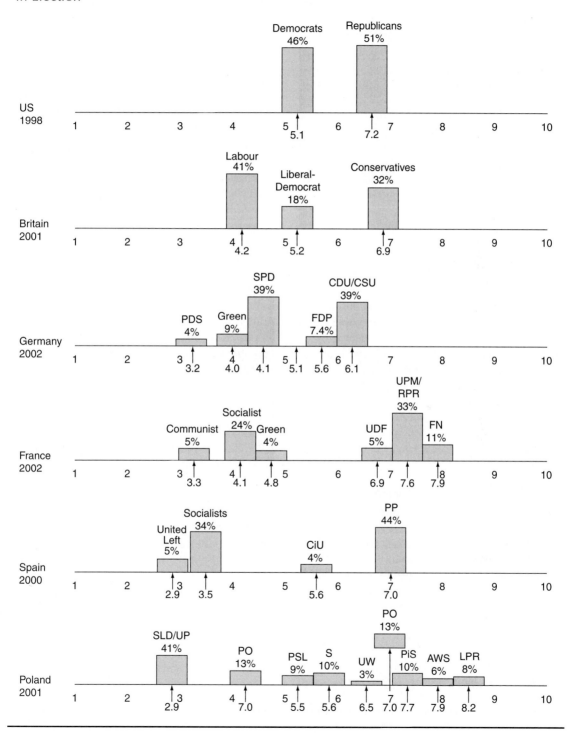

Source: Party positions from the self-placements of party voters; see text note. The height of the bar is the percent of vote won by the party in the parliamentary election shown on the left.

to be prominent in several countries, especially those with Catholic populations. In the last two decades, *Green parties* have challenged the industrialization and pollution associated with economic growth policies. They have often forced older and larger parties to adopt at least some pro-environment programs, even at some cost to jobs and profits. In 1998 the German Green Party joined with the SPD to form the governing coalition (see Chapter 7). Green parties have also participated in governing coalitions in France, Italy, Belgium, and Finland. Because of the serious pollution inherited from Soviet rule, Eastern Europe may offer great potential for Green parties, but these issues have so far been largely overshadowed by those of the economy and democracy.

Another recent issue is the focus on the fear of "foreigners" or minority ethnic groups. These groups have been accused of threatening traditional values, taking scarce jobs from workers, and contributing to crime. Far-right parties focusing on fears and issues of this type have obtained 10 percent or more of the vote in a number of countries (as discussed earlier).

The relationship with the emerging European Union has also been an important and divisive issue in some countries. As the European Union has expanded its power over the trade, monetary, and social policies of the member nations, the consequences of those policies have inevitably helped some groups and hurt others. Whether or not to join the Union, or to participate in each new expansion of its powers is very controversial in Britain and Denmark. In Norway debate over joining the European Union, which Norwegian voters have rejected in referenda, reshaped party competition. In Eastern Europe, many of the newly independent democracies wanted rapid incorporation into the European Union to protect their political independence and encourage their economies. But parties suspicious of EU policies gained surprising support in many of the new EU members (as well as some older members) in the European parliamentary elections in 2004 (see Chapter 12).

In summary, there are still many issues of political contention in contemporary Europe. The party systems in these nations represent these issues, offer a method for deciding between contrasting goals, and offer citizens a way to shape the policies of government.

Key Terms

anomic interest group

associational interest group

civil society

communist parties/ formerly communist parties

corporatist interest group systems

extremist parties

Green parties

institutional groups

left-right continuum

legislatures

mixed electoral rules

multiparty system/majority-electing party system

nonassociational group

number of political parties

pluralist interest group systems

proportional representation (PR)

rightist political parties

single-member districts

social democratic parties

Suggested Readings

Bartolini, Stefano, and Peter Mair. *Identity, Competition and Electoral Availability: The Stabilization of European Electorates.* New York: Cambridge University Press, 1990.

Cox, Gary. *Making Votes Count: Strategic Coordination in the World's Electoral Systems.* New York: Cambridge University Press, 1997.

Dalton, Russell J., and Martin Wattengerg, eds. *Parties without Partisans: Political Change in Advanced Industrial Democracies.* Oxford: Oxford University Press. 2000.

Franklin, Mark, Thomas Mackie, and Henry Valen, et al. *Electoral Change: Responses to Evolving Social and Attitudinal Structures in Western Countries.* New York: Cambridge University Press, 1992.

Hellman, Joel. "Winners Take All: The Politics of Partial Reform in Postcommunist Transitions," *World Politics* 50 (January 1998): 203–34.

Howard, Marc Morje. *The Weakness of Civil Society in Post-Communist Europe.* Cambridge: Cambridge University Press, 2000.

Kitschelt, Herbert. *The Transformation of European Social Democracy.* New York: Cambridge University Press, 1994.

———, Zdenka Mansfedlova, Radoslaw Markowski, and Gabor Toka. *Post-Communist Party Systems: Competition, Representation and Inter-Party Cooperation.* New York: Cambridge University Press, 1999.

LeDuc, Lawrence, Richard G. Niemi, and Pippa Norris, eds. *Comparing Democracies: Elections and Voting in Global Perspective.* Thousand Oaks, CA: Sage, 1996.

Lijphart, Arend. *Patterns of Democracy: Government Forms and Performance in Thirty-Six Countries.* New Haven: Yale University Press, 1999.

Lipset, Seymour M., and Stein Rokkan. *Party Systems and Voter Alignments.* New York: Free Press, 1967.

Powell, G. Bingham. *Contemporary Democracies: Participation, Stability and Violence.* Cambridge: Harvard University Press, 1982.

———. *Elections as Instruments of Democracy: Majoritarian and Proportional Visions.* New Haven: Yale University Press, 2000.

Putnam, Robert, ed. *Democracies in Flux: The Evolution of Social Capital in Contemporary Society.* Oxford: Oxford University Press, 2002.

Rose, Richard, and Neil Munro. *Elections and Parties in the New European Democracies.* Washington: CQ Press, 2003.

Sartori, Giovanni. *Parties and Party Systems: A Framework for Analysis.* New York: Cambridge University Press, 1976.

Webb, Paul, David M. Farrell, and Ian Holiday, eds. *Political Parties in Advanced Industrial Democracies.* Oxford: Oxford University Press, 2002.

 Endnotes

1. These figures are based on the 1999 European Values Study. Fairly similar levels were reported in the European Social Survey from surveys conducted in 2001–2002. As will be seen in Figure 3.1 union membership is, of course, much higher as a percent of the labor force than of the adult population.

2. Calculated from the European Social Survey.

3. Robert Putnam, *Bowling Alone: The Collapse and Revival of American Community* (New York: Simon and Shuster, 2000); Grzegorz Ekiert and Jan Kubik, *Rebellious Civil Society: Popular Protest and Democratic Consolidation in Poland, 1989–1993* (Ann Arbor: University of Michigan Press, 1999); Jean Cohen and A. Arato, *Civil Society and Political Theory* (Cambridge, MA: MIT Press, 1992).

4. Studies of the problems of organizing large groups were stimulated by the now classic work of Mancur Olson, *The Logic of Collective Action* (Cambridge, MA: Harvard University Press, 1965).

5. See Chapters 9–11. Also see Anna Seleny, "Old Political Rationalities and New Democracies: Compromise and Confrontation in Hungary and Poland," *World Politics* 51 (1999): 484–519.

6. Also see Marc Morje Howard, *The Weakness of Civil Society in Post-Communist Europe* (Cambridge: Cambridge University Press, 2000), who reports even sharper differences, based on a slightly earlier set of World Value surveys and a much smaller set of Western European countries.

7. Putnam, *Bowling Alone*: Robert Putnam, "Bowling Alone," *Journal of Democracy* 6 (1995): 65–78.

8. Peter Hall, "Social Capital in Britain," *British Journal of Political Science* 29: 417–61; Bernard Weßels, "Organizing Capacity of Societies and Modernity," in J. van Deth, ed., *Private Groups and Public Life: Social Participation, Voluntary Associations, and Political Involvement in Representative Democracies* (London: Routledge, 1997); Robert Putnam, ed., *Democracies in Flux: The Evolution of Social Capital in Contemporary Society* (Oxford: Oxford University Press, 2002).

9. The classic statements in this very large literature are Philippe Schmitter, "Still the Century of Corporatism," *Review of Politics* 36(1974): 85–131, and Gerhard Lehmbruch, "Liberal Corporatism and Party Government," *Comparative Political Studies* 10(1977): 91–126. Also see, for example, Philippe Schmitter, "Interest Intermediation and Regime Governability," in Suzanne Berger, ed., *Organizing Interests in Western Europe* (New York: Cambridge University Press, 1981), Ch. 12; Peter Katzenstein, *Small States in World Markets* (Ithaca: Cornell University Press, 1985); Arend Lijphart, *Patterns of Democracy: Government Forms and Performance in 36 Countries* (New Haven: Yale University Press, 1999), Ch. 9; Alan Siaroff, "Corporatism in 24 Industrial Countries: Meaning and Measurement," *European Journal of Political Research* 36(1999): 175–205. For a recent review of the evolution of the literature and its response to events of the 1990s see Oscar

Molina and Martin Rhodes, "Corporatism: The Past, Present and Future of a Concept," *Annual Review of Political Science* 5(2002): 305–31.

10. On the earlier relative success of the corporatist systems in economic performance see, for example, Miriam Golden, "The Dynamics of Trade Unionism and National Economic Performance," *American Political Science Review* 87:2(June 1993): 439–54.

11. See Molina and Rhodes, "Corporatism," 2002, and Michael Wallerstein and Bruce Western, "Unions in Decline? What Has Changed and Why?" in *Annual Review of Political Science* 3(2000): 355–77.

12. Barbara Geddes, "A Comparative Perspective on the Leninist Legacy in Eastern Europe," *Comparative Political Studies* 28 (July 1995): 239–74.

13. Paul G. Lewis, *Political Parties in Post-Communist Elections in Eastern Europe* (London: Routledge, 2000); Richard Rose and Neil Munro, *Elections and Parties in New European Democracies* (Washington: CQ Press, 2003), 78–84.

14. Lipset and Rokkan, *Party Systems and Voter Alignments.*

15. See Russell J. Dalton, "Political Cleavages, Issues, and Electoral Change," in Lawrence LeDuc, Richard G. Niemi, and Pippa Norris, eds., *Comparing Democracies 2* (Thousand Oaks, CA: Sage, 2002); Mark Franklin, Tom Mackie, Henry Valen, et al., *Electoral Change: Responses to Evolving Social and Attitudinal Structures in Western Countries* (Cambridge: Cambridge University Press, 1992); and Paul Webb, "Political Parties and Democratic Control," in Paul Webb, David Farrell, and Ian Holiday, eds., *Political Parties in Advanced Industrial Democracies* (Oxford: Oxford University Press, 2002), 438–60.

16. See Herbert Kitschelt, Zdenka Mansfelova, Radoslaw Markowski, and Gabor Toka, *Post Communist Party Systems: Competition, Representation and Inter-Party Competition* (New York: Cambridge University Press, 1999).

17. This number tells us roughly how many parties, of the same size would be the equivalent of the current distributions. From Markku Laakso and Rein Taagepera, "'Effective' Number of Parties: A Measure with Application to West Europe," *Comparative Political Studies* 12 (April 1979): 3–27. See also Arend Lijphart, *Patterns of Democracy* (New Haven: Yale University Press, 1999), Ch. 5. Mathematically, the number is $\dfrac{1}{\sum\limits_{i}^{n} p_i^2}$

P_i is the proportion of votes or seats of the ith party.

18. Because of the working of the single-member districts on the French alignment in 2002, an effective number of voted parties of over five was reduced nearly to two in the Assembly (see Ch. 6). Malta is Western Europe's most purely two-party system.

19. The classic analysis of the incentive for both parties in a two-party system to "converge to the median voter" is Anthony Downs, *An Economic Theory of Democracy* (New York: Harper and Row, 1957).

20. See, for example, Herbert Kitschelt, *The Transformation of European Social Democracy* (New York: Cambridge University Press, 1994); and Wolfgang C. Mueller and Kaare Strom, *Policy, Office or Votes? How Political Parties in Western Europe Make Hard Decisions* (New York: Cambridge University Press, 1999).

21. For example, Duverger, *Political Parties*, 1954, pp. 419–20; see also the discussion in Powell, *Contemporary Democracies*, Ch. 5.

22. Giovanni Sartori, *Parties and Party Systems* (New York: Cambridge University Press, 1976), Ch. 6; and see G. Bingham Powell, Jr., "The Competitive Consequences of Polarized Pluralism," in Manfred Holler, ed., *The Logic of Multiparty Systems* (Dordrecht, Netherlands: Martinus Nijhoff, 1987), pp. 173–90.

23. Paul Warwick, "Economic Trends and Government Survival in West European Parliamentary Democracies," *American Political Science Review* 86(December 1992): 875–87. A very large body of research exists on this topic, beginning especially with Michael Taylor and Valentine Herman, "Party Systems and Government Stability," *American Political Science Review* 65 (March 1971): 28–37; see the reviews in Powell, *Contemporary Democracies*, Ch. 7 and in Warwick.

24. See G. Bingham Powell, Jr., "Extremist Parties, Electoral Polarization, and Citizen Turmoil," *American Journal of Political Science* 30 (1986): 357–78.

25. See discussion in *The Economist*, November 23, 1991, pp. 56–57 and in Chapter 6.

26. For "expert assessment" approaches listing "extreme right" parties in Western Europe, see Cas Mudde, "Defining the Extreme Right Party Family," *West European Politics* 19:2 (April 1996): 225–48; Elisabeth L. Carter, "Proportional Representation and the Fortunes of Right-Wing Extremist Parties," *West European Politics* 25:3 (July 2002): 125–46. On explanations of support for different kinds of extreme right parties, see Herbert Kitschelt, *The Radical Right in Western Europe* (Ann Arbor: University of Michigan Press, 1995); Matt Golder, "Explaining Variation in the Success of Extreme Right Parties in Western Europe," *Comparative Political Studies* 36 (2003): 432–66; Wouter van der Brug and Meindert Fennema, "Protest or Mainstream," *European Journal of Political Research* 42 (2003): 55–76.

27. Grigore Pop-Eleches, "Whither Democracy? The Politics of Rejection in the 2000 Romanian Elections," Berkeley: Berkeley Program in Soviet and Post-Soviet Studies, 2001. The party, which had strongly attacked Hungarian, Jewish, and Gypsy minorities, as well as the failures of the mainstream parties, and called for national expansion, won a fifth of the vote in Romania in the 2000 election.

28. These countries include Bulgaria, Croatia, Estonia, Latvia, Lithuania, and Slovakia, with only slightly less backing in Moldova and Poland. See Grigore Pop-Eleches, "Radicalization or Protest Vote? Explaining the Success of Unorthodox Parties in Eastern Europe" (Princeton, New Jersey, 2004).

29. For an analysis that attempts to explain differences in the role of formerly communist parties in terms of the way the older communist systems were governed and the nature of the transition to democracy, see the discussion in Kitschelt, *Post-Communist Party Systems*. Pop-Eleches, "Radicalization," reports over 10 percent of the voters backing "radical left" parties in Czech Republic, Latvia, Moldova, and Poland. (Note that he classifies Poland's "Self-Defense Party," but not the ex-communist SLD, as a radical left party.) His study does not include Russia.

30. Americans use the terms "liberal" and "conservative" in roughly this sense; "liberal" means something quite different in Europe, so it is safer, as well as regionally correct, to stay with "left."

31. The citizen placements in Britain and Spain are from the *Euro-Barometer 54.1, Nov–Dec. 2000* survey. Those in France, Germany, and Poland are from the *Comparative Election Study* surveys in 2001 and 2002, with the 11-point scale converted to a 10-point scale for comparability. The United States placements are from the 2002 *U.S. National Election Study*, converting the 7-point liberal-conservative scale to a 10 point scale. Roughly similar results derive from a survey of experts in 1993, reported in John Huber and Ronald Inglehart, "Expert Interpretations,"*Party Politics* (1995):73–111 although using the average voter self-placement (as done here) tends to pull placement of the more extreme parties somewhat toward the center.

32. On this idea and the issues involved, see also G. Bingham Powell, Jr., *Elections as Instruments of Democracy: Majoritarian and Proportional Visions* (New Haven: Yale University Press, 2000), esp. Ch. 7 and references.

33. See Ronald Inglehart, "The Changing Structure of Political Cleavages in Western Society," in Russell J. Dalton, Scott C. Flanagan, and Paul Allen Beck, *Electoral Change in Advanced Industrial Societies* (Princeton: Princeton University Press, 1984), pp. 25–69. On the "post-materialist" values, especially associated with generational differences, see Ronald Inglehart, *Culture Shift in Advanced Industrial Society* (Princeton: Princeton University Press, 1990).

34. See Joshua A. Tucker, "*Regional Economic Voting: Russia, Poland, Hungary, Slovakia and the Czech Republic from 1990–99*," N. Y.: Cambridge University Press, 2005; Timothy J. Colton, *Transitional Citizens: Voters and What Influences Them in the New Russia* (Cambridge: Harvard University Press, 2000); Stephen White, Richard Rose, and Ian McAllister, *How Russia Votes* (Chatham: Chatham House, 1997).

Chapter 4

Government
and Public Policy

M ost European governments are liberal democracies in practice, claim, or aspiration. Democratic leaders are supposed to do what their citizens want and be accountable to them through competitive elections. In a *liberal democracy*, citizens
must be free to organize and express their desires, and public policy must be shaped by
these citizen preferences, and not by what some leader or expert claims is the people's
true interest. Moreover, the civil and political rights and liberties of individual citizens,
and the rights of minorities, must be protected. Liberal democracy also depends on the
rule of law. This means that government can take no action that has not been authorized
by law, and that citizens can be punished only if they violate an existing law. The opposite of democratic government is *authoritarianism* or autocracy.

In Western Europe liberal democracy is well established. By the early 1980s, the last
authoritarian governments (in Greece, Portugal, and Spain) had made successful transitions to democracy. Yet, some Western European nations have faced serious conflict, and
some have constrained democratic freedoms in limited ways or in local areas. In the early
1990s, Italian citizens expressed severe dissatisfaction with their country's political performance and attempted to replace most of its politicians and restructure its politics. But despite occasional problems of violence, terrorism, and intolerance, all Western European
countries now have competitive elections, representative assemblies, and civil rights.

The nations of Central and Eastern Europe present a more varied picture. Most of the
successor countries of Yugoslavia have experienced civil war or sharp ethnic tension. The
Soviet Union until 1989 dominated most of the rest of Eastern Europe, where the citizens
endured authoritarian rule and in large part foreign domination. While most citizens
now support their new democratic freedoms and market economies (see Chapter 2), it
has not always been easy to sustain these reforms. Consolidation is hampered not only
by the lack of democratic experience, but also by unfavorable social and economic conditions. Some new democracies, such as Poland and Hungary, have consolidated. Democracy remains provisional or fragile in others, including Russia and Ukraine, while authoritarianism prevails in a few, such as Belarus. History shows that there are many

different ways to run a democracy, with distinct advantages and disadvantages. Despite their occasional shortcomings, the nations of Eastern Europe offer additional experiences in democratic governance and new lessons about why some emerging democracies survive while others fail.

CONSTITUTIONAL ORGANIZATION: RULES FOR MAKING RULES

Working out a *constitution,* which is a general agreement on how laws are made and decision makers chosen, is a critical task for any new democracy. A constitution may be a single written document, a set of statutes and practices, or some combination of these. The choice of constitutional arrangements may shape political decisions for generations. Because constitutional rules are so fundamental, radical changes in them are rare except after massive upheavals.

The most important question in constitutional design is who has authority to make political decisions. Democracies typically mix elements of *direct* governance, in which citizens make political decisions themselves through referendums, initiatives, town hall meetings and the like, and *representative* rule, in which citizens elect politicians that make decisions on their behalf. European democracies are primarily representative. Except for Switzerland, direct democracy is much less common than in many American states. Yet, many European constitutions require or permit referendums on major constitutional changes, such as whether or not to join the European Union or adopt a new Euro constitution.

SEPARATION OF GOVERNMENT POWERS

Since most political decisions in Europe are made by the people's representatives, rather than by the people themselves, it is important to understand what powers different branches of government possess. Whereas authoritarian political systems often lack any effective limitation on the power of the ruler(s), democracies have devised various constraints on politicians. The theory of *separation of powers* has a long and venerable history going back at least to the work of Locke in Britain and

Montesquieu in France.[1] Separation of powers, they argued, can prevent injustices that might result from an unchecked executive or legislature. James Madison and Alexander Hamilton elaborated this theory in *The Federalist,* which described and defended the institutional arrangements proposed by the U.S. Constitutional Convention of 1787. In modern democracies, there are two basic ways to separate power: (1) a *geographic* distribution of authority between the central (national) government and lower levels, such as states, provinces, or municipalities; and (2) a *structural* separation of powers among different branches of government, such as the legislature, the executive, and the judiciary. We shall discuss these dimensions in order.

Geographic Distribution of Government Power

The United States has a long history of geographic separation of power. The Articles of Confederation set up a *confederal* system: ultimate power rested with the states. Under the Constitution of 1787, the American government became *federal:* both central and state governments have since then had separate spheres of authority and the means to implement their power. Most European states are more geographically centralized. Britain, France, Hungary, Poland, and many other European countries are *unitary,* with power concentrated in the central government. Regional and local units have only those powers specifically delegated to them by the central government, which may change or withdraw these powers at will. Thus, confederal systems represent the greatest degree of power dispersion, unitary systems the least, and federal systems are in the middle (see the vertical dimension of Figure 4.1).

There are several federal states in Europe, and especially in the German-speaking region of Central Europe. In Germany and Switzerland, for example, the national government shares power in many policy areas with regional governments (called *Länder* in Germany). Austria and Russia are also federal states, and Belgium became federal in 1993. Moreover, even such unitary countries as France, Italy, and Spain have recently shifted some power from

FIGURE 4.1   Division of Governmental Authority

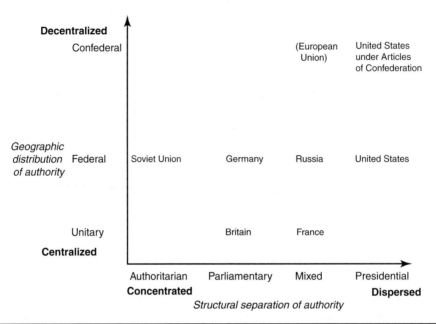

their national governments "downward" to regional ones. The European Union is also becoming increasingly federal, as power is shifted "upward" from the member-states to this supranational body (see Chapter 12).

Federalism can have a number of advantages. In culturally divided societies, it may help protect ethnic, linguistic, or religious minorities, particularly if they are geographically concentrated. In Belgium, federalism was introduced to satisfy the country's two main language communities: the French-speaking Walloons and the Dutch-speaking Flemings. Yet national governments often fear that decentralization of power will put the country on a slippery slope toward a total breakup, as happened in the former Yugoslavia. But even if decentralization leads to a breakup, this is not always undesirable. Czechoslovakia is a more positive example of a federal system that peacefully transformed itself into the separate states of the Czech Republic and Slovakia.

Federalism may also serve as a check on overly ambitious rulers and thus protect the rights and freedoms of the citizens. Moreover, federalism may allow subunits (such as states) to experiment with different policy programs. One government may thus learn from the experiences of others. Besides, citizens can "vote with their feet" and choose the policy environment they like best. However, while federalism promotes choice and diversity, it does so at the expense of equality. Since federalism allows different subnational governments to pursue distinct policies, citizens may get systematically different treatments and benefits. Unitary governments may also be better able than federal ones to redistribute resources from richer to poorer regions.

Parliamentary or Presidential Democracies

The second form of separation of power is *functional*: it runs between the different branches of government. The major distinction is between presidential and parliamentary systems. These alternatives specify the relationship between the *assembly* (or legislature or parliament),[2] which represents the people and has primary authority to make laws, and the *executive*, which carries out these laws. In both parliamentary and presidential democracies the assembly is directly elected by the citizens and has significant authority to make laws, tax, and spend.

In a *presidential democracy*, such as in the United States, the people also elect the president separately. The president is both head of state and chief executive (head of government). He or she appoints a government (cabinet), which helps the president administer all the executive agencies. Both president and assembly have fixed terms; neither can dismiss the other before the next election. (It may be possible to impeach the president or members of the cabinet, but only for serious offenses and after an extraordinary vote that often requires a large majority.) While the primary authority to make laws or raise and spend money usually remains with the assembly, the president often has a veto power. In the United States, for example, Congress can pass legislation over the president's veto only if each House adopts it by a two-thirds majority.

In Western Europe, in contrast, the typical government is some form of *parliamentary democracy*, in which the people do *not* directly elect the chief executive, the *prime minister*. Instead the people elect the assembly (parliament), which then chooses and can dismiss the prime minister. The office of prime minister goes by different names in different countries (prime minister in Britain, premier in France, and chancellor in Germany, for example) but functions in a similar fashion. The prime minister heads the *cabinet*, which consists of the top executive policymakers, primarily the heads of the various executive agencies (known as departments or ministries). The prime minister, his or her cabinet members, and their party-affiliated staff and political advisers are collectively referred to as the "government." The prime minister is the head of government but not the ceremonial head of state. All authority to make and execute laws derives from the elected assembly, but in reality the cabinet dominates policymaking more than it does in presidential systems. Some of the typical features of presidential and parliamentary systems are shown in Table 4.1.

Most parliamentary systems have two critical constitutional provisions that differ from presidential systems. One is the *confidence vote*, and its mirror image, the "vote of no confidence" or "vote of censure." If a parliamentary majority expresses its lack of confidence in the government (the prime

TABLE 4.1   Distinguishing Features of Parliamentary and Presidential Democracies

Distinguishing Features[a]	Parliamentary Democracies	Presidential Democracies
Title of chief executive	Prime minister (head of government)	President (head of state and government)
How is the assembly selected?	By citizens in competitive election	By citizens in competitive election
How is the chief executive selected?	By assembly after election or removal	By citizens in competitive election
Can the chief executive be removed before the end of his/her term?	Yes, by assembly through no-confidence vote	No
Can the assembly be dismissed before the end of its term?	Yes, the prime minister may call for early election[b]	No
Authority to legislate	Assembly only	Assembly plus president (e.g., veto)
Party control of assembly and executive	Same parties control both	Different party control possible
Party cohesion in assembly voting	Strong	Less strong

[a]These define the pure parliamentary and presidential types; as discussed in the text, many constitutional systems, especially in Eastern Europe, "mix" the features of the two types.
[b]Some constitutional systems that are parliamentary in all other ways do not allow for early legislative elections. All parliamentary democracies provide for legislative elections after some maximum time (from three to five years) since the last election.

Box 4.1   The Confidence Vote in Parliamentary Democracies

Confidence votes can be critical and dramatic events in parliamentary democracies, since if they lose the vote, the prime minister and all members of the cabinet have to resign. A confidence vote can be called either by the opposition (a no-confidence motion) or by the the prime minister (a confidence motion). Whether it is a motion of confidence or no confidence, the government must win the vote or resign from office. But why would the prime minister ever voluntarily call for a confidence vote and risk being thrown out of office? The answer is that the confidence motion is typically attached to a bill (a policy proposal) that is favored by the prime minister, but not by the parliamentary majority. By attaching a confidence motion to the bill, the prime minister forces the members of parliament either to adopt the bill or to find another prime minister. This can be a particularly painful choice for dissident members of the prime minister's own party. If they don't vote for the bill, they may bring down their own government, and may perhaps also immediately have to face the voters. Prime ministers can therefore use the confidence motion in order to bring rebellious party members into line. Usually, the threat alone is enough to ensure party discipline and pass important legislation. Thus, the confidence vote helps explain why party discipline tends to be stronger in parliamentary than in presidential systems.

minister and his or her cabinet), then the government must resign.[3] (See Box 4.1.) The second distinctive feature is the possibility of *parliamentary dissolution.* Dissolution allows the government to end the assembly session and hold new elections before they would otherwise be due. In some parliamentary countries, such as Britain, the prime minister can effectively decide to hold new elections whenever he or she wants to. In other countries, the president has to agree, or there are various constitutional restrictions. Votes of no confidence are often followed by parliamentary dissolution. If the government resigns, a new election may be called at the same time. Alternatively, some of the parties in the assembly may try to form a new government without having an election. This depends on the constitutional rules, customs, and the political situation.

The purpose of the confidence vote and the dissolution power is to ensure that the executive branch and the legislature share a common political view, so that they do not work at cross-purposes or get bogged down in gridlock. Rather than a rivalry between government branches, as we often see in the U.S. system, there is strong coordination. This promotes decisive government, but it also means less constraint on those in power.

In almost all parliamentary systems, the executive branch is the major policymaker, while the parliament provides an arena for debate, consent, and final authorization. The assembly thus plays a more limited policymaking role than in presidential systems. In Western Europe the most powerful politician is usually the prime minister.

In the European parliamentary systems most governments depend on disciplined party support to survive. Especially the elected representatives of the governing party tend to vote extremely cohesively. Partisan voting is further encouraged by the fact that members of parliament who want to be appointed to cabinet positions or other prestigious offices depend on the goodwill of their respective party leaders. The tendency of Western Europeans to vote for parties, not individual representatives, both reflects and encourages party cohesion in the assembly. The strong *party cohesion* (often called "discipline") in Western European parliaments is frequently contrasted with the U.S. Congress, where party affiliation is only one of several features shaping voting decisions, along with constituency interests, interest group pressure, and personal opinions. On the average substantive "party" vote in the U.S. Congress in the 1990s, a little more than 80 percent of the party members voted together.[4] In the Western European parliamentary systems, on average over 95 percent of the party members vote together on issues that the parties contest.

Most of the time the major parties enjoy nearly perfect internal cohesion.[5]

A second lesson of European parliamentarism is that the fragmentation of parties in parliament affects the cabinet's stability and strength. When a single party controls a parliamentary majority, it can also control the executive and carry out its election promises in predictable ways. Of course, by the same token it may ignore the interests of minority parties. When elections instead produce a parliament divided between many parties, at least some of them must negotiate with each other to form a government. For better or worse, the resulting government is likely to pursue compromise policies that may not resemble anybody's election platform. If legislative negotiations are difficult, governments may also be unstable (as in Italy, where the average cabinet since World War II has lasted only about a year). For these reasons, election rules that determine how many parties gain representation are especially important in parliamentary systems.

Contrary to presidentialism, parliamentary democracies have a dual (or "split") executive. One person (the prime minister) is the effective leader of the executive branch and someone else the ceremonial representative of the country (the head of state). The head of state may be a president or monarch. A hundred years ago, the overwhelming majority of European heads of state were monarchs, but now there are only eight left (disregarding such micro-states as Monaco and Liechtenstein). The last new European democracy that chose a monarchy was Spain in the 1970s. All the other European monarchies (those in Britain, Scandinavia, and the Low Countries) are at least a century old. And there are no monarchs in Eastern Europe.

Figure 4.2 displays the constitutional structures of Western and Eastern Europe. There are no pure presidential systems. All Western European systems except Switzerland are parliamentary. Typically, the head of state is a president rather than a monarch. But presidents may be selected in many different ways. The most important distinction is between those that are elected by the citizens and those that are selected by parliament.[6]

The power of European heads of state varies a great deal across countries.[7] Nowadays, monarchs have only symbolic or ceremonial functions, though Spain's King Juan Carlos actually played a positive role in consolidating Spain's new democracy in the 1970s and early 1980s. "Parliament-selected" presidents, such as in Germany, Hungary, and Italy, never have much policymaking authority and consistently rank well behind their respective prime ministers in real power. To find powerful heads of state we therefore have to look to countries with popularly elected presidents.

Not all popularly elected presidents are strong, however. Some have largely ceremonial powers, as in Austria, Iceland, and Ireland. But a handful of Western European countries, most notably France, have "mixed" or *semi-presidential systems* that combine parliamentary and presidential features. In such systems, the directly elected president appoints the prime minister. Moreover, the president can usually dissolve parliament and call new elections; he or she may also have some direct policymaking powers. Prime ministers in these countries are "jointly accountable": they depend on majority support in the assembly as well as on the backing of the president. If they fail to retain parliamentary support, they can be removed through a vote of no confidence. If they fail to please the president, they can often be fired.

Table 4.2 compares various powers of the five presidents covered in our text. The Russian president is the strongest of these five executives. He is the only one who names cabinet members directly. Thus, the Russian president, rather than the prime minister, controls the membership of the cabinet. It is also very difficult for the Russian assembly to override presidential vetoes. The German president, on the other hand, is the weakest of the five. He has no veto or decree powers, and he can only dismiss the Assembly (the *Bundestag*) in narrowly defined emergency situations.

As shown in Table 4.2 and Figure 4.2, many Eastern European constitution makers favored a semi-presidential regime. Several countries partly imitated the French constitution. Yet about a third of the Eastern European constitutions (including Hungary) are purely parliamentary and have weak, parliament-selected presidents. A similar number have directly elected, but fairly weak and ceremonial,

FIGURE 4.2   Heads of State in Western and Eastern Europe, as of 2004

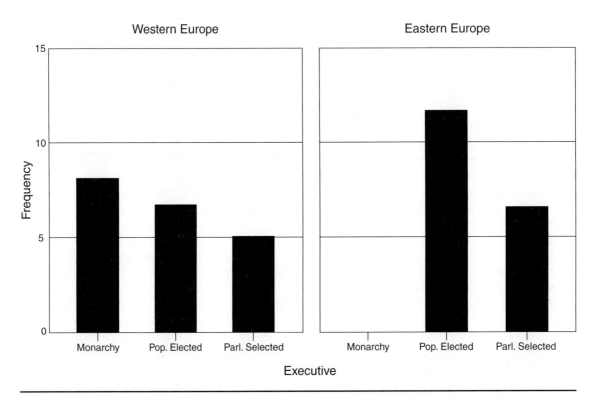

Heads of State in Western and Eastern Europe

Note:
"Popularly Elected" executives include executives that are *directly* elected by the citizens and those that are *indirectly* elected by them. "Parliament Selected" executives may be elected solely by the parliament, or by some combination of the parliament and other government officials.

Source: Central Intelligence Agency. 2004. *CIA World Factbook,* as updated November 30, 2004, from http://www.odci.gov/cia/publications/factbook/fields/2077.html.

presidents. However, the popularly elected presidents in Lithuania, Poland, and Romania have powers at least equal to those of the French president. They appoint prime ministers and cabinets that are accountable to the assembly. The presidents of Croatia, Russia, and Ukraine have even stronger policymaking powers. These are the only European countries in which the president is more powerful than the prime minister. To the extent that these countries are democratic, they come close to being presidential, even though the prime minister is accountable to the national assembly.

A semi-presidential system with a powerful president as well as a prime minister may experience *divided government* (known in France as "cohabitation"). This is where one party (or coalition of parties) holds the presidency, while another party controls the legislature, and typically also the prime ministership. France experienced such "cohabitation" in 1986–1988, 1993–1995, and 1997–2002, and Poland in 1993–1996 and 1997–2001. Divided government can lead to conflict or complex political bargaining. While we are still learning about semi-presidentialism in Eastern

TABLE 4.2   Presidential Powers

Countries	Can the President Veto Laws? If So, How Does Parliament Override?	Can the President Issue Decrees (Regulations Not Passed by the Assembly)?	Can the President Propose a Referendum?	What Is the Role of the President When a Cabinet Is Formed?	Can the President Dissolve the Assembly and Call New Elections?
France (Popularly Elected)	Yes; override by simple majority	The president has limited authority to issue decrees.	Only upon the request of the prime minister or both houses of the Assembly	The president names a prime minister, who must be approved by the Assembly and then names other ministers.	Yes, but not during the first year of the Assembly's term.
Germany (Parliament Selected)	Veto power not clearly established by Constitution	No	No	The president names a prime minister, who must be approved by the Assembly and then names other ministers.	Yes, but only after there has been a vote of no confidence in the prime minister.
Hungary (Parliament Selected)	Yes; override by simple majority	The president has limited authority to issue decrees.	The president has restricted powers to do so, but other institutions may also propose.	The president names a prime minister, who must be approved by the Assembly and then names other ministers.	Yes, but only after there has been a vote of no confidence in the prime minister.
Poland (Popularly Elected)	Yes; override by absolute majority of all representatives	No	Only with the consent of the Senate	The president names a prime minister, who must be approved by the Assembly and then names other ministers.	Yes, but only after there has been a vote of no confidence in the prime minister.
Russia (Popularly Elected)	Yes; override by extraordinary majority	The president has extensive power to issue decrees, as long as they do not conflict with existing laws.	Yes; there are no restrictions on this power.	The president names cabinet ministers directly. They must then be approved by the Assembly.	Yes, but only after there has been a vote of no confidence in the prime minister.

Sources: Albert P. Blaunstein, and Gisbert H. Flanz, ed., *Constitutions of the Countries of the World*, Dobbs Ferry: Oceana; *The Europa World Year Book 2004*, 45th ed., Europa Publications; Taylor and Francis Group: New York, NY; International Institute for Democracy, ed. 1996. *The Rebirth of Democracy: 12 Constitutions of Central and East Europe*, 2nd ed., Council of European Publishers: Netherlands; International Institute for Democracy, ed. 1997. *Transition to Democracy: Constitutions of the New Industrial States and Mongolia*. Council of European Publishers: Germany; Lee Kendall Metcalf, 2000. "Measuring Presidential Power," *Comparative Political Studies* v. 33 (660–85); Matthew S. Shugart and John M. Carey, 1992. *Presidents and Assemblies: Constitutional Design and Electoral Dynamics*, Cambridge University Press: New York, NY.

Europe, the basic lessons from France are that (1) if the president's party controls the assembly, he or she can be the lead policymaker; (2) even without such control a clever president with substantial support can dominate policymaking if the opposition is divided; but (3) if the legislature is controlled by a united opposition, power will tend to shift to the prime minister and the parties controlling the assembly.[8] In Eastern Europe, this third condition has been rare, as fragmented party systems and internally divided parties have facilitated presidential dominance.

There is a heated debate over the advantages of parliamentary versus presidential constitutions. Based on the favorable Western European experience with parliamentarism (and the often unfavorable Latin American experience with presidentialism), scholarly opinion has tended to favor the parliamentary option.[9] Parliamentary systems, their proponents argue, can represent a wide range of public opinion in the assembly and see that these views bear directly on the executive. And if the elected representatives of the people dislike the cabinet's policies, they can change governments.

A presidential system always holds the potential for a confrontation between a strong president who usually initiates a lot of legislation and also implements it—and the assembly that must approve all laws and fund all government programs. Such confrontation is particularly likely when these branches of government are controlled by different political parties. In the United States, divided government has often been associated with deadlock and policy "immobilism," such as the conflict between a Democratic president and a Republican Congress that briefly shut down many government programs in the winter of 1995–1996. When the conflict is very severe, as in Chile in the early 1970s, the strife between these two agents of the people can tear the political system apart. Another problem is that a strong president can also use executive powers to repress democratic competition.

On the other hand, advocates of presidential systems, and many constitution makers in new democracies, point out that direct presidential election and fixed terms improve efficiency and accountability.[10] Election dates are predictable, and citizens

do not constantly have to concern themselves with election campaigns and threats that new elections may be called. These advantages loom especially large when the legislature is divided into multiple parties and factions that cannot consistently support the same government. Under such circumstances, politicians may be especially tempted to call elections to try to improve their standing. Another advantage of presidentialism is that the head of government is chosen directly by the people, not through a process of political "wheeling and dealing," as in parliamentary systems. Independent of a legislative majority for daily survival and elected by the whole nation, the president should be able to take a larger view of national interest than can individual legislators or the prime ministers they choose. Defenders of presidentialism also point out that the instability of many presidential regimes in Latin America may have been due more to unfavorable social conditions than to presidential constitutions. And between the two world wars, parliamentary constitutions in Europe were no more stable than presidential ones in Latin America.

Regrettably, the negative arguments on both sides of the presidential/parliamentary debate can find support in the Eastern European experience. Government stability has been a problem in a number of parliamentary governments and in some mixed systems with moderately strong presidents as well. And all three countries with particularly strong presidents (Croatia, Russia, and Ukraine) have experienced at least temporary limitations on democracy and the freedom of speech. Only about a third of the countries with other types of constitutions have experienced such severe transition problems. The 2004 Freedom House Report of *freedom of the press* tells a very similar tale (see Box 4.2).

The European countries most consistently ranked democratic and free include every constitutional type except the mixed type with a strong president. Yet, this may be because the countries that have adopted strong presidencies are relatively poor and ethnically troubled. Countries with more advanced economies and success in avoiding ethno-nationalist entanglements tend to have an easier transition. Despite the many challenges, so far the transition to democracy has clearly failed only in Belarus, where a

---

Box 4.2 Democratic Failure: An Unfree Press

One of the surest threats to democracy is failure to sustain free broadcast and print media. Freedom House's annual *Press Freedom Survey* evaluates constraints on these freedoms in many countries. Europe scores comparatively high on press freedom, but the region is far from trouble-free. The good news in the most recent report (covering 2003) is that all but one country (Italy) in Western Europe and eight of the countries in Eastern Europe, including Poland and Hungary, were generally classified as having a "free" press.

Yet, Italy and eight Eastern European countries experienced sufficient problems that they were classified as having an only "partly free" press in 2003. Italy's problems lie in "an inadequate legal and institutional framework" and "an unprecedented concentration of media ownership and a resulting increase in and misuse of political pressure on media outlets. Silvio Berlusconi has used his position as prime minister to exert undue influence over the public broadcaster RAI, in addition to manipulating coverage at his family's own sizable media empire, which includes Italy's three largest private television stations."

Finally, the Freedom House analysis classified the media in Belarus, Moldova, Russia, and Ukraine as "not free." These four countries had far to go on the journey toward effective democracy. Concerning Russia, the report notes that "while the constitution provides for freedom of speech and of the press, the Putin administration has increasingly restricted these rights in practice, especially regarding sensitive issues such as criticism of the president, the ongoing conflict in Chechnya, and government corruption." Several independent broadcasting stations and journalists were forced off the air in the run-up to the legislative elections in December 2003. "Independent journalists continue to be harassed, assaulted, kidnapped, and killed."

The most disturbing finding in the Freedom House report may be that for the second successive year press freedom worldwide suffered a substantial decline in 2003. Three European countries were downgraded: Bulgaria and Italy from free to partly free, and Moldova from partly free to not free. Italy's downgrade represents the first time a member-state of the European Union has been classified as anything other than free.

Source: Freedom House, *Press Freedom Survey 2004*, as downloaded November 26, 2004, from www.freedomhouse.org/pfs2004/.

---

strong president has ignored constitutional limits on his power, and in Bosnia-Herzegovina, which was plunged into a civil war before democratic institutions could be consolidated. But even in Russia, Ukraine, and Serbia and Montenegro (the remainder of the former Yugoslavia), democracy seems fragile at best. With so many different risks, the constitutional questions remain open.

LIMITING AND DISPERSING POLICYMAKING POWER

European democracies are embedded in complex constitutional arrangements, many of which require the policymakers to secure the consent of more than a simple parliamentary majority. The British political system is one of the simplest, because a government that controls the House of Commons need not share power with other institutions or political opponents. Most other European countries,

however, feature various constraints on the parliamentary majority.

Besides direct democracy and federalism, many European democracies limit executive power through three different kinds of institutional arrangements: strong legislative committees, bicameralism, and judicial review. The first approach, *strong legislative committees*, requires *power-sharing* with opposition parties within the parliament itself. Such countries as Austria, Germany, and Hungary delegate a large part of the process of drafting laws to parliamentary committees in which the chairmanships are shared proportionally between government and opposition parties. In such committees it is usually necessary for government majorities to take greater account of the parliamentary opposition parties.

Another approach is *bicameralism*—a separation of power between two parliamentary chambers. Germany, Russia, and Switzerland, for example, have (as does the United States) a second legislative chamber with significant power and a different method of election. In some countries, such as Germany, the upper house directly represents regional governments. If different parties control the two chambers, then policymaking may require more extensive bargaining and compromise.

Judicial review by special constitutional courts or councils is another way to constrain the government. Although most European courts are not as active as the U.S. Supreme Court, many have become more assertive in recent years.[11] The constitutions of newly free Eastern European nations generally provide for constitutional courts, many of which have played influential roles in constraining government policies and even defining new constitutional powers. However, in some countries, such as Russia, Belarus, and Albania, the constitutional courts are controversial. For countries that are members of the European Union, the European Court of Justice has become an important check on national legislation.

CONSTITUTIONAL ORGANIZATION: ELECTORAL RULES

European polities operate primarily as representative democracies. Therefore the rules for electing the people's representatives are a critical part of their constitutional arrangements. Although these rules are often established only as ordinary legislation, they play a fundamental part in shaping the policy process and once established are only rarely modified in a substantial way.[12] Most Western European democracies feature *proportional representation (PR)* in parliamentary elections. PR provides for multi-member legislative districts with parties represented in rough proportion to their vote. There are many forms of PR, and none is perfectly proportional. But the larger the number of representatives elected in each district, the easier it is to reach proportionality. For example, it may take up to 33 percent of the vote to gain a seat in a three-member Irish district. In the Netherlands, in contrast, the entire 150-seat legislature is elected from the nation at large, permitting even very small parties to gain representation. Some constitutions also feature so-called *supplementary seats*, which are elected from the na-

tion as a whole and given to parties that would otherwise be underrepresented.

Proportional representation rules with large districts very accurately convert votes into legislative seats, but they can fragment the assembly into a multitude of little parties. Consequently, it may become difficult to build legislative majorities and pass coherent legislation. In order to limit the number of legislative parties, many countries have some minimum "threshold" of votes (for example, 5 percent) that parties must win in order to enter parliament. Such thresholds are often used in combination with supplementary seats. The Swedish Parliament, for example, has 349 seats, out of which 310 are given out in separate districts that have anywhere from 2 to 34 representatives each. The remaining 39 supplementary seats are given to parties that surpass the national threshold of 4 percent but are underrepresented when all the district seats are added up. In this way, Sweden gets highly proportional results for all parties that get at least 4 percent of the vote, whereas parties that fall below this threshold get nothing.

Figure 4.3 shows some features of the election laws in Western and Eastern Europe. The first two bars in each region show countries with PR but different thresholds for representation. Most Western European countries, but only three in Eastern Europe, now have thresholds lower than 4 percent (or no thresholds at all). Most commonly, as shown in the second column, the Eastern European PR systems require parties to win 4 to 9 percent of the vote to enter the national parliament. Although such thresholds seem low, even 4- or 5-percent thresholds can eliminate the representation of many voters (but also help constrain legislative fragmentation) if the party system is extremely splintered. Nonetheless, under PR it is hard for individual parties to win legislative majorities. A few PR countries have small districts or other special rules that raise the effective threshold even higher, making it harder for small parties to enter the legislature and easier for large parties to win majorities.[13]

Single-Member District Plurality Systems

The best-known alternative to proportional representation is the "first-past-the-post" system, in which

FIGURE 4.3   Legislative Election Rules in Western and Eastern Europe, as of 2004

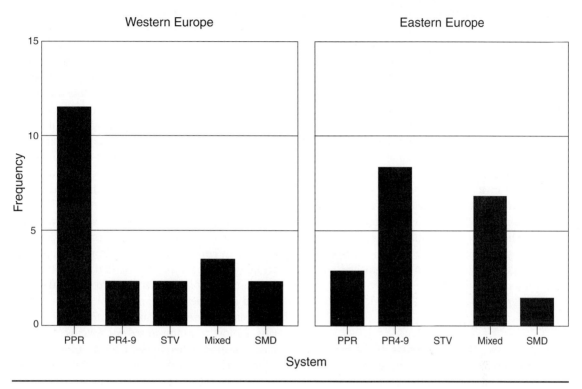

Notes:
"PPR" = Pure proportional representation
"PR4-9" = Proportional representation with a 4–9% electoral threshold
"STV" = Single transferable vote
"Mixed" = Mixed proportional and plurality electoral system
"SMD" = Single-member district system

Sources: Electionworld. 2004. *Elections Around the World,* as updated November 15, 2004, from http://www.electionworld.org/; David Farrell. 2004. *Choosing Electoral Systems.* Presented at the British Columbia Citizens' Assembly in 2004; Harvard University, John F. Kennedy School of Government. 2004. *Kokkalis Program on Southeastern and East-Central Europe,* as updated July 12, 2004, from http://www.ksg.harvard.edu/kokkalis/region; Library of Congress. 2003. *Country Studies U.S.,* as updated in 2003, from http://countrystudies.us.

a country is divided into *single-member districts* and in each district the candidate with the most votes (the plurality) wins. This system is used in legislative elections in the United States and Canada. In Europe, only Britain and Belarus use simple first-past-the-post voting in national parliamentary elections. France uses a similar single-member district system, but with a majority requirement. If no candidate garners an outright majority, the leading candidates go to a second-round runoff. Several other countries, such as Germany and Russia, use single-member district elections for some, but not all, of their legislative seats.

Plurality systems have some attractive features. Districts can be small, and voters can get to know their representative. Voting is simple and easy to understand, and the number of viable candidates is usually low. But plurality elections tend to yield disproportional results. The largest party often gains a majority in parliament even if it does not have a majority of the popular vote. Small parties are shut out unless their votes are concentrated in a few districts. Even medium-sized parties (25 percent or so) whose votes are spread evenly across many districts can come in second nearly everywhere and win few seats. In Britain in 2002, for example, the Liberal Democratic Party won 18 percent of the national vote, but carried only 8 percent of the parliamentary seats. In the same election the Labour Party gained an almost two-thirds parliamentary majority with only 41 percent of the vote (see Chapter 5). The problems of smaller parties are made worse because voters do not want to "waste" their votes on hopeless candidates. Knowing that, such candidates will not run. The tendency for plurality election rules to create two-party systems in the legislature is known as "Duverger's Law," after the distinguished French political scientist who described it.[14]

Mixed Electoral Systems

After World War II, the designers of the new German constitution pioneered a novel electoral system that combines proportional representation and single-member districts (see Figure 4.3). For elections to the German Bundestag (the lower house), the country is divided into single-member districts. Half the members are elected from these districts; the other half are elected by proportional representation from party-lists (with a 5-percent threshold). Each voter casts two votes: one for an individual district candidate and one for a party list of candidates from a larger area. In this way each voter has a representative from his or her geographic district to turn to on local issues, whereas the party-list (PR) seats are allocated so as to achieve partisan proportionality. Parties that are underrepresented in the single-member districts receive a compensatory overrepresentation from the list seats. The result is a very high degree of proportionality. When Italy reformed its electoral system in the 1990s, the country adopted many of the features of the German sys-

tem. However, the Italians opted for a larger share (75 percent) of single-member district seats and a less proportional system.

In the new democracies of Eastern Europe, constitution writers have opted for a variety of electoral systems, as we see on the right side of Figure 4.3. *Mixed electoral rules*, often inspired by the German system, have found wide favor. However, many of these systems lack the compensatory features found in Germany and instead look more like the Italian system.[15] Without such compensation, and where half or more of the seats are single-member districts, as in Hungary and Russia, the results can over- or underrepresent parties very substantially.

In all electoral designs one faces the question of whether representation should be based strictly on the principle of "one person, one vote." Should electoral districts be designed in such a way that each member of the legislature represents an equal number of citizens? Deviations from this principle are known as malapportionment. It may seem obvious that malapportionment should be avoided, and indeed it is generally viewed as undesirable. Yet, in some cases there is malapportionment by design. This is most common in federal systems, where all states (or more generally, subnational units) may be represented equally, regardless of population. Thus, in the U.S. Senate each state, whatever its population, has two seats. The same is true of the upper house of the Russian assembly. In the German upper house, the *Bundesrat*, the biggest states (Länder) have more seats than smaller ones, but not nearly as many as their populations would indicate. Deliberate malapportionment is less common in unitary states or in the lower legislative houses (such as the U.S. House of Representatives, which has very strong rules against it). Yet the Chamber of Deputies in unitary Spain substantially underrepresents some regions and overrepresents others. And Scotland has more seats in the British House of Commons than its population would justify. Overall, though, malapportionment in most European assemblies is modest, though in some countries it systematically benefits particular parties. Serious malapportionment makes it difficult to achieve a high degree of proportionality in party representation.

In countries with directly elected and powerful presidents, the rules for electing the president are just as important as those for the assembly. In Europe the most common method begins with an open contest between candidates from many different parties. If no candidate wins a majority of votes in the first round (as has happened frequently in France, as well as in Poland in 1995 and in Russia in 1996), there is a second-round runoff. Usually only the two leading candidates go on to the second round, which is held a week or two after the first. The relative timing of legislative and presidential elections is important. If the two elections are held at the same time, it is much more likely that the same party or coalition will control both presidency and legislature.[16]

The Effects of Electoral Systems

Election laws and party competition interact to determine the number of parliamentary parties. Since most Western European countries use proportional representation, the number of parties in the legislature is usually only slightly smaller than the number competing in the election. However, in the single-member district systems of Britain and France these discrepancies are quite striking: the number of parties in parliament is much lower than it would be under proportional representation, and single parties often win legislative majorities with far fewer than half of the votes. Some relatively recent electoral systems in Western Europe, such as those of Greece, Italy, and Spain, have some of the basic features of proportional representation, but contain special provisions that reward large parties and often help them secure parliamentary majorities even when they have not won a popular majority.

Eastern Europe is different in two notable ways. First, in about two-thirds of the countries electoral thresholds significantly reduce the number of legislative parties. Often, many parties run unsuccessfully and fall below the electoral threshold. This is because political party leaders (and followers) in many new party systems are only gradually learning enough about the electorate and the electoral rules

to coalesce into viable parties. Eventually the party leaders and organizers in these new democracies may come to build larger and more coherent parties, at least large enough to surmount a barrier of 4 or 5 percent. But there are still quite a few countries in which 10 to 20 percent of the voters support parties that are too small to get any representation.

The second difference is the weakness of national parties in the single-member district elections, which, for example, choose half of the legislators in Ukraine and Russia. To a degree unknown in contemporary Western Europe (except Ireland), many candidates in these elections campaign as independents, representing local rather than national interests. The feeble national parties in these countries have weakened their assemblies and contributed to presidential dominance. However, in smaller countries with mixed electoral systems, such as Hungary, Lithuania, and Macedonia, the single-member district elections predictably reduce the number of legislative parties.

In most of Western Europe the electoral rules, constitutional provisions, and policymaking procedures work together to represent many different groups of citizens through multiple political parties. Only Britain, France, and Greece have rules that typically give unshared political power to directly elected majority governments. The other Western European nations disperse political influence within and/or beyond the national government.

The makers of the Eastern European constitutions were torn between their fear of strong government and their need for it. They were also torn between the desire to involve as many citizens as possible and the concern that dispersed representation would create deadlock. As a result, the emergent constitutions frequently combine diverse elements, such as semi-presidential systems and mixed election rules. Experience with these rules suggests that specific conditions and party strategies can make quite a difference. It can take a number of elections before these effects are fully understood. This is reflected in Eastern Europe in the struggles between legislatures and executives and in the confusions of party competition in the first few elections.

GOVERNMENT FORMATION AND POLICYMAKING

Forming Governments

Since in parliamentary and semi-presidential systems the head of government is not directly elected, parliamentary elections are followed by a period of bargaining over *government formation*. This process is sometimes straightforward, rapid, and simple. When a single political party wins a majority of the parliamentary seats, it almost always forms a government with the party leader as prime minister. The majority party seldom shares cabinet posts with other parties. But as Figure 4.4 shows, after the most recent elections only four Western European countries (Britain, France, Greece, and Malta) have had single-party majority governments. In recent elec-

tions in Eastern Europe, single parties or electoral alliances have won majorities in Albania, Moldova, and Russia.[17]

In most European elections, no single party comes away with a majority. In these cases, a government may form that is a coalition of parties that jointly controls a parliamentary majority. In fact, the tall middle bar in Figure 4.4 shows that such a multiparty majority coalition is the most common type of government in Eastern as well as Western Europe. The task of forming such a coalition can be easy or difficult. It is relatively simple when several parties agree before the election that they would like to govern together and then in fact win a legislative majority. Parties that are already involved in a *coalition government* may simply announce that they will continue to govern together if they collectively win the election. Or parties that are all in op-

FIGURE 4.4 Types of Government Formed After Elections in Western and Eastern Europe, as of 2004

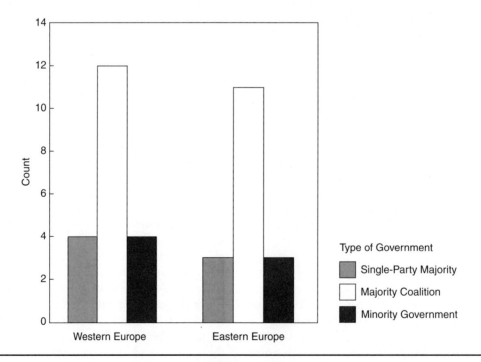

Type of Government
- ▨ Single-Party Majority
- ☐ Majority Coalition
- ■ Minority Government

Source: Keesing's Contemporary Archives, Electoral Studies. Note that "single-party majority" refers to governments containing one party whose representatives constitute a majority in the legislature, even if additional parties also share cabinet seats.

position may agree to present an alternative to the incumbent government. Such preelection agreements have been common in Germany, France, and smaller countries such as Ireland, Denmark, Sweden, and Norway. They may be encouraged by election rules that favor electoral cooperation between parties. All told, about 20 percent of recent Western European governments have been such majority coalitions that were announced before the elections (not shown separately in Figure 4.4).

When there is no parliamentary majority for parties that have already agreed to govern together, the process of forming a government is less straightforward. What happens then depends on constitutional rules as well as circumstances. Typically, the head of state will ask the leader of the largest political party to attempt to negotiate a government. If he or she fails, another party leader will be asked. If it is difficult to anticipate which coalitions may be feasible, the head of state may ask an "informateur" to sound out possible options. Bargaining over government formation is frequent throughout Europe, either immediately after an election or after the breakup of a previous coalition government. Virtually all governments in Belgium, Finland, and the Netherlands (as well as pre-1994 Italy) have been formed in this way.

Sometimes the outcome of coalition bargaining is not what people expect. As shown in Figure 4.4, about a fifth of all European governments are *minority governments,* which consist of parties that do not control a parliamentary majority. Such governments depend on support from a party, or shifting sets of parties, that have no representatives in the cabinet. By the rules of parliamentary democracy, minority governments live dangerously, and in fact they do tend to be shorter-lived than majority governments. But in some countries, minority governments can become a common occurrence. Norway, for example, has had nothing but minority governments since 1985. A minority government can be a stopgap until the next election provides a parliamentary majority (as in Britain in 1974). It can also be an alternative to majority government where the rules permit even the opposition parties to have policy influence (as in Norway), so that they are less keen to defeat the incumbent government. Or minority government may be a sign of parliamentary deadlock in which it is simply not possible to build any majority coalition (as has frequently happened in Italy).[18] As of 2004, seven European countries, including Spain, had minority governments.

After a coalition government has been formed, the cabinet positions are shared among the participating parties, which usually receive such "portfolios" in proportion to their relative strength in parliament. They also tend to demand and receive ministries reflecting their particular interests. Thus, the Ministry of Agriculture tends to go to parties with strong rural support. In semi-presidential systems the president may be able to exert some influence over the composition of the cabinet, even if his or her party does not control the legislature.

Single-party majority governments usually endure until they lose an election, at least in mature party systems such as Britain. Coalition governments that are "minimal winning," which have a parliamentary majority but cannot afford to shed any party without losing their majority, are also usually quite durable. Minority governments, on the other hand, last only about a year and a half on average and less in some countries.[19] When governments fall between elections—either because they lose a confidence vote or because they resign in anticipation of this—the bargaining process must begin anew. In semi-presidential systems, a strong president may be able to use the threat of dissolving the assembly or other policymaking powers to sustain a minority government, as in France (1988–1993) and in Russia before the 1999 election.

Policymaking by Cabinet Governments

Between elections, the policymaking process in parliamentary systems is heavily, but not exclusively, shaped by the composition of the government. In systems with concentrated political power, such as Britain and France, the winning party or coalition expects and is expected to carry out its campaign promises. If the competing parties or coalitions offer contrasting choices, a change of governments usually makes a notable policy difference. When in 1981 a coalition government of Socialists and Communists came to power in France after many years of center-right rule, it made many dramatic policy changes, such as nationalizing private banks and the five largest industrial corporations, as well as raising the minimum wage and social security benefits. In countries that offer more influence to parties outside of government, or where governments are broad coalitions of very different parties, a change of government usually makes less of a dramatic policy difference. Frequent changes in government can also limit the impact of elections and parties on policy, as it takes time for new executives to affect policy.[20]

In semi-presidential systems the president can sometimes play an important role in policymaking. The president may be able to shape the government through his powers of appointment and the influence of his party in the legislature. The president may also have executive powers, for example in foreign and defense policy, directly conferred by the constitution (as in France). Some, like the Russian (but not the French) president, have a legislative veto, which may be difficult for the parliament to override. Some presidents can issue decrees that have the force of law for limited periods or even (as in the Russian case) until replaced by appropriate legislative action. Where the president's powers depend largely on his or her ability to name the government, as in France, policy influence will largely reflect the balance in the legislature. Where the president has powers of veto and decree, as in Russia, the president can have policy influence that depends less on his or her support in the legislature.

All governments are constrained by international conditions and by the economies and societies in which they operate. A government may come to power committed to economic expansion yet be forced to change policies because of the international monetary situation, as was true of the French Socialists in the early 1980s. Governments in most Western European countries since the early 1990s have been frustrated in their ambitions by high levels of unemployment.

DEMOCRATIC POLICIES AND WELFARE IN EUROPE

Economic conditions and public policies jointly affect the welfare of citizens and, in turn, their satisfactions or frustrations with democratic politics. In general, the public policies that have emerged in the wealthy democratic societies of Western Europe have responded to public demand for extensive social "safety nets," substantial public services (that include, for example, government-run public transit systems), and relative economic equality. Governments have also contended with the economic problems of unemployment, inflation, and growth, which tend to worry voters in all modern societies. In recent years governments have also been responding to pressures from citizens and some parties to pay more attention to the environment.

Various social welfare benefits, such as unemployment benefits, social security, and public-sector health care, tend to be more extensive in Western European than in the United States. They also tend to be more thoroughly financed by the government. Historically, the Western European societies developed these policies earlier. In many countries the benefits were markedly expanded during reconstruction after the two world wars. Massive public involvement in housing was also stimulated by postwar reconstruction and remains a prominent, though generally declining, feature in many European nations. Public education, and especially university education, on the other hand, was a priority in the United States before it became one in Europe. Only in recent decades have many Western European countries begun to offer higher education to more than a small elite.

Extensive social services are largely responsible for the comparatively greater size of government relative to the private sector in most of Western Europe. Whereas in the United States, about 15 percent of all workers are in the public sector, this percentage ranges in Western Europe from about the same in Britain to more than 30 in some Scandinavian countries. The median government expenditure in Western Europe is around 45 percent of the gross national product, compared with around 35 percent in the United States or Japan. However, there is again substantial variation across Europe, with Switzerland similar to the United States, but Denmark and Sweden approaching 60 percent of GNP. The welfare state tends to be larger where social democratic parties have frequently been in government, where labor unions are strong, and where there is a tradition of a strong bureaucracy. In the 1990s budgetary pressures resulted in cutbacks in the public sector in some high-spending countries such as Sweden.

Some countries also have large public sectors because the government is directly involved in many large economic enterprises (for example, banks, oil companies, airlines, railroads, or defense industries). Such government ownership is often a hotly contested political issue. For example, in the early 1980s conservative governments in Britain and Germany sold off substantial government enterprises (privatization), while the socialist government in France was acquiring them. Since about the 1980s, market-dominated and competitive economies have yielded superior economic performance, which has led governments in many countries to privatize previously state-owned industries.

The Eastern European countries began their democratic experience in the early 1990s with controlled economies that guaranteed some kind of employment for able-bodied citizens of working age, fixed prices for goods and services, ensured relative income equality, and promised some modest welfare security for the young, the old, and those unable to work. Most of these countries also had great shortages of consumer goods, poor economic productivity, and a standard of living far below their Western European counterparts. Most citizens were disillusioned with the Communist governments.

The newly democratic Eastern European governments began by freeing prices, privatizing industry, and encouraging free competition and investment. Unfortunately, it proved difficult to move swiftly from a controlled economy to a competitive one. In some countries, as in Russia, it has been hard even to dismantle the old system, let alone to build a new one. Even where this was achieved most rapidly and successfully, as in Poland, it came at the cost of short-term drops in living standards and a great deal of confusion as citizens learned to live with economic uncertainties. Debates over the speed of transition and the protection needed for the less fortunate have been bitter and divisive. In several countries the desire to soften the costs of transition brought formerly Communist parties back into power. This policy issue continues to dominate much of Eastern Europe. The region also faces a huge task of cleaning up vast environmental damage created by the Communist

governments' ruthless industrialization, but this is for most citizens a lower priority.

THE RULE OF LAW, CORRUPTION, AND DEMOCRACY

Democracy is a complicated system of government. As noted at the beginning of this chapter, it depends on competitive elections to link government policies to citizen preferences. To ensure that those policies are implemented fairly, democracy also requires the rule of law. The rule of law can fail in many ways, as when the president decides to continue past the end of his term of office or ignore the rulings of a constitutional court (as in Belarus), when ruling parties demand kickbacks from construction firms seeking public works contracts or bribes from interest groups asking for special legislation (which unfortunately happens far too often in too many countries), when tax officials and border authorities take cash payments to overlook tax deficiencies and customs violations, or when corruption opens the way to organized and violent criminal penetration of government.

No democracy is immune to such threats to the rule of law. But some countries suffer much more grievously than others from corrupt government officials. When citizens who must interact with the government find themselves forced to participate in corrupt practices to gain even basic benefits, it surely weakens their confidence in government. In Western Europe the most blatant examples of public corruption emerged in Italy in the early 1990s, when the judicial investigation called "Operation Clean Hands" revealed that the governing political parties had demanded and received huge bribes from business organizations and used them to finance both party organizational activity and lavish lifestyles for their leaders. Other investigations uncovered that organized crime, through bribery as well as violence, had deeply penetrated Italian politics, particularly in the south. These revelations destroyed most of the political parties and leaders that had dominated Italian politics, sparking constitutional change and a new party system.

In Eastern Europe establishing the rule of law has been one of the most difficult parts of the transition to democracy.[21] Communist dictatorships had in many countries coexisted with widespread corruption. Sometimes the governments even encouraged corruption to overcome the inefficiencies of the vast bureaucracies. Abuse of power to gain personal benefits was common at all levels, especially where communism had been imposed upon economically poor societies. Such habits were not easily overcome after democratization, especially in local government. They were sustained by poverty and exacerbated in the short run by the slumping economies and lagging salary payments that made life desperate for many government employees. Privatization of large enterprises that had long been run by the government also created unusual opportunities for insiders to abuse their positions and acquire some of this new wealth, as most dramatically witnessed in Russia.

While it is difficult to study corruption and criminal activity systematically, interesting comparisons are offered by Transparency International, which surveys businesses to estimate corruption levels in different countries. Their "Corruption Perceptions Index" annually rates most countries on a scale from 0 (most corrupt) to 10 (most clean). In 2004 a majority of Western European countries, including Britain and Germany, rated 8 or higher. Finland had the best score of all countries (9.7), followed by New Zealand (9.6) and Denmark (9.5). The Western European average was very similar to that of the United States (7.5). France and Spain (both 7.1) were rated somewhat less "clean" than the United States, but only Italy and Greece were ranked below 5 (the midpoint score).[22] All the Eastern European nations fell well below the Western European average. Slovenia and Estonia were rated highest for the region and above Italy, while Hungary was about level with Italy. Russia scored a discouraging 2.8, whereas at 2.2, Ukraine had the worst perceived corruption problem in Europe.

In Europe and across the world economic development is a very powerful predictor of cleaner politics. Yet, presumably because of the problems of overcoming its communist heritage and managing an economic transition, the Eastern European region scores somewhat more poorly than its economic development would lead us to expect. Corruption is recognized as a serious issue within most

of these countries, but it is easier to raise it as an election issue than to solve the problem.

INTRODUCING AND SUSTAINING DEMOCRACY

Historically, most of the world's democracies have been European. Europe has thus been the source of much of our knowledge of democratic governance. It has also been the site of some of the most famous failures of democracy, most notably the collapse of Germany's Weimar Republic into Nazi dictatorship, with terrible consequences for the entire world. While there are now more democracies outside of Europe, there is little doubt that the experiences of Eastern Europe will add greatly to our understanding of democratization.

In managing democratic conflict, Western European societies have tended to engage in power-sharing through a variety of constitutional and electoral devices, which has encouraged multiple political parties and multiple paths to policy influence. In some European countries the efforts to overcome deep conflicts gave rise to a distinctive form of guaranteed power- and policy-sharing called *consociationalism* (see Chapter 1).[23] The once deeply divided societies of the Netherlands, Austria, Belgium, and Switzerland offer prominent examples of elite-negotiated agreements to share political power. These agreements guaranteed both influence and benefits to all social segments (whether defined by religious, linguistic, or occupational criteria) and were buttressed by formal organizational arrangements. Consociational democracy has proven to be a valuable approach to conflict management in seriously divided societies, although it may work better in the short term than over the longer haul. This is because consociationalism also contributes to the mutual isolation of different social groups. Such isolation can be beneficial in situations of severe conflict, but as social segments become less distinctive and conflicts less intense, the different groups may find consociational arrangements confining and a barrier to fuller integration.

Studies of conflict based largely, but not entirely, on the Western European experience suggest that power-sharing processes can have some success in diminishing riots and protests.[24] Such turmoil is likely to be more intense where there are fewer roads to influence, as in majoritarian democracies. On the other hand, proportional representation and power-sharing strategies may bring turmoil "inside" the institutions, putting extremist parties in the legislature and making stable cabinet government more difficult. Moreover, once violent conflict is underway, elite agreements may be insufficient. Northern Ireland has demonstrated repeatedly that democratic power-sharing agreements cannot be sustained without the assent of the majority of citizens, who will simply replace leaders they view as betraying their interests.

Western Europe has experienced many threats to democracy by violence and military intervention. A common thread in these crises has been the need for organized political parties to rally behind democracy. In the 1930s the bitterly suspicious socialist and middle-class parties failed to unite against the Nazis in Germany, whereas in Austria similar parties careened into civil war. In Greece conservative fears of a new socialist government encouraged the military to overthrow democracy in 1967. In contrast, the fact that all Italian political parties backed government antiterrorist measures in the 1970s helped sustain democracy against intensive bombing and assassination campaigns. In France in 1961 and Spain in 1981, a united front of all major parties helped democratic heads of state defeat attempted coups by rallying citizens and loyal members of the military.

A number of Western European countries must continue to battle against terrorism and violence (especially violence against immigrant groups). In so doing, democratic governments must maintain the critical balance between upholding the security of their residents and protecting their freedoms. This is, of course, easier to do under positive economic conditions and when citizens share common democratic values. In Eastern Europe these conditions were often missing after the collapse of communism, and in many countries the preconditions for democracy are still weak.

Yet, in most of Eastern Europe the revolution that has occurred since 1989 has brought remarkable change with little violence. Democracy is shaky in some nations because of strong ethnic tension, gross corruption in government, and violations of the freedom of speech and other civil liberties (see Box 4.2). In particular, the current decade is a critical time for the region formerly dominated by the Soviet Union; there is great potential, but also great risk. The devastating wars in Chechnya and in the former Yugoslavia show the potential cost of failure.

Democracy seems to be building a firm foundation elsewhere in the former East, perhaps more successfully than we originally expected. Parties are learning to develop internal cohesion and accommodate differences with political opponents. Governments are learning to deal with dissent without suppressing dissenters or the press, to manage economies without taking them over, to provide safety nets for citizens without destroying their incentives. Citizens are demanding a rule of law, and so are many international agencies and nongovernmental organizations. The prospects for democracy are particularly favorable in the eight Eastern European countries that were admitted to the European Union in 2004. This is both because they were selected for membership on the basis of the democratic credentials they had gained, and because the EU itself will insist on and monitor democracy within its member-states.

No one has yet found the perfect political institutions. European democratic institutions are no exception. It is easy to find flaws in constitutional arrangements, party systems, and policymaking processes. It is even easier to criticize the policies of a current government, since democracy does not guarantee good leadership or wise policies. Yet bitter experience in Europe and elsewhere shows that democracy is more likely than any other form of government to sustain personal freedoms, encourage equal treatment under the law, and protect the rights of minorities. Moreover, democracies seldom go to war against each other. Democratic government is the best security for the hard-won personal freedoms of the citizens of Eastern Europe and the newfound peace that has replaced Europe's destructive wars. Building democracy has thus had profound consequences for all Europeans. And the European experiences will continue to hold valuable lessons for the world about the limits and potentials of democratic government.

Key Terms

assembly	federalism	mixed electoral rules	proportional
bicameralism	freedom of the press	parliamentary	representation (PR)
cabinet	government formation	democracy	semi-presidential systems
coalition government	judicial review	power-sharing	single-member districts
confidence vote	liberal democracy	presidential democracy	strong legislative
executive	minority government	prime minister	committees

Suggested Readings

Bowler, Shaun, David M. Farrell, and Richard W. Katz. *Party Cohesion, Party Discipline and the Organization of Parliaments.* Columbus: Ohio State University Press, 1999.

Cox, Gary. *Making Votes Count: Strategic Coordination in the World's Electoral Systems.* New York: Cambridge University Press, 1997.

Doering, Herbert, ed. *Parliaments and Majority Rule in Western Europe.* New York: St. Martin's, 1995.

Hellman, Joel. "Constitutional and Economic Reform in Post-Communist Transitions." *Eastern European Constitutional Review* (Winter 1996): 46–56.

Laver, Michael, and Norman Schofield. *Multiparty Government: The Politics of Coalition in Europe.* New York: Oxford University Press, 1990.

Laver, Michael, and Kenneth A. Shepsle, eds. *Cabinet Ministers and Parliamentary Government.* New York: Cambridge University Press, 1994.

Lijphart, Arend. *Democracy in Plural Societies.* New Haven: Yale University Press, 1977.

———. *Electoral Systems and Party Systems: A Study of Twenty-Seven Democracies, 1945–1990.* New York: Oxford University, 1994.

———. *Patterns of Democracy: Government Forms and Performance in Thirty-Six Countries.* New Haven: Yale University Press, 1999.

Norton, Philip, ed. "Parliaments in Western Europe." *West European Politics* (Special Issue) 13, No. 3 (July 1990).

Powell, G. Bingham, Jr. *Contemporary Democracies: Participation, Stability and Violence.* Cambridge: Harvard University Press, 1982.

———. *Elections as Instruments of Democracy: Majoritarian and Proportional Visions.* New Haven: Yale University Press, 2000.

Rose, Richard. *Do Parties Make a Difference?* 2nd ed. Chatham, NJ: Chatham House, 1984.

Sartori, Giovanni. *Comparative Constitutional Engineering.* New York: NYU Press, 1997.

Shugart, Matthew Soberg, and John Carey. *Presidents and Assemblies: Constitutional Design and Electoral Dynamics.* New York: Cambridge University Press, 1992.

Strøm, Kaare. *Minority Government and Majority Rule.* New York: Cambridge University Press, 1990.

Strøm, Kaare, Wolfgang C. Müller, and Torbjörn Bergman, eds. *Delegation and Accountability in Parliamentary Democracies.* Oxford: Oxford University Press, 2003.

Tsebelis, George. *Veto Players: An Introduction to Institutional Analysis.* Princeton: Princeton University Press and Russell Sage Foundation, 2002.

Volcansek, Mary L., ed. "Judicial Politics and Policymaking in Western Europe." *West European Politics* (Special Issue) 15, No. 3 (July 1992).

Endnotes

1. John Locke, *Two Treatises of Government,* ed. Peter Laslett (Cambridge, England: Cambridge University Press, 1960); Charles de Secondat, Baron de Montesquieu, *The Spirit of the Laws* (London: Hafner, 1960).

2. We occasionally use the term "assembly" rather than the more common "legislature," to emphasize that legislation—making laws—may not be the most important function of this branch of government. The assembly may not have the sole authority to make laws, and it is seldom the most important source of legislation.

3. The German, Hungarian, and Spanish constitutions feature a "constructive" vote of no confidence, under which the government is forced to resign only if a parliamentary majority explicitly designates and supports an alternative government.

4. *Congressional Quarterly,* December 21, 1996, p. 3461. This analysis considers only votes in which the two major parties oppose each other and does not include voting for official House leadership positions (on which voting tends to be strictly along party lines).

5. In the 1987–1992 British House of Commons, both parties were perfectly cohesive on 80 percent of the votes on which these parties took official stands (Philip Norton, "Parliamentary Behavior Since 1945," *Talking Politics*, VIII, 1995–96, p. 112). For evidence of similar cohesion in Germany in the 1970s and 1980s, see Thomas Saalfeld, "The West German Bundestag After Forty Years," *West European Politics* 13, No. 3 (July 1990): 74. On the French Fifth Republic, see Philip E. Converse and Roy Pierce, *Political Representation in France* (Cambridge: Harvard University Press, 1986), pp. 552–61. On party cohesion generally, see Shaun Bowler, David M. Farrell, and Richard W. Katz, *Party Cohesion, Party Discipline and the Organization of Parliaments* (Columbus: Ohio State University Press, 1999).

6. In some countries the president is elected by a special "electoral college" that includes both members of parliament and other public officials, such as representatives of local governments.

7. To avoid confusion, we refer to heads of state as presidents or monarchs and to heads of government in parliamentary systems as prime ministers. The formal titles are sometimes different. Thus, the official title of the head of government is "President of the Council of Ministers" in Spain and "Federal Chancellor" in Germany. See the country chapters for details.

8. See Chapter 6; Roy Pierce, "The Executive Divided Against Itself: Cohabitation in France 1986–1988" *Governance* 4, No. 3 (July 1991): 270–94; and John D. Huber, *Rationalizing Parliament: Legislative Institutions and Party Politics in France* (New York: Cambridge University Press, 1996).

9. See Arend Lijphart, ed., *Parliamentary Versus Presidential Government* (Oxford: Oxford University Press, 1992); Juan Linz and Arturo Valenzuela, eds., *The Failure of Presidential Government* (Baltimore: Johns Hopkins University Press, 1994); G. Bingham Powell, Jr., *Contemporary Democracies: Participation, Stability and Violence* (Cambridge, MA: Harvard University Press, 1982), Chs. 6, 10; Alfred Stepan and Cindy Skach, "Constitutional Frameworks and Democratic Consolidation: Parliamentarism Versus Presidentialism," *World Politics* 46 (October 1993): 1–22.

10. See Shugart and Carey, *Presidents and Assemblies*.

11. See the essays in Mary L. Volcansek, ed., "Judicial Politics and Policymaking in Western Europe," a special issue of *West European Politics* 15, No. 3 (July 1992); and in Martin Shapiro and Alec Stone, "The New Constitutional Politics of Europe," a special issue of *Comparative Political Studies* 26, No. 4 (January 1994).

12. However, in the French Fourth Republic (1947–1958) governments frequently tinkered with the election laws to seek electoral advantage. In France in 1986 and in Greece in 1989 governments introduced proportional representation with low thresholds to try to limit expected losses; these partly successful changes were eventually reversed by their successors. Several of the new Eastern European democracies, including Bulgaria, Macedonia, and Ukraine, have also modified their election rules.

13. These countries are Greece, Ireland, and Spain. For a general discussion of the "effective threshold" for party representation, see Lijphart, *Electoral Systems and Party Systems*, Ch. 2; later in the book Lijphart estimates the effective threshold in each electoral system.

14. Maurice Duverger, *Political Parties: Their Organization and Activity in the Modern State* [1954], trans. Barbara and Robert North (New York: Wiley, 1963).

15. As explained in Chapter 7, the German "mixed" electoral system distributes the party-list seats among the parties so as to make the overall legislative representation (combining single-member district representatives and party-list representatives) correspond as closely as possible to the party vote shares. A party like the Free Democrats, which rarely carries any single-member districts, gets an extra helping of party-list seats to bring its overall proportion into balance with its vote. As discussed in Chapter 9, the Russian version (also used in Japan and elsewhere) gives no such party-list compensation for underrepresentation in the single-member districts. Other European systems use various degrees of compensation. The complicated Hungarian system is discussed in Chapter 11.

16. See Matthew Soberg Shugart, "The Electoral Cycle and Institutional Sources of Divided Presidential Government," *American Political Science Review* 89 (June 1995): 327–43.

17. Belarus and Bosnia have been excluded from Figure 4.4 because government formation in these countries has been constrained by factors other than democratic electoral results.

18. See the discussion of minority governments in Poland in Chapter 10.

19. Governments built on an "excessive" number of parties are also frequently unstable, prone to additional bargaining and to being reduced to the minimum number needed for parliamentary control.

20. See classic analyses of France in the Fourth Republic by Philip Williams, *Crisis and Compromise: Politics in the Fourth Republic* (Hamden, CT: Archon Press, 1964), esp. p. 405. But the issue is controversial; see the discussion and one of the few empirical comparative studies in John D. Huber, "How Does Cabinet Instability Affect Political Performance? Portfolio Volatility and Health Care Cost Containment in Parliamentary Democracies," *American Political Science Review* 92 (1996): 577–91.

21. See, for example, the essays by Stephen Holmes, et al., "Crime and Corruption After Communism," in *East European Constitutional Review* 6 (Fall 1997): 69–98.

22. All scores downloaded from www.transparency.org/cpi/2004/en.html on November 30, 2004.

23. The critical contributor to analysis of this approach has been Arend Lijphart; see especially *Democracy in Plural Societies* (New Haven: Yale University Press, 1977).

24. Powell, *Contemporary Democracies*, Chs. 4, 5, 10.

United Kingdom

0	25	50 mi
0	40	80 km

N

ATLANTIC OCEAN

•Wick

•Inverness

SCOTLAND

Aberdeen•

NORTH SEA

Glasgow• •Edinburgh

Tyne

NORTHERN IRELAND •Belfast

Irish Sea

IRELAND

NORTH

NORTH WEST

Leeds•

Liverpool• •Manchester •Sheffield

Mersey

EAST MIDLANDS

Severn

ENGLAND

Norwich•

EAST ANGLIA

WEST MIDLANDS •Birmingham

WALES

SOUTH EAST

Cardiff•

Thames

London

SOUTH WEST

Portsmouth•

•Plymouth

English Channel

Chapter 5

Politics in England

RICHARD ROSE

Country Bio—United Kingdom

POPULATION: 59.2 million

TERRITORY: 94,525 sq. mi

YEAR OF INDEPENDENCE: from twelfth century

YEAR OF CURRENT CONSTITUTION: unwritten; partly statutes, partly common law and practice

HEAD OF STATE: Queen Elizabeth II

HEAD OF GOVERNMENT: Prime Minister Tony Blair

LANGUAGE(S):   English, Welsh (about 600,000), Scottish form of Gaelic (about 60,000)

RELIGION: Anglican 26.1 million, Roman Catholic 5.7 million, Presbyterian 2.6 million, Methodist 1.3 million, Other Christian 2.6 million, Muslim 1.5 million, Hindu 500,000, Sikh 330,000, Jewish 260,000, Other 300,000, no religion 7,700. The remainder refused to report a religion in the 2001 census.

In a world of new democracies, England is different, because it is an old democracy. Unlike new democracies in Eastern Europe, Latin America, and Asia, England did not become a democracy overnight due to the collapse of a dictatorship. It became a democracy by evolution rather than revolution. Democratization was a slow process that occurred over the centuries. The rule of law was established in the seventeenth century; the accountability of the executive to parliament was established by the eighteenth century; political parties organized in the nineteenth century; and, even though competitive elections had been held for more than a century, the right of every adult man and woman to vote was not recognized until the twentieth century.

The evolution of democracy in England also stands in contrast to the dominant European practice of countries switching between democratic and undemocratic regimes. Whereas the oldest English person has lived under the same constitution all his or her life, the oldest Germans have lived under four or five constitutions, two democratic and two or three undemocratic.[1]

The gradual evolution of political institutions means that at no point in history did representatives of the English people meet together to decide what kind of government they would like to have, as happened in the American constitutional convention of the 1780s, and in dozens of new democracies in the past two decades. Politicians have been socialized to accept institutions as a legacy from their predecessors; these are the rules of the game by which they compete for office. Ordinary citizens have been socialized to accept established institutions too.

The influence of British government can be found in places as far-flung as Australia, Canada, India, and the United States. Just as Alexis de Tocqueville travelled to America in 1831 to seek the secrets of democracy, so might we journey to England to seek the secrets of stable representative government. Yet its limitations as a model are shown by the failure of many of the attempts to transplant its institutions to countries gaining independence from the British Empire, and even more by the failure of its institutions to bring political stability in Northern Ireland.

CURRENT POLICY CHALLENGES

When Tony Blair became prime minister in 1997, he declared a desire to create a New Britain, a "cool Britannia" having more in common with the world of pop stars and Princess Diana than the world of Winston Churchill. Yet rebranding a country is not as easy as rebranding pop groups or designer fashions.

To win office Blair created what he called a "New" Labour party with a vague Third Way philosophy, offered as an alternative to socialism as well as to unfettered capitalism, and modelled on the strategy of President Bill Clinton. In setting out Labour's manifesto, Blair proclaimed, "We are proud now to be the party of modern, dynamic business, proud now to be the party of law and order, proud now to be the party of the family, and proud now to be the party pledged not to increase income tax."[2] He pledged a pragmatic government

that would do "what works," and appealed to the voters to "trust me."

By his lifestyle and rhetoric, Blair has shown that he believes in opportunity for all, and especially for aspiring Britons whose votes are critical for winning reelection. However, winning elections has challenged Blair to deliver campaign promises (Box 5.1). Blair now recognises: "In opposition announcement is the reality. For the first period of time in government, there was a tendency to believe the same situation applied. It doesn't. The announcement is only the intention."[3]

Blair's government has benefited from an abnormally lengthy economic boom, providing additional public revenue without raising taxes. This is important, as an aging population requires more health care, an educated population demands better education for their children, and a more prosperous society wants a better environment to match improved housing. The Labour government has sought to achieve greater efficiency by imposing more centralized controls and performance targets on public sector agencies.

From the right, the *Conservative Party* attacks the government for not being radical enough in promoting private initiatives and for overriding constitutional conventions. The *Liberal Democrats* criticize the government for not raising taxes a little in order to have more money to spend in raising health and education standards and for undermining legal protections of human rights. Tony Blair is content to be attacked from both sides, believing that centrist policies will best maintain the support of most voters.

While the Blair administration has promoted decentralization to Scotland and Wales, critics charge that his "control freak" mentality is centralizing too much power in the hands of prime ministerial advisers who concentrate on promoting favorable headlines in the media and pushing civil servants to produce what makes for good headlines. Moreover, in the wake of terrorist attacks the government's adoption of wide-ranging powers to control the population have been criticized by civil liberties groups as anti-liberal, a charge the prime minister accepts as proof of his toughness.

In a changing world, the big question is: Where does England belong? Geographically, it is an offshore island of Europe. *Insularity* is one of its most

Box 5.1 Accomplishments and Frustrations of Tony Blair

Tony Blair became leader of the Labour Party in opposition with the goal of winning elections. To make the party electable, he abandoned traditional commitments to the trade unions and to socialist values and centralized power in the prime minister's office. The strategy of refashioning the Labour Party has produced three successive election victories.

The Labour government has maintained Margaret Thatcher's principle of avoiding any increase in income tax. Much of the credit for managing the economy went to his Treasury minister, Gordon Brown. The government also implemented Labour's long-standing programme of constitutional reforms, including the devolution of powers to elected assemblies in Scotland and Wales, and enacting human rights legislation.

In foreign policy Blair's chief initiative has been cooperation in military action with the United States. After the 9/11 terrorist attack, he has allied Britain with policies of President George W. Bush, notwithstanding

major opposition in Parliament. Although claiming to want Britain to be at the heart of Europe, Blair has not sought to adopt the euro in place of the pound and has refrained from campaigning for measures to increase British support for the European Union.

Labour won the 2005 election even though it took only 35 percent of the vote. Distrust in Blair was blamed for this fall in vote and it encouraged speculation about when he would resign during his third term in office. Concurrently, Blair has pledged education, health, and pension reforms that can only show their consequences years after he has left office. Blair has explicitly rejected the liberalism of the 1960s and endorsed measures reducing legal and judicial restraints on government action.*

*Cf. Tony Blair, *New Britain: My Vision of a Young Country* (London: Fourth Estate, 1996); Anthony Seldon, *Blair* (New York: Free Press, 2004).

---

striking cultural characteristics. Although the *United Kingdom* is a member of the European Union, the government's commitment to the European Union remains limited. Blair has pledged to put British interests "first, second, and last" in negotiations about the European Union. However, any attempt by Blair to cooperate with the other 24 member states of the European Union will inevitably result in compromises that British critics of the European Union will denounce as "giving away" Britain's sovereignty.

Historically, the country's ties are with English-speaking countries on other continents, including the United States. By deciding to ally himself with President George W. Bush in the war in Iraq, Blair has shown that today, as in Winston Churchill's time, a special relationship with the United States is valued more than ties to Europe.

THE CONSTRAINTS OF HISTORY

The Making of Modern England

The legacy of the past limits current choices, and England has a very long past. For much of its history, England was governed by the rule of law but

the government was not democratic. However, the establishment of lawful procedures to check the arbitrary authority of the King made possible the gradual evolution of a democratic political system.

Compared with its European neighbors, England has been fortunate in solving many of the fundamental problems of governance early. The Crown was established as the central political authority in medieval times. The supremacy of the state's power over the church was settled in the sixteenth century when Henry VIII broke with the Roman Catholic Church to establish the Church of England. The power struggle between Crown and Parliament was resolved by a civil war in the seventeenth century in which Parliament triumphed and a weakened monarch was then restored. Parliament became able to hold the Crown accountable by the eighteenth century, but Parliament represented only a small portion of the population.

There is no agreement among political scientists about when England developed a modern system of government.[4] A constitutional historian might date the change at 1485, the start of the centralizing Tudor monarchy; an economic historian from the beginning of the Industrial Revolution about 1760, and a frustrated reformer might proclaim that it hasn't happened yet. The most reasonable judgment is that modern government developed during the very long reign of Queen Victoria from 1837 to 1901, when government institutions were created to cope with the problems of a society that was increasingly urban, literate, industrial, and critical of unreformed institutions.

The 1832 Reform Act started a gradual process of enfranchising the masses. A majority of English males got the right to vote by 1885. Concurrently, Conservative and Liberal party organizations began to contest elections nationwide. The right to vote was extended to all adult men and women in 1918. The *Labour Party*, founded in 1900 to secure the representation of manual workers in Parliament, first briefly formed a minority government in 1924.

The Industrial Revolution created a demand for government to make cities safe and healthy. In the mid-nineteenth century aristocratic institutions of governance were transformed into a system that could enact and implement laws on public health and education and collect the taxes needed to pay for new public services. The 1906 Liberal government introduced old-age pensions and unemployment insurance; slowly these programs were expanded. The gross national product (GNP) increased greatly, and the share claimed by government increased even more. In 1890 public spending was equal to 8 percent of GNP; in 1910 the share had risen to 12 percent and by 1920 to 26 percent. For the past half century, public spending has fluctuated around two-fifths of the gross national product. The creation of a modern system of government does not make the problems of governing disappear. England emerged on the winning side in two world wars, but its political influence was reduced. Political developments since can be divided into five stages.

First, during World War II an all-party coalition government led by Winston Churchill laid the foundations for a *mixed economy Keynesian welfare state*. The government created full employment to fight the war and rationed food to ensure "fair shares for all." From this coalition emerged the Beveridge Report on social welfare, John Maynard Keynes's Full Employment White Paper of 1944,

and the Butler Education Act of 1944. These three measures—the first two named after Liberals and the third after a Conservative—were landmarks in the development of the British welfare state. The fair shares policy was continued by the Labour government of Clement Attlee elected in 1945 and the National Health Service was established. Coal mines, gas and electricity, railways, and the steel industries were nationalized (that is, taken into government ownership). By 1951 the Labour government had exhausted its catalog of agreed changes.

In the second stage, the Conservatives, in office from 1951 to 1964, maintained a consensus on social policy. Administrations under Winston Churchill, Anthony Eden, and Harold Macmillan were anxious to assure the electorate that they could be trusted to conserve a widely popular welfare state. Keynesian techniques for promoting economic growth, full employment, and low inflation showed evidence of success. Rationing was ended and living standards rose.

The third stage commenced in the early 1960s with a flood of books on the theme "What's wrong with Britain?" Continuities with the past were attacked as the dead hand of tradition. Politicians promoted managerial activism. Labour, Liberal, and Conservative politicians denounced "stagnation" and competed in prescribing activist measures, ushering in what Michael Mora has described as an age of "hyper-innovation."

The Labour Party won the 1964 election under Harold Wilson campaigning with the vague activist slogan, "Let's go with Labour." New titles were given government department offices, symbolizing a desire to change for its own sake. Behind the entrance of these restyled offices, the same people went through the same routines as before. The economy did not grow as predicted, and in 1967 the Wilson government was forced to devalue the pound and seek a loan from the International Monetary Fund. Labour lost the 1970 election.

The major achievement of the 1970–1974 Conservative government under Edward Heath was to make Britain a member of what was then the European Community and is now the European Union. Doing so divided his own party and the opposition. In trying to limit unprecedented inflation by controlling wages, Heath risked his authority in a confrontation with the National Union of Mineworkers. The result was a stalemate, and industry working a three-day week because of a shortage of coal. The prime minister called an election. The "Who Governs?" election of February 1974 showed many voters rejecting both major parties. The Conservative share of the vote dropped to 38 percent and Labour's to 37 percent, while the Liberal vote more than doubled to 19 percent. Due to anomalies in the electoral system, Labour won the most seats in the House of Commons, but no party had an absolute majority there. Labour formed a minority government, with Harold Wilson again prime minister. A second election in October 1974 gave Labour a bare majority. Inflation, rising unemployment, and a contraction in the economy caused this policy to collapse. James Callaghan succeeded Wilson as prime minister in 1976. Keynesian policies were abandoned in 1977 when Labour again relied on a loan from the International Monetary Fund to stabilize the pound.

The 1979 general election was won by the Conservatives under Margaret Thatcher, the first woman to serve as prime minister of a major European country. She ushered in the fourth stage, making a radical break with the past. She regarded the economic failures of previous governments as arising from too much compromise and too little conviction. "The Old Testament prophets did not say 'Brothers, I want a consensus.' They said: 'This is my faith. This is what I passionately believe. If you believe it too, then come with me.'"[5] Above all, she believed that the market rather than government should make the most important decisions in society (Box 5.2).

Divisions among opponents enabled Thatcher to lead her party to three successive election victories although never winning more than 43 percent of the total vote. Militant left-wing activists seized control of the Labour Party. Under Michael Foot its 1983 election manifesto was described by a Labour MP as the longest suicide note in history. In protest, four former Labour Cabinet ministers formed a centrist Social Democratic Party (SDP) in 1981 and made an alliance with the Liberal Party. After Thatcher's third successive election victory in 1987, the SDP leadership merged with the Liberals to form the Liberal Democrats.

While preaching against big government, Thatcher did not court electoral defeat by imposing

---

Box 5.2 The Meaning of Thatcherism

Among British prime ministers, Margaret Thatcher was unique in giving her name to a political ideology, *Thatcherism.* She believed in strong government—as long as it was in her hands. In foreign policy she was a formidable proponent of what she saw as Britain's national interest in dealings with the European Union and in alliance with President Ronald Reagan. The 1982 Argentine invasion of the Falkland Islands, a remote British colony in the South Atlantic, led to a brief and victorious war against Argentina. Thatcher was also quick to assert her personal authority against colleagues in the Cabinet and against civil servants.* The autonomy of local government was curbed by central government, and a property tax on houses replaced by a poll tax on each adult.

Thatcher's central conviction was that the market offered a cure for the country's economic difficulties. As Milton Friedman, the Nobel Prize-winning monetary economist, noted: "Mrs. Thatcher represents a dif-

ferent tradition. She represents a tradition of the nineteenth-century Liberal, of Manchester Liberalism, of free market free trade."[†] In economic policy the Thatcher administration experienced both successes and frustrations. Her anti-inflation policies succeeded but unemployment doubled. Industrial relations acts gave members the right to elect their union's leaders and vote on whether to hold a strike. She introduced what were described as "businesslike" methods for managing everything from hospitals and universities to museums, hoping to reduce public spending and taxation.

*Cf. Dennis Kavanagh, *Thatcherism and British Politics* (Oxford, England: Oxford University Press, 1990); and Margaret Thatcher, *The Downing Street Years* (New York: HarperCollins, 1993).

†"Thatcher Praised by Her Guru," *The Guardian* (London), March 12, 1983.

radical cuts on the biggest spending and most popular programs of the government. In consequence, public spending continued to grow in the Thatcher era. It was 40 percent of the gross domestic product in her last full year in office. While the Conservative majority in Parliament endorsed Thatcher's policies, it did not win the hearts and minds of the electorate. When voters were asked on the tenth anniversary of Thatcher's period in office whether or not they approved of "the Thatcher revolution," less than one-third responded yes.[6]

Within the Conservative Party, Thatcher's increasingly autocratic treatment of Cabinet colleagues created resentment, and during her third term of office this was reinforced by unpopularity in opinion polls. In autumn 1990, disgruntled Conservative members of Parliament (MPs) forced a ballot for the party leadership. In the first round, the prime minister won just over half the votes of Conservative MPs. But under the party's complicated rules for electing a leader, this was not enough to confirm Thatcher in office; she resigned. In the subsequent ballot, Conservative MPs elected a relatively unknown John Major as party leader.

In his first electoral test in 1992, John Major won an unexpected and unprecedented fourth consecutive term for the Conservative government. Shortly after the 1992 election his economic policy of a strong British pound crashed under pressure from foreign speculators. Major was criticized by Thatcherites in the Conservative Party for agreeing to the Maastricht Treaty on expanding the powers of the European Union. Although personally above suspicion, Major's administration was plagued by the exposure of Conservative MPs' *sleazy* behavior, involving sex, money, or both. By 1993 Major reached the lowest popularity rating in the history of the Gallup Poll. The Major government held onto office and Thatcherite economic policies such as the privatization of the coal mines and railways were pursued.

A fifth stage in postwar British politics opened after Tony Blair became Labour leader in 1994. Blair was elected leader because he did not talk or look like an ordinary Labour Party member. Instead of being from a poor background, he was educated at boarding school and studied law at Oxford. Instead

of having grown up in the Labour movement, his parents were Conservatives, and he joined the Labour Party due to the encouragement of a girlfriend, Cherie Booth (now his wife and a very successful lawyer). His qualities appealed to middle-class voters whose support Labour needed to move from opposition to government. Labour won a landslide majority in the House of Commons in the 1997 election, even though it received a smaller share of the popular vote than Margaret Thatcher in 1979, because the Conservative vote fell to its lowest share since 1832. In June 2001, Blair led Labour to another landslide victory over a demoralized opposition. But the longer he has been in office the more he has expressed frustration with the obstacles that British government creates to his hopes for changing Britain overnight.

Blair's decision to commit Britain to go to war in Iraq in 2003 alongside the United States caused a bitter division within his party. Official inquiries into the "spin" that Blair gave for going to war showed that he had exaggerated or misread intelligence briefings, and opinion polls showed that a majority of Britons no longer trusted Blair. Under pressure from Labour critics, Blair has had to interrupt foreign policy forays to show that he is concerned about improving social conditions in Britain.

The continuity of England's political institutions through the centuries is remarkable. Prince Charles, the heir to an ancient Crown, pilots jet airplanes, and a medieval-named Chancellor of the Exchequer pilots the British pound through the deep waters of the international economy. Yet symbols of continuity often mask great changes in English life. Parliament was once a supporter of royal authority. Today Parliament is primarily an electoral college deciding which party leader is in charge of government.

THE ENVIRONMENT OF POLITICS

One Crown but Five Nations

The Queen of England is the best known monarch in the world, yet there is no such entity as an English state. In international law, the state is the United Kingdom of Great Britain and Northern Ireland. The United Kingdom was created in 1801 as the climax of a process of expansion begun in the twelfth century. Great Britain, the principal part of the United Kingdom, is divided into three parts: England, Scotland, and Wales. *Scotland* was once an independent kingdom; since the 1707 Act of Union, there has been a common Parliament for the whole of Great Britain. However, the Scots have retained separate legal, religious, and educational institutions. *Wales* was joined with England in the sixteenth century and administered thereafter as if it were a part of England. Its most distinctive feature is the ancient Welsh language. The fourth part of the United Kingdom, *Northern Ireland*, consists of six counties of Ulster. The remainder of Ireland broke away to form a separate state in 1921 as the culmination of a rebellion against the Crown launched in Dublin in 1916.

In national identity, the United Kingdom is a multinational state as its citizens differ in how they describe themselves (see Table 5.1). In England people often are confused about the difference between being English or British and use the terms interchangeably. When asked to give their national identity, a majority describe themselves as English. In Scotland, more than half see themselves as Scots. In Wales, where three-quarters of the population does not speak Welsh, more than half say they are Welsh. In England, Scotland, and Wales, at least one-third see themselves as primarily British. Just as people in Texas can see themselves as both Texans and Americans, many see themselves as having a secondary British identity as well as well being English, Scots, or Welsh. In Northern Ireland, people divide into two nations. Most Catholics see themselves as Irish while the great majority of Protestants see themselves as British.

The parties competing for seats differ in each nation of the United Kingdom. Northern Ireland is extreme, for British parties do not contest seats there. In Scotland, four parties compete. In the 2005 general election the Labour Party won more than two-thirds of the seats with two-fifths of the vote in competition with the Liberal Party, the pro-independence Scottish National Party, and the fourth-place Conservative Party. In Wales, the nationalist party, Plaid Cymru, came fourth in votes. The most distinctive feature of Welsh politics is the high Labour vote.

Historically, Scotland and Wales have been governed by British Cabinet ministers accountable to the Westminster Parliament. Under pressure from nationalist parties campaigning for independence, the Labour Party adopted a policy of creating elected Assemblies in Scotland and in Wales. Referendums on devolution were held in September 1997. In Scotland, 74 percent voted in favor of a Scottish

TABLE 5.1 National Identity

	England	Scotland	Wales	N. Ireland Prot.	N. Ireland Catholic
THINKS OF SELF AS:					
British	38	35	33	67	15
English	57	2	8	—	—
Scottish	2	52	—	—	—
Welsh	1	—	57	—	—
Ulster	—	—	—	20	6
Irish	1	11	—	8	69
Other, don't know	1	10	2	5	10
Total	100	100	100	100	100

Source: Richard Rose, *The Territorial Dimension in Government: Understanding the United Kingdom* (Chatham, N.J.: Chatham House, 1982), p. 14.

Parliament in Edinburgh while Welsh voters endorsed an Assembly in Cardiff by 50.3 percent.

A Parliament in Scotland with powers to legislate, tax, and spend was first elected in May 1999 under a system of proportional representation. In the second election to the 129-seat Parliament held in May 2003, the Labour Party won 32 percent of the proportional representation vote and 50 seats and the pro-independence Scottish National Party gained 27 seats with 21 percent of the vote. The Conservative Party won 13 percent of the vote and 18 seats, and the Liberal Democrats 10 percent of the vote and 17 seats. The Green Party, Scottish Socialists, and other parties together won 17 seats and almost one-quarter of the vote. As the party with the most seats, Labour provides the First Minister, but to achieve a majority in the Scottish Parliament, it has needed to form a coalition government with the Liberal Democrats.

After the May 1999 Welsh Assembly election, Labour formed a minority government. In the May 2003 election, Labour's share of the vote went up to 37 percent and it won half of the 60 seats in the Assembly. In second place was the Welsh Nationalist Party (Plaid Cymru), with 12 seats and 20 percent of the vote. The Conservatives gained 11 seats with 19 percent of the vote and Liberal Democrats won 6 seats with 13 percent of the vote. Powers over Welsh legislation and total public expenditure remain in the hands of a British Cabinet minister.

Northern Ireland is the most un-English part of the United Kingdom. Formally, it is a secular polity, but differences between Protestants and Catholics about national identity dominate its politics. Protestants, comprising about three-fifths of the population, want to remain part of the United Kingdom. Until 1972 the Protestant majority governed through a home-rule Parliament at Stormont, a suburb of Belfast. Many of the Catholic minority did not support this regime; they wanted to leave the United Kingdom and join the Republic of Ireland, which in its constitution claimed the territory of Northern Ireland.

Since the start of demonstrations by Catholics against discrimination in Northern Ireland in 1968, it has been in turmoil. Demonstrations turned to street violence in August 1969, and the British Army

intervened. The illegal *Irish Republican Army (IRA)* was revived and in 1971 began a military campaign to remove Northern Ireland from the United Kingdom. In retaliation, Protestants organized illegal armed forces too. Since August 1969, more than 3,200 people have been killed in political violence. After adjusting for population differences, the deaths from political violence are equivalent to more than 110,000 political deaths in Britain or more than 500,000 deaths in America.

British policy in Northern Ireland has been erratic. In 1969 the British Army went into action to protect Catholics. In 1971 it helped intern hundreds of Catholics without trial in an unsuccessful attempt to break the IRA. In 1972 the British government abolished the Stormont Parliament, placing government in the hands of a Northern Ireland Office under a British Cabinet minister. In 1985 the British government took the unprecedented step of inviting the Dublin-based government of the Republic of Ireland to participate in institutions affecting the governance of part of the United Kingdom.

A stable agreement about Northern Ireland requires the acceptance by paramilitary organizations on each side of the religious divide as well as of parties solely committed to parliamentary politics. In 1994 the IRA announced a cessation of its military activity, and Sinn Fein, the party political wing of the Irish Republican Movement, agreed to talks. Protestant paramilitary forces also ceased activities. On Good Friday, 1998, an agreement was reached for an elected power-sharing executive and cross-border institutions involving both Dublin and Belfast. The basic principle of the agreement, power-sharing, is the opposite of British government. Whereas in Westminster the majority party in the Commons can form a government on its own, in Northern Ireland government must be a coalition of representatives of both Protestants and Catholics.

The election of a Northern Ireland Assembly in June 1998, led to a power-sharing executive including the Ulster Unionist Party, the nonviolent Social Democratic and Labour Party (SDLP), and Sinn Fein, a party linked politically with the IRA. The Democratic Unionist Party led by Dr. Ian Paisley did not join the administration. When the IRA failed to produce sufficient tangible evidence that it was decommissioning arms, the power-sharing executive collapsed Northern Ireland is once again under "temporary" direct rule from Westminster, and a 45 million dollar bank robber and a brutal murder by the IRA have questioned Sinn Fein's commitment to a non-violent resolution of the conflict. In the 2005 election, the Democratic Unionist Party won the most seats and Sinn Fein came in second.

The United Kingdom is a union—that is, a political system having only one source of authority, the British Parliament. However, institutions governing the United Kingdom are not uniform. Distinctive administrative institutions exist in Scotland and Wales, and *devolution* increases their political legitimacy by creating popularly elected assemblies. Northern Ireland has always been the subject of exceptional legislation.

Even though there is no agreement about what being English means, there is no doubt about which nationality is the most numerous. Politics in England is the focus of this chapter because England dominates the United Kingdom. Its population constitutes five-sixths of the total of the United Kingdom, and the remainder is divided among three different nations. No United Kingdom government will ever overlook what is central to England, and politicians who wish to advance in British government must accept the norms of English society. During the 1997 election campaign, Blair reminded Scottish voters, "Sovereignty rests with me, as an English MP, and that's the way it will stay."[7]

A Multiracial England

Through the centuries England has received a relatively small but noteworthy number of immigrants from other parts of Europe. The Queen herself is descended from royalty who came from Hanover, Germany, to assume the English throne in 1714. Until the outbreak of anti-German sentiment in World War I, the surname of the royal family was Saxe-Coburg-Gotha. By royal proclamation George V changed the family name to Windsor in 1917. Most post–World War II immigrants have been attracted to England by jobs. Since the late 1950s job seekers have been arriving from the West Indies, Pakistan, India, and other parts of what was once the British Empire and is now a multiracial Commonwealth.

In addition, there is a substantial inflow and outflow of people from Australia, Canada, the European Union, and the United States spending a few years in England for study or work.

The new Commonwealth immigrants have only one characteristic in common: they are not white. Beyond that, immigrants share neither culture nor religion. West Indians speak English as their native language and have a Christian tradition; immigrants from India and Pakistan are Hindus, Muslims, or Sikhs and most speak English as a second language. The smaller number of African immigrants are divided by nationality. Chinese from Hong Kong have a distinctive culture too. Altogether, more than half of New Commonwealth immigrants have come from the Indian subcontinent, a quarter are black people from the Caribbean or Africa, and about a tenth are Chinese or other Asians from outside the Indian subcontinent.

The 2001 census estimated the nonwhite population of the United Kingdom had risen from 74,000 in 1951 to 4.6 million, almost 8 percent of the population. Public opinion has opposed unlimited immigration of nonwhites, and both Conservative and Labour governments have passed laws limiting the number of nonwhite immigrants.

With the passage of time the nonwhite population is becoming increasingly British born and educated. This makes the important issue: What is the position of British-born offspring of immigrants? Whatever their country of origin, they differ in how they see themselves: 64 percent of Caribbean origin identify as British, as do more than three-fifths of Pakistanis, Indians, and Bangladeshis, and two-fifths of Chinese. Laws to encourage better race relations and antidiscrimination measures have been enacted. However, provisions for enforcement by the courts are very weak in comparison with American legislation. After the 9/11 terrorist attacks in America, the Labour government has shifted emphasis from promoting multiculturalism to stressing the integration of immigrant families into the British way of life.

Immigrants and their offspring are being integrated into electoral politics, as residential concentration makes local politicians aware of their impact as a voting bloc. There are now hundreds of elected nonwhite councillors in local government; a disproportionate number are Labour. The 15 nonwhite MPs in the Commons today come from diverse backgrounds: India, Pakistan, Aden, Ghana, and the West Indies.

Political disturbances around the world have added a fresh issue, an increasing number of immigrants who claim to be refugees from trouble areas in the Balkans, the Middle East, and Africa. Some have valid credentials as refugees whereas others have been smuggled to England and arrive with false papers. In response to popular concern, the Blair government has promised to be tougher in enforcing asylum laws.

Insularity and Involvement

For centuries the English Channel has represented a literal as well as a symbolic gulf between England and continental Europe. The opening in 1994 of the Channel Tunnel linking England and France has not closed the gap. More than half of Britons say they do not feel at all European, and only 23 percent say that they feel strongly or somewhat European. Depending on circumstances, politicians claim that England is close to the United States, or to the Commonwealth countries scattered around the globe, or to Europe.[8]

Insularity is not to be confused with isolation. Britain is a member of more than 125 different international bodies, including the United Nations, the European Union, and NATO. The British Empire has been replaced by a free association of 54 sovereign states—the Commonwealth—with members on every continent. The independent status of its chief members is shown by the absence of the word "British" from the name of the Commonwealth. Commonwealth countries from Antigua and Australia to Zambia and Zimbabwe differ greatly from each other in wealth, language, culture, and religion, and in their commitment to democracy.

Britain's foreign policy since the end of the Second World War has been a story of contracting commitments. Britain took a lead in establishing NATO to involve the United States in the protection of Western Europe from the Soviet Union. Militarily, it has been dependent on high-tech hardware bought from the United States while retaining an armed force with upwards of 300,000 persons in uniform,

including a major military presence in Iraq since 2003. Blair sees Britain's role as a key link in the creation of "one polar power which encompasses a strategic partnership between Europe and America."[9]

However, there has been limited popular support for the country acting like a global policeman. When a Gallup Poll asked whether people would rather Britain were a leading world power or a small neutral country like Sweden or Switzerland, 49 percent chose being a small power as against 34 percent wanting the country to be a world power.[10] Whereas military force is rarely used, economic transactions are continuous. England depends on world trade, importing much food and many raw materials. To pay for imports, England exports a wide range of manufactured goods, as well as "invisible" services provided by financial institutions in the city of London.

Speeches by the prime minister and head of the Treasury do not determine the foreign exchange value of the pound. This is decided in international markets in which currency speculators play a significant role. The value of the British pound in exchange for the dollar has ranged from above $2.50 to less than $1.25. In spring, 2005 the pound's value fluctuated around $1.90.

As England's world position has declined and the importance of countries such as Germany and France has risen, the government has looked to Europe. In a jet age, the English Channel is no longer a barrier to travel to the European continent. Television and the Internet carry news, sports, and entertainment across national boundaries. Economic ties have grown. For example, the Ford Motor Company links its manufacturing plants in England with factories across Western Europe, just as it links Ford factories between American states. Public opinion and politicians have remained divided about what role Britain can or should play in Europe. When the European Community was established in 1957, Britain did not join, because the government considered the country distant from the problems of continental neighbors ravaged by war. It joined in 1973.

European politics has grown in significance, symbolized by the Community changing its name to the European Union. Powers to promote a Single European Market enable the EU to impose regulations affecting British business and limit the scope for London to give subsidies to industries and firms in trouble. British ministers spend an increasing amount of their time negotiating with their opposite numbers in other countries of the European Union on matters ranging from political fundamentals to whether British beer should be served in metric units or by the traditional measure of a British pint.

The British government cannot insulate the country from changes in the world. English people cannot choose to be a small, rich country like Switzerland or Sweden. The effective choice today is between England being a big, rich country or a big, relatively poor European country. Exchanging nominal sovereignty to participate in the European Union presents no problems to governments in small countries, which have always recognized the influence of bigger neighbors. However, it is a shock to many British politicians who pride themselves on Britain's traditional involvement in three different international settings, the Commonwealth, Europe, and a "special relationship" with the United States.

The diversity of political outlooks within the European Union is so great after its enlargement to 25 member states that government ministers can normally find allies for any British cause. But to do so the government must be fully committed to involvement in the European Union. Seven years after becoming prime minister, Tony Blair has yet to convince fellow EU members that Britain is no longer

an island but an integral part of Europe. The indictment of the American diplomat, Dean Acheson, a generation ago continues to ring true: "Great Britain has lost an empire and has not yet found a role."[11]

THE STRUCTURE OF GOVERNMENT

We must understand what government is as precondition of evaluating what it does. Descriptions of a government often start with its constitution. However, England has no written constitution. At no time in the past was there a break with tradition that forced politicians to write down how the country should be governed.

The *unwritten constitution* of England is a jumble of acts of Parliament, judicial pronouncements, customs, and conventions about the rules of the political game. The vagueness of the constitution makes it flexible, a point that political leaders such as Margaret Thatcher and Tony Blair have been ready to exploit to increase their own power. Instead of giving written guarantees to citizens, as the American Bill of Rights does, the rights of English people are meant to be secured by trustworthy governors. In the words of a constitutional lawyer, J. A. G. Griffith, "The Constitution is what happens."[12]

Comparing the written American and the unwritten English constitution emphasizes how few are the constraints of an unwritten constitution (Table 5.2). The U.S. Constitution gives the Supreme Court the final power to decide what the government may or may not do. In England, by contrast, the final

TABLE 5.2   Comparing an Unwritten and a Written Constitution

	England (unwritten)	United States (written)
Origins	Medieval customs	1787 Constitutional Convention
Form	Unwritten, indefinite	Written, precise
Final power	Majority in Parliament	Supreme Court
Bill of individual rights	No	Yes
Amendment	Ordinary vote in Parliament; unprecedented action by government	More than majority vote in Congress, states
Centrality in political debate	Low	High

authority is Parliament, where the government of the day commands a majority of votes. The Law Lords and the Judicial Committee of the Privy Council can resolve disputes about the interpretation of Acts of Parliament but not declare an Act unconstitutional. The Bill of Rights in the U.S. Constitution allows anyone to seek redress in the courts for infringement of personal rights, whereas in England an individual who believes his or her personal rights are infringed by an act of Parliament had no redress through the courts until the Blair government, instead of preparing a British code of rights, simply incorporated the European Convention of Human Rights into the laws of Britain. Whereas amendments to the U.S. Constitution must receive the endorsement of well over half the states and members of Congress, the unwritten constitution can be changed by a majority vote in Parliament, or by the government of the day choosing to act in an unprecedented manner.

English courts claim no power to declare an act of Parliament unconstitutional. Courts ask whether the executive acts within its statutory powers. Many statutes delegate broad discretion to a Cabinet minister or public authority; the courts hesitate to question how the executive exercises its delegated discretion. Even if the courts rule that the government has improperly exercised its authority, the effect of such a judgment can be annulled by a subsequent act of Parliament retroactively authorizing an action.

The *Crown* rather than a constitution symbolizes the authority of government. However, the monarch is only a ceremonial head of state. The public reaction to the accidental death of Princess Diana was a media event but it was not a political event like the assassination of President Kennedy. Queen Elizabeth II does not influence the actions of what is described as Her Majesty's Government. While the queen gives formal assent to laws passed by Parliament, she may not publicly state any opinion about legislation. The queen is expected to respect the will of Parliament, as communicated to her by the leader of the majority party in Parliament, the prime minister.

What constitutes the Crown? No simple answer can be given. The Crown is a symbol to which people are asked to give loyalty. It does not refer to a particular community of people. The idea of the Crown combines the dignified parts of the constitution, which sanctify authority by tradition and myth, with the efficient parts, which carry out the work of government.

In everyday political conversation, English people talk about government, not the constitution. The term *government* is used in many senses (Figure 5.1). People may speak of the Queen's government, to emphasize enduring and nonpartisan features, or they may refer to Tony Blair's government to stress its personal and transitory features, or to a Labour or Conservative government to emphasize partisanship. The term government officials usually refers to civil servants. Collectively, the executive agencies of government are often referred to as *Whitehall*, after the London street in which many major government offices are located. *Downing Street*, where the prime minister's residence is located, is a short and narrow street off Whitehall. *Parliament*—that is, the popularly elected House of Commons and the nonelected House of Lords—is at the bottom end of the street called Whitehall. Collectively, these institutions are often referred to as *Westminster*, after the district in London in which they are located.

What the Prime Minister Says and Does

Within the Cabinet, the *prime minister* occupies a unique position, sometimes referred to as primus inter pares (first among equals). But as Winston Churchill once wrote, "There can be no comparison between the positions of number one, and numbers two, three or four."[13] However, the preeminence of the prime minister is ambiguous. A politician at the apex of government is remote from what is happening on the ground. The more responsibilities attributed to the prime minister, the less time there is to devote to any one task. Like a president, a prime minister is the prisoner of the political law of first things first. The imperatives of the prime minister are as follows.

1. *Winning elections.* A prime minister may be self-interested but he or she is not self-employed. To become prime minister, a politician must first be elected leader of his or her party. The only election that a prime minister must win is

FIGURE 5.1   Structure of the British Government

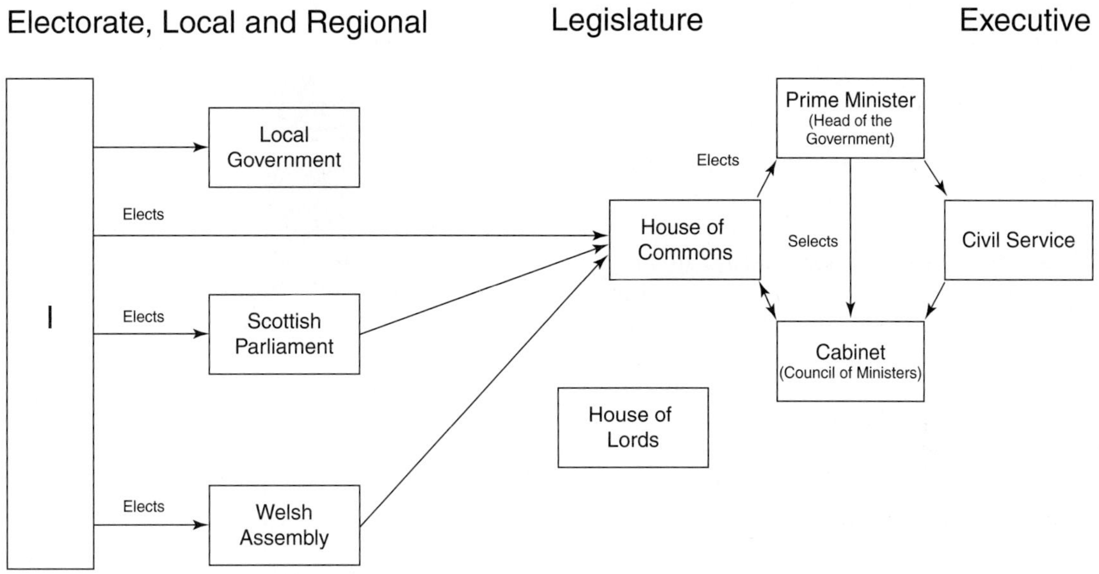

Electorate, Local and Regional   Legislature   Executive

that as party leader. Six of the eleven prime ministers since 1945—Winston Churchill, Anthony Eden, Harold Macmillan, Alec Douglas-Home, James Callaghan, and John Major—initially entered Downing Street during the middle of a Parliament rather than after a national election. In the 17 elections since 1945, the prime minister of the day has ten times led the governing party to victory and seven times to defeat.

2. *Campaigning through the media.* A prime minister does not need to attract publicity; it is thrust upon him or her by the curiosity of television and newspaper reporters. Media eminence is a double-edged sword. When the news is bad, such as rising unemployment or popular concern about crime, the news puts the prime minister in an unfavorable light. While the personality of a prime minister remains relatively constant, during a term of office his or her popularity can fluctuate by as much as 30 or 40 percentage points in public opinion polls.[14]

3. *Patronage.* To remain prime minister, a politician must retain the confidence of his party. He can silence potential critics by appointing a quarter of MPs in the governing party to jobs in the government as ministers or junior ministers; they sit on front bench seats in the House of Commons. MPs not appointed to a post are backbenchers; many ingratiate themselves with the party leader in hopes of becoming a government minister. In making ministerial appointments, a prime minister can use any of four different criteria: (a) personal loyalty (rewarding friends); (b) co-option (silencing critics by giving them an office so that they are committed to support the government); (c) representativeness (for example, appointing a woman or someone from Scotland or Wales); and (d) competence in giving direction to a government department.

4. *Parliamentary performance.* The prime minister appears in the House of Commons weekly for half an hour of questions from MPs, engaging in rapid-fire repartee with a highly partisan audience. Unprotected by a speechwriter's script,

the prime minister must show that he or she is a good advocate of their views or suffer loss of support. He or she occasionally makes statements to the House.

5. *Making and balancing policies.* Leading government is a political rather than a managerial task. When a prime minister asks an awkward question or gives advice, no Cabinet minister can ignore it. Foreign affairs are the overriding concern of a prime minister, because of the need to deal with heads of governments around the world. When there are conflicts between international and domestic policy priorities, the prime minister is the one person who can strike a balance between pressures from the world "out there" and pressures from the domestic electorate. The number of "intermestic" policies (that is, problems combining both an international and domestic element) is increasing.

While the formal powers of the office remain constant, individual prime ministers have differed in how they view their job, and in their political circumstances (see Figure 5.2). Clement Attlee, Labour prime minister from 1945 to 1951, was a non-assertive spokesperson for the lowest common denominator of views within a Cabinet consisting of very experienced Labour politicians. When an aging Winston Churchill succeeded in 1951, he concentrated on foreign affairs and took little interest in domestic policy; the same was true of his successor, Anthony Eden. Harold Macmillan intervened strategically on a limited number of domestic and international issues, while giving ministers great scope on everyday matters. Alec Douglas-Home was weak because he lacked knowledge of economic affairs, the chief problem during his administration.

Both Harold Wilson and Edward Heath were initially committed to an activist definition of the prime minister's job. However, Wilson's major initiatives in economic policy were unsuccessful. In 1974 the electorate rejected Heath's aggressive direction of the economy, and Wilson won office promising to replace confrontation between management and unions with political conciliation. James Callaghan, who succeeded Wilson in 1976, also emphasized consensus.

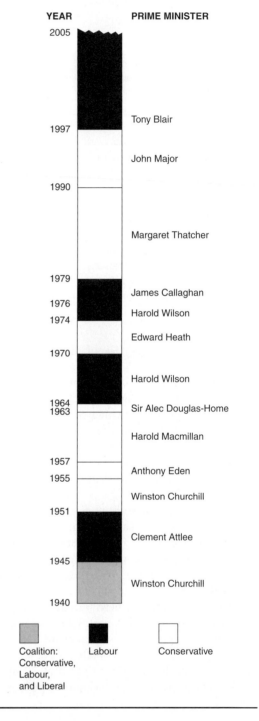

FIGURE 5.2 Prime Minister and Governments Since 1940

Margaret Thatcher had strong views about many major policies; associates gave her the nickname TINA because of her motto: There Is No Alternative. Thatcher was prepared to push her views against the wishes of Cabinet colleagues and civil service advisers by any means necessary. In the end, her "bossiness" caused a revolt of Cabinet colleagues that helped bring about her downfall, and made colleagues welcome John Major in place of a hectoring leader. However, his conciliatory manner was often interpreted as a sign of weakness, and sniping from ministers led Major to refer to his Cabinet colleagues as "bastards."

Tony Blair has carried into Downing Street the priority he gave to campaigning while in Opposition, and brought with him a media staff of "spin doctors" under the leadership of a pro-Labour tabloid journalist, Alastair Campbell. A former editor of *The Times* has charged that Campbell has "imposed the fixations of the press on a compliant government."[15] The media staff are unprecedented in their number, professional skills, and readiness to assert themselves. The emphasis is on "soft" media appearances, for example, on breakfast chat shows, rather than on tough confrontations with the Opposition in the House of Commons. In addition, Blair has brought a large policy staff into Downing Street, and given senior staff formal authority to give orders to civil servants and informal sanction to tell Cabinet ministers what the prime minister wants. This has led to charges of government by "Tony's cronies" and of the politicization of civil servants, who are expected to generate the headlines that Number Ten wants. Producing the policies needed to back up headline-seeking statements is much more difficult, as the prime minister has learned.

Blair's innovations in campaigning and in Downing Street have led to criticisms that he has created a presidential system. However, by comparison with an American president, a British prime minister has less formal authority. The president is directly elected for a fixed four-year term. A prime minister is chosen by colleagues for an indefinite term—no longer than the life of a Parliament—and is thus less secure in office. The president is the undoubted leader of the federal executive and can dismiss Cabinet appointees with little fear of the consequences; by contrast senior colleagues of a prime minister, such as Gordon Brown, are potential rivals for leadership and are kept in Cabinet to prevent them from challenging the incumbent from outside it. With the support of the Cabinet and the majority of the party's MPs, a prime minister can be far more confident than a president that major legislative proposals will be enacted into law. Although the president is the chief executive branch of the federal government, the White House is without authority over Congress, state and local government, and the judiciary. The prime minister is at the apex of a unitary government, with powers not limited by the courts or by a written constitution.

The Cabinet and Cabinet Ministers

The *Cabinet* consists of senior ministers, members of either the House of Commons or House of Lords and appointed by the prime minister. As ministers are leading figures in the majority party in Parliament, they contribute to what Walter Bagehot described as "the close union, the nearly complete fusion of the executive and legislative powers."[16]

The Cabinet has historically been the forum in which the prime minister brought together leading members of the governing party, many with competing departmental interests and personal ambitions, to ensure agreement about major government policies. This was possible because the convention of Cabinet responsibility requires that all Cabinet ministers and their deputies give public support (or at least, refrain from public criticism) of what the government is doing, even if they have opposed a policy in private. A minister who is unwilling to share responsibility has been expected to resign office, and it is rare for a minister to resign because of policy differences.

The Cabinet is no longer a place for collective deliberation in policy. A half century ago there were almost two Cabinet meetings a week with many taking several hours to arrive at a political consensus. By the time of John Major shorter meetings occurred less than once a week. Tony Blair has further reduced meetings and cut their average length to under an hour. Instead of being a forum for consultation, Cabinet meetings are now a forum in which Number Ten exhorts ministers to produce good

Box 5.3   Departmental Organization and Reorganization

British government departments are multipurpose administrative units created as a result of the growth of government and brought together through a series of reorganizations justified by efficiency, policy, fashion, or political expediency.* For example, since 1964 responsibilities for trade, industry, and technology have been placed in departments labelled Trade and Technology, then Trade and Industry, separate departments for Trade and for Industry, and once again reunited as a single Trade and Industry department. Each time that the title on the front door of the department was changed, most officials and programs continued as before. The Cabinet of Tony Blair in January, 2005 had the following departments:

1. External affairs: foreign and commonwealth office; Europe; defence; international development
2. Economic affairs: treasury; trade and industry; transport
3. Law: Lord chancellor and law Officer's department; home office; constitutional affairs
4. Social services: health; social security; education and skills; work and pensions; culture, media, and sport
5. Territorial: environment, food and rural affairs; communities and local government; housing and planning; some parts of constitutional affairs; the Northern Ireland Office
6. Managing government business: Office of Deputy Prime Minister, Leader of the House of Commons; Chief Whip in the House of Commons; Leader of the House of Lords; Chancellor of the Duchy of Lancaster

*See Richard Rose, *Ministers and Ministries: A Functional Analysis* (Oxford, England: Clarendon Press, 1987).

news and bury bad news. Cabinet ministers remain important as department heads, for most decisions of government are taken within departments, and departments are responsible for overseeing all the services of government, which are usually delivered by public agencies distant from Whitehall and subordinate to it (Box 5.3).

The most important departments are the Treasury, which is responsible for taxing, spending, and managing the economy; the Home Office, responsible for police, immigration, and security; and the Foreign Office, although its head often acts as a subordinate to the prime minister. Other departments are prominent when their subject matter is in the news: for example, if there is a rail crash then the minister for Transport answers for what has happened.

Major Whitehall departments differ greatly from each other. For example, the Home Office has a staff approximately ten times larger than the Treasury. Because of the importance of the economy, however, the Treasury has more senior civil servants. The Home Office has more staff at lower levels because of the scale of its routine tasks involving supervision of police, fire, prison, drugs, cruelty to

animals, control of obscene publications, race relations, and so on. The Treasury concentrates on one big task, the management of the economy. The varied tasks of the Home Secretary make him or her much more vulnerable to adverse publicity if, for example, a convicted murderer escapes from prison. But the job of the Chancellor of the Exchequer, the minister in charge of the Treasury, is more important politically, insofar as economic performance affects the governing party's electoral fate. Moreover, Gordon Brown, the current Chancellor, has a power base in the Labour Party independent of Tony Blair and is often described as his potential successor.

A minister has many roles; initiating policies, selecting among alternatives brought forward from within the department, or avoiding a difficult or unpopular decision. A minister is responsible for actions taken by thousands of civil servants nominally acting on the minister's behalf and must answer for agencies to which Whitehall is increasingly contracting out responsibility for delivering public services. In addition, a minister is a department's ambassador to the world outside, including Downing Street, Parliament, the mass media, and pressure groups. Not least, Cabinet ministers are individuals with ambitions to rise in politics.

The typical minister is not an expert in a subject but an expert in parliamentary politics, willing to deal with any department that offers opportunities to further his or her political career. A minister learns on the job. Usually, an MP is first given a junior post as an Under Secretary, with limited policy responsibilities. He or she may then be promoted to Minister of State, a position with broader and more important departmental duties, for example, looking after primary education in the Department of Education. The final step up the career ladder is to become head of a department and a full member of the Cabinet.

The political reputation of Cabinet ministers depends on their success in promoting the interests of their department in parliament, in the media and in battles within Whitehall. Cabinet ministers are willing to go along silently with their colleagues' proposals in exchange for endorsement of their own measures. However, ministers often have to compete for scarce resources, making conflict inevitable between departments. Regardless of party, the defence and education ministers will press for increased spending while treasury ministers oppose such moves. Cabinet ministers prefer to resolve their differences in Cabinet committees including all ministers whose departments are most affected by an issue or by lobbying Downing Street for the prime minister's support.

Tony Blair's concern with continuous campaigning by presenting good news through the media has led him to give his personal staff at Downing Street greater influence over what ministers say and do—insofar as it attracts media attention. However, Blair does not have any more time during the week to go into the details of policy, and because he has never been a departmental minister, his public remarks sometimes show naivete about how government actually works.[17]

The Civil Service

Although government could continue for months without new legislation, it would collapse overnight if hundreds of thousands of civil servants stopped administering laws and delivering public services.

The largest number of civil servants are clerical staff with little discretion; they undertake the routine activities of a large bureaucracy. Only if these duties are executed satisfactorily can ministers have the time and opportunity to make new policies. The most important group of civil servants is the smallest: the few hundred higher civil servants who advise ministers and oversee work of the departments. Top British civil servants deny they are politicians because of the partisan connotations of the term. However, their work is political because they are concerned with formulating, revising, and advising on policies. A publication seeking to recruit bright graduates for the higher civil service declares: "You will be involved from the outset in matters of major policy or resource allocation and, under the guidance of experienced administrators, encouraged to put forward your own constructive ideas and to take responsible decisions."

Top civil servants are not apolitical; they are bipartisan, being ready to work for whichever party is the winner of an election. Their style is not that of the professional American athlete for whom winning is all-important. English civil servants have grown up playing cricket; its motto is that winning is less important than how one plays the game. The relationship between ministers and higher civil servants is critical. Ministers expect higher civil servants to be responsive to their political views and to give advice consistent with their outlook and that of the governing party and Downing Street. Civil servants like working for a political heavyweight who can carry the department's cause to victory in interdepartmental battles. A busy politician does not have time to go into details; he or she wants a brief that can catch a headline or squash criticism. Civil servants prefer to work for a minister who has clear views on policy, but they dislike it when the views proclaimed will get the department into trouble later because they are impractical.

In the traditional Whitehall model, both ministers and civil servants concentrated on political management rather than administrative concerns. Civil servants were expected to think like politicians, anticipating what their minister would want and objections that would be raised by Parliament, pressure groups, and the media. Ministers were also expected to think like civil servants, recognizing all the obstacles to achieving politically desirable goals, and scaling down their ambitions when ways could not be found to overcome these obstacles. The Thatcher government introduced a new phenomenon in Whitehall: a prime minister who believed civil servants were inferior to business people because they did not have to "earn" their living—that is, make a profit. Management was made the buzzword in Whitehall, and departments were supposed to be run in a businesslike fashion, achieving value for money so that the government could profit politically by cutting taxes. Parts of government departments were "hived off" to form separate public agencies, with their own accounts and performance target, However, when an agency's task is politically sensitive, such as the marking of national school examinations, the education minister cannot avoid blame if there are major errors in marking examinations.

The Blair government has continued Thatcherite attempts to make the civil service more businesslike, in hopes it can thereby provide more public services without raising taxes. In addition, it has made political advisers important in formulating policy, leading to criticisms from the independent official Committee on Standards in Public Life. Some civil servants fear that efforts to "modernize" the civil service are a mask for appointing officials who are pliable in the hands of ministers.

After years in office, Tony Blair has attacked the consequences of government by political advisers and spin doctors. In a leaked memo to Cabinet ministers he has criticized them for "too often" rushing out policies "in ignorance of the risks," thus making the government look bad.[18]

The Role of Parliament

The principal division in Parliament is between the party with a majority of seats in the House of Commons and the opposition party. The government gets its way because its members are the leading politicians in the party with a majority in the Commons. If a bill or a motion is identified as a vote of confidence in the government, the government will fall if it is defeated. MPs in the majority party almost invariably vote as the party leadership in-

structs, because only by voting as a bloc can their party maintain control of government. The instrument by which party discipline is imposed is known as a *whip*. This word actually has a double political meaning. It refers, on the one hand, to a member of parliament whose responsibility is to enforce party discipline. Each party will have a number of such offices, with the top officer known as the chief whip. On the other hand, the word "whip" also refers to a document issued by these party officials, on a weekly basis, which tells the party members how to vote on upcoming bills and how important each of these bills is. In nine out of ten votes in the Commons, voting is 100 percent along party lines. If a handful of MPs votes against the party whip or abstains, this is headlined as a rebellion. The government's state of mind is summed up in the words of a Labour Cabinet minister who declared, "It's carrying democracy too far if you don't know the result of the vote before the meeting."[19]

Whitehall departments draft bills presented to Parliament. Only a very small percentage of amendments to legislation are carried without government backing. Moreover, the government rather than Parliament sets the budget for government programmes. The weakness of the British House of Commons stands in marked contrast to the U.S. Congress, where each house controls its own proceedings independent of the White House and can be at loggerheads when different parties control each branch. An American president may ask Congress to enact a bill but cannot compel a favorable vote.

The first function of the Commons is to weigh political reputations. MPs continually assess their colleagues as ministers and potential ministers. A minister may win a formal vote of confidence but lose status if his or her arguments are demolished in debate.

Secondly, MPs in the governing party have private access to government ministers. The whip is expected to listen to the views of dissatisfied backbench MPs and to convey their concerns to ministers. In the corridors, dining rooms, and committees of the Commons, backbenchers can tell ministers what they think is wrong with government policy. However, MPs are unwilling to vote against their party if it threatens to bring down the government. The opposition cannot expect to alter major government decisions because it lacks a majority of votes in the Commons. The opposition accepts the frustrations going with its minority status for the life of a Parliament, because it hopes to win a majority at the next election.

Publicizing issues is a third function of Parliament. Debates in the House of Commons are losing importance; only one-sixth of backbenchers regularly listen to their colleagues' speeches in the House of Commons. An MP has much more access to the mass media than an ordinary citizen. Television has access to Parliament, but news programs usually show only sound bites.

Talking about legislation is a fourth function of the House of Commons. Backbench MPs can demand that the government do something about an issue. The procedures of the Commons force a minister to explain and defend a bill in detail. In theory a government bill can be substantially amended or even withdrawn as a consequence of criticism in Parliament—but such incidents are rare. Laws are described as acts of Parliament, but it would be more accurate if they were stamped "Made in Whitehall."

Fifth, MPs scrutinize how Whitehall departments administer public policies. An MP may write to a minister, questioning a departmental decision called to his or her attention by a constituent or pressure group. MPs can request the parliamentary commissioner for administration (also known as the ombudsman, after the Scandinavian prototype) to investigate complaints about maladministration. Committees scrutinize administration and policy, interviewing civil servants and ministers. However, as a committee moves from discussing details to questions of political principle, it raises the question of confidence in the government. Party loyalty usually guarantees that the government will not lose a committee vote.

A newly elected MP contemplating his or her role as one among 646 members of the House of Commons is faced with many alternatives. An MP may decide to be a party loyalist, voting as the leadership decides, without participating in deliberations about policy. The MP who wishes more attention can make a mark by brilliance in debate, by acting as an acknowledged representative of a pressure group, or in a nonpartisan way—for example, as a wit. An MP is expected to speak for constituency interests, but constituents accept that their MP will not vote against party policy if it is in conflict with local interests. The only role that an MP rarely undertakes is that of lawmaker.

Among modern Parliaments, the House of Lords is unique because none of its members (who are referred to as "peers") are elected. More than one-eighth of the members of this second chamber have inherited a peerage from an ancestor who may have received it several centuries ago. Others serve in the House of Lords because they are senior judges or bishops of the Church of England. But today a large majority of the members of the House of Lords are life peers who have been given a title later in life for achievement in one or another public sphere, including membership in the House of Commons. In 1999 the Labour government abolished the right of all but 92 hereditary peers to sit in the House of Lords. No party has a majority there. Among its 704 members, one-third are Conservative, one-third are Labour, 69 Liberal Democrats, and the remainder divide into a number of nonparty categories.

The government often introduces relatively noncontroversial legislation in the Lords if it deals with technical matters, and it uses the Lords as a revising chamber to amend bills. In addition, the Lords can discuss public issues on matters of partisan controversy or on such cross-party topics as pornography or the future of hill farming. The Lords cannot veto legislation, but it can and does amend or delay the passage of some government bills. The limited influence of both houses of Parliament encourages proposals for reform. Backbench MPs perennially demand changes to make their jobs more interesting and to give them more influence. Labour MPs, especially women elected since 1997, have criticized procedures inherited from past centuries as inappropriate for the new millennium. However, the power to make changes rests with the government rather than the House of Commons. Whatever criticisms MPs made of Parliament while in opposition, once in Cabinet party leaders have an interest in existing arrangements that greatly limit the power of Parliament to influence or stop what ministers do.

While all parties accept the need for some kind of second chamber to revise legislation, there is no agreement about how it should be composed or what its powers should be. Many politicians argue for an elected upper house, but the last thing the government of the day wants is a reform that gives the upper chamber enough legitimacy to challenge a House of Commons that invariably endorses government legislation.

Government as a Network

The ship of state has only one tiller—but more than one pair of hands give it direction. In an era of big government, power does not rest in a single individual or office; it is manifest in a network of relations within and between a network of institutions. Policymaking involves the interaction between prime minister, ministers, and leading civil servants, all of whom share in what has been described as the "village life" of Whitehall—and this English village is far smaller and more intimate than the city full of politicians inside the Washington beltway.[20]

Within the Whitehall network, a core set of political figures are especially important in determining policies. The prime minister is the single most important person in government. Since there is no written constitution, a determined prime minister can challenge the status quo and seek to turn government to fresh ends. For example, Margaret Thatcher entered office with a large agenda of market-oriented policies that she wished to promote, and stamina and determination to push through policies against opposition from Cabinet colleagues as well as civil servants.

To say that the prime minister makes the most important decisions and departmental ministers the secondary decisions begs the question: What is an important decision? Decisions in which the prime minister is not involved affecting such issues as social security are more numerous, require more money, and affect more lives than most decisions taken in Downing Street. Scarcity of prime ministerial time is a major limitation on the influence of the prime minister. In the words of one Downing Street official, "It's like skating over an enormous globe of thin ice. You have to keep moving fast all the time."[21]

The head of the Treasury, the Chancellor of the Exchequer, takes many decisions with broad political ramifications too about measures to promote economic growth, taxation, and public expenditure. Chancellor Gordon Brown is extremely influential on domestic policy because he heads the department deciding how much spending ministers can spend and he has a base of support among Labour MPs independent of the prime minister. Within each department, the permanent secretary, its highest-ranking civil servant, usually has much more knowledge of a department's problems than does a transitory Cabinet minister.

In his first term, Tony Blair emphasized making Whitehall a campaigning organization, trebling the number of policy advisers attached to Downing Street and departments, and raising the priority given to managing news and staging media events. By "loaning" his authority to staff to use in discussions with civil servants and ministers, he has increased the collective influence of Downing Street within government. But the use of the prime minister's name by powerful advisers has also created adverse media publicity due to a "war of leaks" between political advisers.

In his second term, Blair gave priority to supporting antiterrorist actions of President George W. Bush. His argument for going to war in Afghanistan and Iraq invoked high moral principles; the methods that his spin doctors and political advisers used to make the case produced two public inquiries into the use and abuse of military intelligence. The second, chaired by a former head of the civil service, concluded of Blair's method of government: "We are concerned that the informality and circumscribed character of the government's procedures which we saw in the context of policy-making towards Iraq risks reducing the scope for informed collective political judgment."[22]

POLITICAL CULTURE AND LEGITIMACY

Politics is about the articulation of conflicting beliefs about who should govern and what government should do. There are three different political justifications of who should be involved when important political decisions are made.

The *trusteeship theory of government* assumes that leaders should take the initiative in deciding what is in the collective public interest. It is summed up in the epigram, "The government's job is to govern." Tony Blair can argue that as head of the majority party in parliament he has the legitimate right to decide what government does. The trusteeship doctrine is always popular with the party in office because it provides a justification for doing whatever the government wishes. The opposition party rejects this theory because it lacks the power of government.

The *interest group theory of government* sees government's role as balancing the demands of competing groups and classes in society. From this perspective, parties and pressure groups advocating group or class interests are more authoritative than individual voters.[23] Traditional Conservatives emphasized harmony between different classes in society, each with its own responsibilities and rewards. The socialist vision of group politics emphasized class divisions between trade unions and business, each seeking to use government to advance their interests, with the former having more votes and the latter more financial capital. With changes in British society, party leaders have distanced themselves from organized interests as they realize that votes are cast by individuals rather than business firms or trade unions.

The *individualist theory* of representation emphasizes that political parties should represent people rather than organized group interests. In the 1980s Margaret Thatcher was an outspoken advocate of economic individualism, regarding each person as responsible for his or her achievement of welfare through the marketplace. She even went so far as to declare, "There is no such thing as society." Liberal Democrats put more emphasis on individual freedom from collective constraints. Tony Blair has similarly accepted offering individuals more choice in public services. However, individuals are rarely offered a referendum allowing them to vote directly on what government does—and holding a referendum and determining the question put is in the hands of the government of the day. The powers of British government are limited by cultural norms concerning what government should and should

not do. In the words of one High Court judge: "In the constitution of this country, there are no guaranteed or absolute rights. The safeguard of British liberty is in the good sense of the people and in the system of representative and responsible government which has been evolved."[24]

However authority is justified, the great majority of English people find it inconceivable that there should be a fundamental change in the way the country is governed. Even Nationalist parties in Scotland and Wales do not reject parliamentary institutions; what they want is an independent Parliament for Scotland and for Wales.

The unresponsiveness of government to Parliament has encouraged popular protest—but the legitimacy of government means that protest is usually kept within lawful bounds. For example, the latest World Values Survey in Britain found that nearly everyone said they had or might sign a petition and half said they had or might participate in a lawful demonstration, but only one-sixth said they had or might consider an illegal occupation of a building or factor.

The legitimacy of government is evidenced by the readiness of the English people to comply with basic political laws. Law enforcement does not require large numbers of armed police. In proportion to its population, England's police force is smaller than that of America, Germany, or France. The crimes that occur in England are antisocial actions such as street violence, rather than political crimes against the state, such as assassinations. The one notable exception is Northern Ireland, where many major crimes, from murder to bank robbery, are carried out with the political objective of overturning an elected government.

The legitimacy accorded to the government is not the result of economic calculations about whether the British form of parliamentary democracy "pays" best, as rational choice theories propound. During the depression of the 1930s, British Communist and Fascist parties received only derisory votes, while their support was great in Germany and Italy. Likewise, inflation and unemployment in the 1970s and 1980s failed to stimulate extremist politics.

The symbols of a common past, such as the monarchy, are sometimes cited as major determinants of legitimacy. But surveys of public opinion show that the Queen has little political significance; her popularity derives from the fact that she is non-political. The popularity of a monarch is a consequence, not a cause, of political legitimacy. In Northern Ireland, where the minority denies the legitimacy of British government, the Queen is a symbol of divisions between British Unionists and Irish Republicans who reject the Crown.

Habit and tradition appear to be the chief explanations for the persisting legitimacy of authority. A survey asking people why they support the government found that the most popular reason was "It's the best form of government we know." Authority is not perfect or even trouble free: It is valued on the basis of experience. Winston Churchill delivered a very English justification of the country's democracy when he told the House of Commons: "No one pretends that democracy is perfect or all wise. Indeed, it has been said that democracy is the worst form of government, except all those other forms that have been tried from time to time."[25]

Abuses of Power

The government of the day can only claim its authority is legitimate if it acts within the rule of law. In constitutional theory, Parliament can hold ministers accountable for abuses of power by the government. In practice, Parliament is an ineffective check on executive power, because the executive consists of the leaders of the majority party in Parliament. When a member of the government is under attack, the tendency of MPs in the governing party is to close ranks in defense of a colleague. The power of the government to get away with mistakes is supported by official secrecy. The Whitehall view is that information is a scarce commodity that should not be given out freely; publicity about policymaking is not in the "public (sic)" interest, for it can make government appear uncertain or divided about what should be done. Politicians often hide their deliberations behind the veil of collective Cabinet responsibility. The Whitehall view is restrictive: "The need to know still dominates the right to know."[26] Secrecy remains strong because it serves the interests of the most important people in government, Cabinet ministers and civil servants. The Public Information Act of 2005 reduced the executive's power to keep secret the exchange of views within the Whitehall network, but whitehall remains far behind the open government practices of Washington.

Both ministers and senior civil servants are prepared to mislead parliament and the public. William Waldegrave, the Conservative minister nominally responsible for open government, told a Commons select committee in 1994 that "in exceptional cases it is necessary to say something that is untrue in the House of Commons."

When accused in court of telling a lie about the British government's efforts to suppress an embarrassing memoir by an ex-intelligence officer, the then head of the civil service and secretary to the Cabinet, Robert Armstrong, described the government's statements as "a misleading impression, not a lie. It was

---

Box 5.4   Conflicting Loyalties Among Civil Servants

The inability of Parliament to hold the government of the day accountable for palpable misdeeds disturbs senior civil servants who know what is going on and risk becoming accessories before the fact if they assist ministers in producing statements that mislead Parliament. Some even challenge the doctrine that a civil servant must support a minister, whatever the official's personal opinion. In one well-publicized case, a Ministry of Defence official, Clive Ponting, leaked to the House of Commons evidence that questioned the accuracy of government statements about the conduct of the Falklands War. He was indicted and tried for violating the Official Secrets Act. The judge asked the jury to think about the issue this way: "Can it then be in the interests of the state to go against the policy of the government of the day?" The jury concluded that it could be; Ponting was acquitted. However, most senior civil servants are unwilling to become whistle-blowers challenging actions of ministers, thereby jeopardizing their own careers.

*Graham Wilson and Anthony Barker, "Whitehall's Disobedient Servants? Senior Officials' Potential Resistance to Ministers in British Government Departments," *British Journal of Political Science* 27, No. 2 (1997): 223–46.

being economical with the truth." Abuses of executive power have created tensions for civil servants who believe that their job is not only to serve the popularly elected government of the day but also to prevent abuse of the powers of governance. This has led civil servants at times to leak official documents with the intention of preventing government from carrying out a policy that the leaker believes to be unethical or inadvisable (Box 5.4).

Citizens have reacted to changing standards of political behaviour by distrusting their elected representatives. Only a third of Britons report that they have a great deal or quite a lot of confidence in Parliament. The press and trade unions, institutions that theories of civil society describe as important in holding government accountable, are trusted by even fewer people. The most trusted public institutions today are those that maintain authority, led by the armed forces and the police (Figure 5.3).

The decline of ministerial accountability to parliament has encouraged the courts to become more active in making rulings against the elected government of the day. Judges today are ready to find grounds to nullify the way that ministers exercise their powers when they regard actions as going beyond what is authorized in an Act of Parliament. Britain's membership in the European Union and adherence to the European Convention of Human Rights offers additional grounds for nullifying actions by ministers. Such decisions are embarrassing for the government of the day while not involving a frontal challenge to the authority of an Act of Parliament.

Terrorist activities challenge conventional norms of the uses and abuses of power, and successive British governments have faced such challenges since the civil rights demonstrations of 1968–1969 were superseded by violent and murderous actions by illegal Protestant and Catholic groups, including the Irish Republican Army, which regards its use of violence as a legitimate means of liberating Northern Ireland from British rule. Their violence has

FIGURE 5.3 Trust in Political Institutions

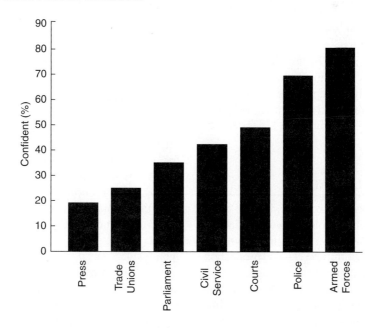

Source: Ronald Inglehart, et al., World Values Survey and European Values Survey, 1999–2001. Ann Arbor: Interuniversity Consortium for Political and Social Research. Interviews conducted in Great Britain, October–November 1999 (N = 1000).

been met by Crown forces "bending" the law. On Bloody Sunday, 1971, British soldiers shot and killed Irish protesters peacefully demonstrating in Londonderry. In England police have fabricated evidence or extracted confessions from some suspected of IRA terrorist violence, with the result that convictions have sometimes been voided subsequently by courts on appeal.

Culture as a Constraint on Policy

English people simultaneously value their form of government while making many specific criticisms about how it works. In the phrase of the English writer E. M. Forster, they give "two cheers for democracy." The values of the political culture impose limitations on the scope of public policy. Cultural norms about freedom of speech prevent political censorship. In the "swinging 1960s," laws against homosexual relations were repealed and abortion legalized, and AIDS has been treated as a disease rather than as a cause of shame or moralizing. Cultural expectations also influence what politicians must do. Regardless of party preference, the great majority of British people believe that government ought to provide education, health services, and social security. Today, the most significant limits on the scope of public policy are practical and political. Public expenditure on popular policies such as the health service is limited by the extent to which the economy grows and the reluctance of the Labour or Conservative governments to raise more money for health care by increasing taxes or by imposing limited charges of some sort for the use of health services.

POLITICAL SOCIALIZATION

Socialization influences the political division of labor. At an early age children learn about social differences relevant to politics; a small proportion become interested in politics, a larger proportion become apathetic, and the median person takes some but not that much interest in politics. The predispositions that a young person forms by the time she or he is old enough to vote are modified by adult experience. A middle-aged English person has voted in five or six general elections and is likely to

evaluate subsequent political events in the light of what has already been learned.

Family and Gender

The family's influence comes first chronologically; political attitudes learned within the family become intertwined with primary family loyalties. A child may not know what the Labour or Conservative party stands for, but if it is the party of Mom and Dad this can be enough to create identification with a party.

The influence of family on voting is limited; 36 percent do not know how one or both of their parents usually voted, or their parents voted for opposing parties. Among those who report knowing which party both parents supported, just over half vote as their parents have done. In the electorate as a whole, only 35 percent say that they know how both parents voted and that they voted for the same party.[27] Children also acquire a religious identification from their parents but except in Northern Ireland, religion no longer has a substantial influence on voting, and there are no groups comparable to the American religious right.

Children learn different social roles according to gender, yet as adult citizens men and women have the same legal right to vote and participate in politics. Bipartisan interest in appealing to women is illustrated by the 1976 Sex Discrimination Act, prohibiting discrimination in employment. It was enacted by a Labour government following a report by a Conservative government.

Today all political parties seek the votes of women, since women are a majority of the electorate. However, parties do not want to offend men, for even though they are a minority, they constitute 48 percent of the electorate. Whether politicians are talking about economic, social, or international issues, they usually stress common concerns of both men and women. At each general election, women divide between parties in much the same way as men (Table 5.3).

Men and women tend to have similar political attitudes. On most political issues women divide into two contrasting groups, and the same is true of men. For example, more than half of women and half of men favor capital punishment and a substantial minority in each group oppose it. Even on the is-

TABLE 5.3   Social Differences and Voting (percentage of voters in 2005)

	Labour	Conservative	Liberal/Democratic	Other
Gender				
Women	37	33	23	7
Men	36	33	23	9
Difference	1	0	0	2
Age				
18–34	37	28	27	8
35–54	41	29	22	8
55+	32	41	20	8
Difference, young/old	5	13	7	1
Class				
Middle	33	36	24	7
Working	41	29	20	9
Difference, top/bottom	8	7	4	2

Source: YouGov post-election online panel survey of 3,749 electors, weighted to represent the British population, and published in the *Daily Telegraph*, London, 9 May 2005.

sue of sex and nudity in the media, which registers a substantial difference of 20 percentage points, both women and men differ among themselves. Gender differences are less important than class, age, or education as an influence on party loyalties.

Gender differences do, however, lead to differences in political participation. Even though women constitute more than half the electorate, men are almost twice as likely as women to be local government councillors. Women constitute almost half the employees in the civil service, but they are heavily concentrated at lower-level clerical jobs; women hold about 10 percent of the top appointments in the civil service. A record number of women candidates stood for the Commons in 2001 but male candidates still outnumbered women by a margin of more than four to one. A total of 125 women were elected to the House of Commons, but it remains more than four-fifths male.[28]

Education

Even though individuals have different IQs, each vote counts equally in the ballot box. Yet education has traditionally assumed inequality. The majority of the population was once considered fit for only a minimum of education; in today's electorate the oldest voters left school at the age of 14 and the median voter by the age of 17. The highly educated are a small fraction of the population; they expect and are expected to play a leading role in politics.

Within the state system, the great majority of pupils attend comprehensive secondary schools, which recruit students of all levels of ability. Within the school, pupils are often divided into an academic stream being taught at a more advanced level than the average American high school education, and many who leave with only a basic education. Less than 6 percent of young persons attend "public" schools, that is, fee-paying schools which are private. Whereas half a century ago England had few universities, today almost one-half of young persons are in post-secondary institutions, many of which lack the facilities of established research universities.

The stratification of English education used to imply that the more education a person had, the more likely a person was to be Conservative. This is no longer the case. People with a university degree or its equivalent are currently less likely to vote Conservative than people with a minimum of education. The minority who are most educated now divide their vote between all three big parties, with the Liberal Democrats doing relatively well.

Education is strongly related to active participation in politics. The more education a person has, the greater the possibility of climbing the political ladder. People with a minimum of education constitute more than half the electorate but less than half of all local government councillors and less than 2 percent of all MPs. Whereas at one time graduates of Eton, Harrow, and other leading public schools predominated in Cabinet, today less than a third of all MPs have attended public schools.

The relatively small percentage of university graduates in the country constitutes 70 percent of all MPs. The expansion of universities has broken the dominance of Oxford and Cambridge; barely one-third of graduate MPs went to these two traditional institutions. The concentration of graduates from many different British universities in top jobs is a sign of a meritocracy, in which governors qualified by education replace an aristocracy based on birth and family. Yet leading posts can still go to those who have a common touch, as indicated by attendance at a state secondary school. John Major attended state secondary schools and did not go to university. Whereas the Labour prime minister Tony Blair went to Scotland's major fee-paying public school, the three Conservative leaders he defeated electorally all went to state schools.

Class

The concept of *class* can refer to occupational status or serve as a shorthand term for income, education, and prestige. Occupation is the most commonly used indicator of class in England. Manual workers are usually described as the working class and nonmanual workers as the middle class.

Historically, party competition has been interpreted in class terms; the Conservative Party has been described as a middle-class party, and Labour as a working-class party. One reason why class appears relatively important in England is the absence of big divisions on race, religion, or language, as in the United States, Canada, or Northern Ireland. Today, the upper class no longer commands deference and celebrities owing their prominence to television and achievements in sports, rock music, or making money are better known than Dukes or Earls. Tony Blair is comfortable mixing with rock musicians and with the new rich from the entertainment industry.

Most Britons have a mixture of middle-class and working-class attributes. The mixed class group has been increasing, as changes in the economy have led to a reduction in manual jobs and an increase in middle-class jobs. Many occupations such as computer technicians and office workers now have an indeterminate status and voting behavior. The relationship between class and party has become limited.

No party now wins as much as half the vote of middle-class electors, and Labour wins just two-fifths the vote of manual workers (Table 5.3). Due to the cross-class appeal of parties, only two-fifths of voters were middle-class Conservatives or working-class Labour voters. The Liberal Democrats and other smaller parties draw a fifth or more of the vote in every class. Less than one in seven voters conforms to the stereotype of a middle-class person (nonmanual occupation, above-average education, homeowner, no trade union membership, and subjective identification with the middle class), or its counterpart working-class stereotype.

Socioeconomic experiences other than occupation also influence voting. At each level of the class structure, people who belong to trade unions are more likely to vote Labour than Conservative. Housing creates neighborhoods with political relevance. About one-sixth of voters live in local government-owned houses clustered together on a housing estate specifically identified as such. Labour wins more than half of the vote of local council tenants, while, regardless of class, Conservatives do relatively well among homeowners.

Mass Media

The mass media tends to reenforce differences arising from class and education. The British press is sharply divided into a few quality papers, such as *The Times, The Guardian, Daily Telegraph, The Independent* and *The Financial Times,* that carry news and comment at an intellectual level higher than American newspapers, and mass circulation tabloids that concentrate on trivia and trash such as *The Sun*, Britain's biggest selling newspaper. Most papers tend to lean toward one party but not uncritically so. When the Conservatives became unpopular with the electorate in the 1990s, some newspapers that were previously pro-Conservative sought to follow their voters in admiring Tony Blair. He actively courted the support of right-wing newspapers but following his fall in popular approval during the Iraq War former press allies became vocal critics.

Historically, radio and television were a monopoly of the British Broadcasting Corporation (BBC). Seeking to educate and to elevate, the BBC was also very respectful of all forms of authority, including government. The introduction of commercial television in the 1950s and commercial radio in the following decade has made all broadcasting channels populist in competing for audiences. There are now five channels plus cable TV and a great variety of radio stations. The law forbids selling advertising to politicians, parties, or political causes.

Current affairs programs often seek audiences by exposing alleged failings of government, and TV personalities make their names by the tough cross-examination of politicians of all parties. However, the government of the day controls the renewal of broadcasting licenses and, in the case of the BBC, the annual fee of about $200 that every viewer must pay for noncommercial BBC programs. Broadcasters try to avoid favoring one party, recognizing that over a period of years control of government and decisions about licenses and fees are likely to change hands between parties. Public opinion polls show that television is the primary source of political news and it is much more trusted than the press. Since political socialization is a lifetime learning process, the loyalties of voters are shaped by an accumulation of influences. In the course of a lifetime, an individual develops values expressing what government ought to do. These political values are independent of family and socioeconomic interests. Economic values concerned with trade unions, the welfare state, business, and privatization influence choices between parties. "New" noneconomic values such as protecting the environment and moral-

ity account for little variation in the vote, because parties usually lack a distinctive and well-established position.

How the government handles current issues affects the economy and public expenditure, but the judgments that people make about government performance reflect their preexisting values, and this is particularly true of popular evaluations of party and leader images. The influence of such current issues and ephemeral personalities is often overrated, for those who focus on today's events forget that voters have had a lifetime to learn which party they prefer.

POLITICAL PARTICIPATION AND RECRUITMENT

Participation

If political participation is defined as paying taxes and drawing benefits from public programs, then everyone is involved, for public policies provide benefits at every stage of life, from maternity allowance to mothers through education, employment and unemployment benefits, health care, and pensions in old age.

An election is the one opportunity people have to influence government directly. Every citizen aged 18 or over is eligible to vote. Local government officials register voters, and the list is revised annually, ensuring that nearly everyone eligible to vote is actually registered. Turnout at general elections has averaged 77 percent since 1950. However, in the 2001 election it fell to 59.4 percent. The Labour government responded by experimenting with voting by post, sending ballots to all persons whose names are on the electoral register. When this was tried in the 2004 European Parliament election, three-fifths of those sent a postal ballot did not send it back and there were well publicized cases of fraud. In 2005 turnout was 61.3 percent.

The wider the definition of political participation, the greater the number who can be said to be at least indirectly or intermittently involved in politics (Figure 5.4). Two-fifths have signed a petition on a public issue; a third say that they feel close to a political party. Political values can also be reflected in refusing to buy a product: one-quarter say that

FIGURE 5.4   Participation in Politics

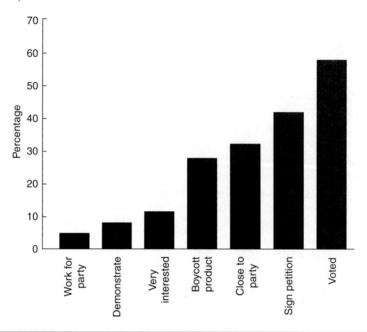

Source: Roger Jowell and the Central Coordinating Team, European Social Survey 2002/03. London: Centre for Comparative Social Surveys, City University. Interviews conducted in the United Kingdom, September 24, 2002 to February 4, 2003 (N = 1908).

politics has affected their shopping by leading them to boycott a product. The most politically involved are a tenth or less of the electorate, those who say they are very interested in politics, took part in a demonstration, or are active in a party or pressure group. If holding or contesting public office is the measure of political participation, the proportion is less than 1 percent of the electorate.

Although political activists are a minority of the electorate, their actions are the focus of much political news. Because of the concentration of the media and politics, a London-based protest with a few thousand people can get press coverage, even though those participating are only one–one-hundredth of 1 percent of the electorate.

Political Recruitment

The most important political roles in Britain are those of Cabinet minister, higher civil servant, and intermittent public person, analogous to informal advisers to an American president. Each group has its own recruitment pattern. To become a Cabinet minister, an individual must first be elected to Parliament and spend years attracting positive attention there. Individuals enter the civil service shortly after leaving university by passing a highly competitive entrance examination; promotion is based on achievement and approval by seniors. Intermittent public persons gain access to ministers and civil servants because of their expertise or position in organizations outside politics, or because they are personally trusted by leading politicians.

In all political roles, starting early on a political career is usually a precondition of success, because experience is positively valued. But aspiring Cabinet ministers are not expected to begin in local politics and work their way gradually to the top at Westminster. Instead, at an early age an individual becomes a "cadet" recruit to a junior position such as a parliamentary assistant to an MP or a "gofer" for a Cabinet minister. This can lead to a central political role after gaining skill and seniority.

Geography is a second major influence on recruitment. Ministers, higher civil servants, and other public persons spend their working lives in London. A change at Downing Street does not bring in policymakers from a different part of the country, as can happen in the White House when a president from Texas succeeds a president from Arkansas. Since London is atypical of the cities and towns in which most British people live, there is a gap between the everyday lives of policymakers and the majority on whose behalf they act.

Cabinet Ministers

For a person ambitious to be a Cabinet minister, becoming an MP is the necessary first step. Nomination for a winnable or safe seat in the House of Commons is in the hands of local party selection committees. A candidate does not have to be resident in the constituency in which he or she is nominated. Hence, it is possible for a young person to go straight from university to a job in the House of Commons or party headquarters, and then look around the country for a nomination for a winnable seat, a process that takes years. Once selected for a constituency in which his or her party has a big majority, the MP can then expect to be reelected routinely for a decade or more.

After entering the House of Commons, an MP seeks to be noticed. Some ways of doing so—for example, grabbing headlines by questioning the wisdom of the party leadership—make it difficult to gain promotion to ministerial rank. Other approaches assist promotion, such as successfully attacking opposition leaders in debate or being well informed about a politically important topic. So too does showing loyalty to the party leader.

Only Members of Parliament can become Cabinet ministers. Yet experience in the Commons does not prepare an individual for the work of a minister. An MP's chief concerns are dealing with people and talking about what government ought to do. A minister must also be able to handle paperwork, relate political generalities to specific technical problems facing a ministry, and make hard decisions when no alternative is popular.

The restriction of ministerial appointments to experienced MPs prevents a nationwide canvass for appointees. A prime minister must distribute about 100 jobs among approximately 200 MPs in the governing party who have had experience in Parliament and not ruled themselves out of consideration for office on grounds of parliamentary inexperience, old age, political extremism, personal unreliability, or lack of interest in office. An MP has a better than even chance of a junior ministerial appointment if he or she serves three terms in Parliament. Exceptionally, Tony Blair has given peerages and ministerial posts to personal supporters who thus depend on loyalty to him rather than to their standing with their constituency electorate and Labour Party.

A minister learns on the job. Usually, an MP is first given a junior post as an Under Secretary and then promoted to Minister of State before becoming a full member of the Cabinet. In the process, an individual is usually shuffled from one department to another, having to learn new subject matter with each shift of departments. The average minister can expect to stay in a particular job for about two years, and never knows when the accidents of politics—a death or an unexpected resignation—will lead to a transfer to another department. The rate of ministerial turnover in Britain is one of the highest in Europe. The minister who gets a new job as the result of a reshuffle usually arrives at a department with no previous experience of its problems. It takes time to learn how to deal with the particular problems of a department. Anthony Crosland, an able Labour minister, reckoned: "It takes you six months to get your head properly above water, a year to get the general drift of most of the field, and two years really to master the whole of a department."[29] A minister's lack of substantial expertise in his or her department has produced criticism of the recruitment system.

Higher Civil Servants

Whereas MPs come and go from ministerial office with great frequency, civil servants have a job in Whitehall for the whole of their working lives. Higher civil servants are recruited without specific professional qualifications or training. They are meant to be the "best and the brightest"—a requirement that has traditionally meant getting a prestigious degree in history, literature, or languages. The Fulton Committee on the Civil Service recommended that recruits should have "relevant" specialist knowledge, but members could not decide what kind of knowledge was relevant to the work of government.[30] The Civil Service Commission tests candidates for ability to summarize lengthy prose papers, to resolve a problem by fitting specific facts to general regulations, to draw inferences from a simple table of social statistics, and to perform well in group discussions of problems of government.

Because bright civil service entrants lack specialized skills and need decades to reach the highest posts, role socialization into Whitehall by senior civil servants is especially important. The process makes for continuity, since the head of the civil service usually starts there as a young official under a head who had himself entered the civil service many decades before.

In the course of a career, civil servants become specialists in the difficult task of managing political ministers and government business. As the television series, *Yes, Minister* shows, they are adept at saying "yes" to a Cabinet minister when they mean "perhaps" and saying "up to a point" when they really mean "no." Increasingly, ministers have tended to discourage civil service advisers from pointing out obstacles to what the government wants to do; they are looking for "can do" advisers from outside the civil service as well as inside. The Blair government has greatly expanded the appointment of two types of political advisers. The largest number are aptly called political advisers, for their job is to mobilize political support for the government and for the Cabinet minister to whom they are assigned. Because their background is in party politics and the media, they bring skills that civil servants often lack. But because they have no prior experience of the civil service, they are often unaware of its conventions and legal obligations. The methods used by political appointees to put a desirable spin on what the government is doing can backfire and cause public controversy.

Another category of political advisers are experts with specialist knowledge about such problems as environmental pollution or experimental medical procedures such as cloning. While they may be inexperienced in the ways of Whitehall, they can contribute expertise that is often lacking in government departments, and they are often long-time supporters of the governing party too.

Most leaders of institutions such as the universities, banks, churches, and trade unions do not think of themselves as politicians and have not stood for public office. They are principally concerned with their own organization. But when government actions impinge on their work, they become involved in politics, offering ministers advice and sometimes criticism. They are thus intermittent public persons.

Selective Recruitment

Nothing could be more selective than a parliamentary election that results in one person becoming prime minister of a country. Yet nothing is more representative, because an election is the one occasion when every adult can participate in politics with equal effect. Traditionally, leaders in English society had high social status and wealth before gaining political office. Today, England has experienced the rise of the full-time professional politician. Aristocrats, business people, or trade union leaders can no longer expect to translate their high standing in other fields into an important political position. As careers become more specialized, a professional politician gains increased expertise in his or her own sphere but becomes increasingly remote from other spheres.

The greater the scope of activities defined as political, the greater the number of people actively involved in government. Government influence has forced company directors, television executives, and university heads to become involved in politics and public policy. Leadership in organizations outside Whitehall gives such individuals freedom to act independently of government, but the interdependence of public and private institutions, whether profitmaking or nonprofit, is now so great that sooner or later they meet in discussions about what constitutes the public interest.

ORGANIZING GROUP INTERESTS

Civil society—that is, institutions independent of government—has flourished in Britain for centuries. So confident are leaders of civil society of their position that they readily discuss public affairs with government officials in expectation that they can exert pressure on behalf of interests they represent.

The Confederation of British Industries is the chief representative organization of British business. As its name implies, its membership is large and varied. The biggest firms or industries usually make direct representations to ministries for trade and industry. The Institute of Directors represents the highest-paid individuals at the top of large and small businesses. Banks and financial institutions in the City of London have their own channels of representation through the Bank of England, the central Bank, and directly to the Treasury. The comparable organization of labour is the Trades Union Congress (TUC); its members are trade unions that sometimes represent workers with conflicting interests, such as between those in low paid jobs and highly paid workers. Most member unions of the TUC are affiliated with the Labour Party, and some leading trade unionists have been Communists or Maoists. None has ever been a supporter of the Conservative Party. The membership of trade unions has shifted from industrial workers in coal and railways to white-collar workers in the public sector, such as teachers and health service employees. Changes in employment patterns have eroded union membership; less than one-third of the British labour force now belongs to unions.

Unlike political parties, interest groups do not seek influence by contesting elections; they want to influence policies regardless of which party wins. Nonetheless, there do remain ties between interest groups and political parties. Trade unions have been institutionally part of the Labour Party since its foundation in 1900. The connection between business associations and the Conservatives is not formal, but its private enterprise philosophy is congenial to business. Notwithstanding common interests, both trade unions and business groups demonstrate their autonomy by criticizing partisan allies acting against the group's interest.

Party politicians seek to distance themselves from pressure groups. Conservatives appreciate that they can only win an election by winning the votes of ordinary citizens, including some trade union members. Tony Blair's success in distancing himself from unions by attracting big donations from multi-millionaires to finance his campaigning activities has led union leaders to attack his government as unsympathetic and threaten to withdraw cash contributions that are vital to meet the costs of the party's organizations. A few small unions have left the Labour Party.

To lobby successfully, interest groups must be able to identify those officials most important in making public policy. They concentrate attention on Whitehall. When pressure groups were asked to rank the most influential offices and institutions, they named the prime minister first by a long distance, Cabinet ministers second, the media third, and senior civil servants fourth (Figure 5.5). Less than 1 percent thought MPs outside the ministerial ranks were of primary importance. However, pressure groups do not expect to spend a lot of time in Downing Street. Most pressure group contacts are with divisions of government departments concerned with issues of little public concern but of immediate interest to the group. Groups that stir up confrontational media publicity make it difficult to gain a sympathetic private hearing from government departments.[31]

What Interest Groups Want

The scope of group demands varies enormously from the narrow concerns of an association for single parents to the encompassing economic policies of organizations such as the Confederation of British Industries and the Trades Union Congress. Groups also differ in the nature of their interests; some are concerned with material objectives, whereas others deal with single causes such as

FIGURE 5.5   Pressure Group View of Who Holds Most Power

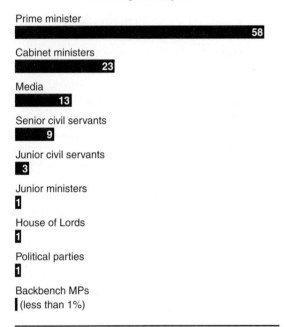

Percentage naming first

Prime minister
58

Cabinet ministers
23

Media
13

Senior civil servants
9

Junior civil servants
3

Junior ministers
1

House of Lords
1

Political parties
1

Backbench MPs
(less than 1%)

Source: Survey of officials of business, labor, and campaign groups, as reported in Rob Baggott. "The Measurement of Change in Pressure Group Politics." *Talking Politics* 5, No. 1 (1992): 19.

violence in the media or race relations. Most interest groups pursue four goals:

1. Information about government policies and changes in policies
2. Sympathetic administration of established policies
3. Influence on policymaking
4. Symbolic status, such as being given the prefix "Royal" in their title

Whitehall departments are happy to consult with interest groups insofar as they can provide government officials with reciprocal benefits:

1. Cooperation in the administration of existing policies
2. Information about what is happening in their field

3. Evaluation of the consequences of policies under consideration
4. Assistance in implementing new policies

As long as the needs of Whitehall and interest groups are complementary, they can bargain as professionals sharing common concerns. Both sides seek a negotiated agreement. This avoids contested decisions being made by politicians who know less and care less about details than interest groups and civil servants involved in departmental administration.

Organizing for Political Action in Civil Society

The more committed members are to a pressure group's goals, the more confidently leaders can speak for a united membership. Consumers are more difficult to organize because they are interested only in goods and services, not in their relations with other customers; they are a category rather than a social group. Changes in the economy, in class structure, and in the life styles of generations have resulted in a decline in the "dense" social capital networks of villages. Individuals are now free to choose among a variety of networks. As a trade union leader has explained, "Our members are consumers too."[32]

Whitehall civil servants find it administratively convenient to deal with united interest groups that can implement agreements. But decades of attempts to plan the British economy demonstrate that business and union leaders cannot guarantee that their nominal followers will carry out bargains that leaders make. Group members who care about an issue may also disagree about what their leaders ought to do. Individuals usually have a multiplicity of identities that are often in conflict—for example, as workers desiring higher wages and as consumers wanting lower prices. The spread of mass consumption and decline in trade union membership has altered the balance between these priorities.

Even if a pressure group is internally united, its demands may be counteracted by opposing demands from other groups. This is normally the case in economic policy, where interests are well defined, well organized, and competing. Ministers can play off producers against consumers or business against unions to increase their own scope for choice and present their policies as "something for everybody" compromises.

The more a group's values are consistent with the cultural norms of society as a whole, the easier it is to equate its interest with the public interest. But in an open society such as England the claims of one group to speak for the public interest can easily be challenged by competing groups.

The centralization of authority in British government means that interest groups must accept as given the political values and priorities of the governing party. Trade unions expect to see their influence increase when a Labour government is in office and business groups have similar expectations when the Conservatives are in power. However, a prime minister seeking to broaden the government's base of support can try to build bridges with nominal opponents too. Tony Blair's Labour government has conspicuously solicited support from business leaders.

Insider pressure groups usually have values in harmony with every party. These groups are often noncontroversial, such as the Royal National Institute for the Blind. The primary concern of permanent insiders is to negotiate on details of administration and finance, and to press for the expansion of programs benefiting the group. They advance their case in quiet negotiations with Whitehall departments. Demands tend to be restricted to what is politically possible in the short term, given the values and commitments of the government of the day.[33]

Outsider pressure groups are unable to negotiate because their demands are inconsistent with the party in power. If they are inconsistent with the views of the opposition as well, then outsider groups are completely marginalized. Excluded from influence in Whitehall, outsider groups often campaign through the media. To television viewers and readers of serious newspapers, their demonstrations appear as evidence of their importance; in fact, they are often signs of a lack of political influence.

Complete outsiders are excluded from Whitehall, whatever the government of the day, because their demands go against prevailing cultural norms. For example, the Ministry of Defence does not consult pacifist groups, for there is nothing to negotiate when principles are mutually exclusive. Green pressure groups face the dilemma of campaigning for fundamental change in hopes that eventually Whitehall departments will turn their way, or working within the system in order to improve the environment to some extent but not as much as ecologists would like.

Keeping Pressure Groups at a Distance

For a generation after World War II ministers endorsed the corporatist philosophy of bringing together business, trade union, and political representatives in tripartite institutions to discuss such controversial issues as dealing with inflation and unemployment, and the restructuring of declining industries. Corporatist bargaining assumed a consensus on political priorities and goals and that each group's leaders could deliver the cooperation of those they claimed to represent. In practice, neither Labour nor Conservative governments were able to maintain a consensus. Nor were interest group leaders able to deliver their nominal followers. By 1979, unemployment and inflation were both out of control.

The Thatcher administration demonstrated that a government firmly committed to distinctive values can ignore group demands and lay down its own pattern of policy. It did so by dealing at arm's length with both trade unions and business groups. Instead of consulting and negotiating with interest groups, it practised state-distancing, keeping the government out of everyday marketplace activities such as wage bargaining and deciding prices and investment.

A state-distancing strategy concentrates on policies that government can carry out without the agreement of interest groups. It emphasizes the use of legislation to achieve goals, since no interest group can defy an act of Parliament. Laws have reduced the capacity of trade unions to frustrate government policies through industrial action. The sale of state-owned industries has removed government from immediate responsibility for the operation of major industries. The Labour government transferred to the Bank of England responsibility for monetary policy. At the same time it kept in the

Treasury's hands the right to set policy goals for which the Bank is responsible.

State-distancing places less reliance on negotiations with interest groups and more on the independent authority of the Crown. Business and labor are free to carry on as they like—but only within the pattern imposed by the government's policy and legislation. Most unions and some business leaders do not like being "outside the loop" when government makes decisions. Education and health service pressure groups like it even less, because they depend upon government appropriations to fund their activities and cannot effectively turn to the market as an alternative source of revenue.

While in opposition, Tony Blair often spoke about the need to achieve "the reinvention of community,"[34] implying endorsement of corporatist institutions of cooperation between representatives of different groups in society. However, since becoming prime minister, Blair has made sure that meetings with groups are on terms laid down by Downing Street. When conflicts are apparent between groups, he avoids taking sides or getting involved in brokering agreements. He prefers to remain on the sidelines, lecturing conflicting groups to cooperate in a vaguely defined public interest.

PARTY SYSTEM AND ELECTORAL CHOICE

British government is party government, for parties nominate parliamentary candidates and elect a leader who is prime minister or in charge of the Opposition. An election gives voters the choice of deciding between parties competing for the right to govern.

A Multiplicity of Choices

A general election must occur at least once every five years; within that period, the prime minister is free to call an election at any time. Although every prime minister tries to pick a date when victory is likely, this desire is often denied. An election offers a voter a very simple choice between several candidates wanting to represent one of the 646 constituencies of the House of Commons. The party leader's name is not on the ballot. Within each con-

stituency, the winner is the candidate who is first past the post—that is, the candidate with the largest number of votes even though his or her plurality falls short of half the vote.

If only two parties contest a constituency, the candidate with the most votes will have an absolute majority. But since three or more candidates now contest each constituency a candidate with the most votes may still have less than half the total vote thanks to multiple competitors dividing the majority of the vote. In a hard-fought contest between four parties in Inverness in 1992, the Liberal Democrats won the seat with only 26 percent of the vote. In hundreds of seats, no candidate gets as much as half the vote and there is no provision for a runoff election, as in France, to produce a winner with majority support.

The winner nationally is the party that gains the most constituency seats. In 1951 and in February 1974, the party winning the most votes did not win the most seats and thus did not form the government. Today, the Labour Party can win an absolute majority in the House of Commons with a smaller share of the vote than the Conservative Party, because its electoral strength is concentrated rather than spread evenly through the country. Between 1945 and 1970 Britain had a two-party system, because the Conservative and Labour parties together took an average of 91 percent of the popular vote and in 1951 as much as 97 percent (Figure 5.6). The Liberals had difficulty fielding candidates to contest most seats and even more difficulty in winning votes. Support for the two largest parties was evenly balanced; Labour won four elections and the Conservatives won four.

In a two-party system the failure of one party tends to benefit its opponent. However, when both the largest parties are discredited, this gives other parties an opportunity to gain support. A *multiparty system* emerged in the elections of 1974. The Liberals won nearly one-fifth of the vote, and the Nationalists did well in Scotland, Wales, and Northern Ireland. Together, the Conservative and Labour parties took only 75 percent of the vote. The 1980s saw the Labour Party vote plummet as the Alliance of Liberals and Social Democrats won almost a quarter of the popular vote. Although the Alliance broke up af-

FIGURE 5.6   Votes Cast in General Elections Since 1945

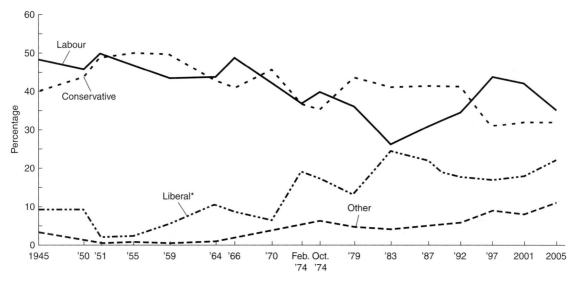

*1945–1979 Liberal Party; 1983–1987 Alliance of Liberals and Social Democratic Party;
since then known as Liberal Democrats.

ter the 1987 election, the fragmentation of voters and parties has continued since.

1. In England, three parties—Labour, Conservatives, and Liberal Democrats—compete for votes and an anti-European Union United Kingdom Independence Party also fights a majority of seats. In Scotland and Wales there are normally four parties, for the Scottish National and Plaid Cymru (Welsh Nationalist) parties win seats too. In Northern Ireland, at least five parties normally contest seats.
2. The two largest parties do not monopolize the vote. Since 1974, the Conservative and Labour parties together have won an average of three-quarters of the vote and in the 2005 election gained just 67 percent of the vote.
3. The two largest parties nationally are often not the two front-running parties at the constituency level. In the 2005 election, the first and second parties in England were Labour and the Conservatives; in Scotland, Labour and the Liberal Democrats; in Wales, Labour and the Conservatives. The Conservatives won only one seat in Scotland and three in Wales. In Northern Ireland the Democratic Unionists and Sinn Fein, which is linked with the IRA, were the largest parties and all 18 seats were won by parties that did not contest seats in Great Britain.
4. More than half a dozen parties consistently win seats in the House of Commons. In 2005 "third" parties won 94 seats in the Commons.
5. Significant shifts in voting usually do not involve individuals moving between the Labour and Conservative parties but in and out of the ranks of abstainers or between the Liberal Democrats and the two largest parties.

To win a substantial number of seats in the House of Commons, a party must either gain at least one-third of the popular vote nationally or concentrate its votes in a limited number of constituencies. Nationalist parties in Scotland, Wales, and Northern Ireland win seats because they concentrate their candidates in one part of the United Kingdom. Although the Liberal Democrats win more than a fifth of the popular vote, because their support is spread relatively evenly across the country, their candidates are far more likely to finish second or third rather than first.

Britain has a system of disproportional representation that manufactures a House of Commons majority for one party with barely two-fifths of the popular vote. The Liberal Democrats are specially disadvantaged by the electoral system. In a totally proportional system of representation, the party's vote share in 2005 would have given it 142 seats; it gained less than half this number. Even more important, in a proportional representation system Labour's vote would have given it 227 seats, far short of a parliamentary majority. In a PR system, forming a government would require a coalition between at least two parties, since none would have a majority of parliamentary seats. In the Scottish Parliament, which is elected with proportional representation, coalition government is the norm.

Defenders of the British electoral system argue that proportionality is not a goal in itself. The *first-past-the-post system* is justified because it places responsibility for government in the hands of a single party. This justification is used in the United States, where the president can be described as representing all the people, even if he has won less than half the vote. By contrast, in countries such as Italy and Belgium proportional representation makes the choice of the parties forming a coalition government the outcome of intensive bargaining between parties that have received anything from one-third to 5 percent of the popular vote.

The strongest advocates of proportional representation are the Liberal Democrats, the party that would benefit most from a change in the electoral system. A change is also supported by those who believe that a coalition government is a better government because it encourages broader interparty consensus.

Successive British governments have altered the electoral system for contests that do not affect the composition of the Westminster Parliament. North-

ern Ireland elections have used proportional representation for more than three decades. The Scottish Parliament and Welsh Assembly are elected by systems involving proportional representation and so are British Members of the European Parliament. The Mayor of Greater London is elected by the alternative vote, ensuring that the winner is the first or second choice of more than half the voters.

Before winning a majority in 1997, Tony Blair encouraged talk about introducing proportional representation and proposals have been put forward by a government-appointed Commission. But this produced a countermobilization in defence of the current system from many MPs elected by first past the post and by trade unions who fear that a coalition government would be less sympathetic to its interests than a government consisting solely of Labour MPs. In Britain the decision about what kind of voting system to have is not determined by reasoning from abstract principles but by the interests of the party in power.

Control of Party Organization

Political parties are often referred to as machines, but this description is very misleading, for parties cannot manufacture votes. Nor can a political party be commanded as an army can be commanded. Parties are like universities; they are inherently decentralized, and people belong to them for a variety of motives.

Much of the work of party organizations is devoted to keeping together three disparate parts of the party: those who vote for it; the small minority who are active in its constituency associations; and the party in Parliament. If the party has a majority in Parliament, the prime minister must make sure that the other parts of the party support his or her actions even if many party activists and MPs do not like what their leader is doing. The London headquarters of each party provides more or less routine organizational and publicity services to constituency parties and to the party in Parliament. Each party has an annual conference to debate policy and to vote on some policy resolutions. Constituency parties are nationally significant because each selects its parliamentary candidate. The *decentralization* of the selection process has allowed the choice of parliamentary candidates with a wide variety of political outlooks and abilities. The Thatcher era encouraged an ideological litmus test on both the right and the left. Under Tony Blair the Labour Party has introduced more central direction in choosing candidates. Left-wing Labour activists argued that central direction has been used to purge socialists and put in Blair loyalists. Blairites justified centralization on the grounds it would promote the adoption of more women candidates in winnable seats; the number of Labour women MPs rose from 37 in 1992 to 98 by 2005.

The Labour Party leader is elected by an electoral college composed of Labour MPs, constituency party members, and trade unions. As part of a drive to prevent criticism of the leadership and public disunity, Tony Blair has created a new party organization that increases his control of the party and reduces the influence of party activists and trade unions.

The Conservative Party in Parliament has been separate from the campaigning arm of the party, Conservative Central Office, and local constituency associations. Until 1965, the party leader was not elected but "emerged" as the result of consultation among senior MPs and peers (members of the House of Lords). Since then, the Conservatives have elected their leader, initially by a ballot of Members of Parliament and today by this ballot identifying two candidates who are then voted on by the party membership at large. The failure of Ian Duncan Smith, chosen as leader by the party membership even though he did not have the support of a majority of Conservative MPs, led to his replacement in 2003 by Michael Howard without a vote, because both MPs and constituency activists saw him as a credible leader in the House of Commons, and in campaigning. He resigned after losing the 2005 election.

The Liberal Democrats have a small central organization, in keeping with their relatively few MPs. Liberal Democrats have sought to build up the party's strength by winning council seats at local government elections. At parliamentary elections, it targets seats where the party is strong locally. This strategy has paid off; it has almost trebled its MPs from 22 in 1987 to 62 in 2005 while its share of the vote fell by 0.6 percent.

The party leader is strongest when he or she is also prime minister. Constitutional principles and Cabinet patronage strengthen a prime minister's hand. Moreover, an open attack on a prime minister threatens electoral defeat as a result of conflict within the party. At the 1998 Labour Party conference Tony Blair told his Labour critics that their choice was not between a Socialist or a Labour government, but between the Labour government or a Conservative government.

Party Images and Appeals

Differences of ideology are often simplified in terms of a left-right scale, with the left representing socialist values and the right the values of Conservatives. While the terminology of left and right is part of the language of elite politicians, it is rejected by the great majority of British voters. When asked to place themselves on a left-right scale, the median voter chooses the central position, and only a tenth place themselves on the far left or far right. Consequently, parties that veer to one or another extreme risk losing votes.

When public opinion is examined across a variety of issues, such as inflation, protecting the environment, spending money on the health service, and trade union legislation, a majority of Conservative, Labour, and Liberal Democratic voters tend to agree for the most part. Tony Blair has proclaimed the goal of making Labour a party that is "the political arm of none other than the British people as a whole." In articulating this view, Blair is denying the existence of politics—that is, debate about what the government of the day ought to do.

Big divisions in contemporary British politics often cut across party lines, for example, attitudes toward the European Union divide both Labour and Conservative MPs and so has the Iraq War. Any attempt to impute a coherent ideology to a political party is doomed to failure, for institutions cannot think, and parties are not organized to debate philosophy but to fight elections. Instead of campaigning in ideological terms or by appealing to collectivist economic interests, increasingly parties stress consensual goals, such as promoting peace and

TABLE 5.4 Consensual Title of Party Election Manifestos

Year	Conservatives	Labour
1964	Prosperity with a Purpose	Let's Go with Labour
1966	Action, Not Words	Time for Decision
1970	A Better Tomorrow	Now Britain's Strong–Let's Make It Great to Live In
1974	Firm Action for a Fair Britain	Let Us Work Together
1974	Putting Britain First	Britain Will Win with Labour
1979	The Conservative Manifesto	The Labour Way Is the Better Way
1983	The Challenge of Our Times	The New Hope for Britain
1987	The Next Moves Forward	Britain Will Win
1992	The Best Future for Britain	Time to Get Britain Working Again
1997	You Can Only Be Sure with the Conservatives	Because Britain Deserves Better
2001	Time for Common Sense	Ambition for Britain
2005	It's Time for Action	Britain Forward not Back

prosperity. They compete in terms of which party or party leader can best be trusted to do what people want. The titles of election manifestos are virtually interchangeable between the Conservative and Labour parties—and so too is much of their content (Table 5.4).

In office, the governing party has the votes to enact any parliamentary legislation it wishes, regardless of protests by the opposition. However, most of the legislation introduced by the government is noncontroversial or so popular that the opposition does not dare vote against the bill's principle. For every government bill that the opposition votes against on principle in the House of Commons, three are adopted with interparty agreement.[35] Prior to the 1997 general election, the Labour Party even pledged that it would not immediately alter the spending limits in the budget of the Conservative government.

Most policies of the government are not set out in its party manifesto; they are inherited from predecessors of the same or a different party. When the Thatcher administration entered office in 1979, it inherited hundreds of programs enacted by preceding governments, including some on the statute books since 1760. The median law was more than half a century old.[36] In more than a decade, the Thatcher administration introduced dozens of new programs. It also repealed programs inherited from its predecessors, and some of its own programs that were

quickly recognized as mistakes. When Margaret Thatcher left office, two-thirds of the programs for which the government was responsible, such as the national health service, were those inherited from previous administrations. When expenditure is analyzed, the influence of the "dead hand" of the past is greater still. Only 11 percent of public expenditure was devoted to programs that Thatcher started and almost three-quarters went to programs based on laws enacted before the end of World War II.

The freedom of action of the governing party is limited by constraints embedded in the obligations of office. Once in office, ministers find that all the laws enacted by their predecessors must be enforced, even if the government of the day would not have enacted them. A newly elected government also inherits many commitments to foreign countries and to the European Union. As a former Conservative minister said of his Labour successors, "They inherited our problems and our remedies."[37]

CENTRAL AUTHORITY AND DECENTRALIZED DELIVERY OF GOVERNMENT POLICIES

In a unitary state, political authority is centralized. Decisions made by central government are of fundamental importance, for they are binding on all public agencies through the Acts of Parliament and regulations prepared in Whitehall. In addition, Whitehall controls taxation and public expenditure to a degree unusual among other member states of the European Union, where coalition government and federalism encourage territorial and functional decentralization.

For ordinary individuals the actions of government are tangible only when services are delivered to them in local schools, a doctor's office, or to their home. However, Whitehall departments usually do not deliver policies themselves. Most public goods and services are delivered by public agencies outside the framework of Whitehall ministries and five-sixths of public employees work for non-Whitehall agencies.[38] Thus, making and delivering public policies involves intragovernmental politics.

There are many reasons why ministers do not want to be in charge of delivering services. Ministers may wish to avoid charges of political interference (for example, tax collection by the Board of Inland Revenue). They may want to allow flexibility in the market (the Bank of England), lend an aura of impartiality to quasi-judicial activities (the Monopolies Commission), show respect for the extragovernmental origins of an institution (Oxford and Cambridge universities), allow qualified professionals to regulate technical matters (the Royal College of Physicians and Surgeons), or remove controversial matters from Whitehall (the Family Planning Association). Leading ministers, and above all the prime minister, prefer to focus upon the glamorous "high" politics of European and foreign affairs and economic management. However, since "low level" services remain important to most voters' lives, ministers are under pressure to do something when there is evidence of declining standards in schools, lengthening queues for hospital admission, and an increase of crime on the streets.

While politicians can make headlines by announcing a good intention, turning popular intentions into a programme that delivers services to citizens requires scarce resources of time and money. Running the Whitehall obstacle race is the first step in intragovernmental politics. Interdepartmental negotiations are required to get ministers to agree how credit and responsibility is to be divided up; how a new programme relates to existing commit-

ments; what agency should administer the programme; and how much money is needed. Since most new policies must take into account the effects of existing policies in a crowded policy "space," negotiations are often time consuming. From the point of view of a prime minister who believes that popular election makes it desirable to do many things, the process of turning desires into practical programmes is often frustrating.

Because of Treasury control of public expenditure, before a bill can be put to Parliament the Treasury must authorize the additional expenditure required. Ministers in charge of spending departments dislike constant Treasury reminders that there are strict cash limits on what they can spend. The limits exist because increased spending implies increased taxation. Gordon Brown has used his position as Chancellor of the Exchequer, the minister in charge of the Treasury, to enforce his priorities on other ministers. Because Brown has a power base in the governing party, he can even enforce Treasury policies against the prime minister. Every Chancellor gains power because limits on public revenue mean that, in the words of a veteran Treasury official, "the Treasury stands for reality."[39]

A departmental minister must pilot a bill through Parliament. While the votes needed to secure passage are assured, if a matter is controversial a minister will face attacks from the Opposition and a host of amendments designed to test the minister's understanding of a policy. In addition to running the Whitehall obstacle race, a minister often must negotiate agreement with public agencies outside Whitehall, and with affected interest groups. The formally centralized authority of the Crown co-exists with a maze of institutions with varying and overlapping territorial and functional responsibilities.

Local government is subordinate to central government, for the latter has the power to write or rewrite the laws that determine what locally elected governments do and spend, or even abolish local authorities and create new units of government with different boundaries. Changes in boundaries have reflected a vain search to find a balance between efficiency (assumed to correlate with fewer councils delivering services to more people spread over a wider geographical area) and

Box 5.5 Delivering Public Services on the Doorstep

The growth of government has caused the primary activities of government to shift from debates in Westminster to the delivery locally of everyday public services such as health care, education, and environmental protection and rubbish collection. Government on the scale that we know it today could not exist if all its activities were concentrated in London, for five-sixths of the country's population lives elsewhere. As the demand for public services has increased, government has grown chiefly through pluralization—that is, the multiplication of familiar institutions delivering such as schools and hospitals. Devolution to Scotland and Wales has added to decentralization, for Westminster gives institutions in Edinburgh and Cardiff the responsibility for delivering many everyday services, while keeping overall financial control in London.

Education is an example of the combination of central authority and localized service delivery. It is authorized by an act of Parliament, financed principally by central government, and the minister in charge of education is a Member of Parliament and Cabinet.

However, the delivery of primary and secondary education has been the responsibility of local government and of the school head and its board of governors. Dissatisfaction with local government has led Whitehall to establish secondary schools independent of local government but dependent on Whitehall.

Control of day-to-day activities within the school is in the hands of the teaching profession. Increasingly, central government seeks to monitor the performance of schools in nationwide examinations. But since the Department of Education employs only 1 percent of the people working in education, success depends on actions taken by others.*

*See Richard Rose, "From Government at the Centre to Government Nationwide," in Y. Meny and V. Wright, eds., *Centre-Periphery Relations in Western Europe* (London: George Allen and Unwin, 1985), pp. 13–32; and Richard Rose, "The Growth of Government Organizations," in C. Campbell and B. G. Peters, eds., *Organizing Government, Governing Organizations* (Pittsburgh: University of Pittsburgh Press, 1988), pp. 99–128.

responsiveness (assumed to require more councils with a smaller territory and fewer people). Local authorities, however organized, have been the chief institution for delivering such public services as education, police protection, refuse collection, housing, and cemeteries (Box 5.5). Collectively, local government accounts for about a fifth of total public expenditure.

Local council elections are fought on party lines. In the days of the two-party system, many cities were solidly Labour for a generation or more, while leafy suburbs and agricultural counties were overwhelmingly Conservative. The Liberal Democrats now win many seats in local elections and when no party has a majority introduce coalition government into town halls. However, being a councillor is usually a part-time job.

The Blair government has assumed that elected mayors are a good way of holding government accountable and effective and, incidentally, breaking the local power base of Labour veterans skeptical of Blair's new Labour Party. Downing Street introduced the direct election of the mayor of Greater London citing New York and Chicago as positive examples. However, it has refused to give it the independence in taxing and spending that American local government enjoys.[40] Blair's political initiative collapsed when a left-wing Labour populist, Ken Livingstone, won election as London's first mayor running as an independent against an official Labour candidate.

Local government in England is usually divided into two tiers of county and district councils, each with responsibility for some local services. The proliferation of public–private initiatives and special-purpose agencies has reduced the services for which local government is exclusively or primarily responsible. The Blair government has proposed an additional tier of regional government in England—but many local Labour councillors oppose this on the grounds that powers would be taken from local government, and a plan for a North-East regional government was rejected by voters in a referendum there. Today there is a jumble of more or less local institutions and uncertainties about surviving a future reorganization.

Acts of Parliament make councils responsible for delivering major services, and central government financial grants and subsidies are the largest source of local government revenue. There is no local income tax, since the central government does not want to give local authorities the degree of fiscal independence that American local government has. The Thatcher government replaced the local property tax with a poll tax on every adult living in a local authority. It believed this would make voters more aware of the costs of local government and keep spending down. In practice, the tax was difficult to implement, and produced a political backlash. The Major government replaced the poll tax with a community charge that once again related local taxation to the value of the house as well as to the number of people living there.[41] The continued squeeze on central government grants to local authorities under the Blair government has pushed up the community charge tax and maintained local government finance as a subject of rancorous intragovernmental politics.

Both Conservative and Labour parties are centralist. *Centralization* is justified in terms of *territorial justice*—that is, the same standards of public policy ought to apply everywhere in the country. For example, schools in inner cities and rural areas should have the same resources as schools in prosperous suburbs. This can be achieved only if tax revenues are collected by central government and then redistributed from well-to-do to poorer parts of England. In addition, ministers emphasize that they are accountable to a national electorate of tens of millions of people, whereas local councillors are only accountable to those who vote in their ward. Instead of small being beautiful, a big nationwide electorate is assumed to be better. The statement—"Local councillors are not necessarily political animals; we could manage without them"—was made by a left-wing law professor.[42]

Devolution has given a degree of autonomy to the delivery of public services in Scotland, Wales, and Northern Ireland. The new Scottish Parliament has the right to enact legislation affecting a large range of social and public services of direct concern to individuals and communities, such as education, health, and roads. It is also responsible for determining spending priorities within the limits set by its block grant of money from the British Treasury. The Welsh Assembly has administrative discretion, but no legislative or taxing powers. Northern Ireland is exceptional, in that the key service is police and security—and this is kept under the control of British ministers, with the Army and intelligence services in the background.

Executive agencies are functional institutions headed by nonelected officials responsible for delivering many major public services. The biggest, the National Health Service (NHS), is not one organization but a multiplicity of institutions. It allocates money to hospitals and to doctors and dentists who operate as self-employed professionals, although nearly all their income is derived from the NHS and they must work to its guidelines. Access to the national health service is provided without charge to every citizen. But health care is not costless; central government picks up the bill. Because of this, the Treasury perennially seeks to limit the increase in health expenditure. The Treasury seeks to drive down prices for supplies, which it can do because it is a monopoly purchaser of many health-related goods and services. It has also sought to restrict the supply of medical services by limiting the number of hospital beds and the number of doctors that it trains and must pay for.

Public demand for more and better health care rises with the ageing of the population, since older people need more health care, and with the development of new and more expensive forms of medical treatment. The government's rationing of supply has led to lengthening queues, involving months of waiting before a person can see a medical specialist and months of additional waiting before a hospital operation is conducted. In its second term of office the Blair government has sought to deal with this problem by management changes intended to increase efficiency and by limited increases in public expenditure. It has not adopted the common practice of most European Union countries, asking patients to pay a limited part of the cost of seeing a doctor or getting hospital treatment.

British government sponsors more than a thousand *Quasi-Autonomous Non-Governmental Organizations (quangos)*. Some quangos simply advise on policy while others deliver public services. All are created by an Act of Parliament or by an executive decision; their heads are appointed by a Cabinet minister; public money can be appropriated to finance their activities; and, when things go wrong, Parliament has difficulty in assigning responsibility for decisions.

Advisory committees draw on the expertise of individuals and organizations involved in programmes for which Whitehall departments are nominally responsible. Ministry of Agriculture officials can turn to advisory committees for detailed information about farming practices; the Department of Trade and Industry can turn to business associations on matters of trade and to industrial associations for information about a particular industry. Because they have no executive powers, advisory committees usually cost very little to run. Representatives of interest groups are glad to serve because this gives them privileged access to Whitehall and an opportunity to influence government in matters in which they are directly interested.

Administrative tribunals are quasi-judicial bodies that make expert judgments in such fields as medical negligence or handle a large number of small claims, such as disputes about whether the rent set for a rent-controlled flat is fair. Ministers may use tribunals to avoid involvement in politically controversial issues, such as decisions about deporting immigrants. Tribunals normally work much more quickly and cheaply than the courts. However, the quasi-judicial role of tribunals has created a demand for independent auditing of their procedures, to ensure that they are fair to all sides. The task of supervising some 70 tribunals is in the hands of a quango, the Council on Tribunals.

Turning to the Market

The 1945–1951 Labour government turned away from the market because its Socialist leaders believed that government planning was better able than private enterprise to promote economic growth and full employment. It nationalized many basic industries, such as electricity, gas, coal, the railways, and airlines. State ownership meant that industries did not have to run at a profit; some consistently made money while others consistently lost money and required big subsidies. Government ownership politicized wage negotiations and investment decisions.

The Thatcher government promoted privatization, selling shares of nationalized industries on the stock market. Profitmaking industries such as telephones, oil, and gas were sold without difficulty. Selling council houses to tenants at prices well below their market value was popular with tenants. Industries that were losing money, such as British Airways, British Steel, and the coal mines, had to be reorganized, and unprofitable activities were shed to make them attractive to buyers. Industries needing large public subsidies to maintain public services, such as the railways, have continued to receive subsidies after *privatization*.

Privatization has been justified on grounds of economic efficiency (the market is better than civil servants in determining investment, production, and prices); political ideology (the power of government is reduced); service (private enterprise is more consumer-oriented than are civil servants); and short-term financial gain (the sale of public assets can provide billions in revenue for government). Although the Labour Party initially opposed privatization, it quickly realized it would be electorally disastrous to take back privatized council houses and shares that people had bought at bargain prices.

Since many privatized industries affect the public interest, new regulatory agencies were established to regulate telephones, gas, electricity, broadcasting, and water. Where there is a substantial element of monopoly in an industry, the government regulatory agency seeks to promote competition and often has the power to fix price increases at a lower rate than inflation. Even though it no longer owns an industry, government cannot walk away from obligations accepted by its Victorian forebears, such as securing public safety and health. When several fatal accidents occurred on railways whose track was the responsibility of a privatized agency, the Blair government took it over.

From Trust to Contract

Historically, the British civil service has relied on trust in delivering policies. British civil servants are much more rulebound than their German counterparts and less worried about being dragged into court to justify their actions than are American officials. Intragovernmental relations between Whitehall departments and representatives of local authorities have been regarded as a discussion in which consensual understandings would be arrived at and upheld by all sides without the force of law, or debate and division in Parliament. However, the Thatcher government considered lengthy deliberations to be inefficient obstructions to its political goals.

The "next steps" inkitiative has made contracts with independent agencies to undertake the day-to-day delivery of such central government services as automobile licenses, patents, and social security benefits from policymaking agencies. In addition, the government has sought to save money on capital expenditure and reduce the size of the public deficit through the private finance initiative, inviting banks and profitmaking companies to loan money for some or all of the costs of investment in public services such as toll bridges that have a capacity to generate revenue. The theory is that government can obtain the greatest value for money by buying services from the private sector, ranging from cleaning the floors or operating staff canteens in government offices to prison services.

Government by contract faces political limits because the departmental minister must answer to Parliament when something goes wrong. The Prison Service is a textbook example. It was established as an executive agency separate from the Home Office in 1993 to bring in private management to reduce unit costs in the face of a rising "demand" for prison services due to changes in crime rates and sentencing policies. However, when prisoners escaped and other problems erupted, the Home Secretary blamed the business executive brought in to head the Prison Service. The Prison Service head replied by attacking the minister's refusal to live up to the terms of the contract agreed between them.

The proliferation of many agencies, each with a distinctive and narrow responsibility for a limited number of policies, tends to fragment government. For example, a single parent may have to deal with half a dozen different agencies to secure all the public services to which she or he is entitled. The Blair government has reacted by endorsing the idea of "joined up" government, linking the provision of related services so that they can more effectively and easily be received by citizens. In order to achieve this goal, Whitehall must centralize powers that it has previously contracted out. Moreover, it must also centralize powers within Whitehall, a measure consistent with Tony Blair's creation of a large staff in Downing Street but inconsistent with the responsibility of individual Cabinet ministers for running their own departments.

The Contingency of Influence

The theory of British government is centralist: All roads lead to Downing Street, where the the prime minister and the Chancellor of the Exchequer have their homes and offices, and the Treasury and the Foreign Office buildings are only a few steps away. In practice, policymaking is multidimensional, for those involved can be divided horizontally between ministries, executive agencies, and other forms of quangos, and vertically between central government and local authorities and other nondepartmental public bodies that deliver services locally and functionally.

Influence is contingent: it varies with the problem at hand. Decisions about war and peace are taken at the very center by the highest-ranking political and military officials. By contrast, decisions about whether a particular piece of land should be used for housing are normally made by local authorities. Most political decisions involve two or more government agencies, and therefore require discussion and bargaining before a decision can be implemented. The making of policy is constrained by disputes within government much more than by differences between the governing party and its opponents. Many tentacles of the octopus of government work against each other, as each public agency claims to represent conflicting definitions of the public interest.

While the center of central government has been pressing harder on other parts of British government, Whitehall itself has been losing influence because of its obligations in the European Union. The Single Europe Act promotes British exports, but it also increases the scope for European Union regulation of the British economy. Whitehall has adopted a variety of strategies in its European Union negotiations, including noncooperation and public dispute. Ironically, it is just these tactics that local government and British executive agencies use when they disagree with Whitehall.

Why Public Policy Matters

However a citizen votes, she or he does not need to look far to see the outputs of government: if there is a school-age child or a pensioner in the house, the benefits to the family are continuous and visible. If a person is ill, the care provided by doctors and hospitals are important outputs of public policy; so too are police protection and tight controls of land use that maintain greenery even in urban landscapes. Today the average household annually receives two significant welfare state benefits, such as education, health care, or a pension. To produce the benefits of public policy, government relies on three major resources: (1) laws, (2) money, and (3) personnel. Most policies involve a combination of these resources, but they do not do so equally. Policies regulating individual behavior, such as marriage and divorce, are law-intensive; measures such as social security, that pay benefits to millions of people, are money-intensive; and the delivery of services such as health care is labor-intensive.

Laws are the unique resource of government, for private enterprises cannot enact laws and the contracts only operate if the laws of the land are respected. The British executive centralizes within it the power to draft laws and regulations that can be approved without substantial amendment by Parliament. Moreover, many laws give ministers significant discretion in administration. For example, an employer may be required to provide "reasonable" toilet facilities rather than having all features of lavatories specified, down to the size and height of a toilet seat.

Public employees are needed to administer laws and deliver major services. Privatizing public services has reduced the number of people counted as civil servants or public employees, but it has not reduced to the same extent the number who depend on public spending for their job. In total, more than a fifth of the entire British labor force depends on government for their job.

To meet the costs of public policy, British government collects almost two-fifths of the gross national product in taxation. Income tax accounts for 28 percent of tax revenue; the top rate of taxation is 40 percent. Social security taxes are paid by deductions from wages and additional contributions of employers; these account for an additional 17 percent of revenue. Since there are no state or local income taxes, a well-to-do English person can be taxed at a lower total rate than a well-off person living in New York City.

Taxes on consumption are important too. There is a value-added tax of 17.5 percent on the sale of almost all goods and services, and gasoline, cigarettes, and alcohol are taxed heavily too. In total, taxes on consumption account for one-quarter of all tax revenue. Since profits fluctuate from year to year, the government prefers businesses to pay taxes on their gross revenues through value-added tax and on their total wages bill, through the employer's contribution to social security. Taxes on the profits of corporations claim an eighth of tax revenue. Additional revenue is generated by the National Lottery, launched in 1993; more people play the lottery than vote in a general election.

Social security is the most costly programme of British government. It accounts for 38 percent of public expenditure (Figure 5.7). It is also the most popular, for it transfers money from government to more than 10 million older people receiving pensions, plus millions of invalids, the unemployed, women on maternity leave, and poor people needing to supplement their limited resources. Spending on health and education are second and third in their claims on the public purse. Together, these three social welfare programmes account for two-thirds of total public expenditure. A classic commitment of government—defence and maintaining public order and safety through the police, fire service, courts, and prisons—are fourth in importance.

FIGURE 5.7   Public Expenditure by Program

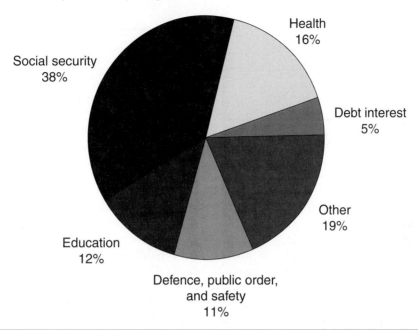

Source: Office for National Statistics, 2004. *United Kingdom National Accounts: The Blue Book.* London: The Stationary Office, pages 276ff.

Since there is no item in the public budget labelled as "waste," any government wanting to reduce public spending must squeeze existing programmes—and big savings can be made only by squeezing popular programmes such as health and education or pensions. But doing so would go against public opinion. When Margaret Thatcher entered office in 1979, the public divided into three almost equal groups: those wanting to spend more and tax more; those wanting to cut taxes even if it means a reduction in public services; and a large middle group wanting to leave things as they are. Thatcher's campaign to cut taxes and public spending produced a reaction in favour of public expenditure. By the time she left office a majority favoured taxing and spending more on social programmes and this has remained the position since (Table 5.5). Tony Blair's government entered office with a pledge not to increase income tax. However, in order to finance increased expenditure on social programmes that are popular with the electorate, it has put up less visible "stealth taxes," such as the employer's contribution to social security, and taxes on insurance funds for pensioners. The effects of these tax increases are passed on to voters—but not in a form that they can easily see.

POLICY OUTCOMES AND CHANGES IN SOCIETY

Although living conditions reflect public policy, only a totalitarian regime claims responsibility for everything that happens in society. In an open society such as England, social conditions are a consequence of the interaction of public policies, the national and international economy, the not-for-profit institutions of civil society, and individual and household activities free of state control. The term welfare state is misleading. Total welfare in society

TABLE 5.5   Public Preference for More Taxing and Spending Rather than Less (in percentages)

	1983	1987	1991	1995	2001
Increase taxes and spending on health, education, and social benefits	32	50	65	61	59
Keep taxes and spending the same as now	54	42	29	31	34
Reduce taxes and spending	9	3	3	5	3
Don't know	5	5	3	3	4

Source: British Social Attitudes surveys, as reported in Alison Park, et al., eds., *British Social Attitudes: The 19th Report* (Thousand Oaks, CA: Sage Publications, 2002), p. 76.

is the sum of a "welfare mix," combining actions of government, the market, and the nonmonetized production of welfare in the household.[43]

Defence against threats to security at home and abroad is a unique responsibility of government. In an interdependent world, British government seeks to guarantee national security by participating in international alliances. Britain was a founder member of NATO, and has fought alongside American forces in the Gulf War in 1991, in Kosovo, and after September 11th, in Afghanistan and Iraq. Maintaining order at home requires the cooperation of others. This is clearest in Northern Ireland, as Whitehall negotiates with leaders of armed paramilitary organizations as well as with elected representatives. Crime prevention depends not only on policing but also on whether or not there are lots of unemployed youths ready to violate the laws in pursuit of money. Over the decades the crime rate has been rising, but it remains lower than in the United States.

Both Conservative and Labour governments accept responsibility for the economy. Most firms are profitmaking, consumers can spend money as they like, and wages and prices are principally decided in the market. Government influences the market through taxing and spending policies, interest rates, and policies for growth and unemployment. Increasingly, what happens to the British economy is also influenced by what happens in other countries of the European Union and on other continents too, and government cannot isolate the country from what happens elsewhere in the global economy.

In each decade since World War II, the British economy has grown, and compounding a small annual rate of growth over many decades cumulatively results in a big rise in living standards. Per capita national income has more than tripled since 1945. Many consumer goods that were once thought of as luxuries, such as owning a car or one's own home, are now mass consumption goods. Things unknown in 1945, such as air travel abroad or VCRs, are now commonplace. Between 1993 and 2003, the British economy grew at a rate of 2.9 percent annually, and over the decade it grew by 24 percent in total. This rate was much higher than France or Germany and almost as high as the United States.

Poverty can be found in Britain; the extent depends on the definition used. If poverty is defined in relative terms such as having less than half the average wage, this is consistent with a rising standard of living in absolute terms. If poverty is defined as being trapped at a low income level for many years, then less than 4 percent are long-term poor.

On all the major indicators of social well-being, the British people enjoy a higher standard of living today than a generation ago. Infant mortality has declined by more than four-fifths since 1951. Life expectancy for men and for women has risen by 12 years. A gender gap remains, as women on average live four years longer than men. The postwar expansion of schools has significantly raised the quantity of education available. Classes are smaller in size, and after leaving secondary school upwards of one-half of British youths go on to some form of further education, usually in institutions that did not exist in 1950. More than two-thirds of families now own their own home and nine-tenths report satisfaction with their housing.

The outputs of public policy play a significant part in the everyday life of all Britons. Everyone makes major use of health and education programs. Children at school or patients seeing a doctor do not think of themselves as participating in politics. Yet the services received are designed and paid for by government. Welfare state benefits—free education, health care, or the guarantee of an income in old age or unemployment—are so taken for granted today that most people see them as nonpolitical. They do not want a change in government after an election to cause radical changes in major social policies.

Popular Expectations

For a century commentators on English society have bemoaned the relative decline in the country's achievements compared with America and leading continental European countries. But ordinary people do not compare their lives with other countries; the most important comparison is with their own past. Evaluating change across time shows great improvements in the living conditions of most English people compared with their parents or grandparents. The longer the time span, the greater the improvements. Furthermore, in the production of such political "goods" as freedom from the state, confidence in the honesty of public officials, and administrative flexibility, British government remains an international leader. The great majority of people are proud of the achievements of Britain and would not want to be a citizen of any other country.

Frustration with government arises only if people expect it to be consistently very successful. But English people tend to have low expectations

of government. In particular, decades of economic difficulties lowered expectations of what government can do to make the economy grow or prevent a rise in unemployment or inflation. Paradoxically, a government presiding over high unemployment and a slow growth economy would be living up to the pessimistic expectations of many. When there are low expectations, any time in which the economy does not get worse can be considered a reprieve from bad news. English people do not hold government responsible for what is most important in their lives; they evaluate their personal circumstances differently from public policy. When people are asked each year whether they think next year will be better or worse personally than the preceding year, on nine-tenths of the occasions a majority say they expect the coming year to be all right for themselves, even when many expect economic difficulties for the country as a whole. National prosperity is desirable but not a necessary condition for personal well-being. When people are asked to evaluate their lives, they are most satisfied with their family, friends, home, and job, and least satisfied with major political institutions of society.[44]

Satisfaction with the present goes along with acceptance of political change in principle. But there are disagreements about the direction of change—for example, whether Westminster should take more responsibility for public services or devolve more responsibilities locally, and whether Britain should align itself more closely with the United States or with the European Union. Even when goals are agreed, there are differences about the particular policy that can best achieve a given goal. Politics in England is thus an ongoing debate about the direction, the means, and the tempo of adapting old institutions and inherited policies to new circumstances in the twenty-first century.

 Key Terms

Cabinet	Conservative Party	devolution	government
centralization	Crown	Downing Street	individualist theory
class	decentralization	first-past-the-post electoral system	

insider and outsider
   pressure groups
insularity
Irish Republican Army
   (IRA)
Labour Party
Liberal Democrats

mixed economy
   Keynesian welfare
   state
multiparty system
Northern Ireland
Parliament
prime minister
privatization

Quasi-Autonomous
   Non-Governmental
   Organizations
   (quangos)
Scotland
sleazy
territorial justice
Thatcherism

trusteeship theory
   of government
United Kingdom
unwritten constitution
Wales
Westminster
Whitehall

Internet Sources

UK Government: www.direct.gov.uk
Parliament website: www.parliament.uk
Prime Minister's Office: www.pm.gov.uk

The BBC News Service: www.news.bbc.co.uk
The Political Studies Association in Britain: www.psa.ac.uk

Suggested Readings

Butler, D. E., and Geraint Butler. *Twentieth Century British Political Facts, 1900–2000,* 8th ed. London: Macmillan, 2000.

Butler, D. E., and Dennis Kavanagh. *The British General Election of 2001.* Basingstoke, England: Palgrave, 2001.

Flinders, Matthew. *The Politics of Accountability in the Modern State.* Aldershot: Ashgate, 2001.

George, Stephen. *An Awkward Partner: Britain in the European Community,* 3rd ed. Oxford, England: Oxford University Press, 1998.

Grant, Wyn. *Pressure Groups and British Politics.* New York: St. Martin's Press, 2000.

Hayward, Jack, Brian Barry, and A. Brown, eds. *The British Study of Politics in the Twentieth Century.* Oxford, England: Oxford University Press, 1999.

Independent Commission on Proportional Representation. *Changed Voting Changed Politics: Lessons of Britain's Experience of PR since 1997.* London: the Constitution Unit.

James, Simon. *British Cabinet Government,* 2nd ed., New York: Routledge, 1999.

Moran, Michael. *The British Regulatory State: High Modernism and Hyper-Innovation.* New York: Oxford University Press, 2003.

Norris, Pippa, ed. *Britain Votes 2001.* Oxford, England: Oxford University Press, 2001.

Norris, Pippa, and Joni Lovenduski. *Political Recruitment: Gender, Race, and Class in the British Parliament.* New York: Cambridge University Press, 1995.

Park, Alison, ed. *British Social Attitudes: The 20th Report.* Thousand Oaks, CA: Sage Publications, 2003.

Pattie, Charles, Patrick Seyd, and Paul Whitele. *Citizenship in Britain.* New York: Cambridge University Press, 2004.

Oliver, Dawn. *Constitutional Reform in the United Kingdom.* New York: Oxford University Press, 2003.

Rose, Richard. *Ordinary People in Public Policy.* Newbury Park, CA: Sage, 1989.

———. *The Prime Minister in a Shrinking World.* Boston: Polity Press, 2001.

Rose, Richard, and Phillip L. Davies. *Inheritance in Public Policy: Change Without Choice in Britain.* New Haven, CT: Yale University Press, 1994.

Saggar, Shamit, ed. *Race and British Electoral Politics.* London: UCL Press, 1998.

Seldon, Anthony. *Blair.* New York: Free Press, 2004.

Smith, Martin J. *The Core Executive in Britain.* London: Macmillan, 1999.

Social Trends. London: Stationery Office, annual.

Trench, Alan. *Has Devolution Made a Difference?* London: Imprint Academic, 2004.

Webb, Paul. *The Modern British Party System.* Thousand Oaks, CA: Sage Publications, 2003.

Whitaker's Almanack. London: J. Whitaker, annual.

Wilson, David, and Game, Chris. *Local Government in the United Kingdom,* 3rd ed. Basingstoke: Palgrave, 2002.

Endnotes

1. See Richard Rose, *What Is Europe? A Dynamic Perspective* (New York: Addison Wesley Longman, 1996), Ch. 3.

2. John Kampfner and David Wighton, "Blair Seals Labour's Switch to Low Tax Party," *Financial Times*, 27 March 1997.

3. Quoted in Krishna Guha, "Labour Escapes from Its Bloody Tower," *Financial Times*, 24 August 2002.

4. See Richard Rose, "England: A Traditionally Modern Political Culture," in Lucian W. Pye and Sidney Verba, eds., *Political Culture and Political Development* (Princeton, NJ: Princeton University Press, 1965), pp. 83–129.

5. Quoted in Richard Rose, *Do Parties Make a Difference?* 2nd ed. (Chatham, NJ: Chatham House, 1984).

6. Cf. Andrew Dilnot and Paul Johnson, eds., *Election Briefing 1997* (London: Institute for Fiscal Studies, Commentary 60, 1997), p. 2.

7. John Kampfner and David Wighton, "Reeling in Scotland to Bring England in Step," *Financial Times*, 5 April 1997.

8. *NOP Social and Political Research*, a nationwide survey of 1,921 respondents, March 17–23, 1995.

9. Philip Stephens and Cathy Newman, "We Need One Power, says Blair," *Financial Times*, 28 April 2003.

10. *Gallup Political and Economic Index*, London No. 390 (February 1993), p. 42.

11. "Britain's Independent Role About Played Out," *The Times* (London), 6 December 1962.

12. Quoted in Peter Hennessy, "Raw Politics Decide Procedure in Whitehall," *New Statesman* (London), 24 October 1986, p. 10.

13. Winston Churchill, *Their Finest Hour* (London: Cassell, 1949), p. 14.

14. See Richard Rose, "A Crisis of Confidence in the Party System or in Individual Leaders," *Contemporary Record* 9, No. 2 (1995): 273–93.

15. Simon Jenkins, "New Dogs, Old Tricks," *Sunday Times* (London), 21 March 2004.

16. Walter Bagehot, *The English Constitution* (London: World's Classics, 1955), p. 9.

17. See Richard Rose, *The Prime Minister in a Shrinking World* (Boston: Polity Press, 2001).

18. David Leppard and Robert Winnett, "Blair Blames Ministers for Policy Gaffes," *Sunday Times*, 18 April 2004.

19. Eric Varley, quoted in A. Michie and S. Hoggart, *The Pact* (London: Quartet Books, 1978), p. 13.

20. Hugh Heclo and Aaron Wildavsky, *The Private Government of Public Money* (London: Macmillan, 1974).

21. Bernard Ingham, press secretary to Margaret Thatcher, quoted in Rose, "British Government: The Job at the Top," in R. Rose and E. Suleiman, eds., *Presidents and Prime Ministers* (Washington, DC: American Enterprise Institute, 1980), p. 43.

22. Lord Butler, *Review of Intelligence on Weapons of Mass Destruction.* House of Commons Document 898. London: The Stationery Office, 2004, p. 160.

23. See Samuel H. Beer, *Modern British Politics*, 3rd ed. (London: Faber and Faber, 1982).

24. Lord Wright, in *Liversidge v. Sir John Anderson and Another,* 1941, quoted in G. Le May, *British Government, 1914–1953* (London: Methuen, 1955), p. 332.

25. House of Commons, *Hansard* (London: Her Majesty's Stationery Office), November 11, 1947, col. 206.

26. Cf. Colin Bennett, "From the Dark to the Light: The Open Government Debate in Britain," *Journal of Public Policy* 5, No. 2 (1985): 209; italics in the original.

27. See Richard Rose and Ian McAllister, *The Loyalties of Voters* (Newbury Park, CA: 1990), Ch. 3.

28. See Joni Lovenduski and Pippa Norris, eds., "Women in Politics," a special issue of *Parliamentary Affairs*, 49, No. 1 (1996).

29. Quoted in Maurice Kogan, *The Politics of Education* (Harmondsworth, England: Penguin, 1971), p. 135.

30. See the Fulton Committee, *Report*, vol. 1, pp. 27ff., and Appendix E, especially p. 162.

31. See Rob Baggott, "The Measurement of Change in Pressure Groups," *Talking Politics* 5, No. 1 (1992): 18–22.

32. Sir Ken Jackson, quoted by Krishna Guha, "Engineers and Electricians Turn Away from Moderate Traditions," *Financial Times*, 19 July 2002.

33. See W. A. Maloney, G. Jordan, and A. M. McLaughlin, "Interest Groups and Public Policy: The Insider/Outsider Model Revisited," *Journal of Public Policy* 14, No. 1 (1994): 17–38.

34. Tony Blair, *New Britain: My Vision of a Young Country* (London: Fourth Estate, 1996), p. 299.

35. For details, see Denis Van Mechelen and Richard Rose, *Patterns of Parliamentary Legislation* (Aldershot, England: Gower, 1986), table 5.2, and more generally, Rose, *Do Parties Make a Difference?*

36. Rose and Davies, *Inheritance in Public Policy*, p. 28.

37. Reginald Maudling, quoted in David Butler and Michael Pinto-Duschinsky, *The British General Election of 1970* (London: Macmillan, 1971), p. 62.

38. See *Better Government Services: Executive Agencies in the 21st Century.* (London: Office of Public Service Reforms and the Treasury, 2002).

39. Sir Leo Pliatzky, quoted in Peter Hennessy, "The Guilt of the Treasury 1000," *New Statesman*, 23 January 1987.

40. See Paul Peterson, "The American Mayor: Elections and Institutions," *Parliamentary Affairs* 53, No. 4 (2000): 667–79.

41. David Butler, Andrew Adonis, and Tony Travers, *Failure in British Government: The Politics of the Poll Tax* (Oxford, England: Oxford University Press, 1994).

42. J. A. G. Griffith, *Central Departments and Local Authorities* (London: George Allen and Unwin, 1966), p. 542. Cf. Simon Jenkins, *Accountable to None: The Tory Nationalization of Britain* (Harmondsworth, England: Penguin, 1996).

43. See Richard Rose, "The Dynamics of the Welfare Mix in Britain," in Richard Rose and Rei Shiratori, eds., *The Welfare State East and West* (New York: Oxford University Press, 1986), pp. 80–106.

44. Rose, *Ordinary People in Public Policy*, pp. 175ff.

France

SPAIN

MEDITERRANEAN SEA

Sardinia

Corsica CORSE

ANDORRA

N

SPAIN

Bay of Biscay

Bordeaux
Garonne
AQUITAINE

MIDI-
PYRÉNÉES
Toulouse

LANGUEDOC

Marseille

PROVENCE-
ALPES-CÔTE
D' AZUR Nice

Toulon

MONACO

Rhône

RHÔNE-
ALPES

Grenoble

ITALY

Lyon

AUVERGNE

LIMOUSIN

Clermont-
Ferrand

POITOU-
CHARENTE

CENTRE

BOURGOGNE

FRANCHE-
COMTE

SWITZERLAND

Nantes

Loire

PAYS DE'
LA LOIRE

BRETAGNE

BASSE

English Channel

HAUTE

RÉGION
PARISIENNE

Paris

Seine

PICARDIE

CHAMPAGNE

LORRAINE

ALSACE

LIECHTENSTEIN

Lille
NORD

BELGIUM

LUXEMBOURG

Rhine

GERMANY

NETHER-
LANDS

UNITED
KINGDOM

NORTH
SEA

Chapter 6

Politics in France

MARTIN A. SCHAIN

Country Bio—France

Population: 60.4 Million

Territory: 211,208 sq. mi

Year of Independence: 486

Year of Current Constitution: 1958

Head of State: President Jacques Chirac

Head of Government: Prime Minister Jean-Pierre Raffarin

Language(s): French 100%, rapidly declining regional dialects and languages (Provencal, Breton, Alsatian, Corsican, Catalan, Basque, Flemish)

Religion: Roman Catholic 90%, Protestant 2%, Jewish 1%, Muslim 1%, unaffiliated 6%

The results of the first round of the presidential elections on April 21, 2002 were supposed to be more or less predictable. The two top contenders—the sitting president, Jacques Chirac, and the sitting prime minister, Lionel Jospin—would win the two top spots for the second round two weeks later. In fact, the candidate of the extreme right National Front, Jean-Marie Le Pen won the second spot, creating what was called a "political earthquake," and throwing the political system into a state of confusion. In the end, Chirac crushed his opponent, winning more than 82 percent of the vote, with the declared support of both the established left and the established right. Thus, Jacques Chirac, whose presidency had been compromised by serious corruption scandals, became a most unlikely savior of republican values. In every legislative election since 1981, the French electorate has favored the opposition, and the legislative elections in 2002 that followed the bizarre presidential election reaffirmed that pattern. Nevertheless,

French citizens now appear to have more confidence in the key institutions of the Republic than they have had at any time in French history. Increasingly, however, they have little confidence in the politicians who are running them. The stability of the Republic has surprised many of the French as well as the outside world. By combining two models of democratic government, the presidential and the parliamentary, the *Fifth Republic* has succeeded in a constitutional experiment that now serves France well. For the first time since the French Revolution, there is no important political party or sector of public opinion that challenges the legitimacy of the regime.

CURRENT POLICY CHALLENGES

At a time in American history when political parties have been deeply divided and the party system highly polarized, and when national government often seems divided, French politics—at least most of the time—seem almost tranquil by comparison. The French have lived with divided government ("cohabitation") for most of the period since 1986 without impeding decision-making effectiveness and without undermining institutional legitimacy. At the same time, the French electorate is clearly concerned about many of the same issues that have concerned Americans during the past decade.

French voters are most worried about rising crime rates and the problems of urban violence. In France, these problems are frequently referred to as problems of the "suburbs," since impoverished neighborhoods, frequently with large immigrant populations, are often found in the old working-class suburbs that surround large cities. These concerns have been related to the success of the radical right, and its endurance since 1983. The electoral importance of the National Front—an anti-immigrant party that advocates strong nationalism—has tended to undermine the stability of the parties of the center-right and support anti-immigrant and racist sentiments among the electorate as a whole. Although the party has never held power at the national level, it maintains strong influence over the political agenda.

Voters also continue to be concerned with high unemployment rates that are more than twice U.S. rates. Anxiety about unemployment is related to deep concern in France about the consequences of European Union. Finally, voters are disturbed about political corruption at every level. During the past decade, hardly a month has passed without a politician being accused of corrupt practices (including the president of the Republic), or another being tried or jailed.

We should emphasize, however, that many of the issues that have been at the heart of American politics today are of little concern to the French electorate. French voters are barely interested in the private lives of their political leaders. Nor is there much concern among voters about the size of the state. There have been considerable efforts in the past decade to reduce the level of public spending. However, there is little support for massive cuts in welfare state programs, which have always been more extensive in France than in the United States. In fact, surveys indicate that French voters are willing to sacrifice a great deal to maintain these programs as well as high levels of state-subsidized social security and long vacations. On the other hand, unlike their American counterparts, French voters are very concerned about the environmental and health consequences of genetically modified organisms.

French voters are also concerned about issues of multiculturalism related to the integration of a large and growing Muslim population. In 2004 the government passed legislation prohibiting students in public schools from wearing conspicuous religious symbols, including Islamic headscarves worn by women. This legislation was far more controversial in the United States than in France, where surveys indicated support for the legislation among all sectors of the French population, including a majority of women of Muslim origin.

Finally, although there was widespread sympathy with the United States just after the attack on the World Trade Center and the Pentagon, there has been a perceptible rise of anti-American sentiment, and distrust of American policy, since then. This distrust has expanded into a major trans-Atlantic crisis, as France took the lead in resisting the American-led military action against Iraq in the Spring of 2003, supported by a broad consensus of public opinion and political party support in favor of French opposition to the war.

A HISTORICAL PERSPECTIVE

France is one of the oldest nation-states of Europe. The period of unstable revolutionary regimes that followed the storming of the Bastille in 1789 ended in the seizure of power by *Napoléon Bonaparte* a decade later. The French Revolution began with the establishment of a constitutional monarchy in 1791 (the First Republic), but the monarchy was overthrown the following year. Three more constitutions preceded Napoléon's seizure of power on the eighteenth day of the revolutionary month of Brumaire (November 10, 1799) and the establishment of the First Empire three years later. The other European powers formed an alliance and forced Napoléon's surrender as well as the restoration of the Bourbon monarchy. Another revolution in 1830 drove the last Bourbon from the French throne and replaced him with Louis Philippe of the House of Orléans, who promised a more moderate rule bounded by a new constitution.

Growing dissatisfaction among the rising bourgeoisie and the urban population produced still another Paris revolution in 1848. With it came the proclamation of the Second Republic (1848–1852) and universal male suffrage. Conflict between its middle-class and lower-class components, however, kept the republican government ineffective. Out of the disorder rose another Napoléon, nephew of the first emperor. Louis Napoléon, crowned Napoléon III in 1852, brought stability to France for more than a decade, but his last years were marked by growing indecision and ill-conceived foreign ventures. His defeat and capture in the Franco-Prussian War (1870) began another turbulent period. France was occupied and forced into a humiliating armistice; radicals in Paris proclaimed the Paris Commune, which held out for two months in 1871, until crushed by the conservative French government forces. In the commune's aftermath, the struggle between republicans and monarchists led to the establishment of a conservative Third Republic in 1871 and to a new constitution in 1875. The Third Republic proved to be the longest regime in modern France, surviving World War I and lasting until France's defeat and occupation by Nazi Germany in 1940.

World War II deeply divided France. A defeated France was divided into a zone occupied by the Germans, while a French government sympathetic to the Germans, lead by Marshall Pétain, governed a "free" zone in the southern half of the country from Vichy. From July 1940 until August 1944, the government of France was a dictatorship. Slowly, a resistance movement that rejected the new order began to emerge under the leadership of General *Charles de Gaulle* and gained greater strength and support after the Allied invasion of North Africa and the German occupation of the "free" zone at the end of 1942. When German forces were driven from occupied Paris in 1944, de Gaulle entered the city with the hope that sweeping reforms would give France the viable democracy it had long sought. After less than two years, he resigned as head of the Provisional Government, impatient as he was with the country's return to traditional party politics. In fact, the *Fourth Republic* (1946–1958) disappointed earlier hopes. Governments fell with disturbing regularity—24 governments in 12 years. At the same time, because of the narrowness of government coalitions, the same parties and the same leaders tended to participate in most of these governments. Weak leadership had great difficulty coping with the tensions created first by the Cold War, then the French war in Indochina, and finally the anticolonialist uprising in Algeria.

When a threat of civil war arose over Algeria in 1958, a group of leaders invited de Gaulle to return to power and help the country establish stronger and more stable institutions. Since then France has lived under the constitution of the Fifth Republic, enacted by a referendum in 1958. De Gaulle was the last prime minister of the Fourth Republic, then the first president of the newly established Fifth Republic.

ECONOMY AND SOCIETY

Geographically, France is at once Atlantic, Continental, and Mediterranean; hence, it occupies a unique place in Europe. In 2004 a total of 60.4 million people, about one-fourth as many as the population of the United States, lived in an area one-fifteenth the size of the United States. It is estimated that more than 3.6 million foreigners (noncitizens) live in France, more than half of whom come from outside of Europe, mostly from North Africa and Africa. In addition, nearly 2 million French citizens are foreign-born. Thus almost 10 percent of the French population is foreign-born, about the same proportion as in the United States.

Urbanization has come slowly to France, in contrast to its neighbors, but it is now highly urbanized. In 1936 only 16 French cities had a population of more than 100,000; they now number 36. Five cities have a population of more than 300,000. Compared with European countries with similar population (Britain and Germany), France has relatively few large cities; only Paris has more than a million people. Yet in 2002, 44 million people (three-quarters of the population) lived in urban areas, compared with half that number in 1936.

Almost one-quarter of the urban population—more than one-sixth of the entire nation and growing—lives in the metropolitan region of Paris. This concentration of people creates staggering problems. In a country with centuries-old traditions of administrative, economic, and cultural centralization, it has produced a dramatic gap in human and material resources between Paris and the rest of the country. The Paris region supports a per capita income about 45 percent higher and unemployment 15 to 17 percent lower than the national average. But the Paris region also has the highest concentration of foreigners in the country (twice the national percentage), and there are deep divisions between the wealthier and poorer towns that comprise the region.

Overall, French economic development, compared with other advanced industrial countries, has been respectable in the recent past. In per capita gross domestic product (GDP) in 2004, France ranks among the wealthiest nations of the world, behind the Scandinavian countries, Ireland, the United States, and Britain, ahead of Germany and Italy, and ahead of the average for the EU 15 (see Chapter 1). During the 1980s, the French economy grew at about the European average but with an inflation rate at half the European average. During this same period, unemployment hovered around 10 percent, slightly above the European average. After the legislative elections in 1997, unemployment

dipped again, as the French economy succeeded in creating new jobs again. Nevertheless, in 2004, with an unemployment rate of 9 percent, France was experiencing some of the same problems as some of the poorer countries of Europe: long-term youth unemployment, homelessness, and a drain on social services. Nevertheless, the level of long-term unemployment (more than one year), still more than 30 percent of those unemployed, had been reduced by almost 25 percent.

The labor force has changed drastically since the end of World War II, in ways that have made France similar to other industrialized countries. During the decade of the 1990s, the labor force grew by more than 1.6 million, continuing a growth trend that was greater than in most European countries. Most of these new arrivals were young people, and an increasing proportion were women. For over a century, the proportion of employed women—mostly in agriculture, artisan shops, and factories—was higher in France than in most European countries. Today, most women work in offices in the service sector of the economy. In 1954 women comprised 35 percent of the labor force; today, they make up 46 percent of a much larger labor force. The proportion of French women working (48 percent) is slightly lower than that of the United States but one of the highest in Western Europe.

In 1938, 37 percent of French labor was employed in agriculture; this proportion was less than 3.5 percent in 2004, and it is still declining. The percentage of the labor force employed in industry was down to about 24 percent, while employment in the service sector rose from 33 percent in 1938 to 71 percent today, somewhat smaller than the United States, and slightly above the average for Western Europe.

By comparison with other highly developed industrial countries, the agricultural sector of France remains important both economically and politically. France has more cultivated acreage than any other country in the European Union. In spite of the sharp decline in the proportion of the population engaged in agriculture, agricultural production has increased massively during the past quarter century. Throughout the 1990s, France was a top producer and exporter of key agricultural products in

Europe (meat, milk, and cereals, for example). Earnings from agricultural exports grew during the past decade. But this impressive performance hides the fact that, although the average income of farmers is about equal to that of a middle-level executive, the disparity of income between the smallest and largest farms is greater than in any other country in the European Union. Nevertheless, French farm incomes are generally higher and more stable than in most EU countries.

Because the political stability of the Third Republic depended on a large and stable peasantry, the government supported French agriculture with protective tariffs that helped farmers (and small businesses) cling to their established routines. Since 1945 there have been serious efforts to modernize agriculture. More attention was paid to the possible advantages of farm cooperatives; marginal farms were consolidated; technical education has been vastly improved; and further mechanization and experimentation are being used as avenues for long-range structural reforms. Particularly after the development of the Common Agriculture Policy (CAP) in the European Community between 1962 and 1968, consolidation of farmland proceeded rapidly. By 1985 the mean size of a French farm was larger than that of any country in Europe except Britain, Denmark, and Luxembourg.

The European Union has paid a large proportion of the bill for agricultural modernization, and subsidies have increased steadily since 1967. As a result, there are pressures (particularly from the British) to reduce CAP expenditures and to deal with the factors that increase them. With the enlargement of the EU in 2004, and the incorporation of more countries in Eastern Europe with large agricultural sectors, these pressures have increased. In addition to requiring the withdrawal of more land from production, major reforms in 1992, 1994, 1999, and 2003 at the European level have gradually moved subsidies away from price supports (that encourage greater production) and toward direct support of farm income. Nevertheless, total subsidies to French farmers increased substantially in the 1990s.

French business has been both highly dispersed and highly concentrated. Even after three decades of structural reorganization of business,

about half of the 2.4 million industrial and commercial enterprises in France belong to individuals. In 1999, 54 percent of the salaried workers in the country worked in small enterprises with fewer than 50 workers, and, as in other advanced industrial societies, this proportion has been slowly increasing, primarily because of the movement of labor into the service sector.

Nevertheless, from the perspective of production, some of the most advanced French industries are highly concentrated, and the few firms at the top account for most of the employment and business sales. Even in some of the older sectors (such as automobile manufacture, ship construction, and rubber), half or more of the employment and sales are concentrated in the top four firms. Among the 200 largest industrial groups in the world in 1997, 21 were located in France, about the same as in Germany.

The organization of industry and commerce in France changed significantly during the decade of the 1990s. In 1997, among the top 20 enterprises in France, only 4 were public, compared with 13 ten years before. During the past 15 years, the process of privatization had reduced the number of public enterprises by 24 percent and the number of those working in those enterprises by 31 percent. To the managerial elite trained in the "grandes écoles" was added a more diverse group of entrepreneurs who had ascended during the period of Socialist governments. Nevertheless, despite a continuing process of privatization, relations between industry and the state remain close.

CONSTITUTION AND GOVERNMENTAL STRUCTURE

The *Constitution of 1958* is the sixteenth since the fall of the Bastille in 1789. Past republican regimes, known less for their achievements than for their instability, were invariably based on the principle that Parliament could overturn a government no longer backed by a majority of the elected representatives. Such an arrangement can work satisfactorily, as it does in most of Western Europe, when the country (and Parliament) embrace two—or a few—well-organized parties. The party or the coalition that gains a majority at the polls forms the government and can count on the almost unconditional support of its members in Parliament until the next elections. At that time, it is either kept in power or replaced by an equally disciplined party or coalition of parties.

The Executive

The constitution that General de Gaulle submitted for popular approval in 1958 offered to remedy previous failings of French political parties and coalition politics. In preceding republics the president was little more than a figurehead. According to the new constitution, the *president of the Republic* became a visible head of state. He was to be placed "above the parties" to represent the unity of the national community. As guardian of the constitution, he was to be an arbiter who would rely on other powers—Parliament, the Cabinet, or the people— for the full weight of government action. He would have the option of appealing to the people in two ways. With the agreement of the government or Parliament, he could submit certain important pieces of legislation to the electorate as a referendum, and, after consulting with the prime minister and the parliamentary leaders, he could dissolve Parliament and call for new elections. In case of grave threat "to the institutions of the Republic," the president also had the option of invoking emergency powers. Virtually all of the most powerful constitutional powers of the president—those that give the president formal power—have been used sparingly. Emergency powers were used only once (by General de Gaulle in 1961), when the rebellion of the generals in Algiers clearly justified such use. The mutiny collapsed after a few days, not because of the constitutional provision, but because de Gaulle's authority was unimpaired and hence left the rebels isolated and impotent. President de Gaulle dissolved Parliament twice (in 1962 and 1968), each time to exploit a political opportunity to strengthen the majority supporting presidential policies (see Figure 6.1).

Upon his election to the presidency in 1981, the Socialist François Mitterrand dissolved the National Assembly. He did so again after his reelection seven years later, in order to open the way for parlia-

FIGURE 6.1 French Presidents and Prime Ministers Since 1958

PRIME MINISTER	YEAR	PRESIDENT
Dominique de Villepin	2005	
Jean Pierre Raffarin	2002	
Lionel Jospin	1997	
Alain Juppé	1995	Jacques Chirac
Edouard Balladur	1993	
Pierre Bérégovoy	1992	
Edith Cresson	1991	
Michel Rocard	1988	
Jacques Chirac	1986	
Laurent Fabius	1984	
Pierre Mauroy	1981	François Mitterrand
Raymond Barre	1976	
Jacques Chirac	1974	Valéry Giscard d'Estaing
Pierre Messmer	1972	
Jacques Chaban-Delmas	1969	Georges Pompidou
Maurice Couve de Murville	1968	
Georges Pompidou	1962	
Michel Debré	1958	Charles de Gaulle

mentary elections. Because of the political momentum of Mitterrand's victories as a presidential candidate, he expected that early parliamentary elections would provide him with reliable majorities in the National Assembly. Finally, President Jacques Chirac dissolved the National Assembly in April 1997 in an attempt to extend the conservative majority into the next century and to gain political support for the reduction of public spending. The president lost his gamble.

The legitimacy and political authority of the president have been greatly augmented by direct popular elections to the office. The 1958 constitution called for the president to be elected indirectly by a college comprised mostly of local government officials. In 1962, however, a constitutional amendment by referendum created a new system of popular election of the president for a renewable term of seven years. In September 2000, the presidential term was reduced to five years—again by constitutional amendment—to coincide with the normal five-year legislative term beginning in 2002. At present, France is one of six countries in Western Europe to select its president by direct popular vote; the others are Portugal, Ireland, Austria, Iceland, and Finland.

President de Gaulle outlined his view of the office when he said that power "emanates directly from the people, which implies that the Head of State, elected by the nation, is the source and holder of this power." Every president who has succeeded de Gaulle has maintained the general's basic interpretation of the office, but there have been some changes in the way the presidency has functioned (for details, see pp. 40–42). The *prime minister* is appointed by the president and has responsibility for the day-to-day running of the government. In actuality, the division of responsibility between the president and his prime minister has varied not only with the personalities of those who hold each of the executive offices but also with the conditions under which the prime minister serves.

The Legislature

The legislature is composed of two houses: the National Assembly and the Senate (see Figure 6.2).

The *National Assembly* of 577 members is elected directly for five years by all citizens over 18. The government may dissolve the legislature at any time, though not twice within one year. The instability of previous regimes had been attributed mostly to the constant meddling of Parliament with the activities of the executive. The Constitution of 1958 strove to end the subordination of government to Parliament. It imposed strict rules of behavior on each deputy and on Parliament as a body. These requirements, it was hoped, would ensure the needed equilibrium.

Now the government, rather than the legislature, is in control of proceedings in both houses and can require priority for bills it wishes to promote. The president rather than the prime minister generally chooses the Cabinet members, although this prerogative tends to be merely formal during periods of cohabitation (see p. 41). Parliament still enacts laws, but the domain of such laws is strictly defined. Many areas of modern life that in other democracies are regulated by laws debated and approved by Parliament are turned over to rule making by the executive in France.

The 19 standing committees of the National Assembly under the Fourth Republic were reduced to six. The sizes of the committees were enlarged to about 73 to 145 members to prevent interaction among highly specialized deputies who could become effective rivals of the ministers. Each deputy is restricted to one committee, and party groups are represented in each committee in proportion to their size in the National Assembly.

It is not surprising that the new constitution detailed the conditions under which the National Assembly could overthrow a government. An explicit motion of censure must be formulated and passed by more than one-half of the members of the house. Even after a motion of censure is passed, the government may resist the pressure to resign: The president can dissolve the Assembly and call for new elections. During the first year after these elections, a new dissolution of Parliament is prohibited by the constitution. The vote of censure is the only way Parliament can condemn the conduct of government, but no government has been censured since 1962. Since that time every government has

FIGURE 6.2   Structure of the French Government

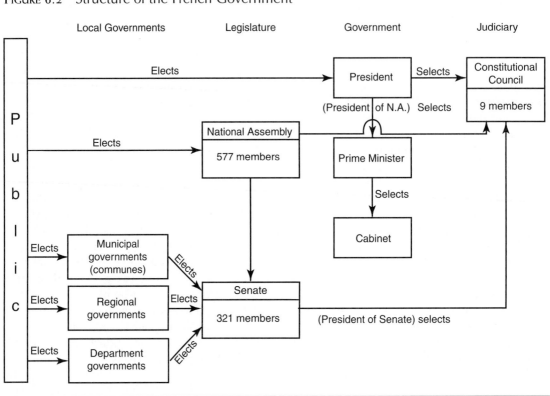

had a working (if not always friendly) majority in the National Assembly.

The National Assembly shares legislative functions with the *Senate*. Not only in France, but in all countries without a federal structure, the problem of how to organize a bicameral legislature is complex. How should the membership of the second chamber be defined if there are no territorial units to represent? The 321 members of the Senate (the "upper house") are elected indirectly for a term of nine years (one-third every three years) by an electoral college of less than 50,000 representatives from municipal, departmental, and regional councils in which rural constituencies are overrepresented. The upper house has the right to initiate legislation and must consider all bills adopted by the National Assembly. If the two houses disagree on pending legislation, the government can appoint a joint committee to resolve the differences. If the views of the two houses are not reconciled, the government may resubmit the bill (either the original bill or as amended by the Senate) to the National Assembly for a definitive vote (Article 45). Therefore, unlike the United States, the two houses are not equal in either power or influence (see again Figure 6.2).

The Judiciary

Until the Fifth Republic, France had no judicial check on the constitutionality of the actions of its political authorities. The *Constitutional Council* was originally conceived primarily as a safeguard against any legislative erosion of the constraints that the constitution has placed on the prerogatives of Parliament.[1] In part because of a constitutional amendment in 1974, however, the council plays an increasingly important role in the legislative process (see pp. 45–46).

POLITICAL CULTURE

Themes of Political Culture

There are three ways that we understand political culture in France: History links present values to those of the past; abstraction and symbolism identify a way of thinking about politics; and distrust in government represents a dominant value that crosses class and generational lines.

THE BURDEN OF HISTORY Historical thinking can prove both a bond and—as the American Civil War demonstrates—a hindrance to consensus. The French are so fascinated by their own history that feuds of the past are constantly superimposed on the conflicts of the present. This passionate use of historical memories, resulting in seemingly inflexible ambitions, warnings, and taboos, complicates political decision making. In de Gaulle's words, France is "weighed down by history."

ABSTRACTION AND SYMBOLISM In the Age of Enlightenment the monarchy left the educated classes free to voice their views on many topics, provided the discussion remained general and abstract. The urge to discuss a wide range of problems, even trivial ones, in broad philosophical terms has hardly diminished. The exaltation of the abstract is reflected in the significance attributed to symbols and rituals. Rural communities that fought on opposite sides in the French Revolution still pay homage to different heroes, two centuries later. They seem to have no real quarrel with each other, but inherited symbols and their political and religious habits have kept them apart.[2] This tradition helps explain why a nation united by almost universal admiration for a common historical experience holds to conflicting interpretations of its meaning.

DISTRUST OF GOVERNMENT AND POLITICS The French have long shared in the widespread ambivalence of modern times that combines distrust of government with high expectations from it. The French citizens' simultaneous distrust of authority and craving for it feed on both individualism and a passion for equality. This attitude produces a self-reliant individual convinced that he is responsible to himself, and perhaps to his family, for what he was and might become. Obstacles are created by the outside world, the "they" who operate beyond the circle of the family, the family firm, and the village. Most of the time, however, "they" are identified with the government.

Memories reaching back to the eighteenth century justify a state of mind that is potentially, if seldom overtly, insubordinate. A strong government is considered reactionary by nature, even if it pretends to be progressive. When citizens participate in public life, they hope to weaken governmental authority rather than encourage change, even when change is overdue. At times this individualism is tainted with anarchism. Yet the French also accommodate themselves rather easily to bureaucratic rule. Since administrative rulings supposedly treat all situations with the same yardstick, they satisfy the sharp sense of equality possessed by a people who have felt forever shortchanged by the government and by the privileges those in power bestow on others.

Although the Revolution of 1789 did not break with the past as completely as is commonly believed, it conditioned the general outlook on crisis and compromise, continuity and change. Sudden change rather than gradual mutation, dramatic conflicts couched in the language of mutually exclusive, radical ideologies—these are the experiences that excite the French at historical moments when their minds are particularly malleable. In fact, what appears to the outsider as permanent instability is a fairly regular alternation between brief violent crises and prolonged periods of routine. The French are accustomed to thinking that no thorough change can ever be brought about except by a major upheaval. Since the great revolution, every French adult has experienced—usually more than once—occasions of political excitement followed by disappointment. This process has led at times to moral exhaustion and widespread skepticism about any possibility of change.

Whether they originated within the country or were brought about by international conflict, most of France's political crises have resulted in a constitutional crisis. Each time, the triumphant forces have codified their norms and philosophy, usually in a comprehensive document. This history explains why constitutions have never played the role of fundamental charters. Prior to the Fifth Republic, their norms were satisfactory to only one segment of the polity and hotly contested by others.

In the years immediately following 1958, the reaction to the constitution of the Fifth Republic resembled that to other constitutions in France. Support for its institutions was generally limited to voters who supported the governments of the day. This began to change after 1962, with the popular election of the president. The election of Mitterrand to the presidency in 1981, and the peaceful transfer of power from a right to a left majority in the National Assembly, laid to rest the 200-year-old constitutional debate among French elites, and proved to be the capstone of acceptance of the institutions of the Fifth Republic among the masses of French citizens.

Confidence in the Fifth Republic constitutional institutions has been strong, and, despite growing disillusionment with politicians, has grown stronger.

Moreover, there is no significant variation among voters by party identity.[3] When French people are asked in which particular institutions they have the most confidence, they invariably give the highest ratings to those closest to them: to local officials, rather than to political parties or national representatives (see Figure 6.3). In recent years distrust in government officials has been high, but expectations of government remain high as well.

Religious and Antireligious Traditions

France is at once a Catholic country—68 percent of the French population identified themselves as Catholic in 2002 (87 percent in 1974)—and a country that the Church itself considers as "dechristianized." Of those who describe themselves as Catholic, only 10 percent attend mass regularly (down from 21 percent in 1974), and 84 percent either never go to church at all or go only occasionally, for such ceremonies as baptism or marriage.[4]

FIGURE 6.3   Feelings of Confidence in Various Political Institutions

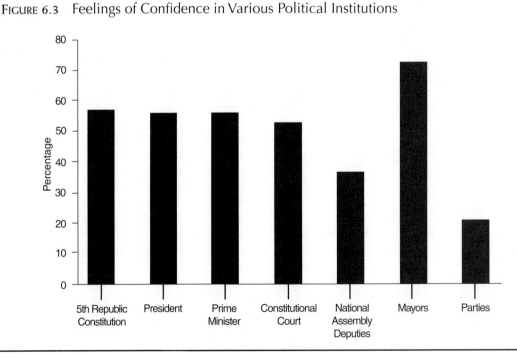

Source: Sofres, L'Etat de L'Opinion 2001 (Paris: Editions du Seuil, 2001), p. 81.

Until well into the present century, the mutual hostility between believers and nonbelievers was one of the main features of the political culture. Since the Revolution, it has divided society and political life at all levels. Even now, there are important differences between the political behavior of practicing Catholics and nonbelievers.

French Catholics historically viewed the Revolution of 1789 as the work of satanic men, and enemies of the Church became militant in their opposition to Catholic forms and symbols. This division continued through the nineteenth century. With the establishment of the Third Republic in 1875, differences between the political subcultures of Catholicism and anticlericalism deepened further. After a few years, militant anti-clericalism took firm control of the Republic. Parliament rescinded the centuries-old compact with the Vatican, expelled most Catholic orders, and severed all ties between church and state, so that "the moral unity of the country could be reestablished." The militancy of the Republican regime was matched by the Pope, who excommunicated every deputy who voted for the separation laws in 1905. As in other European Catholic countries, the difference between the political right and left was largely determined by attitudes toward the Catholic Church.

The gap began to narrow during the interwar period and after Catholics and agnostics found themselves side by side, and sometimes joined together, in the resistance movement during World War II. Nevertheless, the depth of religious practice continues to be the best predictor—with remarkable stability—of whether a voter will support an established party of the right.

Religious practice has been declining in France and many other industrialized countries since the 1950s among all social groups, with only 10 to 12 percent of the French population attending church regularly today. The decline has been greatest among those groups that were the most observant. Farmers are the most observant group in France, but their church attendance is only 23 percent. Blue-collar workers, for most of this century, have been the least observant: Now only 4 percent admit to attending church regularly. In addition to secularization trends, important changes have occurred within the Catholic subculture. Today, the vast majority of self-identified Catholics reject some of the most important teachings of the Church, including its positions on abortion, premarital sex, and marriage of priests. Even among regularly practicing Catholics, there is considerable opposition to the positions of the Church. Only 16 percent of identified Catholics perceive the role of the Church as important in political life, and Catholicism no longer functions as a well-integrated community, with a common view of the world and common social values. In 2000, there were half the number of Catholic priests as in 1960, and a 75 percent decline of ordinations. Most private schools in France are Catholic parochial schools, which the state has subsidized since the Fourth Republic. The status of these schools (in a country in which state support for Catholic schools coexists with the separation of church and state) has never been fully settled. In 1998, 10 percent of primary schools, and 32 percent of secondary schools, were private. Although church attendance continues to decline, there remains considerable support for parochial education.

French Jews (numbering about 600,000 or 1 percent of the population since the exodus that followed Algerian independence in 1962) are sufficiently well integrated into French society so that it is not possible to speak of a Jewish vote. One study demonstrates that, like other French voters, Jews tend to vote left or right, according to degree of religious practice. Nevertheless, Jews have consistently supported the Republic. Recent surveys in 2002 indicate a substantially higher rate of synagogue attendance among French who identify as Jewish, compared with Catholics (24 percent). Although anti-Semitic attitudes and behavior are not widespread in France, attacks against Jews and Jewish institutions—mostly by young maghrebian men in mixed areas of large cities—increased dramatically between the end of 2000 and 2002. Linked to the emergence of the second intifada in the Middle East, these incidents were also related to emerging patterns of urban ethnic conflict in France.

Protestants (just under 1 million or 1.7 percent of the population and growing) have, lived somewhat apart, with heavy concentrations in Alsace, in Paris, and in some regions of central and southeastern France. About two-thirds of Protestants belong to the upper bourgeoisie. The proportion of Protestants in high public positions has been very large. Until recently, they usually voted more leftist than others in their socioeconomic position or in the same region. Although many Protestants are prominent in the Socialist Party, since the 1950s their electoral behavior, like their activities in cultural and economic associations, is determined by factors other than religion.

Islam is now France's second religion. It is estimated that there are 4 to 4.5 million *Muslims* in France, two-thirds of whom are immigrants or their descendants from Muslim countries. The emergence of Islamic institutions in France is part of a larger phenomenon of integrating new immigration into France. In the last decade the affirmation of religious identification coincided with (and to some extent was a part of) the social and political mobilization of immigrants from Muslim countries. There are now over a thousand mosques in France, as well as another thousand rooms set aside for prayer. In 2002 the government created an official representative council (CFCM) to represent Islam with public authorities (similar institutions exist for Jews and Catholics). Nevertheless, a survey in 2002 indicates that regular attendance of services at mosques is about the same as church attendance of Catholics, and that more than 40 percent of those who identify as Muslims say that they never attend services.

The emergence of Islam has challenged the traditional French view of the separation of church and state. Unlike Catholics and Jews, who maintain their own schools, or Protestants, who have supported the principle of secular state schools, some Muslim groups have insisted both on the right to attend state schools and to follow practices considered contrary to the French tradition of secularism by state education authorities. Small numbers of Muslims have challenged dress codes, school curriculum, and school requirements, and have more generally questioned more muscular notions of *laicite*. In response to this challenge, and to reaffirm the secular nature of the public schools, the French Parliament passed legislation in 2004 that banned the wearing of "ostentatious" religious symbols in primary and secondary schools. Although the language was neutral about religion, the law was widely seen as an attempt to prevent the wearing of Islamic head scarves by Muslim girls. Although the new law was widely debated, it was also strongly supported by the French public. A sample of Muslim women surveyed two months before the law was passed also supported it.

Class and Status

Feelings about class differences shape a society's authority pattern and the style in which authority is exercised. The French, like the English, are very conscious of living in a society divided into classes. But since equality is valued more highly in France than in England, deference toward the upper classes is far less developed, and resentful antagonism is widespread.

The number of those who are conscious of belonging to a social class is relatively high in France, particularly among workers. One important study, for example, found a far greater intensity of spontaneous class consciousness among French workers in the 1970s than among comparable groups of British workers.[5] Yet, spontaneous class identity has been declining. In 1994, 61 percent of respondents felt that they belonged to a class, compared with 68 percent 18 years earlier. The decline of class commitments is greatest among blue-collar workers (down to 47 percent) and least among white-collar employees and executives. One survey in 1997 revealed that a majority of workers identified themselves as middle class. Among middle managers, feelings of class identity had actually increased. By the 1990s French workers identified themselves as belonging to a class less frequently than any other major salaried group.

Existing evidence indicates that economic and social transformations have reduced the level of class identification but have not eradicated subjective feelings about class differences and class antagonism. Indeed, the strike movements during the past four years seem to have intensified class feelings. In addition, as the number of immigrant workers among the least qualified workers has grown, traditional class differences are reinforced by a growing sense of racial and ethnic differences.

POLITICAL SOCIALIZATION

The attitudinal patterns that we have analyzed here have been shaped through experience with the political system, as well as through some key institutions and agents. Some agents, such as political associations, act to socialize political values quite directly, while others, such as the family and the media, act in a more indirect manner.

In an old country like France, agents of political socialization change slowly, even when regimes change rapidly. Socializing agents are carriers of a broader cultural tradition. Like any other teaching process, political socialization passes on from one generation to the next "a mixture of attitudes developed in a mixture of historical periods." But "traditions, everyone agrees, do not form a constituted and fixed set of values, of knowledge and of representations; socialization never functions as a simple mechanism of identical reproduction . . . [but rather as] an important instrument for the reorganization and the reinvention of tradition."[6]

Family

For those French who view their neighbors and fellow citizens with distrust, and the institutions around them with cynicism, the family is a safe haven. Concern for stability, steady income, property, and continuity were common to bourgeois and peasant families, though not to urban or agricultural workers. The training of children in bourgeois and peasant families was often marked by close supervision, incessant correction, and strict sanctions.

Particularly during the last 20 years, the life of the French family, the role of its members, and its relationship to outsiders have undergone fundamental, and sometimes contradictory, changes. Very few people condemn the idea of couples living together without being married. In 2001, 44 percent of all births were outside of marriage (compared with 6.4 percent in 1968), a percentage only slightly lower than in the United States, and higher than almost any other European country. The proportion of births outside of marriage is highest among women outside of the labor force and working-class women (with the notable exception of immigrant women). Almost none of these children are in one-parent families, however, since in virtually all cases they are legally recognized by both parents before their first birthday. Nevertheless, 15 percent of children below the age of 19 live with only one of their natural parents, mostly due to divorce. The number of divorces was more than 40 percent the number of marriages in 2000, and it has almost doubled since 1976, when new and more flexible divorce legislation came into effect.

Legislative changes have only gradually modified the legal restrictions on married women that existed in the Napoléonic legal codes. Not until 1970 did the law proclaim the absolute equality of the two parents in the exercise of parental authority and for the moral and material management of the family. Labor-saving devices for house and farm have been described as the "secret agents of modernity" in the countryside.[7] Almost half of all women over the age of 15 are now employed, and 80 percent of French women between the ages of 25 and 49 are now working continuously during their adult years.

The employment of a greater number of married women has affected the role of the family as a vehicle of socialization. Working women differ from those who are not employed in regard to moral concepts, religious practice, political interest, electoral participation, party alignment, and so on. In their general orientations, employed women are far closer to the men of the milieu, the class, or the age group to which they belong, than to women who are not employed.[8]

Although family structure, values, and behavior have changed, the family remains an important structure through which political values broadly conceived are transmitted from generation to generation. Several studies demonstrate a significant influence of parents over the religious socialization and the left-right political choices made by their children.[9]

There is perhaps no greater tribute to the continuing effectiveness of the French family than the results of a survey of French youth taken by the French government in 1994. With 25 percent of 18- to 24-year-olds unemployed, it was hardly surprising that the survey revealed that 78 percent of young people had little confidence in the schools to prepare them for the future. What was more surprising was how much confidence young people had in their families. More than 75 percent felt that their parents had confidence in them, that they were loved at home, and that their families had prepared them well for the future. In a survey taken in 1999, the family was ranked second only to school as a source of deep and durable friendship. The effectiveness of the family as an agent of socialization for general religious and ideological orientations does not mean that succeeding generations do not have formative experiences of their own or that there are no significant differences in the political commitments of different age cohorts. Therefore, political socialization is a product not only of the family experience but also of childhood experiences with peers, education, and the changing larger world. Thus young people of Algerian origin, born in France, are somewhat more likely than their counterparts of French origin to practice, but are far less likely to practice their faith than their counterparts born in Algeria.[10]

Associations and Socialization

The French bias against authority might have encouraged social groups and associations if the egalitarian thrust and the competition between individuals did not work in the opposite direction. The French ambivalence about participation in group life is not merely negativistic apathy but is related to a lack of belief in the value of cooperation. On the one hand, this cultural ambivalence is reinforced by legal restrictions on associational life, as well as by a strong republican tradition hostile to groups serving as intermediaries between the people and the state. On the other hand, the state and local governments traditionally subsidize numerous associations (including trade unions) and give some associations (not always the same ones that were subsidized) privileged access to decision-making power.

After World War II, *overall* membership in associations in France was comparable to other European countries, but lower than in the United States. However, group membership in France was concentrated in politicized associations that reinforced existing social divisions and was less common for independent social and fraternal groups. Membership in key professional organizations, especially trade

unions, was much lower in France than in other European countries.

The number of associations has sharply increased over the past two decades, while the overall percentage of membership among the adult population remained relatively constant. The pattern of association, however, changed considerably. The more traditional advocacy and political groups, politicized unions, and professional associations suffered sharp declines in absolute (and proportional) membership. Sports associations, self-help groups, and newly established ethnic associations now attract larger numbers of people. As more middle-class people have joined associations, working-class people have dropped out.[11] To some extent these changes reflect shifting attitudes about political commitment in France. Although associational life remains strong, *militantisme* (with its implication of deep and abiding commitment) has clearly diminished. Older advocacy and professional associations that were built on this kind of commitment have declined, while newer groups have been built on different and often more limited commitment.

New legislation has also produced changes. A law passed in 1981 made it possible for immigrant groups to form their own organizations. This encouraged the emergence of thousands of ethnic associations. Decentralization legislation passed a few years later encouraged municipalities to support the creation of local associations to perform municipal services.

Even with these changing patterns, there remain uncertainties about the role of associations, old and new, in the socialization process of individuals. Some observers seem to confirm that membership in French organizations involves less actual participation than in American or British organizations and hence has less impact on social and political attitudes. Cultural distrust is manifest less in lower overall membership than in the inability of organizational leaders to relate to their members and to mobilize them for action.

Education

One of the most important ways a community preserves and transmits its cultural and political values is through education. Napoléon Bonaparte recognized the significance of education. Well into the second half of the twentieth century the French educational system remained an imposing historical monument, in the unmistakable style of the First Empire. The edifice Napoléon erected combined education at all levels, from primary school to postgraduate professional training, into one centralized corporation: the imperial university. Its job was to teach the national doctrine through uniform programs at various levels. As the strict military discipline of the Napoléonic model has been loosened by succeeding regimes, each has discovered that the machinery created by Napoléon was a convenient and coherent instrument for transmitting the values—both changing and permanent—of French civilization. The centralized imperial university has therefore never been truly dismantled. The Minister of Education, who presides over a ministry that employs almost a million people, continues to control curriculum and teaching methods, the criteria for selection and advancement of pupils and teachers, and the content of examinations.

Making advancement at every step dependent on passing an examination is not peculiar to France (it is also a pattern in Japan, as well as other countries). What is distinctly French is an obsessive and quite unrealistic belief that everybody is equal before an examination. The idea that education is an effective weapon for emancipation and social betterment has had popular as well as official recognition. Farmers and workers regard the instruction of their children, a better instruction than they had, as an important weapon in the fight against the others in an oppressive world. The *baccalauréat*—the certificate of completion of the academic secondary school, the lycée—remains almost the sole means of access to higher education. But such a system suits and profits best those self-motivated middle-class children for whom it was designed.

During the Fifth Republic, the structure of the French educational system has undergone significant change. The secondary schools, which trained only 700,000 students as late as 1945, now provide instruction for almost 6 million. Between 1958 and 1998, the number of students in higher education rose from 170,000 to 2.1 million. By 1998 the pro-

portion of 20- to 24-year-olds in higher education (40 percent) was as high as that of any other European country.[12]

The introduction of a comprehensive middle school with a common core curriculum in 1963 basically altered the system of early academic selection, and other reforms eliminated rigid ability tracking. However, implementation of reforms, whether passed by governments of the right or the left, has often been difficult because of opposition from middle-class parents and from teachers' unions of the left.[13] Although more than 60 percent of the young passed the baccalauréat in 2001 (double the proportion of 1980), education reforms have altered only slightly the vast differences in the success of children from different social backgrounds.

Because of the principle of open admission, every holder of the baccalauréat can gain entrance to a university. There is, as in some American state universities, a rather ruthless elimination at the end of the first year and sometimes later. Here again students of lower-class background fare worse than the others. In addition, the number of students from such backgrounds is disproportionately great in fields in which diplomas have the lowest value in the professional market and where unemployment is greatest.

The most ambitious attempt to reform the university system at one stroke came in the wake of the student rebellion of 1968, followed by other reforms in the 1970s and 1980s. They strove, by different means, to encourage the autonomy of each university; the participation of teachers, students, and staff in the running of the university; and the collaboration among different disciplines. The government, because of massive protest demonstrations in the streets, though duly enacted, subsequently withdrew some of the reforms. Others failed to be implemented because of the widespread resistance by those concerned. Administrative autonomy has remained fragmentary as the ministry has held the financial purse strings as well as the right to grant degrees. Today the widely lamented crisis of the university system has hardly been alleviated, although the size of the student population appears to have stabilized.

An additional characteristic of the French system of higher education is the parallel system of *grandes écoles*, a sector of higher education that functions outside of the network of universities under rules that permit a high degree of selectivity. As university enrollment has multiplied (by more than 500 percent since 1960), the more prestigious grandes écoles have only modestly increased the number of students admitted upon strict entrance examinations.[14] For more than a century the grandes écoles have been the training ground of highly specialized elites. The schools prepare students for careers in engineering, business management, and the top ranks of the civil service. Their different recruitment of students and of teaching staffs as well as their teaching methods influence the outlook and even the temperament of many of their graduates. In contrast to university graduates, virtually all graduates of the grandes écoles are immediately placed and often assume positions of great responsibility (see pp. 19).

Socialization and Communication

In a country such as France, the political effectiveness of the mass media is often determined by the way in which people appraise its integrity and whether they believe that it serves or disturbs the functioning of the political system. In the past, business firms, tycoons, political parties, and governments (both French and foreign) often backed major newspapers. Today, the press operates under the same conditions as it does in other Western democracies, except that daily press revenue from advertising remains lower than elsewhere. Most newspapers and magazines are owned by business enterprises, many of them conglomerates that extend into fields other than periodical publications.

In spite of a growth in population, the circulation of daily newspapers and their number has been declining since World War II. The decline in readership, a common phenomenon in most European democracies, is due, among other factors, to competition from other media such as television, radio, and the Internet. The number of newspapers has also declined.

Television has replaced all other media as a primary source of political information in France,

and to a greater extent than in Germany, Britain, or the United States.[15] Television is increasingly the primary mediator between political forces and individual citizens, and, as in other countries, it has an impact on the organization and substance of politics. First, a personality that plays well on television (not just a unique personality such as Charles de Gaulle) is now an essential ingredient of politics. As in other countries, image and spectacle are important elements of politics. Second, television helps set the agenda of political issues, by choosing among the great variety of themes, problems, and issues dealt with by political and social forces, and by magnifying them for mass publics. Finally, television is the arena within which national electoral campaigns take place, largely displacing mass rallies and meetings. Nevertheless, confidence in various sources of political information varies among different groups. Young people and shopkeepers are most confident in radio information, while managers are more confident in the written press than television for political information.

Until 1982, all broadcasting and television stations that originated programs on French territory were owned by the state and operated by personnel whom the state appointed and remunerated. Since then, the basic system of state monopoly gradually has been dismantled. As a first and quite important step, the (Socialist) government authorized private radio stations. The move attempted to regularize and regulate more than a thousand pirate radio stations already in existence. Inevitably, this vast network of 1,600 stations is becoming increasingly consolidated—not by the state but by private entrepreneurs who provide programming services, and who in some instances are effectively buying control of a large number of local stations.

The 1982 legislation also reorganized the public television system. It granted new rights of reply to government communications and allotted free time to all political parties during electoral campaigns. During the following years, however, these changes were dwarfed by a process of gradual privatization, begun under the Socialists and continued by the conservatives after 1986, and by the globalization of television broadcasting. Today, well more than 100 television channels are available to French viewers, compared with 30 in 1990 and 3 in 1980.

RECRUITMENT AND STYLE OF ELITES

Until the Fifth Republic, Parliament provided the core of French decision makers. Besides members of Parliament, elected officers of municipalities or departments, some local party leaders, and a few journalists of national renown were counted among what is known in France as the political class, altogether comprising not more than 15,000 or 20,000 persons. All gravitated toward the halls of the National Assembly or the Senate.

Compared with the British House of Commons, the membership of the National Assembly has always been of more modest social origin. From about 1879 on, professionals (lawyers, doctors, and journalists) increasingly dominated the Chamber of Deputies, now called the National Assembly; the vast majority were local notables, trained in law and experienced in local administration.

A substantial change in political recruitment occurred during the Fourth Republic, when for the first time the percentage of self-employed and farmers became a minority. The steadily diminishing share of blue- and white-collar workers during the Fifth Republic is partially due to the professionalization of parliamentary personnel, as well as by the decline of the Communist Party that began in the 1980s.

What is most striking about the professional background of legislators is the number who come from the public sector: almost half the deputies in the 1980s, and 44 percent after the victory of the left in 1997. The number of top civil servants in the National Assembly has risen constantly since 1958, and the left landslide of 1981 only accentuated this process. Although the majority of high civil servants lean toward parties of the right, more than a third of those who sat in the Assembly elected in 1997 were part of the Socialist group. Even more important than their number is the political weight that these deputy-bureaucrats carry in Parliament. Some of the civil servants who run for election to Parliament have previously held positions in the political executive, either as members of the ministerial staffs or as junior ministers. Not surprisingly,

in Parliament they are frequently candidates for a post in the Cabinet.

More than in any other Western democracy, the highest ranks of the civil service are the training and recruitment grounds for top positions in both politics and industry. Among the high civil servants, about 2,300 are members of the most important administrative agencies, the *grands corps*, from which the vast majority of the roughly 500 administrators engaged in political decision making are drawn.[16] The recruitment base of the highest levels of the civil service remains extremely narrow. The knowledge and capability required to pass the various examinations gives clear advantages to the children of senior civil servants. As a result, the ranking bureaucracy forms something approaching a hereditary class. There have been several important attempts to develop a system of more open recruitment into the higher civil service, but all of them have been only marginally successful.

The *Ecole Nationale d'Administration (ENA)* and the *Ecole Polytechnique*, together with the other grandes écoles, play an essential role in the recruitment of administrative, political, and business elites. Virtually all the members of the most prestigious grands corps are recruited directly from the graduating classes of the ENA and the Polytechnique (many of whose graduates have also attended other grandes écoles). What differentiates the members of the grands corps from other ranking administrators is their general competence and mobility. At any one time as many as two-thirds of the members of one of these corps might be on leave or on special missions to other administrative agencies or special assignments to positions of influence.

They might also be engaged in politics either as members of Parliament (46 in the National Assembly elected in 1997) and of local government, or as members of the executive: 11 of the 17 prime ministers who have served since 1959 have been members of a grand corps who attended a grande école. The percentage of ministers in any given government who are members of one of the grand corps has varied between 10 and 60 percent. When Jean-Pierre Raffarin became prime minister in April 2002, he was widely described as an "outsider," in part because his political career had been primarily in the provinces, and because he had *not* been a student at ENA. One study calculates that 40 percent of those who graduated from ENA between 1960 and 1990 served as ministerial advisers. Thus the grandes écoles—grands corps group, though small in membership, produces a remarkable proportion of the country's political elite.

The same system is also becoming increasingly important in recruiting high business executives. Movement from the public sector to the private sector is facilitated because members of the grands corps can go on leave for years, while they retain their seniority and pension rights, as well as the right to return to their job.[17] (Few who leave do in fact return.) In 1993, 47 percent of the directors of the 200 largest companies in France were from the civil service (up from 41 percent in 1985). In the early 1990s, 17 percent of all ENA graduates were working in French industry. Moreover, though the number of ENA graduates is small (about 170 a year), it is three times larger now than in the early 1960s.

Thus the relationship between the grandes écoles and the grands corps, on the one hand, and politics and business, on the other hand, provides structure for an influential elite and survives changes in the political orientation of governments. While this system is not politically monolithic, the narrowness of its recruitment contributes to a persistent similarity of style and operation, and to the fairly stable—at times rigid—value system of its operators.

For outsiders, this tight network is difficult to penetrate. Even during the 1980s—the period when industrial restructuring and privatization of state-run enterprises encouraged a new breed of freewheeling businesspeople in the United States under Reagan and in Britain under Thatcher—a similar process had a very limited impact on the recruitment of new elites in France.

The Importance of Gender

The representation of women among French political elites is close to the lowest in Western Europe. Women comprise well over half the electorate, but barely 12 percent of the deputies in the National Assembly in 2002 and only 6 percent of the members of the Senate are women. Women fare better at

the local level, where they comprised 47.7 percent of the municipal councilors elected in 2001, more than double those elected six years before.

Political parties structure access to political representation far more in France than in the United States, and the left has generally made a greater effort to recruit women than has the right. Thus, when the Socialists and Communists gained a substantial number of seats in the 1997 legislative elections, the proportion of women in the National Assembly almost doubled. In contrast to the United States, political advancement in France has generally required a deep involvement in political parties, with a bias in favor of professional politicians and administrators. However, relatively few women have made this kind of long-term commitment to political life. Nevertheless, despite the losses of the left in the legislative elections of 2002, as a result of the parity legislation passed in 1999 (see following discussion), the number of women in the new assembly actually increased slightly.

Periodically, governments and the political parties recognize this dearth of women's representation, but little has been done. Either the Constitutional Council has rejected the remedies, or the proposed reforms have challenged accepted institutional norms. In 1982, the Constitutional Council overturned legislation that restricted party lists for municipal council elections to no more than 75 percent candidates of one gender. By the 1990s there was a growing consensus among leaders of all political parties in favor of amending the Constitution to permit positive discrimination in favor of greater gender parity in representative institutions. Thus, with support of both the president of the Republic and the prime minister and without dissent, the National Assembly passed an amendment in December 1998 that stipulated that " . . . the law [and not the constitution] determines the conditions for the organization of equal access of men and women to electoral mandates and elective functions." Enforcement legislation requires greater gender parity at least in the selection of candidates. This is a significant departure for the French political system, which has resisted the use of quotas in the name of republican equality.

Perhaps the most important change in the political behavior of French women is in their voting patterns. During the Fourth Republic, a majority of women consistently voted for parties of the right. However, as church attendance among women has declined, their political orientation moved from right to left. In every national election since the 1980s, a clear majority of women have voted for the left.[18]

INTEREST GROUPS

The Expression of Interests

As in many other European countries, the organization of French political life is largely defined within the historical cleavages of class and religious traditions. Interest groups have therefore frequently shared ideological roots and commitments with the political parties with which they have occasionally had organizational connections.

Actual memberships in almost all groups engaged in economic production have varied considerably over time by sector, but they are generally much smaller than comparable groups in other industrialized countries. In 1997 no more than 8 percent of workers belonged to trade unions (a decline of half over 25 years—the greatest decline in Western Europe); about 50 percent of French farmers and 75 percent of large industrial enterprises belonged to their respective organizations (see following discussion).[19] Historically, many of the important economic groups have experienced a surge of new members at dramatic moments in the country's social or political history. But membership then declines as conditions have normalized, leaving some associations with too small a membership to justify their claims of representativeness.

Many groups lack the resources to employ a competent staff, or they depend on direct and indirect forms of state support. The modern interest group official is a fairly recent phenomenon that is found only in certain sectors of the group system, such as business associations.

Interest groups have also been weakened by ideological division. Separate groups that defend the interests of workers, farmers, veterans, schoolchildren, and consumers are divided in France by ideological preferences. The ideological division of representation forces each organization to compete for the same clientele in order to establish their representativeness. Consequently, even established French interest groups exhibit a radicalism in action and goals that is rare in other Western democracies. For groups that lack the means of using the information media, such tactics also become a way to put their case before the public at large. In such a setting, even the defense of purely economic, social, or cultural interests takes on a political color.

The Labor Movement

The French labor movement is divided into national confederations of differing political sympathies, although historical experiences have driven French labor, unlike other European trade unions, to avoid direct organizational ties with political parties.[20] Membership has declined steeply since 1975, but there are indications that the decline has leveled off since 1994. Nevertheless, although union membership is declining in almost every industrialized country, it is now the lowest by far in France (see Chapter 3). Surveys show that the youngest group of salaried workers has virtually deserted the trade union movement. After 1990, candidates supported by nonunion groups in various plant-level elections have attracted more votes than any of the established union organizations.[21] In fact, unions have been losing members and (electoral) support at the very time when the French trade union movement has become better institutionalized at the workplace and better protected by legislation.

Despite these clear weaknesses, French workers still maintain considerable (and increasing) confidence in unions to defend their interests during periods of labor conflict. Strike levels and support for collective action have risen since 1994, as well as confidence in unions and their leadership of strike movements. Indeed, during the massive strikes of public service workers in the fall of 1995, truckers in the fall of 1996, and truckers and taxi drivers (protesting against the rising price of oil) in the fall of 2000, public support for the strikers remained far higher than confidence in the government against which the strikes were directed.[22] However, it is important to keep in mind that, even though there are occasional massive strikes in France, strike levels are declining over the past 30 years.

French labor has had the most difficulty dealing with ideological fragmentation. Indeed, the decline in membership has not encouraged consolidation, but it has resulted in more fragmentation (see following discussion). Unlike the United States, French workers in the same plant or firm may be represented by several union federations. As a result, there is constant competition among unions at every level for membership and support. Even during periods when the national unions agree to act together, animosities at the plant level sometimes prevent cooperation. Moreover, the weakness of union organization at the plant level—which is where most lengthy strikes are called—means that unions are difficult bargaining partners. Unions at this level maintain only weak control over the strike weapon. Union militants are quite adept at sensitizing workers, and in engendering many of the preconditions for strike action as well as channeling strike movements once they begin. However, the unions have considerable difficulty in effectively calling strikes and ending them. Thus unions are highly dependent on the general environment, what they call the social climate, in order to support their positions at the bargaining table. Because their ability to mobilize workers at any given moment is an essential criterion of their representativeness, union ability to represent workers is frequently in question.

Legislation passed by the government of the left in 1982–1983 (the Auroux laws) sought to strengthen the union's position at the plant level. By creating an "obligation to negotiate" for management and by protecting the right of expression for workers, the government hoped to stimulate collective negotiations. In fact, this type of Wagner Act (the basic law of U.S. industrial relations) of French labor brought about some important changes in industrial relations and stimulated collective negotiations. However, given their increasing weakness, unions have not taken full advantage of the potential benefits of the legislation. This law refocused French industrial relations on the plant level without necessarily increasing the effectiveness of unions. The small number of union representatives,

increasingly involved in committees and discussions, appears to have lost much contact with workers on the shop floor.

The oldest and, by some measures, the largest of the union confederations is the *Confédération Générale du Travail* (CGT, General Confederation of Labor). Since World War II, the CGT is identified closely with the Communist Party, with which it maintains a considerable overlap of leadership. Yet by tradition, and by its relative effectiveness as the largest labor organization, it enrolls many non-Communists among its members. Its domination diminished in the 1990s, however, mostly because the CGT lost more members and support than all other unions.

The second strongest labor organization is the *Confédération Française Democratique du Travail* (CFDT, French Democratic Confederation of Labor). In many ways, the CFDT is the most original and the most interesting of all labor movements in Western Europe. An offshoot of a Catholic trade union movement, its earlier calls for worker self-management (*autogestion*) were integrated into the Auroux laws. The leaders of the CFDT see the policy of the confederation as an alternative to the oppositional stance of the CGT. The CFDT now offers itself as a potential partner to modern capitalist management. This movement to the right created splits within several CFDT public service unions, and the establishment of a national rival, the *Solidaire Unitaire et Democratique* (SUD, Solidarity United and Democratic) in 1989. The split was further accentuated by CFDT's opposition to the massive public service strike of 1995. SUD, in turn, was integrated in 1998 into a larger group of militant autonomous unions, *G-10* (le Groupe des dix) in 1998. G-10 now consists of some 27 autonomous unions.

The third major labor confederation, *Force Ouvrière* (FO, Workers' Force), formed at the beginning of the Cold War in 1948 in reaction to the Communist domination of the CGT. It is the only major trade union organization that claims to have gained membership in recent years. This relative success is certainly connected with the steady decline of the Communist Party. The FO adheres to a position that is close to the traditions of American trade unionism and focuses on collective bargaining as a counterweight to employers and the state. Nevertheless, during the strike movements of 1995 and 1996, FO leadership strongly supported the more radical elements of striking workers, and continues to be dominated by trotskyist elements of the left.

One of the most important and influential of the "autonomous" unions is the *Fédération de l'Education Nationale* (FEN, Federation of National Education), the teachers' union. At the end of 1992, as a result of growing internal conflict and declining membership, FEN split. The rump of FEN joined with other independent unions to form the *Union Nationale des Syndicats Autonomes* (UNSA, National Union of Autonomous Unions), and in October 1994, was officially recognized by the government. In legal terms this means that the government places the UNSA on the same level as the other national confederations. Nevertheless, by 1996, FEN (and UNSA) was substantially weakened, when the rival *La Fédération Syndicale Unitaire* (FSU, United Union Federation)—which is close to the Communist Party—gained greater support in social elections, support that was reaffirmed in 1999.

In addition to the fragmentation that results from differences within existing organizations, there are also challenges from the outside. In 1995 the National Front took the initiative to organize several new unions. When the government and the courts blocked these initiatives, the extreme-right party began to penetrate existing unions.

Thus, at a time when strong opposition to government action and growing support for strike mobilization seems to give union organizations an opportunity to increase both their organizational strength and their support, the trade union movement is more fragmented than it has ever been before. As in the past, massive strike movements have accentuated divisions and rivalries rather than provoke unity.

Business Interests

Since the end of World War II, French business has kept most trade associations and employers' organizations within one dominant and exceptionally well-staffed confederation, renamed in 1998 the *Mouvement des Entreprises de France* (MEDEF, The Movement of French Business). However, divergent interests, differing economic concepts, and indeed conflicting ideologies frequently prevent the national organization from acting forcefully and at times hamper its representativeness in negotiations with government or trade unions. Nevertheless, the MEDEF (formerly called CNPF—the National Confederation of French Business) weathered the difficult years of the nationalization introduced by the Socialists, and the restructuring of social legislation and industrial relations, without lessening its status as an influential interest group.

Since the MEDEF is dominated primarily by big business, shopkeepers and the owners of many small firms feel that they are better defended by more movement-oriented groups than by the streamlined modern lobby of the MEDEF.[23] As a result, a succession of small business and shopkeeper movements have challenged the established organization and evolved into organized associations in their own right.

Agricultural Interests

The defense of agricultural interests has a long record of internal strife. However, under the Fifth Republic, the *Fédération Nationale des Syndicats Agricoles* (FNSEA, National Federation of Agricultural Unions), though one of several farm organizations, has dominated this sector. The FNSEA has also served as an effective instrument for modernizing French agriculture. The rural reform legislation of the 1960s provided for the "collaboration of the professional agricultural organizations," and from the outset real collaboration was offered only to the FNSEA. From this privileged position the federation gained both patronage and control over key institutions that were transforming agriculture. It used these instruments to organize a large proportion of French farmers. Thus, having established its domination over the farming sector with the support of a succession of governments, it then periodically demonstrated opposition to government policy with the support of the vast majority of a declining number of farmers.[24]

The principal challenges to the FNSEA in recent years are external rather than internal, as the agricultural sector has suffered from the fruits of its own productive success. Under pressure from the *European Union (EU)*, France agreed in 1992 to major reforms of the Common Agricultural Policy. These reforms took substantial amounts of land out of production and replaced some price supports with direct payments to farmers. That same year, the European Union reached an agreement with the United States to reduce subsidized grain exports and cut back cultivation of oilseed products. France is the largest exporter of these products in the EU, and FNSEA protests (some of them violent) were joined by farm unions from throughout the EU, which ultimately resulted in a face-saving GATT accord in 1994. Pressures to further reduce the budget of CAP have only increased with the process of expansion of the EU toward the east. The substantial opposition in France (and other parts of Europe) to the importation of genetically modified agricultural products has increased the tensions with WTO (formerly GATT).

French organized interests are expressed through an impressive range of different kinds of organizations, from the weak and fragmented trade union movement to the well-organized FNSEA. Overall, what seems to differentiate French groups from those of other industrial countries is their style of expression and their forms of activity.

Means of Access and Styles of Action

In preceding regimes, organized interests found Parliament the most convenient means of access to political power. During the Third and Fourth Republics, the highly specialized and powerful committees of both houses of Parliament often seemed to be little more than institutional facades for interest groups that frequently substituted bills of their own design for those submitted by the government.

Among the reasons given in 1958 for reforming and rationalizing Parliament was the desire to reduce the role of organized interests in the legislative process. By and large this has been accomplished. But interest groups have not lost all influence on rule making and policy formation. To be effective, groups now use the channels that the best equipped groups have long found most rewarding, channels

that give them direct access to the administration. The indispensable collaboration between organized private interests and the state is institutionalized in advisory committees that are attached to most administrative agencies. These committees are composed mainly of civil servants and group representatives. Nonetheless, tendencies toward privileged access, sometimes called *neocorporatism* (see following discussion and Chapter 3), have, with the exception of agriculture and big business, remained weak in France. The weak organization of the labor and small business sectors means that organizations in these sectors are often regarded as unreliable partners. Organized interests also attempt to pressure the political executive. The ministerial staffs—the circle of personal collaborators who support every French minister—are an important target. Inasmuch as the present regime strengthened the position of the political executive, it also enabled both the prime minister and the president to function more effectively as arbiters between competing claims and to exercise stricter control over many agencies and ministries.

It is not surprising that some interests have easier access to governmental bureaus than others. An affinity of views between group representatives and public administrators might be based on common outlook, common social origin, or education. The official of an important trade association or of their well-organized peak association, who already sorted out the raw demands of constituents and submits them in rational fashion, easily gets a more sympathetic hearing in the bureaus than an organization that seeks to defend atomistic interests by mobilizing latent resentment.

High civil servants tend to distinguish between "professional organizations," which they consider serious or dynamic enough to listen to, and "interest groups," which should be kept at a distance. The perspectives of interest representatives tend to reflect their own strength as well as their experience in collaborating with different parts of the state and government. Trade union representatives acknowledge their reliance on the social climate (the level of strike activity) to determine their ability to bargain effectively with the state. Representatives of business claim to rely more on contacts with civil servants, compared with those of agriculture who say that they rely more on contacts at the ministerial level.[25]

Central to the kind of state interest group collaboration described as neocorporatism is the notion that the state plays a key role in both shaping and defining the legitimacy of the interest group universe. The state also establishes the rules by which the collaboration takes place. The French state, at various levels, strongly influences the relationship among groups and even their existence in key areas through official recognition and subsidization. Although representative organizations may exist with or without official recognition, this designation gives them access to consultative bodies, the right to sign collective agreements (especially important in the case of trade unions), and the right to certain forms of subsidies. Therefore recognition is an important tool that both conservative and Socialist governments have used to influence the group universe.

The French state subsidizes interest groups, both indirectly and directly. By favoring some groups over others through recognition and subsidization, the role of the state seems to conform to neocorporatist criteria. However, in other ways the neocorporatist model is less applicable in France than in other European countries. Neocorporatist policymaking presumes close collaboration between the state administration and a dominant interest group (or coalition of groups) in major socioeconomic sectors (agriculture, labor, and employers). Yet, what stands out in the French case, as noted previously, is the unevenness of this pattern of collaboration.[26]

If the neocorporatist pattern calls for interest group leaders to control organizational action and coordinate bargaining, for French interest groups mass action such as street demonstrations, wildcat strikes, and attacks on government property are often poorly controlled by group leadership. Indeed, it can be argued that group protest is more effective in France (at least negatively) than in other industrialized countries because it is part of a pattern of group-state relations. Protests remain limited in scope and intensity, but the government recognizes them as a valid expression of interest. Only in this way can we understand why quite frequently governments backed by a majority in parliament were ready to make concessions to weakly organized interest groups[27] (See Box 6.1.)

Box 6.1   Protest in France

During the early years of Socialist governments, more and more people—farmers, artisans, small businesspeople, truckers, doctors, medical students, all of them organized either by old-established or newly formed interest groups—took to the streets to protest impending legislation or just out of fear for their status. In quite a few cases, the demonstrations led to violence and near riots. The same scenario took place under later conservative governments. Demonstrations by college and high school students forced the withdrawal of a planned university reform under the Chirac government in 1987. A planned imposition of a "youth" minimum wage by the Balladur government in 1994 (with an 80 percent majority in the National Assembly), ostensibly to encourage greater employment of young people, was dropped when high school students opposed it in the streets of Paris and other large cities. After a month of public service strikes, and massive demonstrations in November and December 1995, the new Chirac government abandoned a plan to reorganize the nationalized railway system and revised a plan to reorganize the civil service. A year later, striking truckers won major concessions from a still weakened government. In the autumn of 2000, a protest led by truckers and taxi drivers (that spread to England) against the rising price of oil and gasoline forced the Jospin government to lower consumer taxes on fuel. Until the summer of 2000, the government benefited from unprecedented support in public opinion.

Sources: 1986—*Les Elections législatives du mars 1986* (Paris: *Le Monde*/Supplément aux dossiers et documents du Monde, 1986); 1988—*Les Elections législative du 5 juin et 12 juin 1988*(Paris: *Le Monde*/Supplément aux dossiers et documents du Monde, 1988). *Les Elections législatives du mars 1993* (Paris: *Le Monde*/Supplément aux dossiers du Monde, 1993). CSA, "Les elections legislatives du 25 mai 1997," p. 18. *Le Monde* May 27 and June 3, 1997. *The Economist*, September 16, 2000.

POLITICAL PARTIES

The Traditional Party System

Some analysts of elections see a chronic and seemingly unalterable division of the French into two large political families, each motivated by a different mood or temperament and usually classified as the right and the left. If we view elections from this perspective, political alignments have remained surprisingly stable over long periods of history. As late as 1962, the opposition to de Gaulle was strongest in departments where for more than a century republican traditions had a solid foundation. The alignments in the presidential contest of 1974 and the parliamentary elections of 1978 mirrored the same divisions. Soon thereafter, however, the left's inroads into formerly conservative strongholds had changed the traditional geographic distribution of votes. Majorities have changed at each legislative election since 1981, and few departments now remain solid bastions for either the right or the left.

The electoral system of the Fifth Republic favors a simplification of political alignments. In most constituencies runoff elections result in the confrontation of two candidates, each typically representing one of the two camps. A simple and stable division could have resulted long ago in a pattern of two parties or coalitions alternating in having power and being in opposition, and hence giving valid expression to the voters' opinions. Why has this not occurred?

Except for the Socialists and the Communists, and more recently the RPR, French party organizations have mostly remained as skeletal as political parties were in other democracies in the early nineteenth century. French parties developed in a mainly preindustrial and preurban environment, catering at first to upper-middle-class and later to middle-class elements. Their foremost and sometimes only function was to provide an organizational framework for selecting and electing candidates for local, departmental, and national offices. Even among the better-organized parties, party organization tends to be both fragmentary at the national level, and local in orientation, with only modest linkage between the two levels.

This form of representation and party organization survives largely because voters support it. An electorate that distrusts authority and wants representation to protect it against arbitrary government is likely to be suspicious of parties organized for political reform. For all their antagonism, the republican and anti-republican traditions have one thing in common: their aversion to well-established and strongly organized parties.

Party membership has always been low, except during short and dramatic situations. As late as the 1960s no more than 2 percent of registered voters were party members. In Britain and Germany, for example, some parties have more than a million members, a membership level never achieved by any French political party. Organizational weakness contributes to the endurance of a multiparty system, and a weak multiparty system feeds into the abstract and ideological style of French politics. To avoid the suggestion that they represent no more than limited interests or personalities, these weak parties phrase even the narrowest political issues in lofty ideological terms.

During the Third and Fourth Republics, neither the right nor the left could govern by itself for any length of time, because both lacked a majority and both included extreme parties that contested the legitimacy of the political order. As a normal consequence of this party system, an unstable center coalition was in control of the government most of the time, no matter what the outcome of the preceding elections. Between 1789 and the advent of the Fifth Republic, governments of the center ruled republican France for all but 30 years. In a two- or three-party system, major parties normally move toward the political center in order to gain stability and cohesion. But where extreme party plurality prevails, the center is unable to become a political force. In France, centrist coalitions were an effective, if limited, means of maintaining a regime, but an ineffective means of developing coherent policy.

The Fifth Republic created a new political framework that had a major, if gradual and mostly unforeseen, influence on all parties and on their relationships to each other. The emerging party system, in turn, had an important impact on the way that the institutions of the system actually worked.[28]

The strengthening of parliamentary party discipline in the 1970s gave meaning to strong executive leadership of president and prime minister (who were leaders of the reconstructed parties) and stabilized the political process. The main political parties also became the principal arenas to develop and debate alternative policies.

However, as the national political system became more competitive in the 1980s, the locus of policy debate shifted to political leaders, on one hand, and marginal political organizations, on the other. The main political parties continue to dominate the organization of parliamentary work and the selection of candidates, but are far less important as mass membership organizations. Thus in 2002, at least 79 parties or groups presented 8,424 candidates for 577 seats in the National Assembly, a record for the Fifth Republic. The four main parties were supported by 68 percent of the electorate, with the National Front and the Greens attracting an additional 15 percent. Thus, even if we include the National Front and the Greens, almost 18 percent of the electorate supported an array of issue-based and personality-based parties in 2002. However, only seven parties are represented in the National Assembly in four parliamentary groups, three in the right majority, four allied in the left opposition.

The Main Parties: The Right and Center

UNION FOR A POPULAR MOVEMENT   *The Union for a Popular Movement (UMP)* is the most recent direct lineal descendant of the Gaullist party. The original Gaullist party was hastily thrown together after de Gaulle's return to power in 1958. Only weeks after its birth, it won more than 20 percent of the vote and almost 40 percent of the seats in the first Parliament of the new republic in 1958 (see Table 6.1).

De Gaulle himself, preferring the methods of direct democracy, had little use for any party including his own. But his advisers, foremost among them Georges Pompidou, one of his prime ministers and later his successor, saw the need for a better organized party to win future elections and an orderly succession from the charismatic leader to Gaullism *sans* de Gaulle. In several respects the new party differed from the traditional conservative parties of the right. It appealed directly to a broad coalition of groups and classes, including a part of the working class. The party's leadership successfully built a membership that, according to claims, at one time reached several hundred thousand. Yet the membership's role was generally limited to appearing at mass meetings and assisting in propaganda efforts at election time. An important novelty was that the party's representatives in Parliament followed strict discipline in voting on policy. Electoral success increased with each contest until the landslide election, held after the *events of 1968—* the massive strikes and student demonstrations of May and June—enabled the Gaullists to hold a majority of seats in the National Assembly, a record never before attained under a republican regime in France.

For 16 years (from 1958 to 1974) both the presidency and the premiership were in Gaullist hands. In 1974, after the death of both Charles de Gaulle and Georges Pompidou, with the election of Valéry Giscard-d'Estaing—a prominent conservative who was not a Gaullist—to the presidency (with the help of part of the Gaullist leadership), the party's status deteriorated and electoral support declined.

For a time, Jacques Chirac turned around the decline of the party by restructuring it and renaming it the Rally for the Republic (RPR). His career is typical of the young generation of French political leaders. A graduate of the ENA, he entered on a political rather than a bureaucratic career. He was elected to Parliament at 34 years of age and had occupied important Cabinet posts under Pompidou. After the elections of 1974, he transformed the old Gaullist party into the *Rally for the Republic (RPR)*.

The RPR was quite different from its Gaullist predecessors. Although Chirac frequently invoked Gaullism as his inspiration, he avoided the populist language that had served the movement at its beginnings. The RPR directed its appeal to a more restricted, well-defined constituency of the right, similar to the classic conservative clientele. Its electorate overrepresents older, wealthier voters, as well as farmers (see Table 6.2); its voters are most likely to define themselves as being on the right, anti-left, positive toward business and parochial schools,

TABLE 6.1 First Ballot of French Parliamentary Elections in the Fifth Republic and Seats Won in the National Assembly in Both Ballots[a] (voting in metropolitan France)

Party	1958		1962		1967		1968		1973		1978		1981		1986[a]		1988		1993		1997		2002	
	%	Seats	%	Seats	%	Seats	%	Seats	%	Seats	%	Seats	%	Seats	%	Seats	%	Seats	%	Seats	%	Seats	%	Seats
Registered Voters (in millions)	27.2		27.5		28.3		28.3		29.9		34.4		35.5		36.6		37.9		37.0		39.2		41.0	
Abstentions (%)	22.9		31.3		19.4		19.9		18.7		16.6		29.4		21.5		34.3		31.0		32.0		35.6	
Communists (PCF)	19.1	10	21.8	41	22.5	73	20.0	34	21.2	73	20.5	86	16.2	44	9.7	35	11.3	27	9.1	24	9.9	37	4.8	21
Socialists (PS)	15.5	47	12.5	66	19.0 }	121	16.5 }	41	18.9	89	22.6	107	37.6 }	267	31.6	208	34.8	274	19.2 }	61	23.7	245	25.3 }	141
Left Radicals	—	—	—	—	}		}	8	1.5	12	2.1	10	}	14	3.0	2	1.1	2	}	8	1.5	13	}	8
Radicals	7.3	33	7.8 }																					
Center Outside Government Majority	—	—		39	12.6	41	10.3	33	12.4	31														
MRP	11.6	64	9.1	55																				
Majority	22.1	118	9.6	55																				
UDF (RI and other centrists in government majority)	—	—	4.4	36		42		61	10.6	77	21.4	119	19.2	63		129	18.5	130	18.8	207	14.8	109	4.9	22
Gaullists (RPR)	17.6	212	32.0	233	37.7 }	200	43.65 }	293	23.9	184	22.5	155	20.8	87	42.0 }	145	19.2	128	19.7	242	16.8	140	33.3[f]	362[f]
National Front (FN)	—	—	—	—	—	—	—	—	—	—	—	—	—	—	9.9	35	9.8	1	12.7	0	15.1	1	11.3	—
Others	6.8	0	2.8	17	8.2	10	9.5	16	11.5	24	10.9	14	6.2	16	6.6	23	5.3	15	20.5[b]	37[c]	18.7[d]	32[e]	16.3[g]	13

Note: In the original, curly braces (}) link the first-ballot vote percentages of allied party lists (Socialists–Left Radicals; UDF/Independent Republicans–Gaullists), indicating a combined percentage shown once.

[a] The 1986 election was by proportional representation.
[b] Includes the three Green parties which received 10.9 percent of the vote.
[c] Includes 36 unaffiliated deputies of the right.
[d] Includes the Green parties vote of 6.3 percent, as well as votes for smaller movements of the right and the left.
[e] Includes eight ecologists, seven dissident Socialists, and other unaffiliated deputies.
[f] UMP (Union of the Presidential Majority—new party of center-right organized for 2002 legislative election.
[g] Includes ecologists, dissidents of the right and left, as well as the extreme right party—MNR.
Source: Official results from the Ministry of the Interior.

TABLE 6.2   Sociological Analysis of the Electorate in the First Ballot Legislative Elections of 2002 (percentage of category voting)

	PS/PC/Greens	UMP/UDF + Other Right	FN/MNR
Sex			
Men	38%	42%	13%
Women	40	43	11
Age			
18–24	40	39	6
25–34	45	26	16
35–49	49	35	11
50–64	35	49	13
65+	28	57	13
Profession			
Shopkeepers, craftsmen, and business	31	51	9
Executives, professionals, and intellectuals	43	48	3
Middle management	53	39	3
White collar	38	38	12
Workers	49	21	18
Inactive/retired	30	51	16
Level of Education			
No degree	33	46	16
Vocational degree	41	33	19
High School (academic)	39	43	7
Higher education	41	48	8
Do you feel that you are:			
Socially mobile	42	44	9
In social decline	34	46	16
Total	39	43	12

Source: Louis Harris/Libération Sondage postélectoral, June 10, 2002, p. 8.

more likely to vote for personality rather than ideas, and least supportive of a woman's right to abortion.

Neither as party leader, nor as unsuccessful presidential candidate running against Mitterrand in 1981 and 1988, nor as prime minister between 1986 and 1988 did Chirac show any of the earlier concerns of Gaullism for the role of the state in modernizing the economy and society. Instead, after presiding over a government that dubbed itself neoliberal and that engaged in a round of privatization of previously nationalized industries between 1986 and 1988, he set out to assure those who feared change. Nevertheless, the party's electoral

level slumped after 1973, and in the 1980s its vote remained more or less stagnant. Even in the massive electoral victory for the right in 1993, when the conservative coalition gained 80 percent of the parliamentary seats, the RPR just edged out their conservative rivals with less than 20 percent of the vote in the first round of the elections. In 1997, its vote declined to 16.8 percent, less than two points more than the National Front.

Nevertheless, with an estimated 100,000 members in 1997 (relatively low by European standards), the RPR was the largest party in France.[29] By 2002, the RPR was a long way from the party once dominated

FIGURE 6.4   Political Representation in the National Assembly After the Elections of 1997 and 2002

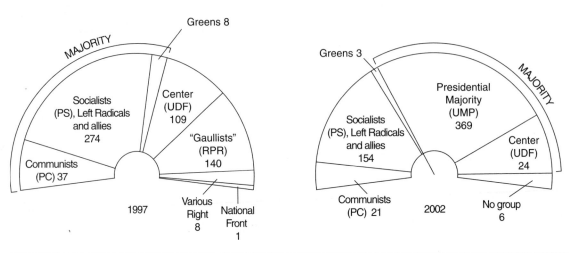

with a firm hand by Gaullist "barons," and defined by the organizing discourse of Gaullism. The victory of Jacques Chirac in the 1995 presidential elections should have given the new president an opportunity to rebuild the RPR as a party of government. However, the seeming unending series of political crises after the summer of 1995, and the disastrous losses in the June 1997 legislative elections, only encouraged and intensified the divisions within the party, and between the RPR and its partners. In 1999, Chirac lost control over the party, when his chosen candidate was defeated in an election for party president. Then, in the fall of 2000, Chirac's candidacy for reelection in 2002 seemed to be undermined by dramatic new evidence of massive corruption in the Paris party machine that directly implicated the president (and former mayor of Paris).

However, the unexpected match against Le Pen in the presidential race of 2002 gave both Chirac and the party a new lease on life. Chirac's massive victory in the second round of the presidential election created the basis for the organization of what became a new successor to the RPR—the *Union pour un Mouvement Populaire, UMP* (originally called the Union for a Presidential Majority (Figure 6.4). The party includes deputies from the RPR, some from the UDF, and some from other small parties of the

right. With more than 60 percent of the new assembly, UMP united the fragmented groups of the right behind the victorious president. However, within two years, the unity began to break down in the run-up to the regional elections of 2004, as the rump of the UDF insisted on maintaining its own lists in the first round of the elections.

THE UNION FOR FRENCH DEMOCRACY (UDF)   Valéry Giscard d'Estaing's foremost concern was to prevent the center's exclusion from power in the Gaullist republic. His small party, the Parti Républicain, the Republican Party (PR), was the typical party, or rather non-party, of French conservatism. It came into existence in 1962, when Giscard and a few other conservative deputies opposed de Gaulle's strictures against European unity and his referendum on direct elections for the presidency. From that time on, the group provided a small complement for the majority in Parliament. Giscard himself, a scion of families long prominent in business, banking, and public service, was finance minister under both de Gaulle and Pompidou before his election to the presidency in 1974. His party never aspired to be a mass party but rather derived its political strength from its representatives in Parliament, many of whom moved in and out of Cabinet posts, and from local leaders who occupied fairly important posts in municipal and departmental councils.

In order to increase the weight of the PR when Chirac was giving a new elan to Gaullism, Giscard, as President of the Republic, chose the way that parties of the right and center have always found opportune: a heterogeneous alliance among groups and personalities organized to support the president in anticipation of the 1978 legislative elections. The result was the *Union for French Democracy (UDF)*, which included, in addition to Giscard's Republicans, remnants of a Catholic party (CDS), the once militant anti-Catholic Radicals, and some former Socialists. The ideological battles of the past within the center had become meaningless, but the parties that formed the UDF found it inopportune to abandon their own weak organizational structures. It is estimated that all of the parties of the UDF combined had no more than 38,000 members in 1995.

Since 1981, the UDF and the RPR had generally cooperated in elections at all levels. However, as the National Front gained in electoral support after 1983, RPR and UDF were compelled to present more and more joint candidates in the first round of parliamentary elections to avoid being defeated by the FN. Nevertheless, even combined, they were incapable of increasing the percentage of their vote beyond 45 percent, even though they won majorities in Parliament in 1986, 1993, and 2002. The two governments organized after the election of Jacques Chirac (in 1995) under Prime Minister *Alain Juppé* were double coalitions: first coalitions of factions within the RPR and the UDF, then coalitions between RPR and UDF. Thus the representatives of the UDF exercised considerable influence over the policymaking process, both as members of the cabinet and as chairs of three of the six permanent committees of the National Assembly. The new government in 2002 was also a double coalition. Prime Minister Jean-Pierre Raffarin is a longtime member of UDF, but with the integration of most of the UDF deputies into the UMP, the UDF as a party appears to have lost most of its independent influence.

The divisions within the UDF deepened after both the 1997 legislative elections, when the UDF became the third party of the right in voter support (just behind the National Front), and the 1998 regional elections, when five (UDF) regional parties accepted the support of the *National Front*. The party split two months later. The liberal (conservative in U.S. terms) minority of the deputies formed a new parliamentary group, Démocratie Libérale (DL, Liberal Democracy), while the RPR, UDF, and DL joined in a loose intergroup in the National Assembly, which they called *L'Alliance* (which has now been restructured into UMP). Only 7 percent of the electorate supported the UDF candidate in the presidential elections in 2002, François Bayrou. In the regional elections of 2004, the party lists attracted a disappointing 8.5 percent of the vote.

THE NATIONAL FRONT Divisions within the right result in part from different reactions to the rise of the *National Front (FN)* during the Mitterrand presidency. Until the 1980s, the FN, founded by *Jean-Marie Le Pen* in 1972, was one of a number of relatively obscure parties of the far right. In none of the elections before 1983 did FN attract more than 1 percent of the national vote. In the 1984 elections for the European Parliament, the National Front built on support in local elections the year before and attracted almost 10 percent of the vote, to the consternation of the established parties of the right and the left.

In the parliamentary elections of 1986 the FN again won almost 10 percent (about 2.7 million votes) of the total vote (and in metropolitan France, more votes than the Communists) and established itself as a substantial political force. Two-thirds of these votes came from voters who previously supported established parties of the right, but the remainder came from some former left voters (mostly Socialists) or from new voters and former abstainers. Profiting from the change to proportional representation elections in 1986, which Mitterrand had introduced partly in order to divide the right, 35 FN deputies entered Parliament. In the 1993 legislative elections, National Front candidates attracted almost 13 percent of the vote in the first round. Because the electoral system was then based on single-member districts, the party elected no deputies. In the 1997 legislative elections, with over 15 percent of the vote, FN became the second conservative party in France and sent a record number of candidates into the second round. However, only one of these candidates was elected.

Nevertheless, FN seemed well on its way to developing a network of local bases. In 1992, the right depended on the party for its majority in 14 out of 22 regions. In 1998 this dependency was translated into a political breakthrough for the National Front when five UDF regional leaders formally accepted FN support to maintain their regional presidencies. In 1995, for the first time FN won municipal elections in three cities and gained some representation in almost half of the larger towns in France. It gained one additional city in a special election in 1997. However this series of breakthroughs brought to a head a growing rivalry between party leader Le Pen and the architect of the party organization, Bruno Mégret, whose coalition strategy was successful in the 1998 regional elections. By the end of 1998, Mégret and his supporters were expelled from the party. In 1999, the two factions became two separate parties, reducing the influence and electoral strength of both. Therefore, the ability of Jean-Marie Le Pen to come in second, with a 17 percent of the vote (and more votes than he had ever attracted) in the first round of the presidential elections of 2002, was a considerable shock to the political system. The FN results in the legislative elections two months later (11 percent) were far lower, but a confirmation that the party—and not simply Le Pen—remained a political force.

The National Front is often compared to a shopkeeper movement that attracted 2.5 million votes in the legislative elections of 1956 (the Poujadist movement) and then faded from the scene.[30] But the FN draws its electoral and organizational support from big-city, rather than small-town, France, and its supporters come more from transfers from the right than had those of Poujade. In addition, the National Front is far more successful than the Poujadist movement in building a strong organizational network. Because of changes in the electoral system, FN has never had more than one deputy in the National Assembly after 1988, but there are still altogether hundreds of elected representatives on the regional, departmental, and local

levels (as well as in the European Parliament). On the eve of the 1998 split, it was estimated that the National Front had 50,000 members (compared with 10,000 in 1985).

Although the influence of the FN has waned since 1998, the party was seemingly given new life by Le Pen's success in 2002, generally confirmed by the results of the regional and European parliamentary elections in 2004. In addition, the process of party emergence and construction over a 15-year period has affected voters of all parties, especially those who would normally vote for the right and young workers who had formerly been mobilized by the now weakened French Communist Party (see following discussion). Approval of the ideas favored by the FN increased dramatically among *all* voters in the 1980s, and, since mid-1999, has increased again. Moreover, the dynamics of party competition systematically force other political parties to place FN issues high on their political agenda.

Although the right now appears to be united behind the president in the UMP alliance, this alliance is a strategic umbrella that papers over the growing fragmentation of party elites. In fact, this tendency toward fragmentation favors the continued influence of the National Front.

The Left

The Socialist Party In comparison with the solid social-democratic parties in other European countries, *le Parti Socialist,* the French *Socialist Party (PS),* lacked muscle almost since its beginnings in 1905. Slow and uneven industrialization and reluctance to organize not only blocked the development of labor unions but also deprived the PS of the working-class strength that other labor parties gained from their trade union affiliations.

Unlike the British Labour Party, the early PS also failed to absorb middle-class radicals, the equivalent of the Liberals in England. The Socialist program, formulated in terms of doctrinaire Marxism, prevented inroads into the electorate of the left-of-center middle-class parties for a long time. The pre–Fifth Republic party was never strong enough to assume control of the government by itself. Its weakness reduced it to being at best one of several partners in the unstable coalition governments of the Third and Fourth Republics.

The emergence of the French Communist Party in 1920 effectively deprived the Socialists of core working-class support. Most of the Socialists' working-class following was concentrated in a few regions of traditional strength, such as the industrial north and urban agglomeration in the center. However, the party had some strongholds elsewhere—among the wine-growers of the south, devotees of republican ideals, of anticlericalism, and of producers' cooperatives. The proportion of civil servants, especially teachers, and of people living on fixed income has been far higher among Socialist voters than in the population at large. This support made for a stable but not particularly dynamic following.

The party encountered considerable difficulties under the changed conditions in the Fifth Republic. After several false starts, the old party dissolved and a new Socialist Party was organized in the summer of 1969, which had considerable success in attracting new members and in reversing its electoral decline. Incipient public disenchantment with conservative governments and new conservative leadership combined with the strong leadership of François Mitterrand to bring about this reversal in Socialist fortunes. Compared with the past, the party membership reached respectable heights in the 1980s (about 180,000 by 1983), though it was still not comparable to the large labor parties of Britain and the continent. In terms of social origin the new membership came predominantly from the salaried middle classes, the professions, the civil service, and especially the teaching profession. Workers rallied to the PS in large numbers in the 1970s, but they were still represented rather sparsely in the party's leadership. But the PS did in the 1970s what other European Socialist parties were unable to do: It attracted leaders of some of the new social movements that emerged in the late 1960s, among them ecologists and regionalists, as well as leaders of small parties of the non-Communist left.[31]

Mitterrand reaped the benefits of the elections of 1981. With the party's leader as president of the Republic and a Socialist majority in Parliament (but also supported by the Communists), the PS found itself in a situation it had never known—and for which it was ill-prepared. The following years of undivided power affected the party's image and outlook. The years in office between 1981 and 1986 were an intense, and painful, learning experience for the PS at all its levels. Under pressure from Mitterrand and a succession of Socialist governments, the classical socialist ideology, which had become rather empty sloganeering even before 1981, was dismantled. What the German Social Democrats had done by adopting a new program at Bad Godesberg in 1959, the French PS did in the early 1980s by its daily practice.

Indeed, by most measures, the Socialist Party was to the 1980s what Gaullists were to the 1960s: a party of government with broad support among most social groups throughout the country (see again Table 6.2). When reelected for a second seven-year term in 1988, Mitterrand carried 77 of the 96 departments of metropolitan France. The Socialists remained strong in most of their areas of traditional geographic strength, and they made inroads in traditionally conservative areas in the west and east of the country. One consequence of this nationalization of Socialist electoral strength, however, was that the party's legislative majority depended on constituencies where voter support was far more conditional. In the legislative elections of 1993 the PS lost a third of its electorate compared with 1988, but far more than that in areas outside of its traditional bastions.

Social trends favored the left for a time. The decline of religious observance, urbanization, the growth of the salaried middle classes (technicians, middle management, etc.) and of the tertiary sector of the economy, and the massive entry of women into the labor market all weakened the groups that provided the right's stable strength: farmers, small businesspeople, the traditional bourgeoisie, and the nonemployed housewives.

Recent studies reveal, however, that the basis of loyalty of large numbers of voters, especially younger voters, was evolving during the 1980s. Voter loyalty became more related to individual attitudes toward specific issues than to collective loyalties based on group or class. Thus the rise of unemployment rates, the growing sense among even Socialist voters that party leadership was worn out, and the mobilization of large numbers of traditional Socialist voters against the government during the campaign for the Maastricht referendum all undermined Socialist support between 1992 and 1994.

During ten years as a governing party (broken by two years of opposition from 1986 to 1988), leadership cohesion came to depend on the prerogatives of power. If the Fifth Republic had become normalized during the 1980s, in the sense that left and right alternated in government with each legislative election, the PS became like other governing parties in France in its dependence on governing power. One index of this normalization was the increased incidence of political corruption within the party. Accusations, investigations, and convictions for corruption swept all parties beginning in the late 1980s. For the Socialists, however, this aspect of normalization undermined the party's image and contributed to the voters' desertion of the party. Estimated membership dropped to about 100,000 in 1995.

Under these circumstances, PS leader *Lionel Jospin* was a remarkably effective presidential candidate, winning the first round before being defeated in the second round by Chirac. Indeed, this was a turning point in the PS electoral fortunes. During the period after the elections, the PS gained in the municipal elections, performed well in by-elections, and made significant gains in the (indirect) Senate elections in September 1995. The real test for Socialist leadership came when President Chirac called surprise legislative elections in April 1997.

Although party leader Jospin and his colleagues were clearly unprepared for the short campaign, they benefited from the rapidly deteriorating popularity and the lack of efficacy of Chirac's majority. After electoral agreements with the Communists and the Greens for the second round, Jospin put together a 31-seat majority (called the *plural left*), was named prime minister, and formed the first cohabitation government of the left in June 1997. The government benefited from declining unemployment and passed a set of important but controversial reforms, including a 35-hour workweek, domestic partnership legislation, and a constitutional amendment requiring parity for women candidacies for elective office. Under pressure from the European Union, the government also passed legisla-

tion establishing a presumption of innocence for those accused in criminal cases, and further limited the French practice of multiple office-holding (*cumul des mandats*). Finally, there were major structural reforms: the presidential term was reduced to five years (with the agreement of the president), and a process began to radically alter the relationship between Corsica and the French state.

Then, with breathtaking rapidity in September 2000, the government lost what appeared to be unusually secure footing. As a result of widespread demonstrations in the streets against rising oil prices and dramatic corruption charges against the RPR that spread to the Socialist and Communist parties, the popularity of Jospin fell to an historic low for the Fifth Republic.

Nevertheless, the elimination of Jospin in the first round of the 2002 presidential elections (by less than 1 percent) was entirely unexpected, and largely resulted from the defection of PS voters to more marginal candidates of the left alliance. Jospin quickly resigned as party leader, leaving the PS without effective leadership. This resulted in the defeat of the left in the legislative elections that followed, as PS representation was cut in half.

However, following a well-established rhythm under the Fifth Republic, the Socialists—together with their allies on the left—rebounded two years later, and swept the regional elections in 2004. They won control of all but one of the 22 regional governments in France. They accomplished this impressive victory without strong leadership at the national level. The victory represented profound public disappointment with—and opposition to—the right, which had used the majority it had gained in 2002 to push through cuts in welfare state benefits.

THE COMMUNISTS   Until the late 1970s *le Parti Communist Français*, the *French Communist Party (PCF)*, was a major force in French politics. This was despite the fact that, except for a short interlude after the war (1944–1947), the party had been excluded since its beginning in 1920 from any participation in the national government. During most of the Fourth Republic, it received more electoral support than any other single party (with an average of just over 25 percent of the electorate). During the Fifth Republic, the party remained, until 1978, electorally dominant on the left, although it trailed the Gaullists on the right (see Table 6.1). In addition to its successes in national elections, the party commanded significant strength at the local level until the early 1980s. Between 1977 and 1983, Communist mayors governed in about 1,500 towns in France, with a total population of about 10 million people.

Over several decades, the party's very existence constantly impinged nationally, as well as locally, on the rules of the political game and thereby on the system itself. The Communists defined (more or less) what left meant, while the Socialists debated the acceptability of that definition. For the parties of the right, the hegemony of the PCF provided an issue (anti-communism) around which they could unite and on which they could attack both the Socialists and the Communists.

The seemingly impressive edifice of the Communists and of its numerous organizations of sympathizers was badly shaken, first by the rejuvenation of the PS under Mitterrand's leadership in the 1970s, and then by the collapse of international communism and the Soviet Union in the 1980s. The association of the French Communist Party with the international communist movement dominated by the Soviet Union had sharply divided communists from socialists in France since 1920, but it provided an important part of the revolutionary identity of the party, especially for its most devoted militants. The international movement also provided considerable financial support for the party organization and its activities, support that disappeared after 1989.

The PCF fielded its leader *Georges Marchais* as a candidate in the first ballot of the presidential election of 1981 with disastrous results: With 15 percent of the vote, the PCF lost one-fourth of its electorate. In the parliamentary elections that followed, the number of its deputies was cut in half.

It turned out that the party's defeats in 1981 were only the beginning of a tailspin of electoral decline.[32] The voters who left the party in 1981 never came back.

Since the legislative elections of 1993, the party has responded to these pressures. In 1994 the PCF revised its statutes to eliminate the principle of democratic centralism and to accept the presence of dissenting factions within the party. Georges Marchais, party leader since 1972, stepped down in favor of *Robert Hue*. Younger, and seemingly more open, Hue apologized to those who were forced out of the party in the past and promoted dialogue and discussion. Nevertheless, the dissidents have not returned, and their numbers have continued to grow.

By 2002, its presidential candidate attracted a mere 3.4 percent of the vote, and just 4 percent of the working-class vote. In the legislative elections, with 4.7 percent of the vote nationally, the PCF was clearly marginal to the left. To win elections, it has grown increasingly dependent on continued (and often difficult) cooperation with the Socialists, as well as on the personal popularity of some of its long-established mayors. Twenty-one of the 37 Communist deputies elected in 1997 were mayors, and others were municipal council members. With their (ever-shrinking) local bases, and the support of PS, the Communists managed to elect 21 deputies in 2002, just enough to maintain their own parliamentary group.

Between 1979 and 1987 the party lost at least 40 percent of its membership. Although claimed membership remains large by French standards, 275,000 according to 1996 party documents—but probably closer to 200,000—the PCF remains the largest mass membership party in the country. However, its organization is increasingly divided, ineffective, and challenged by successive waves of dissidence from within.

What does the marginalization of the PCF mean for the French party system? It has healed the division that had enfeebled the left since the split of the Socialist Party in 1920, in the wake of the Bolshevik seizure of power in Russia. But a price has been paid: The political representation of the French working class has been weakened. Although the fortunes of the PCF have fallen in inverse relation to the rise of the electoral strength of the PS, the proportion of workers actually voting for both parties combined has declined by 30 percent since the 1970s. Perhaps most important, it appears that many young workers, who previously would have been mobilized by Communist militants, are now being mobilized to vote for the National Front.

POLITICAL PARTIES AND PATTERNS OF VOTING

Although France is a unitary state, elections are held with considerable frequency at every territorial level. Councilors are elected for each of the more than 36,000 communes in France, for each of the 100 departments (counties), and for each of the 22 regions. Deputies to the National Assembly are elected at least once every five years, and the president of the Republic is elected (or reelected) at least once every seven years (every five years after 2002). In addition, there are elections for French representatives to the European Parliament every five years since 1979.

France was the first European country to enfranchise a mass electorate, and France was also the first European country to demonstrate that a mass electorate did not preclude the possibility of authoritarian government. The electoral law of 1848 enfranchised all male citizens over the age of 21, but within five years this same mass electorate had ratified Louis Napoléon's coup d'état and his establishment of the Second Empire. Rather than restrict the electorate, Napoléon perfected new modern techniques for manipulating a mass electorate by gerrymandering districts, skillfully using public works as patronage for official candidates, and exerting pressure through the administrative hierarchy.

From the Second Empire to the end of World War II, the size of the electorate remained more or less stable, but it suddenly more than doubled when women 21 years of age and older were granted the vote in 1944. After the voting age was lowered to 18 in 1974, 2.5 million voters were added to the rolls. By 2002, there were more than 40 million voters in France.

Electoral Participation and Abstention

Voting participation in elections of the Fifth Republic has undergone a significant change and fluctuates far more than during previous republics. Abstention tends to be highest in referendums and European elections, and lowest in presidential contests, with other elections falling somewhere in between (see Table 6.1). In 2002, a new record was set for abstention in a presidential election, when 27.9 percent of the registered voters stayed home.[33] During the 1980s, the normal level of abstention in leg-

islative elections increased substantially, and remains high. In the 2002 legislative election, an abstention rate of 35.6 percent set a record for legislative elections for any of the French republics. The elections for the European Parliament always attract relatively few voters, but in 2004 more than 57 percent of the registered voters stayed home (slightly more than in 1999). For referendums, a new record was set in 2000: almost 70 percent of the registered voters chose not to vote in a (successful) referendum to reduce the presidential term from seven to five years (after the elections of 2002).

Rising abstention seems linked to a larger phenomenon of change in the party system. Since the late 1970s, voters' confidence in all parties has declined, and the highest abstention rates in 2002 were among those voters who expressed no preference between parties of the right and left. Nevertheless, in contrast with the United States, among the 90 percent of the electorate that is registered to vote, individual abstention appears to be cyclical and there are few permanent abstainers.[34] In this sense, it is possible to see abstention in an election as a political choice (42 percent of them in 2002 said that they abstained because they had no confidence in politicians).[35] As in other countries, the least educated, the lowest income groups, and the youngest and oldest age groups vote less frequently.

Voting in Parliamentary Elections

Since the early days of the Third Republic, France has experimented with a great number of electoral systems and devices without obtaining more satisfactory results in terms of government coherence. The stability of the Fifth Republic cannot be attributed to the method of electing National Assembly deputies, for the system is essentially the same one used during the most troubled years of the Third Republic. As in the United States, electoral districts (577) are represented by a single deputy who is selected through two rounds of elections. On the first election day, candidates who obtain a majority of all votes cast are elected to parliament; this is a relatively rare occurrence because of the abundance of candidates. Candidates who obtain support of less than 12.5 percent of the registered voters are dropped from the "second round" a week later.

Other candidates voluntarily withdraw in favor of a better-placed candidate close to their party on the political spectrum. For instance, pre-election agreements between Communists and Socialists (and, more recently, the Greens) usually lead to the weaker candidate withdrawing after the first round, if both survive. Similar arrangements have existed between the Rally for the Republic (RPR) and the Union for French Democracy (UDF). Although more recently, the two conservative parties have not competed in the same district even on the first round, and have presented a unified candidate as the Union for a Popular Movement (UMP). As a result, generally three (or at most four) candidates face each other in the second round, in which a plurality of votes ensures election.

This means that the first round is somewhat similar to American primary elections, except that in the French case the primary is among candidates of parties allied in coalitions of the left or center-right. There is considerable pressure on political parties to develop electoral alliances, since those that do not are placed at a strong disadvantage in terms of representation.

The National Front is more or less isolated from coalition arrangements with the parties of the center-right in national elections (though less at the subnational level). Consequently, in 2002, with electoral support of 11.1 percent, none of the Front candidates was finally elected. In comparison, the Communist Party benefited from an electoral agreement with the Socialists: with a mere 4.7 percent of the vote, 21 of their candidates were elected. Not surprisingly, the leading party (or coalition of parties) generally ends up with a considerably larger number of seats than is justified by its share in the popular vote.

Voting in Referendums

Between 1958 and 1969 the French electorate voted five times on referendums (see Table 6.3). In 1958 a vote against the new constitution might have involved the country in a civil war, which it had narrowly escaped a few months earlier. The two referendums that followed endorsed the peace settlement in the Algerian War. In 1962, hardly four years after he had enacted by referendum his "own" constitution, General de Gaulle asked the electorate to endorse a constitutional amendment of great signifi-

cance: to elect the president of the Republic by direct popular suffrage. Favorable attitudes toward the referendum and the popular election of the president, however, did not prevent the electorate from voting down another proposal submitted by de Gaulle in 1969, thereby provoking his resignation.

Since 1969 there have been only four referendums. President Georges Pompidou called a referendum for the admission of Britain to the Common Market. (For the results of referendums and presidential elections between 1958 and 2002, see Table 6.3.) The first referendum during the Mitterrand period, in 1988, dealt with approval for an accord between warring parties on the future of New Caledonia; the referendum was a condition of the agreement. Sixty-three percent of the voters stayed home, but the accord was approved. The electorate was far more extensively mobilized when the question of ratifying the so-called *Maastricht Treaty* on the European Union was submitted to referendum in September 1992, and the results were far more significant for the future of French political life (see Box 6.2). The 2000 referendum—on reduction of the presidential term from seven to five years—was overwhelmingly approved (by 73 percent of those who voted), but the referendum was most notable for the record number of abstentions—almost 70 percent. Finally, 55 percent of those who voted rejected the EU constitutional treaty in May 2005. Public opinion polls indicate that the referendum as a form of public participation is regarded favorably by the electorate. It ranked just behind the popularly elected presidency and the Constitutional Council, among the most highly approved institutional innovations of the Fifth Republic. In one of its first moves, the new government under President Jacques Chirac in 1995 passed a constitutional amendment that expanded the use of the referendum in the areas of social and economic policy.

Voting in Presidential Elections

Presidential elections by direct popular suffrage are for French voters the most important expressions of the general will. After the presidential elections of 1965, it became evident that French voters derived great satisfaction from knowing that, unlike past parliamentary elections, national and not parochial alignments were at stake, and that they were invited

TABLE 6.3 French Referendums (R) and Second Ballots of Presidential Elections (P), 1958–2002 (Voting in Metropolitan France)

Date	Registered Voters (millions)	Abstentions (percentage registered)	"Yes" Votes for Winning Candidate (percentage registered)	(percentage cast)	Winner	"No" Votes for Losing Candidate (percentage registered)	(percentage cast)	Loser
9/28/58(R)	26.6	15.1	66.4	79.2		17.4	20.7	
1/8/61(R)	27.2	23.5	55.9	75.3		18.4	24.7	
4/8/62(R)	27.0	24.4	64.9	90.7		6.6	9.3	
10/28/62(R)	27.6	22.7	46.4	61.7		28.8	38.2	
12/19/65(P)	28.2	15.4	44.8	54.5	de Gaulle	37.4	45.5	Mitterrand
4/18/69(R)	28.7	19.4	36.7	46.7		41.6	53.2	
6/15/69(P)	28.8	30.9	37.2	57.5	Pompidou	27.4	42.4	Poher
4/23/72(R)	29.1	39.5	36.1	67.7		17.2	32.3	
5/19/74(P)	29.8	12.1	43.9	50.7	Giscard d'Estaing	42.8	49.3	Mitterrand
5/10/81(P)	35.5	13.6	43.8	52.2	Mitterrand	40.1	47.8	Giscard d'Estaing
5/8/88(P)	38.2	15.9	43.8	54.0	Mitterrand	37.3	46.0	Chirac
11/6/88(R)	37.8	63.0	26.1	80.0		6.5	20.0	
9/20/92(R)	37.1	28.9	34.9	50.8		33.8	49.2	
5/7/95(P)	39.9	20.1	39.5	52.6	Chirac	35.6	47.4	Jospin
9/24/00(R)	39.6	69.7	18.6	73.2		6.8	26.8	
6/5/02(P)	41.2	20.3	62.0	82.2	Chirac	13.4	17.8	Le Pen
05/29/05 (R)	41.3	30.3	30.7	45.1		37.3	54.9	

Source: Official results from the Ministry of the Interior.

Box 6.2   French Parties and the Maastricht Referendum of 1992

With the support of the president of the Republic, the leaders of the Socialist Party, most (but not all) of the leaders of the conservative opposition, as well as two-thirds of the electorate before the summer, the proposition approving of the treaty to establish a European Union, with European citizenship and (eventually) a single European currency, was expected to achieve an impressive majority in the September referendum. It was also expected to give a boost of support for the Socialist president and government in anticipation of the 1993 legislative elections. The results were far different. The proposed treaty split the electorates of each of the major political parties in unanticipated ways and the summer campaign proved particularly bitter. The Gaullist opposition to the treaty was partly a revolt against the leadership of Jacques Chirac, and it was supported by a clear majority of RPR deputies and voters. The campaign of the Centrist opponents was also

an attack against their leader, former president Giscard d'Estaing, but it did not gain widespread support. Within the left, the Communists proved to be weak but bitter opponents to the approval of the treaty, and Socialist leaders less than enthusiastic proponents. The National Front was united in its opposition. In the end, the treaty was approved on September 20 by a slim majority of the voters, but the results were a political disaster for those who won. For each of the major parties, their "natural" electorates split badly, and the results—in which opposition to the treaty was concentrated among the less privileged voters and in the poorest regions of the country—were widely viewed as a broad rejection of established political leadership.*

*On the referendum, see Andrew Appleton, "The Maastricht Referendum and the Party System," in Keeler and Schain, eds., *Chirac's Challenge*.

to pronounce themselves effectively on such issues. The traditional and once deeply rooted attitude that the only useful vote was against the government no longer made sense when almost everybody knew that the task was to elect an executive endowed with strong powers for seven years. Accordingly, turnout in presidential elections, with one exception, has been the highest of all elections.

The nomination procedures for presidential candidates make it very easy to put a candidate on the first ballot, far easier than in presidential primaries in the United States. So far, however, no presidential candidate, not even de Gaulle in 1965, has obtained the absolute majority needed to ensure election on the first ballot. In runoffs, held two weeks after the first ballot, only the two most successful candidates face each other. All serious candidates are backed by a party or a coalition of parties, the provisions of the law notwithstanding. Nevertheless, with a record number of candidates in 2002 (16), this proposition was stretched to the limit.

Because the formal campaigns are short and concentrated, radio, television, and newspapers are able to grant candidates, commentators, and fore-

casters considerable time and space. The televised duels between the presidential candidates in the last four elections, patterned after debates between presidential candidates in the United States, but longer and of far higher quality, were viewed by at least half of the population.

Informal campaigns, however, are long and arduous. The fixed term of the French presidency means that, unless the president dies or resigns, there are no snap elections for the chief executive as there are from time to time in Britain and Germany. As a result, even in the absence of primaries, the informal campaign begins to get quite intense years before the election. In many ways, the presidential campaign of 2002 began well before the new millennium.

Just as in the United States, electoral coalitions that elect a president are different from those that secure a legislative majority for a government. This means that any candidate for the presidency who owes his nomination to his position as party leader must appeal to an audience broader than a single party. Once elected, the candidate seeks to establish political distance from his party origins. François Mitterrand was the first president in the history of

Box 6.3 The Accidental President

On May 5, 2002, Jacques Chirac was reelected president of France by the largest majority ever obtained by a presidential candidate in a popular election during the Fifth Republic. Yet, until the results of the first round of the presidential elections were tabulated two weeks before, this victory was wholly unexpected. Chirac's first term was marked first by the largest strike movement since 1968, then by an ill-conceived decision to call early legislative elections in 1997 at a time when he controlled an 80 percent majority in the National Assembly. The victory of the left resulted in the installation of a Socialist prime minister, Lionel Jospin, and a new round of cohabitation. After 1997 his leadership of the RPR was challenged, first by fragmentation then by loss of control of the party machine. This was followed by revelations of dramatic new evidence of massive corruption in the Paris party machine that directly implicated the president (the former mayor of Paris). He appeared to be headed for likely defeat in 2002.

Then came the divine surprise of April 2002. With the worst result of any outgoing president in the first round (less than 20 percent of the vote), he edged out his Socialist rival, Lionel Jospin; but Jospin himself was edged out by the resurgent candidate of the extreme right, Jean-Marie Le Pen. With 16 candidates in the first round, Le Pen's considerable achievement was in part an accident of the electoral system, and the inability of voters of the left to anticipate the consequences of their dispersed votes. As a result, the shocked and leaderless left (Jospin resigned from political life) rallied to the support of Chirac to block Le Pen. Confronted with an unhappy choice between one candidate who had been accused of corruption, and a candidate of the extreme right, more than 82 percent of the electorate voted for the former.

---

the Fifth Republic to have been elected twice in popular elections. Jacques Chirac has now accomplished this same achievement. (See Box 6.3)

Although the 2002 presidential election deeply divided all of the major parties, the process of coalition building around presidential elections has probably been the key element in political party consolidation and in the development of party coalitions since 1968. The prize of the presidency is so significant that it has preoccupied the parties of both the right and the left since the 1960s and influences their organization, their tactics, and their relations with one another.

POLICY PROCESSES

The Executive

As we have seen, the French constitution has a two-headed executive: As in other parliamentary regimes, the prime minister presides over the government but unlike other parliamentary regimes, the president is far from being a figurehead. It was widely predicted that such an arrangement would necessarily lead to frequent political crises. During the first 28 years of the Fifth Republic, four presidents, and each of the prime ministers who have served under them, left no doubt that the executive

had only one head, the president (see again Figure 6.1).

The exercise of presidential powers in all their fullness was made possible not so much by the constitutional text as by a political fact: Between 1958 and 1986 the president and prime minister derived their legitimacy from the same Gaullist majority in the electorate—the president by direct popular elections, the prime minister by the support of a majority of deputies in the National Assembly. In 1981 the electorate shifted its allegiance from the right to the left, yet for the ensuing five years the president and Parliament were still on the same side of the political divide. The long years of political affinity between the holders of the two offices solidified and amplified presidential powers and shaped constitutional practices in ways that appear to have a lasting impact. From the very beginning of the Fifth Republic, the president not only *formally appoints* the prime minister proposed to him to Parliament (as the presidents of the previous republics had also done, and as the queen of England does), but he also *chooses* the prime minister and the other Cabinet ministers. In some cases the president has also dismissed a prime minister who was clearly enjoying the continuing confidence of a majority in Parliament.

Hence, the rather frequent reshuffling of Cabinet posts and personnel in the Fifth Republic is different from similar happenings in the Third and Fourth Republics. In those systems the changes occurred in response to shifts in parliamentary support and frequently in order to forestall, at least for a short time, the government's fall from power. In the present system, the president or the prime minister—depending on the circumstances—may decide to appoint, move, or dismiss a Cabinet officer on the basis of his or her own appreciation of the worth (or lack of it) of the individual member. This does not mean that considerations of the executive are merely technical. They may be highly political, but they are exclusively those of the executive.

Since all powers proceeded from the president, the government headed by the prime minister became essentially an administrative body until 1986, despite constitutional stipulations to the contrary. The chief function of the prime minister was to provide whatever direction or resources were needed to implement the policies conceived by the chief of state. This meant primarily that the task of the government was to develop legislative proposals and present an executive budget. In many respects the government's position resembled that of the Cabinet in a presidential regime such as the United States, rather than that of a government in a parliamentary system such as Britain and the earlier French republics.

Regardless of the political circumstances (see following discussion), weekly meetings of the Cabinet always are chaired by the president and are officially called the *Council of Ministers*. They are sometimes a forum for deliberation and confrontation of different points of view, and Cabinet decisions and decrees officially emanate from the council, but in fact real decisions are made elsewhere.

The prime minister, in relation to Cabinet colleagues, is more than first among equals. Among his or her many functions is the harnessing of a parliamentary majority for presidential policies, since according to the constitution the government must resign when a majority in Parliament adopts a motion of censure or rejects the governmental program. This provision distinguishes France from a truly presidential regime such as the United States or Mexico.

The relationship between president and prime minister, however, has operated quite differently during the periods of so-called cohabitation: from 1986 to 1988; between 1993 and 1995 a conservative majority controlled Parliament and the president was a Socialist; and between 1997 and 2002, the left held a parliamentary majority and the president was from a conservative party. Without claiming any domain exclusively as his own, the president (Mitterrand in the first two cases, and Chirac from 1997 to 2002) continued to occupy the foreground in foreign and military affairs, in accordance with his interpretation of his mandate under the constitution. The prime minister became the effective leader of the executive and pursued government objectives, but avoided interfering with presidential prerogatives.

In part because of the experiences of cohabitation, the role of the presidency is now less imposing than it had been before 1986. Even during the interlude of Socialist government between 1988 and 1993, the Socialist prime minister was largely responsible for the main options that were slowly developed for governmental action, with the president setting the limits and the tone. Thus, by the 1990s, the relationship between the president and prime minister was more complicated than during the earlier period of the Fifth Republic, and varied according to the political circumstances in which each had assumed office.

Since the early days of the de Gaulle administration, the office of the chief of state is organized to maximize the ability of the president to initiate, elaborate, and frequently execute policy. In terms of function, the staff at the Elysée Palace, the French White House, composed of a general secretariat and the presidential staff, is somewhat similar to the Executive Office of the U.S. president. Yet it is much smaller, comprising only 40 to 50 persons, with an additional support staff of several hundred people.

As the president's eyes and ears, his staff members are indispensable for the exercise of presidential powers. They are in constant contact not only with the prime minister's collaborators but also directly with individual ministries. Through these contacts the president can initiate, impede, interfere, and assure himself that presidential policies are followed.

The prime minister has a parallel network for developing and implementing policy decisions. The most important method are the so-called interministerial meetings, regular gatherings of high civil servants attached to various ministries. The frequency of these sessions, chaired by a member of the prime minister's personal staff, reflects the growing centralization of administrative and decision-making authority within the office of the prime minister, and the growing importance of the prime minister's policy network in everyday policymaking within the executive.

As we have seen, two different patterns exist for the sharing of executive power. When the presidential and parliamentary majorities are identical (as was the case in 1962–1986, 1988–1993, 1995, 1997, and 2002–), the prime minister is clearly subordinate to the president.[36] Even in this case, however, the president's power is always limited by the fact that he does not control the administrative machinery directly and must work through the prime minister's office and the ministries. Cooperation between the two is thus essential for effective government. Between 1974 and 1981, and again from 1988 to 1993, the prime minister's power was further enhanced by a very narrow majority in the National Assembly, giving him the opportunity to act as a legislative coalition-builder for the executive. Under conditions of cohabitation, the prime minister clearly gains dominant authority at the expense of the president. The power to set the political agenda and to command within the executive is largely transferred to the prime minister. But the president retains the power to bargain, based on his prerogatives to make appointments, to sign ordinances, and to participate in decisions on defense and foreign policy.

Parliament

The constitution severely and intentionally curtails the powers of Parliament both as a source of legislation and as an organ of control over the executive. The fact that both houses of Parliament were confined to sessions of no more than six months in a calendar year until 1995 severely reduced effectiveness. In 1995, maximum sessions were increased to nine months, opening new possibilities for parliamentary leadership to exercise initiative and control.

Despite restrictions on parliamentary activity, the legislative output of the parliaments in the Fifth Republic is quite respectable. The average of only 98 laws per year enacted during the first 35 years of the Fifth Republic (125 per year during the reform period between 1981 and 1986, and down to 72 per year since 1997) is much lower than that during the Fourth Republic. However, it is double the British average for the first 35 years after World War II. Although either the government or Parliament may propose bills, almost all legislation is proposed by the government. The government effectively controls the proceedings in both houses and can require priority for those bills that it wishes to see adopted (see Figure 6.5). Article 44 of the constitution empowers the government to force Parliament by the so-called blocked vote to accept a bill in its entirety with only the amendments agreed to by the government. In recent years the blocked vote is generally used to maintain discipline within the majority, rather than to impose the will of the executive over a chaotic Parliament. Its use has become an index of conflict within the governing party or coalition.[37] After 1986, the conservative government of Jacques Chirac and the Socialist governments of Cresson, Rocard, and Bérégovoy were all tempted to use the blocked vote more often and for the same reason: to make up for their slim majority, and hence their weak support in the National Assembly. For the Jospin government, the blocked vote was a useful tool to maintain a sometimes raucous plural coalition.

Article 38 invites Parliament to abandon "for a limited time" its legislative function to the government if the government wishes to act as legislator "for the implementation of its program." Once Parliament votes a broad enabling law, the government enacts legislation by way of so-called *ordinances*. The government used this possibility of executive lawmaking 22 times between 1958 and 1986, and often for important legislation, sometimes simply to expedite the legislative process. The use of enabling laws is now limited by decisions of the Constitutional Council, which requires that the enabling act spell out the limits of executive lawmaking with some precision.

Another constitutional provision gives the government a unique tool to ensure parliamentary support for any bill that it introduces. According to Ar-

FIGURE 6.5   How a Bill Becomes a Law

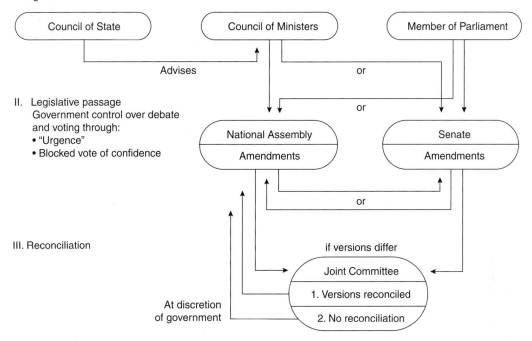

I. Legislative initiative

II. Legislative passage
Government control over debate
and voting through:
• "Urgence"
• Blocked vote of confidence

III. Reconciliation

IV. Review by Constitutional
Council at initiative of:
• President of Republic
• Prime Minister
• President of National Association
• President of Senate
• 60 deputies
• 60 senators

Constitutional Council makes decision:
1. Conforms with constitution
2. Conforms partially   } The bill fails to become a law
3. Does not conform   as adopted by Parliament

ticle 49, Section 3, the prime minister may pledge the "government's responsibility" on any bill (or section of a bill) submitted to the National Assembly. In such a case, the bill is automatically "considered as adopted," without further vote, unless the deputies succeed in a *motion of censure* against the government according to the strict requirements discussed earlier. The success of this motion would likely result in new elections, but so far the threat of having to face new elections has always put sufficient pressure on the incumbent deputies not to support a motion of censure. As a consequence,

whenever the government pledges its responsibility to a bill it introduced, the bill has become law without any parliamentary vote.

Earlier in the Fifth Republic, little use was made of this provision. Between 1981 and 1986, the governments of the left used it for reasons of expediency. It permitted them to enact important legislation quickly, without laying bare conflicts within the ranks of the governing majority. After 1986, governments of both the right and left resorted to this procedure with considerable frequency when they needed to overcome the precariousness of their majorities in Parliament. During the five years between 1988 and 1993, prime ministers engaged the responsibility of their governments 39 times, 9 times each year in 1990 and 1991 alone.

Between June 1997 and the election of a new parliament in 2002, this procedure was not used. This method virtually excludes Parliament from meaningful participation in the legislative process, and is now a permanent, though variable, fixture of governance. The government used it to adopt some of the most important pieces of legislation: France's nuclear strike force, nationalization under the Socialists, and privatization under the conservatives, as well as annual budgets, military planning laws, social security legislation, economic plans—all have become law in this manner.

Some devices for enhancing the role of Parliament, however, are somewhat more effective over the years. In the 1970s, the National Assembly made room for a weekly session devoted to a question period that is similar to the British (and German) version. Two days a week, the party groups select and submit a dozen or more written questions an hour in advance, in rough proportion to membership of each group, and then the relevant minister answers them. The presence of television cameras in the chamber (since 1974) creates additional public interest, and records the dialogue between the government representatives and the deputies.

By using its power to amend, Parliament has vastly expanded its role in the legislative process during the past decades. During the 1980s, proposed amendments averaged almost 5,000 a year. Since 1990, however, this average has more than doubled, which coincides with the doubling of hours devoted to legislative debate each year. About two-thirds of the amendments that are eventually adopted (33 percent of those proposed in 1997–2002) are proposed by parliamentary committees working with the government. Thus committees help shape legislation, and governments have all but abandoned their constitutionally guaranteed prerogative to declare amendments out of order.[38] The long parliamentary session introduced in 1995 has enhanced the role of committee leaders in the legislative process, and will probably increase the bargaining power of the president of the National Assembly.

Finally, the role of Parliament is strengthened by the general support that French citizens give their elected deputies. Better-organized parties both add to the deputy's role as part of a group and somewhat diminish his or her role as an independent actor, capable of influencing the legislative process merely for narrow parochial interests. Nevertheless, individual deputies still command a considerable following within their constituencies. This pattern is enhanced by the fact that 56 percent of the deputies in the National Assembly elected in 1997 were also mayors, while others held other local offices. In 2000, when confidence in political parties was at 24 percent, confidence in deputies had risen to 36 percent, and in mayors to 70 percent (see again Figure 6.3).

Because the electoral college that elects the members of the Senate is composed almost entirely of people selected by small-town mayors, the parties of the center, which are most influential in small towns, are best represented in the Upper House. In 2002, the parties of the center (UDF and DL) still had a few more seats than their RPR rivals in the National Assembly, but RPR is the largest single group within the Senate. The Socialists are the second largest group, a result of the strong roots that the PS has developed at the local level, as well as the initiation of limited proportional representation in senatorial elections. Although the right remains dominant in the Upper House, the Senate has not always been on the right of the political spectrum. Its hostility to social and economic change is balanced by a forthright defense of traditional republican liberties and by a stand against demagogic appeals to latent anti-parliamentary feelings. The Senate, in the normal legislative process, can do little more than delay legislation approved by the government and passed by the National Assembly. There is, however, one constitutional situation in which a majority in the Upper House cannot be overruled: Any constitutional amendment needs the approval of either a simple or a three-fifths majority of senators (Article 89). In the year 2000, lack of support in the Senate forced the president (and prime minister) to withdraw an amendment to create an independent judiciary and to modify significantly the amendment on parity for women (that was passed).

Some legislation of great importance, such as the nuclear strike force, the organization of military tribunals in cases involving high treason, and the reorganization of local government in Corsica and the change in the system of departmental representation (in 1991), was enacted in spite of senatorial dissent. Nonetheless, until 1981 relations between the Senate and the National Assembly were relatively harmonious. The real clash with the Senate over legislation came during the years of Socialist government between 1981 and 1986, when many key bills were passed over the objections of the Senate. However, bills proposed by the government of the left that dismantled some of the "law and order" measures enacted under de Gaulle, Pompidou, and Giscard were supported by the Senate, and the Upper House played an active role when it modified the comprehensive decentralization statute passed by the Socialist majority in the Assembly. Most of the changes were accepted in joint committee.

Criticism of the Senate as an unrepresentative body, and proposals for its reform, have come from Gaullists and Socialists alike (most recently in 1998). All of these proposals for reforming the Senate have failed, though some minor modifications in its composition were passed in 1976 and 1983.

Checks and Balances

France has no tradition of judicial review. As in other countries with civil law systems, and in Britain as well, the sovereignty of Parliament has meant that the legislature has the last word and that a law enacted in constitutionally prescribed forms is not subject to further scrutiny. This principle seemed to be infringed upon when the Constitution of 1958 brought forth an institutional novelty, the Constitutional Council. The council in certain cases must, and in other cases may upon request, examine legislation and decide whether it conforms to the constitution. A legal provision declared unconstitutional may not be promulgated. Each of the presidents of the two houses of Parliament chooses three of the council's members, and the president of the Republic chooses another three for a (nonre-

newable) nine-year term. Those who nominate the council's members were until 1974, together with the prime minister, the only ones entitled to apply to the council for constitutional scrutiny. In 1974 an amendment to Article 61 of the constitution made it possible for 60 deputies or 60 senators also to submit cases to the Constitutional Council. Since then, appeals to the council by the opposition, and at times by members of the majority, are a regular feature of the French legislative process.

Whichever side is in opposition, conservative or Socialist, routinely refers all major (sometimes minor as well) pieces of legislation to the council. In a given year, as many as 28 percent of laws passed by parliament have been submitted for review. A surprisingly high percentage of appeals lead to a declaration of unconstitutionality (see following discussion). Few decisions declare entire statutes unconstitutional, and those that declare parts of legislation unconstitutional (sometimes trivial parts) effectively invite parliament to rewrite the text in an acceptable way.

The impact of the Constitutional Council's decisions is considerable and has sometimes modified short-term, and occasionally long-term, objectives of governments. The council assumes in its practice the role of a constitutional court. By doing so, it places itself at the juncture of law and politics, in a way similar to the U.S. Supreme Court when it reviews the constitutionality of legislation.

In a landmark decision, rendered in 1971, the council declared unconstitutional a statute, adopted by a large majority in Parliament, authorizing the prefects to refuse authorization (needed under the Law on Associations of 1901) to any association which they thought might engage in illegal activities. According to the decision, to require any advance authorization violated the freedom of association, one of "the fundamental principles recognized by the laws of the Republic and solemnly reaffirmed in the preamble of the Constitution." The invocation of the preamble greatly expanded the scope of constitutional law, since the preamble incorporated in its wording broad "principles of national sovereignty" as well as the "attachment to The Declaration of Rights of Man," and an extensive Bill of Rights from the Fourth Republic constitution.

Box 6.4 Judicial Review in France and the United States

Judicial review has become part of the French legislative process, but in a way that is still quite different from that of the United States.* Access remains limited, since citizens have no right to bring complaints before the council. The Constitutional Council, unlike the Supreme Court, considers legislation before it is promulgated. Since 1981, virtually all constitutional challenges have been initiated by legislative petition, a process that does not exist in the United States. A time element precludes the possibility of extensive deliberation: Rulings must be made within a month, and in emergency situations, within eight days. This is surely speedy justice, but the verdicts cannot be as explanatory as those rendered by constitutional courts in other countries. Dissenting opinions are never made public.

*Alec Stone, *The Birth of Judicial Politics in France* (New York: Oxford University Press, 1992).

For introducing a broad view of judicial review into French constitutional law, the decision was greeted as the French equivalent of the U.S. Supreme Court decision in *Marbury v. Madison*. Some of the Constitutional Council's most important decisions, such as those on the nationalization of private enterprises (under the Socialists), on the privatization of parts of the public sector (under the conservatives), or on government control over the media (under both), conform to an attitude which in the United States is called judicial restraint. A few can be qualified as activist, since they directly alter the intent of the law. But as a nonelected body, the council generally avoids interference with the major political choices of the governmental majority. In recent years, the council has nevertheless reviewed about 10 percent of legislation that is passed each year and has found that, on average, 50 percent of this legislation at least in part violates the constitution (63 percent in 1999–2000). In a period in which alternation of governments has often resulted in sharp policy changes, the council decisions have helped define an emerging consensus. By smoothing out the raw edges of new legislation in judicial language, it often makes changes ultimately more acceptable (see Box 6.4).

The approval of the council's activities by a large sector of public opinion (52 percent in 2001, slightly below the popular election of the president and the popular referendum) encourages efforts to enlarge its powers. The proposals aimed at facilitating citizens' direct access to its jurisdiction, greater openness of its procedures, and a strengthening of the council's role in the defense of civil liberties have never succeeded in overcoming opposition to them in the Senate.

The judicial check on policymaking enhances the role of the much older *Council of State*, which in its present form dates back to 1799. The government now consults this council more extensively on all bills before they are submitted to Parliament, and, as it has always done, on all government decrees and regulations before they are enacted. The council also gives advice on the interpretation of constitutional texts. While its advice is never binding, its prestige is so high that its recommendations are seldom ignored. Unlike the Constitutional Council, the Council of State provides recourse to individual citizens who have claims against the administration. The judicial section of the Council of State, acting either as a court of appeal or, in more important cases, as the court of first instance, is the apex of a hierarchy of administrative tribunals. Whenever official acts are found to be devoid of a legal basis, whether those of a Cabinet minister or a village mayor, the council will annul them and grant damages to the aggrieved plaintiff.

THE STATE AND TERRITORIAL RELATIONS

Since the time of the First Republic in the eighteenth century, when the Jacobins controlled the revolutionary National Assembly, the French state has been characterized by a high degree of centralized political and administrative authority. Although there have always been forces that have advocated *decentralization* (of political authority), as

FIGURE 6.6   Subnational Governments in France

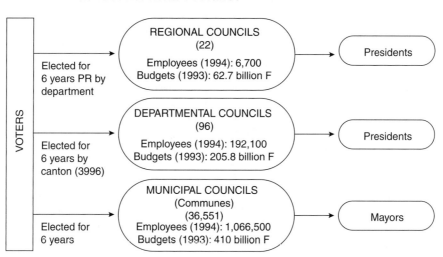

well as deconcentration (of administrative authority), the French unitary state remained (formally) "one and indivisible."[39] Essentially, this meant that subnational territorial units (communes, departments, and regions) had little formal decision-making autonomy. They were dominated by political and administrative decisions made in Paris. Both state action and territorial organization in France depended on a well-structured administration, which during long periods of political instability and unrest was relied on to keep the machinery of the state functioning.

Since the Revolution, France has been divided into 100 *departments* (four of them overseas departments), each about the size of an American county, each under the administrative responsibility of a *prefect*, and (since the Third Republic) with a directly elected general council. Since 1955, departments have been grouped into 22 *regions*, each with its own appointed prefect and, since 1986, with an elected assembly and president (see Figure 6.6).

Centralization has always been more impressive in its formal and legal aspects than it has been in practice, and the practical and political reality has always been more complex. Although France is renowned for its centralized state, what is often ignored is that political localism dilutes centralized decision making (see Box 6.5).

The process of decentralization initiated by the government of the left between 1982 and 1986 was undoubtedly the most important and effective reform passed during that period. The reform reaffirmed, reinforced, and built on the long-established system of interlocking relationships, between central and local authorities, as well as on the patterns of change during the past 25 years. To be sure, the reform altered the formal roles of all the local actors, but the greatest change was that the previously informal power of these actors was formalized.[40]

These powers are based on a system of mutual dependency between them and the prefects, as well as field services of the national ministries, which has existed since the Third Republic. The administrators of the national ministries had the formal power to implement laws, rules, and regulations at the local level. However, they needed the cooperation of local officials, who had the confidence of their constituents, to facilitate the acceptance of the authority of the central state and to provide information to operate the administration effectively at the local level. Local officials, in turn, needed the resources and aid of the administration to help their

Box 6.5   The Political Durability of Local Governments

One manifestation of the political importance of local government in France has been the ability of local units to endure. It is no accident that even after recent consolidations there are still 36,551 *communes* (the basic area of local administration), each with a mayor and council, or about as many as in the original five Common Market countries and Britain together. Almost 33,000 French communes have fewer than 2,000 inhabitants, and of these more than 22,000 have fewer than 500. What is most remarkable, however, is that since 1851 the number of communes in France has been reduced by only 400. Thus, unlike every other industrialized country, the consolidation of population in urban areas has resulted in virtually no consolidation of towns and villages.

constituents and keep their political promises.[41] As in any relationship based on permanent interaction and on cross-functioning controls, it was not always clear who controlled whom. Both the autonomy and the relational power of municipalities were conditioned by the extent of the mayor's contacts within the political and administrative network. These contacts were certainly reinforced by the linkage to national decision making that mayors had established through cumul des mandats—the ability to hold several electoral offices at the same time (limited in 1985 to two major offices, and then in 2000 to prohibit a deputy from holding a local executive office, including mayor). The change in 2000 was particularly important, since combining of the functions of a deputy or senator with those of a mayor or of a member of a departmental council (or both) was traditionally important for a political career. Similarly, a government minister may be, and usually is, a local official as well. Before 2000, this sometimes meant that a mayor's influence in Paris was greater than that of the prefect who held formal administrative authority over him. In 1997, almost 60 percent of the deputies in the National Assembly were also mayors, and perhaps two-thirds or more (and 95 percent of senators) were local officeholders at various levels.

The decentralization legislation transferred most of the formal powers of the departmental and regional prefects to the elected presidents of the departmental and regional councils. In March 1986 *regional councils* were elected for the first time (by a system of proportional representation). In one stroke, the remnants of formal prior administrative authorization of the decisions by local government were abandoned in favor of the decisions of local officials. The department presidents, elected by their department councils, are now the chief departmental executive officers, and they, rather than the prefects, control the department bureaucracy.[42] This accentuates the power of mayors of small and middle-sized towns, who control the departmental councils, to continue to protect the interests of diverse French communes. The representation of the interests of larger French cities is also enhanced by the establishment of elected regional councils, within which big-city mayors have considerable influence.

More broadly, decentralization is replacing the old dependency, which often amounted to complicity, between prefects and mayors, with a new interdependency—this time among elected officials. Interdependence also grows because there is almost no policy area over which one level of government has complete control. What then is left of the role of the central bureaucracy in controlling the periphery? The greatest loss of authority has probably been that of the prefects. Their role now seems to be limited to security (law and order) matters, to the promotion of the government's industrial policies, and to the coordination of the state bureaucracy at the departmental level.

In matters of financing, the principal mechanisms through which the state keeps its hand in local government decisions (financial dependency and standards) have weakened but have not been abandoned. There is still overall financial dependence of subnational governments on the state. Particularly at the commune level, local taxes provide only 40 percent of the annual budget (collected by the state). The price for financial assistance from above is enforced compliance with standards set by the state.

In areas in which the state retains decision-making power—police, education, a large area of welfare, and social security, as well as a great deal of construction—administrative discretion and central control remain important. There is now a consensus in France that the great project of decentralization is a success. This success is marred, however, by financial scandals that exploded in the 1990s. By the fall of 1994, one government minister was in jail, another was on the same path, and 29 members of Parliament had either been convicted or indicted. This total does not include additional local politicians and businesspeople who were in the same predicament. Although each case is somewhat different, the common thread is the corrupt link between public and private complicity at the local level, and the financing of elections and political parties at the local and national levels. Indeed, this corruption is a natural outgrowth of what one scholar terms "the ignorance of conflict of interest, the will, more or less disguised, not to raise problems with regard to situations that are in themselves incompatible."[43]

Decentralization in the 1980s, combined with the system of cumul des mandats, gave a new impetus to local officials to do on a larger scale what they previously had done in a more limited way: to trade influence for private money, to direct kickbacks into party funding operations, and to use their public office for private advantage. The pressures that led to corruption are also linked to more expensive political campaigns and an often poorly demarcated frontier between the public and private arenas in a country in which people who emerge from the grandes écoles-grands corps system move easily between the two.

It is hardly surprising that, confronted with this crisis of corrupt practices, increasingly revealed by a more independent judiciary, there were widespread proposals to limit cumul des mandats, to open the books on party finance, and to impose better controls over public spending and finance at all levels. However, scholars seem to agree that the emphasis must be on major reforms (that seem unlikely) that would better separate private from public interests.

PERFORMANCE AND PROSPECTS

A Welfare State

The overall performance of democracies can be measured by their commitment and ability to distribute the benefits of economic growth. France has a mediocre record for spreading the benefits of the postwar boom and prosperity among all its citizens. In terms of income and of wealth, discrepancies between the rich and the poor remain somewhat greater in France than in other countries of equal development. In 2001 the percentage of income-earners in the top 10 percent of incomes (25 percent) was higher than in Sweden, but lower than in Germany, the UK, or the United States. The percentage in the lowest 10 percent of incomes, on the other hand, was lower than Germany or Sweden, but higher than the UK or the United States. The income gap narrowed significantly between 1976 and 1981, and then even more during the first year of Socialist government. Yet subsequent austerity measures, especially the government's successful effort to hold down wages, have widened the gap again. The emergence of long-term unemployment has increased the number of the new poor, who are concentrated among those who are poorly trained for a rapidly evolving employment market. As opposed to the past, the majority of the lowest income group are no longer the elderly and retired, and heads of households with marginal jobs, but increasingly (particularly since 1990) younger people, many of them long-term unemployed, especially younger single parents.

Since large incomes permit the accumulation of wealth, the concentration of wealth is even more conspicuous than the steepness of the income pyramid. In the 1970s the richest 10 percent controlled between 35 and 50 percent of all wealth in France;

the poorest 10 percent owned not more than 5 percent. In the 1990s it is estimated that the richest 10 percent of the families in the country owned 50 percent of the wealth, while the richest 20 percent owned 67 percent. While income disparities narrowed somewhat until the early 1990s, the gap between the lowest and highest income groups began to grow once again during the past decade.[44]

In spite of some assertions to the contrary, it is not true that the French economy as a whole is burdened with higher taxes than other countries of similar development. Overall tax rates were higher, in 2001, than those in the UK or the United States, but lower than those in Sweden or Germany. What is special about France is the distribution of its taxes: The share of indirect taxes remains far higher in France than in other industrialized countries. Indirect taxes not only drive up prices but also weigh most heavily on the poor. The percentage of revenue collected through regressive indirect taxation was the same in 1986, after five years of Socialist government, as it had been in 1980, and remains about the same now (75 percent in 2001). The French welfare state is most effective in the area of social transfers. Their total amount has risen from 18 percent of GDP in 1970 to 29 percent in 1993, which puts France at about the same level as Germany and Denmark, but ahead of Sweden, Britain, and most other European democracies, and far ahead of the United States. A comprehensive health and social security system, established after World War II and extended since then, and a variety of programs assisting the aged, large families, the handicapped, and other such groups, disburse substantial benefits (Figure 6.7). When unemployment benefits, the cost of job-training programs, and housing subsidies are added, total costs are as high as the remainder of the public budget, with three-fourths of them borne by employers and employees.

In contrast to the United States, there have been fewer cutbacks in welfare state programs in France in recent years—even after the cutbacks of pension benefits in 2003. Indeed the population covered by health insurance has expanded, but financing for these programs has been at the heart of government concerns since 1995 (see Table 6.4). Although, as a percentage of GDP, spending on so-

FIGURE 6.7   The French Budget, 2002

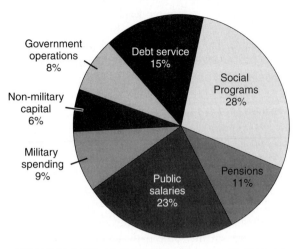

Source: Lois de Reglement, Budget de 2002, AN 24 September 2003.
Note: Military spending excludes pensions.

cial programs has remained stable since 1984, the government cut public spending to reduce its budget deficit in a successful effort to conform to criteria for the common European currency. In 2003 there were important changes in pension entitlements. In addition, some important gaps in benefits remain. For example, full health benefits depend on supplementary insurance coverage generally provided to most (but not all) in the active workforce. In 1994, only 59 percent of unemployed workers and 58 percent of foreign workers had this additional but necessary coverage.

High levels of unemployment and poverty, and problems of homelessness create pressures to expand social programs while diminishing the revenue base that finances them. Since 1998 the French government has confronted many of the same social service problems facing the United States, but resistance to the American-type solutions is widespread. In 1999, for example, as part of the campaign to fight "social exclusion" in France, the Socialist government passed legislation instituting universal medical coverage. This means-tested, tax-financed, and targeted health insurance program represents a departure from the tradition of social insurance in France.

TABLE 6.4   State Spending and Welfare State Spending

	Government Expenditure as Percent of GDP 2001	Government Employment as Percent of Total Employment 1996–2000	State Contributions to Protection Programs as Percent of GDP 2001	State Health Expenses as Percentage of GDP 1994	2001
Britain	40.2	18.7	27.2	5.2	6.2
France	52.5	20.1	30.0	6.6	7.2
Germany	48.3	12.3	29.8	6.3	8.0
Italy	48.5	20.5	25.6	5.3	6.4
Spain	39.3	11.6	20.6	4.7	5.6
Sweden	57.2	6.6	31.3	–	7.4
U.S.	34.9	15.6	16.0	5.2	6.2

Source: OECD, 2003, French Ministry of Finance, 2004, Eurostat 2004, OECD Public Sector Pay and Employment Database.

Nationalization and Regulation

Government-operated business enterprises have long existed in France in fields that are under private ownership in other countries of Western Europe. After several waves of nationalization in the 1930s and after the end of World War II, the government owned and operated all or part of the following: railroads; almost all energy production (mining, electricity, nuclear energy) and much of telecommunication (radio and television); most air and maritime transport; most of the aeronautic industry; 85 percent of bank deposits; 40 percent of insurance premiums; one-third of the automobile industry; one-third of the housing industry. All this is in addition to the old state monopolies of mail services, telephone, telegraph, tobacco, match manufacture, and various less important activities.

By the 1970s public enterprises accounted for about 11 percent of the gross national product. Fifteen percent of the total active population, or 27 percent of all salary and wage earners (excluding agricultural labor), were paid directly by the state either as civil servants as salaried workers or on a contractual basis. Their income came close to one-third of the total sum of wages and salaries.

Legislation enacted in 1981 and 1982, during the first governments of the left, completed the nationalization of the banking sector, expanded state ownership to 13 of the 20 largest firms in France, and controlled interest to many others in such fields as machine tools, chemistry (including pharmaceutical products), glass, metals, and electrical power. In addition, the government obtained majority control of two important armaments firms and several ailing steel companies.

The conservative government that held power in 1986–1988 substantially altered the structure of the nationalized sector in France, accelerating a trend of partial privatization begun during the government of the left. But its ambitious plans for *privatization* were halted (40 percent completed) only a year after their implementation began, in part because of the collapse of the stock market in 1987.[45] Thus some, but not all, of the companies that were nationalized by the Socialist government in 1982 were returned to private stockholders. The conservative government also privatized some companies that had long been controlled by the state. However, both the companies that were returned to private hands and those that remained in the hands of the state were quite different from what they had been a few years before. Recapitalized, restructured, and modernized, for the most part they were, in 1988, the leading edge of the French industrial machine.[46]

Even after privatization, however, about 22 percent of all salary and wage earners received their checks directly or indirectly from the French state in 1997. While this was high compared with the U.S. percentage, it was not out of line from other European countries. If one out of five French citizens depended on the state for their paychecks in the 1990s, so did almost one out of five Britons and one out of eight Germans (see again Table 6.4).

For the actual operation of French business, the move begun by the Socialists and continued by the conservative government toward deregulation of the economy was probably more important than privatization. The deregulation of the stock market, the banking system, telecommunications, and prices has fundamentally changed the way business is conducted in both the private and public sectors.[47] The combination of budgetary rigor and state disengagement meant a real reduction of aid to industry. Sectors in difficulty, including steel, chemicals, shipbuilding, and automobile manufacturing, were therefore forced to accelerate their rationalization plans and their cutbacks in workers.

The conservative government elected in 1993 continued to diminish state holdings in some companies and privatize others, without, however, altering the main lines of industrial and economic policy. As a result, the interventionist and regulatory weight of the state in industry is less important now than it was before the Socialists came to power in 1981. Today, all of the major remaining nationalized industries are either in the process of, or being proposed for, at least partial privatization. In addition, shares have been sold in Air France, and it now competes with other airlines within the French and European markets. The old issue of nationalization and ownership has been bypassed and replaced by more subtle issues of control and regulation in the context of global competition.

In other areas, the regulatory weight of the state has not diminished but has changed during the past 25 years. During the 1970s France expanded individual rights by fully establishing the rights to divorce and abortion. Under the Socialist governments of the 1980s, capital punishment was abolished, the rights of those accused of crimes were strengthened, and detention without trial was checked by new procedures. After much wrangling,

in 1994 the Parliament replaced the obsolete Criminal Code dating from the time of Napoléon. The new code is generally hailed as expressing a consensus across the political spectrum on questions of crime and punishment. Moreover, individual rights in France must now conform to the decisions of the European courts under the general umbrella of the European Union. Finally, in conformity with the Maastricht Treaty, citizenship rights of EU residents in France have increased during the 1990s; a right to the presumption of innocence in criminal cases now exists.

In still other areas, the regulatory weight of the state has increased. One of the most obvious is environmental controls. In the 1990s the French state was making its first significant efforts to regulate individual behavior that has an impact on the environment: The first limitations on smoking, for example, came into effect in the late 1980s and expanded after that. In an effort to deal with the politics of immigration, particularly after 1993, the state increased the regulation of all residents of foreign origin in ways that have diminished individual rights, and most recently France has moved to regulate "ostentatious" religious symbols worn by students in public schools.

Outlook: France and the New Architecture of Europe

The main concerns that dominated French politics three decades ago have changed dramatically. Twenty-five years ago, a coalition of Socialists and Communists was promising a "rupture" with capitalism, and the ideological distance between left and right appeared to be enormous. Today, none of the major parties—including the National Front—is presenting any proposal for dramatic change in society or the political system. As in the United States, political parties are making their commitments as vague and as flexible as possible (with the exception of the National Front). After an experiment with socialism, followed by a reaction of conservative neoliberalism, political parties appeared to be out of fresh ideas on how to deal with the major problems of the French economy and society. The transition away from a smokestack economy has been difficult and painful, and the resulting unemployment continues to dominate public concerns.

Political cleavages based on new conflicts are emerging, even if their outlines are still unclear. Indeed, the issues of the first decade of the twenty-first century may very well be more profound and untenable than those of the past. The political stakes have moved away from questioning the nature of the regime: they are focused much more intensely on the nature of the political community. Between 1986 and the present, this has become evident in a variety of ways.

Immigration has given way to ethnic consciousness, particularly among the children of immigrants from North Africa. Unlike most of the immigrant communities in the past, those of today are more reluctant to assume French cultural values as their own. This, in turn, leads to questioning the rules of naturalization for citizenship, integration into French society, and (in the end) what it means to be French.[48] During the 1980s growing ethnic tensions were given a political voice by the National Front, which mobilized voters and solidified support based on racist appeals. In part because of the growing role of the FN, ethnic consciousness and diversity have grown in France and altered the context of French politics.

Fifteen years ago, the Cold War and the division of Europe was a fact of life and was the basis for much of French foreign, defense, and, to some extent, domestic policy. The Cold War is long over. As a result, Eastern European ethnic consciousness and conflicts previously held in check by Soviet power, and in any case insulated from Western Europe by the Iron Curtain, now have been suddenly liberated. The disintegration of the Soviet Communist experiment (and the Soviet Union) has also had the broader impact of undermining the legitimacy of classic socialism and has thus removed from French (and European) politics many of the issues that have separated left from right for over a hundred years. Parties of the right have lost the anti-Communist glue that has contributed to their cohesiveness, but parties of the left have lost much of their purpose.

Coincidentally, this process of Eastern European disintegration has accelerated at the same time that the countries of the European Union have rein-vigorated the process of European integration, with France in the lead. Membership in the European Union shapes almost every aspect of policy and policy planning and provides the context for the expansion and restructuring of the economy during the Fifth Republic (also see Chapter 12).[49]

At the beginning of his presidency in the early 1980s, François Mitterrand expressed his satisfaction with the existing structures of the Common Market. Having experienced their weakness, however, he increasingly felt that some form of federalism—a federalist finality—was necessary to enable Western Europe to use its considerable resources more effectively. Thus, during the Mitterrand presidency, France supported a larger and a more tightly integrated Europe, including efforts to increase the powers of European institutions and the establishment of a European monetary and political union as outlined in the Maastricht Treaty, approved somewhat reluctantly in 1992. French commitment to a common European currency generated most of the plans to cut public spending plans that many French citizens ferociously resisted. Nevertheless, in 1998 France met all key requirements for European monetary union and is now firmly part of the Euro-12 within the European Union.

The opening of French borders, not only to the products of other countries but increasingly to their people and values (all citizens of the European Union had the right to vote and run for office in the French local elections in 2001), feeds into the more general uneasiness about French national identity. The integration of French economic and social institutions with those of its neighbors will progressively remove key decisions from the French government acting alone. In the past, the French economy reacted to joint decisions made in Brussels. In the future, a broader range of institutions will be forced to do the same. Rumblings of resistance are no longer limited to the fringe parties (the parties of the extreme right and the Communists); opposition exists within all of the major political parties, especially the UMP. Here, too, there is considerable potential for new political divisions.

This chapter, written at the beginning of the twentieth-first century, during the second presidential term of Jacques Chirac, presents a story of a strong and stable political system with an increasingly volatile and unstable party system. The forces that appear to be destabilizing the party system are the major challenges now confronting all of the members of the European Union: the problem of identity in an expanding European union and an independent world; the problem of democratic legitimacy among voters who are less ideologically committed, increasingly skeptical of government and politicians, but who expect more from government.

 Key Terms

baccalauréat
blocked vote
Napoléon Bonaparte
Cabinet (government)
Jacques Chirac
communes
Confédération
    Française
    Democratique du
    Travail (CFDT)
Confédération Générale
    du Travail (CGT)
Constitution of 1958
Constitutional Council
Council of Ministers
Council of State
cumul des mandats
    (accumulation of
    electoral offices)
Charles de Gaulle

departments
Ecole Nationale d'
    Administration
    (ENA)
Ecole Polytechnique
European Union
    (European
    Community before
    1992)
events of 1968
Fédération de'
    Education
    Nationale (FEN)
Fédération Nationale
    des Syndicats
    Agricoles (FNSEA)
Fifth Republic
Force Ouvrière (FO)
Fourth Republic

French Communist
    Party (PCF)
G-10
grandes écoles
grands corps
Robert Hue
Lionel Jospin
Alain Juppé
Jean-Marie Le Pen
Maastricht Treaty
Georges Marchais
François Mitterrand
motion of censure
Mouvement des
    Entreprises de
    France (MEDEF)
Muslims
National Assembly
National Front (FN)

nationalization
neocorporatism
"new" immigration
ordinances
political class
prefects
president of the Republic
prime minister
privatization
Rally for the Republic
    (RPR)
referendum
regions
Senate
Socialist Party (PS)
Union for French
    Democracy (UDF)
Union for a Popular
    Movement (UMP)

 Internet Sources

Office of the President: http://www.elysee.fr/ang/index.shtm
National Assembly: http://www.assemblee-nat.fr

Senate: http://www.senat.fr
Embassy of France in the U.S.: www.info-france-usa.org

 Suggested Readings

Ambler, John, ed. *The Welfare State in France*. New York: New York University Press, 1991.

Baumgartner, Frank R. *Conflict and Rhetoric in French Policymaking*. Pittsburgh, PA: University of Pittsburgh Press, 1989.

Bell, D. S., and Byron Criddle. *The French Socialist Party: The Emergence of a Party of Government*, 2nd ed. Oxford, England: Clarendon Press/Oxford, 1988.

Chapman, Herrick, Mark Kesselman, and Martin Schain. *A Century of Organized Labor in France*. New York: St. Martin's Press, 1998.

Converse, Philip, and Roy Pierce. *Political Representation in France*. Cambridge, MA: Harvard University Press, 1986.

Gallie, Duncan. *Social Inequality and Class Radicalism in France and Britain*. London: Cambridge University Press, 1983.

Gordon, Philip, and Sophie Meunier. *The French Challenge*. Washington, DC: Brookings Institution Press, 2001.

Hall, Peter. *Governing the Economy: The Politics of State Intervention in Britain and France*. New York: Oxford University Press, 1986.

Hall, Peter, Jack Hayward, and Howard Machin, eds. *Developments in French Politics*, rev. ed. London: Macmillan, 1994.

Hayward, Jack. *The State and the Market Economy: Industrial Patriotism and Economic Intervention in France*. New York: New York University Press, 1986.

Hollifield, James. *Immigrants, Markets, and States: The Political Economy of Postwar Europe*. Cambridge, MA: Harvard University Press, 1992.

Hollifield, James, and George Ross, eds. *In Search of the New France*. New York: Routledge, 1991.

Howell, Chris. *Regulating Labor: The State and Industrial Relations in Postwar France*. Princeton, NJ: Princeton University Press, 1992.

Ireland, Patrick. *The Policy Challenge of Ethnic Diversity: Immigrant Politics in France and Switzerland*. Cambridge, MA: Harvard University Press, 1994.

Johnson, R. W. *The Long March of the French Left*. New York: St. Martins Press, 1981.

Keeler, John T. S., *The Politics of Neocorporatism in France*. New York: Oxford University Press, 1987.

Keeler, John T. S., and Martin A. Schain. *Chirac's Challenge: Liberation, Europeanization, and Malaise in France*. New York: St. Martin's, 1996.

Lewis-Beck, Michael. *The French Voter Before and After the 2002 Elections*. Basingstoke: Palgrave 2004.

Mazur, Amy. *Gender Bias and the State: Feminist Policy at Work in France*. Pittsburgh, PA: University of Pittsburgh Press, 1995.

Schain, Martin. *French Communism and Local Power*. New York: St. Martin's Press, 1985.

Schmidt, Vivien A. *Democratizing France*. New York: Cambridge University Press, 1990.

———. *From State to Market: The Transformation of Business and Government*. New York: Cambridge University Press, 1996.

Smith, Rand W. *Crisis in the French Labor Movement: A Grassroots Perspective*. New York: St. Martin's Press, 1988.

Stone, Alec. *The Birth of Judicial Politics in France: The Constitutional Council in Comparative Perspective*. New York: Oxford University Press, 1992.

Suleiman, Ezra. *Elites in French Society*. Princeton, NJ: Princeton University Press, 1978.

———. *Private Power and Centralization in France*. Princeton, NJ: Princeton University Press, 1987.

Wilsford, David. *Doctors and the State: The Politics of Health Care in France and the United States*. Durham, NC: Duke University Press, 1991.

Wilson, Frank L. *Interest Group Politics in France*. New York: Cambridge University Press, 1987.

 Endnotes

1. The best recent book in English on the Constitutional Council is Alec Stone, *The Birth of Judicial Politics in France* (New York: Oxford University Press, 1992).

2. Laurence Wylie, "Social Change at the Grass Roots," in Stanley Hoffmann, Charles P. Kindleberger, Jesse R. Pitts, et al., *In Search of France* (Cambridge, MA: Harvard University Press, 1963), p. 230.

3. See Olivier Duhamel, "Confance institutionnelle et *défrance* politique: *la démocratic* française," in Sofres, *L'État de l'opinion 2001* (Paris: Editions du Seuil, 2001), p. 75.

4. Interesting data on religious practice can be found in extensive opinion polls published in Sofres, *L'Etat de l'opinion 1994* (Paris: Editions du Seuil, 1994), pp. 179–99. These data are taken from an unpublished exit poll dated May 26, 1997.

5. Duncan Gallie, *Social Inequality and Class Radicalism in France and Britain* (London: Cambridge University Press, 1983), p. 34.

6. Annick Percheron, "Socialization et tradition: transmission et invention du politique," *Pouvoirs* 42 (1988): 43.

7. Edgar Morin, *The Red and the White* (New York: Pantheon Books, 1970), Ch. 8, discusses the noisy revolution of the teenagers and the silent one of women.

8. This is the amply documented thesis of Janine Mossuz-Lavau and Mariette Sineau, *Les Femmes françaises en 1978: Insertion sociale, Insertion politique* (Paris: Centre de Documentation Sciences Humaine de CNRS, 1980). The authors also found that women who were no longer working but had been employed previously were likely to express opinions closer to those of working than of nonworking women.

9. Annick Percheron and M. Kent Jennings, "Political Continuities in French Families: A New Perspective on an Old Controversy," *Comparative Politics* 13, No. 4 (July 1981).

10. Ronald Inglehart, *Culture Shift* (Princeton, NJ: Princeton University Press, 1990), Chs. 1–3 and Table 2.4, and Triblat, *Faire France* (Paris: La Découverte, 1995), pp. 93–98.

11. The best summary of the evolution of group membership in France is found in Laurence Haeusler, "Le monde associatif de 1978 1986," in INSEE, *Données Sociales 1990*

(Paris: INSEE, 1990), pp. 369–70. See also Henry Ehrmann and Martin Schain, *Politics in France*, 5th ed. (New York: HarperCollins, 1992), Table 3.6, p. 103.

12. Data on education are taken from *Données Sociales 1996* (Paris: INSEE, 1996), pp. 40–47; *L'Etat de la France 97–98* (Paris: Editions la Découerte, 1997), p. 113; *The Economist*, September 18, 1993, p. 52; *Le Monde*, October 16, 1994, p. 16; and *Tableaux de—l'conomie française*, 1999–2000 (Paris: INSEE, 2000), pp. 52–57.

13. John Ambler, "Constraints on Policy Innovation in Education: Thatcher's Britain and Mitterrand's France," *Comparative Politics* 20, No. 1 (October 1987). See also John Ambler, "Conflict and Consensus in French Education," in John T. S. Keeler and Martin A. Schain, eds., *Chirac's Challenge: Liberalization, Europeanization and Malaise in France* (New York: St. Martins Press, 1996).

14. The restrictive recruitment of the grandes écoles is confirmed by a recent study: "Le recruitment social de l élite scholaire depuis quarante ans," *Education et Formations*, No. 41 (June 1995). Which institutions qualify as grandes écoles is controversial. But among the 140 or so designated as such in some estimates, only 15 or 20, with an enrollment of 2,000 to 2,500, are considered important, prestige schools. The number of engineering and business schools that are generally considered to be grandes écoles has increased in recent years. Therefore the total enrollment of all these schools has increased significantly to well over 100,000.

15. These results are taken from various sources and have been compiled by Russell J. Dalton in *Citizen Politics in Western Democracies* (Washington, DC: CQ Press, 2002), Ch. 2. See Sofres, *L'Etat de l'opinion 1994* (Paris: Seuil, 1994), p. 232.

16. There is no legal definition for any of these terms (nor is there any legal definition for a grande école), although they are widely used by citizens, journalists, and scholars. Thus the figures given here for the early 1980s are approximations, based on positional and reputational definitions given by J-T Bodiguel and J-L Quermonne in *La Haute fonction publique sous la Ve République* (Paris: PUF, 1983), pp. 12–25, 83–94.

17. This system has now been called into question by the *Conseil d'Etat*, the highest French administrative court. In a decision rendered in December 1996, the court annulled the appointment of a high civil servant as the assistant director of a semipublic bank on the grounds of conflict of interest. Indeed the law that was being interpreted dated back to 1919(!), amended in 1994. If broadly applied, this decision would undermine part of the basis of overlap of public and private elites; see "Pantouflage: l'onde de choc," *L'Express*, December 19, 1996, pp. 50–52.

18. Nancy J. Walker, "What We Know About Voters in Britain, France and West Germany," *Public Opinion* (May–June 1988).

19. These percentages are only approximations, since interest groups in France either refuse to publish membership figures or publish figures that are universally viewed as highly questionable. For estimates of interest group member-
ships, see Peter Hall, "Pluralism and Pressure Politics," in Peter Hall, Jack Hayward, and Howard Machin, *Developments in French Politics*, rev. ed. (London: Macmillan, 1994). For the most recent estimates of trade union membership, see Antoine Bevort, "Les effectifs syndiqués à la CGT et à la CFDT 1945–1990," *Communisme*, No. 35–37, 1994. Data indicate that membership decline is continuing. See also the recent study by Dominique Labbé, *La Syndicalisation en France depuis 1945* (Grenoble, France: CERAP, 1995).

20. Herrick Chapman, Mark Kesselman, and Martin Schain, *A Century of Organized Labor in France* (New York: St. Martin's Press, 1998).

21. The most recent studies are reported in *Communisme*, 35–37, 1994, p. 77, and Sofres, *L'Etat de l'opinion 1994*, pp. 264–65. See also Mark Kesselman, "Does the French Labor Movement Have a Future?" in Keeler and Schain, *Chirac's Challenge*.

22. Sofres, *L'Etat de l'opinion 1996*, p. 246; *The Economist*, September 16, 2000; and Roland Cayrol "Unions and French Public Opinion" in Chapman, Kesselman, and Schain, *A Century of Organized Labor*.

23. The most recent serious study of the CNPF and its affiliates by Henri Weber, *Le Parti des patrons: Le CNPF 184–86* (Paris: Editions du Seuil, 1986), analyzes various trends within the patronat and is based on much detailed inside information. One of the earliest studies of the CNPF was written by Henry W. Ehrmann. *Organized Business in France* (Princeton, NJ: Princeton University Press, 1957) presents case studies about the contacts between the administration and the employers organizations, but it is now dated of course.

24. John Keeler, *The Politics of Neocorporatism in France* (New York: Oxford University Press, 1987).

25. Frank Wilson, *Interest-Group Politics in France* (New York: Cambridge University Press, 1987), pp. 151, 153, 162, 164.

26. John T. S. Keeler, "Situating France on the Pluralism-Corporatism Continuum," *Comparative Politics* 17 (January 1985): 229–49.

27. See the articles by John Ambler, Frank Baumgartner, Martin Schain, and Frank Wilson in *French Politics and Society* 12, (Spring/Summer 1994).

28. For a good survey of party developments between 1958 and 1981, see Frank L. Wilson, *French Political Parties Under the Fifth Republic* (New York: Praeger, 1982).

29. For good estimates of party membership, see Colette Ysmal, "Transformations du militantisme et déclin des partis," in Pascal Perrineau, *L'Engagement Politique, déclin ou mutation?* (Paris: Presses de la FNSP, 1994), p. 48. Also see l'Etat de la France (Paris: La Découverte, 1997), pp. 521–26.

30. Stanley Hoffmann, *Le Mouvement Poujade* (Paris: A. Colin, 1956).

31. D. S. Bell and Byron Criddle, *The French Socialist Party: The Emergence of a Party of Government*, 2nd ed. (Oxford, England: Clarendon, 1988).

32. For an analysis of the decline of the Communist vote, see Martin Schain, "The French Communist Party: The Seeds

of Its Own Decline," in Peter Katzenstein, Theodore Lowi, and Sidney Tarrow, *Comparative Theory and Political Experience* (Ithaca, NY: Cornell University Press, 1990). For additional insights into the decline of the PCF electorate, see Jane Jenson and George Ross, *View from the Inside: A French Communist Cell in Crisis* (Berkeley: University of California Press, 1984), part 5.

33. It must be noted—and this is true for all figures on electoral participation throughout this chapter—that French statistics calculate electoral participation on the basis of registered voters, while American statistics take as a basis the total number of people of voting age. About 9 percent of French citizens entitled to vote are not registered. This percentage must therefore be added to the published figures when one wishes to estimate the true rate of abstention and to compare it with the American record.

34. On abstention, see Françoise Subileau and Marie-France Toinet, *Les chemins de l'abstention* (Editions de la découverte, 1993), and Marie-France Toinet, "The Limits of Malaise in France," in Keeler and Schain, *Chirac's Challenge*, pp. 289–91.

35. *Le Monde*, June 15, 2002, p. 8.

36. This analysis is taken from John T. S. Keeler and Martin A. Schain, "Presidents, Premiers and Models of Democracy in France," in Keeler and Schain, eds., *Chirac's Challenge*.

37. One of the very few analyses of the use of the blocked vote, as well as the use by the government of Article 49.3, can be found in John Huber, "Restrictive Legislative Procedures in France and the United States," *American Political Science Review* 86, No. 3 (September 1992); 675–87. Huber's article is also the only attempt to compare such tools with similar procedures in the U.S. Congress.

38. Didier Maus, "Parliament in the Fifth Republic: 1958–1988," in Paul Godt, *Policy-Making in France* (New York: Pinter, 1989), p. 17; and Didier Maus, *Les grands textes de la pratique institutionelle de la Ve République* (Paris: La Documentation Française, 1992).

39. This phrase refers to the first article of the constitution of 1793, which proclaims that "The French Republic is one and indivisible." The constitution of the Fifth Republic repeats it.

40. Vivien A. Schmidt, *Democratizing France* (New York: Cambridge University Press, 1990).

41. The now classic statement of this relationship was written by Jean-Pierre Worms, who years later had major responsi-bilities for developing the decentralization reforms for the government of the left. See "Le Préfet et ses notables," *Sociologie du Travail* 8, No. 3 (1966): 249–75.

42. Mark Kesselman, "The Tranquil Revolution at Clochemerle: Socialist Decentralization in France," in Philip G. Cerny and Martin A. Schain, *Socialism, the State, and Public Policy in France* (New York: St. Martin's Press, 1985), p. 176.

43. Yves Mény, "Les formes discrètes de la corruption," in *French Politics and Society* 11, No. 4 (Fall 1993), special issue on "Etats de la corruption." Mény has also written *La Corruption et la République* (Paris: Fayard, 1992), where he develops many of these ideas on systemic contributions to corruption. In the same issue of *French Politics and Society*, Dominique Lorrain writes about the contribution of local finance to corruption, and Jean-Pierre Worms, the architect of the decentralization legislation, comments on the relationship between corruption and decentralization. See also Ezra N. Suleiman, "The Politics of Corruption and the Corruption of Politics," *French Politics and Society* 9, No. 1 (Winter 1991).

44. See *Le Monde*, October 7, 1999, p. 6.

45. As a result, the number of workers paid indirectly by the state declined. Nevertheless, the proportion of the workforce paid directly by the state (government employment) remained stable at about 23 percent, about a third higher than the United States, Germany, and Italy, but lower than the Scandinavian countries. See Vincent Wright, "Reshaping the State: The Implications for Public Administration," *West European Politics* 17, No. 3 (July 1994).

46. They were also controlled by the same people as when they were nationalized. None of the newly privatized firms changed managing directors. See Michel Bauer, "The Politics of State-Directed Privatization: The Case of France 1986–1988," *West European Politics* 11, No. 4 (October 1988): 59.

47. Philip G. Cerny, "The 'Little Big Bang' in Paris," *European Journal of Political Research* 17, No. 2 (1989).

48. Martin Baldwin Edwards and Martin A. Schain, eds., *The Politics of Immigration in Western Europe* (London: Frank Cass, 1994).

49. See Alain Gayomarch, Howard Machin, and Ella Ritchie, *France and the European Union* (New York: St. Martin's Press, 1998).

Germany

0 50 100 mi
0 80 160 km

DENMARK

BALTIC
SEA

N

NORTH
SEA

Kiel

SCHLESWIG-
HOLSTEIN

Rostock

MECKLENBURG-
WEST POMERANIA

Hamburg

BREMEN

Elbe

Bremen

HAMBURG

NETHER-
LANDS

LOWER   SAXONY

BERLIN

Potsdam

Berlin

Hannover

Weser

Magdeburg

BRANDENBURG

POLAND

NORTH RHINE-
WESTPHALIA

Essen

SAXONY-
ANHALT

Düsseldorf

Leipzig

SAXONY

Cologne

Rhine

Erfurt

Dresden

Bonn

THURINGIA

BELGIUM

HESSE

RHINELAND-
PALATINATE

Wiesbaden

CZECH
REPUBLIC

Mainz

SAAR-
LAND

Nuremberg

LUXEMBOURG

BAVARIA

FRANCE

Stuttgart

Danube

BADEN-
WÜRTTEMBERG

Munich

AUSTRIA

Lake
Constance

LIECHTENSTEIN

SWITZERLAND

ITALY

Chapter 7

Politics in Germany

RUSSELL J. DALTON

Country Bio—Germany

POPULATION: 82.4 Million

TERRITORY: 137,803 sq. mi

YEAR OF INDEPENDENCE: 1871

YEAR OF CURRENT CONSTITUTION: 1949

HEAD OF STATE: President Horst Köhler

HEAD OF GOVERNMENT: Chancellor Gerhard Schröder

LANGUAGE(S):   German

RELIGION: Protestant 34%, Roman Catholic 34%, Muslim 4%, unaffiliated or other 28%

In 2002 German voters selected the government, choosing between continuing the leftist coalition led by *Gerhard Schröder* or changing direction with a new conservative government. On election night the vote projections switched back and forth—much like the U.S. presidential election in 2000.

Schröder's Social Democratic-Green government was returned to power, but the closeness of the election illustrates the uncertainty about which policy courses Germany should follow in the years ahead. The economy continues to stagnate, with GDP growth rates falling below the European average and nearly 4 million workers on the unemployment rolls. There does not appear to be a consensus on the policies that could improve the economy. Germany is struggling to define its international role in the post–Cold War world, and the election illustrated the disagreements among political elites and the public on these roles. Thus the Schröder government retained office, but popular support quickly deteriorated in the public opinion polls.

The elections also reflected the lingering consequences of an even more revolutionary event: with the opening of the Berlin Wall on November 9, 1989, East and West Germany began an amazing process leading toward unification. Since the end of World

War II, Germany was divided between the *Federal Republic of Germany (FRG)* in the West, and the Communist-led *German Democratic Republic (GDR)* in the East. In 1989 "people power" protests rose up in revolution against the Communist regime. The East Germans' willingness to take a stand against the state, and the state's unwillingness to suppress its people with force, brought the communist system to its end. The once formidable East German government collapsed almost overnight and all eyes turned West, toward the Federal Republic of Germany as a source of stability and political reform. Protesters who had chanted "we are the people" when opposing the Communist government in October took up the call for unification with a new refrain: "we are one people."

In less than a year, the unimaginable was a reality. Two German states—one democratic and one communist, one with a market economy and one with a socialist planned economy—were united. German unification has reshaped the map of Europe and it has reshaped how we think about Germany and the lessons of German history. In one sense, this change repeats the pattern of Germany's discontinuous political development that has vacillated between authoritarian states and democratic ones. Germany is building a new nation uniting East and West, and this nation has strong democratic roots. However, many of the problems wrought by unification remain unresolved. There are continuing economic inequalities between East and West, and unemployment is much higher in the East. The policy priorities and positions also differ between regions, with the East favoring more extensive social service programs and a limited military role for Germany. Socially and politically, the "wall in the mind" still divides Westerners and Easterners, even if the Berlin Wall has been destroyed.

The major achievement of contemporary German politics is the creation of a unified, free, and democratic Germany in the heart of Europe. This has contributed to the political stability of Europe, and given millions of Eastern Germans their freedom and new opportunities. Now the challenge facing the new government is to maintain the social and economic vitality of the nation, and build a policy consensus on the reforms to achieve these goals.

CURRENT POLICY CHALLENGES

What political problems do Germans typically read about when they open the daily newspaper or watch their favorite TV newscast—and what political problems preoccupy policymakers in Bonn and Berlin? Often the answer is the same as in most other industrial democracies. News reports analyze the state of the economy, report on crime, and generally track the social and economic health of the nation.

Overshadowing any specific event is a persisting concern about the problems arising from German unification. Unification achieved an important national goal for Germany, brought freedom to the residents of the former German Democratic Republic (GDR), and ended the Cold War conflict. Unification also reflects that old proverbial punishment: "May you get what you wish." Because the economic infrastructure of the East lagged far behind that of the West, severe economic problems resulted from unification. Government agencies and the European Union have invested more than 1,000 billion Euros (€) in the East since unification—raising taxes for all Germans in the process. And still, the nightly news routinely chronicles the continuing economic difficulties in the East, which affect the entire nation (see Box 7.1).

The challenges of unification involve more than economics, however. Different life experiences and different values continue to divide Westerners and Easterners. Indeed, in some ways the psychological gap between the regions has widened since unification. There are growing signs of a "wall in the mind" separating residents in both halves of the country. Even in unified Berlin, Westerners and Easterners read separate newspapers and live separate lives, although they now reside next door to one another.

Another set of concerns involves the general socioeconomic course of the nation. Most Germans agree that their present economic system and social programs need reform—but they cannot agree on the direction the reforms should take. There are mounting concerns that a stagnating economy might threaten the long-term economic

---

Box 7.1   The Curse of Unification?

Germany's attempt to rebuild its once communist East has been an unmitigated disaster and the massive financial transfers from the West endanger the entire nation's economy, according to a government-commissioned report.

A panel of 13 experts headed by former Hamburg Mayor Klaus von Dohnanyi charged with examining the reconstruction of Germany's eastern states has concluded the estimated €1.25 trillion ($1.54 trillion) in aid has done little to help the economically depressed region.

Perhaps even more worrying, the experts fear the €90 billion spent by the government each year is slowly destroying the economy of western Germany, as growth stagnates and the eastern states fail to revive 14 years after German reunification.

Source: The Deutsche Welle Report (April 4, 2004): 62.

---

well-being of the nation. German firms claim they have difficulty competing in a global marketplace because of government and labor restrictions. German labor costs and benefits are quite high by international standards, without a comparable level of productivity to justify these costs. At the same time, efforts to introduce more competitiveness into the economy or pursue labor reforms are criticized by many as creating an "elbow society" where people will push each other aside in pursuit of personal gain. Thus, Schröder's attempt at structural reform—Agenda 2010—is generally seen as failing to take sufficiently decisive action to address these concerns. Most Germans consider themselves economically well off at the present, thus the proposals for structural reform aimed at long-term changes evoke mixed reactions.

Health, pension, and other social welfare costs are also spiraling upward, but there is little agreement on how to address these problems. As the German population ages, the demands being placed on the social welfare system will predictably increase. However, debate has not produced clear policy action. In short, the *Sozialstaat* consensus that typified German politics for the later half of the twentieth century has not carried beyond into the new century.

The challenges of becoming a multicultural nation have also become a new source of political tension. While some argue that "the boat is full" and new immigration should be limited, others claim that continued immigration is essential for Germany's future. Unification has also accentuated the issue of ethnicity in Germany. There are continuing debates about immigration and the policies to address an increasing diverse society. The Schröder government changed citizenship laws in 2000 and reformed immigration legislation in 2002, but the public remains divided on the appropriate policies. Like much of the rest of Europe, Germany is now struggling to address these issues, which is made more difficult because of the legacy of Germany's past.

Finally, Germany's new foreign policy challenges are receiving increased attention. The European Union (EU) is an increasingly visible part of political reporting, and Germans are trying to determine their desired role in an expanding European Union. Germany has been a prime advocate of the expansion of EU membership to Eastern Europe, even though this may dilute Germany's influence within the EU. EU policies such as monetary union and the development of a European currency are creating internal divisions about Germany's relationship to the Union.

In addition, Germany is struggling to define its role in the post–Cold War world. For the first time since World War II, German troops took part in a military action in Kosovo in 1999, and participated in the liberation of Afghanistan in 2001. However, Schröder actively opposed American policy toward Iraq, while still claiming to value the special relationship with the United States. Germany's role in the NATO military alliance and in this changing international context remains a point of policy debate.

Despite these ongoing issues, the Federal Republic is one of the most successful and vibrant democracies in the world today. Its political system is ready to address these challenges, even while it debates the appropriate response to the political transformations in Eastern Europe and increasing unification of East and West Europe. Without a popular consensus on the direction of change, any significant policy advances will be difficult to achieve.

THE HISTORICAL LEGACY

The German historical experience differs considerably from that of most other European democracies. The social and political forces that modernized the rest of Europe came much later in Germany and had a less certain effect. By the nineteenth century when most nations had defined their borders, German territory was still divided among dozens of political units. Although a dominant national culture had evolved in most European states, Germany was torn by sharp religious, regional, and economic divisions. Industrialization generally was the driving force behind the modernization of Europe, but German industrialization came late and did not overturn the old feudal and aristocratic order. German history, even to the present, represents a difficult and protracted process of nation-building.

The Second German Empire

Through a combination of military and diplomatic victories, Otto von Bismarck, the Prussian chancellor, enlarged the territory of Prussia and established a unified Second German Empire in 1871.[1] The empire was an authoritarian state, with only the superficial trappings of a democracy. Political power flowed from the monarch—the *Kaiser*—and the government at times bitterly suppressed potential opposition groups—especially the Roman Catholic Church and the Social Democrats. The government expected little of its citizens: they were to pay their taxes, serve in the army, and keep their mouths shut.

The central government pushed ahead national development during this period. Industrialization finally developed, and German influence in international affairs grew steadily. The force of industrialization was not sufficient to modernize and liberalize society and the political system, however. Economic and political power remained concentrated in the hands of the bureaucracy and traditional aristocratic elites. Democratic reforms were thwarted by an authoritarian state strong enough to resist the political demands of a weak middle class. The state was supreme: its needs took precedence over those of individuals and society.

Failures of government leadership, coupled with a blindly obedient public, led Germany into World War I (1914–1918). The war devastated the nation. Almost 3 million German soldiers and civilians lost their lives, the economy was strained beyond the breaking point, and the government of the empire collapsed under the weight of its own incapacity to govern. The war ended with Germany a defeated and exhausted nation.

The Weimar Republic

In 1919 a popularly elected constitutional assembly established the new democratic system of the *Weimar Republic.* The constitution granted all citizens the right to vote and guaranteed basic human rights. A directly elected parliament and president held political power, and political parties became legitimate political actors. Belatedly, the Germans had their first real experience with democracy.

From the outset, however, severe problems plagued the Weimar government. In the Versailles peace treaty following World War I, Germany lost all its overseas colonies and a large amount of its European territory. The treaty further burdened Germany with the moral guilt for the war and large postwar reparations owed to the victorious Allies. A series of radical uprisings threatened the political system. Wartime destruction and the reparations produced continuing economic problems, finally leading to an economic catastrophe in 1923. In less than a year the inflation rate was an unimaginable 26 billion percent! Ironically, the Kaiser's government that had produced these problems was not blamed for these developments. Instead, many people criticized the empire's democratic successor—the Weimar Republic.

The fatal blow came with the Great Depression in 1929. The Depression struck Germany harder than most other European nations or the United States. Almost a third of the labor force became unemployed, and the public was frustrated by the government's inability to deal with the crisis. Political tensions increased, and parliamentary democracy began to fail. *Adolf Hitler* and his *National Socialist German Workers' Party (the Nazis)* were the major beneficiaries. Their vote share grew from a mere 2 percent in 1928 to 18 percent in 1930 and 33 percent in November 1932. Increasingly, the machinery of the democratic system malfunctioned or was bypassed. In a final attempt to restore political order, President Paul von Hindenburg appointed Hitler chancellor of the Weimar Republic in January 1933. This was democracy's death knell.

Weimar's failure resulted from a mix of factors.[2] The republic's lack of support from political elites and the public was a basic weakness. Democracy depended on an administrative and military elite that often longed for the old authoritarian political system. Elite criticism of Weimar encouraged similar sentiments among the public. Many Germans were not committed to democratic principles. The fledgling state then faced a series of severe economic and political crises. Such strains might have overloaded the ability of any system to govern effectively. These crises further eroded public support for the republic and opened the door to Hitler's authoritarian and nationalistic appeals. The institutional weaknesses of the political system contributed to Weimar's political vulnerability. Finally, most Germans drastically underestimated Hitler's ambitions, intentions, and political abilities. This underestimation, perhaps, was Weimar's greatest failure.

The Third Reich

The Nazis' rise to power reflected a bizarre mixture of ruthless behavior and concern for legal procedures. Hitler called for a new election in March 1933 and then suppressed the opposition parties. Although the Nazis failed to capture an absolute majority of the votes, they used their domination of the parliament to enact legislation granting Hitler dictatorial powers. Democracy was replaced by the new authoritarian "leader state" of the *Third Reich.*

Once entrenched in power, Hitler pursued extremist policies. Social and political groups that might challenge the government were destroyed, taken over by Nazi agents, or co-opted into accepting the Nazi regime. The powers of the police state grew and choked off opposition. Attacks on Jews and other minorities steadily became more violent. Massive public works projects lessened unemployment, but also built the infrastructure for a wartime economy. The government enlarged and rearmed the military in violation of the Versailles treaty. The Reich's expansionist foreign policy challenged the international peace.

Hitler's unrestrained political ambitions finally plunged Europe into World War II in 1939. After initial victories, a series of military defeats beginning in 1942 led to the total collapse of the Third Reich in May 1945. A total of 60 million lives were lost worldwide in the war, including 6 million European Jews who were murdered in a Nazi campaign of systematic genocide.[3] Germany lay in ruins: its industry and transportation systems were destroyed, its cities were rubble, millions were homeless, and even food was scarce. Hitler's grand design for a new German Reich had instead destroyed the nation in a Wagnerian Götterdämmerung.

The Occupation Period

The political division of postwar Germany began as foreign troops advanced onto German soil. At the end of the war, the Western Allies—the United States, Britain, and France—controlled Germany's Western zone and the Soviet Union occupied the Eastern zone. This was to be an interim division, but growing frictions between Western and Soviet leaders increased tensions between the regions.

In the West, the Allied military government began a denazification program to remove Nazi officials and sympathizers from the economic, military, and political systems. The occupation authorities licensed new political parties and democratic political institutions began to develop. These authorities also reorganized the economic system along capitalist lines. Currency and market economy reforms in 1948 revitalized the economic system of the Western zone but also deepened East–West divisions.

Political change followed a much different course in the Eastern zone. The new *Socialist Unity Party (SED)* was a mechanism for the Communists to control the political process. Since the Soviets saw capitalism as responsible for the Third Reich, they sought to destroy the capitalist system and construct a new socialist order in its place. By 1948 the

Eastern zone was essentially a copy of the Soviet political and economic systems.

As the political distance between occupation zones widened, the Western allies favored creation of a separate German state in the West. In Bonn, a small university town along the banks of the Rhine, the Germans began to create a new democratic system. In 1948 a Parliamentary Council drafted an interim constitution that was to last until the entire nation was reunited. In May 1949 the state governments in the West agreed on a *Basic Law (Grundgesetz)* that created the Federal Republic of Germany (FRG), or West Germany.

These developments greatly worried the Soviets. The Soviet blockade of Berlin in 1948, for example, was partially an attempt to halt the formation of a separate German state in the West—though it actually strengthened Western resolve. Once it became apparent that the West would follow its own course, preparations began for a separate German state in the East. A week after the formation of the Federal Republic, the People's Congress in the East approved a draft constitution. On October 7, 1949, the German Democratic Republic (GDR), or East Germany, was formed. As in earlier periods of German history, a divided nation was following different paths (see Figure 7.1). It would be more than 40 years before these paths would converge.

FOLLOWING TWO PATHS

Although they had chosen different paths (or had them chosen for them), the two German states faced many of the same challenges in their initial years. Despite the progress made by the late 1940s, the economic picture was bleak on both sides of the border. Unemployment remained high in the West and the average wage earner received a minimal salary. In 1950 almost two-thirds of the West German public felt they had been better off before the war, and severe economic hardships were still common. The situation was even worse in the East.

West Germany was phenomenally successful in meeting this economic challenge.[4] Relying on a free enterprise system championed by the *Christian Democratic Union (CDU)*, the country experienced sustained and unprecedented economic growth. By

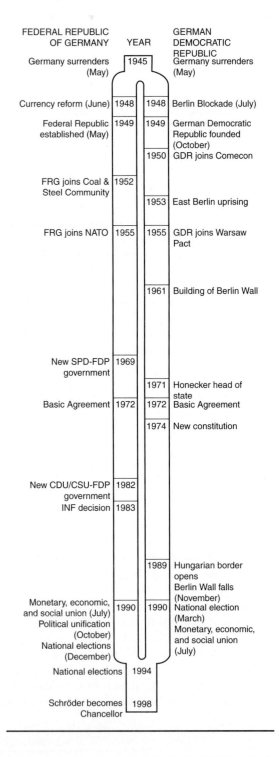

FIGURE 7.1　The Two Paths of Postwar Germany

the early 1950s incomes had reached the prewar level, and growth had just begun. Over the next two decades, per capita wealth nearly tripled, average hourly industrial wages increased nearly fivefold, and average incomes grew nearly sevenfold. By most economic indicators, the West German public in 1970 was several times more affluent than at any previous time in its pre–World War II history. This phenomenal economic growth came to be known as West Germany's *Economic Miracle (Wirtschaftswunder)*.

East Germany experienced its own economic miracle that was almost as impressive. The economic system in the East was based on collectivized agriculture, nationalized industry, and centralized planning.[5] In the two decades after the formation of the GDR, industrial production increased nearly fivefold and per capita national income grew by nearly equal measure. Although still lagging behind its more affluent relative in the West, the GDR became the model of prosperity among socialist states.

The problem of nation-building posed another challenge. The FRG initially was viewed as a provisional state until both Germanies could be reunited. The GDR also struggled to develop its own identity in the shadow of the West, as well as retaining a commitment to eventual reunification. In addition to the problems of division, the occupation authorities retained the right to intervene in the two Germanies even after 1949. Thus both states faced the challenge of defining their identity—as separate states or as parts of a larger Germany—and regaining national sovereignty.

West Germany's first chancellor, *Konrad Adenauer*, steered the nation on a course toward gaining its national sovereignty by integrating the Federal Republic into the Western alliance. The Western powers would grant greater autonomy to West Germany if it was exercised within the framework of an international body. For example, economic redevelopment was channeled through the European Coal and Steel Community and through the European Economic Community. West Germany's military rearmament occurred within the North Atlantic Treaty Organization (NATO).

The Communist regime in the East countered the Federal Republic's integration into the Western alliance with calls for German unification. And yet, the GDR went about establishing itself as a separate German state. In 1952 the GDR transformed the demarcation line between East and West Germany into a fortified border; this restricted Western access to the East and more importantly limited Easterners' ability to go to the West. The GDR integrated its economy into the Soviet bloc through membership in the Council for Mutual Economic Assistance (COMECON), and it was a charter member of the Warsaw Pact. The Soviet Union recognized the sovereignty of the German Democratic Republic in 1954. The practical and symbolic division of Germany became official with the GDR's construction of the Berlin Wall in August 1961. More than a physical barrier between East and West, it marked the formal existence of two separate German states.

Intra-German relations took a dramatically different course once the *Social Democratic Party (SPD)* won control of West Germany's government after the 1969 elections. The new SPD chancellor, Willy Brandt, proposed a policy toward the East (*Ostpolitik*) that accepted the postwar political situation and sought reconciliation with the nations of Eastern Europe, including the GDR. West Germany signed treaties with the Soviet Union and Poland to resolve disagreements dating back to World War II and to establish new economic and political ties. In 1971 Brandt received the Nobel Peace Prize for his actions. The following year the Basic Agreement formalized the relationship between the two Germanies as two states within one German nation. To the East German regime, Ostpolitik was a mixed blessing. On the one hand, it legitimized the GDR through its recognition by the Federal Republic and the normalization of East–West relations. On the other hand, economic and social exchanges increased East Germans' exposure to Western values and ideas, which many GDR politicians worried would undermine their closed system. The revolution of 1989 seemingly confirmed their fears.

After reconciliation between the two German states, both spent most of the next two decades addressing their internal needs. In the West, the SPD-led government initiated domestic policy reforms in the early 1970s that expanded social services and equalized access to the benefits of the Economic

Miracle. Total social spending nearly doubled between 1969 and 1975. But as global economic problems grew in the mid-1970s, Helmut Schmidt of the SPD became chancellor and directed a retrenchment on domestic policy reforms.

The problems of unrealized reforms and renewed economic difficulties continued into the 1980s. In 1982 the Christian Democrats enticed the *Free Democratic Party (FDP)* to form a new government under the leadership of *Helmut Kohl,* head of the Christian Democratic Union. The new government wanted to restore the Federal Republic's economy while still providing for social needs. Kohl presided over a dramatic improvement in economic conditions. The government also demonstrated its strong commitment to the Western defense alliance by accepting the deployment of new NATO nuclear missiles. The public returned Kohl's coalition to office in the 1987 elections.

During the 1970s, the GDR also adapted to its new international status.[6] The GDR expanded its international presence through activities ranging from the Olympics to its new membership in the United Nations. Simultaneously, the GDR tried to insulate itself from the Western influences that accompanied Ostpolitik through a policy of demarcation (*Abgrenzung*) from the West. It revised the constitution in 1974 to strengthen the emphasis on a separate, socialist East German state that was no longer tied to the ideal of a unified Germany. Socialism and the fraternal ties to the Soviet Union became the basis of the GDR's national identity.

Worldwide economic recession also buffeted the GDR's economy in the late 1970s. The cost competitiveness of East German products diminished in international markets, and trade deficits with the West grew steadily. Moreover, the consequences of long-delayed investment in the economic infrastructure began to show in a deteriorating highway system, an aging housing stock, and an outdated communications system. Although East Germans heard frequent government reports about the successes of the economy, their living standards displayed a widening gap between official pronouncements and reality.

As East German government officials grappled with their own problems in the 1980s, they were also disturbed by the winds of change rising in the East. Soviet President Mikhail Gorbachev's reformist policies of *perestroika* and *glasnost* seemed to undermine the pillars on which the East German system was built (see Chapter 9). At one point, an official GDR newspaper even censored news reports from the Soviet Union in order to downplay Gorbachev's reforms. Indeed, the stimulus for political change in East Germany did not come from within, but from the events sweeping across the rest of Eastern Europe.

In early 1989 the first cracks in the Communist system appeared. The Communist government in Poland accepted a series of democratic reforms; the Hungarian Communist Party also endorsed democratic and market reforms. When Hungary opened its border with neutral Austria, a steady stream of East Germans vacationing in Hungary started leaving for the West. East Germans were voting, with their feet. Almost 2 percent of the East German population emigrated to the Federal Republic over the next six months. The exodus also stimulated public demonstrations within East Germany against the regime.

As the East German government struggled with this problem, Gorbachev played a crucial role in directing the flow of events. He encouraged the GDR leadership to undertake a process of internal reform with the cautious advice that "life itself punishes those who delay."

Without Soviet support, the end of the old GDR system was inevitable. Rapidly growing public protests increased the pressure on the government, and the continuing exodus to the West brought the East's economy to a near standstill. The government did not govern; it barely existed, struggling from crisis to crisis. In early November the government and the SED Politburo resigned. On the evening of November 9, 1989, a GDR official announced the opening of the border between East and West Berlin. In the former no-man's land of the Berlin Wall, Berliners from East and West joyously celebrated together.

Once the euphoria of the opening of the Berlin Wall had passed, East Germany had to address the question of "what next?" The GDR government initially followed a strategy of damage control, appointing new leaders and attempting to court public support. However, the power of the state and the vitality of the economy had already suffered mortal wounds. The only apparent source of stability was a policy of unification with the Federal Republic, and the rush toward German unity began.

In March 1990 the GDR had its first truly free elections since 1932. The Alliance for Germany, which included the eastern branch of the Christian Democrats, won control of the government. Helmut Kohl and Lothar de Maiziere, the new GDR leader, both forcefully moved toward unification. An intra-German treaty on July 1 gave the two nations one currency and essentially one economy. The road to complete unification opened when Kohl won Soviet concessions on the terms of unification. On October 3, 1990, after more than four decades of separation, the two German paths again converged.

Unification largely occurred on Western terms. In fact, Easterners sarcastically point out that the only trace of the old regime is the one law kept from the GDR: automobiles can turn right on a red light in the East. Otherwise, the Western political structures, Western interest groups, Western political parties, and Western economic and social systems were simply exported to the East.

Unification was supposed to be the answer to a dream, but during the years that followed it must have occasionally seemed like a nightmare. The Eastern economy collapsed with the end of the GDR; at times unemployment rates in the East exceeded the worst years of the Great Depression. The burden of unification led to inflation and tax increases in the West, and weakened the Western economy. The social strains of unification stimulated violent attacks against foreigners in both halves of Germany. At the end of 1994, Kohl's coalition won a razor-thin majority in national elections.

Tremendous progress had been made by 1998, but many major problems remained. The economy still struggled. Needed reforms in tax laws and social programs were not implemented. When the Germans went to the polls in 1998 they voted for a change and elected a new government headed by Gerhard Schröder. The new coalition government faced many of the same challenges: a stagnant economy, excessive government budget deficits, and growing East–West polarization. The Schröder gov-

ernment made some progress on addressing these challenges—such as a major reform of the tax system and continued investments in the East—but not enough progress. Thus, the closeness of the vote in 2002 signaled of the divisions that exist on how Germany should deal with its current policy challenges. And through the start of 2005, public opinion polls indicated widespread dissatisfaction with the current SPD-led government.

SOCIAL FORCES

Popular accounts of unification sometimes refer to the new Germany as the fourth and richest Reich. The new Germany has about 82 million people, 68 million in the West and 14 million in the East, located in Europe's heartland. The total German economy is the largest in Europe. The combined territory of the new Germany is also large by European standards, although it is small in comparison to the United States—a bit smaller than Montana.

The merger of two nations is more complex than the simple addition of two columns of numbers on a balance sheet, however. Unification creates new strengths, but it also redefines and potentially strains the social system that underlies German society and politics. The merger of East and West holds the potential for reviving some of Germany's traditional social divisions.

Economics

East and West Germany had their own postwar economic miracles, but they followed different courses. In West Germany, economic expansion came in the service and technology sectors, and government employment more than doubled during the later twentieth century. Employment in the Western industrial sector remained fairly constant over time, and agricultural employment decreased markedly. In contrast, economic expansion in the GDR was concentrated in heavy industry and manufacturing. In the mid-1980s about half of the Eastern economy was in these two areas, and the service-technology sector represented a small share of the economy.

By most economic measures, both societies made dramatic economic advances across the postwar decades. However, these advances also occurred at different rates in the West and East. In the mid-1980s the West German standard of living ranked among the highest in the world. By comparison, the purchasing power of the average East German's salary amounted to barely half the income of a Westerner. Basic staples were inexpensively priced in the East, but most consumer goods were more expensive and so-called luxury items (color televisions, washing machines, and automobiles) were beyond the reach of the average family. In 1985 about a third of the dwellings in East Germany still lacked their own baths and toilets. GDR residents lived a comfortable life by East European standards, although far short of Western standards.

German unification meant the merger of these two different economies and social systems: the affluent West Germans and their poor cousins from the East; the sophisticated and technologically advanced industries of the West and the aging rust-belt factories of the GDR. At least in the short run, unification worsened the economic problems of the East. By some accounts, Eastern industrial production fell by two-thirds between 1989 and 1992—worse than the decline during the Great Depression. The government sold Eastern firms, and often the first response by the new owners was to reduce the labor force. Even by 2004, a sixth of the Eastern labor force remained unemployed.

During the unification process politicians claimed that the East would enjoy a modern economic miracle in a few years. This proved overly optimistic. Only massive social payments by the FRG have maintained the living standards in the East. The government also assumed a major role in rebuilding the East's economic infrastructure and encouraging investment in the East. While the personal situation of many Easterners had improved by the early 2000s, many remain pessimistic about economic conditions in the East.[7] The persisting economic gap between East and West creates a basis for social and political division in the new Germany.

Religion

Religious beliefs have divided Germans ever since the Reformation. Religious polarization gradually declined in the postwar FRG, partly because there were equal numbers of Catholics and Protestants,

and partly because of a conscious attempt to avoid the religious conflicts of the past. Secularization also gradually eroded the public's involvement in the churches. In the East, the Communist government sharply limited the political and social roles of the churches.

German unification has unsettled the delicate religious balance in the new Federal Republic. Catholics comprise 42 percent of the Western public but only 7 percent of the East. Thus, Protestants now slightly outnumber Catholics in unified Germany. There is also a small Muslim community that accounts for about 4 percent of the population. Even more dramatic, most Easterners claim to be nonreligious, which may lead to new challenges to FRG policies that benefit religious interests. A more Protestant and secular electorate should change the policy preferences of the German public on religiously based issues such as abortion and may potentially reshape electoral alliances.

Gender

Gender roles are another source of social differentiation. In the past, the three K's—*Kinder* (children), *Kirche* (church), and *Küche* (kitchen)—defined the woman's role, while politics and work were male matters. Attempts to lessen role differences have met with mixed success. The FRG's Basic Law guarantees the equality of the sexes, but the specific legislation to support this guarantee was often lacking. Cultural norms have changed only slowly; cross-national surveys show that West German males are more chauvinist than the average European, and West German women feel less liberated than other Europeans.[8]

The GDR constitution also guaranteed the equality of the sexes, and the government aggressively protected this guarantee. For instance, women's share of seats in the East German People's Congress was nearly twice as high as the percentage of women in the FRG parliament. A larger percentage of Eastern women were employed, although they were underrepresented in the highest level careers. Maternity benefits were more generous in the East, and women had the unlimited right to abortion.

East German women were one of the first groups to suffer from the unification process. Eastern women lost rights and benefits that they had held under East German law. For instance, the Constitutional Court resolved conflicting versions of the FRG and GDR abortion laws in 1993, which essentially adopted the FRG's more restrictive standards. The GDR provided childcare benefits for working mothers that are not provided by the FRG. The greater expectations of Eastern women moved gender issues higher on the FRG's political agenda, and the government passed new legislation on job discrimination and women's rights in 1994. Most Eastern women feel they are better off today than under the old regime because they have gained new rights and new freedoms that were lacking under the GDR. Yet progress lags behind the expectations of many women.

Minorities

Another new social cleavage involves Germany's growing minority of foreigners.[9] When West Germany faced a severe labor shortage in the 1960s, it recruited millions of workers from Turkey, Yugoslavia, Italy, Spain, Greece, and other less developed countries. German politicians and the public considered this a temporary situation, and the foreigners were called *guest workers (Gastarbeiter)*. Most of these guest workers worked long enough to acquire skills and some personal savings, and then returned home.

A strange thing happened, however. Germany asked only for workers, but they got human beings. Cultural centers for foreign workers emerged in many cities. Some foreign workers chose to remain in West Germany, and they naturally brought their families to join them. Foreigners brought new ways of life, as well as new hands for factory assembly lines.

From the beginning, the foreign worker population has faced several problems. They are concentrated at the low end of the economic ladder, often doing work that native Germans will not do. Foreigners—especially those from Turkey and other non-European nations—are culturally, socially, and linguistically isolated from mainstream society. The problems of social and cultural isolation are especially difficult for the children of these foreigners. Foreigners also were a target for violence in reaction to the strains of unification, and there is opposition to further immigration.

The nation has struggled with the problem of becoming a multicultural society, but the solutions are still uncertain. The Federal Republic revised the asylum clause in the Basic Law in 1993 (making it closer to U.S. immigration policy), took more decisive action in combating violence, and mobilized the tolerant majority in German society. The Schröder government changed the citizenship laws in 2000 to better integrate foreign-born residents into German society. But the gap between native Germans and Muslim immigrants seems to be widening. Addressing the issues associated with a permanent racial/ethnic minority (roughly 6 percent of the population) will be a continuing feature of German politics.

Regionalism

Regionalism is another potential source of social and political division. Germany is divided into 16 states (*Länder*), 10 states in the West and 6 new states created in the East, including the city-state of Berlin. Many of the Länder are distinguished by their own historical traditions and social structure. The language and idioms of speech differentiate residents from the Eastern and Western halves of the nation. And no one would mistake a northern German for a Bavarian from the south—their manners and dialects are too distinct.

The decentralized nature of society and the economy reinforce these regional differences. Economic and cultural activities are dispersed throughout the country rather than concentrated in a single national center. There are more than a dozen regional economic centers, such as Frankfurt, Cologne, Dresden, Düsseldorf, Munich, Leipzig, and Hamburg. The mass media are organized around regional markets, and there are even several competing "national" theaters.

Unification has greatly increased the cultural, economic, and political variations between the various states. Indeed, the economic gap between regions is so large that the constitutional guarantees of equal living standards across states were set aside, and the equalization of financial resources across the states remains a source of political tension. German unification also reinforced the social and cultural differences across regions. It is common to hear of "a wall in the mind" that separates *Wessies* (Westerners) and *Ossies* (Easterners). Easterners still draw on their separate traditions and experiences when making political decisions, just as Westerners do. In some terms, the gap between the North and South is also widening. Thus, regional considerations remain an important factor in society and politics.

THE INSTITUTIONS AND STRUCTURE OF GOVERNMENT

The Basic Law adopted in 1949 supposedly created a temporary political system to serve the Federal Republic until both halves of Germany could be united. The preamble, for example, stated the intention "to give a new order to political life for a transitional period."

In actuality, the rapid disintegration of East Germany in 1990 led to the incorporation of the GDR into the existing political, legal, and economic systems of the Federal Republic. In September 1990 the Federal Republic and the German Democratic Republic signed a treaty agreeing to unify their two states, and the government amended the Basic Law to accommodate the accession of new states from the East. Thus the political system of the unified Germany functions within the structure of the Basic Law.

When the Parliamentary Council originally framed the Basic Law in 1949, it wanted to construct a stable and effective democratic political system.[10] One objective was to maintain some historical continuity in political institutions. Most Germans were familiar with the workings of a parliamentary system, and the framers wanted a federal structure of government. Another objective was to design a political system to avoid the institutional weaknesses that contributed to the collapse of Weimar democracy. The framers wanted to establish clearer lines of political authority and to create a new system with extensive checks and balances to prevent the usurpation of power that occurred during the Third Reich. Finally, Germany needed institutional limits on extremist and antisystem forces.

The Basic Law is an exceptional example of political engineering—the construction of a political system to achieve specific goals. It creates a parliamentary democracy that involves the public, encourages elite political responsibility, disperses political power, and limits the influence of extremists. A description of the FRG's institutions will illustrate how these goals were translated into a new constitutional structure.

A Federal System

One way to distribute political power and to build checks and balances into a political system is through a federal system of government. The Basic Law created one of the few federal political systems in Europe (see Figure 7.2). Germany is organized into 16 states (Länder). Political power is divided between the federal government (*Bund*) and the state governments. The federal government has primary policy responsibility in most policy areas. The states, however, have jurisdiction in education, culture, law enforcement, and regional planning. In several other policy areas the states and federal government share responsibility, although federal law takes priority. Furthermore, the states retain residual powers to legislate in areas that the Basic Law does not explicitly assign to the federal government.

The state governments have a unicameral legislature, normally called a *Landtag*, which is directly elected by popular vote. The party or coalition that controls the legislature selects a minister president to head the state government. Next to the federal chancellor, the minister presidents are among the most powerful political officials in the Federal Republic.

The federal government is the major force in the legislation of policy, and the states are primarily responsible for policy administration. The states enforce most of the domestic legislation enacted by the federal government as well as their own regulations. The state governments also oversee the operation of the local governments.

One house of the bicameral federal legislature, the Bundesrat, is comprised solely of representatives appointed by the state governments. State government officials also participate in selecting the federal president and the justices of the major federal courts. This federal system decentralizes political power by balancing the power of the state governments against the power of the federal government.

FIGURE 7.2   The Structure of Germany's Federal Government

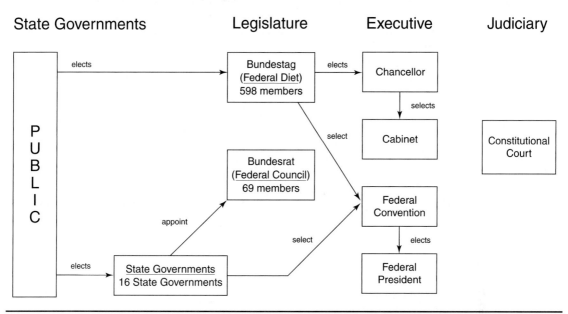

Parliamentary Government

The central institution of the federal government is the parliament. Parliament is bicameral: the popularly elected *Bundestag* is the primary legislative body; the Bundesrat represents the state governments at the federal level.

THE BUNDESTAG   The 598 deputies of the Bundestag (Federal Diet) are the only national government officials who can claim to represent the German public directly.[11] Deputies are selected in elections that normally occur every four years.

The Bundestag's major function is to enact legislation; all federal laws must receive its approval. The initiative for most legislation, however, lies in the executive branch. Like other modern parliaments, the Bundestag evaluates and amends the government's legislative program. Another important function of the Bundestag is to elect the federal chancellor, who heads the executive branch.

Through a variety of mechanisms, the Bundestag also provides a forum for public debate. Its plenary sessions consider the legislation before the chamber. Debating time is allocated to all party groupings according to their size; both party leaders

and backbenchers normally participate. The Bundestag now televises its sessions, including live broadcasts on the Internet, to expand the public audience for its policy debates.[12]

Scrutinizing the actions of the government is another function of the Bundestag. The most common method of oversight is the "question hour" adopted from the British House of Commons. An individual deputy can submit a written question to a government minister: questions range from broad policy issues to the specific needs of one constituent. Government representatives answer the queries during the question hour, and deputies can raise follow-up questions at that time. Bundestag deputies posed more than 17,000 oral and written questions during the 1998–2002 term of the Bundestag.

The Bundestag also boasts a system of strong legislative committees that strengthen its legislative and oversight roles. These committees provide the legislature with expertise to balance the policy experience of the federal agencies; the committees also conduct investigative hearings in their area of specialization.

The opposition parties normally make greatest use of these oversight opportunities; about two-thirds of the questions posed during the 1994–1998 term came from the opposition parties. Rank and file members of the governing parties also use these devices to make their own views known.

Overall, the Bundestag's oversight powers are considerable, especially for a legislature in a parliamentary system. Through committees its members can collect the information needed to understand and question government policymakers. Through question hour and other methods, Bundestag members can raise public issues independent of the government. And through its votes, the Bundestag often prompts the government to revise its legislative proposals to gain passage.

THE BUNDESRAT   The second chamber of the parliament, the *Bundesrat (Federal Council)*, reflects Germany's federal system. The state governments appoint its 69 members to represent their interests. The states normally appoint members of the state cabinet to serve jointly in the Bundesrat; the chamber thus acts as a permanent conference of state ministers. Bundesrat seats are allocated to each state in numbers roughly proportionate to the state's population: from three for the least populous states to six seats for the most. The votes for each state delegation are cast in a block, according to the instructions of the state government.

The Bundesrat's role is to represent state interests. It does this in evaluating legislation, debating government policy, and sharing information between federal and state governments. The Bundesrat is an essential part of the German federal system.

In summary, the parliament mainly reacts to government proposals rather than taking the policy initiative. In comparison to the British House of Commons or the French National Assembly, however, the Bundestag probably exercises more autonomy from the executive branch. Especially if one includes the Bundesrat, the German parliament has more independence and opportunity to revise government proposals. By strengthening the power of the parliament, the Basic Law sought to create a check on executive power. Experience shows that the political system has met this goal.

The Federal Chancellor and Cabinet

A weakness of the Weimar system was the division of executive authority between the president and the chancellor. The Federal Republic still has a dual executive, but the Basic Law substantially strengthened the formal powers of the *federal chancellor (Bundeskanzler)* as the chief executive office. Moreover, the incumbents of this office have dominated the political process and symbolized the federal government by their personalization of power. The chancellor plays such a central role in the political system that some observers describe the German system as a "chancellor democracy."

The chancellor is elected by the Bundestag and is responsible to it for the conduct of the federal government. This situation grants substantial power to the chancellor. He represents a majority of the Bundestag and normally can count on their support for the government's legislative proposals. The chancellor usually heads his own party, directing party strategy and leading the party at elections.

Another source of the chancellor's authority is his control over the Cabinet. The federal government today consists of 13 departments, each headed by a minister. The Cabinet ministers are formally appointed, or dismissed, by the federal president on the recommendation of the chancellor (Bundestag approval is not necessary). The Basic Law also grants the chancellor the power to decide the number of Cabinet ministers and their duties.

The functioning of the federal government follows three principles laid out in the Basic Law. First, the *chancellor principle* says that the chancellor defines government policy. The formal policy guidelines issued by the chancellor are legally binding directives on the Cabinet and the ministries. Thus, in contrast to the British system of shared Cabinet responsibility, the German Cabinet is formally subordinate to the chancellor in policymaking.

The second principle of *ministerial autonomy* gives each minister the authority to direct the ministry's internal workings without Cabinet intervention as long as the policies conform to the government's guidelines. Ministers are responsible for supervising the activities of their departments, guiding their policy planning, and overseeing the administration of policy within their jurisdiction.

The *cabinet principle* is the third organizational guideline. When conflicts arise between departments over jurisdictional or budgetary matters, the Basic Law calls for them to be resolved in the Cabinet. The actual working of the federal government is more fluid than the formal procedures spelled out by the Basic Law. The number and choice of ministries for each party is a major issue in building a multiparty government coalition after each election. Cabinet members also display great independence on policy despite the formal restrictions of the Basic Law. Ministers are appointed because of their expertise in a policy area. In practice, ministers often identify more with their roles as department heads than as agents of the chancellor; their political success is judged by their representation of department interests.

The Cabinet thus serves as a clearinghouse for the business of the federal government. Specific ministers present policy proposals originating in their departments in the hope of gaining government endorsement. The chancellor defines a government program that reflects a consensus of the Cabinet and relies on negotiations and compromise within the Cabinet to maintain this consensus.

The Federal President

Because of the problems associated with the Weimar Republic's divided executive, the Basic Law transformed the office of *federal president (Bundespräsident)* into a mostly ceremonial post. The president's official duties involve greeting visiting heads of state, attending official government functions, visiting foreign nations, and similar tasks.[13] To insulate the office from electoral politics, the president is selected by a Federal Convention composed of all Bundestag deputies and an equal number of representatives chosen by the state legislatures. The president is supposed to remain above partisan politics once elected.

The reduction in the president's formal political role does not mean that an incumbent is uninvolved in the policymaking process. The Basic Law assigns several legal functions to the president, who appoints government and military officials, signs treaties and laws, and possesses the power of pardon. In these instances, however, the chancellor must countersign the actions. The president

also nominates a chancellor to the Bundestag and can dissolve parliament if a government legislative proposal loses a no-confidence vote. In both instances, the Basic Law limits the president's ability to act independently.

Potentially more significant is the constitutional ambiguity over whether the president must honor certain requests from the government. The legal precedent is unclear on whether the president has the constitutional right to veto legislation, to refuse the chancellor's recommendation for Cabinet appointments, or even to reject a request to dissolve the Bundestag. Analysts see these ambiguities as another safety valve built into the Basic Law's elaborate system of checks and balances.

The political importance of the federal president also involves factors that go beyond the articles of the Basic Law. An active, dynamic president can help to shape the political climate of the nation through his speeches and public activities. He is the one political figure who can rightly claim to be above politics and who can work to extend the vision of the nation beyond its everyday concerns. Horst Köhler was elected president in 2004 after serving as Director of the International Monetary Fund.

The Judicial System

The ordinary courts for criminal cases and regular legal disputes are integrated into a unitary system (see Figure 7.3). The states administer the three lower levels of the courts. The highest court, the Federal Court of Justice, is at the national level. These courts hear both civil and criminal cases, and all courts apply the same national legal codes.

The administrative courts hear cases in specialized areas. One court deals with administrative complaints against government agencies, one handles tax matters, and another resolves claims involving government social programs. Another court deals with labor-management disputes. Like the rest of the judicial system, these specialized courts are linked into one system including both state and federal courts.

The Basic Law created a third element of the judiciary: an independent *Constitutional Court*. This court reviews the constitutionality of legislation,

FIGURE 7.3   Organization of the Courts

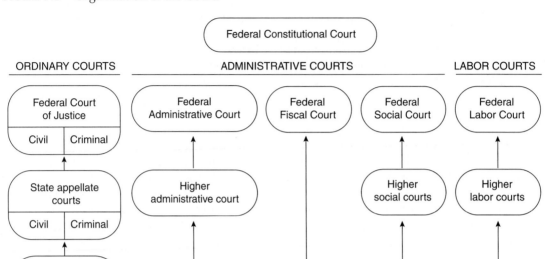

mediates disputes between levels of government, and protects the constitutional and democratic order.[14] This is an innovation for the German legal system because it places one law, the Basic Law, above all others. This also implies limits on the decision-making power of the parliament and the judicial interpretations of lower court judges. Because of the importance of the Constitutional Court, its 16 members are selected in equal numbers by the Bundestag and Bundesrat and can be removed only for abuse of the office.

The Federal Republic's judicial system follows the Roman law tradition that is fundamentally different from the common law Anglo-American system of justice. Rather than relying on precedents from prior cases as in the common law system, the legal process is based on an extensive system of government defined legal codes. The codes define legal principles in the abstract, and specific cases are judged against these standards. The system relies on a rationalist philosophy that justice is served by following the letter of the law.

The Separation of Powers

One of the Basic Law's secret strengths is avoiding the concentration of power in the hands of any one actor or institution. The framers wanted power to be dispersed, so that extremists or antidemocrats could not overturn the system; democracy would thus be a consensus-building process. Each institution of government has strong powers within its own domain, but a limited ability to force its will on other institutions.

In the relationship between the legislative and executive branches, for instance, the chancellor lacks the discretionary authority to dissolve the legislature and call for new elections, something that is normally found in parliamentary systems. Equally important, the Basic Law limits the legislature's control over the chancellor. In a parliamentary system the legislature normally has the authority to remove a chief executive from office by a simple majority vote. During the Weimar Republic, however, extremist parties used this device to destabilize the democratic system by opposing incumbent chancellors. The Basic Law modified this procedure and created a *constructive no-confidence vote*.[15] In order for the Bundestag to remove a chancellor, it simultaneously must agree on a successor. This ensures continuity in government and an initial majority in support of a new chancellor. It also makes removing an incumbent more difficult; opponents cannot simply disagree with the government—a majority must agree on an alternative. The constructive no-confidence vote has been attempted only twice—and succeeded only once. In 1982 a coalition of parties replaced Chancellor Schmidt with a new chancellor, Helmut Kohl.

The Constitutional Court provides another check on government actions, and it has assumed an important role as the guarantor of citizen rights and protector of the constitution. The distribution of power and policy responsibilities between the federal and state governments is another moderating force within the political process. Even the strong bicameral legislature ensures that multiple interests must agree before government policy can be made.

This structure complicates the governing process compared to a unified system such as Britain, the Netherlands, or Sweden. However, democracy is often a complicated process. This system of shared powers and checks and balances has enabled German democracy to grow and flourish.

REMAKING POLITICAL CULTURES

Consider for a minute what the average German must have thought about politics as World War II was ending. Germany's political history was hardly conducive to good democratic citizenship. Under the Kaiser, people were expected to be subjects, not active participants in the political process; this style nurtured feelings of political intolerance. The interlude of the Weimar Republic did little to change these values. The polarization, fragmentation, and outright violence of the Weimar Republic taught people to avoid politics, not to be active participants. Moreover, democracy eventually failed, and national socialism arose in its place. The Third Reich then raised another generation under an intolerant, authoritarian system.

Because of this historical legacy, the development of the Federal Republic was closely linked to the question of whether its political culture was congruent with its democratic system (see discussion in Chapter 2). Initially, there were widespread fears that West Germany lacked a democratic political culture, thereby making it vulnerable to the same problems that undermined the Weimar Republic. Postwar public opinion polls in the FRG presented a negative image of public beliefs that was probably equally applicable to the East.[16] West Germans were politically detached, acceptant of authority, and intolerant in their political views. A significant minority were unrepentant Nazis, sympathy for many elements of the Nazi ideology was widespread, and anti-Semitic feelings remained commonplace.

Perhaps even more amazing than the Economic Miracle was the transformation of West Germany's political culture in little more than a generation. Confronted by an uncertain public commitment to democracy, the government undertook a massive political reeducation program. The schools, the media, and political organizations were mobilized behind the effort. The citizenry itself also was changing—older generations raised under authoritarian regimes were gradually replaced by younger generations socialized during the postwar democratic era. The successes of a growing economy and a relatively smoothly functioning political system also changed public perceptions. These efforts created a new political culture more consistent with the democratic institutions and process of the Federal Republic.

With unification, Germany confronted another serious cultural question. The Communists tried to create a rival culture in the GDR that would support their state and its socialist economic system. Indeed, the efforts at political education in the East were intense and extensive; they aimed at creating a broad "socialist personality" that included nonpolitical attitudes and behavior.[17] Young people were taught a collective identity with their peers, to nurture a love for the GDR and its socialist brethren, to accept the guidance of the Socialist Unity Party, and to understand history and society from a Marxist-Leninist perspective.

German unification meant the blending of these two different political cultures, and at first the consequences of this mixture were uncertain. Without scientific social science research in the GDR, it was unclear if Easterners had internalized the government's propaganda. Western influences also had flowed eastward, and this may have undermined the GDR regime. Furthermore, the revolutionary political events leading to German unification may have reshaped even long-held political beliefs. What does a Communist think after attending communism's funeral?

Unification thus created a new question: could the FRG assimilate 16 million new citizens with potentially different beliefs about how politics and society should function? The following sections discuss the key elements of German political culture and how they have changed over time.

Nation and State

A core element of the German culture is a strong sense of German identity. A common history, culture, territory, and language created a sense of national community long before Germany was politically united. Germany was the land of Schiller, Goethe, Beethoven, and Wagner, even if the Germans disagreed on political boundaries. The imagery of a single *Volk* binds Germans together despite their social and political differences.

Previous regimes had failed, however, to develop a common political identity to match the German society identity. Succeeding political systems were short lived and were unable to develop a popular consensus on the nature and goals of German politics. Postwar West Germany faced a similar challenge: building a political community in a divided and defeated nation.

In the early 1950s large sectors of the West German public remained committed to the symbols and personalities of previous regimes.[18] Most people felt that the Second Empire or Hitler's prewar Reich represented the best times in German history. Substantial minorities favored a restoration of the monarchy or a one-party state. Almost half the pop-

ulation believed that if it had not been for World War II, Hitler would have been one of Germany's greatest statesmen.

Over the next two decades these ties to earlier regimes gradually weakened, and the bonds to the new institutions and leaders of the Federal Republic steadily grew stronger (see Figure 7.4). The number of citizens who believed that Bundestag deputies represent the public interest doubled between 1951 and 1964; public respect shifted from the personalities of prior regimes to the chancellors of the Federal Republic. By the 1970s an overwhelming majority of the public felt that the present was the best time in German history. West Germans became more politically tolerant, and feelings of anti-Semitism declined sharply. Other opinions displayed a growing esteem for the new political system.[19]

Even while Westerners developed a new acceptance of the institutions and symbols of the Federal Republic, something was missing, something that touched the spirit of their political feelings. The FRG was a provisional entity, and "Germany" meant

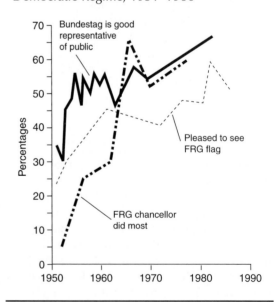

FIGURE 7.4   Increase in Support for the Democratic Regime, 1951–1986

Source: Russell J. Dalton, *Politics in Germany,* 2nd ed. (New York: HarperCollins, 1993), p. 121.

a unified nation. Were citizens of West Germany to think of themselves as Germans, West Germans, or some mix of both? In addition, the trauma of the Third Reich burned a deep scar in the Western psyche, making citizens hesitant to express pride in their nation or a sense of German national identity. Because of this political stigma, the Federal Republic avoided many of the emotional national symbols that are common in other nations. There were few political holidays or memorials; the national anthem was seldom played; and even the anniversary of the founding of the FRG received little public attention. This legacy means that even today Germans are hesitant to openly express pride in the nation (see Box 7.2).

The quest for a national identity also occurred in the East. The GDR claimed to represent the "pure" elements of German history; it portrayed the Federal Republic as the successor to the Third Reich. Most analysts believe that the GDR succeeded in creating at least a sense of resigned loyalty to the regime because of its political and social accomplishments. Thus a 1990 study found that Eastern youth most admired Karl Marx (followed by the first president of the GDR), while Western youth were most likely to name Konrad Adenauer, the first Chancellor of the Federal Republic.[20]

By the late 1980s, however, the GDR lacked a popular consensus in support of the state.[21] There were repeated purges against those who might oppose the GDR. The secret police (*Stasi*) kept files on more than 6 million people, government informers seemed omnipresent, and the Berlin Wall stood as a constant reminder of the nature of the East German state. The government found it necessary to use coercion and the threat of force to sustain itself. Once socialism failed, the basis for a separate East German political identity also evaporated.

Unification began a process by which the German search for a national political identity might finally be resolved. The opening of the Berlin Wall created positive political emotions that were previously lacking. The celebration of unification, and the designation of October 3 as a national holiday, finally gives Germans a positive political experience to celebrate. Germans in East and West remain somewhat hesitant to embrace an emotional attachment to the nation, and Easterners retain a lingering tie to their separate past (see Figure 2.2). Yet, the basic situation has changed. For the first time in over a century, nearly all Germans agree where their borders begin and end. Germany is now a single nation—democratic, free, and looking toward the future.

Democratic Norms and Procedures

A second important element of the political culture involves citizen attitudes toward the system of government. In the early years of West Germany, the rules of democratic politics—majority rule, minority rights, individual liberties, and pluralistic debate—were new ideas that did not fit citizens' experiences.

Box 7.2   Can One Be Proud, and German?

Could anyone imagine a French president or a British prime minister or indeed just about any other world leader refusing to say he was proud of his nationality? Yet this is a contentious statement in Germany because expressions of nationalism are still linked by some to the excessive nationalism of the Third Reich. Thus, when in 2001 the general secretary of the CDU declared: "I am proud to be German," this set off an intense national debate. A Green member of the SPD-Green Cabinet replied that this statement demonstrated the mentality of a right-wing skinhead. President Rau tried to sidestep the issue by declaring that one could be "glad" or "grateful" for being German, but not "proud." Then Chancellor Schröder entered the fray: "I am proud of what people have achieved and our democratic culture . . . In that sense, I am a German patriot who is proud of his country." It is difficult to imagine such exchanges occurring in Washington, D.C. or Paris.

Source: The Economist (March 24, 2001): 62.

To break this pattern, the leaders of the Federal Republic constructed a system that formalized democratic procedures. Citizen participation was encouraged and expected, policymaking became open, and the public gradually learned democratic norms by continued exposure to the new political system. Political leadership provided a generally positive example of competition in a democratic setting. Consequently, a popular consensus slowly developed in support of the democratic political system. By the mid-1960s agreement was nearly unanimous that democracy was the best form of government. More important, the Western public displayed a growing commitment to democratic procedures—a multiparty system, conflict management, minority rights, and representative government.

Political events occasionally have tested the long-term growth in democratic values in West Germany. For instance, during the 1970s a small group of extremists attempted to topple the system through a terrorist campaign.[22] In the early 1980s the Kohl government faced a series of violent actions by anarchic and radical ecology groups. In both instances, however, the basic lesson was that the political system could face the onslaughts of political extremists and survive with its basic procedures intact, and without the public losing faith in their democratic process.

The propaganda of the East German government also stressed a democratic creed. In reality, however, the regime tried to create a political culture that was compatible with a communist state and socialist economy. The culture drew on traditional Prussian values of obedience, duty, and loyalty: people were again told that obedience was the responsibility of a good citizen, and support of the state (and the party) was an end in itself. Periodically, political events—the 1953 Berlin uprising, the construction of the Berlin Wall, and the expulsions of political dissidents—reminded East Germans of the gap between the democratic rhetoric of the regime and reality.

One reason the popular revolt may have grown so rapidly in 1989 was that citizens no longer supported the principles of the regime. For instance, studies of young Easterners found that identification with Marxism-Leninism and belief in the inevitable victory of socialism dropped off dramatically during the mid-1980s.[23] At the least, the revolutionary changes that swept through East Germany as the Berlin Wall fell nurtured a belief in democracy as the road to political reform. A 1990 public opinion survey found nearly universal support for the basic tenets of democracy among both West and East Germans, and these parallels persisted over the decade.[24]

The true test of democracy, of course, occurs in the real world. Some initial studies suggested that Easterners' understanding of the democratic creed was limited, or at least different from the West.[25] Yet, Eastern orientations toward democracy in 1989 were markedly different from the situation in Germany in 1945. Rather than remaking this aspect of the East German culture, the greater need was to transform Eastern support for democracy into a deeper and richer understanding of the workings of the process and its pragmatic strengths and weaknesses. And now, more than a decade after unification, Easterners have largely demonstrated their commitment to the principles of democracy.

Social Values and the New Politics

Another area of cultural change in West Germany involves a shift in public values produced by the social and economic accomplishments of the nation. Once West Germany addressed traditional social and economic needs, the public broadened their concerns to include a new set of societal goals. New issues such as the environment, women's rights, and increasing citizen participation attracted public attention. In the early 1980s a vibrant peace movement rekindled the debate on West Germany's international role.

Ronald Inglehart introduced a theory of value change to explain the development of these new political orientations in the West.[26] He maintains that a person's value priorities reflect the family and societal conditions that prevail early in life. Older generations socialized before World War II lived at least partially under an authoritarian government, experienced long periods of economic hardship, and felt the destructive consequences of war. These older individuals are preoccupied with economic security, law and order, religious values, and a strong national defense—despite the economic and political advances of postwar Germany. In contrast, because younger generations grew up in a democratic political setting during a period of unprecedented economic prosperity, relative international stability, and now the collapse of the Soviet Empire, they are shifting their attention toward *New Politics* values. These new values emphasize self-expression, personal freedom, social equality, self-fulfillment, and maintaining the quality of life.

Although only a minority of Westerners hold these new values, they represent a "second culture" embedded within the dominant culture of FRG society. These values are even more limited among Easterners. Still, the evidence of political change is apparent. Public interest in New Politics issues has gradually spread beyond its youthful supporters and developed a broader base. Even in the East, many of the early demonstrations for democracy had supporters calling for *"Freiheit und Umwelt"* (freedom and the environment).

Two Peoples in One Nation?

Citizens in the East and West share a common German heritage, but 40 years of separation created cultural differences that now are being integrated into a single national culture.

Because of these different experiences, the broad similarities in many of the political beliefs of Westerners and Easterners are surprising. Easterners and Westerners espouse support for the democratic system, its norms, and institutions. There is also broad acceptance of the principles of the market economy of the West. Thus the Federal Republic's second transition to democracy features an agreement on basic political and economic values that is markedly different from the situation after World War II.

Yet, other aspects of cultural norms do differ between regions. For instance, although residents in both the West and East endorse the tenets of democracy, it is harder to reach agreement on how these ideals translate into practical politics. The open, sometimes confrontational style of Western politics is a major adjustment for citizens raised under the closed system of the GDR. In addition, Easterners endorse a broader role for government in providing social services and guiding social development than is found among Westerners.[27]

There are also signs of a persisting gap in regional identities between East and West. The passage of time and harsh postunification adjustments created a nostalgia for some aspects of the GDR among its former residents. Easterners do not want a return to communism or socialism, but many miss the slower and more predictable style of their former lives. Even while expressing support for Western capitalism, many Easterners have difficulty adjusting to the idea of unemployment and to the competitive pressures of a market-based economy. There is a nostalgic yearning for symbols of these times, ranging from the Trabant automobile to consumer products bearing Eastern labels. The popularity of the recent movie "Goodbye Lenin" is an indication of these sentiments—and a good film for students interested in this phase of German history. In fact, public opinion surveys show that the percentage of Easterners who think of themselves as "East German" rather than "German" grew after unification. Easterners are developing a distinct regional identity that is similar to the feelings of Southerners in the United States.

Unification may have also heightened New Politics conflicts within German society. The GDR had struggled to become a materialist success, while West Germany was enjoying its postmaterial abundance. Consequently, Easterners give greater weight to goals such as higher living standards, security, hard work, and better living conditions. Most Easterners want first to share in the affluence and consumer society of the West, before they begin to fear the consequences of this affluence. The clash of values within West German society has now been joined by East–West differences.

Germans share a common language, culture, and history—and a common set of ultimate political goals—although the strains of unification may magnify and politicize the differences. The nation's progress in blending these two cultures successfully will strongly affect the course of the new Germany.

POLITICAL LEARNING AND POLITICAL COMMUNICATION

If a congruent political culture helps a political system to endure, as many political experts maintain, then one of the basic functions of the political process is to create and perpetuate these attitudes. The process of developing the beliefs and values of the public is known as political socialization. Researchers normally view political socialization as a source of continuity in a political system, with one generation transmitting the prevailing political norms to the next. The preceding discussion of political cultures described how socialization produced political change in postwar Germany. Now, German unification creates a need for political relearning among the citizenry.

Family Influences

During their early years, children have few sources of learning comparable to their parents—normally the major influence in forming basic values. Family discussions can be a rich source of political information and one of the many ways that children internalize their parents' attitudes. Basic values acquired during childhood often persist into adulthood.

In the early postwar years, family socialization did not function smoothly on either side of the German border. Many adults hesitated to discuss politics openly because of the depoliticized environment of the period. Many parents also did not discuss politics with their children for fear that the child would ask: "What did you do under Hitler, Daddy?" Furthermore, parents in West Germany were ill prepared to tell their children how to be good democrats, and Eastern parents were equally uncertain of the new communist system.

The potential for parental socialization grew steadily since the immediate postwar years.[28] The frequency of political discussion increased in the West, and family conversations about politics became commonplace. Moreover, young new parents raised under the system of the Federal Republic could pass on democratic norms and party attachments held for a lifetime. The family also played an important role in the socialization process of the GDR. Family ties were especially close in the East, and most young people claimed to share their parents' political opinions. The family also provided one of the few settings where people could openly discuss their beliefs, a private sphere where individuals could be free of the watchful eyes of others.

Here one could express praise—or doubt—about the state.

Despite the growing socialization role of the family, both Germanies have experienced a widening generation gap in recent years. Youth in the West are more liberal than their parents, more oriented toward noneconomic goals, more positive about their role in the political process, and more likely to challenge prevailing social norms.[29] East German youth are also a product of their times; an autonomous peace movement and other counterculture groups flourished as part of the youth culture of the 1980s. The youthful faces of the first refugees exiting through Hungary or the democracy protests in Leipzig and East Berlin highlighted the importance of the youth culture within East Germany. Clearly, young people's values and goals are changing, often putting them in conflict with their elders.

Education

After World War II the FRG government enlisted the school system to reeducate the young into accepting democratic norms. Instruction aimed at developing a formal commitment to the institutions and procedures of the Federal Republic. Civics classes stressed the benefits of the democratic system, drawing sharp contrasts with the communist model. The educational system helped to remake the West German political culture.

Growing public support for the FRG's political system gradually made this program of formalized political education redundant. The content of civics instruction changed to emphasize an understanding of the dynamics of the democratic process—interest representation, conflict resolution, minority rights, and the methods of citizen influence. The present system tries to prepare students for their adult roles as political participants.

In the East, the school system also played an essential role in the political education program, although the content was very different. The schools tried to create a socialist personality that encompassed a devotion to communist principles, a love of the GDR, and participation in state-sponsored activities. Yet again, the rhetoric of education conflicted with reality. Government publications claimed that "education for peace is the overriding principle underlying classroom practice in all schools." However, paramilitary training was compulsory for ninth and tenth graders. The textbooks told students that the GDR endorsed personal freedom, but then they stared from their school buses at the barbed wire strung along the border. Many young people accepted the rhetoric of the regime, but the education efforts remained incomplete.

The GDR used several other methods of political education. A cornerstone of the GDR's socialization efforts was a system of government-supervised youth groups. Nearly all primary school students enrolled in the Pioneers, a youth organization that combined normal social activities—similar to those in the Boy Scouts or Girl Scouts in the United States—with a heavy dose of political education. At age 14, about three-fourths of the young graduated into membership in the Free German Youth (FDJ) group. The FDJ was a training and recruiting ground for the future leadership of East Germany. The politicization of social life even extended to sports. Like other communist states, the GDR staged mass sporting events that included an opportunity for political indoctrination, and used the Olympic medal count as a measure of the GDR's societal progress. In summary, most aspects of social, economic, and political relations came under the direction of party and state institutions. From a school's selection of texts for first grade readers to the speeches at a sports awards banquet, the values of the regime touched everyday life.

SOCIAL STRATIFICATION Another important effect of education involves its consequences for the social stratification of society, which differs in basic ways between West and East. The secondary school system in the West has three distinct tracks. One track provides a general education that normally leads to vocational training and working-class occupations. A second track mixes vocational and academic training. Most graduates from this program are employed in lower middle-class occupations. A third track focuses on academic training at a Gymnasium (an academic high school) in preparation for university education.

These educational tracks reinforce social status differences within society. Students are directed into one track after only four to six years of primary schooling, based on their school record, parental preferences, and teacher evaluations. At this early age family influences are still a major factor in the child's development. This means that most children assigned to the academic track come from middle-class families, and most students in the vocational track are from working-class families. Sharp distinctions separate the three tracks. Students attend different schools, minimizing social contact. The curricula of the three tracks are so different that once a student is assigned, he or she would find it difficult to transfer between tracks. The Gymnasia are more generously financed and recruit the best-qualified teachers. Every student who graduates from a Gymnasium is guaranteed admission to a university, where tuition is free.

There have been numerous attempts to reform West Germany's educational system to lessen its class bias, which determines children's educational future at an early age and produces inequalities in the content of education.[30] There is a clear tendency for middle-class children to benefit under the tracked educational system. Some states have a single comprehensive secondary school that all students may attend, but only about 10 percent of Western secondary school students are enrolled in these schools. Reformers have been more successful in expanding access to the universities. In the early 1950s only 6 percent of college-aged youths pursued higher education; today this figure is over 30 percent. The FRG's educational system retains an elitist accent, though it is now less obvious.

The socialist ideology of the GDR led to a different educational structure. Ten-year comprehensive polytechnic schools formed the core of the educational system. Students from different social backgrounds, and with different academic abilities, attended the same school—much like the structure of public education in the United States. The schools emphasized practical career training, with a heavy dose of technical and applied courses in the later years. Those with special academic abilities could apply to the extended secondary school during their twelfth year, which led to a university education.

The differences between the educational systems of the two states illustrate the practical problems posed by German unity.[31] Beyond the important differences in the content of education, the West lags in equalizing access to higher education. The Western educational system perpetuates social inequality and thus conflicts with the stated social goals of the Federal Republic. In contrast, the formal structure of the GDR's comprehensive schools was closer to the educational system of other European democracies, such as Britain or France, and was less elitist than the FRG's educational system. The unification treaty called for the gradual extension of the Western educational structure to the East, but the dissolution of comprehensive schools has generated dissatisfaction among Easterners. Ironically, unification is leading to new pressures for liberal reform within the Federal Republic's educational system.

Mass Media

The mass media have a long history in Germany: the world's first newspaper and first television service both appeared on German soil. Under previous regimes, however, political authorities frequently censored or manipulated the media. National socialism showed what a potent socialization force the media could be, especially when placed in the wrong hands.

The mass media of the Federal Republic were developed with the legacy of Nazi propaganda in mind.[32] After the war the Allied occupation forces licensed only newspapers and journalists who were free of Nazi ties. The Basic Law also guaranteed freedom of the press and the absence of censorship. There were two consequences of this pattern of press development. First, this created a new journalistic tradition, committed to democratic norms, objectivity, and political neutrality. This marked a clear departure from past journalistic practices, and it contributed to the remaking of the political culture.

A second consequence is the regionalization of the media. The Federal Republic lacks an established national press like that of Britain or France. Instead, each region or large city has one or more newspapers that circulate primarily within that locale. Of the several hundred daily newspapers, only a few—such as the *Frankfurter Allgemeine Zeitung, Welt, Süd-*

deutsche Zeitung, or *Frankfurter Rundschau*—have a national following.

The electronic media in the Federal Republic also follow a pattern of regional decentralization. Even in this age of new electronic media, public corporations organized at the state or regional levels manage the public television and radio networks. These public broadcasting networks still are the major German media sources. To ensure independence from commercial pressures, the public media are financed mostly by taxes assessed on owners of radio and television sets.

The mass media are a primary source of information for the public and a communications link between elites and the public. The higher quality newspapers devote substantial attention to domestic and international reporting, although the largest circulation newspaper, *Bild Zeitung,* sells papers through sensationalist stories. The public television networks are strongly committed to political programming; about one-third of their programs deal with social or political issues. The most important development is the expansion of privately owned cable and satellite television stations. Today, most German households receive these stations. This development steadily erodes the government's control of the electronic media and pressures public stations to devote more attention to consumer preferences. Many analysts see these new media offerings as expanding the citizen's choice and the diversity of information, but others worry that the quality of German broadcasting will suffer as a result.

Public opinion surveys show that Germans have a voracious appetite for the political information provided by the mass media. A 2001 survey found that 59 percent of the public claimed to read news in the newspaper on a daily basis, 56 percent listened to news on the radio daily, and 68 percent said they watched television news programs daily.[33] These high levels of usage indicate that Germans are attentive media users and well informed on the flow of political events.

CITIZEN PARTICIPATION

Developing public understanding and acceptance of democratic rules was an important accomplishment for the Federal Republic in the post–World

War II period. At first, however, the public did not participate in the new process; they acted like political spectators who were following a soccer match from the grandstand. German history in the early twentieth century certainly had not been conducive to developing widespread public involvement in politics. The final step in remaking the political culture was to involve citizens in the process—to have them come onto the field and participate.

From the start, both German states tried to engage their citizens to participate in politics, although with different expectations about the citizen's appropriate role. The democratic procedures of West Germany induced many people to become at least minimally involved in politics. Turnout in national elections was uniformly high. Westerners became well informed about the democratic system and developed an interest in political matters. After continued experience with the democratic system, people began to internalize their role as participants. Most Westerners thought their participation could influence the political process—people believed that democracy worked.[34]

Changing perceptions of politics led to a dramatic increase in involvement. In the 1950s almost two-thirds of the West German public never discussed politics; today about three-quarters claim they talk about politics regularly. This expansion in citizen interest created a participatory revolution in the Federal Republic, as involvement in campaign activities and political organizations increased. Perhaps the most dramatic evidence of rising participation levels has been the growth of *citizen action groups (Bürgerinitiativen)*. Citizens interested in a specific issue form a group to articulate their political demands and influence decision makers. These groups often resort to petitions, protests, and other direct-action methods to dramatize their cause and mobilize public support. Parents organize for school reform, homeowners become involved in urban redevelopment projects, taxpayers complain about the delivery of government services, or residents protest the environmental conditions in their locale. These groups expand the means of citizen influence significantly beyond the infrequent and indirect methods of campaigns and elections.

Under the GDR system, political involvement was widely encouraged, but people could only be active in ways that reinforced their allegiance to the state. For example, elections were not measures of popular representation but offered the Communist leadership an opportunity to educate the public politically. More than 90 percent of the electorate cast ballots, and the government parties always won nearly all the votes. People were expected to participate in government-approved unions, social groups (such as the Free German Youth or the German Women's Union), and quasi-public bodies such as parent-teacher organizations. However, participation was not a method for citizens to influence the government but for the government to influence its citizens.

Although they draw on much different experiences, Germans from both the East and West have been socialized into a pattern of high political involvement (see Figure 7.5). Voting levels in national elections are among the highest of any European democracy. Over 80 percent of Westerners turned out at the polls in the 2002 Bundestag elections, as well as 78 percent of voters from the East. This turnout level is high by American standards, but it has declined from the nearly 90 percent voting in West German elections of the 1980s. High turnout partially reflects the belief that voting is part of a citizen's duty. In addition, the electoral system encourages turnout: elections are held on Sunday when everyone is free to vote; voter registration lists are constantly updated by the government; and the ballot is always simple—there are at most two votes to cast.

Beyond the act of voting, many Germans participate in other aspects of politics. Data from a survey conducted in 2002 illustrate the participation patterns of Easterners and Westerners (see again Figure 7.5). Almost a third of the public in West and East have signed a petition within the previous year, and a quarter have boycotted some product on political grounds. These are high levels by cross-national standards (see Chapter 2). After the tumult of the GDR's collapse and the transition to democracy, political participation has decreased in the East. This underscores the point that the Western public is integrated into the democratic process, while Easterners are still learning to be democratic and participatory citizens.

FIGURE 7.5   Participation Levels in West and East Germany

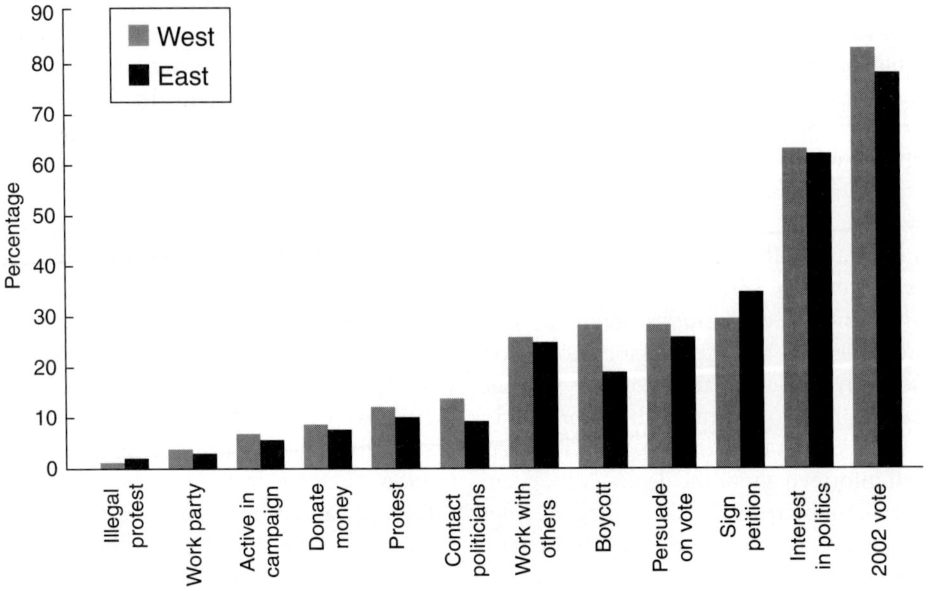

Source: 2002 Comparative Study of Electoral Systems Survey, Germany and 2002 European Social Survey, Germany. Berlin residents are excluded from East/West comparison; vote turnout is from government statistics.

There is also an interesting comparison between working with political parties and citizen-action groups. A significant proportion of Westerners (4 percent) and Easterners (3 percent) said they had worked for a political party during the 2002 election, and nearly twice as many had participated in the campaign or donated money. Yet, participation in a legal demonstration or working with others on a community problem is much more common among both Westerners and Easterners. This indicates the expansion of political involvement to new modes of action.

Thus, the traditional characterization of the German citizen as quiescent and uninvolved is no longer appropriate in either the West or the East. Participation has increased dramatically over the past 50 years, and the public is now involved in a wide range of political activities. The spectators have become participants.

POLITICS AT THE ELITE LEVEL[35]

The Federal Republic is a representative democracy. Above the populace is a group of a few thousand political elite who manage the actual workings of the political system. Elite members, such as party leaders and parliamentary deputies, are directly responsible to the public through elections. Civil servants and judges are appointed to represent the public interest, and they are at least indirectly responsible to the citizenry. Leaders of interest groups and political associations participate in the policy process as representatives of their specific clientele groups. Although the group of politically influential elites is readily identifiable, they do not constitute a homogeneous elite class. Rather, elites in the Federal Republic represent the diverse interests in German society. Often there is as much heterogeneity in policy preferences among the political elites as there is among the public.

Paths to the Top

Individuals may take numerous pathways to elite positions. Party elites may have exceptional political abilities; administrative elites are initially recruited because of their formal training and bureaucratic skills; and interest group leaders are selected for their ability to represent their group.

One feature of elite recruitment that differs from American politics is the long apprenticeship period that precedes entry into the top elite stratum. Candidates for national or even state political office normally have a long background of party work and officeholding at the local level. Similarly, senior civil servants spend nearly all their adult lives working for the government. The biography of the present chancellor, Gerhard Schröder, is a typical example of a long political career (see Box 7.3). Not all political careers are as illustrious as Schröder's, but they often are as long.

A long apprenticeship means that political elites have extensive experience before attaining a position of real power; elites also share a common basis of experience built up from interacting over many years. National politicians know each other from working together at the state or local level; the paths of civil servants frequently cross during their long careers. These experiences develop a sense of trust and responsibility in elite interactions. For instance, members of a chancellor's Cabinet are normally drawn from party elites with extensive experience in state or federal government. Seldom can top business leaders or popular personalities use their outside success to attain a position of political power quickly. This also contributes to the cohesion of elite politics.

The prerequisites for elite positions in the GDR—loyalty to the Socialist Unity Party and its communist ideology—conflicted with the values of the Federal Republic. Consequently, most governmental elites from the old GDR regime left office, by choice or expulsion. Thus, the initial political leadership in the East was heavily drawn from the ranks of church leaders, dissident intellectuals, low-level Eastern officials, and Western politicians. Gradually a new class of political elites is developing in the East, trained under the democratic institutions of the Federal Republic.

Elites in East and West also differ in many of their policy priorities. For instance, Eastern elites are more likely to emphasize the need for greater social and economic equality, social security, and the integration of foreigners.[36] Creating a new political consensus is one of the challenges of unification.

INTEREST GROUPS

Interest groups are an integral part of the German political process, even more so than in the United States. Some specific interests may be favored more than others, but interest groups are generally welcomed as necessary participants in the political process.

German interest groups are connected to the government more closely than groups in the United States Doctors, lawyers, and other self-employed

---

Box 7.3 Schröder's Political Career

Born in 1944, Gerhard Schröder is part of the new generation of German political leaders raised after World War II. When he was 19 years old, he joined the Social Democratic Party and became active in its youth organization. He attended night school to earn admission to the university, and worked as he studied for his law degree. In 1978 he became the national chairman of the Young Socialists, and two years later was elected to the Bundestag. He gained notoriety in his initial parliamentary speech when he became the first deputy to ever address the Bundestag without wearing a necktie. According to a well-known story, after a late night of drinking in Bonn he stopped outside the chancellor's residence to shout, "I want in there!" He became Minister-President of Lower Saxony in 1990. In 1998 he fulfilled his earlier wish, gaining entry into the Chancellory by winning the Bundestag elections as the head of the SPD-Green coalition.

professionals belong to professional associations that are established by law and receive government authorization of their professional activities, making them quasi-public bodies. These associations, which date back to the medieval guilds, enforce professional rules of conduct.

The German system of formally involving interest groups in the policy process reaches further. Administrative law requires that government officials contact groups when formulating new policies that may affect their interests. These consultations ensure that the government can benefit from the expertise of interest group representatives. Other legislation gives interest groups a formal advisory role in the management of public broadcasting, or in other elements of policy administration.

In some instances the pattern of interest group activity approaches the act of governance. For example, when the government recognized the need for structural reform in the steel industry, it assembled interest group representatives from the affected sectors to discuss and negotiate a common plan. Group officials attempted to reach a consensus on the necessary changes, and then implemented the agreements, sometimes with the official sanction of the government.

This cooperation between government and interest groups is described as *neocorporatism*, a general pattern having the following characteristics:[37]

- Social interests are organized into virtually compulsory organizations.
- A single association represents each social sector.
- These associations are hierarchically structured.
- Associations are accepted as formal representatives by the government.
- Associations may participate directly in the policy process.

Policy decisions are reached in discussions and negotiations among the relevant association and the government—then the agreements are implemented by government action.

This neocorporatist pattern solidifies the role of interest groups in the policy process. Governments feel that they are responding to public demands when they consult with these groups, and the members of interest groups depend on the organization

to have their views heard. Thus, the leaders of the major interest groups are important actors in the policy process. Neocorporatist relations also lessen political conflict; for instance, strike levels and political strife tend to be lower in neocorporatist systems.

Another major advantage of neocorporatism is that it makes for efficient government; the involved interest groups can negotiate on policy without the pressures of public debate and partisan conflict. However, efficient government is not necessarily the best government, especially in a democracy. Decisions are reached in conference groups or advisory commissions, outside of the representative institutions of government decision making. The "relevant" interest groups are involved, but this assumes that all relevant interests are organized, and that only organized interests are relevant. Decisions affecting the entire public are often made through private negotiations, as democratically elected representative institutions—state governments and the Bundestag—are sidestepped and interest groups deal directly with government agencies. Consequently, interest groups play a less active role in electoral politics as they concentrate their efforts on direct contact with government agencies.

Although interest groups come in many shapes and sizes, we focus our attention on the large associations that represent the major socioeconomic forces in society. These associations normally have a national organization, a so-called *peak association*, that speaks for its members.

Business

Two major organizations represent business and industrial interests within the political process. The *Federation of German Industry (BDI)* is the peak association for 35 separate industrial groupings. The BDI-affiliated associations represent nearly every major industrial firm, forming a united front that enables industry to speak with authority on matters affecting their interests.

The *Confederation of German Employers' Associations (BDA)* includes an even larger number of business organizations. Virtually every large or medium-sized employer in the nation is affiliated with one of the 68 employer and professional associations of the BDA.

Although the two organizations have overlapping membership, they have different roles within the political process. The BDI represents business on national political matters. Its officials participate in government advisory committees and planning groups, presenting the view of business to government officials and Cabinet ministers.

In contrast, the BDA represents business on labor and social issues. The individual employer associations negotiate with the labor unions over employment contracts. At the national level, the BDA represents business on legislation dealing with social security, labor legislation, and social services. It also nominates business representatives for a variety of government committees, ranging from the media supervisory boards to social security committees.

Business interests have a long history of close relations with the Christian Democrats and conservative politicians. Companies and their top management provide significant financial support for the Christian Democrats, and many Bundestag deputies have strong ties to business. Yet both Social Democrats and Christian Democrats readily accept the legitimate role of business interests within the policy process.

Labor

The *German Federation of Trade Unions (DGB)* is the peak association that incorporates eight separate unions—spanning a range from the metalworking and building trades to the chemical industry and the postal system—into a single organizational structure.[38] The DGB represents more than 7 million workers. However, union membership has declined and today barely a third of the labor force belongs to a union. This membership includes many industrial workers and an even larger percentage of government employees.

As a political organization, the DGB has close ties to the Social Democratic Party, although there is no formal institutional bond between the two. Most SPD deputies in the Bundestag are members of a union, and about one-tenth are former labor union officials. The DGB represents the interests of labor in government conference groups and Bundestag committees. The large mass membership of the DGB also makes union campaign support and

the union vote an essential part of the SPD's electoral base.

In spite of their differing interests, business and unions have shown an unusual ability to work together. The Economic Miracle was possible because labor and management implicitly agreed that the first priority was economic growth, from which both sides would prosper. Work time lost through strikes and work stoppages has been consistently lower in the Federal Republic than in most other Western European nations.

This cooperation is encouraged by joint participation of business and union representatives in government committees and planning groups. Cooperation also extends into industrial decision making through *codetermination (Mitbestimmung)*, a federal policy that requires half of the board of directors in large companies to be elected by the employees. The system was first applied to the coal, iron, and steel industries in 1951; a 1976 law extended a modified form to large corporations in other fields. When codetermination was introduced, there were dire forecasts that it would destroy German industry. The system generally has been successful, however, in fostering better labor-management relations and thereby strengthening the economy. The Social Democrats also favor codetermination because it introduces democratic principles into the economic system.

Religious Interests

Religious associations are the third major organized interest in German politics. Rather than being separated from politics, as in the United States, church and state are closely related. The churches are subject to the rules of the state, and in return they receive formal representation and support from the government.

The churches are financed mainly through a church tax collected by the government. The government adds a surcharge (about 10 percent) to an employee's income tax, and the government transfers this amount to the employee's church. A taxpayer can officially decline to pay that tax, but social norms discourage this step. Similarly, Catholic primary schools in several states receive government funding, and the churches accept government subsidies to support their social programs and aid to the needy.

In addition to this financial support, the churches are often directly involved in the policy process. Church appointees regularly sit on government planning committees that deal with education, social services, and family affairs. By law, the churches participate on the supervisory boards of the public radio and television networks. Members of the Protestant and Catholic clergy occasionally serve in political offices, as Bundestag deputies or as state government officials.

Although the Catholic and Protestant churches receive the same formal representation by the government, the two churches differ in their political styles. The Catholic Church has close ties to the Christian Democrats, and at least implicitly encourages its members to support these parties and their conservative policies. The Catholic hierarchy is not hesitant to lobby the government on legislation dealing with social or moral issues. With its abundant resources and tightly structured organization, the Catholic Church often wields an influential role in policymaking.

The Protestant Church is a loose association of mostly Lutheran churches spread across Germany. The pattern of the church's political involvement varies with the preferences of local pastors and bishops and their respective congregations. In the West, the Protestant churches have minimized their involvement in partisan politics, although they are seen as favoring the Social Democrats. Protestant groups also work through their formal representation on government committees or function as individual lobbying organizations.

The Protestant Church in the GDR played a more significant political role because it was one of the few organizations that retained its autonomy from the state. Churches were meeting places for people who wanted to discuss freely the social and moral aspects of contemporary issues. As the East German revolution gathered force in 1989, churches in Leipzig, East Berlin, and other cities granted sanctuary for citizens' groups. Weekly services acted as a rallying point for opposition to the regime. Religion was not the opiate of the people, as Marx had feared, but one of the forces that swept the Communists from power.

Despite their institutionalized role in the Federal Republic's formal system of interest group representation, the influence of both the Catholic and Protestant churches has gradually waned over the past several decades. Declining church attendance in both West and East marks a steady secularization of German society. About one-tenth of Westerners claim to be nonreligious, as are nearly half the residents in the East. The gradual secularization of German society suggests that the churches' popular base will continue its slow erosion.

New Politics Movement

In recent years, a new set of political groups has emerged as part of the New Politics movement. Challenging business, labor, religion, agriculture, and other established socioeconomic interests, these new organizations have focused their efforts on the lifestyle and quality-of-life issues facing Germany.[39] Environmental groups are the most visible part of the movement. Following the flowering of environmental interests in the 1970s, antinuclear groups popped up like mushrooms around nuclear power facilities, local environmental action groups proliferated, and new national organizations formed. Another part of the New Politics network has been the women's movement. That movement developed a dualistic strategy for improving the status of women: changing the consciousness of women and reforming the laws. A variety of associations and self-help groups at the local level nurture the personal development of women, while other organizations focus on national policymaking.

These New Politics groups have distinct issue interests and their own organizations, but they are also parts of a common movement unified by their shared interest in the quality of life for individuals, whether it is the quality of the natural environment, the protection of human rights, or peace in an uncertain world. They draw their members from the same social base: young, better-educated, and middle-class citizens. These groups also are more likely to use unconventional political tactics, such as protests and demonstrations.

The New Politics movement does not wield the influence of the established interest groups, although their membership now exceeds the size of the formal membership in the political parties. These groups have become important and contentious actors in the political process. Moreover, the reconciliation of women's legislation in the united Germany and the resolution of the East's nearly catastrophic environmental problems are likely to keep these concerns near the top of the political agenda.

THE PARTY SYSTEM

The party system presents one of the clearest examples of the different political histories of the FRG and the GDR. Following World War II, the Western Allies created a democratic, competitive party system as part of the new political process in the West. The Allies licensed a diverse set of parties that were free of Nazi ties and committed to democratic procedures. The Basic Law further required that parties support the constitutional order and democratic methods of the Federal Republic. Because of these provisions, the FRG developed a strong system of competitive party politics that was a mainstay of the new democratic order. Elections focused on the competition between the conservative Christian Democrats and the leftist Social Democrats, with the small Free Democratic Party often holding the balance of power. Elections were meaningful; control of the government shifted between the left and right as a function of election outcomes. When New Politics issues entered the political agenda in the 1980s, a new political party, the Greens, emerged to represent these concerns. And in the late 1980s, a small extreme-right party, the *Republikaner (REP)*, formed as an advocate of nationalist policies and antiforeigner propaganda.[40] However, this party has failed to win seats in the Bundestag.

Although the GDR ostensibly had a multiparty system and elections, this presented only the illusion of democracy—the Socialist Unity Party (SED) firmly held political power. In advance of an election, the SED would assemble a National Front list of candidates that would include representatives from the other parties and various social groups. The SED decided the members of this list and each party's allocation of parliamentary seats before the poll. Thus, the elections in the East were largely symbolic acts.

When the GDR collapsed, its party system was drawn into this void. Support for the SED plummeted, and the party distanced itself from its own history by changing its name to the *Party of Democratic Socialism (PDS)*. Many antigovernment opposition groups tried to develop into parties in order to compete in the March 1990 elections. Other new political parties represented interests ranging from the Beer Drinkers Union to a women's party. Very soon, however, the West German parties usurped the electoral process, taking over the financing, tactics, organization, and substance of the campaign. The consolidation of the Western and Eastern party system was essentially completed with the 1990 Bundestag election. Today the party system of the new Germany largely represents an extension of the Western system to the East.

Christian Democrats

The creation of the Christian Democratic Union (CDU) in postwar West Germany signified a sharp break with the tradition of German political parties. The CDU was founded by a mixed group of Catholics and Protestants, businesspeople and trade unionists, conservatives and liberals. Rather than representing narrow special interests, the party wanted to appeal to a broad segment of society in order to gain government power. The party's unifying principle was to reconstruct West Germany along Christian and humanitarian lines. Konrad Adenauer, the party leader, developed the CDU into a conservative-oriented catchall party (*Volkspartei*)—a sharp contrast to the fragmented ideological parties of Weimar. This strategy succeeded; within a single decade the CDU emerged as the largest party, capturing 40 to 50 percent of the popular vote (see Figure 7.6).

The CDU operates in all states except Bavaria, where it allies itself with the *Christian Social Union (CSU)*, whose basic political philosophy is more conservative than the CDU. These two parties generally function as one in national politics (CDU/CSU), forming a single parliamentary group in the Bundestag and campaigning together in national elections.

The CDU/CSU's early voting strength allowed the party to control the government, first under the

FIGURE 7.6   Shares of the Party Vote (Second Vote), 1949–2002

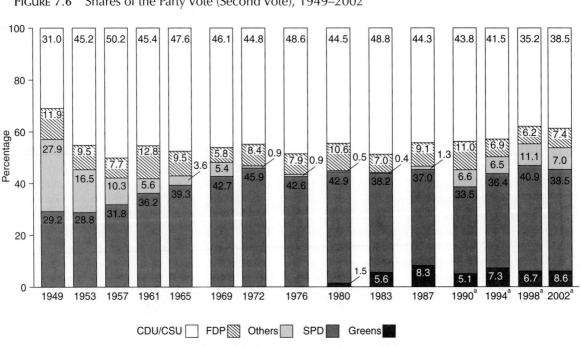

CDU/CSU ☐   FDP ▨   Others ▤   SPD ▦   Greens ■

[a] 1990–2002 percentages combine results from Western and Eastern Germany.

leadership of Adenauer (1949–1963) and then under Ludwig Erhard (1963–1966), as shown in Table 7.1. In 1966, however, the party lost the support of its coalition partner, the Free Democrats, and formed a Grand Coalition with the Social Democrats. Following the 1969 election, the Social Democrats and Free Democrats formed a new government coalition; for the first time in the history of the Federal Republic, the CDU/CSU became the opposition party.

In the early 1980s the strains of a weak economy increased public support for the party and its conservative economic program. In 1982 the Christian Democrats and the Free Democrats formed a new conservative government through the first successful constructive no-confidence vote that elected Helmut Kohl as chancellor. Public support for Kohl's policies returned the governing coalition to power following the 1983 and 1987 elections.

The collapse of the GDR in 1989 provided a historic opportunity for the CDU and Kohl. While others looked on the events with wonder or uncertainty, Kohl quickly embraced the idea of closer ties between the two Germanies. Thus, when the March 1990 GDR election became a referendum in support of German unification, the Christian Democrats were assured of victory because of the party's early commitment to German union. Kohl emerged victorious from the 1990 Bundestag elections, but his government struggled with the policy challenges produced by German unification. The governing coalition lost more than 50 seats in the 1994 elections, but Kohl retained a slim majority. By the 1998 elections, the accumulation of 16 years of governing and the special challenges of unification had taken their toll on the party and Helmut Kohl. Many Germans looked for a change. The CDU/CSU fared poorly in the election, especially in the Eastern Länder that were frustrated by their persisting

TABLE 7.1   Composition of Coalition Governments

Date Formed	Source of Change	Coalition Partners[a]	Chancellor
September 1949	Election	CDU/CSU, FDP, DP	Adenauer (CDU)
October 1953	Election	CDU/CSU, FDP, DP, G	Adenauer (CDU)
October 1957	Election	CDU/CSU, DP	Adenauer (CDU)
November 1961	Election	CDU/CSU, FDP	Adenauer (CDU)
October 1963	Chancellor retirement	CDU/CSU, FDP	Erhard (CDU)
October 1965	Election	CDU/CSU, FDP	Erhard (CDU)
December 1966	Coalition change	CDU/CSU, SPD	Kiesinger (CDU)
October 1969	Election	SPD, FDP	Brandt (SPD)
December 1972	Election	SPD, FDP	Brandt (SPD)
May 1974	Chancellor retirement	SPD, FDP	Schmidt (SPD)
December 1976	Election	SPD, FDP	Schmidt (SPD)
November 1980	Election	SPD, FDP	Schmidt (SPD)
October 1982	Constructive no-confidence	CDU/CSU, FDP	Kohl (CDU)
March 1983	Election	CDU/CSU, FDP	Kohl (CDU)
January 1987	Election	CDU/CSU, FDP	Kohl (CDU)
December 1990	Election	CDU/CSU, FDP	Kohl (CDU)
October 1994	Election	CDU/CSU, FDP	Kohl (CDU)
September 1998	Election	SPD, Greens	Schröder (SPD)
September 2002	Election	SPD, Greens	Schröder (SPD)

[a]CDU: Christian Democratic Union. CSU: Christian Social Union. DP: German Party. FDP: Free Democratic Party. G: All-German Bloc Federation of Expellees and Displaced Persons. SPD: Social Democratic Party.

second-class status. The CDU's poor showing in the election was a rebuke to Kohl and he resigned the party leadership.

The CDU made some gains after the election and seemed poised to win several state elections in 1999 and 2000—and then lightning struck. Investigations showed that Kohl had accepted illegal campaign contributions while he was chancellor. Kohl's allies within the CDU were forced to resign, and the party's electoral fortunes suffered. To change its popular image, in 1999 the CDU selected a party leader who was nearly the opposite of Kohl: Angela Merkel (an Easterner, a relative newcomer to politics, a Ph.D. in physics, and a woman).

The CDU/CSU chose Edmund Stoiber, the head of the Christian Social Union, as its chancellor candidate in 2002. Stoiber's campaign stressed the struggling German economy, and under his leadership the CDU/CSU gained the same vote share as the Social Democrats and nearly as many seats in the Bundestag (see Figure 7.7). Although an SPD-led coalition retained control of the government, the CDU/CSU reemerged from the election as a renewed force in German politics. It has led the SPD in the polls since 2002 and is demonstrating its influence in the Bundesrat and state politics.

Social Democrats

The postwar Social Democratic Party (SPD) in West Germany was constructed along the lines of the SPD in the Weimar Republic—an ideological party, primarily representing the interests of unions and the working class.[41] In the early postwar years the Social Democrats espoused strict Marxist doctrine and consistently opposed Adenauer's Western-oriented foreign policy. The SPD's image of the nation's future was radically different from that of Adenauer and the Christian Democrats.

The SPD's poor performance in early elections (see again Figure 7.6) generated internal pressures for the party to broaden its electoral appeal. At the 1959 Godesberg party conference, the party

FIGURE 7.7   The Distribution of Bundestag Seats in 1998 and 2002

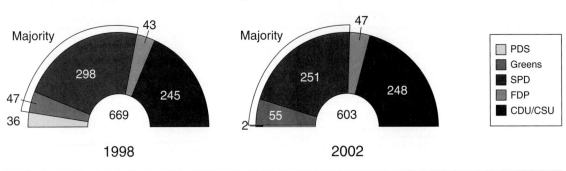

renounced its Marxist economic policies and generally moved toward the center on domestic and foreign policies. The party continued to represent working-class interests, but by shedding its ideological banner the SPD hoped to attract new support from the middle class. The SPD transformed itself into a progressive catchall party that could compete with the Christian Democrats.

An SPD breakthrough finally came in 1966 with the formation of the Grand Coalition (see again Table 7.1). By sharing government control with the CDU/CSU, the Social Democrats alleviated lingering public uneasiness about the party's integrity and ability to govern. Political support for the party also grew as the SPD played an active part in resolving the nation's problems.

Following the 1969 election, a new Social Democrat–Free Democrat government formed with Willy Brandt (SPD) as chancellor. After a period of economic recession, Helmut Schmidt replaced Brandt as chancellor in 1974, and the SPD turned its attention toward the faltering economy. Although the SPD retained government control in the 1976 and 1980 elections, these were trying times for the party. The SPD and the Free Democrats frequently disagreed on economic policy, and political divisions developed within the SPD. For example, many young middle-class SPD members opposed nuclear energy and large-scale economic development projects that were favored by the unions.

These policy tensions eventually led to the breakup of the SPD-led government in 1982. Once

again in opposition, the SPD faced an identity crisis. In one election they tried to appeal to centrist voters, in the next election to leftist/Green voters—but neither strategy succeeded. In 1990 the SPD campaign was overtaken by events in the East.

Perhaps no one (except perhaps the Communists) was more surprised than the SPD by the course of events in the GDR in 1989–1990. The SPD had been normalizing relations with the SED as a basis of intra-German cooperation, only to see the SED ousted by the citizenry. The Social Democrats were ambivalent about German unification and stood by quietly as Kohl spoke of a single German *Vaterland* to crowds of applauding East Germans. The party's poor performance in the 1990 national elections reflected its inability either to lead or to follow the course of the unification process. Frustrated by the course of German politics and the economy after unification, the public came to the brink of voting the SPD into office in 1994, and then pulled back.

In the spring of 1998 the Social Democrats selected Gerhard Schröder to be their chancellor candidate. Representing the moderate wing of the party, Schröder attracted former CDU/CSU and Free Democratic voters who were disenchanted with the government's performance. The SPD made broad gains in the 1998 election and formed a new coalition government with the environmental Green Party. Schröder pursued a middle course, balancing the centrist and leftist views existing within the governing coalition. For instance, overdue reductions in tax rates and government spending were paired with a new environmental tax advocated by the Greens. The government allowed German troops to play an active role in Kosovo and Afghanistan, while mandating the phasing out of nuclear power.

As the 2002 election approached, however, the German economy was struggling and the SPD-led government was behind in the polls. Schröder deflected criticism of his economic policy and opposed American policy toward Iraq to gain new votes from Easterners and erode the voter base of the PDS. This strategy succeeded, and the SPD-Green government was returned to office with a narrow majority (see Figure 7.7).

The SPD now faces a growing need for economic and social reforms in a nation divided on these issues—including deep divisions within the governing coalition. It has suffered a series of losses in state elections, indicating the public's dissatisfaction with the government's policies so far.

Free Democratic Party

Although the Free Democratic Party (FDP) is far smaller than the two major parties, it has often wielded considerable political influence. Government control in a multiparty, parliamentary system normally requires a coalition of parties, and the FDP often held enough seats to have a pivotal role in forming the government.

The FDP—created to continue the liberal tradition from the prewar party system—was initially a strong advocate of private enterprise and drew its support from the Protestant middle class and farmers. Its economic policies made the FDP a natural ally of the CDU/CSU (see again Table 7.1). In the mid-1960s the Free Democrats emphasized their liberal foreign and social programs, opening the way for the SPD-FDP coalition that began in 1969. Worsening economic conditions in the early 1980s led to a new coalition with the CDU/CSU that began in October 1982.

The FDP has generally acted as a moderating influence, limiting the leftist leanings of the SPD and the conservative tendencies of the CDU/CSU. This places the party in a precarious position, however,

because if it allies itself too closely with either major party it may lose its political identity. The party struggled with this problem for the past several elections.

In January 2001 Guido Westerwelle won the party leadership; his goal is to return the FDP to a role in the national government. The party fared well in early preelection polls in 2002, and was seen as the clearest advocate for many of the economic and social reforms that many analysts favored. However, internal party divisions harmed the party's standing in 2002, and its poor showing kept the conservative CDU/CSU-FDP coalition from winning the election. Now the party needs to redress its internal divisions and decide the future program of the party.

The Greens

Environmental issues began to attract public attention in the 1970s, and the established parties generally were unresponsive to environmental concerns. The environmental movement therefore developed its own party representative: *the Greens*.[42] The party addresses a broad range of New Politics issues: opposition to nuclear energy and Germany's military policies, commitment to environmental protection, support for women's rights, and further democratization of society. The Greens initially differed so markedly from the established parties that one Green leader described them as the "antiparty party."

The party won its first representation in the Bundestag in 1983, becoming the first new party to enter parliament since the 1950s. Using the legislature as a political forum, the Greens campaigned vigorously for an alternative view of politics, seeking much stronger measures to protect the environment and showing staunch opposition to the government's nuclear power program. The Greens also added a bit of color and spontaneity to the normally staid procedures of the political system. The typical dress for Green deputies was jeans and a sweater, rather than the traditional business attire of the established parties; their desks in parliament often sprouted flowers, rather than folders of official-looking documents. The party's loose and open internal structure stood in sharp contrast to the hierarchic and bureaucratized structure of the established parties. Despite initial concerns about the impact of the Greens on the governmental system, most analysts now agree that the party brought necessary attention to political viewpoints that previously were overlooked.

German unification caught the Greens unprepared. The Western Greens opposed the simple eastward extension of the FRG's economic and political systems. Moreover, to stress their opposition to the fusion of both Germanies, the Western Greens refused to form an electoral alliance with the Eastern Greens in the 1990 elections. The Eastern Greens/Alliance' 90 won enough votes to enter the new Bundestag in 1990, but the Western Greens fell under the 5 percent threshold and did not win any parliamentary seats on their own. The Greens' unconventional politics had caught up with them. After the 1990 election loss, the Greens charted a more moderate course for the party. Their commitment to the environment and an alternative agenda remained, but they tempered the unconventional style and structure of the party. The party reentered the Bundestag in 1994.

By 1998 the moderates had won control of the Green Party and asked voters to support a new Red-Green coalition of SPD and the Greens. This Red-Green coalition received a majority in the election, and for the first time the Greens became part of the national government. It is difficult to be an outsider when one is inside of the establishment, however. The antiparty party struggled to balance its unconventional policies against the new responsibilities of governing—and has steadily given up its unconventional style. For instance, the party supported military intervention into Kosovo, despite its pacifist traditions; it supported tax reform that lowered the highest rates in exchange for a new environmental tax. It pressed for the abolition of nuclear power, but agreed to wait 30 years for this to happen. In the 2002 campaign, the anti-elitist Greens ran a campaign heavily based on the personal appeal of their leader, Joschka Fischer. The Greens' success in 2002 is what returned the Schröder government to power. The Greens have become a conventional party in terms of their style, now pursuing unconventional and reformist policies.

Communists to the Party of DemocraticSocialism

The Communists were one of the first political parties to form in postwar Germany, and the party's history reflects the two paths Germany followed. In the West, the Communist Party (KPD) suffered because of its identification with the Soviet Union and the GDR. The party garnered a shrinking sliver of the vote in the early elections, and then in 1956 the Constitutional Court banned the party because of its undemocratic principles. A reconstituted party began contesting elections again in 1969 but never attracted a significant following.

The situation was obviously different in the East. As World War II was ending, Walter Ulbricht returned to Berlin from exile in Moscow; he reorganized the Communist Party in the Soviet military zone. In 1946 the Soviets forced a merger of the Eastern KPD and SPD into a new Socialist Unity Party of Germany (SED), which became the ruling institution in the East. The SED controlled the government apparatus and the electoral process; party agents were integrated into the military command structure; the party supervised the infamous state security police (*Stasi*); and party membership was a prerequisite to positions of authority and influence. The state controlled East German society, and the SED controlled the state.

In 1989 the SED's power collapsed along with the East German regime. Party membership plummeted, and local party units abolished themselves. The omnipotent party suddenly seemed impotent. To save the party from complete dissolution and to enable it to compete in the new democratic environment in the East, the party changed its name in February 1990 and became the Party of Democratic Socialism (PDS). The old party guard was ousted from positions of authority, and new moderates took over the leadership.

The PDS has campaigned as the representative of those who opposed the economic and social course of German unity. In the 1990 Bundestag elections the PDS won 11 percent of the Eastern vote, although it captured only 2 percent of the national vote. The PDS shared in the proportional distribution of Bundestag seats in the 1994 and 1998 elections (see the following discussion of the electoral system).

The future role of the PDS is uncertain following the 2002 election. The party holds only two seats in the Bundestag and gained less than 5 percent of the national vote. The PDS suffered partly because of internal party divisions and partly because the SPD consciously sought the support of former PDS voters in the East. Although the PDS is still very active in state and local politics in the East, the lack of national standing will limit the party's influence and the lack of effective leaders may weaken the party in the future.

THE ELECTORAL SYSTEM

The framers of the Basic Law had two goals in mind when they designed the electoral system. One was to create a *proportional representation (PR)* system— a system that allocates legislative seats based on a party's percentage of the popular vote. If a party receives 10 percent of the popular vote, it should receive 10 percent of the Bundestag seats. Other individuals saw advantages in the system of single-member districts used in Britain and the United States. They thought that this system would avoid the fragmentation of the Weimar party system and ensure some accountability between an electoral district and its representative.

To satisfy both objectives, the FRG created a mixed electoral system. On one part of the ballot citizens vote for a candidate to represent their district. The candidate with the most votes in each district is elected to parliament.

On a second part of the ballot voters select a party. These second votes are added nationwide to determine each party's share of the popular vote. A party's proportion of the second vote determines its total representation in the Bundestag. Each party receives additional seats so that its percentage of the combined candidate and party seats equals its percentage of the second votes. These additional seats are distributed according to lists prepared by the state parties before the election. Half of the Bundestag members are elected as district representatives and half as party representatives.[43]

One major exception to this PR system is the 5-percent clause, which stipulates that a party must win at least 5 percent of the national vote (or three district seats) to share in the distribution of party-list seats.[44] The law is designed to withhold representation from the type of small extremist parties that plagued the Weimar Republic. In practice, however, the 5-percent clause handicaps all minor parties and contributes to the development of a few large parties.

This mixed system has several consequences for electoral politics. The party-list system gives party leaders substantial influence on who will be elected to parliament by the placement of candidates on the list. The PR system also ensures fair representation for the smaller parties. The FDP, for example, has won only one direct candidate mandate since 1957, and yet it receives Bundestag seats based on its national share of the vote. In contrast, Britain's district-only system discriminates against small parties; in 2001 the British Liberal Democrats won 18.3 percent of the national vote but only 7.8 percent of the parliamentary seats. The German two-vote system also affects campaign strategies. Although most voters cast both their ballots for the same party, the FDP traditionally encourages supporters of its larger coalition partner to "lend" their second votes to the Free Democrats. In recent federal elections these split ballots kept the FDP above the 5-percent hurdle. Perhaps because of its mixed features, variations of the German electoral system have been used in the new democracies of Hungary and Russia; Italy, Japan, and New Zealand introduced versions of this system in the early 1990s.

The Electoral Connection

One of the essential functions of political parties in a democracy is interest representation. Elections provide individuals and social groups with an opportunity to select political elites who share their views. In turn, this choice leads to the representation of voter interests in the policy process because a party must be responsive to its electoral coalition if it wants to retain its support.

The ideological and policy differences among parties are reflected in the patterns of support across social groups. Social differences in voting have

TABLE 7.2   Electoral Coalitions of the Parties in the 2002 Federal Elections

	SPD	Greens	CDU/CSU	FDP	Total Public
Region					
West	78.3	89.0	85.3	81.0	80.9
East	21.7	11.0	14.7	19.0	19.1
Occupation					
Worker	34.4	17.1	22.3	21.1	27.1
Self-employed	6.4	18.3	19.5	23.7	13.8
White collar/government	59.2	64.1	58.2	55.3	59.1
Education					
Primary	41.0	22.5	34.3	31.7	35.3
Secondary	36.5	21.6	37.4	35.4	35.4
Advanced	22.5	55.9	28.3	32.9	29.4
Religion					
Catholic	29.3	35.6	47.2	21.2	35.3
Protestant	41.8	33.9	38.1	44.7	36.4
Other, none	28.9	30.5	14.7	34.1	28.3
Size of town					
less than 5,000	31.7	28.0	31.3	28.9	30.8
5,000–20,000	22.2	26.3	27.2	25.3	24.7
20,000–100,000	20.6	15.3	21.2	27.7	20.5
more than 100,000	25.5	30.5	20.2	18.1	24.0
Age					
Under 40	36.1	46.6	32.5	39.3	37.2
40–59	32.5	32.2	32.0	35.7	32.0
60 and over	31.4	21.2	35.5	25.0	30.8
Gender					
Male	46.1	52.5	48.1	49.4	47.9
Female	53.9	47.5	51.9	50.6	52.1

Source: September 16–20, 2002 German Election Study; conducted by the Forschungsgruppe Wahlen for the Zweite Deutsche Fernsehen (weighted N=1277). Some percentages do not total 100 because of rounding or missing cases. Dieter Roth provided access to these data.

gradually narrowed in the Federal Republic, and unification has added several million new voters and partially changed the composition of the electorate. Still, the voting patterns for the combined German electorate in 2002 reflect the traditional social divisions in German society and politics (see Table 7.2).[45]

The SPD's electoral coalition draws more voters from the liberal sectors of society, with greater support from workers, the less-educated, and Protestants. The party's strength is concentrated in central and north Germany, especially in the cities; the SPD gained significantly among Eastern voters in 2002.

The CDU/CSU's base is almost the reverse of the SPD's voters: a large share of CDU/CSU voters comes from the middle class, seniors, and residents of rural areas and small towns. Catholic voters also give disproportionate support to the party.

The Greens have a very distinct electoral base heavily drawn from groups that support New Politics movements: the new middle class, the better educated, and urban voters. Even more striking are the age differences in party support; many (46.6 percent) Green voters are under 40, though this is down markedly from previous elections. In 2002 the Greens' voter balance became more like the electorate overall, perhaps indicating its less distinctive image as a result of its more conventional image and reliance on Fischer's personality as an attraction for voters.

The FDP's voter base in 2002 illustrates the party's new electoral appeal. The FDP voters include new young voters; the party also increased its vote share beyond its traditional base among Protestant members of the middle class. In addition, the FDP was more successful in 2002 in appealing to Eastern voters.

The incorporation of the new voters from the East is still producing strains within the German party system. The SPD's appeal to Easterners will give them a new voice within the government, but the losses for the PDS may leave other views unrepresented. At the same time, the Greens and FDP have become distinctly Western parties in their voter appeal. The 2002 results suggest that East–West political divisions are continuing.

Party Government

Political parties in Germany deserve special emphasis because they are such important actors in the political process, perhaps even more important than in most other European democracies. Some observers describe the political system as government for the parties, by the parties, and of the parties.

The Basic Law is unusual because it specifically refers to political parties (the American Constitution does not). Because the German Empire and the Third Reich suppressed political parties, the Basic Law guarantees their legitimacy and their right to exist—if they accept the principles of democratic government. Parties are also designated as the primary institutions of representative democracy. They act as intermediaries between the public and the government and function as means for citizen input on policy preferences. The Basic Law takes the additional step of assigning an educational function to the parties, directing them to "take part in forming the political will of the people." In other words, the parties should take the lead and not just respond to public opinion.

The centrality of parties in the political process appears in several ways. There are no direct primaries that would allow the public to select party representatives in Bundestag elections. Instead, district candidates are nominated by a small group of official party members or by a committee appointed by the membership. Party-list candidates are selected at state party conventions. Thus, the leadership has discretion in selecting list candidates and their ordering on the list. This power can be used to reward faithful party supporters and discipline party mavericks; placement near the top of a party list virtually ensures election, and low placement carries little chance of a Bundestag seat.

The dominance of party is also evident throughout the election process. Most voters view the candidates merely as party representatives rather than as independent political figures. Even the district candidates are elected primarily because of their party ties. Bundestag, state, and European election campaigns are financed by the government, with the parties receiving public funds for each vote they get. Again, government funding and access to public media are allocated to the parties, not the individual candidates. Government funding for the parties also continues between elections, to help them perform their informational and educational functions as prescribed in the Basic Law.

Within the Bundestag, the parties are even more influential. Organizationally, the Bundestag is structured around party groups (*Fraktionen*) rather than individual deputies. The important legislative posts and committee assignments are restricted to members of a party Fraktion. The size of a Fraktion determines its representation on legislative committees, its share of committee chairs, and its participation in the executive bodies of the legislature. Government funds for legislative and administrative support are distributed to the Fraktion, not to the deputies.

Because of these forces, the cohesion of parties within the Bundestag is exceptionally high. Parties caucus before major legislation to decide the party position, and most legislative votes follow strict party lines. This is partially a consequence of a parliamentary system and partially a sign of the pervasive influence parties have throughout the political process.

THE POLICY PROCESS

The policymaking process may begin from any part of society—an interest group, a political leader, an individual citizen, or a government official. Because these elements interact in making public policy, it is difficult to trace the true genesis of any policy idea. Moreover, once a new policy is proposed, other interest groups come into play and become active in amending, supporting, or opposing the policy.

The pattern of interaction among policy actors varies with time and policy issues. One set of groups is most active on labor issues, and they use the methods of influence that are most successful for their cause. A very different set of interests may assert themselves on defense policy and use far different methods of influence. This variety makes it difficult to describe policymaking as a single process, although the institutional framework for enacting policy is relatively uniform in all policy areas.

The growing importance of the European Union has also changed the policymaking process for its member states (see Chapter 12).[46] Now, policies made in Brussels often take precedence over German legislation. Laws passed by the German government must conform to EU standards in many areas. The European Court of Justice also has the power to overturn laws passed by the German government. Thus policymaking is no longer a solely national process.

This section describes the various arenas in which policy actors compete within the German political process, and clarifies the balance of power between the institutions of the German government.

Policy Initiation

Most issues reach the formal policy agenda through the executive branch. One reason for this predominance is that the Cabinet and the ministries manage the affairs of government. They are responsible for preparing the budget, formulating revenue proposals, administering existing policies, and the other routine activities of government. The nature of a parliamentary democracy further strengthens the policymaking influence of the chancellor and the Cabinet. The chancellor acts as the primary policy

spokesperson for the government and for a majority of the Bundestag deputies. In speeches, interviews, and formal policy declarations, he sets the policy agenda for the government. It is the responsibility of the chancellor and Cabinet to propose new legislation to implement the government's policy promises. Interest groups realize the importance of the executive branch, and they generally work with the federal ministries—rather than Bundestag deputies—when they seek new legislation.

This focus on the executive branch means that the Cabinet proposes about two-thirds of the legislation considered by the Bundestag. Thirty members of the Bundestag may jointly introduce a bill, but only about 20 percent of legislative proposals begin in this manner. Most of the Bundestag's own proposals involve private-member bills or minor issues. State governments also can propose legislation in the Bundesrat, but they do so infrequently.

The Cabinet attempts to follow a consensual decision-making style in establishing the government's policy program. Ministers seldom propose legislation that is not expected to receive Cabinet support. The chancellor has a crucial part in ensuring this consensus. The chancellor's office coordinates the legislative proposals drafted by the various ministries. If the chancellor feels that a bill conflicts with the government's stated objectives, he may ask that the proposal be withdrawn or returned to the ministry for restudy and redrafting. If a conflict on policy arises between two ministries, the chancellor may mediate the dispute. Alternatively, interministerial negotiations may resolve the differences. Only in extreme cases is the chancellor unable to resolve such problems; when such stalemates occur, policy conflicts are referred to the full Cabinet.

In Cabinet deliberations the chancellor also has a major part. The chancellor is a fulcrum, balancing conflicting interests to reach a compromise that the government as a whole can support. His leadership position gives him substantial influence as he negotiates with Cabinet members. Very seldom does a majority of the Cabinet oppose the chancellor. When the chancellor and Cabinet agree on a legislative proposal, they occupy a dominant position in the legislative process. Because the Cabinet also represents the majority in the Bundestag, most of its initiatives are eventually enacted into law. In the twelfth Bundestag (1994–1998), more than 90 percent of the government's proposals became law; in contrast, about 30 percent of the proposals introduced by Bundestag members became law. The government's legislative position is further strengthened by provisions in the Basic Law that limit the Bundestag's authority in fiscal matters. The parliament can revise or amend most legislative proposals. It cannot, however, alter the spending or taxation levels of legislation proposed by the Cabinet. Parliament cannot even reallocate expenditures in the budget without the approval of the finance minister and the Cabinet.

Legislating Policy

When the Cabinet approves a legislative proposal, the government sends it to the Bundesrat for review (see Figure 7.8). After receiving the Bundesrat's comments, the Cabinet formally transmits the government's proposal to the Bundestag. The bill receives a first reading, which places it on the agenda of the chamber, and it is assigned to the appropriate committee.

Much of the Bundestag's work takes place in these specialized committees. The committee structure generally follows the divisions of the federal ministries, such as transportation, defense, labor, or agriculture. Because bills are referred to the committee early in the legislative process, committees have real potential for reviewing and amending their content. Committees evaluate proposals, consult with interest groups, and then submit a revised proposal to the full Bundestag. Research staffs are small, but committees also use investigative hearings. Government and interest group representatives testify on pending legislation, and committee members themselves often have expertise in their designated policy area. Most committees hold their meetings behind closed doors. The committee system thus provides an opportunity for frank discussions of proposals and negotiations among the parties before legislation reaches the floor of the Bundestag.

When a committee reports a bill, the full Bundestag examines it and discusses any proposed revisions. At this point in the legislative process, how-

ever, political positions already are well established. Leaders in the governing parties participated in the initial formulation of the legislation. The parties have caucused to decide their official position. Major revisions during the second and third readings are infrequent; the government generally is assured of the passage of its proposals as reported out of committee.

Bundestag debate on the merits of government proposals is thus mostly symbolic. It allows the parties to present their views to the public. The successful parties explain the merits of the new legislation and advertise their efforts to their supporters. The opposition parties place their objections in the public record. Although these debates seldom influence the outcome of a vote, they are nevertheless an important part of the Bundestag's information function.

A bill that passes the Bundestag is transmitted to the Bundesrat. The Bundesrat represents the state governments in the federal policy process. The legislative authority of the Bundesrat equals the Bundestag in areas where the states share concurrent powers with the federal government or administer federal policies. In these areas the approval of the Bundesrat is necessary for a bill to become law. In the remaining policy areas that do not involve the states directly, such as defense or foreign affairs, Bundesrat approval of legislation is not essential. About two-thirds of legislative proposals now require Bundesrat approval.

The sharing of legislative power between the state and federal governments has mixed political consequences. State leaders can adapt legislation to local and regional needs through their influence on policymaking. This division of power also provides another check in the system of checks and balances. With strong state governments, it is less likely that one leader or group could control the political process by usurping the national government.

The Bundesrat's voting procedures give disproportionate weight to the smaller states; states representing only a third of the population control half the votes in the Bundesrat. Thus, the Bundesrat cannot claim the same popular legitimacy as the proportionally represented and directly elected Bundestag. The Bundesrat voting system may encourage

FIGURE 7.8   The Legislative Process

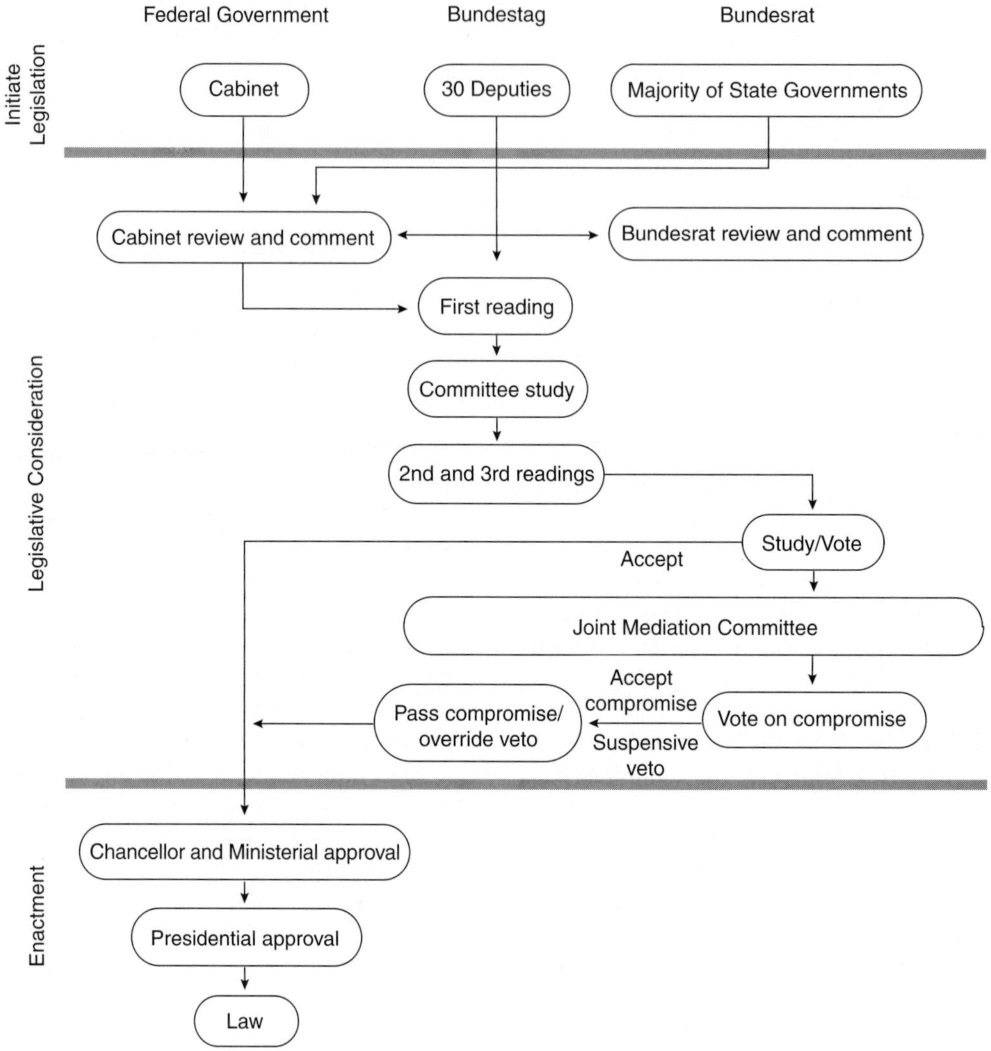

parochialism by the states. The states vote as a bloc; therefore, they view policy from the perspective of the state, rather than the national interest or party positions. The different electoral bases of the Bundestag and Bundesrat make such tensions over policy an inevitable part of the legislative process.

During most of the 1990s and into the 2000s, different party coalitions controlled the Bundestag and the Bundesrat. In one sense, this division strengthened the power of the legislature because the federal government had to negotiate with the opposition in the Bundesrat, especially on the sensitive issues of German union. But divided government also prevented necessary new legislation in a variety of areas.

As in the Bundestag, much of the Bundesrat's work is done in specialized committees where bills are scrutinized for both their policy content and their administrative implications for the states. After committee review, a bill is submitted to the full Bundesrat. If the Bundesrat approves of the measure, it transmits the bill to the chancellor for his signature. If the Bundesrat objects to the Bundestag's bill, the representatives of both bodies meet in a joint mediation committee and attempt to resolve their differences.

The mediation committee submits its recommendation to both legislative bodies for their approval. If the proposal involves the state governments, the Bundesrat may cast an absolute veto and prevent the bill from becoming a law. In the remaining policy areas, the Bundesrat can cast only a suspensive veto. If the Bundestag approves of a measure, it may override a suspensive veto and forward the proposal to the chancellor. The final step in the process is the promulgation of the law by the federal president.

Throughout the legislative process, the executive branch is omnipresent. After transmitting the government's proposal to the Bundestag, the federal ministers work in support of the bill. Ministry representatives testify before Bundestag and Bundesrat committees to present their position. Cabinet ministers lobby committee members and influential members of parliament. Ministers may propose amendments or negotiate policy compromises to resolve issues that arise during parliamentary deliberations. Government representatives may also attend meetings of the joint mediation committee between the Bundestag and Bundesrat; no other nonparliamentary participants are allowed. The government frequently makes compromises and accepts amendments proposed in the legislature. The executive branch, however, retains a dominant influence on the policy process.

Policy Administration

In another attempt to diffuse political power, the Basic Law assigned the administrative responsibility for most domestic policies to the state governments. As one indicator of the states' central administrative role, the states employ more civil servants than the federal and local governments combined.

Because of the delegation of administrative responsibilities, federal legislation normally is fairly detailed to ensure that the actual application of a law matches the government's intent. Federal agencies may also supervise state agencies, and in cases of dispute they may apply sanctions or seek judicial review.

Despite this oversight by the federal government, the states retain discretion in applying most federal legislation. In part, they do so because the federal government lacks the resources to follow state actions closely. Federal control of the states also requires Bundesrat support, where claims for states' rights receive a sympathetic hearing. This decentralization of political authority provides additional flexibility for the political system.

Judicial Review

As in the United States, legislation in Germany is subject to judicial review. The Constitutional Court has the authority to evaluate the constitutionality of legislation and to void laws that violate the provisions of the Basic Law.[47]

Constitutional issues are brought before the court by one of three methods. The most common involves constitutional complaints filed by individual citizens. Citizens may appeal directly to the court when they feel that their constitutional rights were violated by a government action. More than 90 percent of the cases presented to the court arise from citizens' complaints. Moreover, cases can be filed without paying court costs and without a lawyer. The court is thus like an ombudsman, assuring the average citizen that his or her fundamental rights are protected by the Basic Law and the court.

The Constitutional Court also hears cases based on "concrete" and "abstract" principles of judicial review. Concrete review involves actual court cases that raise constitutional issues and are referred by a lower court judge to the Constitutional Court. In an abstract review the court rules on legislation as a legal principle, without reference to an actual case. The federal government, a state government, or one-third of the Bundestag deputies can request review of a law. This procedure is sometimes used by groups that fail to block a bill during the legislative process. In recent years various groups have challenged the constitutionality of the unification treaty with the GDR (upheld), abortion reform law (overturned), the involvement of German troops in UN peacekeeping roles (upheld), the new citizenship law (upheld), and several other important pieces of legislation. Over the last two decades, the court received an average of two or three such referrals a year.[48] Judicial review in the abstract expands the constitutional protection of the Basic Law. This directly involves the court in the policy process and may politicize the court as another agent of policymaking.

POLICY PERFORMANCE

By most standards, the two Germanies could both boast of their positive records of government performance. The Federal Republic's economic advances in the 1950s and early 1960s were truly phenomenal, and the progress in the East was nearly as remarkable. By the 1980s West Germany had one of the strongest economies in the world and its living standard was among the highest of any nation. Other government policies improved the educational system, increased workers' participation in industrial management, extended social services, and improved environmental quality.

Although economic and social development in the East lagged that of the West, the GDR had its own impressive record of policy accomplishments. East Germany developed a network of social programs, some of which were even more extensive than in the West. The GDR was the economic miracle of the Eastern bloc and the strongest economy in COMECON. Despite this progress, the political and social systems in the East crumbled when the opportunity for change became apparent. Now, a unified Germany faces the challenges of maintaining the advances in the West and improving conditions in the East.

At this point, the outcomes are still uncertain. The integration of two different welfare systems, two different legal systems, two different military systems, and two different social systems cannot simply be resolved by the decision to unify. Perhaps the best forecasts we can make for the future are based on the present policy programs and outputs of the Federal Republic, since these systems have been gradually extended to the East. Then after discussing the Federal Republic's policy record, we can consider the major policy challenges facing the nation.

The Federal Republic's Policy Record

For Americans who hear politicians rail against "big government" in the United States, the size of the German government gives greater meaning to this term. Over the past half century the scope of German government has increased both in total public spending and in new policy responsibilities. Today, government spending accounts for almost half of the total economy, the federal government manages many economic enterprises, and government regulations touch many areas of the economy and society. Germans are much more likely than Americans to consider that the state is responsible for addressing social needs and to support government policy activity. In summary, total public expenditures—federal, state, local, and the social security system—have increased from less than 15 billion Euro (€) in 1950 to 269 € billion in 1975, and over 987 € billion for a united Germany in 2002, which is nearly 50 percent of the gross domestic product.

It is difficult, however, to describe the activities of government in precise terms of revenue and budgets. A major complicating factor is Germany's extensive network of social services. Social security programs are the largest part of public expenditures; however, they are managed in insurance programs that are separate from the government's normal budget.

Another complicating factor is Germany's federal system. The Basic Law distributes policy responsibilities among the three levels of government. Local authorities provide utilities (electricity, gas, and water), operate the hospitals and public recreation facilities, and administer youth and social assistance programs. The states manage educational and cultural policies. They also hold primary responsibility for public security and the administration of justice. The federal government's responsibilities include foreign policy and defense, transportation, and communications. Consequently, public expenditures are distributed fairly evenly over the three levels of government. In 2003 the federal budget's share was 28.3

Figure 7.9   The Distribution of Total Public Expenditures, 1998[a]

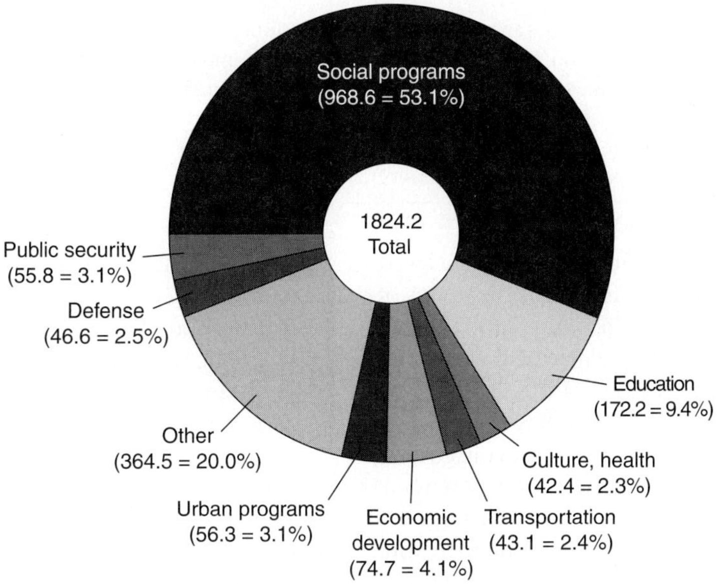

Social programs
(968.6 = 53.1%)

1824.2
Total

Public security
(55.8 = 3.1%)

Defense
(46.6 = 2.5%)

Education
(172.2 = 9.4%)

Other
(364.5 = 20.0%)

Culture, health
(42.4 = 2.3%)

Urban programs
(56.3 = 3.1%)

Economic
development
(74.7 = 4.1%)

Transportation
(43.1 = 2.4%)

[a]In DM billions.

Source: Statistisches Jahrbuch für die Bundesrepublik Deutschland 2001, p. 506.

percent, the state governments spent 25.9 percent, and the local governments spent 25.9 percent.

Figure 7.9 describes the activities of government, combining public spending by local, state, and federal governments, as well as the expenditures of the social insurance systems in 1998. Public spending on social programs alone amounted to DM 968.6 billion, more than was spent on all other government programs combined. Because of these extensive social programs, analysts often describe the Federal Republic as a welfare state, or more precisely a social services state. A compulsory social insurance system includes nationwide health care, accident insurance, unemployment compensation, and retirement benefits. Other programs provide financial assistance for the needy and individuals who cannot support themselves. Finally, additional programs spread the benefits of the Economic Miracle regardless of need. For instance, the government provides financial assistance to all families with children and has special tax-free savings plans and

other savings incentives for the average wage earner. The unemployment program is a typical example of the range of benefits available (see Box 7.4). For much of the history of West Germany, politicians competed to extend the coverage and benefits of such programs. Despite efforts by the CDU government in the 1980s to scale back the scope of government activity, the basic structure of the welfare state has endured.

Unification has put this system (and the federal budget) to a new test. Unemployment, welfare, and health benefits for the East provided basic social needs during the difficult economic times following unification. However, this came at a cost of several hundred billion Deutschmarks (now Euros). This places new strains on the political consensus in support of these social programs, as well as the government's ability to provide these benefits (see following discussion).

The federal government is, of course, involved in a range of other policy activities. Education, for

Box 7.4 German Unemployment Benefits

An unemployed worker receives insurance payments that provide up to 67 percent of normal pay (60 percent for unmarried workers or those without children) for up to a year. After a year, unemployment assistance continues at a reduced rate for a period depending on one's age. The government pays the social insurance contributions of individuals who are unemployed, and government labor offices help the unemployed worker find new employment or obtain retraining for a new job. If the worker locates a job in another city, the program partially reimburses travel and moving expenses.

example, is an important concern of all three levels of government, accounting for about one-tenth of all public spending (see again Figure 7.9). The federal government is also deeply involved in communications and transportation. Much of the electronic media, television, and radio, are owned or managed by the government. The federal government also owns and operates the railway system.

In recent years the government's policy agenda has expanded to include some new issues; environmental protection is the most visible example. Several indicators of air and water quality show real improvements in recent decades, and Germany has an ambitious recycling program. The SPD-Green government developed stronger policies for environmental protection, such as phasing out nuclear power and programs to limit global warming.

Defense and foreign relations are another important activity of government. More than for most other European nations, the FRG's economy and security system are based on international interdependence. The Federal Republic's economy depends heavily on exports and foreign trade; in the mid-1990s over one-fourth of the Western labor force produced goods for export, a percentage much higher than that for most other industrial economies.

The FRG's international economic orientation has made the nation's membership in the *European Union (EU)* a cornerstone of its economic policy. The FRG was an initial advocate of the EU and has benefitted considerably from its EU membership. Free access to a large European market was essential to the success of the Economic Miracle, and it is a continuing basis of the FRG's export-oriented economy. Germany's integration into the EU has gradually grown over recent decades, most recently illus-

trated by the currency shift from the Deutschmark (DM) to the EURO (€) in 2002. At the same time, participation in EU decision making gives the Federal Republic an opportunity to influence the course of European political development.

The Federal Republic is also integrated into the Western military alliance through its membership in the North Atlantic Treaty Organization. Among the Europeans, the Federal Republic makes the largest personnel and financial contribution to NATO forces, and the German public supports the NATO alliance. In the post–Cold War world, however, the threats to Germany's national security no longer come from the Warsaw Pact in the East. This has led to a reduction in overall defense spending to less than 3 percent of total public spending.

Public expenditures show the policy efforts of the government, but the actual results of this spending are more difficult to assess. Most indicators of policy performance suggest that the Federal Republic has been relatively successful in achieving its policy goals. Standards of living have improved dramatically, and health statistics show similar improvement. Although localized shortages of housing still appear in the West, overall housing conditions have steadily improved. Even in new policy areas such as energy and the environment, the government has made real progress. The opinions of the public reflect these policy advances (see Table 7.3). In 1998 most Westerners were satisfied with most aspects of life that might be linked to government performance: housing, living standards, work, income, social security, environmental quality, and public security.[49] Easterners are not as positive about their circumstances, but their evaluations have improved during the 1990s. By 1998, the gap between East and

TABLE 7.3   Satisfaction with Life Areas

Area	Westerners	Easterners
Housing	90%	82%
Work	88	86
Living standard	84	75
Leisure	83	73
Health	80	76
Household income	77	63
Social security	70	56
Environment	64	61
Physical security	58	41
Average	77	68

Source: 1998 Socioeconomic Panel; this survey is available from the Zentralarchiv für empirische Sozialforschung, University of Cologne. Table entries are the percent satisfied with each area.

West has narrowed, but there are still considerable differences separating the two regions.

Paying the Costs

The generous benefits of government programs are not, of course, due to government largesse. The taxes and financial contributions of individuals and corporations provide the funds for these programs. Therefore, large government outlays inevitably mean an equally large collection of revenues by the government. These revenues are the real source of government programs.

Three different types of revenue provide the bulk of the resources for public policy programs.[50] Contributions to the social security system represent the largest source of public revenues (see Figure 7.10). The health, unemployment, disability, retirement, and other social security funds are primarily self-financed by employer and employee contributions. For example, contributions to the pension plan amount to about 19.5 percent of a worker's gross monthly wages; health insurance is 14 percent of wages; unemployment is 6.5 percent; and long-term disability premiums are 1.7 percent. The various insurance contributions combined account for more than a third of the average worker's income, which is divided between contributions from the worker and from the employer.

The next most important source of public revenues is direct taxes—that is, taxes that are directly assessed by the government and paid to a government office. One of the largest portions of public revenues comes from a personal income tax that the federal, state, and local governments share. The rate of personal taxation rises with income level, from a base of 15 percent to a maximum of 42 percent. The 2000 tax reforms significantly reduced tax rates, but these rates are still significantly higher than in the United States. The German government taxes corporate profits at a lower rate than personal income to encourage businesses to reinvest their profits in further growth, and the corporate rates were also reduced in the 2000 reform.

The third major source of government revenues is indirect taxes. Like sales and excise taxes, indirect taxes are based on the use of income rather than wages and profits. The most common and lucrative indirect tax is the *value-added tax (VAT)*—a charge that is added at every stage in the manufacturing process and increases the value of a product. The standard VAT is 16 percent for most goods, with lower rates for basic commodities such as food or books. Other indirect taxes include customs duties, liquor, and tobacco taxes. In 1999 the government introduced a new energy tax on the use of electricity and other energy sources. This tax creates incentives for energy savings and provides an alternative source of government revenue. Altogether, indirect taxes account for about two-fifths of all public revenues. Indirect taxes—one of the secrets to the dramatic growth of government revenues—are normally "hidden" in the price of an item, rather than explicitly listed as a tax. In this way people are not reminded that they are paying taxes every time they purchase a product; it is also easier for policymakers to raise indirect taxes without evoking public awareness and opposition. Revenues from indirect taxes automatically rise with inflation, too. Indirect taxes are regressive, however; they weigh more heavily on low-income families because a larger share of their income goes for consumer goods.

The average German obviously has deep pockets to fund the extensive variety of public policy programs; U.S. taxation levels look quite modest by comparison. The marginal tax rate for the average

FIGURE 7.10   The Sources of Public Revenues, 1998 (in DM billions)

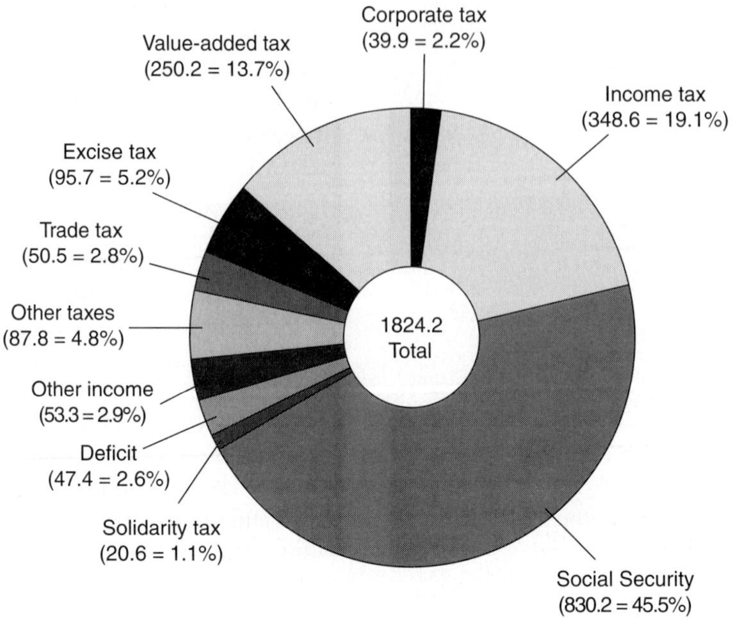

Corporate tax
(39.9 = 2.2%)

Value-added tax
(250.2 = 13.7%)

Income tax
(348.6 = 19.1%)

Excise tax
(95.7 = 5.2%)

Trade tax
(50.5 = 2.8%)

Other taxes
(87.8 = 4.8%)

1824.2
Total

Other income
(53.3 = 2.9%)

Deficit
(47.4 = 2.6%)

Solidarity tax
(20.6 = 1.1%)

Social Security
(830.2 = 45.5%)

Source: Statistisches Jahrbuch für die Bundesrepublik Deutschland 1999, pp. 486, 487, 508.

German worker, including taxes and social security contributions, is over 50 percent, compared with a marginal rate in America of about 40 percent.

Even with these various revenue sources, public expenditures repeatedly have exceeded public revenues in recent years. To finance this deficit, the government draws on another source of "revenue"—loans and public borrowing—to maintain the level of government services. The costs of unification inevitably increased the flow of red ink. A full accounting of public spending would show deficits averaging more than 50 billion Euros a year since union.

The German taxpayer seems to contribute an excessive amount to the public coffers, and Germans are no more eager than other nationalities to pay taxes. Thus, one of the major policy accomplishments of the Schröder government was new legislation in 2000 that broadly reduced income and corporate taxes. Still, the question is not how much citizens pay, but

how much value is returned for their payments. In addition to normal government activities, Germans are protected against sickness, unemployment, and disability; government pension plans furnish livable retirement incomes. Moreover, the majority of the public expects the government to take an active role in providing for the needs of society and its citizens.

ADDRESSING THE POLICY CHALLENGES

The last decade has been a time of tremendous policy change and innovation for the Federal Republic as it has adjusted to its new domestic and foreign policy circumstances. While a government faces policy needs in many areas, two themes dominate the current political debate. The first is to accommodate the remaining problems flowing from German unification. The second is to reform the German economic and social systems. This section outlines the challenges the government faces in both areas.

The Problems of Unification

As we noted at the outset of this chapter, one of the major policy challenges facing contemporary Germany flows from the unification of East and West. Given the GDR's apparent policy accomplishments, most observers were surprised by the sudden and dramatic collapse of the East German economic and social systems in the wake of the November 1989 revolution. During the first half of 1990, for instance, the gross national product of the GDR decreased by nearly 5 percent, unemployment skyrocketed, and industrial production fell off by nearly 60 percent.[51]

The most immediate economic challenge after unification was the need to rebuild the economy of the East, integrating Eastern workers and companies into the social market economy of the West. The GDR economy looked strong in the sheltered environment of the Socialist economic bloc, but it could not compete in a global marketplace. The GDR's impressive growth statistics and production figures often papered over a decaying economic infrastructure and outdated manufacturing facilities. Similarly, the GDR was heavily dependent on trade with other COMECON nations. When COMECON ended with the collapse of communism in Eastern Europe, a major portion of the GDR's economy was destroyed.

The Currency Union in July 1990 was an experience in "cold turkey capitalism"—overnight the Eastern economy had to accept the economic standards of the Federal Republic. Even with salaries one-third lower in the East, productivity was still out of balance. Matching the Western economy against that of the East was like racing a Porsche against the GDR's antiquated two-cylinder Trabant— a race in which the outcome is foreordained.

The FRG took several steps to rebuild the economy of the East and then raise it to Western standards. The government-directed Trust Agency (*Treuhandanstalt*) privatized the 8,000 plus firms that the GDR government had owned. All of these firms were sold off or closed by 1994, when the Treuhand itself was disbanded. However, privatization did not

generate the capital for investment; and disputes about property ownership further slowed the pace of development. The sale of the GDR's economic infrastructure generated a net loss for the nation.

The economic by-products of German unification affected other policy areas as well. The high levels of unemployment created great demands on the FRG's social welfare programs. Unemployed Eastern workers drew unemployment compensation, retraining benefits, and relocation allowances. The Federal Republic also assumed the pensions and health insurance benefits of Easterners. The government also spent massive amounts: from rebuilding the highway and railway systems of the East, to upgrading the telephone system to international standards, to moving the capital from Bonn to Berlin. In 1991, for example, the combined payments to the new Länder from official sources amounted to DM 113 billion (almost DM 7,000 per capita); this was more than twice Poland's per capita disposable income for the same year.[52] Government statistics for 1999 showed that the net payments to the East had increased to DM 140 billion. All Germans still pay an extra "solidarity surcharge" on their income tax that funds part of the investment in the East.

Economic progress is being made. Recent economic growth rates in the East often exceed those in the Western states by a comfortable margin. However, the East–West gap is still wide. Unemployment rates in the East are still more than double the rates in the West, and even after years of investment, productivity in the East still lags markedly behind the West. Although standards of living in the East have rapidly improved since the early 1990s, they remain significantly below Western standards. Furthermore, the gap will continue. Even if the economy in the Eastern states grows at double the rate of the West, it will take decades for full equality to be reached.

German unification also creates new challenges for noneconomic policy areas. For example, the GDR had model environmental laws, but these laws were not enforced. Consequently, many areas of the East resembled an environmentalist's nightmare: untreated toxic wastes from industry were dumped into rivers, emissions from power plants poisoned the air, and many cities lacked sewage treatment plants. The unification treaty called for raising the environmental quality of the East to Western standards—a difficult and expensive task. The price tag that is required to correct the GDR's environmental legacy competes against economic development projects for government funding. Thus, unification intensified the political debate on the trade-offs between economic development and environmental protection.

Agenda 2010

The *Wirtschaftswunder* (Economic Miracle) is a central part of the Federal Republic's modern history—but these miraculous times are now in the distant past. Contemporary Germany faces a series of new problems as its economy and social programs must compete in the modern world.

For instance, business interests repeatedly criticize the uncompetitiveness of the German economy in a globalized economic system. Labor costs are higher than in many other European nations, and dramatically higher than labor costs in Eastern Europe and other regions. The generous benefits that create liberal social services programs come at a cost in terms of employee contributions and regulations on employment. Other regulations impede the creation of new jobs or temporary employment. Thus German firms have been slow to produce new job positions, productivity is stagnating, and Germany is losing its competitive position in the global economy.

A related issue is the economic viability of Germany's social service programs. The changing demographic mix of the population—a rapidly aging population—means that the demand for health care and pension benefits will steadily increase over time, but there are fewer employed workers to contribute to these social insurance systems. For instance, in the 1950s there were roughly 4 employees for every person receiving a pension; by 2010 there will be less than 2 employees for every pensioner. Similar demographic and economic issues face Germany's other social programs. Public debates about these problems have grown in the past several years—as economic growth has slowed and unemployment rates remain unacceptably high. Germany once had one of the highest living standards in Europe; now it falls below the average of other West European nations.

The Schröder government commissioned a series of studies and blue-ribbon commissions to formulate policy reforms, but it has been unable to develop a consensus on what actions are needed. Business interests want to reduce government taxes and regulations on businesses, while labor unions oppose a reduction in these hard-won benefits of the past. There is also disagreement between the SPD and Greens within the government. There is little willingness to compromise between contending forces, so the problems persist.

In 2004 the Schröder government enacted a new reform program known as "Agenda 2010." The reforms are a three-pronged effort to revitalize the economy. One set of measures reforms the labor market by easing employment rules, reducing the nonwage labor costs, and reforming the unemployment system. A second set of measures reforms the pension and health care systems by reducing benefits. The third reforms were to continue the restructuring of the tax system begun during Schröder's first term.

While these reforms have moved in the right direction, many critics claim they are too little, too late. The Schröder reforms are far short of what the CDU/CSU and FDP advocated in the 2002 election. Because Germany remains an affluent nation, few are willing to make hard choices that might lead to more fundamental reforms, which many economists claim are needed. The struggle to modernize the German economy is likely to continue for the years ahead.

A New World Role

Paralleling its domestic policy challenges, the new Germany is redefining its international identity and its foreign policy goals. The Federal Republic has linked its role in international politics to its participation in the NATO alliance and the European Union. Both relationships are changing as a result of German unity.

In mid-1990 Gorbachev agreed to continued German membership in NATO in return for concessions on the reduction of combined German troop levels; the definition of the GDR territory as a nuclear-free zone; and Germany's continued abstention from the development or use of atomic, biological, and chemical weapons. With unification, Germany became a fully sovereign nation and now seeks its own role in international affairs.

The new Germany will likely play a different military and strategic role as a result of these agreements and the changing international context. NATO existed as a bulwark of the Western defense against the Soviet threat; the decline of this threat will lessen the military role of the alliance. Moreover, Germany wants to be an active advocate for peace within Europe, developing its role as a bridge between East and West. The Federal Republic was thus one of the strongest proponents of the recent expansion of EU membership to several East European nations.

The new Germany is also assuming a larger responsibility in international disputes outside the NATO region. In 1993 the Constitutional Court interpreted the Basic Law to allow German troops to serve outside of Europe as part of international peacekeeping activities—as they did in Somalia, the Balkans, and Afghanistan.

At the same time, Schröder's vocal opposition to U.S. policy toward Iraq demonstrated a new independence in Germany's foreign policy, and has been a source of tension in U.S.-German relations. Germany is now increasingly likely to exercise an independent foreign policy, within a framework of partnership with its allies.

Unification is also reshaping the Federal Republic's relationship to the European Union.[53] The new Germany outweighs the other EU members in both its population and gross national product; thus, the parity that underlies the consensual nature of the Union will change. Moreover, Germany will have to walk a narrow line between being too active and too inactive in EU affairs. Some economic partners worry that Germany will attempt to dominate the European Union, pursuing its own national interests more aggressively. Other nations worry that Germany will turn its attentions eastward, diminishing its commitment and involvement in the EU's ambitious plans for the future.

Germany has attempted to address these fears: working to expand the powers of the EU, developing a common European currency (the Euro) and other integrationist policies, and expanding the Union's membership to other European states. Worries about German goals and commitments remain, however. At the least, it is clear that a united Germany will approach the process of European integration based on a different calculus than that which guided its actions for the previous 40 years.

AFTER THE REVOLUTION

Revolutions are unsettling, both to the participants and the spectators. Such is the case with the German revolution of 1989. Easterners realized their hopes for freedom, but they also have seen their everyday lives change before their eyes, sometimes in distressing ways. Westerners saw their hopes for German union and a new peace in Europe answered, but at a substantial political and economic cost to the nation. The Federal Republic is now forging a new social and political identity that will shape its domestic and international policies. Many Germans on both sides of the former border are hopeful, but still uncertain, of what the future holds for their nation. The Federal Republic's neighbors wonder what role the new Germany will play in European and international affairs. Addressing these questions will test the strength of the Federal Republic and its new residents in the East.

Unification has clearly presented new social, political, and economic challenges for the nation. One cannot merge two such different systems without experiencing problems. However, these strains were magnified by the inability or unwillingness of elites to state the problems honestly and to deal with them in a forthright manner. Even as voters were turning Kohl out of office in 1998, they differed on the new direction they wanted the government to follow. The nation must reforge the social and political consensus that was a foundation for the Federal Republic's past accomplishments.

Once this has been accomplished, Germans finally may be able to answer the question of their national identity. Unification has created a new German state linked to Western political values and social norms. Equally important, unity was achieved through a peaceful revolution (and the power of the DM), not blood and iron. The trials of the unification process are testing the public's commitment to these values. The government's ability to show citizens in the East that democracy and the social market economy can improve the quality of their lives may be necessary to solidify their democratic aspirations. If the revolution succeeds, this aspect of the German question may finally be answered.

Key Terms

Konrad Adenauer
Basic Law (*Grundgesetz*)
Bundesrat
Bundestag
Christian Democratic
   Union (CDU)
Christian Social Union
   (CSU)
citizen action groups
   (*Bürgerinitiativen*)
codetermination
   (*Mitbestimmung*)
Confederation of
   German Employers'
   Associations (BDA)
Constitutional Court

constructive no-
   confidence vote
Economic Miracle
   (*Wirtschaftswunder*)
European Union (EU)
federal chancellor
   (*Bundeskanzler*)
federal president
   (*Bundespräsident*)
Federal Republic of
   Germany (FRG)
Federation of German
   Industry (BDI)
Free Democratic Party
   (FDP)

German Democratic
   Republic (GDR)
German Federation of
   Trade Unions
   (DGB)
the Greens
guest workers
   (*Gastarbeiter*)
Adolf Hitler
Kaiser
Helmut Kohl
National Socialist
   German Workers'
   Party (the Nazis)
neocorporatism
New Politics

Ostpolitik
Party of Democratic
   Socialism (PDS)
peak association
proportional
   representation (PR)
Republikaner (REP)
Gerhard Schröder
Social Democratic Party
   (SPD)
Socialist Unity Party
   (SED)
Third Reich
value-added tax (VAT)
Weimar Republic

Internet Sources

Bundestag: http://www.bundestag.de
Federal Government: http://www.bundesregierung.de
German Information Center: http://www.germany-info.org

German politics and society websites, compiled at the University of California, Irvine: www.democ.uci.edu/germany.html

Suggested Readings

Anderson, Christopher, and Karsten Zelle, eds. *Stability and Change in German Elections: How Electorates Merge, Converge, or Collide.* Westport, CT: Praeger, 1998.

Ash, Timothy Garton. *In Europe's Name: Germany in a Divided Continent.* New York: Random House, 1993.

Bark, Dennis, and David Gress. *A History of West Germany,* 2 vols., 2nd ed. London: Blackwell, 1993.

Childers, Thomas, and Jane Caplan, eds. *Reevaluating the Third Reich.* New York: Holmes & Meier, 1993.

Dalton, Russell. *Politics in Germany,* 2nd ed. New York: HarperCollins, 1993.

Fulbrook, Mary. *Anatomy of a Dictatorship: Inside the GDR, 1949–1989.* New York: Oxford University Press, 1995.

———. *History of Germany, 1918–2000.* Oxford: Blackwell, 2002.

Hampton, Mary, and Christian Soe, eds. *Between Bonn and Berlin: German Politics Adrift?* Lanham, MD: Rowman & Littlefield, 1999.

Hancock, M. Donald, and Helga Welch, eds. *German Unification: Process and Outcome.* Boulder, CO: Westview, 1994.

Hanreider, Wolfram. *Germany, America, Europe: Forty Years of German Foreign Policy.* New Haven, CT: Yale University Press, 1989.

Huelshoff, Michael, Andrei Markovits, and Simon Reich, eds. *From Bundesrepublik to Deutschland: German Politics After Unification.* Ann Arbor, MI: University of Michigan Press, 1993.

Jarausch, Konrad. *The Rush to German Unity.* New York: Oxford University Press, 1994.

Katzenstein, Peter. *Policy and Politics in West Germany: The Growth of a Semisovereign State.* Philadelphia: Temple University Press, 1987.

Kolinsky, Eva. *Women in Contemporary Germany.* New York and Oxford, England: Berg, 1993.

Kopstein, Jeffrey. *The Politics of Economic Decline in East Germany, 1945–1989.* Chapel Hill: University of North Carolina Press, 1997.

Krisch, Henry. *The German Democratic Republic: The Search for Identity.* Boulder, CO: Westview, 1985.

Maier, Charles. *Dissolution: The Crisis of Communism and the End of East Germany.* Princeton, NJ: Princeton University Press, 1997.

Markovits, Andrei, and Philip Gorski. *The German Left: Red, Green and Beyond.* New York: Oxford University Press, 1993.

McAdams, James. *Germany Divided: From the Wall to Unification.* Princeton, NJ: Princeton University Press, 1993.

———. *Judging the Past in Unified Germany.* New York: Cambridge University Press, 2001.

Merkl, Peter. *German Unification in the European Context.* University Park: Pennsylvania State University Press, 1993.

———, ed. *The Federal Republic at Fifty: The End of a Century of Turmoil.* New York: New York University Press, 1999.

Orlow, Dietrich. *A History of Modern Germany,* 3rd ed. Englewood Cliffs, NJ: Prentice Hall, 1995.

Padgett, Stephen. *Organizing Democracy in Eastern Germany.* Cambridge: Cambridge University Press, 2000.

Rohrschneider, Robert. *Learning Democracy: Democratic and Economic Values in Unified Germany.* New York: Oxford University Press, 1999.

Sheehan, James. *German History 1770–1866.* New York: Oxford University Press, 1989.

Sinn, Gerlinde, and Hans-Werner Sinn. *Jumpstart: The Economic Unification of Germany.* Cambridge, MA: MIT Press, 1992.

Smith, Gordon, et al. *Developments in German Politics 3.* London: Palgrave, 2003.

Spielvogel, Jackson. *Hitler and Nazi Germany: A History.* Englewood Cliffs, NJ: Prentice Hall, 1988.

Turner, Henry. *Germany from Partition to Unification.* New Haven: Yale University Press, 1992.

 Endnotes

1. The First German Empire was formed in the ninth century through the partitioning of Charlemagne's empire; see Kurt Reinhardt, *Germany: 2000 Years,* Vol. 1 (New York: Ungar, 1986).

2. Karl Dietrich Bracher, *The German Dictatorship* (New York: Praeger, 1970); Martin Broszat, *Hitler and the Collapse of Weimar Germany* (New York: St. Martin's Press, 1987).

3. Raul Hilberg, *The Destruction of the European Jews,* rev. ed. (New York: Holmes and Meier, 1985); Sarah Gordon, *Hitler, Germans and the "Jewish Question"* (Princeton, NJ: Princeton University Press, 1984).

4. Karl Hardach, *The Political Economy of Germany in the Twentieth Century* (Berkeley: University of California Press, 1980); Eric Owen Smith, *The German Economy* (London: Routledge, 1994).

5. Gregory Sandford, *From Hitler to Ulbricht: The Communist Reconstruction of East Germany, 1945–1946* (Princeton, NJ: Princeton University Press, 1983).

6. James McAdams, *East Germany and the West: Surviving Detente* (New York: Cambridge University Press, 1985); Stephen Larrabee, ed., *The Two German States and European Security* (New York: Macmillan, 1989).

7. Forschungsgruppe Wahlen, *Politbarometer* (monthly publications of the Forschungsgruppe Wahlen, Mannheim, 2000).

8. Eva Kolinsky, *Women in Contemporary Germany* (Oxford, England, and New York: Berg, 1993); Pippa Norris and Ronald Inglehart, *A Rising Tide* (New York: Cambridge University Press, 2003); Russell Dalton, *Citizen Politics* (Washington, DC: CQ Press, 2005): Ch. 6.

9. Christian Joppke, *Immigration and the Nation-State: The United States, Germany, and Great Britain* (New York: Oxford University Press, 1999); James Hollifield, *Immigrants, Markets and States* (Cambridge, MA: Harvard University Press, 1993).

10. The Allied occupation authorities oversaw the drafting of the Basic Law and held veto power over the final document; see Peter Merkl, *The Origins of the West German Republic* (New York: Oxford University Press, 1965).

11. The membership of the Bundestag was reduced in 2002 from its previous size of 656. This reduction was a result of a redistricting to equalize the number of voters in each district.

12. The URL for the Bundestag is: http://www.bundestag.de

13. Ludger Helms, "Keeping Weimar at Bay: The German Federal Presidency since 1949," *German Politics and Society* 16 (Summer 1998): 50–68.

14. Donald Kommers, *Constitutional Jurisprudence of the Federal Republic* (Durham, NC: Duke University Press, 1989); Donald Kommers, "The Federal Constitutional Court in the German Political System," *Comparative Political Studies* 26 (1994): 470–91.

15. A second type of no-confidence vote allows the chancellor to attach a no-confidence provision to a government legislative proposal. If the Bundestag defeats the proposal, the chancellor may ask the federal president to call for new Bundestag elections; see Russell J. Dalton, *Politics in Germany,* 2nd ed. (New York: HarperCollins, 1993), p. 62.

16. Anna Merritt and Richard Merritt, *Public Opinion in Occupied Germany* (Urbana: University of Illinois Press, 1970);

Ralf Dahrendorf, *Society and Democracy in Germany* (New York: Doubleday, 1967).

17. Christiane Lemke, "Political Socialization and the 'Micromilieu,'" in Marilyn Rueschemeyer and Christiane Lemke, eds., *The Quality of Life in the German Democratic Republic* (New York: M. E. Scharpe).

18. Gabriel Almond and Sidney Verba, *The Civic Culture* (Princeton, NJ: Princeton University Press, 1963); David Conradt, "Changing German Political Culture," in Gabriel Almond and Sidney Verba, eds., *The Civic Culture Revisited* (Boston: Little Brown, 1980).

19. Conradt, "Changing German Political Culture," pp. 229–31; Kendall Baker, Russell J. Dalton, and Kai Hildebrandt, *Germany Transformed: Political Culture and the New Politics* (Cambridge, MA: Harvard University Press, 1981).

20. Deutsches Jugendinstitut, *Deutsche Schüler im Sommer 1990* (Munich, Germany: Deutsches Jugendinstitut, 1990).

21. Henry Krisch, *The German Democratic Republic: The Search for Identity* (Boulder, CO: Westview, 1985); Gebhard Schweigler, "German Questions of the Shrinking of Germany," in Larabee, *The Two German States.*

22. Gerald Braunthal, *Political Loyalty and Public Service in West Germany* (Amherst: University of Massachusetts Press, 1990).

23. Walter Friedrich and Hartmut Griese, *Jugend und Jugendforschung in der DDR* (Opladen, Germany: Westdeutscher Verlag, 1990).

24. Russell Dalton, "Communists and Democrats: Democratic Attitudes in the Two Germanies," *British Journal of Political Science* 24 (1994): 469–93; Frederick Weil, "The Development of Democratic Attitudes in Eastern and Western Germany in a Comparative Perspective," in Frederick Weil, ed. *Democratization in Eastern and Western Europe* (Greenwich, CT: JAI Press, 1993).

25. Hans-Dieter Klingemann and Richard Hofferbert, "Germany: A New 'Wall in the Mind?'" *Journal of Democracy* 5 (1994): 30–44; Robert Rohrschneider, *Learning Democracy: Democratic and Economic Values in Unified Germany* (New York: Oxford University Press, 1999).

26. Ronald Inglehart, *Modernization and Postmodernization* (Princeton, NJ: Princeton University Press, 1997); Ronald Inglehart, *Culture Shift in Advanced Industrial Society* (Princeton, NJ: Princeton University Press, 1990).

27. See Chapter 3; Dalton, *Citizen Politics,* Ch. 6.

28. Dalton, *Politics in Germany,* Ch. 5; Christiane Lemke, "Political Socialization and the 'Micromilieu,'" in Rueschemeyer and Lemke, eds., *The Quality of Life in the German Democratic Republic.*

29. Meredith Watts, et al., *Contemporary German Youth and Their Elders* (New York: Greenwood, 1989); Elizabeth Noelle-Neumann and Renate Köcher, *Die verletze Nation* (Stuttgart, Germany: Deutsche Verlag, 1987); Deutsches Jugendinstitut, *Deutsche Schüler im Sommer 1990.*

30. Max Planck Institute, *Between Elite and Mass Education* (Albany: State University of New York Press, 1982).

31. Rosalind Pritchard, *Reconstructing Education: East German Schools and Universities After Unification* (New York: Berghahn Books, 1999).

32. Peter Humphreys, *Media and Media Policy in Germany: The Press and Broadcasting Since 1945,* rev. ed. (New York and Oxford, England: Berg, 1994).

33. *Eurobarometer 55* (Brussels: Commission of the European Communities, 2001).

34. Dalton, *Politics in Germany,* Ch. 6; Max Kaase, "Partizipative Revolution: Ende der Parteien?" in Joachim Raschke, ed., *Bürger und Parteien* (Opladen, Germany: Westdeutscher Verlag, 1984).

35. Wilhelm Bürklin, Hilke Rebenstorf, et al., *Eliten in Deutschland: Rekutierung und Integration* (Opladen, Germany: Leske and Budrich, 1997); Dietrich Herzog, Hilke Rebensstorf, and Bernhard Wessels, eds., *Parlament und Gesellschaft: Eine Funktionsanalyse der repräsentativen Demokratie* (Opladen, Germany: Westdeutscher Verlag, 1993).

36. Wilhelm Bürklin, "Einstellungen und Wertorientierungen ost-und westdeutscher Eliten 1995," in Oskar Gabriel, ed., *Einstellungen und politisches Verhalten in Transformationsprozess* (Opladen, Germany: Leske und Budrich, 1996); Rohrschneider, *Learning Democracy.*

37. See Chapter 3; also; Volker Berghahn and Detlev Karsten, *Industrial Relations in West Germany* (New York and Oxford, England: Berg, 1989); Claus Offe, "The Attribution of Political Status to Interest Groups," in Suzanne Berger, ed., *Organizing Interests in Western Europe* (New York: Cambridge University Press, 1981), pp. 123–58.

38. Kathleen Thelen, *Union in Parts: Labor Politics in Postwar Germany* (Ithaca, NY: Cornell University Press, 1991).

39. Ruud Koopmans, *Democracy from Below: New Social Movements and the Political System in West Germany* (Boulder, CO: Westview Press, 1995).

40. Hans-Joachim Veen, Norbert Lepszy, and Peter Mnich, *Die Republikaner Party in Germany: Right-Wing Menace or Protest Catchall?* (Westport, CT: Praeger, 1993); Hans-Georg Betz, *Rightwing Populism in Western Europe* (New York: St. Martin's Press, 1994).

41. Gerard Braunthal, *The German Social Democrats Since 1969,* 2nd ed. (Boulder, CO: Westview Press, 1994).

42. Thomas Poguntke, *Alternative Politics: The German Green Party* (Edinburgh, Scotland: University of Edinburgh Press, 1993); E. Gene Frankland and Donald Schoonmaker, *Between Protest and Power: The Green Party in Germany* (Boulder, CO: Westview, 1992).

43. If a party wins more district seats in a state than it should have based on its proportion of the second vote, the party is allowed to keep the additional seats and the size of the Bundestag is increased. In 2002 the actual Bundestag membership was 603.

44. The electoral system also provides that a party that wins at least three district seats shares in the PR distribution of seats. In 1994 and 1998 the PDS won four district seats in East Berlin, which earned them additional seats through the PR distribution. In 2002 the PDS won only two direct seats.

45. For evidence of voting patterns in prior elections, see Christopher Anderson and Karsten Zelle, eds., *Stability and Change in German Elections: How Electorates Merge, Converge, or Collide* (Westport, CT: Praeger, 1998); Russell Dalton, "Voter Choice and Electoral Politics" in Gordon Smith, et al., *Developments in German Politics III* (London: Palgrave, 2003).

46. Vivien Schmitt, *The Futures of European Capitalism* (Oxford: Oxford University Press, 2002); Alec Stone Sweet, Wayne Sandholtz and Neil Fligstein, eds., *The Institutionalization of Europe* (Oxford: Oxford University Press, 2001).

47. The European Court of Justice also has the power to evaluate German legislation against the standards of the European Union agreements.

48. Alec Stone, "Governing with Judges: The New Constitutionalism," in Jack Hayward and Edward Page, eds., *Governing the New Europe* (Oxford, England: Polity Press, 1995).

49. Statistiches Bundesamt, *Datenreport 1999: Zahlen und Fakten über die Bundesrepublik Deutschland* (Bonn, Germany: Bundeszentrale für politische Bildung, 2000), pp. 432–33.

50. Arnold Heidenheimer, Hugh Heclo, and Carolyn Adams, *Comparative Public Policy*, 3rd ed. (New York: St. Martin's Press, 1990), Ch. 6.

51. Gerlinde Sinn and Hans-Werner Sinn, *Jumpstart: The Economic Unification of Germany* (Cambridge, MA: MIT Press, 1992).

52. Sinn and Sinn, *Jumpstart*, pp. 24–25.

53. Maria Cowles, Thomas Risse, and James Caporaso, eds., *Transforming Europe* (Ithaca: Cornell University Press, 2001); Desmond Dinan, *Ever Closer Union? An Introduction to the European Community*, 2nd ed. (Boulder, CO: Lynne Rienner, 1999).

Spain

	0	50	100 mi
	0	80	160 km

Bay of Biscay

BASQUE COUNTRY

FRANCE

ANDORRA

ASTURIAS

CANTABRIA

Bilbao

GALICIA

NAVARRA

CASTILE y LEÓN

LA RIOJA

CATALONIA

CASTILE-LEÓN

Ebro

Duero

Saragossa

Barcelona

ATLANTIC OCEAN

ARAGÓN

MADRID

Madrid

Minorca

Balearic Sea

PORTUGAL

Tagus

VALENCIA

Majorca

BALEARIC ISLANDS

ESTREMADURA

CASTILE-LA MANCHA

Valencia

Guadiana

Ibiza

Lisbon

Formentera

MEDITERRANEAN SEA

Córdoba

Guadalquivir

Murcia

Sevilla

MURCIA

ANDALUSIA

Málaga

Strait of Gibraltar

ALGERIA

CANARY ISLANDS

La Palma

Lanzarote

Fuerteventura

Gomera

Tenerife

Hierra

Gran Canaria

MOROCCO

N

Chapter 8

Politics in Spain

DONALD SHARE

Country Bio—Spain

POPULATION: 42.7 Million
TERRITORY: 194,896 sq.mi
YEAR OF INDEPENDENCE: 1492
YEAR OF CURRENT CONSTITUTION: 1978
CHIEF OF STATE: King Juan Carlos
HEAD OF GOVERNMENT: José Luís Rodríguez Zapatero
LANGUAGE(S): Castilian Spanish 74%, Catalan 17%, Galician 7%, Basque 2%
RELIGION: Roman Catholic 99%, other 1%

Spain has largely overcome the legacy of 40 years of authoritarian rule. Spain was one of the first nations in the Third Wave of democratization beginning in the 1970s, and its political future was initially uncertain. Spanish democracy is flourishing today, and is arguably as healthy as any European political system. This chapter analyzes Spain's development over this period, and the challenges that remain.

CURRENT POLICY CHALLENGES

Early in the twenty-first century Spanish democracy faces two serious policy challenges—terrorism and chronic unemployment—that are at least partly related to that authoritarian legacy, and a third challenge that can be associated with democratization.

Twenty-five years after its transition to democracy, Spain continues to suffer from violence perpetrated by ETA, the pro-independence Basque terrorist organization that has killed over 800 Spaniards since 1975. Spanish governments have so far been unable to either crush ETA or persuade it to lay down its arms. When conservative Prime Minister José María Aznar announced the start of government-ETA negotiations in late 1998, there were high hopes that peace could be achieved. For about a year, Spain was free of terrorist violence. But negotiations broke down in late 1999 as ETA negotiators refused to abandon their demand that the Basque Country be given the right to self-determination. A wave of terrorist killings ended the cease-fire and destroyed any hope for immediate peace. During the 2000 general election campaign Spanish courts appeared to threaten the right to free speech when they banned campaign material that was seen as supportive of ETA. More recently, the courts have upheld a ban on political parties that are believed to support ETA.

Basque terrorism has its roots in the particular brutality with which Francisco Franco treated the Basque Country during his dictatorship (1939–1975). It has been sustained by a deeply polarized political environment within the Basque Country, and the electoral success of Basque parties who support the goals (an independent Basque Country), if not the tactics, of ETA. Continued terrorist acts could undermine the legitimacy of Spanish democracy.

An equally vexing problem facing Spanish policymakers is an unemployment level that stubbornly remains well above the European average. In large part the high levels of unemployment are the result of Spain's transition from a highly protected economy under Franco to an increasingly global one. Franco had achieved labor quiescence and near-full employment through a combination of repression, laws that prevented layoffs of workers, protectionism, and massive emigration. With Spain's democratization and integration into the European Union, governments of the right and left have cautiously (some argue too cautiously) liberalized the economy, reducing the state role, making labor laws more "flexible," and ending subsidies to Spain's many inefficient industries. Despite these efforts, by 2000 Spanish labor laws were still among the most restrictive in Europe, and vestiges of Franco's statist economy were still evident. The results were predictable: Unemployment rose from 4.5 percent on the eve of the transition, to 20.8 percent 10 years later and has remained in double-digits since then. Only in the late 1990s did Spain start to create new jobs at a pace sufficient to reduce unemployment. Current levels of unemployment (about 11 percent in 2004) are among the highest in Europe, and they pose a formidable challenge to Spanish policymakers. In monthly polling conducted by the Centro de Investigaciones Sociológicas, unemployment is regularly named as Spain's most pressing problem.[1]

A third challenge that has emerged since democratization is the dramatic growth of immigration into Spain. Franco's isolated dictatorship severely limited immigration, and as late as 1990 immigrants comprised under 1 percent of the population. Since Spain's entry into the European Union in 1986 there has been a rapid increase in immigration, mostly from Africa, Latin America, and Eastern Europe. Immigrants now make up 6.2 percent of the population. Spain's Muslim population has grown rapidly as large numbers of illegal immigrants have crossed the 13-mile Straits of Gibraltar in search of employment. Moroccans now make up about a quarter of all Spanish immigrants. They played a crucial role in Spain's recent economic boom but also pose new challenges to a traditionally homogenous Spanish society.

The terrorist railway bombings of March 2004, in which 191 Spaniards perished and over 1,400 were injured, have drawn greater attention to the challenge of immigration. A network of mostly Moroccan Islamic terrorists carried out the bombing, and many of the terrorists were residents in Spain. To date Spain has not seen the emergence of the type of anti-immigrant political parties that have arisen in other European societies. Although some acts of violence have been aimed at immigrants, Spaniards have generally reacted with tolerance. However, polling data reveal a growing hostility toward immigrants that could be a source of future concern. Both major parties in the 2004 electoral campaign called for reform of Spain's immigration laws.[2]

THE HISTORICAL LEGACY

All U.S. schoolchildren learn the significance of 1492 in American history. That date is even more significant for Spain. In the events of that year we can observe the major themes that dominated Spanish history from the fifteenth century to the present.

First and foremost, the date represented the victory of the *Reconquista*, the Catholic reconquest of the Iberian Peninsula from the Moors. The Moors were nomadic African Muslims who crossed the Straits of Gibraltar in A.D. 711 and occupied most of the peninsula for more than seven centuries. Their presence added immeasurably to Spanish culture and society. The Moorish influence on architecture, music, cuisine, and language is still evident 500 years after their forced expulsion (along with Spain's Jews) in 1492. Spain's long isolation from the rest of Christian Europe led many Spaniards (including Francisco Franco, Spain's dictator from 1939–1975) to argue that Spain was (and should remain) fundamentally distinct from its European neighbors. This legacy also frames the current debate over how Spain should view its growing Moslem minority.

Second, the expulsion of the Moors was made possible by the political unification and centralization of a previously fragmented Iberian Peninsula. Ferdinand and Isabel, the monarchs of Spain's most important independent kingdoms, were married in 1492, uniting much of the peninsula in a single, centralized state. This unification is often credited with facilitating the building of Spain's vast global empire from the fifteenth to nineteenth centuries. However, a centralized Spain was never completely accepted by some Spaniards. Many formerly independent peoples, including the Basques and the Catalans, stubbornly resisted centralization and maintained separate languages, cultural identities, and even some political institutions, as noted in Chapter 1. The struggle between center and periphery in Spanish politics continues to this day.

Third, the fierce military struggle by Catholics to unify Spain and expel the Moors set a precedent for repressive authoritarian rule. The victorious Catholic monarchs immediately expelled all religious minorities from Spain and established the notorious *Spanish Inquisition*, a tribunal established in 1478 to enforce strict moral, religious, and political uniformity throughout Spain's empire. The dominant role given military leaders in the Reconquista and in the creation of Spain's vast American empire set the stage for numerous *pronunciamientos* (military uprisings) during the nineteenth and twentieth centuries.

Finally, 1492 marked the start of Spain's imperial experience with the arrival of Columbus in the New World. The immensity and wealth of Spain's empire gave rise to a national pride (some would say arrogance) that rivaled British nationalism. When the rigidly centralized and overly bureaucratized empire began a slow and painful decline in the eighteenth century, many Spaniards were unable to accept that reality. The loss of Spain's last colonies, Cuba and the Philippines, in 1898, marked the end of the Spanish Empire. By then Spain had become an impoverished and peripheral European nation, but many Spaniards continued to wallow in Spain's past glory rather than accept the need for political and economic change. Some Spaniards blamed the forces of modernity for having accelerated the loss of empire and the subsequent economic decline. Others argued that the backwardness of Spain's economy and the rigidity of its political structures were responsible for Spain's demise. They called for economic reform and the democratization of Spanish political structures. This dispute between what have been dubbed the *two Spains* partly explains the political chaos of the nineteenth century, during which progressives (who tended to favor republican forms of government) and conservatives (who tended to favor authoritarian monarchies) repeatedly dislodged each other from power. The Constitution of 1812, for example, was one of Europe's earliest constitutions, and it embodied very progressive and democratic ideas for its time. It was short lived, however, and was abolished by Ferdinand VII in 1814. Between 1812 and 1931 Spain had seven different constitutions, four of which were progressive and three conservative.

During the *Spanish Second Republic (1931–1936)*, the forces of the two Spains met head on. Antimonarchical progressives founded the Republic, and its constitution contained protections for democracy, regional decentralization, and secularism. Conservative forces immediately felt threatened by the rapid political changes, especially measures that weakened the Catholic Church and the central state. Progressives controlled government from 1931 to 1933, while conservatives governed from 1934 to 1935. When a progressive coalition won the 1936 elections, forces of the right, led by a sector of the Spanish military, launched a rebellion against the Republic.

The *Spanish Civil War (1936–1939)* was the defining event of twentieth-century Spanish history,

Box 8.1 Spain's Unusual Transition to Democracy

Spain's transition to democracy was unique. It occurred fairly rapidly and without major bloodshed. Moreover, leaders of the Francoist regime carried out a controlled and methodical transition, negotiating with the democratic opposition over the new rules of the game. As a result of this transition there were never any attempts to punish Francoist leaders for human rights abuses during authoritarian rule. Political scientists were quick to coin terms for this unique transition such as *transition through transaction, transition from* *above, negotiated transition,* and *pacted transition.* Spain's model of transition presents a nice contrast to neighboring Portugal, where in 1974 democracy was brought about by a coup of junior military officers. A social revolution and considerable violence followed. Spain also differs from Eastern Europe, where authoritarian regimes quickly disintegrated. The Spanish model of transition remains unique in Europe, but it was followed rather closely in countries on other continents such as Chile and South Africa.

and the brutality of that conflict traumatized an entire generation of Spaniards. When the rebels under the leadership of *Francisco Franco* declared victory they set out to destroy the progressive movement in Spain once and for all. Franco was particularly vindictive when it came to identifying and punishing the losers of the war. He imposed laws that made it a crime to have supported the Republic, and his regime executed thousands of the Republic's supporters and exiled hundreds of thousands more. The government banned political parties and independent trade unions and imposed strict censorship on the press. The regime centralized all political power in Madrid; fused executive, legislative, and judicial power; and made Franco dictator for life. The Catholic Church's official status and privileges were restored, and manifestations of regional culture, including the speaking of regional languages, were banned. The severe repression during the first three decades of Francoist rule quashed the democratic opposition. Franco eased the repression in the 1960s, and protest activity increased, but rapid economic growth during that period helped preserve the regime's strength.

Many feared that the death of Franco in 1975 would rekindle a conflict between the two Spains. Instead, Spain's transition to democracy between 1975 and 1978, after four decades of authoritarianism, evolved as what has been hailed as a model of peaceful regime change. The transition to democracy was not only peaceful, but it appears to have resolved two of the historical cleavages, regime type and church and state, that formed the basis of

the struggle between the two Spains. The center-periphery cleavage persists but no longer directly threatens democratic rule (see Box 8.1).

DEMOCRACY AND SPAIN'S HISTORICAL CLEAVAGES

Monarchy Versus Republic, or Both?

The transition to democracy was accomplished peacefully because of several factors. First, members of the Franco regime, not the democratic opposition, initiated it. Opposition to Franco was strong and growing, but it alone could not force the regime to democratize. The transition to democracy was stewarded by *King Juan Carlos*, Franco's handpicked successor as head of state, and *Adolfo Suárez*, a former Francoist bureaucrat and Juan Carlos' second prime minister. Second, the transition to democracy was carried out within the existing legal framework of the Franco regime. The laws that called for the first democratic elections and the dissolution of the Francoist legislature, for example, were passed according to the Francoist legal framework. Third, key leaders of the transition not only promoted democratic change, but they assumed a leading role in the early years of the new democracy. Adolfo Suárez, the last authoritarian prime minister, became the first democratically elected prime minister. The last authoritarian head of state, Juan Carlos, became the first head of state under the democratic Constitution of 1978.

Finally, many aspects of the transition to democracy were negotiated between the Francoist reformers and the democratic opposition, giving rise to what has been elsewhere termed a "transition through transaction."[3] The negotiated nature of the transition helps explain why the Constitution of 1978 was purposely vague on a number of key issues, including regional devolution and certain social issues. Moreover, the negotiated nature of the transition meant that there were never any purges or prosecution of Francoist officials for human rights abuses or corruption, nor were there any official attempts to attack the Francoist past or to erase the symbols of Franco's regime. Herein lies what may be the chief asset of Spain's transition to democracy. The historical enmity between advocates of different types of political regimes was virtually eliminated by Spain's transition. Francoist loyalists were assured that the Franco regime implemented (indeed legislated) the transition to democracy, and were assuaged by the continued presence of Franco's handpicked successor in the role of head of state. Today democrats can take comfort from the fact that Spain's democracy is now fully established and widely supported, even by the historically antidemocratic Spanish right. As will be noted later, Spain has a progressive constitution and a legitimate political system. Both sides can be relieved that the change of regimes took place without much bloodshed, in marked contrast to the bitter precedent set during the Spanish Civil War.

Church and State: Bridging the Religious Divide

The feud over the proper role of the Catholic Church in society has been an explosive Spanish historical cleavage. Maintaining a key role in Spain's history, the Church was a central actor in the counterreformation, and Spain was the birthplace of the Jesuit order. The Spanish Inquisition, an institution that epitomized religious intolerance, was run by the Spanish Church and was not abolished until the 1830s. Many liberals and progressives viewed Spain's decline as the result of its cultural and economic backwardness, and the dominant historical

role of the Church was seen as a chief culprit. Church supporters rallied to defend their privileges and blamed the forces of secularism for Spain's problems. From the Napoleonic Wars of the early nineteenth century to the 1930s Spain experienced a protracted and often violent struggle between the Church and political liberals. During this period the Church begrudgingly accepted the end of the old regime and a loss of much of its power, but it was able to secure generous state financial support from weak liberal regimes, and dominance in important areas, like education. The religious cleavage reached its apogee during the Spanish Second Republic when a radical republican regime attempted to secularize Spain and limit the Church's role in Spanish politics. The religious cleavage became highly dramatized and exaggerated during the Second Republic. Liberals and leftists, angered over historic Church support for authoritarian rule, and convinced of the need to modernize Spain, advanced a highly antagonistic anticlerical agenda that was deeply offensive to many Spaniards, and it turned many against democracy. Repression of the Church (including expulsion of religious orders and attacks on clergy) during the republic quickly turned the Church into one of the major supporters of Franco's Nationalist rebels.

Church support for Franco paid off handsomely. A thoroughly united Church emerged "triumphant" from the Spanish Civil War, and it no longer needed to seek compromises with liberal regimes. The Franco regime was unabashedly confessional from the start, and all other religions were initially banned and repressed. The Church was given control over marriage, was allowed to run about half of all Spanish schools, and was handed the reigns of state censorship. The Francoist state lavished the Church with generous economic benefits.

The Church was a pillar of Franco's regime, but by the mid-1950s growing sectors of the Church began to distance themselves from authoritarian rule. Socially progressive currents of thought in Rome began to influence the Spanish Church, and in the 1960s sectors of the Church represented one of the most serious sources of opposition to Franco. The Church was thus divided on the eve of Spain's transition to democracy. Some conservative Catholic organizations (like the secretive lay society, the Opus Dei) had advocated the continuation of authoritarian rule while other sectors of the Church wholeheartedly endorsed democratization. Given the historical intensity of the religious cleavage, many observers were surprised by the relatively neutral role assumed by the Church during the transition to democracy. However, as noted later in this chapter, there is lingering evidence of the presence of the religious factor in Spanish politics.

RESOLVING THE CENTER-PERIPHERY CLEAVAGE

Another historical trademark of Spanish politics has been the center-periphery cleavage. In the twentieth century this issue was associated with contending attempts to explain Spain's decline. Many readers may think of Spain as a single nation with a single language. However, most people in Barcelona, for example, would take issue with this characterization. They would note that Spain currently contains many regional ethnic identities (*Basques, Catalans, Galicians, Castilians,* etc.), and that there are many Spanish languages (Basque, Catalan, Galician, etc.) including Castilian (what most people incorrectly call "Spanish"). An ardent advocate of centralism would likely flinch at this characterization of Spain. The role of regionalism in contemporary Spanish politics will be discussed in more depth later, but the composition of Spain and the degree of centralization and decentralization have long been subject to different interpretations.

There has been much speculation about the causes of Spain's intense regionalism. Many observers have noted that for centuries Spaniards have been more loyal to their families, towns, and regions than to the central state. Spain is one of Europe's largest countries, and its mountainous terrain and poor infrastructure historically isolated communities from one another. Car travel between Madrid and Barcelona (about 300 miles), Spain's two largest cities, took nine hours up until the late 1970s. There may also be historical reasons for the intensity of Spanish regionalism. The invasion of the Moors from North Africa in A.D. 711 shattered a budding national identity, and it forced the retreat-

ing Christians into isolated "statelets." During much of the long struggle to retake the Iberian Peninsula from Moslem forces, these isolated regions retained significant autonomy. Attempts to unify Spain under a centralized monarchy during the fifteenth century were far from complete. The image of a unified Catholic Spain that built a vast global empire ignores the reality of persistent regional identity.

Another foreign invasion, this time by Napoleon at the start of the nineteenth century, was also unable to extinguish regionalism despite the Napoleonic penchant for centralization. Attempts to abolish historic privileges of the Basque Country, for example, gave rise to a fierce, politically conservative Basque nationalism, known as Carlism. Two bitter and protracted wars waged by Carlist forces (1841 and 1876) were unable to restore regional privileges in the Basque Country, and they helped intensify the center-periphery cleavage. By the end of the nineteenth century, there was considerable popular support in the Basque Country and Catalonia, two of the wealthiest and most industrialized regions of Spain, for greater political autonomy from Madrid.

During the Spanish Second Republic, the center-periphery cleavage intensified. Republican leaders actively supported statutes guaranteeing autonomy to the Basque Country and Catalonia. These moves, and calls by radical nationalists in both regions for outright independence, frightened the Spanish right and helped precipitate the Spanish Civil War. Basques and Catalans were cruelly punished for their support of the Republic, and both regions experienced some of the harshest repression during and after the Civil War. Perhaps the most famous symbol of this repression is Pablo Picasso's *Guernica*, a painting depicting the aerial bombardment of the Basque town of Guernica in 1937. Franco immediately revoked political and economic autonomy and harshly circumscribed the use of regional languages—street names were "Castilianized"—and cultural practices. This repression, particularly ruthless in the Basque Country, gave rise in the 1950s to new Basque separatist and terrorist movements, which constituted the single greatest threat to the survival of the Franco regime.

The regional cleavage remained potentially explosive on the eve of Spain's transition to democracy.

Strong regional movements existed in Catalonia and the Basque Country. Spain's military and much of the Spanish right vehemently opposed any kind of federal system, and they steadfastly opposed threats to the "unity of Spain." As described later, the Constitution of 1978 struck some unusual and not completely successful compromises in an attempt to resolve the regional question in Spanish politics.

Economics and the Weakening of Historical Cleavages

To a remarkable extent, Spain's transition to democracy overcame the cleavages of regime type, church and state, and center-periphery. By Franco's death in 1975, however, economic growth and the concomitant social and cultural changes had already done much to erode the passions these schisms aroused. In comparative perspective, Spain stands out because its transformation from an underdeveloped, largely agrarian country to a modern urban country occurred in a very short time. At the turn of the century, most of the population lived in villages and small towns. By the 1960s, an economic "miracle" turned Spain into a largely urban country; by 2004, 78 percent of Spaniards were living in urban settings. The economic boom also contributed to a more secular and less isolationist culture. During the 1960s, the inability of the Francoist economy to employ much of its population led to a massive emigration of labor. Simultaneously, hordes of foreign tourists began to discover Spain's beaches. Tourist development, combined with industrialization and economic growth, thus created a new politically and socially tolerant middle class.

STRUCTURE AND PROCESS OF THE POLITICAL SYSTEM

The Constitution of 1978: The Constitution of Consensus

As noted earlier, members of the Franco regime initiated Spain's democratization after his death. The emerging regime, embodied in the Constitution of 1978, resulted from a set of complex negotiations between political forces. The writing of the Constitution was officially entrusted to the *Cortes*—the Spanish legislature—elected in June 1977. A committee of the Lower House of the Cortes appointed a seven-member subcommittee of "experts" to write the document. This contrasted markedly from previous Spanish constitutions, which were more partisan documents. The subcommittee operated secretly, and it produced a document that was full of compromises. A joint session of the legislature approved the Constitution of 1978 with more than 90 percent voting affirmatively; there was some opposition and abstention by parliamentarians of the right and regional groups. The Constitution gained considerable legitimacy in a referendum held in November 1978, when 87.8 percent of the voters approved it, and it became law on December 27, 1978.

The Constitution borrows heavily from other European countries. It is the longest and most complex constitution in Spanish history, and some aspects of it are imprecise and vague, in part due to compromises required by Spain's unusual transition. Figure 8.1 provides an overview of the institutions of Spanish government as established by the Constitution.

The Monarchy

The Constitution defines Spain as a constitutional monarchy, which initially drew strong opposition from the Spanish left. In principle the creation of a monarchy in the 1970s should have been anathema to the left not only because it was an unabashedly elitist institution, but because it installed as king Juan Carlos de Borbón, Franco's handpicked successor. Worse, Juan Carlos was not even the legitimate Bourbon heir to the throne. He was the grandson of Alfonso XIII, the last reigning Bourbon monarch and the son of the legitimate heir, Don Juan de Borbón. During the Francoist regime, Don Juan lived in exile and openly opposed the dictator. Curiously, he allowed his son Juan Carlos, from the age of 10, to be educated in Spain under Franco's tutelage. Under the close supervision of Franco, Juan Carlos was thoroughly socialized in the practices and protocol of authoritarian Spain. Despite the fact that in 1969 Franco designated Juan Carlos to be his successor, Juan Carlos' father did not renounce his right to the throne until after Franco died, when the democratic

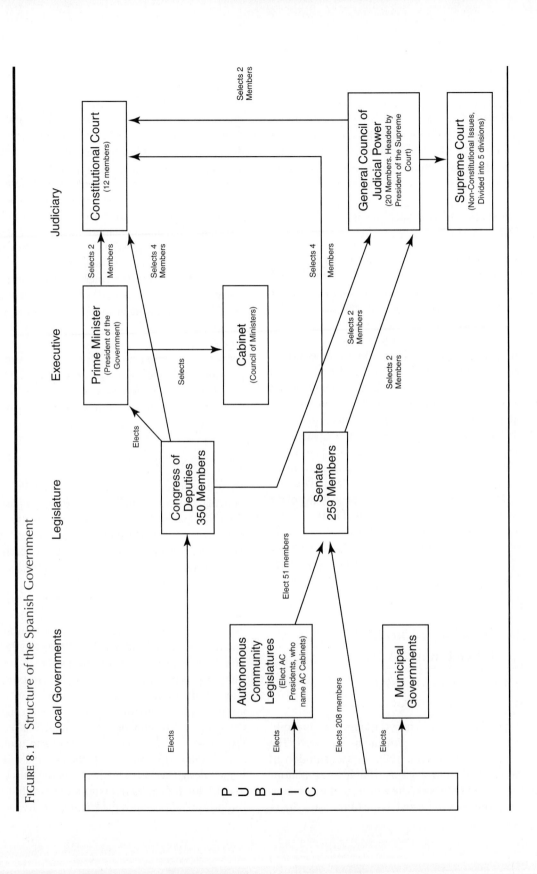

FIGURE 8.1   Structure of the Spanish Government

reform was well underway. Juan Carlos' early willingness to be Franco's designated successor and his accession to the throne after Franco's death in 1975 (despite the opposition of his exiled father) "tainted" the young prince in the eyes of the democratic opposition.

In addition to being hereditary, Spain's monarchy is sexist: The Constitution adopts the rule of primogeniture, which gives the firstborn son of the monarch the right to accede to the throne and allows for a queen only if there are no male heirs. In 2004 the newly elected Socialist government pledged to introduce legislation that would give females an equal right to inherit the throne.

Much of the left's initial resistance to a monarchy was mitigated by the strict limits placed on the institution, clearly spelled out in Articles 56–65 of the Constitution. Spain's monarchy is today largely symbolic, and the powers of the monarch leave little room for discretion. The monarch is head of state but more of an arbiter than a key actor. The monarch has no power to legislate but is entitled to a weekly meeting with the head of government in order to keep abreast of current affairs. The head of state does promulgate laws and issue decrees, but only those already approved by the parliament. One of the greatest powers enjoyed by the monarch, especially during Spain's transition to democracy, is that he is commander in chief of the armed forces.

As in the United Kingdom, Spain's monarch can, under certain circumstances, exercise a degree of discretion. The monarch is charged with appointing the prime minister from among the top candidates for the post, but except in rare circumstances the choice is strictly limited. The monarch must designate the leader of the largest party in the lower house as candidate for the prime minister's office. Ultimately, the legislature, not the monarch, determines who is to be head of government. The monarch's chief role is to act as Spain's ambassador to the world, a job in which Juan Carlos has excelled.

For a variety of reasons the monarchy, and Juan Carlos in particular, initially had an authoritarian image. Juan Carlos' chief accomplishment has been to cautiously but deliberately democratize the monarchy in the eyes of a vast majority of Spaniards. His behavior during the February 1981

attempted military coup (see Box 8.4) was crucial in safeguarding the new democracy and validating the monarchy's democratic image. The King generally avoids controversy, and his public statements are usually a masterpiece of diplomacy. He is an advocate of political compromise, calm, and common sense. He has denounced terrorism and is an outspoken advocate of the democratic system. Opinion polls show that Juan Carlos is immensely popular and that a majority of Spaniards support the monarchy and view it as an essential component of democracy.

Perhaps as a reflection of the King's popularity, the Spanish press treated the royal family with kid gloves up until about 1990, when some questions were raised about the "jet-setting" royal family. Spain's leading newspaper even suggested that the King might be having an affair. Still, the Spanish press has not savaged the monarchy to the extent witnessed in the United Kingdom (see Box 8.2).

Juan Carlos has established a monarchy that is one of the world's most modern, least ostentatious, and least controversial. There is no royal court. The royal family pays taxes and lives relatively modestly, having refused to live in the Palacio de Oriente, a huge eighteenth-century palace in Madrid. By some estimates, Spain's monarchy is the least costly in Europe, costing less than half of that of the UK. Juan Carlos is a very visible monarch who regularly visits towns throughout Spain, occasionally addressing audiences in local languages.

The Legislature

Spain's Constitution specifies that the *Cortes Generales*, or parliament, is the repository of national sovereignty (Article 1.3). However, although Spain is formally a parliamentary system, its legislature has not been the most powerful political institution. The framers of the Constitution took great pains to create a strong executive and in the process weakened the legislature.

The negotiated transition to democracy also initially weakened the Cortes. In order to avoid potentially dangerous political confrontation, most key policies during the first years of democracy resulted from an informal consensus among party

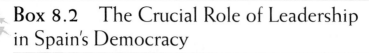

Box 8.2   The Crucial Role of Leadership in Spain's Democracy

The King's identification with democracy was further enhanced during the attempted coup of February 1981. Despite initial concerns (and obvious hopes from sectors of the military) that the King might support the coup, his actions to defend democracy were unambiguous. He forcefully ordered the military back to the barracks and was widely hailed by political leaders of every stripe. Had King Juan Carlos wavered the coup might have ended Spain's young experiment with democracy. His behavior underscores the importance of effective leaders in the consolidation of new democracies. Moreover it underscores the fact that undemocratic institutions like the monarchy can sometimes contribute to modern democracies. The King's role during the crisis strengthened the democratic system and gave the monarchy additional legitimacy.

elites. This consensus came to an end in 1979, and from 1979 to 1982 there was a precarious minority government. However, the failed military coup of 1981 delayed any resurgence of an independent parliament, and party leaders made agreements during this period without much regard for parliament. By 1982, when the Spanish Socialist Workers Party (PSOE) won the first ever absolute majority in the young democracy, the party easily controlled the Cortes because of its voting strength and extraordinary party discipline. From 1982 to 1989, and again from 2000 to 2004, there were a majority of governments that had no effective political opposition, so they could ignore the opposition and further weaken parliamentary life. After 1989, when the Socialists lost their majority, and under the 1996–2000 conservative minority government, the Cortes became more assertive and adversarial.

Spain's legislature consists of two houses: the *Congress of Deputies* (lower house) and the *Senate* (upper house) (see again Figure 8.1). Each house elects a president, and the president of the Congress of Deputies is the equivalent of the Speaker of the British House of Commons. The chamber presidents have the power to enforce the rules of their respective houses. The King formally proposes prime ministerial candidates to the lower house president.

Both houses are organized around "party groups" comprised of a minimum of 15 deputies (10 in the lower house), or 5 or more deputies who won at least 15 percent of the vote in a given region. Most parliamentary groups are made up of deputies from the same party. Members who do not have a party group to join (members of small, mostly regional parties) are forced to join the "mixed group." Party groups, in turn, dominate the running of each chamber. They determine who is allowed to participate in debate, and who sits on committees. Party group leaders become the big hitters within the legislature, and in each house they sit on the Council of Party Spokesmen, chaired by the chamber president. This group sets the agenda for the legislature and assigns tasks to committees.

CONGRESS OF DEPUTIES   The lower house and more powerful house of the legislature contains 350 members elected to four-year terms. The Congress of Deputies must pass all national laws and budgets. Yet, compared with their European counterparts, Spain's parliamentarians are on the weaker end of the spectrum. Ninety percent of the laws passed by the Cortes originate with the government.[4] The Cortes strictly limits the activities of individual members, and officially designated parliamentary groups introduce almost all legislation that originates within the Congress.

Spain's legislature has yet to play much of a "watchdog" role and has generally been ineffective in controlling the executive. The Constitution's framers saw to it that the Cortes could not assert itself too boldly vis-à-vis the executive branch. The *constructive vote of no confidence,* similar to that used in Germany, requires the Congress of Deputies to agree on a replacement for the prime minister before they can vote out the incumbent. To date no prime minister has been removed from office by such a vote. In its first 20 years the Congress of Deputies produced few investigative commissions of real importance. However, in the last years of Socialist government, the Cortes began to assert itself more. As in the United Kingdom, Spanish members of parliament question cabinet members during a weekly question time. Parliamentary groups may force a public debate on key policy issues in order to embarrass or challenge the government. Either house of parliament can require cabinet members to testify at hearings.

Parliamentary committees do play a crucial role in the legislative process. Every proposed law must be scrutinized and approved and can be amended by standing committees. Since the majority party in the Cortes has always dominated the committees, governments get their way with most legislation, but committees can and sometimes do substantially alter legislative bills.

The role of the Cortes as a recruiting mechanism for executive positions is limited because cabinet members do not need to be members of Parliament, though in fact about 60 percent are. There is higher turnover in the Spanish legislature than in most Western European legislatures. This is partly due to the low prestige and few incentives attached to being a deputy. The Cortes is not well connected to the organized interests or decision-making centers, and a 1983 law prohibits a member of parliament from holding certain jobs. In addition, salaries are very low, and resources available to deputies are strictly controlled by leaders of the parliamentary groups. Individual deputies thus have relatively little power.

The day-to-day weakness of the Cortes should not obscure the crucial legitimating function it performed in the consolidation of democracy in June 1977, when it was the only elected body in the country. The relative balance among parliamentary forces encouraged cooperation among them. Initially, the Cortes played a key role in ratifying agreements, such as the Moncloa Pacts, a key set of macroeconomic accords agreed upon in 1978. Regional autonomy accords were pushed through by the parliamentary representatives from different regions. The Constitution was in fact written by a small number of parliamentarians representing most political groups.

THE SENATE   Spain's upper house is composed of 259 members, 208 elected under a plurality system that has made it far less representative than the lower house, and 51 indirectly elected through Spain's 17 *Autonomous Communities*, identified in the map at the beginning of this chapter. The Senate was originally intended to be representative of Spain's regions, but the parliaments of the Autonomous Communities, rather than the Senate, have performed this function. The Senate suffers because it is widely regarded as a superfluous body. Its main power is that it has two months to review bills passed by the Congress of Deputies. Several Spanish governments and Senators themselves have called for an overhaul of the chamber to make it truly representative of the Autonomous Communities, but such reform will require a constitutional amendment, and to date the political will has been lacking.[5]

Spain's lower house, the Congress of Deputies, is charged with the most important duties—formally electing the prime minister, approving or rejecting votes of confidence submitted by the prime minister, passing censure motions against the government, ratifying decrees or laws, passing the government budget, and authorizing states of emergency. The Senate can initiate legislation, but this rarely happens, and it can amend lower house laws but the amendments must always be hammered out in a joint Congress of Deputies-Senate committee. A simple majority in the Congress can override Senate amendments and vetoes of Congress legislation. The Senate can delay legislation for a maximum of 2 months for ordinary bills, and 20 days for urgent ones.

The Legislative Process

Most laws originate as Council of Ministers–sponsored *proyectos de ley* (government bills),

FIGURE 8.2   How Bills Become Law in Spain

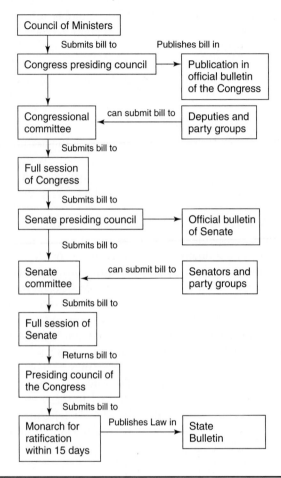

Source: Peter J. Donaghy and Michael T. Newton, *Spain: A Guide to Political and Economic Institutions* (Cambridge, England: Cambridge University Press, 1987) p. 59.

although *proposiciones de ley* (private-member bills) occasionally pass. Figure 8.2 illustrates how such proposals become law. Once sent to the Congress of Deputies leadership and published in the official bulletin of Congress, a bill is sent to legislative committees for amendments. A legislative proposal that survives this scrutiny must then be approved by a majority of the Congress. The Senate is given 15 days to consider and amend the bill. Once it has obtained a majority in the Senate, the bill is submitted to the monarch (who must ratify it within 15 days) and published in the official State Bulletin.

The Head of Government

Spain's head of government is officially called the *President of the Government*, although the office-holder is actually a prime minister. The "presidential" designation is significant since the framers of Spain's 1978 Constitution created one of the most powerful executives in Europe, clearly seeking to avoid the impotence of prime ministers of both previous republics. In both cases weak heads of government led to weak government and political instability.

TABLE 8.1   Spanish Heads of Government, 1975–2004

Head of Government	Term	Party	Elected by Cortes After General Elections?	Minority, Coalition, or Majority Government
Carlos Arias Navarro	1974–1975	Appointed by Franco		n/a
Carlos Arias Navarro	1976–1976	Appointed by King		n/a
Adolfo Suárez	1976–1977	Appointed by King		n/a
Adolfo Suárez	1977–1979	UCD	yes	minority
Adolfo Suárez	1979–1981	UCD	yes	minority
Leopoldo Calvo Sotelo	1981–1982	UCD	no	minority
Felipe González	1982–1986	PSOE	yes	majority
Felipe González	1986–1989	PSOE	yes	majority
Felipe González	1989–1993	PSOE	yes	minority
Felipe González	1993–1996	PSOE	yes	minority
José María Aznar	1996–2000	PP	yes	minority
José María Aznar	2000–2004	PP	yes	majority
José Rodríguez Zapatero	2004–	PSOE	yes	minority

Source: Adapted from Paul Heywood, "Governing a New Democracy: The Power of the Prime Minister in Spain," *West European Politics* 14, No. 2 (April 1991): p. 98.

The 1978 Constitution created a prime minister responsible only to the Cortes, which has generally been a meek institution, especially under majority governments. Moreover, Spain's prime minister has unusually strong powers vis-à-vis the legislature. Article 98.2 gives the prime minister broad powers to form and lead a government and to appoint anybody to the cabinet, whether or not a member of the Cortes, and whether or not a member of the governing party. The prime minister can without parliamentary approval add cabinet members "without portfolio." The prime minister can also ask the monarch to dissolve the legislature (though only once per year, and not while a motion of censure against the government is being considered).

After parliamentary elections, the monarch selects a prime minister-designate who must then win a vote of investiture in the Congress of Deputies. Once elected, prime ministers may serve for a maximum of four years, but there are no limits to the number of times that a prime minister may be reelected. Prime ministers can request a vote of confidence at any time during their term of office. *Felipe González*, prime minister between 1982 and 1996, called and won such a vote in April 1990. As noted earlier, prime ministers may be ousted by the legislature only if legislators can agree on a replacement (Article 113). The legislature cannot, however, remove an unpopular head of government alone: The entire government falls whenever a head of government is ousted, making the constructive vote of no confidence a measure that is likely to be employed rarely.

Table 8.1 lists the 12 governments and 6 prime ministers since the death of Franco. Three heads of government, Adolfo Suárez, Felipe González, and José María Aznar, have dominated the office and shaped its powers. Adolfo Suárez (1976–1981), despite having immense prestige associated with his stewardship of the transition to democracy, was a very weak head of government beholden to the leaders of his coalition's factions. The minority status of both of his governments exacerbated his dependence on his squabbling coalition partners. Suárez's more conservative successor, Leopoldo Calvo Sotelo (1981–1982), was equally weak due to his lack of charisma, his coalition's rapid disintegration, and the continuing minority status of his government.

Felipe González, a Socialist, was elected in 1982 in the first alternation of power in the young democracy. From 1982 to 1989 he presided over the first single-party majority government in Spanish history and was thus in a perfect position to enhance the powers of his office. Moreover, during much of that time he faced a disorganized and demoralized political opposition. Beginning with the elections of 1989, González's strength slowly began to erode, and from 1993 to 1996 he governed with a minority in the legislature. Many observers argued that the immense powers granted to the government, the meekness of the legislature, and the Socialists' long tenure in power had created the conditions under which corruption thrived. Indeed, the corruption scandals that plagued Socialist administrations in the 1990s were largely responsible for their fall from power.

The conservative José María Aznar (1996–2004) was first elected in 1996 but lacked a parliamentary majority. He was forced to work with regional parties in order to maintain a parliamentary majority until his party obtained an absolute majority in the March 2000 elections. Aznar was the first post–Franco era conservative to govern Spain. He clearly established the democratic credentials of a modern conservative party. He presided over an extraordinary economic boom, but his foreign policy was extremely controversial, especially his support of the Iraqi war. Aznar set an important precedent by deciding not to seek a third term in office, choosing to leave the party in the hands of his hand-picked successor.

Spanish heads of government are strongest when their parties are unified. Indeed, given the constitutional advantages enjoyed by prime ministers, it is fair to say that the most significant limits to their power come from within their own parties. Thus from 1982 to 1990 the Socialists maintained iron (some would say quasi-authoritarian) internal party discipline, and this greatly enhanced the power of Felipe González.[6] After 1990, due to a series of corruption scandals, internal party dissent increased, there were calls for an internal democrati-

zation of the PSOE, and González lost some power. José María Aznar was an even more successful party manager, and he maintained strong discipline within his ranks during both of his terms.

Two prime ministers, Adolfo Suárez and Felipe González, used their immense personal charm and charisma to enhance their power in office. Unlike some parliamentary systems, Spain's prime ministers have generally remained aloof vis-à-vis the legislature and the prime minister's own party. González, for example, went long periods without appearing in the Cortes (there is no constitutional requirement for the prime minister to appear before the legislature). Near the end of his stint in power he was clearly much more interested in foreign than domestic affairs.

Even though the Cortes does not exercise much control over the head of government, it would be a mistake to argue that Spain's prime minister has limitless power. During the first two decades of Spain's democracy, prime ministers often appeared to make decisions that represented compromises with entrenched political interests, both domestically and internationally. As late as the 1980s, for example, Prime Minister González reversed his own (and his party's) position on taking Spain out of the North Atlantic Treaty Organization (NATO). He did so in part to mollify the Spanish military, which favored NATO membership, and in part to satisfy business interests, who viewed NATO membership and Spain's desired membership in the European Union (EU) as conjoined. On the domestic level, the unwillingness of the Socialists to liberalize Spain's restrictive abortion law, despite a legislative majority and widespread public support, suggests that the Church can exercise some limits on the government's power. José María Aznar's decision, despite overwhelming popular opposition, to support the U.S.-led invasion of Iraq (breaking with France and Germany, Spain's traditional European allies), contributed to the Conservatives' upset loss in the 2004 general elections.

The Judicial System[7]

Reforming Spain's judicial system was one of the greatest challenges facing the democratic regime.

Under the Franco regime, the courts had little independence, and most judges were appointed directly by the government. The courts were identified with harsh repression against those who opposed the dictatorship. As late as September 1975, and despite an international outcry, Francoist courts sanctioned the execution without trial of Basque terrorists arrested under martial law.

In an attempt to depart from this authoritarian legal tradition, the 1978 Constitution established a *Constitutional Court* as the supreme arbiter in political disputes and attempted to give it independence from the state. The Court consists of 12 members, all of them professional lawyers or judges. The Cortes selects eight of the judges (four per house, approved by three-fifths of both chambers), the government proposes two names, subject to the legislature's approval, and the General Council of the Judiciary (discussed later) names the final two. Its members must be independent of any party and cannot actively participate in them. Members are appointed to nine-year terms, with a third of the court renewed every three years. The government or legislature cannot dismiss Constitutional Court judges, and the Court controls its own budget and organization.

The Constitutional Court can declare any law or government decree unconstitutional; it has the power to rule on a direct appeal by the prime minister, 50 members of either house, assemblies of Spain's Autonomous Communities, or lower court judges. In some cases, individual citizens may appeal to the Court if they feel that their constitutional rights have been violated. The legislature or the government may also ask the Court to rule on the constitutionality of pending legislation.

To date, the Constitutional Court has played a significant role in limiting Spain's powerful majoritarian government. For example, in 1983 it ruled unconstitutional a major law intended to rationalize (and in some cases slow down) the devolution of power to Spain's Autonomous Communities. In 1993 it struck down key provisions of a government antiterrorism bill that would have facilitated police search of private homes. Despite this record of opposition to government measures, the Court has been criticized for lacking the political neutrality for which it was designed.

During the long Socialist reign (1982–1996), the Socialist legislature was accused of packing the Court with its cronies. The massive backlog of cases and the lack of resources have hampered the effectiveness of the Court and the entire Spanish judiciary. The Constitution's ambiguity with regard to regional devolution has meant that the Court has been bogged down adjudicating countless disputes between the Autonomous Communities and the central government.

For matters that are not of a constitutional nature, the highest court is the *Supreme Court (Tribunal Supremo)*. This court has existed since 1834, but was completely overhauled in 1978 to rid it of its Francoist legacy. The powers of the Supreme Court have been eroded by the creation of the Constitutional Court (generally seen as the most powerful court in Spain), and by the devolution of many of its powers to the Autonomous Communities. Still, the Supreme Court has the final word in the enforcement of the penal code. In July 1988 the Supreme Court demonstrated its power and independence when it sentenced a former Socialist cabinet member to prison for his role in a government-sponsored antiterrorist death squad.

Each of the 17 Autonomous Communities has its own High Court of Justice *(Tribunales Superiores de Justicia)*, which oversees the administration of justice in each region. These are the highest courts at the regional level and are charged with, among other things, resolving electoral disputes. Each high court has three chambers dealing with civil/penal, administrative, and social matters.

One of the most interesting offices created by the 1978 Spanish Constitution is the *Defensor del Pueblo*, or Ombudsperson, appointed by the Cortes for a period of five years. Because the appointment requires the approval of a three-fifths majority in each house, the Defensor is intended to be a nonpartisan individual. The position was designed to be a watchdog over the administration and to investigate citizen complaints in their dealings with officialdom. The Defensor reports yearly to the Cortes with a summary of complaints against state agencies. Despite the initial appointment of a prestigious lawyer, Joaquín Ruíz Giménez, the Defensor's office has been a disappointment to date. Like the attorney general's office, it lacks a sufficient budget and staff. Its functions, broadly outlined in the Constitution, are not yet clearly defined. Early on, the office was deluged with a huge number of cases, obviously reflecting the pent-up frustration of Spaniards with the bureaucracy. During the Socialist administration, the opposition complained that the position was overly partisan. Eyebrows were raised when the Defensor refused to challenge the government in the courts over the controversial Public Security Law, an antiterrorist measure that severely restricted civil liberties.

The Spanish judiciary is supervised by the General Council of the Judiciary, created in an attempt to insulate judges from political pressure. The Council has 20 members, 10 approved by each house of the legislature, for 5-year terms. The Spanish judiciary has clearly made a lot of progress since the Franco regime. Spanish judges cannot be easily removed by the government, are forbidden from holding any other public office, and cannot be members of any political party or trade union. Since the 1980s the judiciary has played an increasingly aggressive role in combating corruption, and limiting the government. In a number of highly publicized corruption scandals beginning in 1990, Spanish judges were put in the spotlight, investigating and prosecuting cases against a variety of top Spanish officials. These investigations greatly enhanced the prestige of Spain's judiciary, converting some judges into national heroes with name recognition and popularity ratings rivaling the top political leaders (see Box 8.3).

While many Spaniards suspected that the Socialist government manipulated the judiciary, the government tended to view the judiciary and its increasingly assertive behavior as conservative and anti-Socialist. During the long Socialist tenure in office, the judiciary attempted to prevent government incursions against civil liberties. In the context of rapidly rising crime and the continued war against terrorism, and as an attempt to mollify the police and military, the Socialists passed the Public Security Law and gave permanent status to a controversial 1977 antiterrorism law. These measures, among other things, gave police broad powers to enter private homes without a court order if they suspected criminal activity and to hold suspects incommunicado for long periods of time. In 1995 Prime Minister González admitted that police units had top political leaders under surveillance, increasing demands on the courts for protection of civil liberties against a powerful government. Spanish civil libertarians sought protection from the courts and were partly successful in weakening the law. In 1999 Spain's Constitutional Court dealt a blow to the Aznar government when it overturned the conviction of 23 Basque politicians who had been jailed for airing an election broadcast that allegedly supported Basque terrorists. In short, a healthy tension between the government and the judiciary has been an important feature of Spain's political culture.

The most serious obstacle to the Spanish judiciary has been financial deprivation, not govern-

---

Box 8.3   Spain's Assertive New Judiciary

Some Spanish judges have become celebrities in the international arena as well as at home. Baltazar Garzón, a young, independent, and aggressive investigative judge of Spain's National Court, has become an international phenomenon due to his attempt to bring former Latin American military rulers to justice for human rights abuses committed against Spanish citizens during the 1970s and 1980s. Garzón formally requested the extradition of former Chilean dictator Pinochet (who was receiving medical treatment in the United Kingdom) to Spain in 1998, provoking strong opposition from the Chilean government. Despite obvious opposition to Garzón's action (the Aznar government did not want to endanger Spain's close rela-

tions with Latin America) the government made no attempt to stop the extradition. The British ultimately refused to extradite Pinochet, but the incident was another sign of the growing independence and prestige of Spain's judiciary. In April 2005 Garzón sentenced a former Argentine naval officer to 640 years in prison for human rights abuses under the Argentine military junta in the 1970s and 1980s.

Garzón has also waged a long-standing campaign against Basque terrorism, seizing assets from the radical Batasuna party and ordering organizations associated with terrorism to pay damages for terrorist attacks. In late 2003 Garzón brought charges against international terrorist Osama Bin Laden.

ment manipulation. Spain's judiciary is allocated a far smaller share of the budget than its European counterparts. As a result, there is a chronic backlog of cases. The inefficiency of the Spanish legal system has damaged its prestige, and only encourages the Spanish tendency to ignore laws and expect little from the administration of justice. Spain's democracy has so far been only partly successful in narrowing the gap between the citizen and the justice system. After two decades of delay, the first implementation of the constitutionally sanctioned jury system in June 1996 may be a first move toward involving Spanish citizens in the administration of justice.

Spain's Autonomous Communities

Despite the long history of regional nationalism, Spanish history offers no precedent for a successful decentralization of power. Past attempts to give autonomy to Spain's regions (usually Catalonia and the Basque Country) alienated the Spanish right, and attempts at decentralization during the Second Republic helped provoke the Spanish Civil War and precipitated the destruction of democracy. Under Franco all power was centralized in Madrid. Provincial governors, appointed by the dictator and under direct orders of the Ministry of the Interior, ran local government and appointed local officials. Thus the founders of Spain's democracy after Franco's death addressed this issue with caution. After protracted debate and much compromise, the 1978 Constitution attempted to establish a middle ground between federalism (favored by the left and by regional nationalists) and a unitary state (favored by the right). The result, agree almost all observers, is a confusing and often contradictory arrangement.

Spain's 1978 Constitution recognizes the right to regional autonomy through the Autonomous Communities (ACs), carefully avoiding the terms "state" or "nation," and without defining the meaning of that term or specifying the exact powers to be enjoyed by these communities. The Constitution left the nuts and bolts of the autonomy-granting process to future legislatures. Moreover, as a result of the interparty bargaining process (in which the Catalans, but not the Basques, were directly represented), the Constitution

provided for a faster route to autonomy for "historic" regions like Catalonia, the Basque Country, and Galicia, which had a history of separate languages and national identity. While all regions aspiring to AC status had to apply for it and complete a tedious set of procedures, the historic regions faced far fewer obstacles.

By 1979 autonomy statutes had been approved for Catalonia and the Basque Country, setting off a frenzy in which every region of Spain demanded autonomy. This resulted in the formation of 17 ACs through *devolution*, a chaotic process that frustrated regional nationalists and centralizing rightists alike, and may have encouraged the attempted coup of February 1981 (the *golpistas* had plans to rein in the devolution process). As a result of the attempted coup, the governing center-right Union of the Democratic Center (UCD), together with the opposition Socialists, passed a controversial measure designed to slow down the devolution process. The measure gave Spanish law priority over AC law, even in the historic regions. Infuriated Basques and Catalans got the Constitutional Court to throw out about one-third of the law in 1983, effectively killing the measure. By then the governing Socialists were not as jittery about a military coup, and they began to expedite devolution. By February 1983 all 17 Autonomous Communities were in place, and by the end of that year all had held a regional election. (Catalonia, the Basque Country, Galicia, and Andalusia, the first four to obtain autonomy statutes, had held their first regional parliamentary elections earlier.) In most AC elections the Socialists mirrored their earlier success in general elections. With the Socialists a major player in most AC governments, the transfer of power from Socialist-dominated center to Socialist-dominated periphery was facilitated.

Currently all ACs have their own statutes of autonomy, and each has its own unicameral legislature, a president, an AC public administration, and an AC high court of justice. However, unlike purely federal systems each AC has slightly different powers depending on the negotiations between Madrid and the AC, and the timing and route to autonomy taken by the AC. The outcome has been referred to as "asymmetric federalism." The AC government of the Basque Country, for example, had the greatest amount of power. By the early 1990s the Socialist government made efforts to transfer identical powers to all ACs, raising fears from Catalans and Basques that they were being stripped of their special privileges as "historic" Autonomous Communities. Under current rules, regional and central governments share powers in many areas (education, health, law and order, civil service, among others), except for those specifically reserved for the central government (defense, foreign policy, and economic policy, among others). In practice the exact nature of the powers enjoyed by the central government and the ACs remains vague. However, even under the conservative Aznar governments, the process of devolution, though uneven, continued, and AC governments today have more power than ever.

SPANISH POLITICAL CULTURE

During Franco's traditional authoritarian regime, Spaniards were encouraged to stay out of politics and to focus their attentions on their families, their work, and other diversions such as sports and the state-censored television. Spain became a political desert, and fear of police repression kept it that way for the vast majority of Spaniards. Public opinion research conducted during Franco's rule documented the consequences of authoritarian rule for Spain's political culture. In 1966 when Spaniards were asked whether "it is better for one person to have all the authority and make all the decisions for us, or for a group of people elected by all citizens to make the political decisions," only 35 percent opted for the more democratic answer.[8] At the time of the democratic transition about one-half of Spanish respondents gave authoritarian responses on this and other questions.

By the 1960s, however, Spain's isolation from the democratic world had ended due to emigration, tourism, increasing exposure to European ideas, and the concomitants of economic growth. Studies conducted in the 1960s and 1970s began to document the modernization of Spain's political culture. Still, on the eve of the transition, many scholars pondered whether a modern democracy could be constructed with Spain's authoritarian culture. The transition to democracy coincided with a severe economic recession that threatened to undermine the fragile legitimacy of the new democracy.

Such fears have proved to be unfounded. After two decades of democracy, and with a few exceptions, the political culture of Spaniards is no longer very different from other European countries. By 1977, more than two-thirds of Spanish respondents disagreed with the notion that one person should rule, while a vast majority approved of allowing political parties to compete for power. According to polling data gathered by Spain's Centro de Investigaciones Sociológicas, by 1980 50 percent of respondents agreed that "democracy is preferable to any other form of government," and by 2000 that figure had risen to 88 percent, a figure that is on par with other European democracies.[9] A 1999 survey showed that 68 percent of Spanish respondents were very or fairly satisfied with democracy, the fourth highest level within the European Union (the EU average was 56 percent).[10] Twenty-eight percent claimed to be unsatisfied with democracy in Spain, far less than the EU average of 40 percent. The fear that the economic crisis of the mid-1970s and the persistence of extraordinarily high levels of unemployment might erode the legitimacy of democratic rule proved unwarranted. Indeed, Spanish survey results demonstrate that "support for democracy rose despite poor state performance" and they confirm the conclusion of other scholars that the behavior of Spanish political elites and the centrist orientation of Spain's party system were able to prevent political polarization that might otherwise have overwhelmed Spain's young democracy.[11] A recent European Union study developed an aggregate indicator of support for and trust in national political systems. The results show that Spaniards' view of their political system is close to the European average.[12] Germans, Britons, and Danish citizens all had considerably more negative views of their political systems.

Spain may have a democratic political culture, but legacies of authoritarian rule remain, and in some important ways Spain's political culture deviates from the European norm. Spaniards continue to express much less interest in politics than their Western European counterparts.[13] Perhaps a sign of the years under Franco and the elite-led transition, Spaniards still participate less in politics than their

European counterparts. Spanish political parties and trade unions have the lowest per capita membership in Western Europe, and confidence in those institutions is especially weak (see Figure 8.3). According to the World Values Survey, the percentage of Spaniards in 1996 who reported membership in any organized group was only 36 percent.[14] Fewer Spaniards identified with a political party than in most other industrial democracies. Younger Spaniards, who were not subjected to Franco's depoliticization, score roughly the same as their European counterparts, suggesting that they have a different, more democratic political culture than their elders. Moreover, despite Spaniards' lack of political participation, voter turnout has remained relatively robust (though somewhat lower than elsewhere in Europe), and is certainly higher than in some established democracies like the United States. Spaniards interviewed for opinion research continue to express very low levels of trust in their politicians, and very low levels of political efficacy.

The global sociopolitical orientations in Spain are broadly similar to European societies. Spaniards are moderately inclined toward social reformism, and very few take extreme positions on any issue. Indeed, in 1985 Spanish respondents were far less inclined toward conservative or extreme positions than in most other European Union countries. Spaniards generally rank the values of liberty and equality about equal.

A number of researchers have studied the major political cleavages in Spanish society. One study concluded that region, religion, and class, together with generational conflict, are the "master cleavages of Spanish politics."[15] However, in contrast with the Second Republic, Spain is now overwhelmingly urban, literate, and industrialized. Reduced church attendance, greater geographical mobility, emigration, and exposure to mass media have made Spain a less parochial society. The intensity of these "master cleavages," therefore, has diminished considerably, and they no longer threaten democratic rule.

FIGURE 8.3   Political Confidence in Various Institutions

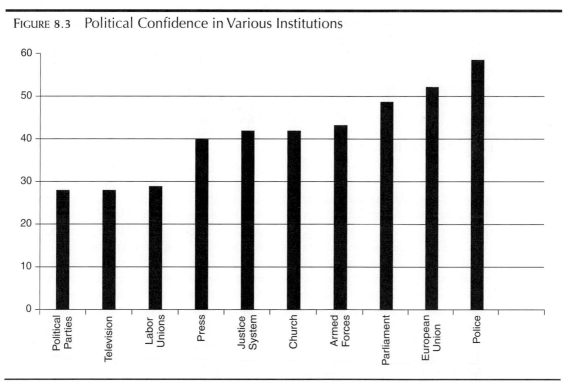

Source: World Values Survey 1999–2001. Figure presents the percentage of respondents expressing "great deal" or "quite a lot" of confidence.

Moreover, none of the cleavages are closely linked with partisan identification, a factor that has facilitated the consolidation of democracy.

The regional cleavage, initially feared to be the intractable schism most likely to undermine Spanish democracy, is less important than expected. This has partly been the result of the massive internal demographic shift within Spain that brought many immigrants to the Basque Country and Catalonia. These immigrants are less parochial and more attached to a Spanish national identity. Only in the Basque Country, and to a lesser extent, Catalonia, are there significant feelings of alienation toward the Spanish state. Because the regional cleavage is not strongly related to left and right (there is a weak relationship between regionalism and leftism), the danger posed by the regional cleavage has been lessened.

Moreover, the intensity of regional nationalism is not even easily related to the attachment to a regional language.[16] Indeed, in the Basque Country, where radical and violent nationalism has been strongest, 57 percent of those polled claim that they cannot understand Euskera, the regional language. In Catalonia 97 percent of respondents claim to understand Catalan, but nationalism there has been far more moderate than in the Basque Country. In Galicia 99 percent of respondents claim to understand the regional language but radical nationalism has been virtually nonexistent.

POLITICAL SOCIALIZATION

Education

Contemporary Spain is a highly educated and literate nation. Only 2 percent of Spaniards (mostly older citizens) are illiterate. Franco invested significant resources in education during the economic boom of the 1960s, and since democratization Spain's educational system has received a considerable boost. Unlike the United Kingdom, education in Spain has been remarkably accessible to people of all social classes, and to women (there are more women students than men in Spanish universities), and there is little of the elitism surrounding education that exists in the UK. The desire to obtain a college education, for example, does not vary considerably among classes. There is no Spanish equivalent of Britain's Oxford or Cambridge, and no well-established hierarchy among Spain's universities.

About one-third of Spanish schoolchildren are educated at private schools, one-half of which are owned by religious orders and the rest are secular. Because of the shortage of schools in Spain, UCD governments, like their predecessors from the Franco regime, allowed some Catholic private schools to provide state-subsidized places for students. This practice was expanded under the PSOE, and currently about 90 percent of secular private schools and 98 percent of religious schools are run with taxpayers' money. In return, the Socialists required private schools to set standardized admissions procedures and form representative governing bodies. In addition, teachers in these private schools had to be paid directly by the state, giving the state greater control. Students in these schools were given the option of not taking religion classes. These and other measures were deeply resented by many middle-class parents, and by the Catholic Church, as state encroachment on their educational freedom. Protests over Socialist educational policy produced some of the largest mass demonstrations of the democratic period, but the protests and an appeal to the Constitutional Court failed to stop the reforms.

The Socialists made educational reform one of their chief priorities, and in the early 1990s they overhauled the entire structure of Spanish education. The government attempted to alleviate a significant source of educational inequality by providing free preschool for children ages 4 to 6. Since the recent reforms, Spanish children start primary education at age 6, and then progress to secondary education (ages 13 to 16). Students can then leave school or pursue a *Bachillerato* (high school diploma), from ages 16 to 18. After completing this degree, students can either enter university or attend state-funded vocational schools. The Socialists modernized the curriculum of Spanish schools as well. Foreign language training (English is now the predominant foreign language) is mandatory beginning at age 8. The Socialists added such topics as peace studies and environmental conservation, and eliminated gender discrimination from the traditional curriculum. New class size limits were imposed to reduce overcrowding.

About 30 percent of Spanish youth attend university, a higher percentage than in the UK and some other EU states. However, given the high rate of course repetition (due to the high failure rate in Spanish university courses), the real figure is probably quite a bit lower.[17] The relatively open access to higher education produces serious overcrowding at the relatively small number of Spanish universities. The Socialists tripled the number of university scholarships, but this has only exacerbated overcrowding. The Socialists tried to clear the logjam by facilitating the establishment of more private universities.

Aznar's conservative governments enacted a number of controversial educational reforms, especially after the PP gained a parliamentary majority in 2000. In 2002 the Aznar government devolved power to individual universities, including their ability to control admissions, eliminating the national selection exam for university admission. The measure was criticized by some as being too favorable to private religious universities.

The Role of the Media

Visitors to Spain often note the plethora of periodicals on news kiosks and are impressed with their variety and sophistication. However, a 2004 survey showed that only 27 percent of Spaniards read a newspaper daily, well below the EU average of 41 percent.[18] Yet, newspaper readership has grown quickly since the birth of democracy. Moreover, the relative absence of tabloids that are so popular in other European countries partly explains the low readership statistics. Even the most sensationalistic Spanish dailies contain serious news coverage. Despite small readership, the Spanish press has often played an important role in politics. During the PSOE tenure in office, when there was little parliamentary opposition and scrutiny, the press brought a number of important scandals to the public's attention.

Television, however, is the most important medium in Spain, and it has been argued that "Spain is a nation of TV addicts."[19] After the British, Spaniards spend more time than any other Europeans watching TV. One study showed that about 70 percent of Spaniards formed their political views based on what they see on television.[20] Nearly all Spanish homes have TV sets, even if they lack other amenities: In Andalusia, despite the torrid heat, as late as the 1980s more homes had televisions than refrigerators.

Given the importance of television, control of that medium has been a political tempest since 1977. Prime Minister Suárez, a former director of the Francoist television monopoly, RTVE (Spanish Radio and Television), dragged his feet when it came to relinquishing state control of the electronic media. Parliamentary oversight has been mostly ignored. Once in office, the PSOE continued to manipulate the electronic media, and state television was unabashedly pro-government in the 1986 NATO referendum.

Slowly, however, the state monopoly of the electronic media has been reduced, in part because of the creation of regional television channels. Spain's state television monopoly ended in 1990 with the birth of private television channels. According to one expert on the media, the Socialists begrudgingly granted privatization of television and "is likely to be seen with hindsight as one of their most valuable contributions to the consolidation of democracy, comparable with their taming of the army."[21] Despite the proliferation of private television and radio since that time, two full decades after Franco's dictatorship the state is still the biggest owner of mass media. Private television has eroded the state monopoly, possibly contributing to the erosion of support for the PSOE, but by 2002 TVE-1 (the main state network) still topped the ratings (with about a 32 percent market share).[22] After his 2004 election, Prime Minister Zapatero pledged to reform the state media, perhaps creating an autonomous agency similar to the British BBC.

The Importance of Family

The declining importance of the Church, the expansion and secularization of education, and the emergence of a modern media have all weakened traditional forms of socialization in Spain. However, the importance of family is one traditional value that remains surprisingly strong. Opinion research demonstrates that Spaniards value their families far more than work, friends, leisure, religion, or politics. The continued strength of the family is partially caused by the high rates of unemployment among youth, which has forced about 70 percent of 18- to 29-year-olds to live with their parents. The strength of family may have helped cushion the succession of changes that have swept over Spanish society in recent years, especially the dislocation caused by Spain's integration into the European Union.

INTEREST GROUPS

Under Franco, the state controlled virtually all interest groups and incorporated both employees and employers in a state-dominated organization. Even the Catholic Church was subject to state control. During the transition, organized interests played a secondary role and were not a crucial force pressuring for democratization.

Trade Unions

Franco's regime depended on labor repression and exclusion, despite some liberalization in the 1960s. Opposition trade unions differed in their approach to the Francoist trade union structure. The Communist *Workers' Commissions (CC.OO)* sought to infiltrate the official trade unions, while the PSOE-affiliated *General Confederation of Workers (UGT)* boycotted them. In the democratic period, these two trade union organizations became the chief rivals for the allegiance of Spanish workers.

Spain has the lowest unionization rate in Europe, and unions are divided ideologically, tactically, and regionally. Today only about one-tenth of salaried workers are unionized, down from a high of 57.8 percent in 1978; much higher figures are found in Italy, Greece, and Turkey.[23] The weakness of trade unions would lead one to expect a high level of labor conflict, and indeed over the last decade Spain has had the second highest strike rate in Europe (see Figure 8.4).

Although organizationally weak, Spanish trade unions have considerable influence. The 1980 Workers Statute codified worker representation in the workplace and gave trade unions a role in the process. In firms with 10 to 50 employees, workers are represented by up to 3 elected delegates. In

larger firms workers' councils are elected. Unions that elect at least 10 percent of council delegates are entitled to participate in collective bargaining negotiations. Workers can vote for representatives even if they do not belong to a union, an unusual feature that contributes to low levels of union membership. Thus, even though union membership is low, 80 percent of Spanish workers vote in workers' council elections. According to Schmitter, "Spanish unions have few members (and, therefore, precarious finances), but they exercise impressive power. They negotiate collective contracts that cover a very substantial proportion of the workforce; they regularly win most of the elections held for representatives at the enterprise level."[24] The best measure of union strength comes from workers' council elections conducted in the workplace. In the 1999 union elections, the UGT and CC.OO each won just under 40 percent of the workplace delegates, with the remainder of the votes going to small (often regional) trade unions.

The role of trade unions has changed during the first two decades of democracy. The UGT and the CC.OO entered the democratic period as "transmission belts" for the leftist parties with which they were affiliated. The desire to consolidate democracy took precedence over worker demands. The *Moncloa Pacts* of October 1977, a landmark economic accord between the center-right UCD government and the leftist political parties, required trade unions to toe the party line and accept major sacrifices. Ties between the UGT and the PSOE were especially strong. PSOE members were required to join the UGT and to work with the union. A similar but somewhat looser relationship existed between the CC.OO and the PCE, the Spanish Communist Party.

The UGT hoped to be compensated for its moderation and patience when the Socialists were elected to office in 1982. The PSOE program called for the creation of 800,000 new jobs. Instead, the Socialists embarked on a harsh austerity policy designed to internationalize the economy and to create labor-market "flexibility." In the first four years of PSOE government, about three-quarters of a million people lost their jobs, and by 1987 Spain's unemployment rate reached 22 percent. The Socialists passed laws making it easier for Spanish businesses to lay off workers and hire part-time labor. By the

FIGURE 8.4   Labor disputes

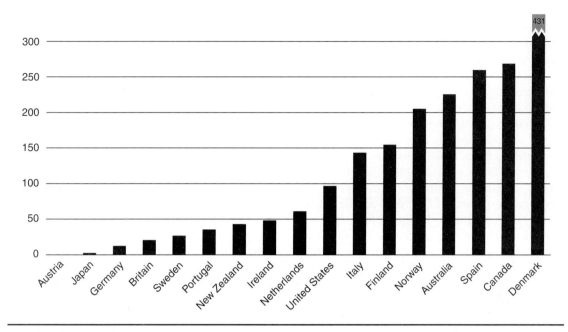

Source: Office for National Statistics.

mid-1980s, the UGT rejected the PSOE government's neoliberal economic policies. The CC.OO (Communist-affiliated Workers Commissions) and workers' councils at the factory level had long been actively opposed to Socialist economic policy. Massive strikes throughout the 1980s failed to alter PSOE policy. The consistently high rates of unemployment under the Socialists tested the patience of the UGT, but government attempts to cut welfare and unemployment benefits in 1988 further alienated the UGT. By 1986 the UGT and PSOE were in open conflict. The UGT leader quit his PSOE seat in the Cortes and formally broke links with the Socialists. In the 1989 elections the UGT refused to endorse the Socialists. Since the late 1980s the UGT and CC.OO have often coordinated activities.

Socialist economic policy not only infuriated the trade unions; it also ended the tripartite wage accords that from 1979 to 1987 had involved the government, unions, and employers. The general strike of December 1988, supported by all major trade unions, was the largest such protest since 1934: Some 8 million workers refused to work for a day. The strike pitted organized labor against the Socialist government. Despite its impressive size, it failed to reverse Socialist policy although it undoubtedly weakened the PSOE in the 1989 general elections. Strikes called since then have been even less effective, and during Aznar's two terms in office the government viewed general strikes with even less sympathy.

Business Organizations

Business associations are stronger and more unified than organized labor. Near the end of the Francoist regime, a number of entrepreneurial organizations were tolerated, and the *Spanish Confederation of Entrepreneurial Organizations (CEOE)* emerged as the most important of these. The CEOE claims to incorporate 75 percent of firms and an even larger percentage of Spain's total production. It is probably the most successful peak business organization in Southern Europe. Founded in 1977, the CEOE has 133 affiliated associations and 1.3 million affiliated firms. It includes a very wide spectrum of businesses. In 1983 it incorporated the main small and medium business organization, and most regional business groups belong to the CEOE.

The CEOE took a hands-off approach to the democratic transition. Only after the attempted coup of 1981 did the CEOE make clear commitments to the democratic system. However, the organization played an important role as spokesperson for business interests in the tripartite wage agreements during the late 1970s and early 1980s. The CEOE has tended to maintain its distance from political parties. It supports parties of the right and center, but its relationship with the PSOE has been far better than the PSOE–trade union relationship. The CEOE has been a pro-free market force, complaining about high energy costs and foreign competition. It opposes tax policies that it believes hurt business and limit investment, and it steadily assails "unproductive" public spending. A constant goal of the CEOE is to revise what it views as overly restrictive laws regarding the hiring and firing of workers, many of which date from the Francoist era. Employers claim that they need more flexibility in hiring workers in order to compete with foreign enterprise.

Agricultural lobbies are very weak in Spain, a reflection of the fact that the importance of agriculture in Spain has steadily declined. By 2003 agriculture employed only 7 percent of the population and accounted for 3.6 percent of the GDP. Agricultural lobbies are divided between high-tech interests that want further EU integration and smaller farmers who fear European competition.

The Armed Forces

Spain's military has a long history of political involvement. Since the early nineteenth century, military officers regularly tried to depose governments in support of both conservative monarchist and liberal agendas: From 1820 to 1936 there were 44 pronunciamientos (military uprisings), culminating with the antidemocratic rebellion led by General Franco. The humiliating defeats suffered by the military as Spain lost the last pieces of its empire, from Cuba to Morocco, made the armed forces defensive and sensitive to criticism by civilians. For most of the twentieth century, civilians accused of offending the military's honor were subject to military courts, a measure repealed only in 1978 after democracy's restoration.

The Spanish Civil War was a turning point in the history of the armed forces. A significant minority of the military remained loyal to the democratic Republic, and this faction was purged when Franco won control of the government. The armed forces became a far more conservative institution. Under Franco the military had a prominent political role, although the regime was never a pure military dictatorship: Members of the armed forces held 32 out of 114 Francoist cabinet posts. Military men sat on the boards of state-owned companies. Most importantly, the military gained control over all police forces, intelligence organizations, and customs. As a result of this beneficial treatment, the military was the group most consistently loyal to Franco.

During the transition, the military begrudgingly accepted the authority of Franco's designated successor, King Juan Carlos, and his prime minister, Adolfo Suárez. Military leaders, however, vigorously opposed aspects of the democratization process, especially the legalization of the Communist Party. Military hard-liners felt increasingly uneasy during the first UCD governments because of increased terrorism (usually directed against military members), rapid devolution of powers to Spain's regions, and squabbling and chaotic governments. Weak UCD governments failed to act decisively in the face of repeated acts of military insubordination.

Ironically, it was the Socialist Party that finally tamed the military. The strength and determination of the PSOE allowed it to act decisively vis-à-vis the military, and most observers would rank the Socialists' reform of the military as their single most important achievement in office. The Socialists streamlined and modernized the army. The PSOE decision to join NATO gave the Spanish military an international role and reduced its focus on domestic security. Most importantly, the PSOE consistently imposed severe punishment on members of the military for acts of insubordination. Spanish law

Box 8.4   The Last *Pronunciamiento?*

On February 23, 1981, a detachment of Spain's *Civil Guard*, a militarized police force, burst into Congress and stopped a debate on the selection of a new prime minister. Millions of Spaniards following this debate on radio and television heard the gunshots and screams as members of the armed forces attempted to end Spain's democracy. Spain's outgoing prime minister and leader of the transition was pushed to the ground when he tried to resist the rebels. In Valencia, tanks occupied the streets and troops surrounded the Socialist Party headquarters. Most of the armed forces did not support the coup attempt, and King Juan Carlos ordered the rebellious soldiers back to their barracks. The coup attempt fizzled and democracy was saved, but the dramatic events of February 1981 reminded Spaniards that the military remained a serious obstacle to democratic consolidation. Since that time democratic leaders worked hard to discipline, reform, and reorient the Spanish armed forces. These measures have been highly successful, and the modernization and democratization of Spain's military is arguably the greatest achievement of Spain's democracy.

now prohibits political or union activity by active military personnel, who must permanently leave the armed forces if they wish to run for office. The Spanish police forces have been thoroughly civilianized. The military presence in Spanish politics is now negligible.

During the first decades of democracy, a constant point of contention was the requirement that all Spanish males complete military service. In the 1980s several political parties (though not the PSOE) advocated abolition of the draft. The PSOE liberalized provisions for conscientious objections and cut the length of military service. One of the first acts of the conservative Aznar government in 1996 was to announce a gradual elimination of conscription. Defense spending rose steadily as a percentage of GDP from 1975 to 1985, a reflection of attempts to modernize the armed forces. Since 1985, however, the military budget has fallen steadily as a percentage of GDP. Spain currently spends only 1.2 percent of its GDP on the military, the second lowest in NATO (see Box 8.4).

The Catholic Church

Religion is still the strongest cleavage dividing Spaniards. The intensity of the religious question reflects the prominent role of the Catholic Church in Spanish history, and the resentment that this role has often created. During the transition to democracy, the Catholic Church did not play an active political role. This neutrality reflected the fact that the Church had long ceased to be a unified supporter of authoritarian rule. By the mid-

1950s, Catholic progressives began using the Church's autonomy to engage in social activism. By 1975, much of the Church, though not most of the top leadership, actively opposed the continuation of authoritarian rule. The bystander role taken by the Church during the transition was one reason that a successful Catholic political party never emerged.

In the democratic regime the Catholic Church has gradually become a more vocal participant in the political process. Church representatives weighed in during the writing of the Constitution, expressing their concerns on issues such as abortion and divorce. In the 1979 elections the Church fought hard to prevent a Socialist victory, publishing a number of documents warning of the dangers of a PSOE government. The Church's pugnacious stance on divorce helped spark the breakup of the UCD in the early 1980s. During the Socialist tenure, the Church reacted strongly to proposed changes in education. On the eve of the March 2000 general election the Church angered many Spaniards when it openly endorsed the Popular Party.

Much of the defensive posture adopted by the Church results from its weakening presence in Spanish society.[25] In a survey conducted in 1990, 87 percent of respondents said they were members of a religion (of whom 99 percent were Catholic). However, the data reveal a dramatic decline in religious practice. Only 19 percent of Spaniards in 2002 said they were practicing Catholics and regular churchgoers.[26] Moreover, church attendance is dropping quickly in most urban and wealthy areas and among younger Spaniards. The number of Spaniards dedicating themselves to become priests or nuns is falling precipitously.

Democracy has meant a considerable loss of influence and wealth for the Church. Since 1976 Spanish heads of state no longer appoint Spanish bishops, and the revision of the Spanish-Vatican Concordat in 1979 prepared the groundwork for the separation of Church and state. State support for the Church will eventually be phased out, but no Spanish government has yet been willing to pull the plug entirely. Currently, Spanish taxpayers may opt to dedicate part of their taxes to the Church, but only about one-third of taxpayers do so.

The ability of the Church to influence voter choice appears to be very weak. Few Spaniards believe that religious issues should be considered when voting.[27] Research has also shown that large percentages of Spaniards opposed the official Church policy on a variety of issues. Religion continues to be a very strong cleavage in Spanish politics, but the relationship between religiosity and voting is strongest at the political extremes: The PP does best among the most religious and the United Left does best among atheists. The relationship is weaker in the political center. Indeed, about one-third of the most religious Catholics vote for the PSOE.

The Church, however, continues to be an important actor in Spanish politics. Pronouncements by the Bishops Conference, a top Church leadership body, carry considerable weight and are followed closely by the press. The Church continues to administer about one-third of Spanish schools, though it now has less control over curriculum in many of them. The Church publishes a daily newspaper and owns a radio network. For decades Spaniards have also speculated about the power of *Opus Dei* (God's Work), a secretive Catholic lay organization founded in 1928. During the Francoist regime, this organization rose to prominence in Spanish business and education. Opus Dei members supposedly occupied about a quarter of university professorships during the Franco period. The Opus Dei still runs an important private university, the University of Navarre, and a prestigious business school in Barcelona. Several members of Prime Minister José María Aznar's cabinet had close ties to Opus Dei. In 2001 the Aznar government passed a controversial law requiring that all students in Spanish schools take a graded course on either Catholicism or "world religions." The law was opposed by parent groups, teachers, and unions, and was repealed by the Socialist government elected in 2004.

Other Groups

Since the return of democracy many interest groups have formed, and some have acquired significant political and economic power. One of the most fascinating and unusual examples is the Spanish Organization of the Blind (ONCE). Created by Franco's government in 1939 to employ the many who lost their vision while fighting in the civil war, ONCE was allowed to run tax-exempt lotteries throughout Spain. By 1950, ONCE used the profits to set up a welfare system for its own members. The organization was forced to reorganize and democratize after 1977 but has still managed to control Spanish lotteries. The wealth of ONCE has become immense, and the organization now invests in a plethora of Spanish businesses, including one of Spain's top private television stations. The wealth and power of the organization has led some to question the organization's tax-exempt status.

As in much of Europe, Spaniards have been attracted to a whole host of "single issue" interest groups. However, environmental, peace, and feminist groups, to mention a few, are less developed in Spain than in their European counterparts. The Franco regime's promotion of demobilization and apathy is partly responsible for the relative weakness of these organizations in Spain. Many political activists in the 1960s and 1970s focused their energy on the struggle against Franco, and this tended to weaken single-issue groups. In the 1980s a strong peace movement arose in opposition to Spain's participation in the North Atlantic Treaty Organization, but the decision of the governing Socialists to remain in NATO dealt the movement a major blow.

Polls show that awareness of environmental issues is growing rapidly in Spain. Nevertheless, Spain had no major environmental party until the

1993 creation of *Los Verdes* (Greens), and the Spanish environmental movement has yet to have the kind of impact that has occurred in other parts of Europe in large part because of a lack of strategic and organizational unity in the movement.[28] As noted later in this chapter, Spanish women's groups have had significant success in the 1980s and 1990s, but the results have come more through the efforts of women in the established political parties (especially the Socialist Party) than through independent feminist groups.

ELECTORAL COMPETITION IN SPAIN

The Political Party System

Political parties were banned during the four decades of authoritarian rule in Franco's Spain. The official Francoist National Movement never functioned as a mobilizing party; rather it operated bureaucratically, preempting the political space. Franco vilified modern political parties as parasitic organizations unable to act in the common interest. To a considerable extent, the nature of political parties in contemporary Spain—weak organizations with scant membership—can be explained by this long hiatus in party politics.

Spanish parties have the lowest percentage of the electorate as members in Western Europe. Spain's two largest parties, the PP and PSOE each have only about half a million members.[29] They make relatively little effort to recruit new members. With the exception of the Spanish Communist Party (PCE), no party emerged from Francoism with a strong membership base. Given the clandestine conditions under which parties had to operate during the dictatorship, mass membership was not a goal pursued by Spanish parties. During the transition, hundreds of parties emerged on the left, right, and center of the political system. There were several parties claiming to be Socialist, several Christian Democratic organizations, and numerous parties of the extreme right. In the first elections in 1977, what distinguished these parties most was the popularity and name recognition of key leaders, not the size of their membership. It is also important to remember that the Spanish party system was created

in the 1970s, well into the age of modern mass media. Unlike other European party systems, where traditions of mass membership parties predated the age of electronic media, Spain's party system emerged in an era when image mattered far more than organizational strength. Finally, given the negotiated nature of Spain's transition, the politics of mobilization was discouraged. Party leaders entered into a series of "bargains" with each other, and the building of mass party membership was not seen as facilitating such elite-level bargaining. Spain's political leaders remembered that in the Second Republic radicalized party masses had made such political compromise impossible.

The personalism of Spanish politics and the weak ideological content shares much in common with the trend in European politics as a whole. However, the same factors that limit party membership in Spain exaggerate personalism. Memories of the Spanish Second Republic and the Civil War, still reasonably fresh among older Spaniards, emphasize the dangers of ideology. Four decades of authoritarianism stripped most Spaniards of ideological passion: The regime inculcated Spaniards with an apolitical orientation more than any particular ideological vision. During the transition, the emergence of hundreds of "new" political parties all competing for electoral survival meant that name recognition and simple slogans, rather than complex ideological messages, were at a premium. Personalism was better suited for political campaigns that depended largely on television advertising. Finally, Spanish political leaders purposely restrained themselves from presenting an ideologically charged image, fearing that ideological polarization would threaten the transition to democracy. As a result, political parties espoused vague commitments and once in office wandered far from their official platforms.

The hierarchical and rather authoritarian internal workings of Spanish political parties of today are partially related to the characteristics noted earlier. Low membership facilitates strong internal control by party leaders. The importance of personalism, itself facilitated by ideological weakness, gives party leaders (especially charismatic ones) excessive influence over their parties. Lack of ideology often facilitates the formation of internal factions seeking to impose a stronger ideological vision on the party. Such internal ideological struggles have destroyed a number of political parties, including the Union of the Democratic Center (UCD), the governing party from 1977 to 1981, and have severely weakened others, such as the Spanish Communist Party (PCE). The electorate has consistently punished parties that display internal turmoil. Spain's most successful parties, consequently, have limited internal dissent and imposed strict party discipline. Hierarchical control within parties is facilitated by Spain's closed-list electoral system that gives party leaders (not the voters) control over the order in which party candidates for office appear on electoral lists. The electoral system also discriminates against small nationwide parties, making it more costly for dissatisfied party factions to bolt and form separate organizations. Finally, within the Cortes, there are procedural rules that severely penalize small parties, and that give almost no voice to party backbenchers.

The Major Parties

Spain's political parties have undergone widespread and pervasive changes since the first elections in 1975. In order to simplify the discussion here, the parties are organized into several broad categories: the Communist left, the Socialists, parties of the center and right, and regional parties.

THE COMMUNIST LEFT   During the Second Republic, the *Spanish Communist Party (PCE)* was a marginal electoral force, but it came to play an important role during the Civil War. Under Franco, the PCE, though illegal, was the only opposition force with any real presence inside Spain, conducting some guerrilla operations against the regime in the 1940s and 1950s. As a result, it was singled out for extremely harsh repression by the dictator. By the mid-1950s, the party had almost been eliminated within Spain and many of its leaders were in exile.

In 1956 Santiago Carrillo, the PCE leader, changed the party's strategy to encourage alliances with other democratic forces in order to topple Franco. By the early 1970s, Carrillo was one of Europe's foremost proponents of *Eurocommunism:* He distanced his party from the Soviet Union and from Marxist-Leninist ideology and accepted democratic electoral politics. Carrillo rejected the authoritarianism of both the Franco regime and the Soviet Union. Adolfo Suárez surprisingly legalized the PCE on the eve of the first democratic elections, which infuriated the military and much of the right. However, during the transition the PCE exhibited exemplary behavior. It supported the monarchy, acted moderately and responsibly, and participated in the elite compromises that were required to write the Constitution. The moderate behavior of the PCE undoubtedly aided the consolidation of democracy, but it also alienated many party rank and file who saw the PCE as overly compromising.

The PCE had hoped to dominate the left after the 1977 elections. Instead it polled just under 10 percent, well behind the Socialists. Spanish voters were not entirely convinced of the democratic credentials of the Communists. At the same time, the moderation of the PCE program made it appear similar to the Socialists, robbing the Communists of their distinctiveness. The PCE's electoral failure led to internal dissent. Despite its ideological moderation, the party under Carrillo remained very centralized. Ideological dissidents or critics of Carrillo's leadership style were purged from the party in 1981. Consequently, the PCE lost some of its most talented members, many of whom joined the Socialists. The definitive blow to the PCE occurred in the 1982 general elections. The Communists were drubbed and won only 4 percent of the vote, which was down from almost 11 percent in the previous election. Carrillo stepped down as Communist leader, but the damage had been done. Bitter internal infighting began in 1983 and by 1985 Carrillo had left the party. The pro-Soviet faction of the party bolted as well. As a result of these schisms, PCE membership plummeted from a high of 240,000 in 1978 to only 55,000 in 1991.[30]

The remains of the Eurocommunist wing of the party, together with other leftist parties, formed a coalition called *United Left (IU)*. This coalition was initially formed as an anti-NATO protest movement, uniting Communists, environmentalists, and feminists. After 1986, the IU became the only real leftist opposition to the Socialists, operating as a relentless and sometimes very effective critic of their economic policies. It argued that Socialist neoliberal economic policies disproportionately hurt the poor. The coalition's "green" and feminist emphasis also made it a strong critic of the Socialists in these areas.

After 1986 the IU gradually increased its number of seats, but there was still discontent within the PCE. In February 1988 Julio Anguita, the charismatic head of the PCE in Andalusia (a Communist stronghold), became the PCE leader. Under Anguita the PCE left, the Communists, mounted an energetic attack on the Socialist government over corruption charges. At the same time, Anguita purged most of the Marxist rhetoric from his public discourse. The new image for the PCE and IU paid off. In the 1996 election the IU polled over 10 percent of the vote and won 21 seats, which came close to the 23 seats that the PCE had won at its zenith in 1979. However, given the troubles of the governing Socialists, the failure of the IU to gain more ground is puzzling. Moreover, the success proved short lived: The IU was the biggest loser of the 2000 general elections, dropping 13 of its 21 seats, and ceding its third-place status to the Catalan Minority. The decline continued in 2004, when the IU won only 5 seats and under 5 percent of the vote.

As has been the case for all European Communist parties, the fall of Eastern European communism presented a crisis for PCE. Spain's Communists had long established independence from (and were often openly opposed to) those parties, but many within the PCE began to question whether the party should adopt a new name (as occurred in Italy) and alliance strategy. With its dismal 2004 electoral results, the IU has been relegated to a marginal political role.

THE SOCIALISTS   The *Spanish Socialist Workers Party (PSOE)* has been a dominant force during the first two and a half decades of Spanish democracy.[31] Its long tenure in government—from 1982 to 1996—and its internal unity and discipline have made it highly successful.

During the Second Republic the PSOE became the largest single party in Spain. However, it was badly divided between reformist social democrats (who were strongly anti-Communist and deeply committed to democratic procedures) and revolutionary socialists (whose main commitment was to the working class, and whose loyalty to the democratic Republic was "conditional"). The behavior of many Socialist leaders during the Republic was, in the words of Juan Linz, "accidentalist": They supported democracy only if it delivered the specific policy outcomes (workers' rights and the building of socialism) that they desired.[32] When the right won the elections of 1934, many of these leaders turned against the Republic and called for revolution. The PSOE spearheaded a protracted armed uprising by workers in northern Spain. In the eyes of many contemporary Spanish socialist intellectuals, the divisions within the PSOE and the weak commitment to parliamentary rule contributed to the downfall of democracy and the rise of authoritarian rule. As a result, the PSOE suffered four decades of repression and exile during Franco's rule.

Throughout most of the Franco regime, the bulk of the Socialist leaders remained in exile, mainly in France and Mexico. The Socialists who remained in Spain attempting to reorganize were eclipsed by the better organized PCE. Beginning in the 1950s, however, a new generation of PSOE leaders based inside Spain began to revive the party. In 1974 a group of young militants, led by Felipe González, wrested control of the PSOE. Under its new leaders, the party made spectacular gains in organizational strength from 1974 to the first elections in 1977. During that period its membership grew from 3,500 to 51,000, and then doubled again by 1979.[33]

Between 1974 and 1977 the PSOE's young leadership espoused radical Marxist beliefs. Stylistically, these leaders were trained in the combative rhetoric of the underground struggle against Franco, and they appeared far more leftist than the conservative PSOE in exile. As long as Franco's regime was intact, the radicalism of the PSOE platform was almost unavoidable. The rapid growth of PSOE membership had pushed the party rank and file to the left, and the December 1976 Party Congress adopted a radical socialist platform. Yet, the young PSOE leadership moved toward the center. After four decades of Francoist rule, the PSOE leadership came to realize that a highly ideological campaign would not win votes. The PSOE leaders, unlike their predecessors in the Second Republic, recognized that the consolidation of democracy was more important than ideological purity.

The PSOE's success in the first general elections exceeded all expectations: The Socialists took second place, with 28.5 percent of the vote and 33.7 percent of the seats in the Congress of Deputies (see Table 8.2). It trounced the PCE and clearly established itself as the hegemonic force on the left. Thus, the PSOE earned the right to play a large role in the writing of the new constitution. During the elite-level negotiations over the Constitution and the economy, the PSOE leadership abandoned much of its official platform, angering the party's left. PSOE leaders were convinced that a moderation of party ideology and tighter party discipline were needed to achieve an electoral breakthrough. Such changes were imposed at an Emergency Congress in 1979. Most important was the elimination of the Marxist, proletarian, and class-based definition of the party, and the affirmation of ideological pluralism within the PSOE. The party purged some of its more radical proposals from its electoral platform and pledged to become more of an interclass "catch-all" party. At the party's Twenty-Ninth Congress in October 1981, the PSOE presented itself as a unified, moderate political party. Delegates included far fewer members of the working class, and the party left was virtually excluded from the Congress. González and his entire executive committee were reelected with almost no opposition.

The more moderate party platform and the PSOE's virtual elimination of internal dissent (especially when contrasted with the internal chaos in Spain's other major parties) paid huge dividends in the 1982 elections. The PSOE victory was the first instance of party alternation in the new democracy and produced the first government that contained no former Francoist leader. It also was the first single-party majority government in Spain's history. The dimensions of the victory were unprecedented. The PSOE won 48.4 percent of the valid votes and 57.7 percent of the seats in the Congress of Deputies.

The new Socialist government gained an unprecedented degree of control in a system that gives majoritarian governments extraordinary power. From the start of its term, the Socialists moved quickly to pursue a controversial neoliberal macroeconomic policy that clearly favored integration of Spain into the world economy, economic growth, and the building of infrastructure over full employment. The Socialists spent lavishly for the 1992 World's Fair in Seville and the Barcelona Olympics, including a controversial high-speed train from Seville to Madrid.

The hegemony enjoyed by the PSOE resulted in an aloofness and arrogance on the part of the government. Scandals involving the abuse of public offices continued to surface. Spaniards were shocked when in 1985 González and his family vacationed on Franco's former yacht. Throughout the 1980s the PSOE was dogged by accusations that it had raised funds illegally. In 1988 the government-appointed head of state radio and television was accused of

TABLE 8.2 Seats in the Congress of Deputies, 1977–2004

	1977	1979	1982	1986	1989	1993	1996	2000	2004
AP/CP/PP	16	9	106	105	106	141	157	183	148
UCD/CDS	166	168	12	19	14	0	—	—	—
PSOE	118	121	202	184	176	159	140	125	164
PCE/IU	20	23	4	7	17	18	21	8	5
CIU	2	8	12	18	18	17	16	15	10
PNV	2	7	8	6	5	5	5	7	7
Others	26	14	6	11	14	10	11	15	13
Total seats	350	350	350	350	350	350	350	350	350

Source: www.elpais.es

spending tax dollars to buy clothes and jewelry for herself and for friends. In 1989, the deputy prime minister (and deputy leader of the PSOE) resigned because his brother was accused of influence peddling. Perhaps the most damaging scandal involved a secret government-run death squad aimed at Basque terrorists, for which a number of top Socialist officials were jailed. By the 1993 elections, the PSOE's majority was in jeopardy. The Socialists kept their status as the largest party but fell 17 seats short of a majority. The PSOE had to depend on centrist regional parties to prop up a minority government, and a third of the members of the new cabinet did not even belong to the PSOE.

The PSOE is structured much like other Social Democratic parties in Europe, but it is unusually centralized. It is formally federal, with the local *agrupación* (party branch) as its primary structure, electing provincial and regional bodies. In 1979 the party leadership embraced a shift to a much more disciplined party structure. Rule changes were enacted to inhibit factionalism and to reinforce party stability. After the PSOE defeat in the 1996 elections many members felt that the Socialist leadership had gotten out of touch with the rank and file. Consequently, the PSOE's 1997 Party Congress adopted a primary election system for candidates for local and regional posts, and this was later extended to the selection of Socialist candidates for head of government. The use of party primaries to select candidates was a first for Spanish political parties, and it augured well for an internal democratization of the PSOE. After the Socialists lost power in 1996 the party continued to struggle at the polls.

The PSOE was drubbed in the 2000 elections—it lost 15 seats in the lower house, and over 1 million votes—leading to an internal struggle for power. In July 2000, the Socialists elected 39-year-old *José Luis Rodríguez Zapatero* as their new leader. Zapatero, who in 1986 had become the youngest member of parliament ever, represents a new generation of Socialist "whiz kids" who seek to further democratize party institutions and to resuscitate the PSOE's image. He quickly moved to bring in new blood to the PSOE leadership team and to repair damaged relations with the socialist trade unions. His party's upset victory in the March 2004 elec-

tions propelled him to the forefront of Spanish politics rather quickly. After nine years of conservative rule, the new prime minister pledged to undertake a series of social reforms, including the legalization of gay marriage and the easing of abortion restrictions. His first foreign policy move was to withdraw Spanish troops from Iraq.

PARTIES OF THE CENTER On the eve of Spain's first elections in 1977, the political center was in disarray, with countless groups claiming to be "centrist." These included timid Francoist reformers who emerged in the twilight of the Franco regime, anti-Franco opposition figures, Christian Democrats, liberals, monarchists, and Social Democrats. In early 1977 a weak coalition of these groups was organized, to compete with both the Francoist political right and the democratic left. The coalition lacked a well-known leader and was beset by political squabbling. On the eve of the historic June 1977 elections, Adolfo Suárez, the Francoist bureaucrat responsible for stewarding the transition to democracy, agreed to lead this coalition, which took the name *Union of the Democratic Center (UCD)*.

The UCD experiment was initially very successful. Backed by the still powerful state media and bureaucracy, and fronted by Spain's most popular and charismatic leader, the UCD easily won the first two democratic elections. Running campaigns based solely on the image of its popular leader, the UCD advocated a cautious support for devolution of power to the regions, a separation of church and state, military reform, and economic restructuring. It polled well among rural voters, women, and Catholics. In retrospect, these victories were extremely important for the viability of Spanish democracy. The UCD brought to power a coalition of Francoist reformers and moderate democratic opposition members, thus bridging the gap between authoritarianism and democracy. It proved that those who had played a role in the Francoist regime could have a place in the new democracy. Indeed, in the first democratic legislature 44 UCD members of the Congress of Deputies were former members of the Francoist legislature, and 44 percent of the party's members were officeholders (mostly middle-level bureaucrats) under Franco.[34] Suárez and the UCD were thus in an ideal position to negotiate a democratic constitution that could appeal to a wide range of voters.

Once in power, however, the UCD proved to be unwieldy. The ideological diversity of "centrists" was a fatal flaw, especially for a party that had to oversee constitutional compromise. The tension between the Christian Democratic UCD right and the Social Democratic left eventually tore the party apart. Suárez had alienated sectors of the military because of his role in the transition, and his government was unable to discipline the increasingly restive armed forces. Suárez resigned in January 1981, after he failed to acquire greater control over squabbling party leaders. The attempted military coup of February 23, 1981, accelerated the intramural chaos in the UCD. Soon the UCD Social Democrats bolted the party, some joining the PSOE, while some UCD Christian Democrats joined the rightist Popular Alliance. The 1982 elections marked one of the largest electoral defeats of a governing party in Spain's electoral history and dealt the UCD, which dropped from 168 seats to only 11, a deathblow.

Since the demise of the UCD, no centrist party has been able to achieve electoral success. The main reason has been that after the Socialist victory in 1982 the centrist political space grew smaller. The PSOE's move toward the center deprived other parties of that space, and the right's moderation and drift toward the political mainstream had a similar effect.

Parties of the Right   Spanish parties of the right have a long history of weakness and disunity. Some have argued that the Spanish right has never had to organize given that its historical interests have usually been well protected. When its interests were threatened the Spanish right supported authoritarian rule. During the Second Republic, the main party of the right eventually supported Francoist authoritarianism.

After 1977 the Spanish right was confronted with a difficult problem. It was initially unable and unwilling to distance itself from the Franco regime, and that identification hurt it at the polls. Attempts by rightist leaders to draw on the legacy of Spanish conservatism in the late nineteenth and early twentieth centuries had little resonance.

Spain's main conservative party, the Partido Popular (Popular Party, PP) began as the Popular Alliance (AP) in October 1976, drawing recruits largely from the former top-level apparatus of the Francoist state. Manuel Fraga, a well-known minister under Franco, led the party. The well-organized and well-funded AP had high hopes for electoral success until Adolfo Suárez and UCD entered the 1977 electoral campaign. Compared with the UCD and the youthful Suárez, Fraga and his party appeared more authoritarian and less committed to democracy. The AP campaign stressed the need for order and continuity. It accepted regional autonomy but rejected federalism or regional independence. It opposed divorce and abortion, and advocated support for the police and armed forces. The AP performed poorly in the first democratic elections, winning only 16 seats of 350 in the Congress of Deputies, with only 8 percent of the vote. In the Basque Country and Catalonia, the AP won almost no support.

In retrospect it is clear that the post-Francoist right faced some serious obstacles. The right might have expected active support from the Catholic Church, but the Church (itself divided) refused to endorse any one political party. A more serious obstacle was the regional question. The Spanish right has a long history of opposing political decentralization, and therefore conservatives in Spain's most important regions have backed regional instead of Madrid-based conservative parties. The absence of a single party capable of representing national and regional conservatives has weakened the right.

The dismal electoral results of 1977 encouraged the AP to ally with two small centrist parties (one Liberal and one Christian Democratic), under the name Popular Coalition (CP). Despite the reorganization, the CP won only nine seats in the Congress of Deputies and 6 percent of the vote in 1979, leading many observers to predict the disappearance of the right altogether. This might have been the outcome had the governing UCD not suddenly disintegrated in the 1982 elections. The Popular Coalition in alliance with regional conservative parties reaped the benefits, winning 26 percent of the vote and 107 seats in the Congress of Deputies. About half of former UCD voters switched to the AP in 1982.[35] Despite the raised expectations, the CP failed to improve on its 1982 performance in the

1986 general elections, and the rightist coalition disbanded.

In 1988 the AP once again attempted to polish its image. It took a new name, the *Popular Party (PP)*, and sought to integrate former UCD leaders, but it failed to improve its percentage of the vote much in the 1989 elections. In 1990 the PP selected a new leader, *José María Aznar*, the young president of the Castilla-León Autonomous Community. Aznar promoted a modern Christian Democratic image and tried to purge the party of its extreme right. He also waged a relentless campaign against PSOE corruption. His steady, if not flamboyant, leadership of the PP paid dividends in the 1993 elections when the party made significant gains, and in the 1996 elections when the PP finally took power. In the 1980s the right had moved from being a vehicle for former Francoist elite to a more mainstream party. The PP's membership rose from 5,000 members in 1979 to 220,000 by October 1986, and younger Spaniards made up much of the new membership. The PP victory in the 1996 general elections finally enabled the Spanish right to demonstrate its credentials as a modern, democratic party.

Aznar's first term in office allayed any fears that Spanish conservatives could not be trusted to uphold democratic rule. Under the PP Spain prospered, with annual growth rates averaging 3 percent, and unemployment fell by 8 percent. Aznar's willingness to enter into negotiation with Basque nationalists, coupled with his hard line during the bargaining process, won him much support. Voters in the March 2000 elections rewarded the PP. It became the first conservative party in Spanish history to win an absolute majority of legislative seats (see Table 8.2).

During his eight years in office Aznar provided a stark contrast to his flamboyant predecessor. However, like González, Aznar kept an iron grip on his party, even handpicking his successor (Mariano Rajoy) to head the PP ticket in the 2004 elections after Aznar decided not to pursue a third term. Aznar can take credit for almost a decade of rapid economic growth and real progress in the war against Basque terrorism. His aloof style, his conservative social policies, and especially his support for the invasion to remove Saddam Hussein's regime in Iraq, all contributed to a decline in his popularity and the PP's loss in the 2004 elections.

CATALONIAN PARTIES Spain's regional parties have played an important role in its democratic system, both within the Autonomous Communities, and to a lesser extent in the national party system. It is impossible here to cover all the regional groups, but it is important to touch on the major parties in the two most important regions, Catalonia and the Basque Country.

As is clear from Table 8.3, the Catalonian party system has been fairly stable from the start, dominated by the Democratic Convergence of Catalonia (CDC), which has run in elections together with a smaller group, the Democratic Union of Catalonia (UDC) in a coalition called *Convergence and Union*, or *CiU*. The CDC was founded in 1974 near the end of the Francoist regime, when political associations were being tolerated. CiU was until recently the leading

TABLE 8.3 Percentage of Votes (and Number of Seats) in the Catalonian Legislature, 1980–2003

	1980	1984	1988	1992	1995	1999	2003
CiU (Centrist Nationalists)	28 (43)	47 (72)	46 (69)	41 (70)	41 (60)	38 (56)	30.9 (46)
PP (National Conservatives)	13 (18)	8 (11)	9 (9)	7 (7)	15 (17)	10 (12)	11.8 (15)
ERC (Republican Left of Catalonia)	9 (14)	4 (5)	4 (6)	8 (11)	10 (13)	9 (12)	16.4 (23)
PSC-PSOE (Catalonian Socialists)	22 (33)	30 (41)	30 (42)	28 (40)	25 (34)	38 (52)	31.1 (42)
PSUC/IC/ICV (Catalonian Communists-United Left and Greens)	19 (25)	6 (6)	8 (9)	7 (7)	10 (11)	3 (3)	7.3 (9)

Source: Anuario El País, various years and www.elmundo.es.

electoral force in Catalonia, and it is currently the third largest electoral force in the national legislature.

The CiU has operated very much as a Catalonian "catch-all" party of the center. Its founder, Jordi Pujol, dominated it from the start. Pujol spent two years in jail under Franco, and he later became a leading force behind the Banca Catalana, a regional bank. Pujol won the first elections to the restored *Generalitat* (Catalonian Government) in 1980, and five subsequent elections. Pujol's political longevity gave him immense prestige within Catalonia and considerable respect nationwide. However, his active promotion of Catalonian interests abroad often angered Madrid. After the March 1996 elections, he lent his party's support to the PP government of Aznar despite the Spanish right's historical opposition to regional devolution. He was able to exact promises from the PP regarding regional devolution. However, Pujol always kept his distance from the national government, steadfastly refusing to accept cabinet positions.

The CiU is best viewed as a centrist political party with a blend of Christian Democratic and nationalist ideology. It advocates a more formally federal system but has come to accept the system of Autonomous Communities. It is a party that has also represented the small- and medium-sized Catalonian bourgeoisie. Despite its early flirtation with social democratic ideas, it has generally promoted market economics and free enterprise. A main emphasis of the CiU, and an area where it has had a significant impact, is its policy to restore the Catalan language to a position of dominance in Catalonia. By the mid-1980s, over 85 percent of the schools in the region offered some classes in Catalan, compared with about 3 percent at the start of the democratic period. In 2003 the Catalan Socialists, led by former Barcelona mayor Pascal Maragal, were able to unseat the CiU and form a regional coalition government with the left-nationalist Esquerra Republicana de Catalunya (Catalan Republican Left, ERC).

Basque Parties Unlike the Catalonian party system, the situation in the Basque Country has been very volatile and extremely polarized. As in Catalonia, the dominant party in the region has been a centrist force, the *Basque Nationalist Party (PNV)*.

The PNV was an important regional force during the Second Republic, and it had a long history of opposition to and fierce repression by Franco during the authoritarian regime. Partially due to this painful history, and partially due to a strong and violent pro-independence movement, the PNV has been less accepting of the Autonomous Community status than the CiU in Catalonia. Unlike the CiU, the PNV formally opposed the Constitution of 1978.

The PNV president of the Basque Country since 1999, Juan José Ibarretxe has proposed a referendum on the right to self-determination (though not necessarily independence) for the Basque Country, and has called for the unilateral creation of a "free associated state" with ties to Spain. That plan was strongly opposed by both the PP and the PSOE. The PNV has governed the Basque Country since the approval of the Basque Autonomy Statute in 1979, but since 1986 it has done so in coalition with other parties. The PNV was badly weakened by a party split in 1985. In national elections, the PNV has consistently made a strong showing, and like the CiU in Catalonia, it has done best when national centrist parties are weakest (see Table 8.4). In the 2001 elections it experienced a breakthrough, winning 42.7 percent of the vote in the Basque Country. However, the PNV and the planned referendum on independence were dealt a severe blow in the April 2005 regional elections. The PNV lost its majority in the regional legislature, and the anti-referendum opposition made important gains.

In contrast to Catalonia, there has been a consistently strong nationalist left presence in the Basque Country. The Euskadiko Euskerra (EE), or Basque Left, represented the regional left until it split during the transition to democracy. It lost much of its support to the Radical Basque Left party, *Herri Batasuna (HB)*, the political arm of the terrorist organization ETA. Unlike the other Basque parties, the HB (renamed Euskal Herritarrok, or EH, in 1998) is an antisystem party, and like ETA it promotes the independence of the region from Spain. It has done surprisingly well in regional and national elections, and won seats in every national election between 1979 and 1996, peaking with five deputies in 1986. Initially its elected members of the national parliament refused to occupy their

TABLE 8.4   Percentage of Votes (and Number of Seats) in Basque Elections, 1980–2005

	1980	1984	1988	1992	1994	1998	2001	2005
PNV (Basque National Party)	38 (25)	42 (32)	24 (17)	29 (22)	29 (22)	30 (21)	42.7 (33)	38.6 (29)
EE (Basque Left)	10 (6)	8 (6)	11 (9)	8 (6)	—(—)	—	—	
HB (Radical Basque Left)	17 (11)	15 (11)	18 (13)	18 (13)	16 (11)	18 (14)	10.1 (7)	12.5 (9)
EA (Moderate Breakaway from PNV)	—(—)	—(—)	16 (13)	11 (9)	10 (8)	9 (6)	—	
PSE-PSOE (Socialists)	14 (9)	23 (19)	22 (19)	20 (16)	17 (12)	18 (14)	17.8 (13)	22.6 (18)
PCE/IU (Communists)	4 (1)	1 (0)	1 (0)	1 (0)	9 (6)	6 (2)	5.5 (3)	5.4 (3)
National Right (PP)	13 (8)	9 (7)	8 (4)	9 (6)	14 (11)	20 (16)	23.0 (19)	17.3 (15)

Source: Anuario El País, various years, www.elmundo.es, and www.elpais.es.

seats as a sign of protest against the Spanish state. When HB deputies finally agreed to take their seats in 1989, they were expelled from the legislature for refusing to take the required oath to the Constitution. After 1986 the HB strength in national elections waned, and it won only two seats in the 1993 and 1996 elections. HB's successor, EH, boycotted the 2000 general elections and encouraged voters to abstain. Shortly before the 2001 Basque elections Spain's highest court upheld a government ban of EH. In the 2005 regional elections the radical Basque left, running under yet another moniker, continued to garner about a tenth of the vote.

The Electoral System

Spain's electoral system was one of the many compromises that resulted from the negotiated transition to democracy. Adolfo Suárez negotiated the electoral laws with major opposition groups on the eve of the transition to democracy. The 1978 Constitution made some minor changes to the electoral law, but left it mostly intact. The left insisted on the use of proportional representation, while the right advocated a single-member district/plurality system. The compromise called for proportional representation for the Congress of Deputies, but with strong "corrective" measures to favor the major parties and to prevent excessive fragmentation of the legislature. Conservatives won some additional victories. A plurality system was adopted for the Senate, and the voting age was set at 21, though it was reduced to 18 in 1979.

Spain's Congress of Deputies employs a modified system of proportional representation, using Spain's 50 unevenly sized provinces (generally smaller than the ACs) as constituencies. All provinces, regardless of size, receive a minimum of two deputies in the lower house, then additional seats for each 144,500 citizens. Conservatives initially saw this electoral system as favorable, since urban areas that were thought to favor the left were underrepresented. In the first democratic elections the small size of electoral districts and the overrepresentation of conservative rural districts made it easier for the UCD to win elections. Spain's electoral system favors large parties over small ones, especially in smaller electoral districts. It also favors small parties whose vote is concentrated geographically, as is the case with Spain's many regional parties. Spanish parties must win over 3 percent of the vote to win seats in the legislature, a measure that also limits the success of small parties. Spain's electoral system is, in the words of one scholar, "strikingly unproportional."[36]

Elections for the Congress of Deputies employ the closed list system of presenting candidates: The order and content of party lists are set by party leaders, not by voters. Moreover, candidates on party lists are not required to be members of that party. Both these provisions have weakened party rank and file vis-à-vis party leaders. For elections to the Senate, voters select up to three names from a single list of all candidates who run in a given province, and the recipients with the most votes are elected.

In addition, some Senators are appointed directly by the Autonomous Communities.

The electoral system for the Cortes has had its intended outcome. It has often produced governments with a majority or plurality large enough to govern alone. Spain's party system is still highly fragmented, but it would undoubtedly be more so were it not for the electoral laws. Small parties find it difficult to survive on the national level as a result of both the electoral system and Spain's system of party finance. On the national level at least, two large parties have dominated.

Strict laws govern the financing of political parties, but these laws have not been followed very closely during the first two decades of Spanish democracy. Spain's political parties can raise their funds through public financing, membership dues, and strictly limited donations. The state reimburses parties for electoral expenses based on the number of seats they win in an election. The system clearly favors large incumbent parties, since campaign funds must be raised up front, often by bank loans. Since 1987, a parliamentary Audit Commission inspects party finances, but critics have argued that financing rules have been only sporadically enforced.[37] A series of party financing scandals made headlines in the 1980s and early 1990s as Spanish parties ran up gigantic debts. The incessant schedule of elections (national, regional, municipal, and European) began to take its toll on party coffers. With few dues-paying members and almost no unpaid volunteers, both major parties were tempted to trade political favors for campaign contributions.

Sources of Party Support

Most scholars have argued that social class is not an important basis of party support in Spanish democracy, despite the fact that inequality in Spain ranks among the highest in Europe. They noted that the growth of a large middle class, the increased social mobility since the 1960s, and the long tenure in power of the Socialist Party (which enjoyed strong support from all social classes) have all helped to weaken this once divisive cleavage. As noted in Table 8.5, the income levels of party supporters is not dramatically different across parties, although slightly more PP supporters are in the highest income level than are PSOE supporters.

Several studies point to the surprising continued strength of the religious cleavage in Spanish politics. McDonough and his colleagues found that religion is a much stronger cleavage than class or region, even though the latter two are still important, and the religious cleavage appears to have been somewhat resistant to economic and social modernization. Table 8.5 reveals that PSOE supporters are almost twice as likely as PP supporters to say that they never or hardly ever attend church, while supporters of the left-wing IU are three times as likely to give that response. At the same time, Spanish society has rapidly become more secularized. The percentage of Spaniards who described themselves as either "very good Catholics" or "Practicing Catholics" dropped from 64 percent in 1970 to 32 percent in 2002.[38] About one-half of Spaniards report going to church only once a year or less. Moreover, when it comes to politics, religious values no longer are of concern to the overwhelming majority of the public. Religion no longer polarizes Spanish political culture as it once did. By the mid-1990s, McDonough and his colleagues concluded that "religious attachments have little do with popular attitudes toward democracy or toward government in Spain. . . . The day of mobilization against the political system on the basis of religion seems to be over."[39] Moreover, the importance of the religious cleavage is mitigated by the fact that those who are most religious tend to participate less both in conventional political behavior (such as voting and party militancy) and also in protest activities. Finally, most studies of Spanish public opinion have shown that the intensity of social cleavages diminishes among younger Spaniards. A more secular and less divided Spain appears to be the way of the future.

Campaigns and Elections

Unlike the United States, Spanish citizens of voting age are automatically registered to vote. The Central Electoral Junta is responsible for drawing up a list of eligible voters. An Electoral College, made up by cit-

TABLE 8.5   Social Bases of Party Support in Spain, 2000

		PP	PSOE	IU	CIU	PNV	Others	Abstain or No Vote
Gender	Male	47.2	52.8	66.7	40.7	52.0	45.3	49.7
	Female	52.8	47.2	33.3	59.3	48.0	54.7	50.3
	Total	100.0	100.0	100.0	100.0	100.0	100.0	100.0
Age	18–29	16.7	20.4	30.9	18.5	4.0	27.6	35.4
	30–49	33.5	36.6	48.0	27.8	40.0	23.5	38.5
	50+	49.8	43.1	21.1	53.7	56.0	39.9	26.1
	Total	100.0	100.0	100.0	100.0	100.0	100.0	100.0
Income Level	Lower	33.1	40.4	23.7	23.5	6.3	44.3	24.8
	Middle	38.9	40.4	36.1	50.0	62.5	33.1	38.2
	Higher	28.0	25.4	40.2	26.5	31.3	22.6	23.8
	Total	100.0	100.0	100.0	100.0	100.0	100.0	100.0
Education Level	Lower	53.5	56.1	39.0	57.4	32.0	46.5	43.8
	Middle	30.7	32.8	38.3	38.9	56.0	38.2	35.6
	Higher	15.8	11.1	22.8	3.7	12.0	15.3	20.6
	Total	100.0	100.0	100.0	100.0	100.0	100.0	100.0
Church Attendance	Seldom or Never	28.3	49.5	70.7	43.4	32.0	44.2	52.8
	Occasionally	20.1	21.3	19.5	24.5	20.0	19.6	18.9
	Regularly	51.7	29.2	9.8	32.1	48.0	36.2	28.3
	Total	100.0	100.0	100.0	100.0	100.0	100.0	100.0

Source: Calculated from data contained in World Values Survey, 1999–2001.

izens chosen randomly, counts the votes and oversees elections. Ultimately, the Constitutional Court is responsible for ensuring that elections are free and fair. As can be seen in Figure 8.5, Spaniards turn out to vote in large numbers, despite the daunting frequency with which elections are held. In 2004 voter turnout was a very high 77.2 percent.

Spanish electoral campaigns are short affairs. Until 1994, campaigns lasted three weeks, but since then they have been reduced to only two weeks, in order to save time and money. The day before elections is designated a "day of reflection," and all advertisements and campaign activities are banned. In the early years of Spanish democracy, parties used mass rallies to build enthusiasm. In recent years, such mass electoral events have become rarities, and parties rely heavily on the mass media to get out the word. Spanish parties are allocated free time on tele-

vision according to their performance in the last election, thus favoring incumbents. Both the UCD and PSOE were criticized when in office for using the state media to enhance their political fortunes. The recent appearance of private television and radio would appear to have limited somewhat the ability of governments to manipulate the media in their favor. A recent innovation that reflects the growing importance of television in electoral campaigns is the televised debate between party leaders. In the 1993 electoral campaign, Felipe González and José María Aznar engaged in a series of debates that drew a huge national audience, and that did much to enhance the image of the little-known Aznar.

Spain's first electoral campaign in 1977 was a mild affair. Given the fragility of the transition to democracy, political elites from the major parties went out of their way not to polarize the political

FIGURE 8.5   Voting Turnout, 1977–2004

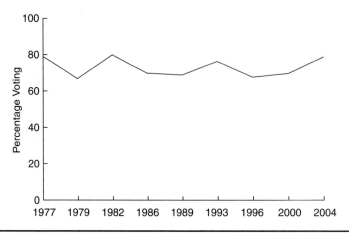

Source: *Anuario El Pais* (1994, 1995); the figure presents the actual voters as a percentage of potential voters.

environment. Campaigns seemed drab and devoid of much content. There was relatively little in the way of personal attacks. In the 1979 electoral campaign Suárez shocked the opposition by launching a last-minute attack on the PSOE aimed at creating fears about a leftist victory. Since then, campaigns have tended to be more hard-nosed. During the Socialist tenure in office, opposition candidates harped on PSOE abuses of power, and there was more mudslinging. As its majority slipped away, the PSOE attempted to raise fears about a victory of the right, linking that group to the Francoist era.

The 2000 electoral campaign was relatively lackluster. The PP electoral slogan was *vamos a mas* ("Let's Take It to the Next Level"). The PP bitterly attacked the last-minute electoral pact between the PSOE and the IU, charging that a leftist government would damage Spain's relations with the EU and threaten Spain's economic growth. Moreover, during the campaign Aznar predicted that the coalition partners would be unable to work together. Resting on a comfortable lead in the polls, Aznar refused to engage in televised debates. The leftist coalition adopted the slogan *lo próximo* ("Coming Soon"), blamed Aznar for a growing concentration of income, called for a 35-hour work week, and proposed a tax on windfall profits accrued by privatized enterprises.

The 2004 campaign featured new candidates at the head of two leading parties. Counting on his comfortable lead in the polls, PP candidate Mariano Rajoy refused to debate his Socialist opponent, a move that some believe damaged Rajoy's candidacy. Meanwhile, Socialist leader José Luis Rodríguez Zapatero hammered the governing conservatives on a whole host of issues ranging from the U.S.-led invasion of Iraq to PP's controversial National Water Plan. The Madrid terrorist bombings, only three days before the elections, cast a pall over what had been a hard-fought campaign.

The Party System

During the first two decades of democracy, there was constant change in Spain's party system, with parties rising and falling almost overnight. The presence of separate regional party systems in some of Spain's most important Autonomous Communities makes any simple characterization of the Spanish party system very elusive. In several recent elections these regional parties have played a crucial role in supporting minority governments of one of the two major parties.

However, it is possible to point to some constant features of Spain's party system. First, since 1979 two major parties (though not always the same two) have dominated the electoral landscape (see again

Table 8.2). In every general election between 1977 and 2004, the two largest parties have won over 80 percent of the seats (the figure in 2004 was 89 percent). Between 1977 and 1981, the UCD and PSOE were dominant; since then the PP and PSOE have dominated. This trend appears to consolidate with the PP victory of 1996, which put to rest fears that the Spanish right was incapable of contributing to democracy.

Second, there has been a growing fragmentation of the vote and a steady rise in regional parties throughout Spain. The success of such parties, which are largely middle-of-the-road, goes hand in hand with the inability of a national centrist party to achieve electoral success since the demise of UCD. Regional parties won only 7 percent of seats in the lower house in 1977, but in recent elections this percentage has risen to about 10 percent.

Third, despite the fluctuation in the party system, the Spanish electorate has remained remarkably stable. Opinion research consistently shows that Spanish voters are clustered just to the right or left of center.[40] With the exception of the Basque Country (where antisystem parties have consistently drawn significant support), Spain's party system is less polarized than those of many other European countries.

Consequently, a fourth feature of the party system is the failure of national parties that are perceived to be on the political extremes. The PCE (and later the IU) was unable to convince voters that it had moved toward the center, and as a result was condemned to no more than one-tenth of the vote (in the 2004 elections it received under 5 percent). The PP, in contrast, has left behind an older generation of leaders identified with Franco and moderated its image. Even in the Basque Country only a relatively small minority (about 10 percent) has backed radical nationalist parties.

Fifth, as noted earlier, Spaniards are not very attached to political parties, and they have comparatively weak party identification, partly a result of the changing party landscape during the first decades of democracy.[41] Spanish political parties have very few members and are organizationally very weak. Consequently, Spaniards place great weight on the popularity of party leaders, and image means a great deal.

Studies of electoral volatility (shifts in individual voting behavior from one election to the next) show that the change in Spanish parties has not mirrored a change in voter orientation. Morlino found that, excluding the watershed election of 1982, the volatility of the Spanish voters was not much higher than the average in other European elections.[42] A more specific measure of voting change is "interbloc" volatility, which is a shift from right-center to left voting, or vice versa. Spain has had high total volatility, but very low levels of interbloc volatility. Even in the party system realignment of 1982, relatively few voters crossed the divide between left and right.

The 1996 electoral results did little to change this description of the Spanish party system. The PSOE actually received more votes than in 1993, but failed to win enough seats to form a government with the IU or the Catalan CiU. The PP gained 4 percent in its vote, but fell 19 seats short of a majority. Regional parties, like the CiU in Catalonia and the National Galician Bloc (BNG) in Galicia, made important gains. The IU lost three seats and fell below 10 percent of the vote, confirming that most Spaniards view it as being too far left.

The 2000 elections consolidated the PP's control of government (Figure 8.6). The Conservatives won an absolute majority, and the PSOE and IU both suffered serious setbacks. The PP even won a number of electoral districts in Andalusia, the traditional Socialist stronghold. The Basque PNV gained two seats, and a number of small regional parties gained seats in the legislature. The 2004 elections, held three days after Spain's worst-ever terrorist attack, ended the PP's eight-year control of government. The PP lost almost 7 percent of its 2000 vote and dropped 35 seats. The Socialists were the biggest winners but fell 12 seats short of a majority in the lower house. The PSOE formed a minority government that depends on the support of regional (especially Catalan) parties. The leftist IU continued its decline, losing half its 2000 vote and half its seats.

POLICY PERFORMANCE AND OUTCOMES

Do politics matter? Does public policy change when there is a change in political regime? The transition from Francoist authoritarianism to democracy in Spain provides an opportunity to examine this question. There has been a dramatic

FIGURE 8.6   Vote Shares in Congress of Deputies Elections, 2000 and 2004

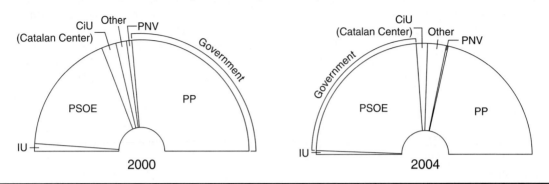

Source: Ministerio del Interior.

Box 8.5   Terrorism and Democratic Elections

Early in the morning of March 11, 2004, a series of explosions destroyed several commuter trains in Madrid. The acts of terror killed 191 people and injured over 1,500. In a country all too accustomed to terrorist acts perpetrated by Basque nationalists, the March 2004 attacks stood out as the worst single act of terrorism in Spanish history. The Aznar government, backed by the state-owned media, initially blamed ETA for the massacre, and it stubbornly stuck to this interpretation even as evidence mounted that Islamic radicals were responsible. On the eve of general elections many Spaniards suspected that Aznar's government was trying to capitalize on his party's tough anti-ETA policies while diverting attention away from his very unpopu-

lar support for the U.S.-led invasion and occupation of Iraq. Only three days after the attacks, Spanish voters handed Aznar's Conservatives a stunning defeat. Some foreign observers called the vote a victory for terrorism, arguing that the violence had provided a last-minute boost for Spain's Socialist Party, which had openly opposed Spain's role in the occupation of Iraq. Others countered that the Conservatives were punished for having falsely blamed ETA for the bombings and for having long pursued a foreign policy that was opposed by a vast majority of Spaniards. Still others questioned whether democracies should conduct national elections in the immediate aftermath of such traumatic attacks.

shift in public policy outputs between the two regimes. Under Franco, Spain was far below other Western industrialized states in its levels of taxation and state public spending. As a result, the provision of many public services approached third world levels. By the mid-1980s, after only a decade of democracy, Spain's public policy outputs were very close to the European norm. Figure 8.7 compares some measures of public policy outputs during two regimes.

The Size and Scope of Spanish Government

Spain is often identified with strong leaders like Ferdinand and Isabel, and Francisco Franco. Historically, however, the Spanish state was weak compared to other European nations. It often was unable to collect taxes or enforce laws. Even dictatorships were far from all-encompassing in their power. Franco shelved the totalitarian project pro-

FIGURE 8.7   Patterns of Policy
Development Across Regimes

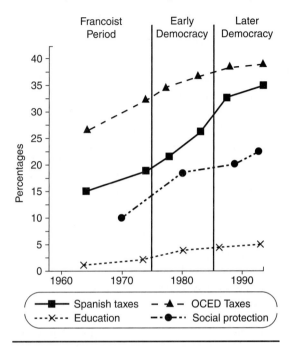

Source: Richard Gunther, "The Impact of Regime Change on Public Policy: The Case of Spain," *Journal of Public Policy* 16, No. 2 (1996): 177, 179.

posed by some of his supporters early in his regime. Part and parcel of this legacy is Spain's long history of bureaucratic inefficiency and stagnation, and the inability of governments to enact civil service reform has plagued authoritarian and democratic regimes alike.

From 1982 to 1996 Spain's Socialist government tried hard to tame the bureaucracy. Under the Socialists the *reforma de los relojes* (reform of the clocks) required civil servants to work strict schedules, mandated that government offices remain open between 9 A.M. and 2 P.M., and attempted to streamline the bureaucratic maze facing Spaniards who sought government services. In 1984 the Socialists formally banned the practice of *pluriempleo* (multiple job holding). These reforms have been only partially successful. Moreover, with regional

devolution state bureaucracies have often been replaced with Autonomous Community offices that may operate no more efficiently.

In 1990 there were about 2 million people dependent in some way on the public purse. About one-third were employed in the state's central administration (including the military, police, legal corps, and social security staff); about one-quarter were employed by Autonomous Communities. By 1993 public sector employees represented just over 20 percent of the country's salaried workers, a figure that may seem large but is actually in line with other European nations.

Due in part to the Francoist legacy, the Spanish state owns and operates many business enterprises and plays an important role in many traditional (and declining) industries such as mining, iron, steel, and shipbuilding. In 1986 there were 180 companies in which the state held a direct majority share through three large state holding companies, along with 300 subsidiaries and more than 500 minority holdings. Together they accounted for about 5 percent of the total labor force and about 9 percent of the industrial sector labor force, which in comparative perspective is rather insignificant. Spanish governments of the left and right have undertaken a gradual and carefully controlled privatization of state holdings, beginning in 1986 with the privatization of the automobile maker SEAT (later sold to Germany's Volkswagen), and including, more recently, the state airline IBERIA.

Economic Performance

The economy in Spain stagnated for the first two decades of Franco's regime, and only in 1963 did real wages recover to the pre–Civil War level of 1936. After World War II, Spain's regime was ostracized from the international community. The dictator initially pursued a policy of autarky (self-sufficiency through high levels of protectionism) that led to widespread suffering. By the early 1950s this policy had failed and Spain was going bankrupt. Franco switched course and began to liberalize the economy in order to attract foreign capital. The result was the economic "miracle" of the 1960s.

Spain's cheap labor (due to repression of unions) and low taxes, combined with state protection of key industries, produced extraordinarily rapid industrial development.

By 1975 Spain was suffering from the side effects of this rapid growth. The OPEC oil crisis of the 1970s hit oil-dependent Spain particularly hard. Inflation, historically very low under Franco, was beginning to increase. Wages that had been kept artificially low during decades of authoritarian rule were now under pressure to rise. Spain's traditionally low budget deficit began to rise as governments during the transition to democracy sought to satiate pent-up demand for public services. Most ominous, however, was the widespread economic crisis symbolized by many of Spain's overprotected and increasingly obsolete industrial plants.

The first governments of the democratic period were unable to address the impending economic crisis. The UCD governments were too weak, and major economic policies were implemented through neocorporatist pacts negotiated between the UCD and parties of the left. The desire to consolidate democracy took precedence over economic reform. As a result, the economy stagnated from 1975 to 1982 as growth slowed to only 1.5 percent. Inflation soared, unemployment climbed, and industrial production and investment declined. The budget deficit skyrocketed. Spain's economic crisis at the time was the most severe in all of Western Europe.

The rapid rise in unemployment since the transition to democracy is the most alarming economic problem facing Spain. Unemployment rose from under 5 percent in 1975 to 16 percent in 1982. For most of the Socialist's tenure in office, unemployment consistently topped 20 percent (the 1996 rate was 22.7 percent). The Aznar government received much credit for reducing that rate to just over 11 percent by 2004, but Spain continues to have a very serious unemployment problem. There are many causes for this. Franco avoided high unemployment because of the massive migration of Spaniards to other European nations and the low number of women in the workforce. Europe's economic crisis in the 1970s and the return of democracy reversed this outflow of the labor force. Democratization brought a rapid entry of women into the workforce.

The delayed effects of the 1960s baby boom that accompanied the economic "miracle" also swelled the labor market. Franco's use of state protectionism prolonged the life of many industries, but Spain's entry into the Common Market made continued state support for inefficient enterprises untenable. The Socialists' policy of closing down and streamlining such industries threw many Spaniards out of work. The rapid rise in wages after democracy was not accompanied by a rise in productivity, and as a result many firms became less competitive.

Between 1982 and 1996 the Socialists attempted to restructure Spain's economy and prepare it for a full integration into the international economy.[43] In order to carry out this policy, the government implemented tough austerity measures, many of which hurt poor Spaniards the most. On its first day in office, the PSOE announced a devaluation of Spain's currency and a dramatic rise in energy prices. The 1983 Law of Re-conversion and Reindustrialization started the process of closing down the most inefficient of Spain's industries. As noted earlier, the Socialists liberalized labor laws, giving employers more freedom to hire and fire workers and thus infuriating Spain's trade unions. Spain's deficit was cut in half between 1982 and 1990, and the rate of growth in public expenditure fell dramatically. Tax reform increased the state's revenue, and inflation fell considerably. In the second half of the 1980s, the economic growth rate was about 5 percent annually, on average twice that of the European Community. In short, the Socialists were remarkably effective in reforming the Spanish economy. Ironically, some of those neoliberal measures were similar to those adopted by Thatcher's Conservative Party in Britain. The Socialists defended their record in office by noting the dramatic growth between 1982 and 1989 in expenditures on public pensions, public health, unemployment benefits, and education. Indeed, the Socialists unquestionably made vast improvements in Spain's welfare state, even though their main concern was economic growth and European integration. The real wages of workers improved more than 6 percent during the Socialist period in office.[44] It is also true that once Spain joined the European Union in 1986 and endorsed the European Monetary System in 1989, it had little leeway in its macroeconomic policy.

However, critics have attacked the Socialist policies as hurting the poor and failing to reduce inequality. The percentage of Spaniards living in poverty stayed constant during their period in office, at about 20 percent of the population, far above the European Union average of 14 percent. GINI index data (measuring income inequality) show that inequality declined sharply at the start of the democratic period but held constant (with a very slight decline) during the 14 years of Socialist government. However, as was shown in Table 1.2 in Chapter 1, it is clear that income in Spain is more equally distributed than in the United Kingdom, France, Germany, and Russia.

After 1996 the conservative government continued most of the Socialist economic policies, and it accelerated the privatization for state industries to include some of the most profitable pieces of the public sector. Parts of the state telephone and energy-generating monopolies were sold. The PP announced drastic budget cuts of $1.6 billion and called for the elimination of over 6,000 public sector jobs. The conservatives reduced taxes on small and medium-sized enterprise and cut capital gains taxes to 20 percent. In 2003 Spain's overall rate of taxation (35.4 percent of GDP) was the lowest in the European Union, where the average was 41 percent.[45] Aznar reduced Spain's budget deficit, limit the public debt, and tamed inflation so as to comply with the EU standards required for participation in the proposed single European currency. By May 1997 Spain had met EU goals and by 1998 it qualified for participation in the new European currency (see Chapter 12).

In recent years the trend of continued growth, declining inflation, and a dropping deficit, has been maintained (see Table 8.6). For much of Aznar's eight years in power Spain had the fastest growing economy among the four largest nations in the Eurozone. Aznar imposed substantial cuts in spending on social programs, and Spain's level of spending on social programs dropped to one of the lowest in Europe.[46]

The Spanish Welfare State

By the 1980s Spain was spending a greater proportion of national income on social security than did the United States, Britain, Canada, Switzerland, or

TABLE 8.6   Recent Spanish Economic Performance

	1993	1996	1999	2004
Real GDP growth	−1.2	2.4	3.7	2.8
Inflation (consumer prices)	4.6	3.6	2.9	2.8
Unemployment (% of labor force)	23.7	22.2	15.4	11.1
Government deficit as % of GDP	7.0	4.6	1.4	0.3

Source: Anuario El País 1999, various years and 2004 estimates by economist.com.

Australia, and it is currently in the middle of the pack among OECD nations.[47] This largesse is a relatively recent phenomenon and is mostly the result of the democratic regime. In 1960 Spain spent about 2 percent of its GDP on social security, but by 1990 that figure had risen to about 15 percent, and peaked at about 19 percent in 1995. Likewise, education spending, which lagged during the Francoist regime, doubled between 1975 and 2001, as noted in Figure 8.7.

Democratic governments have overhauled and enhanced the welfare system. All citizens are now entitled to receive welfare benefits. A basic pension is guaranteed to all Spanish citizens regardless of the amount they have paid into the system. Spain's Social Security agency has seen its share of the national budget grow steadily, while the amount of its budget contributed by employers and employees has gradually declined (the state currently contributes about one-third of the total cost of social security, similar to other European countries). Social security payments include health care, old age pensions, family support, and support to the disabled.

The National Health System created in 1986 replaced a variety of insurance schemes with an integrated public system that provides universal medical coverage. Universal coverage for all but the wealthiest 1 percent of the population was achieved by 1991. About one-quarter of Spanish health care is private, and private providers are often contracted by the state to perform health services. A drawback to the extended coverage is the increase in waiting lists, and investment in health care that has not kept up with increased demand. Still, Spain is one of the healthiest societies in the world and has the highest life expectancy in the EU. Infant mortality has plummeted and is lower than in the United States and most EU countries. In addition, the PSOE established a fairly extensive rural subsidy and jobs program, targeting Andalucia and Extremadura, the poor southern provinces. Though criticized for their inefficiency, these programs have significantly improved living standards in the south.

Spain's benefits for the elderly are among the most generous in the world. As a percentage of former earnings, only Sweden's are higher. With the economic crisis of the 1970s and 1980s, the pension system teetered on the verge of bankruptcy. The Socialists overhauled the system, restricting access to disability pensions and imposing stricter limits on the value of retirement benefits.

Spain's alarmingly high unemployment rate has focused attention on unemployment benefits. At the end of the Franco regime, only 62 percent of Spaniards were eligible for such benefits.[48] The Socialists steadily tightened up the criteria for receiving benefits, but in one of the few areas where they responded to trade union pressure, they raised that figure to about 70 percent by 1993. Under the Socialists, the number of Spaniards receiving unemployment benefits rose dramatically. In 2002 the Aznar government restricted those benefits. The government did not give in to union pressure, even after a nationwide general strike. Unlike many European countries, there is no safety net for those who do not qualify for benefits. These individuals are forced to depend on their families for support. Spain's unemployment rate has been especially high among young people, and first-time job seekers do not qualify for unemployment benefits. Workers who qualify for benefits receive an amount that varies according to how much a worker has contributed to unemployment insurance over his or her career, but which is limited to six years. After six years, a very small unemployment "subsidy" (about $5,000 per year) is available.

Regional Devolution

Spain's democracy has gone a long way toward solving the historical conflict between center and periphery. But the constitutional solution has involved compromise, and a small minority of Spaniards remains dissatisfied. There can be no doubt that democratization has created a genuine devolution of power. A look at the shift in public expenditures from center to periphery clearly reveals that Spain's 17 Autonomous Communities get an increasingly large share of the pie (see Figure 8.8). The percentage of public employees who work for regional and local governments instead of the central government has grown steadily, although in Spain the balance is still tilted toward the center when compared with federal systems in Germany and the United States.[49]

Between 1981 and 1991 the central government lodged Constitutional Court appeals against the ACs 120 times, while the regional government made appeals against the central government 127 times.[50] Most of these disputes involved the "historic" regions of Catalonia and the Basque Country.

FIGURE 8.8   Growth in Regional Shares of Government Expenditures, 1983–1994

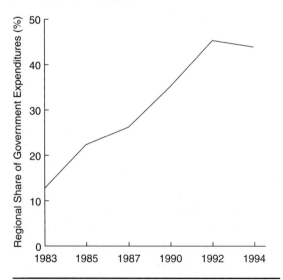

Source: *Anuario El País* (1991, 1993, 1994).

The steady decline of such appeals in recent years (dropping from a high of 131 in 1985 to only 16 by 1993) suggests that a *modus vivendi* is slowly emerging.[51] However, the slow process of devolution and the ambiguous nature of the entire process give rise to some serious tensions between center and periphery (see Box 8.6).

The most contentious issue between the central and AC governments concerns funding. The ability to receive revenue from Madrid and to raise it locally varies considerably from region to region. Under the Socialists a gradual transfer of funds, especially in the areas of education and health care, began to take place, often raising cries of favoritism. The ability of ACs to levy their own taxes has not been fully resolved, and little AC revenue is now generated from internal taxes. With the exception of the Basque Country and Navarre, which tax their citizens and then repay the central government for the cost of its services, most of the AC budgets come from a portion of central government taxes collected in each region. Currently, the exact percentage of such taxes going to AC governments is determined by a complex and controversial formula that considers population, area, industrialization, migration patterns, and poverty levels. The bottom line, however, is that ACs remain heavily dependent on the central state for their budgets, and far more so than states in Germany or the United States.

One problem faced by the central government is income disparities among regions. Since the transition to democracy, many leaders in Madrid have sought to finance ACs in a way that would equalize the wealth among Spanish regions, similar to the European Union's policies toward its poorest members. Article 2 of the Spanish Constitution calls for a leveling of income between regions, and the Inter-Territorial Compensation Fund was established to achieve this. Since 1975, Spanish regions have become more equal, though this has in part resulted from equalization efforts of the European Union. However, Spain's two wealthiest regions and the regions with the greatest autonomy (the Basque Country and Catalonia) view such leveling as a drain on their economies. In addition, such solidaristic policies exacerbate the deep-seated view in both regions that Madrid has historically taken from these regions more than it has given back.

A more localized but still serious tension between center and periphery concerns the minority of individuals in the Basque Country (and to a much smaller extent, Catalonia) who continue to desire independence from Spain. In the Basque Country, the political wing of the pro-independence Basque terrorist organization ETA (Basque Homeland and Liberty) regularly receives between 10 and 15 percent of the vote in elections. Those favoring independence through violent means are clearly in a small minority, but the persistence of pro-independence sentiment alarms many observers. The most prominent Basque leadership often lacks the unified political will to confront and marginalize terrorism. In contrast to Catalonia, the major

---

Box 8.6   The Persistence of Center-Periphery Issues in Spain

The center-periphery cleavage no longer threatens Spanish democracy, but it is still the source of serious tensions. For example, in 1992 the president of Catalonia, Jordi Pujol, infuriated the government in Madrid when he created a foreign policy delegate (similar to a foreign minister) within his government. Ads placed in foreign periodicals by the *Generalitat* (the Catalan government) affirmed "we are a nation." Pujol claimed that the 1992 Olympics were a victory for the Catalan nation. In his trips abroad Pujol was often received more like a head of state than a state governor. More recently, the Aznar government angered regional officials when it claimed that school curriculums established by regional governments diminished the importance of Castile in Spain's history. In Catalonia the most recent regional elections produced large gains for parties that favor independence (though not through violent means).

Basque political forces are ambiguous in their support for Spain's constitution. The centrist Basque National Party has called for a referendum that would give Basques the power to decide whether or not to remain part of Spain. Demands for independence in Catalonia have always been weaker. And in the Basque Country as well as Catalonia, the percentage of those polled favoring independence has steadily dropped. In the 2003 regional elections in Catalonia, the sole party advocating independence (though not through violence) received an unprecedented 16 percent of the vote.

Opinion research makes it clear that only in these two regions, Catalonia and the Basque Country, is there a large population with a truly dominant ethnic identity.[52] In other regions, citizens clearly accept both national and regional identifications.[53] Even in the Basque Country and Catalonia, however, a sizable group, though not a majority, feel equally attached to Spain and the region. In Catalonia a significant percentage (13 percent) view themselves as only Spanish.

The trend toward devolution now appears to be unstoppable. The central government in 1997 controlled only 61 percent of all public spending compared with 89 percent in 1979, one clear sign that the ACs are increasingly important.[54] There is now a growing realization that Spain is moving toward a federal model of government, even if the delicate transition to democracy was not able to acknowledge this at the outset. As a result, there are renewed calls for revamping the Senate into a genuinely regional body. Concerns that the electoral victory of José María Aznar in 1996 would stem the devolution process were unfounded. Lacking a parliamentary majority, Aznar cut political deals with centrist regional groups that virtually guarantee a continuation of the devolution process.

The ability of the Spanish right to accommodate regional autonomy is one of the crowning achievements of Spanish democracy. After the 1996 elections, the PP's dependence on regional parties to sustain the Aznar government has facilitated this rapprochement. Aznar pledged to double the AC's share of the national income tax, and to give ACs far greater control over education (see Box 8.7). Socialist Prime Minister Zapatero was similarly dependent on the support of the Catalan nationalists after the 2004 elections and can be expected to support some aspects of the nationalists' agenda.

Terrorism

Terrorism—one of the most intractable problems of democracy in Spain—had its origins in the Francoist regime. The two main terrorist groups, *Basque Homeland and Liberty* (*ETA*—Euskadi ta Askatassuna) and the October First Revolutionary Antifascist Group (GRAPO), both emerged in opposition to Francoist repression. ETA carried out about 70 percent of the terrorist acts from 1976 to 1980, and about 90 percent after then. GRAPO, a tiny radical leftist group, was responsible for 14 percent of all acts before 1980, but has since disappeared.

Democracy has not solved the problem of domestic terrorism, but there has been a decline in the incidence of terrorism over the past decade. As a result of democratization and devolution of powers to the regions, a major faction of ETA quit the armed struggle in 1977, backing a leftist Basque political party. Curiously, however, ETA continued to grow rapidly, and terrorist acts did not cease. Most targets of ETA terrorism have been members of the state security forces, but innocent bystanders are regularly murdered in ETA attacks. Attacks on hotels in 2004 sought to damage Spain's tourist industry.

Box 8.7   Devolution in Action

The success of Spain's devolution can be seen on many levels. In Catalonia, street signs appear in Catalan and a majority of children learn both Catalan and Castilian. The large majority of citizens in Catalonia now speak Catalan. In Catalonia and the Basque Country there are regional police forces and television and radio stations that broadcast in regional languages. All 17 ACs have their own elected governments and court systems, and each has control over territorial planning, social services, and cultural policy.

ETA's constant attacks on military personnel were a source of frustration for the armed forces and may have precipitated the attempted coup of 1981. ETA's strategy, in fact, has been to provoke a military coup in an attempt to demonstrate the underlying authoritarian nature of Spanish democracy.

There is much speculation about why democratization did not eliminate Basque terrorism. Although it is thought to have no more than 500 members, ETA's continued existence has been aided by its secretive structure (it is organized into small cells) and its constant campaign of robbery and extortion that give the organization substantial resources. Popular support for ETA and the behavior of Basque political elites are also important factors. The Constitution's failure to recognize the Basque Country's right to self-determination alienated many Basques. Until fairly recently political leaders at both the central and regional level lacked the unity and resolve to combat terrorism. Many leftists, and Basques of all political stripes, sympathized with ETA during the dictatorship and found it hard to denounce the organization after 1977. The Basque Nationalist Party (PNV), for example, refused to refer to ETA as "terrorist." The Basque clergy condemn ETA, but often equate it with police repression. In addition, ETA receives support from foreign terrorist groups, and the French government tolerated the presence of Basque terrorists within its borders until the mid-1980s. ETA's political front, Herri Batasuna (HB), and its various successors have fared well in regional elections.

Nevertheless, democratic leaders, while unable to stop Basque terrorism, may be slowly winning the political battle. An accord between Spain and France in 1984 tightened the screws on ETA. Spain's entry into the European Union and NATO, and the September 11, 2001 attacks in the United States gave Spain important allies in the fight against terrorism. Most importantly, the tide of popular opinion within the Basque Country appears to have turned decidedly against ETA. The new Basque police force has improved the image of government. In January 1988 all Basque political forces, except the pro-ETA HB, signed an antiterrorism pact. The leading Basque political party, the PNV, has been more openly critical of ETA, even though it often dis-

agrees with the government in Madrid over how to best stop terrorism. Polls now regularly show that an overwhelming majority of Basques favor the disarming of ETA. In recent years, massive demonstrations against terrorism have become commonplace. Indeed, ETA's sudden announcement of a unilateral cease-fire in September 1988 (see Box 8.7) likely resulted from its growing isolation within the Basque Country. ETA's attempt to drive a wedge between political forces with the Basque Country has clearly failed. Unfortunately, just as the threat of domestic terrorism appeared to subside a new terrorist threat surfaced with the March 2004 Madrid bombings, carried out by Islamic radicals (see Box 8.7).

Women in Spain

During the Franco regime, discrimination against women was blatant. Males had statutory power over women within Spanish families, and women needed permission from their husbands for a wide variety of activities. Women had no control over family assets. Penalties for adultery were far harsher for women than for men. Contraception, divorce, and abortion, to which many women wanted access, were all strictly illegal. The government banned women's organizations, except for the patronizing "Women's Section" of the official party (which sponsored courses on how to be a good wife and mother).

How successful has democracy been in promoting equality for Spain's women? The answer to this question is generally encouraging, but not without some important qualifications.[55] Much of the struggle for women's rights after 1975 was subordinated to the struggle to consolidate democracy. The first UCD governments abolished some of the most egregious legislation from the Francoist period, and the Constitution gave women and men legal equality, but many aspects of the document disappointed the women's movement and particularly those on the left. For example, on the issue of abortion the framers of the Constitution rejected the wording proposed by the left and instead stated that "All have the right to life," possibly implying constitutional protection of the fetus. As noted earlier, the Constitution gives male heirs to the throne precedence over females.

The consolidation of democracy did, however, facilitate the passing of laws that gave basic rights to women. By 1978 parliament had abolished some sexist laws, like criminalization of adultery for women, and had legalized contraceptives. Divorce was legalized only in 1981, and only after a bitter struggle that helped destroy the governing UCD. Other reforms had to await the election of the Socialists. After 1982, the PSOE government actively sought to promote women's causes, and feminists were able to obtain important political positions. The most important innovation was the creation of the Spanish Women's Institute, the most powerful governmental institution to which Spanish women had access. With cabinet backing, it pursued myriad actions to improve the lot of women. It attempted to eliminate all legislation that discriminated against women, improve women's health (a landmark 1985 health bill included provisions for state-funded family planning), promote women's participation in society, and encourage equal sharing of domestic responsibilities.

As a result, the lives of Spanish women in the first two decades of democracy have improved considerably. But as women have had increased opportunities to enter the labor market and as contraception has become widely available, there has been a rapid decline in birthrates: By 1990 Spain's birthrate was one of the lowest in Europe. Publicly funded preschool for 3- to 6-year-olds, a crucial issue for women, has been extensively implemented through Socialist policies. Spanish women have made enormous strides in higher education. By the end of the Francoist regime, only about one-third of university students were women. Today over one-half of university students are women, one of the highest numbers in Europe in this respect.

The Socialist record on abortion was far more mixed. Surveys show that most Spaniards favor access to abortion, although the Catholic Church and many Catholic women do not. Though pledging to legalize abortion, the PSOE introduced legislation in 1983 that legalized abortions only if a woman's life or health was in danger, if the pregnancy resulted from rape, or if the fetus was gravely deformed. In practice abortions are hard to obtain in the National Health System. While doctors at private health clinics often interpret the law

liberally (citing emotional distress to the mother as a health danger), many women seek illegal abortions or travel to other European countries where abortions are permitted. The Socialist plan to further liberalize abortion was shelved after the PSOE lost its majority in the 1993 elections and was forced to rely on support from more conservative regional forces.

Unemployment has been a matter of particular concern for women, who work disproportionately in lower paying and less secure jobs. In 1992 women on average earned only 72.5 percent of what men were paid, reflecting the lower skill levels and often part-time nature of their jobs. These jobs are also less secure, as the unemployment rate for women (about 30 percent) is almost double that of men and the highest in Europe.[56]

Spain's Socialists can take credit for increasing the role of women in politics, a profession reserved for men until very recently. The PSOE introduced a quota system requiring that a quarter of all party-controlled public posts be given to women. At the start of the Socialists' tenure in office, only 5 percent of political appointments went to women; by 1991 this figure had increased to 13 percent. About 25 percent of the members of the Spanish legislature elected in 2004 were women, well above the European average of 16 percent.[57] Despite the continued strength of Spanish *machismo* and the persistence of discrimination against women, signs of change are everywhere. Women judges, cabinet ministers, and (since 1993) bullfighters have changed the traditional image of Spanish women. José Luis Zapatero took office in 2004 pledging to make women's issues a priority. He called for tough new laws against domestic violence, relaxed restrictions on abortion, and a constitutional change to allow females to occupy the throne. One-half of Zapatero's cabinet, including the deputy prime minister, are women.

Foreign Policy

Spain was not an important international actor during the Franco regime. The international community ostracized authoritarian Spain during the first part of Franco's rule. The isolation was partly broken in the 1950s, when the United States began to value Spain's role as an anti-Communist bulwark. A 1953 agreement between Spain and the United States gave the United States valuable military facilities on Spanish soil in exchange for American economic aid and political support. Membership in the United Nations came soon after, in 1955, and relations with Spain's European neighbors began to thaw (a trade agreement with the EEC was signed in 1970) but remained cool until after the death of the dictator in 1975.

Under the first UCD governments, Spain's relations with the world rapidly normalized. Spain applied for membership in the European Community and NATO, improved relations with its neighbors, and formally renounced its last colonial claims in North Africa. After Spain's four decades of isolation the decision to join the European Union was supported by almost every Spanish political force and took on almost mythical significance. Spain, along with Portugal, joined the EU in 1986 after intense and protracted negotiations. Spain quickly became one of the strongest proponents of monetary integration. Despite the enormous sacrifices required over the last two decades in order to integrate into the EU, Spaniards continue to be among the strongest supporters of European integration and a common foreign policy. Opinion research conducted in 2004 showed that 64 percent of Spaniards believed that EU membership has been good for Spain, far above the average European level.[58] Spaniards were also among the most enthusiastic backers of the new European currency, the euro.

Integration into NATO proved far more controversial. Much of the left and a sector of the governing UCD were opposed to NATO membership when the government first proposed it in 1977, but they were unable to stop the process and Spain was formally admitted in May 1982. The PSOE opposed NATO membership and promised to hold a referendum on the issue if elected to power. The Socialists' resounding electoral victory in 1982 put Spain's membership in the Atlantic Alliance in question, as the new government froze military integration into NATO. However, Prime Minister González began to back

away from his party's opposition to NATO. The reasons for this change of heart are complex, but fear of endangering Spain's EC application and a desire to democratize and modernize Spain's military were key factors. By mid-1984, González proposed a "compromise" whereby Spain would remain within NATO (but would not integrate into the military command structure), reduce the U.S. military presence in Spain, and ban nuclear weapons from Spanish territory. The PSOE kept its promise to hold a referendum on NATO—but now called on voters to ratify membership! Despite considerable popular opposition to NATO membership (many Spaniards favored neutrality, which had been the official policy of the PSOE in the 1982 electoral campaign), Spanish voters narrowly supported continued NATO membership in a March 1986 referendum. In 1988 the Socialists carried through on the pledge to reduce the U.S. military presence by renegotiating Spain's military agreement with the United States. The 1995 appointment of Javier Solana, a former Socialist cabinet minister, as the first Spanish NATO Secretary General, ended doubts about Spain's commitment to the organization. In 1996 the conservative government of Prime Minister Aznar guided a bill through the Cortes that fully integrated Spain into NATO's military command. Despite strong domestic opposition, Spain sent 1,000 troops to participate in NATO's Kosovo operation in 1999 and later sent small contingents to both Afghanistan and Iraq. Aznar's uncompromising support for the U.S.-led invasion of Iraq proved extremely unpopular from the start. Polls showed that about 90 percent of the public opposed the invasion at the start, and a similar percentage continued to oppose the war by early 2004. After his 2004 electoral victory, Socialist Prime Minister Zapatero immediately fulfilled a campaign pledge to withdraw Spain's 1,300 troops from Iraq, while offering to beef up Spain's contingent in Afghanistan.

Spain's relationship with its southern neighbor Morocco remains a source of tension. Morocco, a former Spanish colony, resents Spain's continued occupation of two enclaves on Morocco's Mediterranean coast. Spain is concerned about the growing flood of illegal immigrants who cross the Straits of Gibraltar to seek employment in Europe. Racial tensions between African migrant workers and Spanish citizens exploded in southern Spain in February 2000, leading to considerable violence. In 2002 Moroccan forces briefly occupied a Spanish islet off Morocco's coast. The 2004 Madrid railway bombings, carried out largely by Moroccan-born terrorists, convinced the newly elected Socialist prime minister of the need to improve Spanish-Moroccan relations, and his first foreign visit was to Morocco.

One unresolved foreign policy issue concerns the status of *Gibraltar*, a tiny (just over two square miles) British dependency on the southwest portion of the Iberian Peninsula that juts out into the Mediterranean Sea. Great Britain won the "rock" from Spain in 1704 but Spain claims sovereignty over Gibraltar. In protest over Britain's refusal to "return" Gibraltar, Franco closed the border between Gibraltar and Spain in an attempt to cut off and strangle the enclave. Instead, the policy only strengthened the resolve of Gibraltar's residents to remain British citizens. Only after the election of a Socialist government in 1982 was the border between Spain and Gibraltar normalized, but Spain continues its claim over the rock. Fortunately, this issue no longer endangers Spain's relations with Britain—indeed Spain and the UK both backed the invasion of Iraq to depose Saddam Hussein—and the dispute is no longer imbued with the emotion that was present during the Franco years. An April 1999 accord between Spain and the United Kingdom has opened the way for future negotiations over the territory and promises to further ease tensions.

Spain enjoys special ties to its former colonies in Latin America, having assumed the role of cultural leader of the 300 million Spanish speakers worldwide. It attempts to represent the interests of Latin America within the European Union. In addition, Spanish governments have been harsh critics of human rights violations in Latin America. Socialist support for Sandinista Nicaragua and Castro's Cuba created friction with the Reagan and Bush administrations during the 1980s. One of the first foreign policy acts of the conservative Aznar government was to cut off official Spanish aid to Cuba, an act that drew praise from the United States. However, in 1997 the new conservative government locked horns with the Clinton administration over U.S. Cuban policy. PP Foreign Minister Abel Matutes blasted U.S. attempts to penalize European investors in Cuba, threatening the United States with retaliation. Spain has played an active role in the negotiation and enforcement of peace proposals in Nicaragua and El Salvador, and has played a key role in United Nations missions in both countries.

THE PEACEFUL DISAPPEARANCE OF THE TWO SPAINS

For students of comparative politics, Spain's remarkable transition to democracy and its ability to overcome dangerous historical cleavages offer numerous lessons. Most importantly, the transition to democracy demonstrates that the art of politics—especially creative leadership and political compromise—can solve seemingly intractable political problems. The transition was successful in large part because of the ability of Juan Carlos and Adolfo Suárez to use Francoist political structures to promote democratic reform, and the willingness of democratic opposition leaders to tolerate such a strategy. Skilled political leadership was not the only explanation for Spain's successful democratization. As noted in Chapter 1, the relationship between economic development and democracy is a complex one, and this is certainly illustrated in the Spanish case. Rapid economic development under Franco after 1960 began to change Spanish society in ways that the dictator could not have foreseen. The urbanization, secularization, greater education, and increasing wealth of Spaniards all eroded historical cleavages. The opening of Spain to foreign investment ignited the economic boom, and the opening of Spanish society to foreign influence began to foster a democratic political culture.

Not all political cleavages have been mitigated by skilled leadership and economic modernization. As we have seen, the center-periphery issue continues to challenge Spanish democracy, but by 2004 only Basque terrorism remained as a reminder of this persistent problem. Small sectors of Spain's armed forces still admire Spain's authoritarian past, but the vast majority have accepted democratic rule. On the whole, however, the historic divide between the "two Spains" has been replaced by a united, vibrant, and modern democracy that is undergoing a successful integration with its European neighbors.

Key Terms

Autonomous
   Communities
José María Aznar
Basque Homeland and
   Liberty (ETA)
Basque Nationalist
   Party (PNV)
Basques
King Juan Carlos
Castilians
Catalans
Civil Guard
Congress of Deputies
Constitutional Court

constructive vote of no
   confidence
Convergence and
   Union (CiU)
Cortes
Defensor del Pueblo
devolution
Francisco Franco
Galicians
General Confederation
   of Workers (UGT)
Gibraltar
Felipe González
Herri Batasuna (HB)
Opus Dei

Popular Party (PP)
President of the
   Government
Reconquista
José Luis Rodríguez
   Zapatero
Senate
Spanish Civil War
   (1936–1939)
Spanish Communist
   Party (PCE)
Spanish Confederation
   of Entrepreneurial
   Organizations
   (CEOE)

Spanish Inquisition
Spanish Second
   Republic
   (1931–1936)
Spanish Socialist Workers
   Party (PSOE)
Adolfo Suárez
Supreme Court
two Spains
Union of the Democratic
   Center (UCD)
United Left (IU)
Workers' Commissions
   (CC.OO)

Suggested Readings

Gibbons, John. *Spanish Politics Today*. Manchester, UK: Manchester University Press, 1999.

Gunther, Richard, J. Montero, and J. Botella. *Democracy in Modern Spain*. New Haven, CT: Yale University Press, 2004.

Gunther, Richard, G. Sani, and G. Shabad. *Spain After Franco*. Berkeley: University of California Press, 1986.

Heywood, Paul. *The Government and Politics of Spain*. New York: St. Martin's Press, 1995.

Hooper, John. *The New Spaniards*. London: Penguin, 1995.

Lieberman, Sima. *Growth and Crisis in the Spanish Economy, 1940–1993*. London: Routledge, 1995.

McDonough, Peter, Samuel H. Barnes, and Antonio López Pina. *The Cultural Dynamics of Democratization in Spain*. Ithaca, NY: Cornell University Press, 1998.

Pérez-Díaz, Víctor M. *Spain at the Crossroads: Civil Society, Politics, and the Rule of Law*. Cambridge, MA: Harvard University Press, 1999.

Share, Donald. *Dilemmas of Social Democracy: The Spanish Socialist Workers Party in the 1980s*. Westport, CT: Greenwood Publishers, 1989.

———. *The Making of Spanish Democracy*. New York: Center for the Study of Democratic Institutions/Praeger Publishers, 1986.

Threlfall, Monica. "Feminist Politics and Social Change in Spain." In Monica Threlfall, ed., *Mapping the Women's Movement*. London: Verso, 1996, pp. 115–51.

Internet Sources

Office of the President: www.la-moncloa.es/
Spain's lower house: www.congreso.es/
Spanish Socialist Workers Party: www.psoe.es/
Partido Popular: www.pp.es/
Izquierda Unida: www.izquierda-unida.es
CiU, leading Catalan Party: www.convergencia.org/
PNV, leading Basque Party: www.eaj-pnv.com/

Directory of Spanish politics resources on the Web: www
.sispain.org/SiSpain/english/index.html
El País, Spain's leading daily newspaper: www.elpais.es/
El Mundo, leading Spanish daily newspaper: www
.elmundo.es/
La Vanguardia, leading daily from Barcelona: www
.lavanguardia.es/

 Endnotes

1. A May 2004 CIS Barometer reported that 63 percent of Spaniards named unemployment as one of the biggest problems facing Spain, followed by terrorism, at 52 percent.

2. According to a CIS poll in May 2004, 53 percent of Spaniards feel there are too many immigrants in Spain.

3. Donald Share, *The Making of Spanish Democracy* (New York: Praeger Publishers and the Center for the Study of Democratic Institutions, 1986), pp. 86–118.

4. For a good overview, see Richard Gillespie, "The Break-up of the 'Socialist Family': Party-Union Relations in Spain, 1982–1989," *West European Politics* 13, No. 1 (January 1990): pp. 47–62.

5. On the reform of the Senate see Elisa Roller, "Reforming the Senate: Mission Impossible?" *West European Politics* 25, No. 4 (October 2002): pp. 69–72.

6. Donald Share, *Dilemmas of Social Democracy: The Spanish Socialist Workers Party in the 1980s* (Westport, CT: Greenwood, 1989).

7. An outstanding overview is Thomas Lancaster and Michael Gates, "Spain," in Alan Katz, ed., *Legal Traditions and Systems* (New York: Greenwood Press, 1986), pp. 360–80.

8. Frederick Weil, "The Sources and Structure of Legitimation in Western Democracies," *American Sociological Review* 54 (October 1989): 691.

9. From Richard Gunther, J. Montero, and J. Botella, *Democracy in Modern Spain* (New Haven, CT: Yale University Press, 2004), p. 163.

10. *Eurobarometer,* 52, April 2000, p. 12.

11. Frederick Weil, "The Sources and Structure of Legitimation in Western Democracies," *American Sociological Review* 54 (October 1989): 696.

12. *Eurobarometer,* 47.1, December 1997.

13. The discussion below draws heavily on Gunther, Montero, and Botella, *Democracy in Modern Spain,* pp. 146–97.

14. Gunther, Montero, and Botella, *Democracy in Modern Spain,* p. 147.

15. Peter McDonough, Samuel H. Barnes, and Antonio Lopez Pina, "Social Identity and Mass Politics in Spain," *Comparative Political Studies* 21, No. 2 (July 1988): 200–30.

16. Gunther, Montero, and Botella, *Democracy in Modern Spain,* p. 180.

17. Hooper, *The New Spaniards,* p. 269.

18. Centro de Investigaciones Sociológicas, "opinión publica ante la Unión Europea" (Spring 2004).

19. *Eurobarometer,* 52, April 2000, p. 15.

20. Hooper, *The New Spaniards,* p. 307.

21. Hooper, *The New Spaniards,* p. 306.

22. Karen Sanders with María José Canel, "Spanish Politicians and the Media: Controlled Visibility and Soap Opera Politics," *Parliamentary Affairs* 57, No. 1 (January 2004): p. 200.

23. Heywood, *Government and Politics of Spain,* p. 250; Philippe Schmitter, "Organized Interest and Democratic Consolidation in Southern Europe," in Richard Gunther et al., *The Politics of Democratic Consolidation* (Baltimore: Johns Hopkins University Press, 1995), p. 294.

24. Schmitter, "Organized Interest and Democratic Consolidation," p. 295.

25. Hooper, *The New Spaniards,* p. 133.

26. *New York Times* (December 21, 2003): p. 15.

27. José Ramón Montero, "Religiosidad, ideología y voto en españa," *Revista de Estudios Políticos* 83 (January–March 1994): 85.

28. John Karamichas, "Developments in Spanish Greens: Change of Course or Repetition?" *Environmental Politics* 11, No. 1 (Spring 2002): pp. 178–83.

29. Gunther, Montero, and Botella, *Democracy in Modern Spain,* pp. 147 and 263.

30. Heywood, "The Spanish Left: Towards a Common Home?" in Martin Bull and Paul Heywood, eds., *West European Communist Parties After the Revolutions of 1989* (London: St. Martins, 1994).

31. On the PSOE, see Donald Share, *Dilemmas of Social Democracy.*

32. Juan J. Linz, "From Great Hopes to Civil War: The Breakdown of Democracy in Spain," in Juan J. Linz and Alfred Stepan, eds., *The Breakdown of Democratic Regimes: Europe* (Baltimore, MD: Johns Hopkins University Press, 1978), p. 166.

33. See Share, *Dilemmas of Social Democracy*, p. 28.
34. Kenneth Medhurst, "Spanish Conservative Politics," in Zig Layton-Henry, ed., *Conservative Parties in Western Europe* (London: MacMillan, 1982), p. 313.
35. Heywood, *Government and Politics of Spain*, p. 204.
36. Richard Gunther, "Electoral Laws, Party Systems, and Elites: The Case of Spain," *American Political Science Review* 83, No. 3 (September 1989): 840.
37. Heywood, *Government and Politics of Spain*, p. 183.
38. Gunther, Montero, and Botella, *Democracy in Modern Spain*, p. 143.
39. McDonough, Barnes, and Lopez Pina, "The Nature of Political Support," pp. 335–36.
40. Gunther, Montero, and Botella, *Democracy in Modern Spain*, pp. 170–71.
41. Morlino, "Political Parties and Democratic Consolidation in Southern Europe," in Richard Gunther, P. Nikiforous Diamandorous, and Hans-Jurgen Puhle, eds., *The Politics of Democratic Consolidation* (Baltimore: Johns Hopkins Press, 1995), pp. 331–32.
42. Morlino, "Political Parties," p. 319.
43. Sebastián Etchemendy, "Revamping the Weak, Protecting the Strong, and Managing Privatization," *Comparative Political Studies* 37, No. 4 (August 2004): pp. 623–51.
44. Maravall, "Politics and Policy," p. 108, argues that despite huge crisis and unemployment, earnings per worker actually rose from 1983 to 1991, up 6.2 percent in real earning power.
45. OECD, *Economic Survey, Spain* (2003).
46. Gunther, Montero, and Botella, *Democracy in Modern Spain*, p. 370.
47. Francis G. Castles, "Welfare State Development in Southern Europe," *West European Politics* 2 (April 1995): 292. This is an excellent overview of the Spanish welfare state, from which this section draws heavily.
48. Hooper, *The New Spaniards*, p. 245.
49. Gunther, Montero, and Botella, *Democracy in Modern Spain*, p. 298.
50. Heywood, *Government and Politics of Spain*, p. 147.
51. *Anuário El País* (1995), p. 96.
52. Eduardo López-Aranguren and Manuel Garcia Ferrando, "Nacionalismo y regionalism en la España de los autonomias," in José Beneyto Vidal, ed., *España a debate* (Madrid: Teenos, 1991), pp. 177–90.
53. Luis Moreno, *The Federalizaton of Spain* (London: Frank Cass, 2001).
54. Gunther, Montero, and Botella, *Democracy in Modern Spain*, p. 300.
55. The best overview of the women's movement in Spain, from which this section borrows heavily, is Monica Threlfall, "Feminist Politics and Social Change in Spain," in Monica Threlfall, ed., *Mapping the Women's Movement* (London: Verso, 1996), pp. 115–51.
56. Threlfall, "Feminist Politics," p. 141.
57. Based on information gathered from The Inter-parliamentary Union, http://www.ipu.org/.
58. European Commission, *Eurobarometer*, 52 (April 2000), p. 26, and Centro de Investigaciones Sociológicas, "opinión ante la unión Europea."

Russia

0 25 50 mi
0 40 80 km

ARCTIC OCEAN

Barents Sea

East Siberian Sea

Laptev Sea

Bering Sea

Kara Sea

DENMARK
NORWAY
SWEDEN
FINLAND
LATVIA
POLAND
ESTONIA
BELARUS
LITHUANIA
UKRAINE
St. Petersburg
Moscow

Volga

Ob

Ob

Yenisey

Lena

Magadan

Yakutsk

N

Sea of Okhotsk

GEORGIA
ARMENIA

Caspian Sea

AZERBAIJAN

TURKMENISTAN

UZBEKISTAN

Aral Sea

Lake Balkash

K A Z A K H S T A N

Omsk
Novosibirsk
Tomsk

Krasnoyarsk

Irkutsk

Lake Baikal

Khabarovsk

JAPAN
Sea of Japan

IRAN

AFGHANISTAN

TAJIKISTAN

KYRGYZSTAN

C H I N A

M O N G O L I A

NORTH KOREA

Chapter 9

Politics in Russia

THOMAS F. REMINGTON

Country Bio—Russia

POPULATION: 145 Million

TERRITORY: 17 million square kilometers

YEAR OF INDEPENDENCE: 1991

YEAR OF CURRENT CONSTITUTION: 1993

CHIEF OF STATE: President Vladimir Vladimirovich Putin

HEAD OF GOVERNMENT: Premier Mikhail Efimovich Fradkov

LANGUAGE(S):   Russian, other

RELIGION: Russian Orthodox 70–80%, Muslim 8–9%, Buddhist 0.6%, Jewish 0.3%

REBUILDING RUSSIA

The year 2000 opened with a dramatic change of leadership in Russia. On December 31, 1999, President *Boris Yeltsin* appeared on Russian national television to announce that he was resigning as president of Russia as of midnight. Although Yeltsin's term was not due to expire until June 2000, he had decided to leave office early and turn the powers of the presidential office over to his prime minister, Vladimir Putin, who under the constitution was Yeltsin's successor. Just completed parliamentary elections had confirmed Putin's political strength. Yeltsin's departure gave Putin a strong advantage in the upcoming presidential election, which according to the constitution had to be held within three months of the president's leaving office. Putin's very first decree as acting president was to grant Yeltsin and his family lifetime immunity from all criminal prosecution. The manner in which the succession occurred was not illegal, but it reflected an unseemly bargain: Yeltsin was giving Putin the presidency in return for security for himself and his family.

Yeltsin's departure marked the end of a turbulent decade during which Russia struggled to shed its Communist past and create a new political and economic system. The change in regime from communism to democracy occurred largely without bloodshed, but produced an intense and protracted behind-the-scenes fight over power and property. Social inequality exploded: a handful of people grew fabulously wealthy from the privatization of state assets. At the same time, over 40 percent of the population sank into poverty as unemployment rose and high inflation destroyed incomes and savings. The social safety net wore thin. Crime and corruption proliferated. Discipline and accountability in the state bureaucracy—which had deteriorated in the late Communist period—broke down still further. The government attempted to carry out a far-reaching program of fiscal and monetary reform, but with only limited success. Entrenched bureaucratic interests fought at every turn to subvert the government's plans. Many people bitterly reflected that the expansion of democratic freedoms had brought more misery than progress.

Meantime Russians had to adjust to the fact that their country was no longer a great empire consisting of 15 ethnically diverse, nominally sovereign republics forming a single union. Now it was an independent state and its neighbors were likewise free and independent under international law. The political controls that the Communist Party had exercised over the economy, property, culture, and political decision making were gone. New institutions for coordinating the behavior of the citizens and territories of the country had not yet taken hold. The state was extremely weak, a problem made all the more serious because even after the dissolution of the Soviet Union, Russia was still by far the largest country in the world in physical expanse. Maintaining the unity of the country under those conditions was a severe challenge. President Putin's first priority, therefore, has been to restore order by recentralizing state power.

Russia's transition posed an especially serious challenge to governance because the breakdown of the Communist regime ended many of the political structures that had held the state together. The very identity of the state was in question because the Soviet Union itself dissolved in December 1991 and the 15 republics of the federal union became independent. Russians therefore had to redefine their political community around a smaller, national state, and to generate new bonds of loyalty to it. Creating a post-Communist state that was both gov-ernable and democratic was extremely difficult because the Soviet regime had left behind so few of the political prerequisites of legitimate democratic authority, such as developed political parties, an honest and professional bureaucracy, an independent judiciary, encompassing social interest groups, and a democratically oriented political culture. Finally, putting the country on a path of self-sustaining economic development after decades of stagnation and decline required the replacement of the old centralized planning system with an economy based on the market system and private property. In all three areas, Russia entered the new century having made halting, partial steps forward in some respects, but major steps backward in the quality of life and quality of government.

CURRENT POLICY CHALLENGES

Vladimir Putin, Yeltsin's successor as president, faces an agenda of enormous proportions. He seeks to rebuild the power of the central government after a decade in which power slipped away to powerful economic magnates and entrenched regional bosses. To do this he has worked hard to tighten administrative discipline in the state. He has had some success. After nearly 10 years of steady economic contraction, the economy began to grow again in 1999, and has registered steady growth since then. Putin has enjoyed high levels of popular confidence, giving him wide latitude in choosing his policies. Gradually his general policy course has become clearer. It has three main elements. In foreign policy, he seeks to integrate Russia more deeply into the international system economically and politically. In the economy, he is trying to put Russia on a course of high and self-sustaining economic growth through the discipline of the market and incentives for investment. In politics, he is quietly but steadily imposing a centralized system of rule that relies on police controls and allows little more than a symbolic role for political opposition. Observers call his ideal model of rule "managed democracy." He wants to preserve the formal trappings of constitutional democracy, but also to manipulate political processes to ensure the outcomes he wants. His strategy has been to remove or neutralize potential sources of opposition to his power while creating an environment conducive to business investment and economic growth. Like previous Russian rulers, he has consolidated his own power by replacing officials considered loyal to the previous leadership with new people tied to him personally. He made his career in the security police and he has filled a strikingly large proportion of senior state positions with officials from the police, secret services, and armed forces (see Box 9.1).

Putin has only been partially successful in realizing his goals. Much of the credit for the economic recovery goes to the high world market prices for oil and gas. Most of the ambitious fiscal and administrative reforms he has introduced have been blunted in implementation. Some of Putin's actions, such as the suppression of independent media and the campaign against the oil giant *Yukos*,

have discouraged business investment and fueled capital flight, leading to slower economic growth. Putin's heavy reliance on the country's "power structures" (the interior ministry with its police and security troops, the regular armed forces, the law enforcement system, and the secret services) to remove or intimidate his rivals and to reinforce central control has chilled open public discourse and judicial independence. This makes it harder for the center to monitor bureaucratic performance. Actual improvements in the quality of governance under Putin have been modest. Putin has been much more successful in undercutting democratic checks and balances on central power than in making the new authoritarian system work effectively. Putin appears to believe that by centralizing power and eliminating opposition he can make the bureaucracy a more effective instrument for achieving his goals. However,

---

Box 9.1   Who Is Mister Putin?

Vladimir Putin's rise to power was so rapid that when he succeeded to the presidency, he was virtually unknown. A question often asked by Russians and foreigners alike was "Who is Mr. Putin?"

Vladimir Vladimirovich Putin was born on October 7, 1952, in Leningrad (called St. Petersburg since 1991), and grew up in an ordinary apartment. From early on, he took an interest in martial arts and became expert at judo. Inspired by heroic tales of the secret world of espionage, at the age of 16 he paid a visit to the local headquarters of the KGB, hoping to become an agent. There he was told, however, that he needed to go to university first. In 1970 he entered Leningrad State University and specialized in civil law. Upon graduation in 1975, Putin went to work for the KGB and was assigned to work first in counterintelligence, and then in its foreign intelligence division. Proficient in German, he was sent to East Germany in 1985. In 1990, after the Wall fell, Putin went back to Leningrad, working at the university but in the employ of the KGB. When a former law professor of his, Anatolii Sobchak, became mayor of Leningrad in 1991, he went to work for Sobchak. In the mayor's office he handled external relations, dealing extensively with foreign companies interested in investing in the city, and rose to become deputy mayor.

In 1996, Putin took a position in Yeltsin's presidential administration. He made a rapid career. In 1998, Yeltsin named Putin head of the FSB, (the Federal Security Service-successor to the KGB), and in March 1999, secretary of the Security Council as well. In August 1999, President Yeltsin appointed him prime minister. Thanks to his decisive handling of the military operation in Chechnia, Putin's popularity ratings quickly rose. On December 31, 1999, Yeltsin resigned, making Putin acting president. Putin ran for the presidency and, on March 26, 2000, won with an outright majority of the votes.

As time passed, Putin's political persona became somewhat clearer. Uncomfortable with the give and take of public politics, he prefers the hierarchical style of organization used in the military and police. He is a pragmatist with no particular affection either for the Soviet or tsarist order. He recognizes that Russia must participate in the contemporary world economy rather than burden itself with new international conflicts. Skilled at projecting an affable, relaxed demeanor, he is also self-possessed and disciplined, and reveals little of himself in dealing with others. Like many previous Russian rulers, he has made the consolidation of his own political power his first priority.

history suggests that administrative over-centralization usually ends up not strengthening but weakening state capacity.

HISTORICAL LEGACIES

The Tsarist Regime

The Russian state traces its origins to the princely state that arose around Kiev (today the capital of independent Ukraine) in the ninth century. For nearly a thousand years, the Russian state was autocratic. That is, it was ruled by a hereditary monarch whose power was unlimited by any constitution. Only in the first decade of the twentieth century did the Russian tsar agree to grant a constitution calling for an elected legislature—and even then, the tsar soon dissolved the legislature and arbitrarily revised the constitution. In addition to autocracy, the historical legacy of Russian statehood includes absolutism, patrimonialism, and Orthodox Christianity. Absolutism meant that the tsar aspired to wield absolute power over the subjects of the realm. *Patrimonialism* refers to the idea that the ruler treated his realm as property that he owned rather than as a society with its own legitimate rights and interests.[1] This conception of power continues to exert an influence over state rulers today.

Finally, the tsarist state identified itself with the Russian Orthodox Church. In Russia, as in other countries where it is the dominant religious tradition, the Orthodox Church ties itself closely to the state, considering itself a national church. Traditionally it has exhorted its adherents to show loyalty and obedience to the state in worldly matters, in return for which the state treated it as the state church. This legacy is still manifested in the post-Communist rulers' efforts to associate themselves with the heritage of Russia's church, and in many Russians' impulse to identify their state with a higher spiritual mission.

Absolutism, patrimonialism, and Orthodoxy have been recurring elements of Russian political culture. But alternate motifs have been influential as well. At some points in Russian history, the country's rulers have sought to modernize its economy and society. Russia imported Western practices in technology, law, state organization, and education in order to make the state competitive with other great powers. Modernizing rulers such as Peter the Great (who ruled from 1682 to 1725) and Catherine the Great (1762–1796) had a powerful impact on Russian society, bringing it closer to West European models. The imperative of building Russia's military and economic potential was all the more pressing because of Russia's constant expansion through conquest and annexation of neighboring territories, and the ever-present need to defend its borders. The state's role in controlling and mobilizing society rose with the need to govern a vast territory. By the end of the seventeenth century, Russia was territorially the largest state in the world. But for most of its history, Russia's imperial reach exceeded its actual grasp.

By comparison with the other major powers of Europe, Russia's economic institutions remained backward well into the twentieth century. However, the trajectory of its development, especially in the nineteenth century, was toward that of a modern industrial society. By the time the tsarist order fell in 1917, Russia possessed a large industrial sector, although it was concentrated in a few cities. The country had a sizable middle class, although it was greatly outnumbered by the vast and impoverished peasantry and the radicalized industrial working class. As a result, the social basis for a peaceful democratic transition was too weak to prevent the Communists from seizing power in 1917.

The thousand-year tsarist era left a contradictory legacy. The tsars attempted to legitimate their absolute power by appealing to tradition, empire, and divine right. They treated law as an instrument of rule rather than a source of authority. The doctrines that rulers should be accountable to the ruled and that sovereignty resides in the will of the people were alien to Russian state tradition. Throughout Russian history, state and society have been more distant from each other than in Western societies. Rulers and populace regarded one another with mistrust and suspicion. This gap has been overcome at times of great national trials such as the war against Napoleon and later World War II. Russia celebrated victory in those wars as a triumphant demonstration of the unity of state and people. But

Russia's political traditions also include a yearning for equality, solidarity, and community, as well as for moral purity and sympathy for the downtrodden. And throughout the Russian heritage runs a deep strain of national identification based on pride in the greatness of the country and the endurance of its people.

The Communist Revolution and the Soviet Order

The tsarist regime proved unable to meet the overwhelming demands of national mobilization in World War I. Tsar Nicholas II abdicated in February 1917 (March 1917, by the Western calendar). He was replaced by a short-lived provisional government which in turn fell when the Russian Communists— Bolsheviks, as they called themselves—took power in October 1917 (November, by our calendar). Their aim was to create a socialist society in Russia and, eventually, to spread revolutionary socialism throughout the world. Socialism, the Russian Communist Party believed, meant a society without private ownership of the means of production, where the state owned and controlled all important economic assets, and where political power was exercised in the name of the working people. *Vladimir Ilyich Lenin* was the leader of the Russian Communist Party and the first head of the Soviet Russian government. (Figure 9.1 lists the Soviet and post-Soviet leaders since 1917.)

Under Lenin's system of rule, the Communist Party controlled all levels of government. At each level of the territorial hierarchy of the country, full-time Communist Party officials supervised government. At the top, final power to decide policy rested in the CPSU (Communist Party of the Soviet Union) Politburo. Under *Joseph Stalin*, who took power after Lenin's death in 1924, power was even further centralized. Stalin instituted a totalitarian regime intent upon building up Russia's industrial and military might. The state survived the terrible test of World War II, ultimately pushing back the German army all the way to Berlin. But, the combined cost of war and terror under Stalin was staggering. The institutions of rule that Stalin left behind when he died in 1953 eventually crippled the

FIGURE 9.1   Timeline of Russian Rulers Since 1917 and the Periods of Their Rule

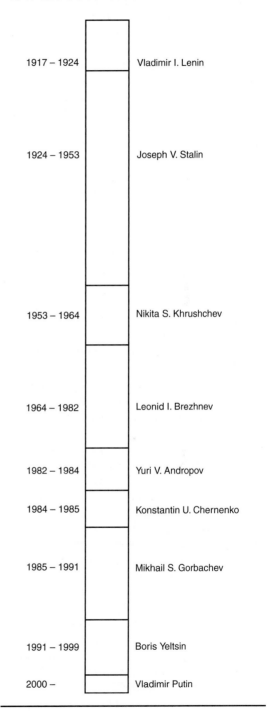

1917 – 1924	Vladimir I. Lenin
1924 – 1953	Joseph V. Stalin
1953 – 1964	Nikita S. Khrushchev
1964 – 1982	Leonid I. Brezhnev
1982 – 1984	Yuri V. Andropov
1984 – 1985	Konstantin U. Chernenko
1985 – 1991	Mikhail S. Gorbachev
1991 – 1999	Boris Yeltsin
2000 –	Vladimir Putin

Soviet state. They included personalistic rule, insecurity for rulers and ruled alike, heavy reliance on the secret police, and a militarized economy. None of Stalin's successors could reform the system without undermining Communist rule itself.

As vast as the Soviet state's powers were, they were frustrated by bureaucratic immobilism. As in any organization, overcentralization undermined actual power, through distortions of information flow, tacit resistance to the center's orders by officials at lower levels, and the force of inertia. Bureaucratic officials were generally more devoted to protecting and advancing their own personal and career interests than in serving the public interest. By the time *Mikhail Gorbachev* was elected General Secretary of the CPSU in 1985, the political system of the USSR had grown top heavy, unresponsive, and corrupt. The regime had more than enough power to destroy any budding political opposition. However, it was unable to modernize the economy or improve living standards for the population. By the early 1980s, the economy had stopped growing and the country was unable to compete militarily or economically with the advanced countries of the West.

The youngest member of the Politburo at the time he was named party leader—he was only 54 when he took over—Gorbachev quickly grasped the levers of power that the system granted the General Secretary. He moved both to strengthen his own political base, and to carry out a program of reform.[2] Emphasizing the need for greater openness—*glasnost*—in society, Gorbachev stressed that the ultimate test of the party's effectiveness lay in improving the economic well-being of the country and its people. By highlighting such themes as the need for market relations, pragmatism in economic policy, and less secretiveness in government, he identified himself as a champion of reform. Gorbachev not only called for political democratization, but he pushed through a reform bringing about the first contested elections for local soviets in many decades. He legalized private enterprise for individual and cooperative businesses and encouraged them to fill the many gaps in the economy left by the inefficiency of the state sector. He called for a "law-governed state" (*pravovoe gosudarstvo*) in which state power—including the power of the Communist Party—would be subordinate to law. He welcomed the explosion of informal social and political associations that formed. He made major concessions to the United States in the sphere of arms control. This resulted in a treaty which, for the first time in history, called for the destruction of entire classes of nuclear missiles.

Using to the full the General Secretary's authoritarian powers, Gorbachev quickly railroaded his proposals for democratization through the Supreme Soviet. In 1989 and 1990, Gorbachev's plan for free elections and a working parliament was realized as elections were held, deputies elected, and new soviets formed at the center and in every region and locality. When nearly half a million coal miners went out on strike in the summer of 1989, Gorbachev declared himself sympathetic to their demands.

Gorbachev's radicalism received its most dramatic confirmation through the astonishing developments of 1989 in Eastern Europe. All the regimes making up the Socialist bloc collapsed and gave way to multi-party parliamentary regimes in virtually bloodless popular revolutions. The Soviet Union stood by and supported the revolutions. The overnight dismantling of communism in Eastern Europe meant that the elaborate structure of party ties, police cooperation, economic trade, and military alliance that had developed with Eastern Europe after World War II vanished. Divided Germany was allowed to reunite.

In the Soviet Union itself, meantime, the Communist Party faced a critical loss of authority. The newly elected governments of the national republics making up the Soviet state one by one declared that they were sovereign. The three Baltic Republics declared their intention to secede from the union. Over 1989–1990, throughout the Soviet Union and Eastern Europe, Communist Party rule was breaking down.

Political Institutions of the Transition Period: Demise of the USSR

Gorbachev's reforms had consequences he did not intend. The 1990 elections of deputies to the Supreme Soviets in all 15 republics and for local soviets stimulated popular nationalist and democratic movements in most republics. In the core republic—Russia itself—Gorbachev's rival Boris Yeltsin won election as Chairman of the Russian Supreme Soviet in June 1990. As chief of state in the Russian Republic, Yeltsin was well positioned to challenge Gorbachev for preeminence.

Yeltsin's rise forced Gorbachev to alter his strategy. Beginning in March 1991, Gorbachev sought terms for a new federal or confederal union that would be acceptable to Yeltsin and the Russian leadership, as well as to the leaders of the other republics. In April 1991 he reached an agreement on the outlines of a new treaty of union with 9 of the 15 republics, including Russia. A weak central government would manage basic coordinating functions. But the republics would gain the power to control the economies of their territories.

Gorbachev had underestimated the strength of his opposition. On August 19, 1991, his own vice-president, prime minister, defense minister, KGB chairman, and other senior officials preempted the signing ceremony of the treaty by placing Gorbachev under house arrest and seizing state power. This was a fateful moment for Russia. In Moscow and St. Petersburg, thousands of citizens rallied to the cause of democracy and Russian sovereignty. The coup collapsed on the third day and Gorbachev returned to office again as president. But his power was now fatally weakened. Neither union nor Russian power structures heeded his commands. Through the fall of 1991, the Russian government took over the union government, ministry by ministry. In November 1991, President Yeltsin issued a decree formally outlawing the Communist Party of the Soviet Union. By December, Gorbachev was president without a country. On December 25, 1991, he resigned as president and turned the powers of his office over to Boris Yeltsin.[3]

Political Institutions of the Transition Period: Russia 1990–1993

The Russian Republic followed the example of the USSR and adopted its own constitutional amendments creating a Congress of People's Deputies and Supreme Soviet, and soon after, a state presidency.

Boris Yeltsin was elected president of the Russian Federation in June 1991. Unlike Gorbachev, Yeltsin was elected in a direct, popular, competitive election, which gave him a considerable advantage in mobilizing public support against Gorbachev and the central USSR government (see Box 9.2).

Like Gorbachev before him, Yeltsin demanded extraordinary powers from parliament to cope with the country's economic problems. Following the August 1991 coup attempt, he sought from the Russian Congress of People's Deputies, and was given, the power to carry out a program of radical market-oriented reform by decree. Yeltsin named himself acting prime minister and formed a government led by a group of young, Western-oriented leaders determined to carry out a decisive economic transformation. The new government's economic reforms took effect on January 2, 1992. Their first results were felt immediately as prices skyrocketed. Quickly many politicians began to distance themselves from the program: even Yeltsin's vice-president denounced the program as "economic genocide." Through 1992, opposition to the reforms grew stronger and more intransigent. Increasingly, the political confrontation between Yeltsin and the reformers on the one side, and the opposition to radical economic reform on the other, became centered in the two branches of government. President Yeltsin demanded broad powers to carry out the reform program, but parliament refused to adopt a new constitution that would give him the powers he demanded. In March 1993 a motion to remove the president through impeachment nearly passed in the parliament.

On September 21, 1993, Yeltsin declared the parliament dissolved, and called for elections to a new parliament. Yeltsin's enemies barricaded themselves inside the parliament building. After a 10-day standoff, the dissidents joined with some loosely organized paramilitary units outside the building and attacked the Moscow mayor's offices adjacent to the Russian White House. They even called on their followers to "seize the Kremlin." Finally, the army agreed to back Yeltsin and suppress the uprising by force.

The circumstances of the December 1993 parliamentary elections were hardly auspicious. Yeltsin's

Box 9.2   Boris Yeltsin: Russia's First President

Boris Yeltsin, born in 1931, graduated from the Urals Polytechnical Institute in 1955 with a diploma in civil engineering, and worked for a long time in construction. From 1976 to 1985 he served as first secretary of the Sverdlovsk oblast (provincial) Communist Party organization.

Early in 1986 he became first secretary of the Moscow city party organization but was removed in November 1987 for speaking out against Gorbachev. Positioning himself as a victim of the party establishment, Yeltsin made a remarkable political comeback. In the 1989 elections to the Congress of People's Deputies, he won a Moscow at-large seat with almost 90 percent of the vote. The following year he was elected to the Russian republic's parliament with over 80 percent of the vote. He was then elected its chairman in June 1990. In 1991, he was elected president of Russia, receiving 57 percent of the vote. Thus, he had won three major races in three successive years. He was reelected as president in 1996 in a dramatic, come-from-behind race against the leader of the Communist Party.

Yeltsin's last years in office were notable for his lengthy spells of illness, and for the carousel of prime ministerial appointments he made. The entourage of family members and advisers around him, dubbed colloquially "the Family," seemed to exercise undue influence over him. Yet, infirm as he was, he judged that Russia's interests and his own would be safe in Vladimir Putin's hands. Instead of turning against Putin when Putin gained in power and popularity, Yeltsin chose to resign and turn the presidency over to Putin. His resignation speech was full of contrition for his failure to bring a better life to Russians. In retirement, Yeltsin entered a dignified private life, resurfacing with his old rival Mikhail Gorbachev for President Putin's inauguration on May 7, 2000.

Yeltsin's legacy is mixed. He was most effective when engaged in political battle, whether he was fighting for supremacy against Gorbachev, or fighting against the Communists. Impulsive and undisciplined, he was gifted with exceptionally keen political intuition. He regarded economic reform as an instrument in his political war with the Communist opposition, and used privatization to make it impossible for any future rulers to return to state socialism. Imperious and willful, he also regarded the adoption of the 1993 constitution as a major achievement and willingly accepted the limits on his presidential power that it imposed.

---

decree meant that national elections were to be held for a legislature that did not, constitutionally, exist, since the constitution establishing these institutions was to be voted upon in a referendum held in parallel with the parliamentary elections. Yet for all the violence surrounding its inception, the constitution approved in the December referendum has stayed in force since then.

THE CONTEMPORARY CONSTITUTIONAL ORDER

The Presidency

The 1993 constitution combined elements of presidentialism and parliamentarism. (See Figure 9.2 for a schematic overview of the Russian constitutional structure.) Although it provided for the separation of executive, legislative, and judicial branches and for a federal division of power between the central and regional levels of government, it gave the president wide power. The president is popularly elected for a four-year term (under the constitution, he is limited to two terms). The president names the prime minister to head the government. Yet the government must have the confidence of parliament to remain in power. Although the constitution does not call the president the head of the executive branch, he is so in fact by virtue of his power to appoint the prime minister and the rest of the government, and his right to issue *presidential decrees* with the force of law. (The decree power is limited, however, because decrees may not violate existing law and can be superseded by legislation.)

Over the decade since the constitution was approved, some informal practices have come to govern the exercise of central power. For example, the president and government divide executive respon-

FIGURE 9.2   Russian Political System Under the 1993 Constitution

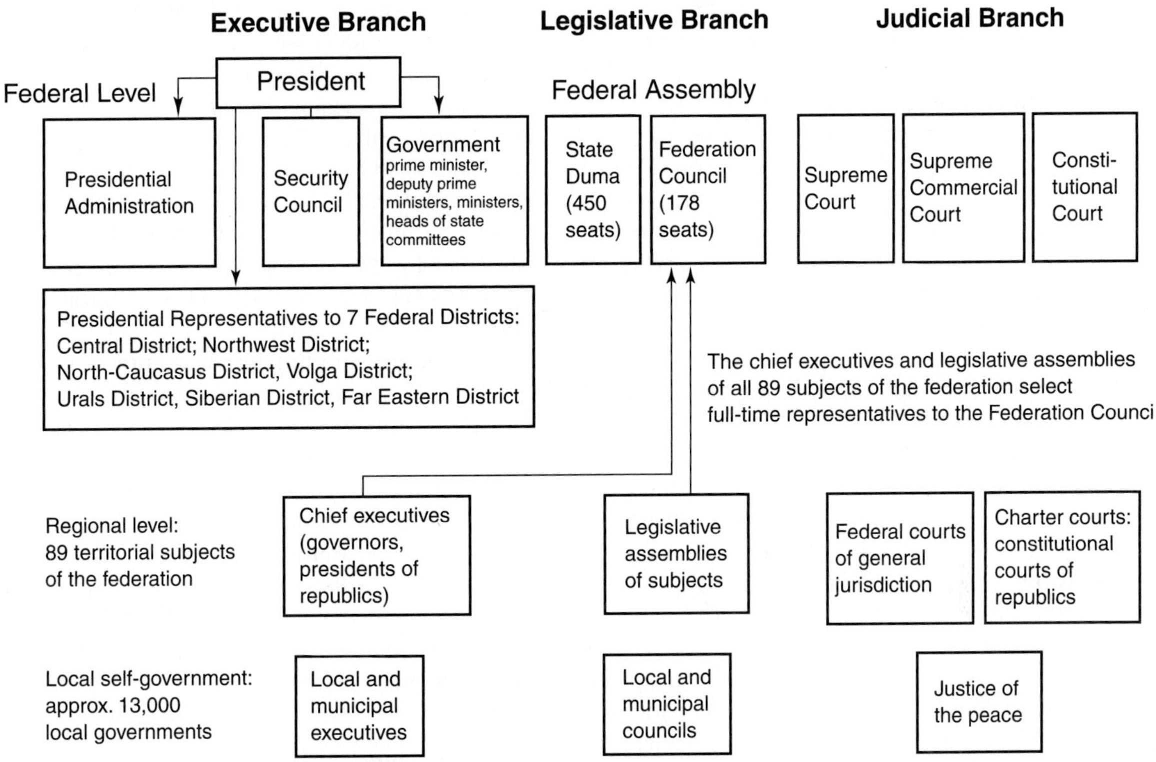

Executive Branch **Legislative Branch** **Judicial Branch**

Federal Level — President

Federal Assembly

| Presidential Administration | Security Council | Government prime minister, deputy prime ministers, ministers, heads of state committees | State Duma (450 seats) | Federation Council (178 seats) | Supreme Court | Supreme Commercial Court | Constitutional Court |

Presidential Representatives to 7 Federal Districts:
Central District; Northwest District;
North-Caucasus District, Volga District;
Urals District, Siberian District, Far Eastern District

The chief executives and legislative assemblies of all 89 subjects of the federation select full-time representatives to the Federation Council

Regional level: 89 territorial subjects of the federation

| Chief executives (governors, presidents of republics) | | Legislative assemblies of subjects | Federal courts of general jurisdiction | Charter courts: constitutional courts of republics |

Local self-government: approx. 13,000 local governments

| Local and municipal executives | Local and municipal councils | Justice of the peace |

---

sibility. The government, headed by the prime minister, is primarily responsible for economic and social policy. The president directly oversees the ministries and other bodies directly concerned with coercion, law enforcement, and state security—the "power ministries." These include the Foreign Ministry, Defense Ministry, Ministry of Internal Affairs (which controls the regular police and security troops), Federal Security Service (FSB—formerly the KGB), and several other security and intelligence agencies. The president and his staff set overall policy in foreign and domestic domains, and the government develops the specific proposals and rules carrying it out. In practice, the government answers to the president, rather than to parliament. The government's base of support is the president rather than a particular coalition of political forces in parliament.

Despite the asymmetrical constitutional balance, the parliament does have some power. Its approval is required for any bill to become law. The State Duma (the lower house of parliament) must confirm the president's nominee for prime minister. If, upon three successive votes, the Duma refuses to confirm the nomination, the president must dissolve the Duma and call new elections. Likewise the Duma may vote to deny confidence in the government. If a motion of no confidence carries twice, the president must either dissolve parliament or dismiss the government. During Yeltsin's tenure as president, the Duma was able to block some of Yeltsin's legislative initiatives. Under Putin, however, it has largely been a rubber stamp. Conceivably, future presidents may have less of a free hand in their dealings with parliament than Putin does. The constitution allows for a wide range of types of relationship between president, government, and parliament, depending on the degree to which the president dominates the political system.

In addition to these powers, the president has a large array of other formal and informal powers in his constitutional capacity as "head of state," "guarantor of the constitution," and commander-in-chief of the armed forces. He oversees a large presidential administration which supervises the federal government and keeps tabs on regional governments. Informally, the administration also manages relations with the parliament, the courts, big business, the media, political parties, and major interest groups. A good indication of the degree to which Putin has revived Russia's traditional authoritarian style of rule is the informal rule that no significant political undertaking in Russia is possible without prior clearance from the presidential administration.

The president also oversees many official and quasi-official supervisory and advisory commissions. One of the most important is the *Security Council*, chaired by the president, which consists of a permanent secretary, the heads of the power ministries and other security-related agencies, the prime minister, and, more recently the finance minister and chairs of the two chambers of parliament. Its powers are broad but shadowy. Another prominent body advising the president is the *State Council*, which comprises the heads of regional governments. Both Yeltsin and Putin have regularly created and dissolved new institutions answering directly to the president. These improvised structures can be politically useful as counterweights to constitutionally mandated bodies such as parliament, as well as providing policy advice and feedback. They help ensure that the president is always the dominant institution in the political system, but they undermine the authority of formal institutions.

The Government

In contrast to most parliamentary systems, the makeup of the Russian government is not directly determined by the party composition of the parliament. Indeed, there is scarcely any relationship between the distribution of party forces in the Duma and the political balance of the government. Nearly all members of the government are career managers and administrators rather than party politicians. Overall, the government is not a party government, but reflects the president's calculations about how to balance considerations such as personal loyalty, professional competence, and the relative strength of major bureaucratic factions. When President Putin chose Mikhail Fradkov to be prime minister on March 1, 2004—two weeks *ahead* of presidential elections—the political establishment was taken by surprise. Fradkov was a relatively obscure figure who had headed the Federal Tax Police for two years. His very lack of independent political clout underscored the fact that Putin would be the main source of policy direction for the country.

Following a major restructuring in 2004, the Cabinet comprises 15 ministries and 3 state committees that in turn oversee dozens of other state committees and agencies responsible for managing the federal executive branch. The reform sought to replace the many ministries responsible for managing specific branches of the economy with a smaller number of ministries performing broad functions. Skeptics noted that although the aim was to streamline the structure of government, the total number of federal-level executive bodies rose from 57 to 72.[4]

The Parliament

The parliament—called the Federal Assembly—is bicameral. The lower house, the *State Duma*, combines single-member district representation and party-list proportional representation. The upper house, the *Federation Council*, represents each of Russia's 89 federal regions on an equal basis. Party factions dominate the proceedings of the State Duma, while the Federation Council avoids forming partisan groups.

Under President Yeltsin, the Federal Assembly was a modestly authoritative body. President Putin, however, has a degree of influence over both chambers that has turned them nearly into a rubber stamp for his legislative agenda. Whether this present state of affairs will last, however, is open to question. President Putin's domination of the political system may prove temporary, and popular demands for policy change and political representation may again make parliament a source of opposition influence. Russia's constitution can accommodate a variety of possible arrangements. In any case, the actual power of parliament will depend more on the evolution of the party system and other structures for aggregating popular demands than on formal constitutional rules.

The Duma has the right to originate legislation except for certain categories of policy which are under the jurisdiction of the Federation Council. As Figure 9.3 shows, upon passage in the State Duma, a bill goes to the Federation Council for consideration. The Federation Council can only pass it, reject it, or reject it and call for forming an agreement commission comprising members of both houses to iron out differences. If the Duma rejects the up-

per house's changes, it can override the Federation Council by a two-thirds vote and send the bill directly on to the president.

When the bill has cleared parliament, it goes to the president for signature. If the president refuses to sign the bill, it returns to the Duma. The Duma may pass it with the president's proposed amendments by a simple absolute majority, or override the president's veto, for which a two-thirds vote is required. The Federation Council must then also approve the bill, by a simple majority if the president's amendments are accepted, or a two-thirds vote if it chooses to override the president. On rare occasions, the Duma has overridden the president's veto

---

FIGURE 9.3   The Legislative Process: Three Readings

The Legislative Process: Three Readings

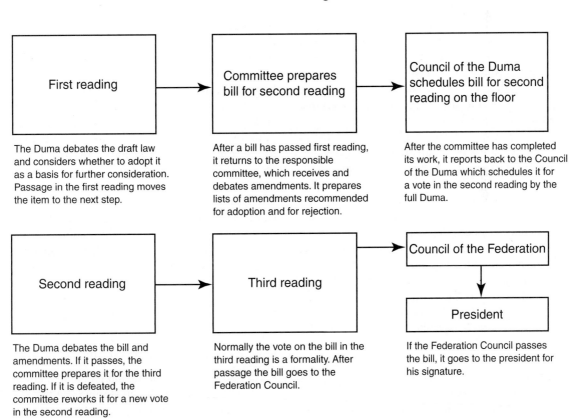

| First reading | Committee prepares bill for second reading | Council of the Duma schedules bill for second reading on the floor |

The Duma debates the draft law and considers whether to adopt it as a basis for further consideration. Passage in the first reading moves the item to the next step.

After a bill has passed first reading, it returns to the responsible committee, which receives and debates amendments. It prepares lists of amendments recommended for adoption and for rejection.

After the committee has completed its work, it reports back to the Council of the Duma which schedules it for a vote in the second reading by the full Duma.

| Second reading | Third reading | Council of the Federation → President |

The Duma debates the bill and amendments. If it passes, the committee prepares it for the third reading. If it is defeated, the committee reworks it for a new vote in the second reading.

Normally the vote on the bill in the third reading is a formality. After passage the bill goes to the Federation Council.

If the Federation Council passes the bill, it goes to the president for his signature.

and it has overridden Federation Council rejections more frequently. In other cases, the Duma has passed bills rejected by the president after accepting the president's amendments. Under President Yeltsin, political forces opposed to Yeltsin, particularly Communists and nationalists, held the majority in the Duma. But parliament and president generally worked to head off major confrontations.

The Duma's 450 members are elected in two ways. Half, or 225, are elected in *single-member districts* by a first-past-the-post, plurality rule. The other 225 are elected on party lists. A party receiving at least 5 percent of the vote on the party-list ballot is entitled to as many of the 225 party-list seats in the Duma as its share of the party-list vote. As in other proportional representation systems, votes cast for parties that fail to clear the 5 percent threshold go to winning parties. In the fall of 2004, however, President Putin proposed reforming the electoral system so as to eliminate all single-member district seats and elect all 450 deputies proportionally from party lists.

Nearly all Duma deputies either join party factions or form their own groups. Factions and groups enjoy desirable privileges in the Duma, including the right to committee chairmanships, office space, and recognition in floor debate. Faction leaders are represented on the governing body of the Duma, the Council of the Duma.

The December 2003 elections gave the forces aligned with President Putin an overwhelming majority in the Duma, which they have used to centralize power. The pro-Putin party is called *United Russia*, and it holds two-thirds of the seats in the Duma. Around 80 percent of all single-member district deputies joined the United Russia faction—a good indication of its drawing power. The new Duma that convened in January 2004 gave nearly all committee chairmanships to members of United Russia, and 8 out of the 11 members of the Council of the Duma are from United Russia. Since United Russia votes with a high degree of discipline, the Duma consistently delivers the president legislative majorities. Other factions have very little opportunity to influence the agenda, let alone the outcomes of legislative deliberations.

Each deputy is a member of 1 of 29 standing committees with specific policy jurisdictions. As bills are submitted to the Duma, they are assigned to particular committees, which collect and review proposed amendments before reporting out the bills for votes by the full chamber with the committee's recommendations.

The Federation Council is designed as an instrument of federalism in that (as in the United States Senate) every constituent unit of the federation is represented by two representatives. Thus the populations of small ethnic-national territories are greatly overrepresented compared with more populous regions. The Federation Council has important powers. Besides acting on bills passed by the lower house, it also approves presidential nominees for high courts such as the Supreme Court and the Constitutional Court. It must approve presidential decrees declaring martial law or a state of emergency, or any acts altering the boundaries of territorial units. It must consider any legislation dealing with taxes, budget, financial policy, treaties, customs, and declarations of war.

Until a major reform pushed through by President Putin in the spring of 2000, its members were the heads of the executive and legislative branches of each constituent territory of the federation. Now, however, each governor and each regional legislature names a representative to the Federation Council to serve on a full-time basis. The governors appoint their representatives, who are then confirmed by the legislatures. The regional legislatures elect their representatives. They can recall their representatives at any time.

There is great deal of dissatisfaction over the current role of the Federation Council. Many believe that the composition of the chamber should be replaced with one providing that the members are popularly elected. This must be reconciled, however, with the constitutional requirement that the 2 members of the chamber from each of Russian 89 territorial subjects must represent the executive and legislative branches.

Executive-Legislative Relations

Relations between president and parliament during the Yeltsin period were often stormy. The first two Dumas, elected in 1993 and in 1995, were dominated by the Communist and other leftist factions hostile to President Yeltsin and the policies of his government. This was particularly true in areas of economic policy and privatization. On other issues, however, such as matters concerning federal relations, the Duma and president often reached agreement—sometimes against the resistance of the Federation Council, whose members fought to protect regional prerogatives.

The 1999 election produced a Duma with a pro-government majority. President Putin and his government built a reliable base of support in the Duma for their legislative initiatives comprising a coalition of four centrist political factions. The 2003 election produced a still wider margin of suppport for the president in the Duma and an overwhelming majority for the United Russia party. This means that the president does not need to expend much effort in bargaining with the Duma to win its support for his policies. Generally speaking, the pro-presidential deputies in the Duma need the Kremlin much more than the Kremlin needs them. As a result, the balance of power in the political system under Putin has shifted steadily away from the parliament and toward the president.

The Constitutional Court

The 1993 constitution provides for judicial review by the *Constitutional Court.* Its 19 members are nominated by the president but are subject to confirmation by the Council of the Federation. The Court is empowered to consider the constitutionality of actions of the president, the parliament, and lower-level governments. The court has carefully avoided issuing any decisions restricting presidential powers in any significant way. However, it has decided a number of thorny constitutional issues, including the relations between the two chambers of parliament and the delineation of powers between the central and regional governments. It has also consistently defended the rights of individual defendants in the criminal justice system. The court has also tended to uphold the sovereignty of federal law over the rights of the constituent territories of the federation. In 2000 the court ruled, for instance, that the national republics within Russia may not call themselves "sovereign" or claim ownership of the natural resources on their territories.

Central Government and the Regions

Following the breakup of the Soviet Union, many Russians feared that Russia would break up as well into a patchwork of independent fiefdoms. Certainly Russia's territorial integrity was subjected to serious strains. Under President Yeltsin, the central government granted wide autonomy to regional governments in return for political support. Under Putin the pendulum has swung back sharply toward centralization.

Demographic factors also affect Russia's territorial integrity. Eighty percent of Russia's population is ethnically Russian. None of its ethnic minorities accounts for more than 4 percent of the total (the Tatars form the largest of the ethnic minorities, constituting about 5.5 million of the 146 million total population). Rebuilding national community in post–Soviet Russia has been helped by Russia's thousand-year history of statehood. Yet until 1991, Russia was never constituted as a nation-state: under the tsars it was a multinational empire, and under Soviet rule it was nominally a federal union of socialist republics. State policy toward nationality has also varied over the centuries. In some periods, Russia recognized a variety of distinct ethnic-national communities and tolerated cultural differences among them. In other periods the state pressured non-Russian groups to assimilate to Russian culture.[5]

Russia was formally established as a federal republic under the Soviet regime. In contrast to the Soviet Union of which it was the largest component, only some of its constituent members were ethnic-national territories. The rest were pure administrative subdivisions, populated mainly by Russians. The non-Russian ethnic-national territories were classified by size and status into autonomous republics, autonomous provinces, and national districts. In many of them, the indigenous ethnic group comprised a minority of the population. Since 1991, the names and status of some of the constituent units have changed. As of 2004, Russia comprises 89 constituent territorial units. In Russian constitutional law, these are called the "subjects of the federation." They represent 6 different types of unit: 21 are republics, 6 are *krais* (territories), 10 are autonomous districts (all but one of them located within other units), 1 is an autonomous *oblast*, 2 are cities, and 49 are *oblasts*. Republics, autonomous districts, and the one autonomous oblast are units created specifically to give certain political rights to populations living in territories with significant ethnic minorities. Oblasts and krais are simply administrative subdivisions with no special constitutional status.

One of the centralizing measures President Putin has pursued is the merger of smaller ethnic regions into larger territorial units. The first such merger is between Perm' oblast and its neighbor, the Komi-Permyak autonomous district. Persuaded by a combination of pressures and material inducements from the central government, voters and officials in both regions approved the merger in December 2003. It will take effect in December 2005. Several similar mergers are now being negotiated, including the incorporation of Tiumen' oblast with two oil-rich autonomous districts that border it. Most observers believe that the Putin administration seeks to eliminate most or all of the smaller ethnic units by merging them into larger neighboring regions and reducing the patronage rights that come with their status as separate territorial units.[6]

The ethnic republics jealously guard their special status. From 1990 to 1992, all the republics adopted declarations of sovereignty and two made attempts to declare full or partial independence of Russia. In the mountainous region of the North Caucasus, between the Black and Caspian Seas, there lies a belt of ethnic republics that includes the Chechen Republic (*Chechnia*). Its leadership declared independence of Russia in 1991, an act Russia refused to recognize but did not initially overturn by force. The Tatar Republic also sought to separate itself from Russia. It is situated on the Volga, in an oil-rich and heavily industrialized region. Eventually Russia and Tatarstan worked out a treaty satisfactory to both sides, and the separatist movement in Tatarstan gradually subsided. In Chechnia, however, armed opposition failed to unseat the secession-minded leader. In December 1994 Russian forces attacked the republic directly,

subjecting its capital city, Groznyi, to devastating bombardment. This forced tens of thousands of Chechen and Russian residents to flee the city and led to a protracted, destructive war. Fighting ceased in summer 1996 but resumed in 1999. Federal forces had established control over most parts of Chechnia by early 2000, but Chechen guerrillas continue to carry out ambushes and suicide attacks against federal units and have impeded the restoration of political order. Chechen terrorist groups have attacked civilian targets both in the North Caucasus region and in Moscow. One of the most shocking of these incidents was the seizure of a school in the town of Beslan, near Chechnia, in September 2004 (see Box 9.3). The brutal methods used by federal forces to suppress the uprising have fueled continuing hatred on the part of many Chechens against the federal government, which in turn facilitates recruitment by the terrorists. The 21 ethnic republics have the constitutional right to determine their own form of state power so long as their decisions do not contradict federal law. All 21 have established presidencies. In many cases, the republic presidents have constructed personal power bases around appeals to ethnic solidarity and the cultural autonomy of the indigenous nationality. In many cases they have used this power to establish personalistic dictatorships in their regions.

President Putin has made clear his intention to reassert the federal government's authority over the regions. The reform of the Federation Council was one step in this direction. In 2000 Putin pushed a law through parliament that gave him the ability to remove a governor if a court found that the governor had refused to act in line with the federal constitution and law. Needless to say, the governors strongly opposed these changes. But the Duma supported the proposal and, with some modifications, it was passed into law.

Putin's decree of May 13, 2000, also created seven new "federal districts." He appointed a special presidential representative to each district who monitors the actions of the regional governments within that district. This reform sought to strengthen central control over the activity of federal bodies in the regions. Often, in the past, local branches of federal agencies had fallen under the

Box 9.3   Beslan

September 1 is the first day of school each year throughout Russia. Children, accompanied by their parents, often come to school bringing flowers to their teachers. A group organized by the Chechen warlord Shamil Basaev chose September 1, 2004, to carry out one of the most horrific incidents in the history of the Chechen wars. A group of heavily armed militants stormed a school in the town of Beslan, located in the republic of North Osetia, next door to Chechnia. Over 1,000 schoolchildren, parents, and teachers were taken hostage. The terrorists crowded the captives into the school gymnasium, which they filled with explosives to prevent any rescue attempt. Negotiations over the release of the hostages failed; the terrorists even refused to allow water and food to be brought into the school to relieve the hostages' suffering. Reports on the terrorists' demands varied. Some indicated that the terrorists demanded the release of some of their comrades who had been captured earlier that summer; other reports said that the terrorists called for the withdrawal of federal troops from Chechnia.

On the third day of the seige, something triggered the detonation of one of the bombs inside the school. In the chaos that followed, many of the children and adults rushed to escape. The terrorists fired at them. Federal forces stormed the school, trying to rescue the escaping hostages and to kill the terrorists. Many of the bombs planted by the terrorists exploded. Ultimately around 350 of the hostages died, along with all the terrorists, and an unknown number of security troops.

The media covered the events extensively. The Beslan tragedy had an impact on Russian national consciousness comparable to that of September 11 in the United States. While there had been a number of previous attacks tied to Chechen terrorists, none had cost so many innocent lives. Although many Russians blamed corruption and poor organization among the police for allowing the terrorists to take over the school initially and for failing to prevent the destruction at the end, they also recognized that the terrorists had made it impossible for the security forces to attempt a rescue for fear of provoking a massacre of the children.

Putin and other senior government officials claimed that the terrorists were part of an international terrorist movement aimed ultimately at the dismemberment of Russia itself. Putin studiously avoided linking the incident to Russian policy in Chechnia. In response to the crisis, Putin called for measures to reinforce national security, particularly in the North Caucasus, and to improve the effectiveness of federal police, security, and military agencies. He also called for several reforms of the political system, including an end to the institution of direct popular election of governors. Instead, he proposed that the president would nominate candidates for governor, and the regional legislatures would confirm them. This step, he said, would make governors more accountable for the safety and well-being of their regions. He also proposed eliminating single-member district seats in the Duma elections in favor of filling all Duma seats by party-list proportional representation. Most observers assumed that Putin wanted to make these changes anyway, and that the Beslan tragedy simply gave him a political opening to enact them. By the same token, however, Putin has placed his own political reputation on the line by tying his strategy of centralizing power to the goal of strengthening state security.

influence of powerful governors. Critics of Putin's reform complained that it was a step in the direction of creating a hypercentralized, authoritarian system of rule. Defenders argued that many regions had effectively become personal dictatorships and that decisive steps were needed to bring them back under central control. Putin has moved carefully but steadily to limit the autonomy of governors. He has replaced most of the heads of regional police and security service administrations. But he has refrained from forcibly removing governors. The governors have generally avoided direct confrontations with Putin. Moreover, once Putin enacts the reform replacing direct election of governors with a system of appointed governors, they will be still more careful to appear politically loyal to the president.

Below the tier of regional government is a tier of units that are supposed to enjoy the right of self-government—municipalities and other local government units. There are some 13,000 of these local entities. Local governments have almost no independent sources of revenue. On average, they receive 90 percent of their budget funds from the regional and federal governments. Regional governments resist allowing local governments to exercise any significant powers of their own, and federal laws have been unable to alter this situation. In many cases, the mayors of the capital cities of regions are political rivals of the governors of the regions. Moscow and St. Petersburg are exceptional cases because they have the status of federal territorial subjects like republics and regions. Other cities lack the power and autonomy of Moscow and St. Petersburg, and must bargain with their superior regional governments for shares of power.

Before 2005, regional chief executives (generally called *governors*) were chosen by direct popular election. Since the enactment of Putin's recent reforms, however, the president appoints governors. Many citizens supported this change, believing that the institution of local elections had been discredited by corruption and fraud and that elections were more often determined by the influence of wealthy insiders than by public opinion (see Box 9.4). Putin clearly hopes that appointed governors will be more accountable and effective, but past experience suggests that centralizing power by itself is unlikely to improve state performance in the regions in the absence of other mechanisms for enforcing federal law.

Box 9.4   The 2004 Vladivostok Mayor's Race[*]

Even by the standards of Russian elections, the race for mayor of the city of Vladivostok in 2004 stood out for the scale of corruption. Vladivostok is the capital city of the Far East region. Governance in the region has been corrupt and incompetent, often resulting in disruptions in the supply of heat, electric power, and water. There has been a chronic power struggle between the governor of the region and the mayor of Vladivostok.

In February 2001 President Putin finally succeeded in dislodging the powerful governor of the region. Many thought that the destructive conflict between governor and mayor would finally end. However, the new governor, Sergei Darkin, continued to fight with the Vladivostok mayor. Darkin sponsored his own candidate for mayor in the 2004 election, Vladimir Nikolaev, who was a deputy in the local legislature and controlled a major fishing company. Nikolaev also had been convicted in 1999 of beating one local official and threatening to murder another (he began serving a three-and-a-half-year jail term, but was soon amnestied). Russian press reported that he heads a major organized crime group and bears the underworld nickname of "Winnie the Pooh."

The mayoral race was bitterly fought. During the campaign there were physical attacks on candidates, threats, abductions of newspaper distributors, and copious disinformation. No candidate won an outright majority in the first round, so a second round was

scheduled. The two top finishers—Nikolaev, who received 26.8 percent and a former mayor, Viktor Cherepkov, who received 26.3 percent—entered the runoff. Nine days before the election, a bomb reportedly exploded at Cherepkov's headquarters. What finally forced Cherepkov off the ballot was not the bombing, however, but a court decision six days before the election that disqualified him from running for using illegal campaign methods.

Under normal procedures, Kopylov, who had received the next highest vote total in the first round, would have entered the runoff, but he refused. So did the person who received the fourth highest total. In the end, the man who came in fifth, with 3 percent, was Nikolaev's opponent. Nikolaev went on to win with 53 percent of the vote; 37 percent voted "against all."

Many observers wondered how to interpret the Kremlin's passivity in dealing with Vladivostok: Does it reflect Putin's indifference to local power struggles? Or is it a sign of Moscow's powerlessness in the face of entrenched corruption? Some cynics have even speculated that elections so scandalous are actually intended to discredit the very institution of elections in order to prepare the way for direct presidential rule.

[*]This account is based on a report by Vyachaslav Shirokov in *Russian Regional Report*, Vol. 9, No. 13, 20 July 2004; and Julie Corwin, "Vladivostok Sees Its Wildest Election Yet," RFE/RL Newsline, July 28, 2004.

Russia's post-Communist constitutional arrangements are still evolving. The political system allows considerable room for the arbitrary exercise of power and even, as under President Putin, the evisceration of democracy. Both Yeltsin and Putin have interpreted their presidential mandates broadly. President Yeltsin used his decree power to carry out a massive privatization program. He signed bilateral treaties with almost 50 individual regional governments. He also launched a brutal military campaign to suppress an independence movement in the Chechen Republic. He carried out all of these actions without seeking parliamentary approval. In one 18-month period between 1998 and 1999, he named and dismissed his prime minister four times.

President Putin has also used his powers expansively. In 2000 he issued a decree creating seven federal super-districts to facilitate central supervision of regional governments and he appointed representatives to oversee them. By decree he also created a new consultative structure of regional governors called the State Council. This was an effort to mollify the governors, whom he had deprived of seats in the Federation Council. Both institutional changes were not envisioned by the constitution, but also not specifically prohibited by it. The constitutional arrangements established under President Yeltsin had the potential to evolve toward democracy. A successful democratic transition, however, depends on more than a democratic constitution. The web of political institutions surrounding formal constitutional rules strongly shapes the way officeholders wield power. Informal rules can be far more important than formal rules. If rulers can circumvent formal limits on their power, constitutional structures may become irrelevant to the actual exercise of power.

Russia somewhat resembles the pattern that political scientist Guillermo O'Donnell has called "delegative democracy."[7] In such a system, common in Latin America, a president may win an election and then proceed to govern as if he were the sole source of authority in the country. The president exercises so much power over other political structures, thanks to his control of the police and military and his access to patronage, that he can negate the nominal separation of powers written into the constitution. In such a system, parliamentarians may use their positions not to represent constituents or craft legislation but to trade favors and enrich their friends and family. Judges may deem it safer to tailor their decisions to the wishes of powerful state officials. The editors of major newspapers bury stories unfavorable to the authorities. Interest groups curry favor with officials rather than mobilizing their supporters around particular policy positions. The leaders of opposition parties learn to accept their role on the sidelines.

Under Putin this pattern of "hollowed out democracy" has become evident. Without explicitly violating any constitutional limits on his power, and without abolishing elections or other democratic institutions, Putin has effectively negated the constitutional limits on his power built into the constitution. Using the president's extensive powers over the executive branch, he has neutralized and marginalized nearly all independent sources of political authority, while observing formal constitutional procedures. For example, he enacts his policy program by passing legislation through parliament rather than by relying on his decree power. But having used his control over electoral processes to secure overwhelming majority support in both chambers, parliamentary approval of his agenda is assured. As observers have pointed out, Putin appears to dislike the open give and take of democratic politics, preferring more familiar methods of behind-the-scenes bureaucratic maneuvering.[8] Putin's use of presidential power presents a sharp contrast to the Yeltsin period. Yeltsin used his presidential powers erratically and impulsively. But Yeltsin respected certain limits on his power: he did not suppress media criticism, and he tolerated political opposition. Faced with an opposition-led parliament, Yeltsin was willing to compromise with his opponents to enact legislation. However, Yeltsin grew dependent on a coterie of powerful financial-media-industrial *oligarchs* for support and let them acquire substantial influence. Likewise, Yeltsin allowed regional bosses to flout federal authority with impunity because he found it much less costly to accommodate them than to fight them.

The loss of state capacity under Yeltsin illustrates one danger of an overcentralized political system. When the the president does not effectively command the powers of the office, power drifts to other centers of power. Putin's presidency illustrates the opposite danger. When Putin took over, he was faced with the task of reversing the breakdown of political control and responsibility that had accelerated under Yeltsin. Although he has repeatedly called for a system based on respect for the rule of law, he has also steadily restored authoritarian rule. He captured the contradictory quality of this vision in his 2004 message to parliament, when he said that creating "a free society of free people is the very most important of our tasks" but at the same time warned that any attempts to effect a significant change in policy "could lead to irreversible consequences. And they must be absolutely excluded."[9]

Russian Political Culture in the Post-Soviet Period

Russian political culture is the product of centuries of autocratic rule, rapid but uneven progress of educational and living standards in the twentieth century, and rising exposure to Western standards of political life. The result is a contradictory bundle of values and beliefs: a sturdy core of commitment to democratic values is accompanied by pronounced disillusionment with the way democratization and market reforms have worked out in Russia. Russians rate the Soviet regime before perestroika positively as a time of relative security and prosperity, but reject the notion of bringing back communism. Forty-one percent of Russians say they would support a return to the Brezhnev era, but only 5 percent think that such an event is possible.[10] Over 70 percent of Russians regret the breakup of the Soviet Union, but 72 percent say that restoring it is neither possible nor necessary.[11]

Support for some features of a market economy is high but low for others. For example, surveys consistently find substantial support for the idea that the state should own all major industrial enterprises (about half the population expresses this opinion).[12] Only 21 percent of the population supports private ownership of land. On the other hand, the number of people who agree with the proposition that "it is immoral to be wealthy in a poor country" is declining with time, and more people now disagree with the idea (47 percent) than agree with it (39 per-

cent).[13] Seventy percent of the population oppose ending the policy of allowing tenants to acquire their state apartments as private property at no charge.[14]

James Gibson sums up the findings of a number of studies by drawing three conclusions: there is rather extensive support in Russia for democratic institutions and processes so long as people see these as rights for themselves; there is much less support for extending rights to unpopular minorities; and the segments of the population who are the most exposed to the influences of modern civilization (younger people, more educated people, and residents of big cities) are also those most likely to support democratic values. This suggests that as Russia becomes more open to the outside world, support for democratic values will grow.[15]

Contemporary values and beliefs have been shaped by both long-term factors such as the rise in educational levels over the decades of Soviet rule, and by short-term factors such as the powerful impact of glasnost in raising popular aspirations for a standard of living close to that of the developed West. Public values were also shaped by the wrenching loss of familiar bearings as the old regime collapsed and with it, the very Soviet Union.

In his struggles with the Communist opposition, Yeltsin encouraged people to imagine that his leadership would usher in a new era of prosperity and freedom. Instead, poverty, unemployment, and inequality rose sharply, and privation led to the enrichment of a small class of ultra-rich tycoons who flaunted their quickly amassed fortunes. Organized crime flourished. The modest but universal social safety net of the Communist regime disintegrated. Little wonder that many Russians came to regard "democracy" as a bitter joke and the market economy as a mechanism for exploitation—just as Communist propaganda had taught. Democratization and economic liberalization became associated in Russians' minds with the breakdown of social and economic order since the late 1980s. Although Russians generally value the idea of democratic rights and freedoms, most people tend to consider them remote and unattainable in Russia.

Both nostalgia for the old order and aspirations for a better future set standards by which people judge the current regime harshly. Most Russians are

TABLE 9.1 How Do You Regard the People Currently in Power? (in %)

They are people concerned only with their own material and career well-being.	53
They are honorable but weak people, unable to use power and ensure order and a consistent policy.	14
They are honorable but incompetent people who do not know how to lead the country out of its economic crisis.	9
They are a good team of politicians who are leading the country in the right direction.	13
Hard to answer.	11

February 2004, N=1600.
Source: Yuri Levada, "Svoboda ot vybora? Postelektoral'nye razmyshleniia," published on website Polit.ru, May 18, 2004.

highly critical of the performance of the current regime—apart from Putin. Russians think that the country's leaders are mainly concerned with their own power and wealth rather than with the country's well-being. A 2004 survey suggests the low esteem in which citizens hold their leaders (see

Table 9.1). Although they have a low opinion of the authorities in general, Russians have varying levels of trust in different institutions. Table 9.2 indicates that the army and regional governors enjoy somewhat higher confidence than most other institutions; the table also confirms that Putin towers over all other structures. It is striking, however, that Russians ascribe the greatest power to some of the institutions in which they have the lowest confidence. This is particularly notable in the case of banks, industrial managers, and the State Duma.

Survey after survey shows that citizens have little faith in the current political system, although there is a good deal more confidence in Putin than in any other individual leaders or institutions. Since he has come into power, Putin's approval ratings have consistently remained between 70 and 80 percent, higher by far than any other leader or institution.[16] The number of Russians who approve of the activity of the prime minister (as of June 2004) is only 37 percent (44 percent disapprove) and only 38 percent give a favorable rating to the activity of the government as a whole, while 54 percent give it an unfavorable rating.[17] Russians give Putin credit above all for reversing the deterioration of living

TABLE 9.2 Trust in Institutions; Assessed Influence of Institutions

Institution	% Expressing Trust	% Ascribing Influence
Bankers, financiers	6	59
Governor of region	34	54
Television	29	43
Federal Security Service (FSB)	26	42
Army	34	38
Directors of industrial enterprises	8	36
Duma members	8	36
Newspapers	25	33
Parties	6	29
Constitutional Court	24	29
Police	15	28
SMD representative	11	23
President Putin	53	79

Source: New Russian Barometer X. Nationwide survey 17 June–3 July 2001. N=2000. Figures represent percentage of respondents giving each institution a rating of at least 5 on a 7-point scale. Cited in Richard Rose and Neil Munro, *Elections Without Order: Russia's Challenge to Vladimir Putin* (Cambridge: Cambridge University Press, 2002), p. 226.
Note: Question: To what extent do you trust each of these institutions to look after your interests?
Question: How much influence do you think each of the following groups has on Russian life today?

TABLE 9.3 Assessments of Current Political System

	Better (in %)	Same (in %)	Worse (in %)	Difference Between Better and Worse (%)
Everybody has freedom of choice in religious matters	79	16	5	74
One can join any organization one likes	75	18	7	68
Everybody has a right to say what they think	73	21	6	67
Everyone can decide individually whether or not to take an interest in politics	66	27	7	59

Source: New Russian Barometer VII. Nationwide survey, 6 March–13 April 1998. N=1904. Cited in Richard Rose and Neil Munro, *Elections Without Order: Russia's Challenge to Vladimir Putin* (Cambridge: Cambridge University Press, 2002), p. 67.
Note: Question: Compared to our system of government before perestroika, would you say that our current system is better, much the same, or not so good as the old system in the following respects.

standards: 24 percent of the population cite this as his main achievement.[18] These figures show how successful Putin has been at taking credit for positive developments in the country and allowing the government to take the blame for continuing problems. Not surprisingly, Putin's popularity leads Russians to want to give him sweeping power over the political system. After the March 2004 presidential election, a nationwide survey found that 68 percent agreed with the statement that concentrating nearly all state power in Putin's hands "would be beneficial to Russia." Fifty-four percent believed that the best system would be one in which the government "is fully subordinate to the president and his administration."[19] After the series of terrorist incidents in summer 2004, culminating with the Beslan school siege in September, the public supported Putin and his handling of the crisis while expressing sharp criticism of the police and security forces for allowing the terrorists to strike with impunity at civilian targets.

Russians' impatience with a separation of powers system, and their faith in Putin, does not mean that they do not also want democratic rights and freedoms for themselves. Indeed, paradoxically, many associate Putin with democracy. Over half of the population (55 percent) thought that following Putin's reelection as president in 2004 the country would develop as a democracy; the comparable figure in 2000 was only 35 percent.[20] Russians prize their right to criticize the authorities: 76 percent of respondents think it is permissible to criticize Putin, and 86 percent think criticism of the government is permissible.[21] And as skeptical as they are of elections, they nonetheless value the opportunity elections give them to choose representatives. Russians also value the freedoms that democratization has brought. Comparing the present system with the Soviet regime before Gorbachev, Russians recognize that they are much freer of state controls (see Table 9.3).

The political culture thus combines contradictory elements. Russians do value democratic rights, but experience has taught them that under the banner of democracy, politicians can abuse their power to the detriment of the integrity of the state and the well-being of society. They also feel powerless to affect state policy. Little wonder that a leader such as Putin can command such widespread support despite the general mistrust Russians have for the post-Soviet political institutions. Russians see him as restoring order following a protracted period of social and political breakdown. Faced with a hypothetical choice between democratic freedoms and a guaranteed income, Russians are closely divided (see Table 9.4).

The survey results reported here illustrate the contradictory influences on Russian political culture.

TABLE 9.4   Democratic Freedoms vs. Guaranteed Income

Agree	26%
More agree than disagree	17%
More disagree than agree	23%
Disagree	25%

Source: New Russian Barometer VII. Nationwide survey, 6 March–13 April 1998. N=1904. Cited in Richard Rose and Neil Munro, *Elections Without Order: Russia's Challenge to Vladimir Putin* (Cambridge: Cambridge University Press, 2002). Note: Question: Are you agreed with the following opinion: If state guarantees to me a normal wage and decent pension, I am prepared to give up freedom of speech and the right to travel freely abroad.

On the one hand, Russians associate democratization with loss and breakdown: the loss of the Soviet Union, the breakdown of familiar principles of political and economic organization, the deterioration of employment and social safety nets. On the other hand, Russians value democratic freedoms. There is considerable continuity with the past in support for the idea that the state should ensure society's prosperity and the citizens' material security.[22] More than in Western Europe or the United States, Russians believe that the state is responsible for providing a just moral and social order, with justice being understood as social equality more than as equality before the law.[23] This pattern reflects the lasting influence of traditional conceptions of state and society on Russian political culture. Still, few would support the reestablishment of Soviet rule or a reversion to a military dictatorship. Most people think that the tremendous upheavals they have experienced since the late 1980s will result in an improved life—not soon, but "eventually."[24]

Political culture is also shaped by slower-acting but more lasting influences, including the succession of generations, rising educational levels, and urbanization.[25]

The shift in values and beliefs has accelerated as new generations of young people are exposed to fundamentally different influences than those to which their parents were exposed. The older generation, for instance, views Stalin much more favorably than among the younger generations.[26] To a large extent, these differences are mutually reinforcing: the older generations tend to have lower levels of education and less exposure to the more cosmopolitan way of life of cities.

Political Socialization

The Soviet regime devoted enormous effort to political indoctrination and propaganda. The regime controlled the content of school curricula, mass media, popular culture, political education, and nearly every other channel by which values and attitudes were formed. The heart of Soviet doctrine was the Marxist belief that the way in which a society organizes its production—feudalism, capitalism, socialism, and so forth—determines the structure of values and beliefs prevalent in the society. The idea was that the ruling class in each society determines the basic ideology of the society. Therefore, Soviet propaganda and indoctrination emphasized that Soviet citizens were part of a worldwide working class movement to overthrow capitalism and replace it with socialism, in which there would be no private property. Needing to knit together a highly diverse multinational state, the Soviet regime downplayed national feeling and replaced it with a sense of patriotic loyalty to the Soviet state and to the working class's interests in the worldwide class struggle.

Today the ideology of Russian education has changed significantly. In place of the idea of the class struggle and the international solidarity of the working class, textbooks stress love for the Russian national heritage. Historical figures who in the Communist era were honored as heroes of the struggle of ordinary people against feudal or capitalist masters are now held up as great representatives of Russia's national culture.[27] There is still a strong emphasis on loyalty to Russia as a state, but now it is wedded to Russian nationalism. This is logical, in view of Russia's effort to create a new sense of national community within the new post-Soviet state boundaries.

There is also a strong undercurrent of desire for some sort of restored union among at least some of the former Soviet republics. Russian television broadcasts pay considerable attention to activities in the "near abroad," as Russians term the other former Soviet republics. Russians continue to feel tied to the other republics by decades of shared social, economic, cultural, and political experience. Putin and other politicians actively play on this sentiment, calling for the reinforcement of ties between Russia and its neighbors in the Commonwealth of Independent States (CIS). Sergei Shoigu, the relatively popular minister for Emergency Situation, noted during the parliament election campaign in November 2003 that he hoped "to live to see the day when we have one big country within the borders of the [former] Soviet Union." A former KGB chairman went so far as to say that "if we do not reassemble the Soviet Union, we have no future at all."[28] Putin rarely goes so far as to call for rebuilding the Soviet Union, but he regularly declares that it is a strategic imperative for Russia to strengthen the CIS.[29] The neo-imperial currents running through Russian political culture undercut the effort to create a new post-Soviet national community based on democratic values.

The contradictory forces acting on political culture reflect both the dislocations of the transition from Soviet rule as well as aspirations awakened by the longer-term process of modernization. Support for democratic principles coexists with severe discontent with the way reform turned out in practice, nostalgia for the certainties of the Soviet order, and regret at the breakup of the Soviet Union. Russians value highly their right to vote, and they have exercised it actively in recent elections. Overwhelming majorities of the public rate the present regime preferable to the old Communist regime with respect to freedom of speech, freedom of religion, and freedom of association.[30] Russians are skeptical about their ability to influence the current political system but most regard Putin favorably, and if his efforts to raise economic growth rates and living standards are successful, confidence in the system as a whole will gradually rise. As Richard Rose argues, the reason Russians generally approve the current regime is not because they consider it to be ideal, but because it has improved economic well-being and they see little prospect for changing it.[31]

Political attitudes are relatively independent of citizens' evaluations of the performance of the current regime, but attitudes about the market economy have shifted markedly as the economic situation worsened in the 1990s. As time passes, support for democracy will therefore rest on two interacting forces: the turnover of generations, and the performance of the regime. The collapse of Communist rule and the promise of democratic equality awakened expectations that have been cruelly disappointed. Many Russians consider democracy an ideal that is unattainable for Russia at present, and are willing to settle for a regime that provides basic order and well-being.

POLITICAL PARTICIPATION

In a democracy, citizens take part in public life both through direct forms of political participation, such as voting, party work, organizing for a cause, demonstrating, lobbying, and more indirect forms of participation, such as membership in civic groups and voluntary associations. Both kinds of participation influence the quality of government. By means of collective action citizens signal to policymakers what they want government to do. Through these channels of participation activists rise to positions of leadership. But, despite the legal equality of citizens in democracies, levels of participation across groups in the population vary with differences in resources, opportunities, and motivations. The better-off and better-educated are disproportionately involved in political life everywhere, but in some societies the disproportion is much greater than in others.[32]

The Importance of Social Capital

A healthy fabric of voluntary associations has been recognized since de Tocqueville's time as an important component of democracy. As Robert Putnam has shown, participation in civic life builds social capital—reciprocal bonds of trust and obligation among citizens that facilitate collective action. Where social capital is greater, people treat one another as equals rather than as members of social hierarchies. They are more willing to cooperate in ways that benefit the society and improve the quality of government by sharing the burden of making government accountable and effective.[33] For example, where people feel less distance and mistrust toward government, governments are better able to float bonds to provide improvements to community infrastructure. People are more willing to pay their taxes, so that government has more revenue to spend on public goods—and less ability and less incentive to divert it into politicians' pockets. Both capitalism and democratic government rest on people's ability to cooperate for mutual benefit.

In Russia, however, social capital has historically been scarce compared with West European societies, and participation in civic activity has been extremely limited (see Chapter 2). Moreover, state and society have generally been separated by mutual mistrust and suspicion. State authorities have usually stood outside and above society, extracting what resources they needed from society but not cultivating ties of obligation to it. To a large extent, the gap between state and society still exists today in Russians' attitudes and behavior. Thus, although Russians turn out to vote in elections in relatively high numbers, participation in organized forms of political activity (that is, not simply talking about politics with others or engaging in protest) is low. Opinion polls show that most people believe that their involvement in political activity is futile, and have little confidence that government serves their interests.

Since the late 1980s, political participation, apart from voting, has seen a brief, intense surge followed by a protracted ebb. Membership in voluntary associations in contemporary Russia is extremely low. According to survey data, 91 percent of the population do not belong to any sports or recreational club, literary or other cultural group, political party, local housing association, or charitable organization. Four percent belong to sports or recreation groups, and 2 percent each say that they belong to a housing bloc, neighborhood association, or cultural group. Only half a percent report being a member of a political party. About 9 percent report attending church at least once a month, and about 20 percent say that they are members of trade unions. Attending religious services and trade union membership are very passive forms of participation in public life. Yet even when these and other types of participation are taken into account, almost 60 percent of the population still are outside any voluntary public associations.[34]

This is not to say that Russian citizens are *psychologically* disengaged from public life or that they are socially isolated. Half of the Russian adult population reports reading national newspapers "regularly" or "sometimes" and almost everyone watches national television "regularly" (81 percent). Sixty-nine percent read local newspapers regularly or sometimes. Sixty-six percent discuss the problems of the country with friends regularly or sometimes and 48 percent say that people ask them their opinions about what is happening in the country. A similar percentage of people discuss the problems of their city with friends.[35] Russians do vote in high proportions in national elections—higher, in fact, than their American counterparts.[36]

Moreover, Russians prize their right *not* to participate in politics.[37] Today's low levels of political participation are a reflection of the low level of confidence in political institutions and the widespread view that ordinary individuals have little influence over government. In one 2000 survey, 85 percent of the respondents expressed the opinion that they have no influence to affect the decisions of the authorities.[38] In another survey, 60 percent said that their vote would not change anything; only 14 percent of the respondents thought that Russia was a democracy while 54 percent said that "overall" it is not a democracy.[39]

The withdrawal from active political participation today results from the shattering of the expectations for change that rose to unrealistic levels in the late 1980s and early 1990s. Gorbachev's policy of relaxing controls on political expression and political participation stimulated a short-lived surge of involvement in many forms of public activity, including mass protests such as strikes and demonstrations, as well as the creation of thousands of new informal organizations. But this wave subsided in the early 1990s. The disengagement and skepticism reflected in public life today certainly reflects disillusionment with how conditions have turned out.

Elite Recruitment

Elite recruitment refers to the institutional processes in a society by which people gain access to positions of influence and responsibility. Elite recruitment is closely tied to political participation, because it is through participation in community activity that people take on leadership roles, learn civic skills such as organization and persuasion, develop networks of friends and supporters, and become interested in pursuing political careers.

In the Soviet regime, the link between participation and elite recruitment was highly formalized. The Communist Party recruited the population into a variety of officially sponsored organizations, such as the Communist Party, youth leagues, trade unions, and women's associations. Through such organizations, the regime identified potential leaders and gave them experience in organizing group activity. The party reserved the right to approve appointments to any position which carried high administrative responsibility or which was likely to affect the formation of public attitudes. The system for recruiting, training, and appointing individuals for positions of leadership and responsibility in the regime was called the *nomenklatura* system. Those individuals who were approved for the positions on nomenklatura lists were informally called "the nomenklatura." Many citizens regarded them as the ruling class in Soviet society.

The democratizing reforms of the late 1980s and early 1990s made two important changes to the process of elite recruitment. First, the old nomenklatura system crumbled along with other Communist Party controls over society. Second, although most members of the old ruling elites adapted themselves to the new circumstances and stayed on in various official capacities, the wave of new informal organizations and popular elections brought many new people into elite positions. Today the contemporary Russian political elite consists of a mixture of career types: some people have worked their way up through the state bureaucracy while others have entered politics through other channels, such as elective politics or business.

As in other areas of political life, old Soviet institutional mechanisms for recruitment are being restored under Putin. In the Communist regime, the party maintained schools for training political leaders, where rising officials were given a combination of management education and political indoctrination. Today most of those schools serve a similar function as academies for training civil servants and are overseen by Putin's presidential administration. Moreover, elements of the old nomenklatura system

are being restored with a view to ensuring that competent and politically reliable cadres are available for recruitment not only to state bureaucratic positions but even for management positions in major firms.[40]

There are two major differences between elite recruitment in the Communist regime and the present. The nomenklatura system of the Soviet regime ensured that in every walk of life, those who held positions of power and responsibility were approved by the party. They thus formed different sections of a single political elite and owed their positions to their political loyalty and usefulness. Today, however, there are multiple elites (political, business, scientific, cultural, etc.), reflecting the greater degree of pluralism in post-Soviet society.

Second, there are multiple channels for recruitment to today's *political* elite. Many of its members come from positions in the federal and regional executive agencies. Putin in particular has recruited officials for his administration heavily from among the police (the regular police and the security services) and from the military.[41] Other prominent political figures climbed the ladder by winning local or national elections, or after making successful business careers.

The formation of a business elite, in fact, is one of the most remarkable phenomena since the end of the Soviet regime. Many of today's successful businesspeople came out of the old Soviet nomenklatura, as old guard bureaucrats discovered ways to cash in on their political contacts and get rich quickly. Money from the Communist Party found its way into the establishment of many new business ventures, including several of the first commercial banks.[42] As early as 1987 and 1988, officials of the Communist Youth League (Komsomol) saw the possibilities of using the organizations' assets to set up lucrative business ventures, such as video salons, banks, discos, tour agencies, and publishing houses.[43] They took advantage of their insider contacts, obtaining business licenses, office space, and exclusive contracts with little difficulty. Some bought (at bargain basement prices) controlling interests in state firms that were undergoing privatization, and a few years later found themselves millionaires or billionaires.

Other members of the new business elite rose through channels outside the state. Many, in fact, entered business in the late 1980s, as new opportunities for legal and quasi-legal commercial activity opened up. A strikingly high proportion of the first generation of the new business elite comprised young scientists and mathematicians working in research institutes and universities. The new commercial sector sprang up very quickly. By the end of 1992 there were nearly 1 million private businesses registered, with some 16 million people working in them.[44]

The new business elite is closely tied to the state, sometimes in order to capture benefits, and sometimes because state officials keep business on a short leash. Financial-industrial conglomerates often cultivate strategic alliances with well-placed officials in the government. Both under Yeltsin and Putin, bureaucratic factions form around particular enterprises and industries. Businesses need licenses, permits, contracts, exemptions and other benefits from government. Political officials, in turn, need financial contributions to their campaigns, political support, favorable media coverage, and other benefits that business can provide. In the 1990s, the close and collusive relations between many businesses and government officials nurtured widespread corruption and the meteoric rise of a small group of business tycoons popularly known as oligarchs. The oligarchs took advantage of their links to President Yeltsin's administration to acquire control of some of Russia's most valuable companies. The prominence of the newly rich fed a strong public backlash that made it politically viable for President Putin to suppress some of them and destroy their business empires by police methods. The notion that businesspeople can make money honestly and benefit society by doing so strikes many people as a hopelessly naive proposition. Many therefore welcome a heavy-handed state to protect them from the power of the wealthy. But often when the state cracks down on a particular business empire, it is a maneuver by one bureaucratic faction to acquire control of a lucrative business asset from another, not a step toward the rule of law.

INTEREST ARTICULATION: BETWEEN STATISM AND PLURALISM

The political and economic changes of the last decade in Russia have had a powerful impact on the way social interests are organized. A far more diverse spectrum of interest associations has developed than existed under the Communist regime. There are tens of thousands of non-governmental organizations—a phenomenon that could not exist in the Communist society, when the Communist Party oversaw all organizations. The pattern of interest articulation, however, still reflects the powerful impact of state control over society as well as the sharp disparities in wealth and power that formed during the transition period. A few organizations have considerable influence in policymaking, while other groups have little. Patron-client networks between state officials and their patrons and their clients remain a persistent feature of political life. The old regime did not tolerate the open pursuit of any interests except those authorized by the state. Interest organizations such as trade unions, youth groups, professional societies and the like were closely supervised by the Communist Party. This statist model of interest articulation was upset by glasnost. Glasnost stimulated an explosion of political expression which in turn prompted groups to form and to make political demands and participate in elections. It is hard today to imagine how profound was the impact of glasnost on Soviet society. Suddenly it opened the floodgates to a growing stream of startling facts, ideas, disclosures, reappraisals, scandals, and sensations. Gorbachev was clearly surprised by the range and intensity of the new demands that erupted. In loosening the party's controls over communication sufficiently to encourage people to speak and write freely and openly, Gorbachev also relinquished the controls that would have enabled him to limit political expression when it went too far.

As people voiced their deep-felt demands and grievances, others recognized that they shared the same beliefs and values, and made common cause with them, sometimes forming new, unofficial organizations. Therefore, one result of glasnost was a wave of participation in "informal"—that is, unlicensed and uncontrolled—public associations. Daring publications in the media allowed people with common interests to identify one another and encouraged them to come together to form independent associations. When the authorities tried to limit or prohibit such groups, they generated still more frustration and protest. Associations of all sorts formed: groups dedicated to remembering the victims of Stalin's terror; ultra-nationalists who wanted to restore tsarism; nationalist movements in many republics. The devastating explosion of the nuclear reactor at Chernobyl in 1986 had a tremendous impact in stimulating the formation of environmental protest, linked closely to nationalist sentiment in Belarus and Ukraine.[45]

The elimination of the state's monopoly on productive property resulted in the formation of new interests, among them those with a stake in the market economy. No longer does the state demand that organized groups serve a state-defined political agenda, as was the case under the old regime. Now groups can form freely to represent a diversity of interests, compete for access to influence and resources, and define their own agenda. By 2001, there were over 300,000 non-governmental, non-commercial organizations registered with the government, of which around 70,000 were active.[46] Over 2 million people work in these organizations as activists and employees, and around 12–13 percent of the population receive assistance in some form from them.[47]

As new interest organizations have formed, they have entered into a variety of relationships with the state. Some organizations have survived into the new regime, clinging to their organizational assets and legacies and continuing to seek "insider" access to the state. Others that have sprung up from scratch also work closely with legislative and executive authorities, but others play "outsider" roles, trying to influence government by mobilizing public attention and support. The pattern of interest group activity is more pluralist than corporatist because the very rapidity with which new associations have formed has defeated efforts by both government and interest groups to form monopolistic, stable, comprehensive umbrella organizations that the state could treat as the official voice of a particular interest. In most cases, interest associations are too numerous, too weak internally, and too competitive for corporatism to succeed.

Let us consider three examples of associational groups: the *Russian Union of Industrialists and Entrepreneurs (RUIE)*, the *League of Committees of Soldiers' Mothers*, and the *Federation of Independent Trade Unions of Russia (FITUR)*. They illustrate different strategies for organization and influence.

The Russian Union of Industrialists and Entrepreneurs

Most formerly state-owned industrial firms are now wholly or partly privately owned. More and more industrial managers respond to the incentives of a market economy rather than those of a state socialist economy. Under the old regime, managers were told to fulfill the plan regardless of cost or quality. Profit was not a relevant consideration.[48] Now, more managers seek to maximize profits and increase the value of their firms. Although many still demand subsidies and protection from the state, more and more would prefer an environment where laws and contracts are enforced by the state, regulation is reasonable and honest, taxes are fair (and low), and barriers to foreign trade are minimized. These gradual changes are visible in the changing political interests of the association that represents the interests of big business in Russia, the Russian Union of Industrialists and Entrepreneurs, or RUIE. The RUIE is the single most powerful organized interest group in Russia. Its members comprise both the old state industrial firms (now mostly private or quasi-private) and the newer financial-industrial conglomerates headed by the oligarchs. Its long-time president is Arkadii Vol'skii, who had been a senior CPSU official. In the early 1990s the RUIE's lobbying efforts were aimed at winning continued state support of industrial firms and planning for a slow transition to a market economy. The RUIE also helped broker agreements between business and labor, and was a source of policy advice for government and parliament.

With time, the RUIE's political goals have shifted and its clout has grown. Policymakers in the Putin administration have institutionalized consultation with the RUIE in developing economic policy. The improvement in economic conditions at the end of the 1990s made the RUIE's members more interested in improving the business environment for Russia generally, rather than in capturing industry-specific privileges. The RUIE expanded its in-house capacity for working with the government and the parliament in drafting legislation. On a wide range of issues such as land reform; tax law; pension policy; bankruptcy legislation; reform of the natural gas, energy, and railroad monopolies; regulation of the securities market; and the terms of Russia's entry to the WTO, the RUIE has been active and influential in shaping policy. A measure of its stature is the fact that at its annual conference in June 2001, the prime minister, two deputy prime ministers, the minister of economic development, the head of the state pension fund, several governors, and officials from more than 50 regions attended.

Yet the limits of RUIE's power as the collective voice of big business are clear. When the Putin regime began its campaign to destroy the Yukos oil firm starting in July 2003 (see subsequent discussion), RUIE confined itself to mild expressions of concern. Its members, evidently fearful of crossing Putin, chose not to defend Yukos' head, Mikhail Khodorkovsky, or to protest the use of police methods to destroy one of Russia's largest oil companies. Instead, they promised to meet their tax obligations and to do more to help the country fight poverty. Putin pointedly avoided meeting with RUIE and other business association leaders from November 2003 to July 2004—and then agreed to meet with them only on the condition that the subject of Yukos not be discussed. Perhaps if big business had taken a strong and united stand, they could have influenced state policy. But the desire by each individual firm to maintain friendly relations with the government and fear of government reprisals undercut business's capacity for collective action.

THE YUKOS AFFAIR   One of the most widely publicized episodes of the Putin era concerns the state's drive to break up the powerful oil company Yukos, whose head, Mikhail Khodorkovsky, was one of the most prominent of Russia's new post-Communist magnates. Khodorkovsky began as one of a group of young Komsomol activists working in the Moscow city government in the late 1980s who used their Komsomol resources and connections to start a bank called Menatep. Financing from the Menatep bank enabled them to acquire—at a bargain basement price—80 percent of the shares of the Yukos oil company when the government privatized it in

1995. At first, Khodorkovsky sought to squeeze maximum profit from the firm. Soon, however, his business strategy changed, and he made Yukos the most dynamic of Russia's oil companies. Khodorkovsky discovered that by emulating Western business practices the company could increase its net worth and productive capacity. At its peak in 2002, the company's assets were worth about $20 billion, and Khodorkovsky owned nearly $8 billion. He was Russia's wealthiest citizen.

Meantime, Khodorkovsky created a foundation called Open Russia and launched several charitable initiatives. Khodorkovsky also was active in Russian politics, funding democratic parties, and sponsoring the election campaigns of several deputies to the State Duma. Detractors accused him of wanting to control parliament and even of wanting to change the constitution to turn it into a parliamentary system. There was talk that he intended to seek the presidency.

Without consulting with the Kremlin, he began talks with foreign oil companies on selling a significant share of Yukos stock. In April 2003, Yukos announced an agreement to merge with another Russian oil company, which would have created Russia's largest oil company. In June 2003 he signed an agreement with China for Yukos to build a major oil pipeline that would supply a quarter of China's oil imports. At a meeting at the Kremlin in February 2003, Khodorkovsky even crossed swords with President Putin over a deal by which a state-owned oil company had acquired a private firm, complaining openly to Putin that the deal was corrupt.

At some point in spring 2003, the Putin administration evidently decided that Khodorkovsky and Yukos had grown too independent and must be destroyed. In a series of actions beginning in July 2003, several top figures in Yukos and associated companies were arrested and charged with fraud, embezzlement, tax evasion, and even murder. One case involved a privatization deal going back to 1993. The police raided the offices of the company and a number of its affiliates. They even raided the office of an orphanage sponsored by Open Russia. In October 2003, Khodorkovsky was arrested and charged with fraud and tax evasion. The courts refused to release him on bail. At the end of December, the government opened another front against the company, charging it with failure to pay taxes in the years from 1998 to 2003. The tax ministry demanded that the company pay 100 billion rubles (about $3.4 billion) in unpaid taxes from 2000 and declared that more claims from 2001, 2002, and 2003 were pending. The government froze the company's bank accounts as collateral against the claims. In July 2004 the company defaulted on payments to foreign banks for loans and claimed that it could not meet the government's demands. It threatened that it would have to begin laying off workers. The government continued to step up its campaign against Yukos. In December 2004 it seized control of the company's largest production subsidiary (responsible for about 60 percent of Yukos' total oil output) and auctioned it off to an obscure company which the next day was bought by Rosneft', a fully state-owned oil company headed by one of President Putin's top aides.

Analysts have suggested many reasons for the government's relentless campaign against Yukos, which has harmed Russia's economy. Yukos had been Russia's fastest-growing and most forward-looking energy company. It was responsible for the rapid growth of Russian oil exports, and was a model of the transformation of the "robber barons" of the 1990s into entrepreneurial capitalists. Indirectly, the government's campaign had a chilling effect on Russian and foreign investment. Some have suggested political motives, arguing that Khodorkovsky, through his refusal to kowtow to the authorities and his liberal spending in the political arena, was challenging Putin. Some have taken the authorities' explanations at face value, accepting the argument that Yukos had indeed engaged in shady tax-avoidance schemes and that it was getting no more than its just desserts. The problem with this explanation is the selective and coordinated nature of the campaign against Yukos. All major Russian companies had behaved as Yukos had, seeking to take advantage of legal loopholes in order to minimize taxes and maximize profits. But only Yukos was singled out for attention. The dismantling of Yukos and destruction of Khodorkovsky were very similar in this respect to the authorities' successful campaigns to break up the business empires of two other oligarchs in 2000, Boris Berezovsky and Vladimir Gusinsky, who had turned against Putin. In those cases as well, criminal and civil prosecutions were used as weapons to dismantle their companies and drive their leaders into exile overseas.

Another, more plausible, explanation for the Yukos affair is that it is part of a struggle among intra-bureaucratic factions over the distribution of control over profitable business assets. Whatever the motives for the authorities' actions, the Yukos affair shows that the regime will manipulate the legal system for political purposes, and that many of the most important political contests in Russia are fought out within the state bureaucracy rather than in the open arena of public politics.

The League of Committees of Soldiers' Mothers

The Soviet regime sponsored several official women's organizations, but these mainly served propaganda purposes. During the glasnost period, a number of unofficial women's organizations sprang up. One such group was the Committee of Soldiers' Mothers. It formed in the spring of 1989 when some 300 women in Moscow rallied to protest the end of student deferments from military conscription. In response to their actions, Gorbachev agreed to restore the deferments. Since then the movement has grown, with local branches forming in hundreds of cities, joined together in the League of Committees of Soldiers' Mothers. Their focus has expanded somewhat but remains centered on the problems of military service. The league presses the military to eliminate the use of soldiers' labor in its construction battalions and to end the brutal hazing of recruits which results in the deaths (in many cases by suicide) of hundreds of soldiers each year. The league also helps young men avoid being conscripted.[49]

The onset of large-scale hostilities in Chechnia in 1994–1996 and 1999–2000 stimulated a new burst of activity by the league. It helped families locate soldiers who were missing in action or captured by the Chechen rebel forces. It sent missions to Chechnia to negotiate for the release of prisoners and to provide proper burial for the dead. It collected information about the actual scale of the war and of its casualties. It also continued to advise families on ways to avoid conscription and to lobby for decent treatment of recruits. Through the 1990s, it became one of the most sizable and respected civic groups in Russia. It can call upon a network of thousands of active volunteers for its work. They visit wounded soldiers in hospitals and help military authorities in identifying casualties. One of the movement's greatest assets is its moral authority as mothers defending the interests of their children. This stance makes it hard for their opponents to paint them as unpatriotic or power-hungry.

The league actively lobbies parliament (for example, it fought to liberalize the law on alternative civil service for conscientious objectors but with only modest success), but for the most part it concentrates on helping soldiers and their families deal with their problems. Thus it performs multiple functions, combining political goals with services to clients. Unlike many Russian associational groups, the league has chosen to remain independent of government, not seeking any special privileges or recognition.

Like many non-governmental organizations, the League of Committees of Soldiers' Mothers cultivates ties with peace and women's groups in Europe and North America, and has won widespread international recognition for its work. For some groups, such ties are a source of dependence, as organizations compensate for the lack of mass membership with aid and knowhow from counterpart organizations abroad. However, these dilemmas of organizational development have not been a serious problem for the soldiers' mothers movement, which has a vital and self-sustaining base of support for its activity despite the sometimes-hostile attitude of the authorities.[50]

The Federation of Independent Trade Unions of Russia

The Federation of Independent Trade Unions of Russia (FITUR) is the successor of the official trade union federation under the Soviet regime. Unlike RUIE, however, it has poorly adapted itself to the post-Communist environment even though it inherited substantial organizational resources from

the old Soviet trade union organization. In the Soviet era, virtually every employed person belonged to a trade union. All branch and regional trade union organizations were part of a single labor federation, called the All-Union Central Council of Trade Unions. With the breakdown of the old regime, some of the member unions became independent, while other unions sprang up as independent bodies representing the interests of particular groups of workers. Nonetheless, the nucleus of the old official trade union organization survived, and is called the Federation of Independent Trade Unions of Russia. It remains by far the largest trade union federation in Russia. Around 95 percent of all organized workers belong to unions which at least formally are members of FITUR. The independent unions are much smaller. By comparison with big business, however, the labor movement is fragmented, weak, and unable to mobilize workers effectively for collective action.

FITUR inherited valuable real estate assets from its Soviet-era predecessor organization, including thousands of office buildings, hotels, rest homes, hospitals, and children's camps. It also inherited the right to collect workers' contributions for the state social insurance fund. Control of this fund enabled the official trade unions to acquire enormous income-producing property over the years. These assets and income streams give leaders of the official unions considerable advantages in competing for members. But the FITUR no longer has centralized control over its regional and branch members. In the 1993 and 1995 parliamentary elections, for instance, member unions formed their own political alliances with parties. Thus internal disunity is another major reason for the relative weakness of FITUR as an organization. Much of its effort is expended on fighting other independent unions to win a monopoly on representing workers in collective bargaining with employers rather than in joining with other unions to defend the interests of workers generally.[51]

The ineffectiveness of the FITUR is also illustrated by the tepid response of organized labor to the severe deterioration in labor and social conditions in the 1990s. There has been much less labor protest than might be expected. Unrest did increase through the 1990s, mainly because of wage arrears. Surveys find that in the 1990s, in any given year, three-quarters of all workers received their wages late at least once.[52] Teachers were particularly hard hit by the problem of unpaid wages and organized numerous local strikes. Waves of strikes by teachers shut down thousands of schools in the late 1990s. After 1999, teachers' protests subsided somewhat as wage arrears gradually were paid off thanks to the beginning of the economic recovery.[53]

We might wonder why there has not been more labor protest. One reason is workers' dependence on the enterprises where they work for a variety of social benefits which are administered through the enterprise, such as pension contributions, cheap housing, and access to medical clinics and day care facilities.[54] Another, however, is the close, clientelistic relationship between the leadership of the FITUR and government authorities. Like business, organized labor for the most part prefers to cultivate a clientelistic relationship with the political authorities rather than to stand independently of them.

New Sectors of Interest

In a time when people's interests themselves are changing rapidly, interest groups search for new roles. Some old groups decline, while new organizations form. In Russia, many new associations have formed around the interests of new categories of actors. Bankers, political consultants, realtors, mayors of small cities, mayors of large cities, judges, attorneys, auditors, television broadcasters, political consultants, and numerous other professional and occupational groups have all formed associations to seek favorable policies or regulate professional standards. Environmental groups, women's organizations, human rights activists, and many other cause-oriented groups have organized. Most of these operate in a particular locality, but a few have national scope.

The rules of the game for interest articulation are not well established. In the Yeltsin period, lobbying frequently took corrupt forms, including bribery of parliamentary deputies and government officials. By the end of the 1990s, more collective action by business and other sectors of interest was evident and there was more open bargaining over

the details of policy.[55] Under Putin, however, policy-making is more centralized again, and interest groups are more dependent on the goodwill of the president for access. Still, organized interests still press their demands through the mass media, the parliament, and the government, and public pressure does have some impact on policymaking.

PARTIES AND THE AGGREGATION OF INTERESTS

Interest aggregation refers to the generalization of the demands of various groups of the population into programmatic options for government. Although other political institutions also aggregate interests, parties are the quintessential structure for this vital task. How well parties aggregate interests, define choices for voters, and hold politicians accountable is of critical importance to democracy (see Chapter 3).

In Russia, despite over a decade of post-Communist political development, the party system remains tenuous and fluid. There is considerable turnover in the parties that run in parliamentary elections from election to election. Politicians are constantly starting new parties, only to abandon them after the election. Voters have little sense of attachment to parties and more often associate them with particular politicians' personalities than with specific ideological stances. In the Duma, deputies do organize their political activity around party factions, but most of these parties have very weak roots in society. Party activity in Russia is organized more around *patronage*—the delivery of particularistic benefits to favored client groups—than around mobilizing support for the achievement of *programmatic* goals.

The struggle between democratic reformers and their Communist opponents, which defined the politics of 1989–1991, helped shape the party system in the first half of the 1990s. Some parties allied themselves with the democratic movement, while others remain wedded to Marxist-Leninist ideology. Still others identify themselves with Russian nationalism. All three tendencies—democratic, communist, and nationalist—can still be found in the spectrum of Russia's political parties today.

Since the mid-1990s, however, ideological conflict has faded in importance. Instead there have been repeated efforts to create patronage parties with strong official sponsorship. Such a party is known as a *party of power*. It is a party that both state officials and voters recognize as enjoying the favor of power-holders. To the voters, such a party presents an image of continuity and stability. For officeholders, it is a vehicle for career advancement. At present United Russia embodies the model perfectly. However, in the 1990s there were several less successful predecessors that formed and faded away before United Russia came to dominate the political scene.

Each parliamentary election brings a new impetus to the formation of political parties. Presidential elections, however, have not had a similar effect. Because Russia's presidential system encourages the president to avoid making commitments to parties, presidential elections have tended to concentrate attention on the candidates' personalities rather than their policy programs, and therefore have undermined party development. Yet even in parliamentary elections, each new election presents voters with a substantially new set of party choices, making it hard for voters to develop any lasting attachments to parties or to make sensible judgments about parties' past or future performance.

Elections and Party Development

THE 1989 AND 1990 ELECTIONS The development of parties began with the elections under Gorbachev to the reformed USSR and Russian Republic parliaments. Democratically oriented politicians coalesced to form legislative caucus in the USSR Congress of People's Deputies in 1989, and in turn helped a broad coalition of democratic candidates run for the Russian Congress in 1990. In parliament, democratic factions competed for influence with communist, nationalist, agrarian, and other political groups. These parliamentary factions became the nuclei of political parties in the parliamentary election of December 1993.

Table 9.5 indicates the results of the party-list voting in the 1993, 1995, 1999, and 2003 elections, and Figure 9.4 shows the distribution of parliamentary parties' seats in the Duma following the 1999 and 2003 elections.

Parliamentary factions vary in their composition. A few have substantial numbers of both list and single-member district (SMD) deputies, but most are composed predominantly of one type of member or the other. Some factions are "start-up" groups made up of independents elected in SMD races who do not wish to affiliate themselves with the party factions, while for others, the core of their membership are deputies elected on the party list. In the case of United Russia in the current Duma, about 60 percent of the members are from single-member districts—which means that 80 percent of single-member district deputies elected in 2003 chose to join the United Russia faction. This is a good indication of the power of the United Russia bandwagon.

THE 1993 AND 1995 ELECTIONS The 1993 election produced a shock—the pro-reform, pro-Yeltsin party, Russia's Choice, did unexpectedly poorly, while Vladimir Zhirinovsky's misleadingly named Liberal Democratic Party of Russia (LDPR) did unexpectedly well. The Communists (*Communist Party of the Russian Federation*, or CPRF) took about 10 percent of the seats. Altogether the democratic factions received about 38 percent of the seats in the Duma, the left about 20 percent, and centrist factions about 20 percent. No political camp had a majority, but Zhirinovsky's oppositional stance meant the anti-Yeltsin forces had a narrow majority.

In the 1995 elections a wide array of political groups competed—far more than could possibly be accommodated given that the same 5 percent threshold rule was kept. Some 43 organizations registered and won a spot on the ballot. In the end, only four parties crossed the 5 percent threshold: the Communists, Zhirinovsky's LDPR, the "Our Home Is Russia" bloc formed around Prime Minister Chernomyrdin, and the Yabloko party. Of these, the Communists were the most successful, winding up with nearly a third of the seats in the Duma. Altogether, half of the votes were cast for parties that failed to win any seats on the party-list ballot.

THE 1996 PRESIDENTIAL ELECTION The 1995 parliamentary election was a test of strength for Russia's parties and leaders. The big unknown was how

TABLE 9.5   Party-List Vote in Duma Elections, 1993, 1995, 1999, and 2003

Party	1993	1995	1999	2003
Democratic Parties				
Russia's Choice	15.51	3.9	—	—
Union of Rightist Forces (SPS)	—	—	8.52	4.0
Yabloko	7.86	6.89	5.93	4.37
Party of Russian Unity and Concord (PRES)	6.76	—	—	—
Democratic Party of Russia (DPR)	5.52	—	—	.2
Centrist Parties				
Women of Russia	8.13	4.6	2.04	—
Civic Union[a]	1.93	1.6	—	—
Parties of Power				
Our Home Is Russia	—	10.1	1.2	—
Fatherland—All Russia (OVR)	—	—	13.33	—
Unity/United Russia[b]	—	—	23.32	38.2
Nationalist Parties				
Liberal Democratic Party of Russia (LDPR)[c]	22.92	11.2	5.98	11.6
Congress of Russian Communities (KRO)[d]	—	4.3	.62	—
Motherland (Rodina)	—	—	—	9.2
Leftist Parties				
Communist Party of the Russian Federation (CPRF)	12.4	22.3	24.29	12.8
Agrarian Party	7.99	3.8	—	3.69
Other parties failing to meet 5% threshold	10.98	26.81	12.55	11.1
Against all	4.36	2.8	3.34	4.8

Source: Compiled by author from reports of Central Electoral Commission.
[a]In 1995, the same alliance renamed itself the Bloc of Trade Unionists and Industrialists.
[b]In 2003, Unity ran under the name United Russia following a merger with the Fatherland party.
[c]In 1999, the LDPR party list was called the Zhirinovsky bloc.
[d]In 1999, this party was called "Congress of Russian Communities and Yuri Boldyrev Movement."

Yeltsin would perform in the 1996 presidential race. At the beginning of 1996 his approval was in the single digits.[56] During the campaign, Yeltsin succeeded in persuading voters that the election was about a choice between him and a return to communism.

This strategy worked. Yeltsin's displays of vigor during the campaign, his lavish promises to voters, and his domination of media publicity, all contributed to a remarkable surge in popularity and a victory over Gennadii Ziuganov, his Communist rival (see Table 9.6).[57] The campaign took its toll on Yeltsin, however. Soon afterward he had major heart surgery and for much of his second term he was in poor health.

THE 1999 ELECTIONS   The 1999 election was dominated by the question of who would succeed Yeltsin as president. Many federal and regional officeholders wanted to rally around a new "party of power" in order to protect their positions. A group of backroom Kremlin strategists formed a movement called Unity in late summer 1999. They wanted to create a political movement that state officials throughout the country could rally around in the parliamentary election. The party would serve as a political vehicle for Vladimir Putin, whom Yeltsin had just named prime minister and anointed as his successor. Conveniently, at the same time as Unity's formation and Putin's appointment, Chechen rebels launched raids

FIGURE 9.4   Seat Shares of Parliamentary Parties in State Duma, 2000 and 2004

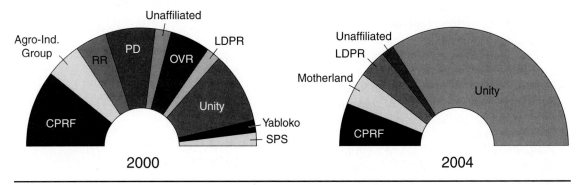

2000   2004

Source: Compiled by author from reports of State Duma.
Note: Figures taken as of January 2000 and May 2004. Percentages shift with time as members change factional affiliations. Note that United Russia was the result of a merger of the Fatherland party with Unity.
*These were groups made up of deputies elected in single-member districts who chose not to affiliate with any of the party-based factions, but were registered as official deputy groups on the basis of having at least 35 members. In the 2004 Duma, there were no such groups.

TABLE 9.6   Presidential Election Results (in percent)

	First Round (June 16, 1996)	Second Round (July 3, 1996)
Boris Yeltsin	35.28	53.82
Gennadii Ziuganov	32.03	40.31
Aleksandr Lebed'	14.52	
Grigorii Yavlinskii	7.34	
Vladimir Zhirinovsky	5.70	
Svyatoslav Fedorov	0.92	
Mikhail Gorbachev	0.51	
Martin Shakkum	0.37	
Yurii Vlasov	0.20	
Vladimir Bryntsalov	0.16	
Aman Tuleev	0.00	
Against all candidates	1.54	4.83

into the neighboring region of Dagestan. Bombings of apartment buildings attributed to Chechen terrorists also occurred in Moscow and other cities. Putin's decisive handling of the military operations against the Chechen guerrillas gave him and the Unity movement a tremendous boost in popularity during the campaign. Unity, which had not even existed until late August, won 23 percent of the party-list vote.

PUTIN AND THE 2000 PRESIDENTIAL RACE   The presidential election of 2000 occurred ahead of schedule due to President Yeltsin's early resignation. Under the constitution, the prime minister automatically succeeds the president upon the premature departure of the president, but new elections for the presidency must be held within three months. Accordingly, the presidential election was scheduled for March 26, 2000. The early election gave the front-runner and incumbent, Putin, an advantage because he could capitalize on his popularity and the country's desire for continuity. Putin ran the Russian equivalent of a "rose garden" campaign, preferring to be seen going about the normal daily business of a president rather than going out on the hustings and asking for people's votes. He counted on the support of officeholders at all levels, a media campaign that presented a "presidential" image to the voters, and the voters' fear that change would only make life worse. His rivals, moreover, were weak. Several prominent politicians prudently chose not to run against him. In the event, Putin won an outright majority on the first round. Table 9.7 shows the results.

THE 2003 AND 2004 ELECTIONS Under Putin the ideological divide between Communists and democrats that had marked the transition era disappeared. The political arena was dominated by the president and his supporters. The loyal pro-Putin party Unity was renamed United Russia after it merged with a rival party, Fatherland (headed by Moscow mayor Yuri Luzhkov). United Russia held almost a monopolistic position in the party spectrum, squeezing other parties to the margins. The magnetic attraction of a successful party of power was demonstrated vividly in the 2003 parliamentary election, when United Russia won 38 percent of the party-list vote and wound up with two-thirds of the seats in the Duma. The Communists suffered a severe blow, losing almost half their vote share, and the democrats did even worse. For the first time, none of the democratic parties won seats on the party-list vote. The result underscored Putin's drive to eliminate any meaningful political opposition. Such an impressive showing for United Russia assured Putin's reelection as president. The March 2004 race was a landslide. Putin won easily with 71.31 percent of the vote (see Table 9.8). European observers commented that the elections were "well administered" but hardly constituted "a genuine democratic contest" in view of the president's overwhelming control of media coverage of the race and the absence of genuine competition.[58]

TABLE 9.7 Presidential Election Results, March 26, 2000 (in percent)

Vladimir Putin	52.94
Gennadii Ziuganov	29.21
Grigorii Yavlinskii	5.8
Aman Tuleev	2.95
Vladimir Zhirinovsky	2.70
Konstantin Titov	1.47
Ella Pamfilova	1.01
Stanislav Govorukhin	0.44
Yuri Skuratov	0.43
Alexei Podberezkin	0.13
Umar Dzhabrailov	0.10
Against all candidates	1.88

TABLE 9.8 Russian Presidential Election Results, 2004 (as % of valid vote)

Vladimir Putin	71.31
Nikolai Kharitonov	13.74
Sergei Glaz'ev	4.1
Irina Khakamada	3.84
Oleg Malyshkin	2.02
Sergei Mironov	.75
Against all	3.45
Turnout	64.4

Source: Central Electoral Commission.

Party Strategies and the Social Bases of Party Support

Survey researchers have found differences in party support among various categories of the population. Factors such as household income, age, urban or rural residence, and education levels are related to differences in party preferences.[59]

Table 9.9 indicates how the parties differed in the social bases of their support in the 2003 Duma elections. Note that the table should be read downward. For example, it tells us that 64.5 percent of the Communist voters were 55 and over. The table shows that age, gender, education, and economic situation all influence party choice. For example, the Communists depended much more on older

TABLE 9.9   Social Bases of Support for Parties, Duma Parliamentary Election, December 2003 (in %)

Party Support by Age Group	Motherland	LDPR	United Russia	CPRF	Other Party	Against All	Did Not Vote	Total
18–24	3.8	19.2	13.9	1.8	9.6	10.3	17.3	13.7
25–39	14.1	31.3	22.8	9.1	23.9	33.8	36.1	28.5
40–54	37.2	38.4	29.3	24.5	31.4	33.8	25.5	28.7
55+	44.9	11.1	34.0	64.5	35.1	22.1	21.2	29.1
Total	100	100	100	100	100	100	100	100
By sex								
Male	43.6	60.6	38.0	49.5	44.1	43.3	46.6	45.3
Female	56.4	39.4	62.0	50.5	55.9	56.7	53.4	54.7
Total	100	100	100	100	100	100	100	100
By education								
Incomplete secondary	35.9	20.2	29.9	43.1	25.1	16.7	26.8	28.0
Secondary, specialist	47.4	65.7	55.6	45.9	49.2	65.2	58.4	56.0
Incomplete higher, higher	16.7	14.1	14.5	11.0	25.7	18.2	14.9	16.0
Total	100	100	100	100	100	100	100	100
By household economic situation								
Barely make ends meet	12.7	14.1	12.1	24.8	12.9	9.0	17.2	15.4
Enough for food	38.0	38.4	36.5	45.0	36.0	28.4	36.8	37.0
Enough for clothes	38.0	37.4	40.6	24.8	37.1	47.8	35.5	36.8
Enough for durables+	11.4	10.1	10.8	5.5	14.0	14.9	10.4	10.8
Total	100	100	100	100	100	100	100	100

Key: LDPR: Liberal Democratic Party of Russia (Zhirinovsky's party)
   CPRF: Communist Party of the Russian Federation
Source: New Russia Barometer XII, 12–22 December 2003, N=1601. From website: www.russiavotes.org accessed July 19, 2004.
Note: In each table, figures read downward. Each cell entry is the share of a given party's supporters represented by a given social category. Thus, of the supporters of the party Motherland, 3.8% were in the 18–24 age group; 29.1% of all voters were in the 55 years or older age group, but of Communist voters, 64.5% were in this age category.

voters than do other parties, and on voters with lower levels of education and lower income levels. In contrast, United Russia drew its support from across the political spectrum. United Russia voters are distinctive because women predominate: 62 percent of their supporters were female. This fact is consistent with the observation that female voters in Russia tend to support parties promising stability and continuity in policy. In other respects, however, United Russia's base of social support is strikingly broad, suggesting that the party is successful in positioning itself as a nonideological catch-all party.

Following their poor performance in the 2003 and 2004 elections, most parties have fundamentally rethought their strategies. Traditionally, the Communists have relied on their inherited organizational networks, their habits of party discipline, a clear-cut ideological profile, and their association with the socialist legacy of the old regime to attract voters. Some party strategists, however, believe that they must change their message and their leadership in view of their dismal showing in 2003. Likewise, the democratic parties, such as the Union of Rightist Forces and Yabloko, are considering a merger. By competing against each other in 2003, they both fell below the 5 percent threshold. The nationalists found it difficult for them to identify any winning issues in the face of Putin's skillful manipulation of the idea of a strong state and continuity with Russia's past. Most politicians have recognized that career success today requires hitching their wagon to the dominant party of power—United Russia.

Toward Consolidation of the Party System?

Party development in Russia has been hampered by institutional factors, such as the powerful presidency. Strong presidentialism undermines the ability of parties to promise that electoral success will translate into policy influence, since the president can choose a government largely of his own liking. Moreover, both Yeltsin and Putin have avoided party affiliations, preferring to remain above the partisan fray. Under these circumstances, politicians have little incentive to invest their efforts in building up party organizations. As a result, parties are weak at performing the functions of aggregating the interests of citizens and formulating practical policy options. In turn, voters have little basis on which to form definite opinions and attachments about parties. There are also short-term reasons for the arrested development of political parties. Under Yeltsin, the power of regional political bosses and large business firms offered candidates and voters more useful resources for winning elections than parties could.[60] Moreover, under Putin, there was little room for any party other than United Russia.

The current situation is not likely to last indefinitely, however. The strongly presidential tilt to the constitution is not likely to change soon. But it is hard to predict what will happen once Putin no longer occupies the dominant political institution. If the system evolves in the direction of a European democracy, future presidents will need to consider the balance of political forces in the parliament in choosing a government. There will be a greater balance between president and parliament, and a greater role for parties and party competition. If, in contrast, Putin's authoritarian methods survive him, party competition will be nominal at best.

THE POLITICS OF ECONOMIC REFORM

The Dual Transition

Russia's transition was so wrenching because the country had to remake both its *political* and *economic* institutions following the end of communism. The move to a market economy created opportunities for some, and hardships for many more. Democratization opened the political system to the influence of groups that could organize to press for advantages for themselves. Many people who had modest but secure livelihoods under the Communist regime were ruined by inflation and unemployment when the planned economy broke down. A smaller number took advantage of opportunities for entrepreneurship or exploited their connections with government to amass sizable fortunes. The Russian case illustrates the danger that a transition to democracy and a market economy can get stuck partway, as power is captured by powerful entrenched interests that take advantage of the initial steps toward reform, only to block any further steps toward competition and an open economy.

STABILIZATION Russia pursued two major sets of economic reforms in the early 1990s, macroeconomic stabilization and privatization. Stabilization, also called structural adjustment (and sometimes *shock therapy*), is an austerity program for the economy. The government seeks to restore a macroeconomic balance between what society consumes and what it produces. It requires a painful dose of fiscal and monetary discipline. Stabilization gives the national currency real value, which requires eliminating chronic sources of inflation by cutting state spending, raising taxes, lifting price controls, and ending protectionism. Structural reform of this kind always lowers the standard of living for some groups of the population, at least in the short run.

Initially it was believed stabilization would be opposed by those whose living standards suffered as a result of the higher prices and lower incomes, such as workers in state enterprises, government employees, and pensioners. In practice, however, those who benefitted from the early steps to open the economy and privatize state assets then opposed any subsequent measures to carry economic reform through to its conclusion. This includes officials who acquired ownership rights to monopoly enterprises and then worked to shut out potential competitors from their markets. It also includes state officials who benefited from collecting "fees" to issue licenses to importers and exporters or permits for doing business, and entrepreneurs whose firms monopolize the market in their industry.[61] A fully competitive market system, with a level playing field for all players, would threaten their ability to profiteer from their privileged positions.

FROM COMMUNISM TO CAPITALISM   Communist systems differed from other authoritarian regimes in ways that made their economic transitions more difficult. This has been particularly true for the Soviet Union and its successor states. For one, the economic growth model followed by Stalin and his successors concentrated much production in large enterprises. This meant that many local governments are entirely dependent on the economic health of a single employer. The heavy commitment of resources to military production in the Soviet Union further complicates the task of reform in Russia, as does the country's vast size. Rebuilding the decaying infrastructure of a country as large as Russia is staggeringly expensive.

The economic stabilization program began on January 2, 1992, when the government abolished most controls on prices, raised taxes, and cut government spending sharply. Almost immediately, opposition to the new program began to form. Economists and politicians took sides. The "shock therapy" program was an easy target for criticism, even though there was no consensus among critics about what the alternative should be. It became commonplace to say that the program was all shock and no therapy.

By cutting government spending, letting prices rise, and raising taxes, the stabilization program sought to create incentives for producers to increase output and to look for new niches in the marketplace. In theory, increases in production should have driven down prices. But Russian producers did not respond by raising productivity. As a result, so-

ciety suffered from a sharp, sudden loss in purchasing power. People went hungry, bank savings vanished, and the economy fell into a protracted slump. Firms that were politically connected were able to survive by winning cheap credits and production orders from government, which dampened any incentive for improving productivity. Desperate to raise operating revenues, the government borrowed heavily from the IMF and issued treasury bonds at ruinously high interest rates. IMF loans came with strings attached—the government pledged to cut spending further and step up tax collections as a condition of accepting IMF assistance, which fueled the depression further. Communists and nationalists got a rise out of audiences by depicting the government as the puppets of a malevolent, imperialist West.

PRIVATIZATION   Stabilization was followed shortly afterward by the mass *privatization* of state firms. In contrast to the shock therapy program, privatization enjoyed considerable public support, at least at first. Privatization transfers the legal title of state firms to private owners. Economic theory holds that under the right conditions, private ownership of productive assets is more efficient for society as a whole than is state ownership because in a competitive environment owners are motivated by an incentive to maximize their property's ability to produce a return. Under the privatization program, every Russian citizen received a voucher with a face value of 10,000 rubles (around $30 at the time). People were free to buy and sell vouchers, but they could only be used to acquire shares of stock in privatized enterprises or shares of mutual funds investing in privatized enterprises. The program sought to ensure that everyone became a property owner instantly. Politically, the program aimed to build support for the economic reforms by giving citizens a stake in the outcome of the market transition. Economically, the government hoped that privatization would eventually spur increases in productivity by creating meaningful property rights. Beginning in October 1992, the program distributed 148 million privatization vouchers to citizens. By June 30, 1994, when the program ended, 140 million vouchers had been exchanged for stock out of 148 million originally distributed.[62] Some 40 million citizens were, in theory, share owners. But these shares were often of no value, because they paid no dividends and shareholders could not exercise any voting rights in the companies.

The next phase of privatization auctioned off most remaining shares of state enterprises for cash. This phase was marked by a series of scandalous sweetheart deals in which banks owned by a small number of Russia's wealthiest tycoons—the so-called oligarchs—wound up with title to controlling packages of shares in some of Russia's most lucrative oil, gas, and metallurgy firms for bargain basement prices.[63]

A small group of such magnates devised a scheme in 1995 under which the government auctioned off packages of shares in several major state-owned companies in return for loans to the government. Under the plan, called *loans for shares*, if the government failed to repay the loans in a year's time, the shares would revert to the banks that made the loans. The government, not surprisingly, defaulted on the loans, letting a small number of oligarchs acquire controlling stakes in some of Russia's largest and most lucrative companies.

CONSEQUENCES OF PRIVATIZATION   On paper, privatization was a huge success. By 1996, privatized firms produced around 90 percent of industrial output, and around two-thirds of all large and medium-sized enterprises had been privatized.[64] In fact, however, the actual transfer of ownership rights was far less impressive than it appeared. For one thing, the dominant pattern was for managers to acquire large shareholdings of the firms they ran. As a result, management of many firms did not change. Moreover, many nominally private firms continued to be closely tied to state life-support systems such as cheap state-subsidized loans and credits.[65]

The program allowed a great many unscrupulous wheeler-dealers to prey on the public through a variety of financial schemes. Some investment funds promised truly incredible rates of return. Most investors in Western companies would have regarded these claims as outrageous and fraudulent. Many people lost their savings by investing in funds that went bankrupt or turned out to be simple pyramid schemes. The Russian government lacked the

capacity to protect the investors. Many people were disenchanted with the entire program as a result. Privatization was carried out before the institutional framework of a market economy was in place. Markets for stocks, bonds, and commodities were, and still are, small in scale and weakly regulated. The legislative foundation for a market economy has gradually emerged, but only after much of the economy was already privatized. Banks do a very poor job of mobilizing private savings into investment in Russian companies. For much of the 1990s, the lack of liquidity in the economy meant that enterprises failed to pay their wages and taxes on time, and traded with one another using barter. By 1998, over half of enterprise output was being "sold" through barter trade.

The government fell into an unsustainable debt trap. Unable to meet its obligations, it grew increasingly dependent on loans. As lenders became increasingly certain that the government could not make good on its obligations, they demanded ever higher interest rates, deepening the trap. Ultimately the bubble burst. In August 1998, the government declared a moratorium on its debts and let the ruble's value collapse against the dollar. Overnight, the ruble lost two-thirds of its value and credit dried up.[66] The government bonds held by investors were almost worthless. The effects of the crash rippled through the economy. The sharp devaluation of the ruble made exports more competitive and gave an impetus to domestic producers, but also significantly lowered people's living standards.

As Table 9.10 shows, economic output in Russia fell for a decade before beginning to recover in 1999. The recovery is not due to a structural reform of the economy. There has not been a substantial overhaul of the banking system or the way industry is managed. The economy is still vulnerable to a downturn in the international economic situation, because Russia remains highly dependent on exports of natural resources: exports of oil and gas make up over half of Russian exports and a fifth of Russian GDP.[67] Still, a number of industries are showing real vigor. The oil industry has increased investment and output sharply and several oil companies have expanded their international distribution and marketing efforts. They have even invested

TABLE 9.10   Russian Annual GDP Growth and Price Inflation Rates, 1991–2003 (in %)

	1991	1992	1993	1994	1995	1996	1997	1998	1999	2000	2001	2002	2003
GDP	−5.0	−14.5	−8.7	−12.6	−4.3	−6.0	0.4	−11.6	3.2	7.6	5.0	4.0	7.3
Inflation	138.0	2323.0	844.0	202.0	131.0	21.8	11.0	84.4	36.5	20.2	18.6	15.1	12.0

Note: GDP is measured in constant market prices. Inflation is measured as the percentage change in the consumer price index from December of one year to December of the next.
Source: Press reports of Russian State Statistical Service (www.gks.ru).

in agriculture and food processing, which are also showing signs of recovery. Several domestic industries got a boost from the steep increase in the prices of imported goods. In an economy that was as deeply depressed as Russia's, even a small infusion of cash has a multiplier effect, as enterprises are able to pay off arrears in back wages and taxes. In turn, these taxes allowed government to pay off its backlog of wages and pensions, in turn allowing consumer demand for industry's products to rise, and so on. These trends have raised living standards noticeably. Unemployment has fallen since the August 1998 crisis and the number of people living in poverty has declined by about one-third. President Putin has expressed satisfaction with the favorable trends in the economy, but has warned that they are not sufficient to achieve sustained and balanced development. He has called for doubling GDP in 10 years, which would require average annual economic growth of 7 percent per year for the next decade.[68] However, some of Putin's actions—such as the moves to drive the oil firm Yukos into bankruptcy and the jailing of its founder, Khodorkovsky—are having a chilling effect on business investment and make it that much harder for Russia to achieve high sustainable economic growth.

SOCIAL CONDITIONS Living standards fell deeply during the 1990s. A small minority became wealthy, and some households improved their lot modestly. Most people, however, suffered a net decline in living standards as a result of unemployment, lagging income, and nonpayment of wages and pensions.

A much larger share of the populace lives in poverty than during the Soviet era. As of 2004, about 30 million people, or about 20 percent of the population, live in poverty. High poverty rates are

the result of unemployment and the lag of incomes behind prices. Unemployment, at about 8 percent, is much lower than its crisis level of 13 percent, but still is high for a country that was accustomed to nearly full employment in the Soviet period, and where the state-funded social safety net is weak.

As elsewhere in the former Communist countries, unemployment has affected women more severely than men. In Russia two-thirds of the unemployed are women and young people (and these are, of course, overlapping categories).[69] Also vulnerable to the economic trends of the past few years have been groups whose incomes are paid directly out of the state budget, such as those living on pensions and disability payments, as well as teachers, scientists, and health care workers. Although they received periodic increases in pay, these usually were insufficient to keep up with increases in prices.

Inequality has also grown sharply since the end of the Soviet era. One commonly used measure of inequality is the Gini index, which is an aggregate measure of the total deviation from perfect equality in the distribution of wealth or income. In Russia, the Gini index nearly doubled during the early 1990s, rising from 26 in 1987–1990 to 48 in 1993–1994. Inequality in Russia was higher than any other post-Communist country except for Kyrgyzstan.[70] As the economy began to recover and poverty has declined, the gap between rich and poor has closed somewhat.

The erosion of public health is also tied to deteriorating economic performance. Mortality rates have risen, especially among males. In 2003, the president of the Russian Academy of Medical Sciences reported that mortality among men of working age had risen 80 percent in 10 years.[71] At present rates, he declared, of boys aged 16 in 2004, only half would survive to age 60. Life expectancy for males is only 58 while for females it is 72, a remarkable discrepancy, generally attributed to the higher rates of abuse of alcohol and tobacco among men. Other demographic indicators are equally grim. Every year Russia's population declines by a half a million people or more due to the excess of deaths over births. The rate of deaths per year is 70 percent higher than the rate of births.[72] Rates of incidence of HIV and other infectious disease, murders, suicides, drug addiction, and alcoholism are rising. Policy makers consider the demographic crisis to be one of the gravest threats to the country's national security.

Setting the country on a path of self-sustaining economic growth, where workers and investors are confident in their legal rights, requires a complete overhaul of the relationship of the state to the economy. The Soviet state used central planning to direct enterprises on what to produce and how to use resources. Much of the economy was geared to heavy industry and defense production, and government ministries directly administered each branch of the economy. The post-Communist state must have an entirely different relationship to the economy in order to stimulate growth. It must set clear rules for economic activity, regulate markets, enforce the law, supply public goods and services, and promote competition. Shifting the structure of the state bureaucracy and the attitudes of state officials has been a herculean task.

We can get some idea of the legacy of the Communist system in the way the state was intertwined with the economy by looking at the structure of the state budget. Figure 9.5 shows the breakdown graphically. As a proportion of federal spending, defense (at 15.5 percent) is lower than in the United States (18.7 percent of federal spending in 2003). So is spending to service the federal debt (11 percent in Russia as opposed to 14.7 percent in the United States). The large spending for aid to regions and law enforcement makes it difficult for Russia to maintain an adequate social safety net or to maintain its education and health systems. Moreover, under Putin, defense and national security spending is rising, while education spending is falling.[73] The budget

surpluses of the last four years made it possible for the government to meet its basic obligations, but spending was pared back so severely in the 1990s that many critical needs continue to go unmet. Only sustained economic growth will allow the government to rebuild the country's physical and social infrastructure.

Rule Adjudication: Toward the Rule of Law

The Law-Governed State

One of the most important goals of Gorbachev's reforms was to make the USSR a *law-governed state (pravovoe gosudarstvo)* rather than one in which state bodies and the Communist Party exercised power arbitrarily. Since 1991, the Russian leaders have asserted that the state must respect the primacy of law over politics—even when they took actions grossly violating the constitution. The difficulty in placing law above politics testifies to the lingering legacy of the old regime's abuse of the legal system. President Putin too has emphasized the rule of law (in a strange but memorable phrase, he once called for the "dictatorship of law") even while his actions have sometimes flagrantly infringed on the independence of the judiciary.

The struggle for the rule of law began well before Gorbachev.[74] After Stalin died, his successors ended mass terror and took significant steps to reduce the use of law for political repression. Still, throughout the late Soviet era, the Communist Party and the KGB often used legal procedures to give the mantle of legal legitimacy to acts of political repression. Although the prosecution of political dissidents has ended, the use of the legal system for political purposes by state authorities continues. Changes since 1991 represented some movement toward establishing an independent judicial branch, but under Putin political control over the legal system has started to grow again.

The major institutional actors in the legal system are the *procuracy,* the *judiciary,* and the *bar.* Each has undergone substantial change in the post-Communist period.

FIGURE 9.5   2004 Russian State Budget (in %)

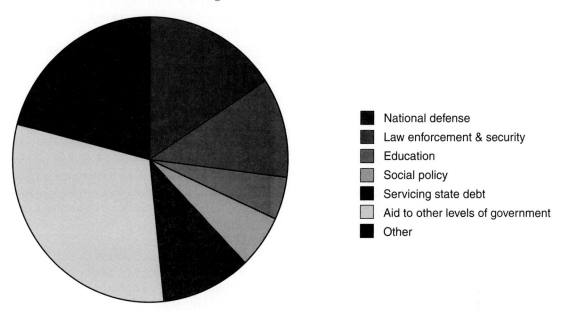

- National defense
- Law enforcement & security
- Education
- Social policy
- Servicing state debt
- Aid to other levels of government
- Other

THE PROCURACY   Russia's legal system traditionally vested a great deal of power in the procuracy; the procuracy was considered to be the most prestigious branch of the legal system. The procuracy is comparable to the system of federal and state attorneys-general in the United States, but has more wide-ranging responsibilities and is organized as a centralized hierarchy headed by the Procurator-General. The procuracy is charged with fighting crime, corruption, and abuses of power in the bureaucracy. It investigates crimes and official malfeasance and seeks to ensure that all state officials and public organizations observe the law. Moreover, the procuracy oversees the entire system of justice. The procuracy has traditionally been the principal check on abuses of power by state officials. But it is inadequately equipped to meet the sweeping responsibilities that the law assigns to it, because of the difficulty of effectively supervising the vast state bureaucracy and overcoming the entrenched political machines of party and state officials.

THE JUDICIARY   In contrast to the influence that the procuracy has traditionally wielded in Russia, the bench has been relatively weak. Trial judges are usually the least experienced and lowest paid of the members of the legal profession, and the most vulnerable to external political and administrative pressure. Successful judicial reform requires greater independence and discretion on the part of courts. Judges are being asked to raise their standards of professionalism at a time of rapid change in law, legal procedure, and social conditions. In a few instances, judges have been murdered when they attempted to take on organized crime. Many judges have left their positions to take higher paying jobs in other branches of the legal profession, but caseloads have risen substantially.

Policymakers pay lip service to the ideal of an independent judiciary but often violate it in practice. A number of reforms have the potential to increase judicial independence. Putin, for example, has backed a reform that will allow defendants in major criminal cases to request a trial by jury. Trial by jury has been tried out in several regions on an experimental basis and now will be implemented nationwide. It is opposed by the procuracy, because the prosecution has to work much harder to present a convincing case. It is also expensive, because court facilities must be expanded and jurors must be selected and paid. The goal of the jury system, however, is to make the judicial system more adversarial, so that the prosecution and the defense have equal status in the courtroom, and the judge becomes a neutral arbiter between them.

The Russian judiciary is a unitary hierarchy. All courts of general jurisdiction are federal courts, except for local justices of the peace. Most trials are held in district and city courts, which have original jurisdiction in most criminal proceedings. Higher-level courts, including regional and republic-level courts, hear appeals from lower courts and have original jurisdiction in certain cases. In turn, the Russian Supreme Court hears cases referred from lower courts and also issues instructions to lower courts on judicial matters. The Supreme Court does not have the power to challenge the constitutionality of laws and other official actions of legislative and executive bodies. The constitution assigns that power to the Constitutional Court. Under the constitution, the judges of the Supreme Court are nominated by the president and confirmed by the Federation Council.

There is a similar hierarchy of courts hearing cases arising from civil disputes between firms or between firms and the government called *commercial courts (arbitrazhnye sudy)*. Like the Supreme Court, the Supreme Commercial Court is both the highest appellate court for its system of courts as well as the source of instruction and direction to lower commercial courts. As with the Supreme Court, the judges of the Supreme Commercial Court are nominated by the president and confirmed by the Federation Council. In recent years, the Supreme Commercial Court has handed down a number of major decisions that clarify the new rules of the economic game.

The Ministry of Justice oversees the court system and provides for its material and administrative needs. Its influence over the judiciary is limited, however, because it lacks any direct authority over the procuracy.

THE BAR   Change of another sort has been occurring among those members of the legal profession who represent individual citizens and organizations in both criminal and civil matters: "advocates" (*advokaty*). They are comparable to defense attorneys in the United States. Their role has expanded considerably with the spread of the market economy. They have long enjoyed some autonomy through their self-governing associations, through which they elect officers and govern admission of new practitioners. In the past, their ability to effectively use their rights was limited, but in recent years their opportunities have risen markedly. Private law firms are proliferating. The profession is attractive for the opportunities it provides to earn high incomes.

CONSTITUTIONAL ADJUDICATION   One of the most important reforms in post-Communist Russia's legal system is the establishment of a court for constitutional review of the official acts of government. The Constitutional Court has authority to interpret the constitution in a variety of areas. It has ruled on several ambiguous questions relating to parliamentary procedure. It has overturned some laws passed by national republics within Russia, and struck down several provisions of the Russian Criminal Code that limited individual rights. Generally, in disputes between individuals and state authorities, the court finds in favor of individuals, thus reaffirming the sphere of individual legal rights. It has consistently upheld the sovereignty of the federal constitution over regional governments.

However, the most important challenge for the court is the huge domain of presidential authority. The court has been reluctant to challenge the president. One of its first and most important decisions concerned a challenge brought by a group of Communist parliamentarians to President Yeltsin's decrees launching the war in Chechnia. The court ruled that the president had the authority to wage the war through the use of his constitutional power to issue decrees with the force of law. In other, less highly charged issues, the court established legal limits to the president's authority. For instance, the court ruled that Yeltsin could not refuse to sign a law after parliament had overridden his veto. However, in the more authoritarian climate under Putin, the court has not issued any rulings restricting the president's powers. Generally the court is sensitive to the political climate surrounding it, and takes care not to issue a ruling that would be ignored or opposed by the president.

Obstacles to the Rule of Law

Movement toward the rule of law continues to be hampered by the abuse of legal institutions by the political authorities and endemic corruption in state and society.

In the post-Soviet state the security police continue to operate autonomously. In the Soviet period, the agency with principal responsibility for maintaining domestic security was called the KGB (State Security Committee). The KGB exercised very wide powers, including responsibility for both domestic and foreign intelligence. Since 1991 its functions are split up among several agencies. The main domestic security agency is called the Federal Security Service (FSB). Although the structure and mission of the security agencies have changed, they have never undergone a thorough purge of personnel. No member or collaborator of the Soviet-era security services has been prosecuted for violating citizens' rights.

The security police are regarded as one of the more professionally competent and uncorrupted state agencies. However, despite being assigned new tasks such as fighting international narcotics trafficking and terrorism, they still demonstrate a Soviet-style preoccupation with controlling the flow of information about the country. For example, in 2001 the security police sent a directive to the Academy of Sciences demanding that scholars report all contacts with foreigners. Many similar Soviet-era police practices have been revived under Putin.

Another grounds for concern about the impartiality of the judicial system is a series of actions taken against independent media beginning in 2000. These combined a variety of judicial tactics that included police harassment and criminal prosecution as well as civil actions such as bankruptcy proceedings. These actions forced the owners of two television companies to divest themselves of their media holdings and transfer ownership to compa-

nies loyal to the administration. As a result, Russia's two relatively autonomous national television companies, NTV and TV-6, lost their political independence; one respected liberal newspaper was shut down; and the entire media establishment was sent a strong signal that it would be wise to avoid crossing the current administration.

CORRUPTION Another serious obstacle to the rule of law is endemic corruption. Corruption increased substantially after the Soviet period. It is widespread both in everyday life and in dealings with the state. A recent large-scale survey by a Moscow research firm gives some indication of the nature and scale of corruption. At least half the population of Russia is involved in corruption in daily life.[75] For instance, the survey found that the probability that an individual will pay a bribe to get an automobile inspection permit was about 60 percent. The likelihood of paying a bribe to get one's child into a good school or college, or to get good grades, was about 50 percent. There was a 26 percent chance of paying a bribe to get a favorable ruling in a court case. The areas where the largest sums are spent are health care, education, courts, and automobile inspections; these alone make up over 60 percent of the money spent on bribes.[76]

Bribery in the dealings between business and the state is of a far larger magnitude. The survey's authors estimate that 82 percent of business firms engage in giving bribes to government officials, particularly those involved in licensing, taxation, and regulation. They calculated that the total annual cost of such corruption is $33.5 billion, a sum equivalent to about half of the federal budget.[77]

Corruption is hardly unique to Russia or to the former Communist world. However, it is especially widespread in Russia and the other former Soviet states. Corruption on this scale imposes a severe drag on economic development, both because it diverts resources away from public needs, and because it undermines people's willingness to invest in productive activity.[78] Moreover, much corruption is tied to organized crime, which bribes government officials for protection, and drives out legal businesses. For example, in a number of cases, criminal organizations have forced owners of legitimate businesses to sell out. The payment of protection money by businesses to organized crime groups is very widespread. The corruption of the police and courts ensures that such crimes go unpunished and forces legal businesses to compete in the corruption market with illegal ones.

Corruption in Russia has deep roots and many Russians assume that it is ineradicable. Comparative studies of corruption demonstrate, however, that a culture of corruption can be changed by changing the expectations of the public and the government.[79] The key is for the political leadership to make a serious effort to combat corruption, and to back their commitment up with institutional reform and sustained attention to the problem. In Russia, corruption is so pervasive that it is a significant drag on the economy and the political system.

Reforms of the legal system have made some progress toward realizing the goal of the rule of law. Putin has taken a number of steps which, if fully implemented, would strengthen the judiciary's independence from both political pressure and corruption. At the same time, Putin's willingness to use the courts as weapons against his political opponents, and the powerful corrosive effect of corruption, continue to subvert the integrity of the legal system.

RUSSIA AND THE INTERNATIONAL COMMUNITY

Russia's thousand-year history of expansion, war, and state domination of society has left behind a legacy of autocratic rule and a preoccupation with defending national borders. The collapse of the Soviet regime required Russia to rebuild its political institutions, economic system, national identity, and relations with the outside world. During the Soviet period, state propaganda used the image of an international struggle between capitalism and socialism to justify its repressive control over society and its enormous military establishment. Now the country's leaders recognize that only through international integration can Russia hope to prosper. The return to authoritarian methods of rule, however, contradicts this aim.

Gorbachev, Yeltsin, and Putin all believed that integration of Russia into the community of developed democracies was strategically important for Russia. Gorbachev was willing to allow Communist regimes to fall throughout Eastern Europe for the sake of improved relations with the West. Yeltsin accepted the admission of East European states into NATO as a necessary condition for close relations with the United States and Europe. Putin has repeatedly emphasized that he regarded Russia's admission to the World Trade Organization (WTO) as critical for Russia's long-term economic success. Following the September 11, 2001, terrorist attacks on the United States, Putin immediately telephoned President Bush to offer his support. Putin clearly saw an advantage for Russia in aligning itself with the United States against Islamic terrorism, which it identified as an immediate threat to its own security. Putin cited Russia's own war in Chechnia as part of the global struggle against Islamic terrorists.

Many elements of the political establishment criticized Gorbachev, Yeltsin, and Putin for making concessions to the United States and the West without receiving any benefits in return. Neither trade nor investment has blossomed as Russia had hoped, and Russia still depends on its raw materials exports to maintain a positive trade balance.

Russia has not fully embraced integration into the international community. It has expanded its military presence in several former Soviet republics, pressuring them to become satellites of Russia. In its brutal military campaigns in Chechnia, from 1994 to 1996, and then again from 1999 to the present, it has insisted that the war is a matter of domestic sovereignty and refused to allow international human rights organizations to monitor Russian practices. The regime has forced the mass media to report a sanitized picture of the situation. Corruption and inefficiency in government, both at the central level and in many regions, deter foreign investors from making a serious commitment of resources. Russian leaders constantly urge foreign business to invest in Russia. But, as many foreign investors point out, why should they take a greater risk than Russia's own business community, which has sent some $300 billion to off-shore havens?

Russia thus has some distance to go before it is fully integrated into the international community politically or economically. Yet it is far more open than it was under Soviet rule and its leaders recognize that they cannot retreat into isolation and autarky. Whether Putin is fully ready to embrace international standards of democracy, human rights, and the rule of law, however, is another matter.

Russia's post-Communist transition has been difficult and incomplete. Within Russia, many are disenchanted with the promise of democracy. At the same time, the end of communism has stimulated groups to organize for the protection of their interests. New institutions for articulating and aggregating these interests remain fragile. The spread of political and property rights has resulted in the emergence of a more pluralistic environment. Democratization in the post-Communist era succeeded in establishing some democratic institutions, such as competitive elections and a more open press. The accumulation of power by large financial-industrial conglomerates and by regional political bosses under Yeltsin, however, and the drive toward centralization of administrative and police power by Putin, have negated much of the progress Russia made in moving toward democracy. Russia's vast size and formidable climate have always challenged its rulers' ability to administer the state effectively. Throughout Russian history, rulers have relied on mobilization and centralization to accomplish their objectives. Today their challenge is to reconcile honest and efficient governance with democratic institutions for aggregating popular demands and making policy decisions.

Key Terms

bar
Chechnia
commercial courts
Communist Party of the
    Russian Federation
Constitutional Court
Federation Council
Federation of
    Independent Trade
    Unions of Russia
    (FITUR)

glasnost
Mikhail Gorbachev
governors
judiciary
law-governed state
League of Committees
    of Soldiers' Mothers
Vladimir Ilyich Lenin
loans for shares
nomenklatura

oligarchs
party of power
presidential decrees
privatization
procuracy
Vladimir Putin
Russian Union of
    Industrialists
    and Entrepreneurs
    (RUIE)

Security Council
shock therapy
single-member districts
Joseph Stalin
State Council
State Duma
United Russia
Boris Yeltsin
Yukos

Suggested Readings

Aslund, Anders. *Building Capitalism: The Transformation of the Former Soviet Bloc.* Cambridge, MA: Cambridge University Press, 2002.

Bahry, Donna. "Comrades into Citizens? Russian Political Culture and Public Support for the Transition." *Slavic Review* 58, No. 4 (1999): 841–53.

Breslauer, George W. *Gorbachev and Yeltsin as Leaders.* Cambridge, MA: Cambridge University Press, 2002.

Bunce, Valerie. *Subversive Institutions: The Design and the Destruction of Socialism and the State.* Cambridge, MA: Cambridge University Press, 1999.

Colton, Timothy J. *Transitional Citizens: Voters and What Influences Them in the New Russia.* Cambridge, MA: Harvard University Press, 2000.

Fish, M. Stephen. *Democracy from Scratch: Opposition and Regime in the New Russian Revolution.* Princeton, NJ: Princeton University Press, 1995.

Hellman, Joel S. "Winners Take All: The Politics of Partial Reform in Postcommunist Transitions." *World Politics* 50, No. 1 (1998): 203–34.

Hill, Fiona, and Clifford Gaddy. *The Siberian Curse: How Communist Planners Left Russia Out in the Cold.* Washington, DC, Brookings Institution, 2003.

Huskey, Eugene. *Presidential Power in Russia*. Armonk, NY: M. E. Sharpe, 1999.

McFaul, Michael. *Russia's Unfinished Revolution: Political Change from Gorbachev to Putin*. Ithaca, NY: Cornell University Press, 2001.

Rose, Richard, and Neil Munro. *Elections Without Order: Russia's Challenge to Vladimir Putin*. Cambridge: Cambridge University Press, 2002.

Sakwa, Richard. *Putin: Russia's Choice*. London: Rutledge, 2004.

Shleifer, Andrei, and Daniel Treisman. *Without a Map: Political Tactics and Economic Reform in Russia*. Cambridge, MA: MIT Press, 2000.

Sperling, Valerie. *Organizing Women in Contemporary Russia: Engendering Transition*. Cambridge, MA: Cambridge University Press, 1999.

Stoner-Weiss, Kathryn. *Local Heroes: The Political Economy of Russian Regional Governance*. Princeton, NJ: Princeton University Press, 1997.

White, Stephen, Richard Rose, and Ian McAllister. *How Russia Votes*. Chatham, NJ: Chatham House Publishers, Inc., 1997.

Internet Sources

An invaluable source for daily news about Russia and neighboring countries is the Radio Free Europe-Radio Liberty Newsline: www.rferl.org/newsline

A useful daily e-mail newsletter containing news stories and commentary is Johnson's Russia list: www.cdi.org/russia/johnson/

A portal to a wide range of political resources on the Web is: www.politicalresources.net/russia.htm

The University of Pittsburgh links to Web-based resources on Russia at: www.ucis.pitt.edu/reesweb

This is the home of "Friends and Partners," a joint Internet project by a team of Russians and Americans: www.friends-partners.org

The *Moscow Times* is an English-language daily newspaper published in Moscow, primarily for the expatriate community: www.themoscowtimes.com

The portal for the main institutions of the federal government—the president, the parliament, the government, and others—is: www.gov.ru/index.html

The University of Strathclyde's Center for the Study of Public Policy provides a wealth of public opinion and electoral information from Russia: www.RussiaVotes.org

Endnotes

1. Richard Pipes, *Russia Under the Old Regime*, 2nd ed. (New York: Penguin Books, 1995).

2. Archie Brown, *The Gorbachev Factor* (New York: Oxford University Press, 1996).

3. For a comparison of the leadership styles of Gorbachev and Yeltsin, see George W. Breslauer, *Gorbachev and Yeltsin as Leaders* (Cambridge, MA: Cambridge University Press, 2002); see also Archie Brown and Lilia Shevtsova, eds., *Gorbachev, Yeltsin, and Putin: Political Leadership in Russia's Transition* (Washington, DC: Carnegie Endowment for International Peace, 2001); Lilia Shevtsova, *Putin's Russia*. (Washington, DC: Carnegie Endowment for International Peace, 2003).

4. Konstantin Smirnov, "Vse pravitel'stvo: ekonomicheskii blok," *Vlast'*. 28 June 2004, pp. 63–78; World Bank. Russian Economic Report, June 2004. No. 8. From website: www.worldbank.org.ru

5. On the challenges of reconstructing national communities and loyalties in Russia and other post-Soviet successor states, see Ian Bremmer and Ray Taras, eds., *New States,* *New Politics: Building the Post-Soviet Nations* (Cambridge, MA: Cambridge University Press, 1997); Pal Kolsto, *Political Construction Sites: Nation Building in Russia and the Post-Soviet States* (Boulder, CO: Westview, 2000.)

6. J. Paul Goode, "The Push for Regional Enlargement in Putin's Russia," *Post-Soviet Affairs* 20, No. 3 (July–September 2004): 219–57.

7. Guillermo O'Donnell, "Delegative Democracy." *Journal of Democracy* 5, No. 1 (1994): 55–69.

8. For an alternative interpretation of Putin and his policies, see Richard Sakwa, *Putin: Russia's Choice* (London: Rutledge, 2004).

9. Quoted from text published on website Polit.ru, May 26, 2004.

10. Yuri Levada, "Svoboda ot vybora? Postelektoral'nye razmyshleniia," published on website Polit.ru, May 18, 2004. Levada heads a respected public opinion survey firm currently called the Levada Center. Until recently the center was called the All-Russian Center for Public Opinion Research (VTsIOM, according to its Russian language ini-

tials). However, the authorities maneuvered to take it over from Levada in 2003. Levada then founded his own firm under his own name.

11. Nationwide survey results conducted by the Public Opinion Foundation, reported by RFE/RL Newsline, December 10, 2001.

12. VTsIOM survey reported on website Polit.ru, May 16, 2002.

13. From a survey conducted by the Russian firm Ekspertiza, cited by Robert Coalson, "Russia's Evolving Liberalism," in RFE/RL Political Weekly, April 2, 2004.

14. From a national survey conducted by the Levada Center, "Sotsial'naia reforma dlia strany i naseleniia, September 22, 2004, Accessed September 30, 2004. http://www.levada.ru/press/2004092702.html.

15. James L. Gibson, "The Resilience of Support for Democratic Institutions and Processes in the Nascent Russian and Ukrainian Democracies," in Vladimir Tismaneanu, ed., *Political Culture and Civil Society in Russia and the New States of Eurasia* (Armonk, NY: M. E. Sharpe, 1995), p. 57.

16. L. Sedov, "Obshchestvenno-politicheskaia situatsiia v Rossii v iune 2004," from website of Levada Center http://www.levada.ru/press/2004071402.print.html.

17. Ibid.

18. Levada, "Svoboda ot vybora?

19. Ibid.

20. Ibid.

21. Sedov, "Obshchestvenno-politicheskaia situatsiia."

22. James R. Millar and Sharon L. Wolchik, "Introduction: The Social Legacies and the Aftermath of Communism," in James R. Millar and Sharon L. Wolchik, eds., *The Social Legacy of Communism* (Washington, DC and Cambridge: Woodrow Wilson Press and Cambridge University Press, 1994), p. 16.

23. Marcia A. Weigle, *Russia's Liberal Project: State-Society Relations in the Transition from Communism* (University Park, PA: Pennsylvania State University Press, 2000), pp. 432–41.

24. Richard Rose and Neil Munro, *Elections Without Order: Russia's Challenge to Vladimir Putin* (Cambridge: Cambridge University Press, 2002), p. 237.

25. Donna Bahry, "Society Transformed? Rethinking the Social Roots of Perestroika," *Slavic Review* 52, No. 3 (1993): 512–54.

26. William M. Reisinger, Arthur H. Miller, Vicki L. Hesli, and Kristen Hill Maher, "Political Values in Russia, Ukraine and Lithuania: Sources and Implications for Democracy," *British Journal of Political Science* 24 (1994): 200.

27. Lisovskaya, Elena and Vyacheslav Karpov, "New Ideologies in Postcommunist Russian Textbooks." *Comparative Education Review* 43, No. 4 (1999): 522–32.

28. RFE/RL Newsline, December 1, 2003.

29. For example, in July 2004 he warned that Russia must either work to strengthen the CIS or it will disappear. The fact that he made this statement at a meeting of the Security Council highlighted the strategic importance that he assigned to this task.

30. Reported on website www.russiavotes.org/ July 3, 2002.

31. Richard Rose, Neil Munro, and William Mishler, "Resigned Acceptance "Resigned Acceptance of an Incomplete Democracy: Russia's Political Equilibrium," *Post-Soviet Affairs* 20, No. 3 (2004): 195–218.

32. Sidney Verba, Norman H. Nie, and Jae-on Kim, *Participation and Political Equality: A Seven-Nation Comparison* (Cambridge, MA: Cambridge University Press, 1978).

33. Robert D. Putnam, *Making Democracy Work: Civic Traditions in Modern Italy* (Princeton, NJ: Princeton University Press, 1993).

34. Richard Rose and Neil Munro, *Elections Without Order: Russia's Challenge to Vladimir Putin* (Cambridge: Cambridge University Press, 2002), pp. 224–225; Richard Rose, *Getting Things Done with Social Capital: New Russia Barometer VII* (Glasgow, Centre for the Study of Public Policy, University of Strathclyde, 1998), pp. 32–33.

35. Rose, *Getting Things Done.*

36. Turnout in the December 2003 parliamentary elections was reported to be 55.45 percent and for the presidential election in March 2004, 64.4 percent. In the United States, turnout of the voting-age population in the closely contested presidential election in 2000 was 51.3 percent.

37. Rose and Munro, *Elections Without Order*, p. 66.

38. VTsIOM survey findings, as reported on Polit.ru website, January 10, 2001.

39. From a survey in *Novoe vremia*, No. 34, 2001, as reported in RFE/RL Newsline, September 4, 2001.

40. Eugene Huskey, "Nomenklatura Lite? The Cadres Reserve (*Kadrovyi reserv*) in Russian Public Administration," NCEEER Working Paper, October 24, 2003, Washington, DC, National Council for Eurasian and East European Research.

41. Olga Kryshtanovskaya and Stephen White, "Putin's Militocracy," *Post-Soviet Affairs* 19, No. 4 (2003): 289–306.

42. Igor M. Bunin, ed., *Biznesmeny Rossii: 40 istorii uspekha* (Moscow: OKO, 1994), p. 373.

43. Steven L. Solnick, *Stealing the State: Control and Collapse in Soviet Institutions* (Cambridge, MA: Harvard University Press, 1998), pp. 112–24.

44. Bunin, *Biznesmeny Rossii*, p. 366.

45. Jane I. Dawson, *Eco-Nationalism: Anti-Nuclear Activism and National Identity in Russia, Lithuania, and Ukraine* (Durham, NC: Duke University Press, 1996).

46. RFE/RL Newsline, June 13, 2001.

47. EastWest Institute, *Russian Regional Report*, Vol. 6, No. 42, November 28, 2001.

48. In a system where all prices were set by the state, there was no meaningful measure of profit in any case. Indeed, relative prices were profoundly distorted by the cumulative effect of decades of central planning. The absence of accurate measures of economic costs is one of the major reasons that Russia's economy continues to be so slow to restructure.

49. Article 59 of the 1993 constitution provides that young men of conscription age who are conscientious objectors to war may do alternative service rather than being called up to army service, but legislation that would specify how this

right is to be exercised still only passed in 2002, due to the strong opposition from the military itself. Thus would-be conscientious objectors and courts were in a legal limbo.

50. Several authors have examined the effect of Western aid on NGOs in Russia and other post-Communist countries. See Sarah L. Henderson, *Building Democracy in Contemporary Russia: Western Support for Grassroots Organizations* (Ithaca, NY: Cornell University Press, 2003); Thomas Carothers and Marina Ottaway, eds., *Funding Virtue: Civil Society Aid and Democracy* (Washington, DC, Carnegie Endowment for International Peace, 2000); Sarah E. Mendelson and John K. Glenn, eds., *The Power and Limits of NGOs: A Critical Look at Building Democracy in Eastern Europe and Eurasia* (New York: Columbia University Press, 2002.)

51. The FITUR reached a Faustian bargain with the government over the terms of a new Labor Relations Code which was adopted in 2001. Under the new legislation, employers no longer have to obtain the consent of the unions to lay off workers. But collective bargaining will be between the largest union at each enterprise and the management unless the workers have agreed on which union will represent them. Thus the new labor code favors the FITUR at the expense of the smaller independent unions.

52. Richard Rose, *New Russia Barometer VI: After the Presidential Election* (Glasgow: Centre for the Study of Public Policy, University of Strathclyde, Studies in Public Policy no. 272), p. 6; Richard Rose, *Getting Things Done*, p. 15. In 1996, the question was: At any point during the past 12 months, have you received your wages or pension late? In 1996, 78 percent responded yes, 21 percent no. In 1998, the question was: At any point during the past 12 months, have you received your wages late? 75 percent responded yes, 25 percent no.

53. RFE/RL Newsline, January 13, 1997; January 17, 1997; February 18, 1997; November 25, 1998; January 14, 1999; January 27, 1999; September 15, 1999; June 26, 2000.

54. Linda J. Cook, *Labor and Liberalization: Trade Unions in the New Russia* (New York: The Twentieth Century Fund Press, 1997), pp. 76–77.

55. Pauline Jones Luong and Erika Weinthal, "Contra Coercion: Russian Tax Reform, Exogenous Shocks, and Negotiated Institutional Change." *American Political Science Review* 98, No. 1 (2004): 139–52.

56. Stephen White, Richard Rose, and Ian McAllister, *How Russia Votes* (Chatham, NJ: Chatham House, 1997), p. 254.

57. White, Rose, and McAllister, *How Russia Votes*, pp. 241–70.

58. Quoted from a press release of the election observer mission of the Organization for Security and Cooperation in Europe posted to its website immediately following the election, as reported by RFE/RL Newsline, March 15, 2004.

59. Survey researchers have found that younger and better-educated voters are likelier to respond "yes" to the question, "Is there a party which represents your interests?" See Arthur H. Miller, Gwyn Erb, William M. Reisinger and Vicki L. Hesli, "Emerging Party Systems in Post-Soviet Societies: Fact or Fiction," *Journal of Politics* 62, No. 2 (May 2000): 464–66.

60. Henry Hale argues that "nonparty substitutes" such as governors' machines and big business began squeezing political parties out of the political arena in the mid-1990s, stunting the development of a party system. See Henry Hale, *Elections, Parties, and Democratization in Russia*, Cambridge, Cambridge University Press (forthcoming).

61. Joel S. Hellman, "Winners Take All: The Politics of Partial Reform in Postcommunist Transitions." *World Politics* 50, No. 1 (1998): 203–34.

62. Radio Free Europe/Radio Liberty Daily Report, July 1, 1994.

63. An excellent account of the "loans for shares" program, based on interviews with many of the participants, is Chrystia Freeland, *Sale of the Century: Russia's Wild Ride from Communism to Capitalism* (New York: Crown Publishers, 2000), pp. 169–89.

64. Joseph R. Blasi, Maya Kroumova, and Douglas Kruse, *Kremlin Capitalism: Privatizing the Russian Economy* (Ithaca, NY: Cornell University Press, 1997), p. 50.

65. Blasi, Kroumova, and Kruse, *Kremlin Capitalism;* Michael McFaul, "State Power, Institutional Change, and the Politics of Privatization in Russia," *World Politics* 47 (1995): 210–43.

66. Thane Gustafson, *Capitalism Russian-Style* (Cambridge, MA: Cambridge University Press, 1999), pp. 2–3, 94–95.

67. "OECD Economic Survey of the Russian Federation, 2004: The Challenge of Sustaining Growth" (Paris: OECD, 2004). From website: http://www.oecd.org/document/62/0,2340, en_2649_201185_32474302_1_1_1,00.html.

68. President's annual message to parliament, from Polit.ru, May 26, 2004.

69. OMRI Daily Digest, January 12, 1995.

70. The World Bank, *Transition: The First Ten Years: Analysis and Lessons for Eastern Europe and the Former Soviet Union* (Washington, DC: World Bank, 2002), p. 9.

71. RFE/RL Political Weekly, May 29, 2003.

72. RFE/RL Newsline, March 23, 2000; March 20, 2002.

73. Oksana Yablokova and Francesca Mereu, "Social Spending Takes a Back Seat," *Moscow Times*, June 21, 2004.

74. A seminal study of the influences on the development of law in the Soviet Union is Harold J. Berman, *Justice in the U.S.S.R.*, rev. ed. (Cambridge, MA: Harvard University Press, 1963).

75. G. A. Satarov, *Diagnostika rossiiskoi korruptsii: Sotsiologicheskii analiz* (Moscow: Fond INDEM, 2002).

76. Satarov, *Diagnostika*, pp. 16–17.

77. Ibid, p. 21.

78. Joel S. Hellman, Geraint Jones, and Daniel Kaufmann, "'Seize the State, Seize the Day': State Capture, Corruption, and Influence in Transition," Policy Research Working Paper, no. 2444 (Washington, DC: World Bank Institute, September 2000).

79. Susan Rose-Ackerman, *Corruption and Government: Causes, Consequences, and Reform* (Cambridge, MA: Cambridge University Press, 1999), pp. 159–74.

Poland

SWEDEN

LATVIA

BALTIC
SEA

LITHUANIA

RUSSIA

0   50   100 mi
0   80   160 km

N

GERMANY

BELARUS

• Slupsk   Gdynia
             • Gdańsk
• Koszalin   • Elblag
                        • Olsztyn   • Augustów

• Szczecin   • Grudziadz   Narew • Lomża   • Bialystok

        Notéc   • Bydgoszcz   • Toruń

                    Vistula   • Plock   Bug

        • Poznań   ✪ Warsaw

        Warta   • Siedlce

• Zielona   • Kalisz   • Lódz
  Góra
                        • Piotrków   • Radom   • Lublin
        • Wroclaw   Trybunalski   • Chelm

        Odra   • Częstochowa   • Kielce   • Zamość
                • Opole

                • Katowice   San

                        • Cracow   • Rzeszów
                            • Tarnów

CZECH REPUBLIC

UKRAINE

SLOVAKIA

Chapter 10

Politics in Poland

RAY TARAS

Country Bio—Poland

POPULATION: 38.2 Million (2003)

TERRITORY: 120,700 sq. mi

YEAR OF INDEPENDENCE: 1918

YEAR OF CURRENT CONSTITUTION: 1997

CHIEF OF STATE: President Aleksander Kwaśniewski

HEAD OF GOVERNMENT: Prime Minister Marek Belka

LANGUAGE(S):   Polish

RELIGION: Roman Catholic 95%, Eastern Orthodox, Protestant, and other 5%

If 1989 remains a remarkable year, an *annus mirabilis* in recent Central and Eastern European history, it now has to share the limelight with 2004, the year that yielded the fruits of the victory over communism—membership in the European Union. The 15-year interlude was marked by rising popular expectations about what democracy and the market would bring to the region, then disappointment that an economic turnaround was not in the making. Being invited to join the EU after fulfilling many stringent legal, political, and economic conditions for entry was a historic breakthrough for Poland and other states in the region, even if it was met by widespread skepticism about prospects for change.

When 1989 began, Communist parties ruled in eight East European countries: Poland, Czechoslovakia, East Germany, Hungary, Bulgaria, Romania, Yugoslavia, and Albania. By Christmas day, when Romanian dictator Nicolae Ceausescu and his wife Elena were executed, Communist leaders remained firmly in control of only Albania. With the opening of the Berlin Wall in November, communist East Germany was about to disappear, and the breakup of socialist Yugoslavia into separate nation-states had become irreversible. The year 1989 marked not only a historic regime change in the region, therefore, but a reconfiguration of countries and borders as well.

EU enlargement in May 2004 institutionalized the geopolitical shift in Central and Eastern Europe. By far the largest of the ten countries acceding to the EU was Poland, but it was the inclusion of the three small Baltic republics that illustrated how differently Europe was now configured. The year 2004 was a "minor miracle" for some countries, then, if not for all of them.

A saying that captures the character of political change in Central Europe is that if it took Poland 10 years to overthrow communism, it took Hungary 10 months and Czechoslovakia 10 days (the so-called "velvet revolution"). Poland had indeed to struggle longer to end Communist rule, but it was precisely by virtue of this fact that the other overthrows were swifter. Similarly, Poland drove the hardest bargain with the EU's enlargement commissioner allowing other applicants to gain concessions too.

The breakthroughs of 1989 and 2004 originated in an earlier development that took place in Poland—the birth of *Solidarność (Solidarity)* in August 1980. Starting off as a trade union and led by a fiery shipyard electrician, *Lech Wałęsa*, Solidarity grew into a 10-million member national movement that expressed public discontent with the Polish Communist regime. Its dramatic rise, and fall—martial law imposed in December 1981 made the organization illegal—drew the attention of the Communist leadership in the Soviet Union, which feared that its control over the Communist parties of Eastern Europe could unravel. Without Solidarity, therefore, there may never have been Mikhail Gorbachev, a man selected to revitalize the USSR but who inadvertently brought about its demise.

If Poland was pivotal to the chain of events that produced the 1989 and 2004 breakthroughs in the region, can we say that Poland serves as the model democracy and market economy in today's Central Europe? What problems does Poland face in raising its political and economic development to the level found in the long-standing EU member-states? Is Poland's exceptionalism—as a trigger of change in the region—a thing of the past?

CURRENT POLICY CHALLENGES

Even with EU membership secured, democratic Poland faces a series of challenges that will determine the health and stability of its political system. The job of finding the right institutional tools to forge ahead is largely complete, but a glaring exception is a political party system that remains chaotic and unpredictable. Policy is difficult to formulate when key political actors are in constant flux. Where most European states have fairly stable two- or multiparty systems that rarely undergo major change, Poland's has displayed little continuity from one election to the next. True, we can conceptualize electoral battles as regular showdowns between a left-of-center secular political bloc and a more conservative, nationalist camp. Until 2005 the makeup of the left-of-center, social democratic bloc was unproblematic: it was anchored by the very successful offshoot of the former Communist Party that transformed itself in the 1990s into a credible democratic party. The lynchpin of the conservative camp, by contrast, was different from one election to the next as right-wing parties scrambled to form viable electoral alliances. By 2005 the social democrats had fragmented, too, adding a degree of complexity to the political system that had not existed before. Effective policies are the product of an effective party system, and Poland seemed to be grappling with this fundamental systemic problem.

A second policy challenge is fine-tuning free market reforms. While Poland's progress toward a flourishing capitalist system is impressive (as we describe in the section on policy outcomes later), this very progress has engendered a new set of problems centered on growing social and economic inequalities. Economic transformation has deepened the gap between those who have emerged under capitalism as the winners (largely well-educated urbanites) and those who find themselves the losers—the poorly educated, blue-collar workers, inhabitants of less prosperous regions, rural dwellers. The problems of Polish agriculture in particular—heavily labor-intensive and inefficient—are chronic and have resulted in regular, sometimes violent social protests. Many citizens remain leery of the possibility of extensive foreign ownership of Polish land and companies—even more so now that the country is in the EU.

A third policy challenge, crafting new security arrangements in a changing geopolitical environment, has been a constant overriding concern to Polish policymakers since breaking out of the Soviet bloc. Joining NATO in 1998 appeared to have been a giant step guaranteeing national security but an unexpected series of developments has eroded the luster of NATO membership. First, the responsibilities of alliance membership have triggered new challenges. NATO's interventionism in conflicts in the Balkans, its peacekeeping commitments there and in Afghanistan, the backlash to an enlarged NATO in Russia, and the ambiguous security status of Poland's large eastern neighbor, Ukraine, add up to new security dilemmas for the country. Secondly and more important, Poland was forced to choose between the U.S. and EU positions on intervention in Iraq in 2003. Instead of fudging the choice or playing both sides against the other, Polish leaders came out categorically in favor of President George W. Bush's decision to wage war in Iraq. Indeed, after Britain, Poland represented the most important ally the United States had in "stabilizing" Iraq after the invasion. The fallout from that decision has been extensive. Senior EU member-states have belittled and ridiculed Poland's decision, the country's fellow-traveler in the Iraq intervention, Spain, reversed its policy, the threat of domestic terrorism has risen, popular resentment that Poland gained far fewer contracts from engaging in Iraq than had been thought has spread, and mounting Polish casualties in Iraq have alarmed the political establishment. Bandwagoning with the world's only superpower seemed the unassailably rational thing to do in 2003. But by the end of 2004 politicians across the political spectrum expressed doubts whether that had been the prudent choice, especially since the country had had the option of taking a lower profile under an EU umbrella. The extent to which Poland's international reputation has been tarnished, and the speed with which it can be mended,

are important issues facing the new president, prime minister, and parliament chosen in 2005.

The final policy challenge is to meet the criteria Europeanness—that is, Poland's effort to assume a twenty-first century European identity. This entails many things: constructive cooperation with EU member-states in finalizing a European constitution and then applying its provisions, aligning its institutions and legal practices in accordance with EU criteria, joining the Euro monetary zone and the Schengen curtain controlling population movement, and becoming more secular as well as less pro-American in terms of popular values and orientations. As we shall see next, Poles claim that their history proves that they have always been European. From the perspective of Brussels or Strasburg, however, where Western European politicians have a much shorter memory and may still think in terms of a sovietized Slavic bloc of nations only now attempting to embrace Europe, the case is not self-evident. How easily Polish policymakers will work with their counterparts from the longer-standing EU member-states is an intriguing question to consider.

THE MAKING OF MODERN POLAND

Every nation takes a selective approach to its own history: it focuses on a handful of recorded events, great leaders, and rival nations, and transforms them into a core history. Often this core history establishes the political traditions of a nation and weaves credible myths that help shape contemporary political attitudes and behavior.[1] Especially if a country has undergone regime change, as Poland did after 1989, there will be efforts to legitimate the new system by reference to past traditions. What are the most salient aspects of Polish history that have popular currency today and help give legitimacy to (or bring into question) the country's present path of political development?

Defining Features and Historical Development

Today's Poland occupies a location centered in the lowlands of the Northern European Plain that is remarkably similar to the first Polish state established a millennium ago. Geographically it is the "heart of

Europe"[2] and, therefore, it is correct to view Poland as a Central European nation. But because the eastern part of the country was ruled by Russia throughout the nineteenth century, and the Polish communist state between 1945 and 1989 formed part of the Soviet bloc, Poland has also been described as Eastern European. In terms of surface area Poland is large by European standards, just slightly smaller than unified Germany.

The vast majority of Poland's population of about 40 million is Roman Catholic. About one-third of the population is rural even though the country was industrialized under Communist rule and, after 1989, the service sector grew exponentially. The capital, Warsaw, has become a major European financial center as well as the seat of the national government. Other major cities are Łódź, Kraków, Wroclaw, Poznań, and Gdańsk. Greater trade with the West has transformed much of Poland, especially the cities, and it is visibly more cosmopolitan than a few decades ago.

Poles form part of the Slavic world. Their language belongs to the western Slavic group that includes Czech and Slovak. Some historical evidence indicates that the original home of all Slavs was the territory ruled by Polish kings in the fourteenth century. Even today, Poles frequently give the impression that they—rather than the larger Russian nation—represent the heart of the Slavic world. Most Poles would certainly argue that they, not the Russians, form an integral part of the European tradition.

Poland's first king, *Mieszko I*, converted to Christianity in 966 in order to bolster the country's alliances in the face of a Germanic threat. But it was a Rus invasion in 981 that stripped the country of much of its lands. The dilemmas Mieszko faced presaged those of a thousand years later—an observation not lost on Poles who have cursed their disastrous geopolitical position. That is why EU membership in 2004 is considered so historic.

An important historical debate touches on whether Poland has constituted an ethnically homogeneous or a multinational state. History provides ambiguous evidence on this matter. For the first four centuries Poland consisted largely of related tribes, but in 1370 a Polish-Lithuanian union was created that transformed the country into a multinational state. The union's expansive borders stretched from the Baltic Sea in the north to the Black Sea in the south. The adage that to be Polish means to be Catholic is, therefore, inaccurate given the ethno-religious diversity of Poland in medieval times. Thus, about 80 percent of the world's Jews lived in Poland in the Middle Ages, causing one writer to note that "in no other country than ancient Israel, have Jews lived continuously for as many centuries, in as large numbers, and with as much autonomy as in Poland."[3] During his 1997 pilgrimage to his home country, Pope John Paul II celebrated the culture that Catholic and Jewish Poles had helped forge over the centuries. He drew attention to the idea that Polishness was not the sole possession of Catholic Poles.

The ecumenical approach of Pope John Paul II departs from a more proprietary attitude traditionally taken by the Catholic Church toward Poland. The role of Catholicism in the making of the Polish nation is evident from the time of Mieszko, but in the mid-fifteenth century the ruling gentry began to define Poland's role in Europe in terms of an *antemurale christianitatis*—that is, the easternmost bulwark of Roman Catholicism. Poland was regarded as a nation lying on the fault line of Western and Eastern civilizations. In the following centuries a Polish version of manifest destiny was elucidated that highlighted the country's role as defender of Western Christian civilization. No better example of successfully pursuing this role can be found than the defeat inflicted by King Jan Sobieski in 1683 on the Turkish armies outside of Vienna, thereby saving Europe from Islam.

Internally, Poland's political system came to be increasingly decentralized, offering a spectacular exception to the rule of absolute monarchies found in most European states of the late Middle Ages. The nobility, or *szlachta*, embraced a radical new formula: "one nobleman, one vote." Power became vested in this class, not in the monarchy, leading to a crude kind of proto-democracy—what was to be known as *szlachta democracy*. Constitutional laws were enacted that incorporated the ideas of liberty, equality, and government based on the consent of a significant part of the nation. The system of elective kings became the political cornerstone of this so-called Republican Commonwealth that lasted until the partitions of Poland in the late eighteenth century.

Fear of absolutist government rather than a precocious commitment to democratic ideas led to constitutional arrangements fostering "unrule" in the country. It was behind the adoption of the best known principle of the Commonwealth, the *liberum veto*, which allowed a single member of the *Sejm* (or parliament) to veto any act presented to this body. The szlachta's rationale was that "The liberum veto would defend the sovereignty of the individual. God and Europe would defend that of the Republic."[4] The flaw in the logic was that God and Europe did not rescue Poland from the partitions. Although the Polish state had devised an ingenious system of checks-and-balances to preserve the democracy of the gentry, when skillfully exploited by Poland's foes, it led to the destruction of the Commonwealth.

Between 1772 and 1795 Polish lands were *partitioned* among its powerful neighbors until an independent Polish state ceased to exist. Stanislaw Kosciuszko's national insurrection of 1794 was a romantic highpoint of resistance but it foundered and led to bloody reprisals by Russian troops. By the third partition signed by Russia, Prussia, and Austria in October 1795, all remaining Polish lands were divided up, the king was forced to abdicate, and the name Poland was supposed to disappear from world maps forever.

How did Poles respond to the loss of statehood? Adam Mickiewicz, a nineteenth-century romantic writer acclaimed as national poet, compared Poland to Christ, destined to suffer on the cross to redeem the sins of other nations so that they, too, might become worthy of liberty. Mickiewicz broached an important theme running through modern Polish history, that of *romantic insurrectionism*. During the partitions Poles staged a series of uprisings, the most extensive taking place in 1830 and 1863. All were crushed by the partitioning powers.

As a result, an alternative, more pragmatic approach to rebuilding the Polish nation was charted.[5] Positivism involved the belief that reason, intelligence, and "organic work"—a spirit of industriousness raising the social, economic, and cultural level of the nation—would promote Poland's economic and therefore political development. Positivism was influential in the struggle of Poles to forge a civil society—fusing an individual's private and public spheres while remaining outside the reach of alien state structures. "Poland never had an autonomous State in modern times," wrote one scholar. "The idea of civil society thus provided the only ideological alternative to foreign domination."[6] The task of constructing an independent civil society was resumed almost a century later when Poles organized resistance to the Communist regime.

Interwar and Communist Poland

When Poland regained independence in November 1918, it had less to do with romantic insurrectionism, positivism, or the building of a civil society. It owed more to the collapse of empires and to the role played by the Western Allies. The tsarist empire in Russia disintegrated in November 1917 when the Bolsheviks seized power, and Austria and Germany were defeated a year later to end World War I. For a time at least, Poland's nemeses were gone. To be sure, in 1920 Polish leader *Józef Pilsudski*, considered the father of the reborn Polish state, faced off against Russian armies intent on bringing Bolshevism to the country. His forces stymied the Soviet advance, then moved eastward and conquered large parts of Ukraine and Belorussia for the new Polish state.

This expanded state turned out to be ethnically more heterogeneous than Woodrow Wilson had anticipated in his Fourteen Points, announced in January 1918. The thirteenth point referred to a "united, independent and autonomous Poland with free unrestricted access to the sea" and situated on "territories inhabited by an indubitably Polish population." Nevertheless, in 1921 about 30 percent of the population was made up of minority groups. These included up to 6 million Ukrainians, 3 million Jews, 1.5 million Belorussians, and more than 1 million Germans.

Deprived of statehood for over a century, Poland's new leaders gave priority to nation-building over safeguarding the rights of minorities. If anti-Semitism never became official government policy, it was not energetically resisted by successive interwar governments.

Pilsudski's regime was a personal dictatorship concealed in a parliamentary guise. After the *May 1926 coup* that he orchestrated, even that role for parliament was eliminated as rigged elections, internment of opposition officials, and widespread censorship brought his misnamed *sanacja* ("purification") regime into disrepute. After his death in 1935, the "colonels' regime" abandoned all pretense of democracy and fascist tendencies surfaced. Fear of communism increased, strikes were violently suppressed, and living conditions of the peasantry worsened. Poland's foreign policymakers were at a loss to forge alliances that would counter the dual threats emanating from Nazi Germany and Stalinist Russia.

Poles' historical anxiety about partition was reawakened by two insidious international agreements signed just prior to and toward the end of World War II. In August 1939 a secret protocol of the *Ribbentrop-Molotov pact*, officially announced as a nonaggression treaty between Hitler's Germany and Stalin's Soviet Union, partitioned Poland again. When the Germans invaded on September 1, 1939 and the Russians on September 17, each claimed their prearranged spoils.

The very survival of the Polish nation was in question during the subsequent German occupation lasting until 1945. One-fifth of Poland's prewar population, more than 6 million people, was killed, the highest casualty rate of any nation in the war. Some 3 million Polish Jews (90 percent) were exterminated, together with 3 million other Poles. Resistance to German occupation was relentless but two insurrections stand out. It took one month of savage repression for German forces to liquidate the Jewish ghetto of Warsaw in April and May of 1943. In all, 60,000 Jews were killed. In the 63-day long Warsaw uprising of 1944, nearly 200,000 Poles lost their lives. Russian forces remained on the other side of the river as the capital was destroyed, offering no help.

Russian occupation of eastern Poland during the war added to the nation's suffering. From the experience of World War II, Poles learned that insurrections did not lead to national independence; agreements concluded among the great powers, as happened at Yalta, did.

The *Yalta agreement* was the second destructive international event for Poland in the twentieth century. The February 1945 meeting of Churchill, Roosevelt, and Stalin at the Crimean resort of Yalta informally incorporated Poland into the Soviet bloc and deprived it of political independence. Churchill was persuaded that "free and unfettered elections" called for by the Yalta accord would indeed take place. By summer 1945, Poland's provisional government was stacked with Communists and the prospect of free elections was an illusion. The United States and Britain extended diplomatic recognition to the Communists anyway.

The sovietization of Poland began when the Red Army entered the country in 1944 to liberate it from German occupation. The process accelerated during Stalin's last years when all political freedoms and political opposition had been erased, and Poland's system—its institutions, processes, ideology, economy—resembled that of the USSR. A communist party—called the *Polish United Workers' Party (PUWP)*—headed by an all-powerful Politburo and its leader, the first secretary, had a monopoly over decision making.

The post-Stalin thaw in the Soviet Union provided a chance for Polish Communist leaders to ease the Kremlin's hold on the country and effect some political liberalization. In 1956, workers in Poznań staged protests demanding bread and freedom. While swiftly quashed, the unrest ushered in the celebrated *Polish October*, with a new Communist leadership promising a Polish road to socialism, political reform, and expanded cultural freedoms. By 1960 the bleakness, austerity, and repressiveness of life under communism had returned.

In an uncanny repeat of 1956, strikes in shipyards on the Baltic coast in December 1970—again brutally repressed by the Communist authorities—triggered another change in Communist leadership and another promise of liberalization. Even if the promise was again not kept, strike organizers like Wałęsa mastered the art of organizing resistance. The Catholic Church was no longer alone in standing up to the Communist rulers even though the much-loved Primate of the Catholic Church,

Cardinal Stefan Wyszyński, continued to personify opposition to Marxist ideology. He died in 1981, shortly after Solidarity was organized, and Wałęsa became the natural candidate to succeed him as de facto leader of a national anti-Communist movement. Another famous opposition organization, established in 1976 to defend workers who had gone on strike that year and faced reprisals, was the *Committee for Workers' Self-Defense (KOR).* It brought together a score of dissidents—like *Adam Michnik* and *Jacek Kuroń*—who figured prominently in the Solidarity organization in 1980, at the 1989 roundtable talks that paved the way for democracy, and in the politics of the *Third Republic*—the name of Poland's political system after 1989.

Before the historic years of 1989 and 2004 there was 1980. That summer strikes spread throughout the country. Initially the demands were only economic (higher wages, lower prices for food products), but by August the strikers, led by Wałęsa, demanded recognition of an independent trade union. The union chose Solidarity for its name and presented 21 demands, economic and political, to the Communist authorities. After a tense standoff when even the threat of a Soviet invasion seemed imminent, Wałęsa prevailed and a political revolution followed. The Communist monopoly on power had been broken, and Solidarity quickly transformed itself into a social movement.

Under pressure from the Kremlin, the Communist leadership drew up contingency plans to crush Solidarity. *General Wojciech Jaruzelski* was put in charge of preparing *martial law.* When it was imposed on December 13, 1981, Solidarity leaders seemed taken by surprise. Most were rounded up and interned, and the trade union was declared illegal. Scores of people lost their lives during the first months of martial law, but a Soviet invasion that might have produced a catastrophe was averted. For the next seven years Jaruzelski did not allow Solidarity and its leaders back into political life.

In sum, the communist system could boast of some successes between 1945 and 1989. The proportion of the labor force employed in the agricultural sector was halved, from 54 percent in 1950 to 27 percent in 1990.[7] Longitudinal data presented in Table 10.1 on such factors as GNP per capita, urbanization, educational attainment (number of students enrolled in primary, secondary, and higher education), and media diffusion (numbers of radio and television sets, telephones, and passenger cars)

TABLE 10.1   Indices of Economic and Social Change, 1946–2000

	1946	1950	1960	1970	1980	1990	2000
Economy							
Per capita gross domestic product	—	$271	$564	$955	$4,276	$4,099	$9,844
Urban population (%)	33.9	36.8	48.3	52.3	58.8	61.8	61.8
Workforce outside of agriculture (%)	—	46.4	56.7	65.7	70.3	73.2	72.0
Education							
Students in primary schools (000s)	3,322	3,360	4,963	5,389	4,260	5,276	3,221
High school graduates (000s)	26	111	105	365	552	440	554
College graduates (000s)	4	15	21	47	84	52	261
Communications and Transport							
Registered radios (000s)	—	1,464	5,268	5,658	8,666	10,944	9,313
Registered televisions (000s)	—	—	426	4,215	7,954	9,919	9,069
Telephone (000s; includes cell for 2000)	—	194	535	1,070	1,943	3,293	17,695
Registered passenger automobiles (000s)	—	40	117	479	2,383	5,261	9,991

Source: Główny Urząd Statystyczny, *Mały Rocznik Statystyczny Polski 2004* (Warsaw: GUS, 2004). Net material product rather than GDP before 1980; GDP based on purchasing power parity after 1990.

also reveal some modest achievements in the communist period. Overall, the population was increasingly better educated and more informed (the falloff in the number of high school and college graduates in the 1980s was largely the result of demographic factors).

Other successes claimed by the Communist regime were that per capita GDP had increased tenfold, and real income nearly tripled, between 1955 and 1981—the peak year. Undoubtedly people's living standards improved in this period, evidenced by an estimated threefold increase in the consumption of meat—historically a reliable indicator of living standards—and about a halving of the consumption of potatoes—a staple food for the poorer off. The best evidence that the Polish economy was in crisis in the 1980s and early 1990s was that the average Pole was again substituting potatoes for meat in his or her diet. Indeed, if we focus on data from the late communist period we find that poverty was affecting all social groups. Between 1981 and 1990 (which corresponds to the Jaruzelski years), real income fell by one-third—a bottom line that more than anything explains the Communists' desperate effort to persuade Solidarity to share political responsibility.[8]

Resistance to communism, of course, was driven by noneconomic factors, too, not least of which was the moral bankruptcy of Marxism.[9] Organized resistance reflected the contrasting political traditions of the country: revolutionary romanticism versus political pragmatism; a multinational, civic understanding of the state versus an ethnic, religious one; an orientation toward Western Europe versus self-consciousness about lying on the eastern edge of Western civilization. In her poem, "Possibilities," 1996 Nobel Prize-winning poet Wislawa Szymborska captured the eternal moral choices that have pervaded Polish history.

I prefer when I like humans,
Than when I love humanity.
I prefer not to believe,
That reason is responsible for everything.
I prefer moralists, who promise me nothing.
I prefer conquered to conquering countries.
I prefer the hell of chaos than the hell of order.[10]

The Democratic Transition

A paradoxical aspect of the democratic breakthrough in Poland is that it was not the result of popular unrest. We have noted the social upheavals of 1956, 1970, and 1980 but, in 1989, little or no mass political mobilization took place. Strikes had recurred in the summer of 1988 but they were not on the scale of the summer of 1980. If the year 1989 is associated in Eastern Europe with images of large-scale popular rallies in Prague, Bucharest, Vilnius and, of course, Berlin, Warsaw is conspicuous by its absence.

Regime change was the product, instead, of a pacted transition between Communist and opposition elites. The first indication of a shift in the Communist leadership's approach to resolving crises came in August 1988 when the Interior Minister (responsible for state security) publicly called for *roundtable talks* with representatives of various social groups. "I stipulate no preconditions regarding the subject of the talks nor regarding the composition of participants," he announced.[11] "Talks about talks" commenced in August 1988 and soon included an informal meeting between the Minister and Wałęsa. Soon afterwards, a debate took place on state television between Wałęsa (a "non-person" not allowed to appear in public after Solidarity was banned) and the head of the Communist trade union. Wałęsa scored a resounding debating victory, and Solidarity was set to return to center stage.

In January 1989 the PUWP leadership, prodded by a now reform-minded Jaruzelski, voted in favor of political and trade union pluralism, thereby giving a green light to full-scale roundtable talks. Jaruzelski's role in the transition was crucial; he was reported to have said: "Please remember that only General de Gaulle was capable of getting France out of Algeria."[12]

The roundtable of February-April 1989 consisted of representatives of the Communist leadership, called the "coalition-government" side, and those of the democratic movement, the "opposition-Solidarity" side. The leadership of the Catholic Church was officially not involved in the roundtable talks and declared its neutrality, though its representatives invariably backed positions advocated by Solidarity. Six hundred individuals participated in the roundtable negotiations but the most important discussions, centering on establishing conditions for a *pacted transition,* involved private meetings between top party and Solidarity leaders held at a villa in Magdalenka. The secretive nature of discussions at Magdalenka led some observers to claim that a secret deal was worked out between the elites. Accordingly, an allegation repeated throughout the 1990s was that in exchange for withdrawing from politics, the ruling Communist class (the *nomenklatura*) would have a free hand in privatizing state assets.

At the center of roundtable negotiations was the return of Solidarity to politics. A compromise was worked out under which 35 percent of Sejm seats would be contested and the remaining 65 percent set aside for the Communists and their allies. The elections for the 35 percent of seats were to be "nonconfrontational," which meant that the Communists should not be the target of a negative campaign. Finally, this *contract Sejm* was to be a one-time arrangement and the following legislative elections were to be fully free.

An important political institution that was reestablished by the roundtable agreement was the presidency (abolished in 1952). Both sides agreed that a president could serve as a stabilizing force and a symbol of continuity during the transition. The obvious Communist candidate was Jaruzelski, and even much of Solidarity recognized the advantage of having the long-serving leader preside over the transition. When Solidarity won all the contested Sejm seats in the June 1989 election, the arrangement it proposed—"your President, our Prime Minister"—seemed both sensible and generous.

The roundtable agreement also restored an upper house of parliament, the Senate, abolished in 1948. Since it was not invested with much power, elections to it were to be free. The Senate contest thus offered Solidarity the chance to demonstrate its strength throughout the country. The final roundtable pact contained many mutual checks and balances and, it appeared, could not possibly produce a lopsided defeat for the Communists. It was crafted so as to ensure that the transition would be gradual and would pose no risk to either the old or new elite. But all those premises changed once the

elections results were in and when events in other communist countries outpaced the speed of the Polish transition.

In terms of the popular vote in the June election, the government (Communist) side obtained just over one-quarter of all valid votes cast (26.8 percent) while Solidarity tallied 69.9 percent (the remainder went to independents). Solidarity swept all contested Sejm seats and 99 out of 100 Senate seats. Worse for the Communist side, of the 65 percent of seats set aside for it the majority of its candidates did not win 50 percent of the votes, thereby necessitating a second round of elections.

Turnout for the first round of this historic election was an unimpressive 63 percent of eligible voters. One explanation for this was that the public might have viewed the election as a deal cut by two establishment parties—the Communists and Solidarity. The same suspicions aroused by the talks in Magdalenka—"elites talking to elites"[13]—may have spread to sections of the population as they contemplated whether voting really was meaningful.

The election results produced a domino effect on other provisions of the roundtable agreement. Jaruzelski announced he would not be a candidate for the presidency, but after Wałęsa announced that he did not wish to stand at this time (partly to allay Kremlin fears that too much change was happening too quickly), the General reversed his decision and in July was elected by a slim majority of the two houses.

This left one other issue to be resolved in the summer of 1989—the formation of a government. Since the Communist bloc held a working majority in the contract Sejm, Jaruzelski nominated his Interior Minister to the post. This, however, would have left both major offices in the hands of the electorally repudiated Communist Party. The surprise defection of two small pro-Communist parties from the government camp sealed the fate of the Communists. In August Tadeusz Mazowiecki—Catholic intellectual, editor of an important Solidarity newspaper, and long-time Wałęsa adviser—was appointed prime minister—the first non-Communist one in East Europe since Stalin's time. With all but hardline Communists accepting the new political reality, his nomination was endorsed in the Sejm by 378 to 4, with 41 abstentions.

Eleven of twenty-three ministerial posts in Mazowiecki's government were taken by Solidarity, only four were given to the PUWP (admittedly these included the pivotal defense and security portfolios), and the rest went to small parties. Few participants at the roundtable talks a few months earlier could have foreseen this dramatic change in the course of events.

STRUCTURE OF THE POLITICAL SYSTEM

What distinguishes a democracy from an authoritarian system of government? According to one think tank, Freedom House, political rights and civil liberties are basic to democracy. "Political rights enable people to participate freely in the political process, including through the right to vote, compete for public office, and elect representatives who have a decisive impact on public policies and are accountable to the electorate." In turn "civil liberties allow for the freedoms of expression and belief, associational and organizational rights, rule of law, and personal autonomy without interference from the state." Since 1995 a panel of Freedom House experts has been giving Poland its top ranking of 1 (on a scale to 7) on its political rights and 2 on civil liberties.[14]

Another important feature of democracy is that political outcomes should be determined by rules of the game designed and accepted by the main political actors. These rules are outlined in a country's constitution, they can be found in laws passed by an elected assembly or approved in a general referendum, and they can be based on conventions and traditions that have developed over time. Rules identify the jurisdiction and powers of various governmental institutions—president, prime minister, cabinet, parliament. Rules also determine how officeholders of such institutions are to be picked.

The interwar experience influenced the design of the post-1989 democratic system. Indeed, continuity was highlighted by naming the new system the Third Republic. Interwar Poland had been the *Second Republic* while the Communist regime was not numbered because it was not regarded as an independent Polish state (though some facetiously called it the Second-and-a-Half Republic).

The structure of the new government, illustrated in Figure 10.1, did, however, have to incorporate vestiges of its Communist predecessor. Democratizing the political system meant designing new institutions and formulating legal provisions in place of Communist ones. Among the institutional changes were: (1) replacing the constitution of July 22, 1952; (2) introducing an electoral law for a multiparty system; (3) changing the official symbols and terms of the communist system (the country's official name, coat of arms, flag, and anthem); (4) reintroducing such political institutions as the presidency, the Senate, and a reformed local government system; (5) providing the legal framework for private ownership; (6) safeguarding the independence of the judiciary; and (7) enshrining principles incorporating political rights and civil liberties.

Adopting a new constitution was the most urgent issue since other changes would follow from it. Because the stakes were high, however, it took seven years of wrangling before a draft was passed by parliament and then approved in a national referendum. There was widespread disagreement about what the new constitution should include. Just the preamble proved contentious because opinions differed whether it was the Polish nation (an ethnic category) or the citizens of Poland (a civic understanding) that were the subjects of the document. There was disagreement, too, about whether the special role of Catholicism in the country should be explicitly mentioned (as was the case in the Irish constitution). The constitution adopted in 1997 avoided making choices on these matters and instead contained references to both the Polish nation and its citizens, and to Catholicism and other religious faiths. The noncontroversial approach taken contributed to a low turnout in the referendum when only 43 percent of the electorate turned out at the polls. Just 53 percent voted in favor of its adoption. Those opposing it wanted primarily to deprive the left-of-center government that had cobbled the document together of a success; their substantive disagreement was minor.

Before this constitution was passed the distribution of power between the branches of government resembled that of the interwar republic up to 1926. The power of the executive branch—defined

FIGURE 10.1   The Structure of Poland's Political System

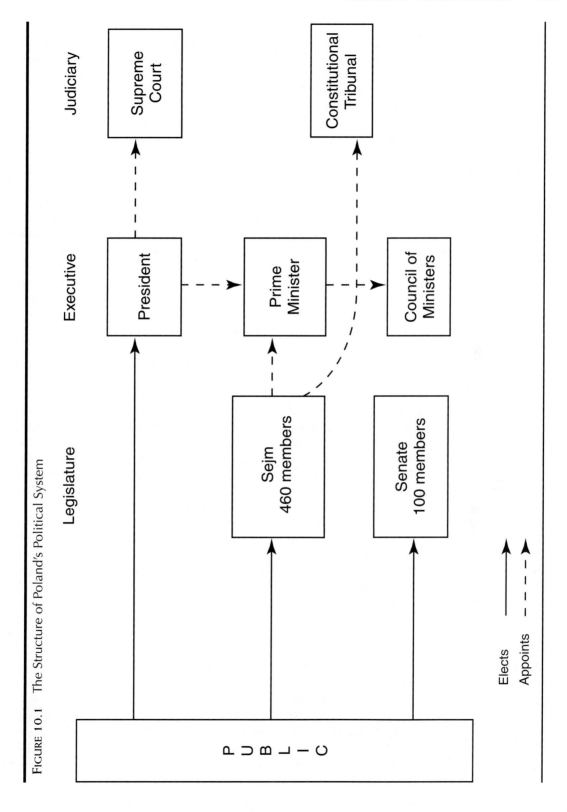

as including both president and prime minister—was circumscribed. A form of "Sejmocracy" emerged in which little could get done without the legislature's approval. Even the momentous *Balcerowicz plan* of January 1990 which created a free market would not have passed had not its author, finance minister Leszek Balcerowicz, surprised the Sejm with a bill he demanded immediate approval of.

Wałęsa, who became president in December 1990 after direct elections for the office, fought hard against this Sejmocracy and often invoked the interwar experience. The chaos and paralysis that a powerful legislature had produced then had convinced Pilsudski that a strong executive was essential to political efficacy and stability; that was why he undertook the 1926 coup. While no evidence exists that Wałęsa was plotting a coup, he clearly favored a strong presidential system. Accordingly, during his five-year term as president, he undermined the authority of a succession of prime ministers, in the process heightening the political instability he condemned. He did his best to prevent a parliamentary system from being institutionalized, but the Sejm just as effectively rebuffed his attempts to expand presidential powers. When in 1995 the Sejm began to consider various drafts of a new constitution, Wałęsa's was the only version of seven that proposed a presidential system. His failure to get reelected that year was in good measure a popular vote against establishing a strong executive branch. The new president, *Aleksander Kwaśniewski*, was quick to emphasize that he was a "parliamentarian" and was content to preside over rather than dominate Polish politics. Wałęsa's defeat signified not only a shift in power from Solidarity to ex-Communist forces but also a change from an activist to a deliberative presidency.

The President

The constitutional role of the presidency in the new system is circumscribed. An interim constitution adopted in 1992 termed Poland "a Presidential-parliamentary system of government," but the *constitution of 1997* dropped this phrasing. Article 10.1 of Chapter 1 declares that "the system of the Polish Republic is based on the separation and balance of legislative authority, executive authority, and judicial authority." The presidency is considered a part of the executive branch which also includes the government, or *Council of Ministers* (Article 10.2).

The president is elected directly by majority vote. If no candidate obtains a majority, a second round of elections is held two weeks later between the top two vote-getters from the first round. The term of office is five years, with a two-term limitation. There is no vice-president, and in the event of the president's incapacity or death the Marshal of the Sejm (similar to Speaker of the House) temporarily holds the office until new elections are held.

The constitution designates the president as head of state and commander-in-chief of the armed forces. A political convention has emerged that the president should not formally belong to a political party. Chapter 5 of the 1997 constitution enumerates the specific powers of the president. Article 126.1 declares that the president is "the supreme representative of the Polish Republic and guarantees the continuity of state authority." Enumerated powers include the right to designate the prime minister (though not cabinet ministers), initiate legislation, veto bills (which the Sejm can override by a three-fifths majority), refer bills to the Constitutional Court for a ruling as to their constitutionality, under certain conditions dissolve parliament and call early elections, call a referendum, oversee defense (indirectly through the defense ministry and through appointing the Chief of the General Staff of the armed forces) and national security matters (together with the National Security Council), declare martial law if the Sejm is unable to meet quickly, and represent the state in foreign relations. The president can issue decrees and administrative acts, the latter requiring the prime minister's countersignature. The officeholder also has a constitutionally recognized Presidential Chancellory (Article 142.2b) to help his or her carry out duties.

Despite these diverse formal powers, the Polish president does not seem to have the political clout that his counterpart in France, who heads a semi-presidential system, has. This may be due in part to the diffidence and discretion exercised by

Kwaśniewski during his two terms as president. It may be that even with a divided parliament for much of this period, it and the president shared similar political values and goals. Indeed only in the last two years of Kwaśniewski's presidency have serious rifts arose over such fundamental questions as the direction of Polish foreign policy and the country's role in the EU. Finally, parties in the Sejm were reluctant to stake their political capital by challenging an extremely popular president. They were content to let Kwaśniewski act as "the supreme representative of the Polish Republic" who "guarantees the continuity of state authority." His successor in 2006 may want to be more involved in the shaping of domestic policy. Especially if he or she has no communist pedigree (as Kwaśniewski had in the PUWP), the new president may feel less of a need to act in a conspicuously nonpartisan manner.

The Legislature

The legislative branch is made up of two chambers: the lower house (Sejm) consists of 460 deputies and the upper house (Senate) is made up of 100 members (Chapter IV of the constitution). On some occasions the two meet together as the National Assembly. Direct elections to both houses must be held no more than four years apart. Early elections can be held if (1) a government cannot be formed; (2) a vote of no confidence in an existing government is passed (however, the notion of a "constructive" no-confidence vote, which is not mentioned in the constitution but has been used in Poland and resembles that found in Germany, would mean that the present government would be replaced or reconstitute itself—not that elections should follow); or (3) the president decides, under certain conditions, to dissolve the legislature. As in most parliamentary systems, the prime minister, or head of the government, seeks to influence the timing of elections so as to coincide with an upswing in his or her party's fortunes.

The Sejm enacts legislation through three readings of a bill, after which it is sent to the Senate for approval. The Senate can make changes to the bill or even vote it down, but the Sejm can have its way by enacting the bill again with a simple majority vote. The bill becomes law when the president signs it. The power of the Senate is limited and there have been calls for its abolition. We should remember that it was little more than a bargaining chip, rather than an issue of substance, at the roundtable talks.

The Sejm is at the center of Polish politics, then. It is where the competitive party system functions for most of the year (the Sejm recesses briefly in summer). The extended, often-heated debates on legislative bills give the lower house the constant visibility that the presidency does not possess. The most controversial issues of Polish politics after 1989 have been debated in extenso in the Sejm: enacting a new constitution, defining the official place of the Catholic Church in society, determining women's access to abortion, drafting legislation on the privatization of state-owned industry, clarifying the public role that former Communist officials could play in a democratic Poland (through the so-called lustration law that required a "background check" of candidates for high office to determine whether they had worked secretly with the former security apparatus), reorganizing local government (from 47 to 16 regions), ratifying membership in NATO, agreeing to hold a national referendum to approve EU membership and, of course, the passing of government budgets.

If the Sejm makes or breaks prime ministers and their cabinets, it can also serve as the stage where the performance of a backbench parliamentarian is noticed, leading to possible promotion to a ministerial post. Deftness as chair of a Sejm committee is also a basis for political advancement. Each of the major parties has a parliamentary caucus that to a great degree determines who will hold positions of leadership, and it looks to a deputy's Sejm record (attendance, speeches, bills proposed, voting) for guidance. One of the most overlooked factors smoothing the process of democratic transition was the shift in power in 1989 within the Communist Party from its own bureaucratic apparatus to its representatives in the Sejm. The PUWP caucus was the forum that allowed future President Kwaśniewski and several Social Democratic prime ministers to rise to prominence. It is no exaggeration to claim that in addition to its all-important legislative function, the Sejm can serve as a "kingmaker."

Prime Minister and Cabinet

According to Article 146.1 of the constitution, "The Council of Ministers carries out the domestic and foreign policies of the Polish Republic"; Article 146.2 also gives it residual powers—that is, those not explicitly assigned to other bodies. Another key function of the Council of Ministers (synonymous with the government, or cabinet) is determining the annual budget. Article 157 introduces the principle of the collective responsibility of this body to the Sejm, and of the individual responsibility of each minister for the work of his or her department, also to the Sejm. By the 1997 constitution, both the government and the prime minister can issue decrees within their own areas of jurisdiction.

Fifteen years into the new political system, it has become clear that the office involving the highest stakes is that of prime minister. The prime minister is officially nominated by the president but, in practice, is usually the leader or a high-ranking member of the largest party in parliament. It has happened that the candidate was not drawn from the ranks of the strongest party. Thus, in 1992 the Solidarity camp and in 1993 the ex-Communist bloc, called the *Alliance of the Democratic Left (SLD)*, opted for the leader of the pivotal Polish Peasant Party (PSL) to be prime minister. A party's hold on the prime ministership places it at an advantage in the political system. This is illustrated by the fact that from 1993 to 1995 President Wałęsa's power was neutralized by a prime minister emanating from the ranks of the opposing SLD camp. Similarly for several years after 1997 President Kwaśniewski's power was weakened by the presence of a prime minister from the opposing Solidarity Electoral Action (AWS) bloc.

Throughout much of the 1990s no one party was able to obtain an absolute majority of parliamentary seats so prime ministerial turnover and cabinet reshuffles were commonplace (see Figure 10.2). Between 1989 and the end of 1997, nine persons were nominated to be prime minister. Following the victory of *Solidarity Electoral Action*

FIGURE 10.2   Presidents and Prime Ministers of Poland, 1989–2004

Prime Minister	Year	President
Marek Belka	2004	
Leszek Miller	2001	
Jerzy Buzek	1997	
Wlodzimierz Cimoszewicz	1996	
Józef Oleksy	1995	Aleksander Kwaśniewski
Waldemar Pawlak	1993	
Hanna Suchocka	1992	
Waldemar Pawlak	1992	
Jan Olszewski	1991	
Jan Krzysztof Bielecki	1990	Lech Wałęsa
Tadeusz Mazowiecki	1989	Wojciech Jaruzelski

(AWS) in the 1997 elections, Jerzy Buzek managed to keep the job of prime minister for four years.

We cannot say for certain that this turnover of governments produced real political instability. The democratic system had widespread support, whether measured by public opinion polls or by party leaders' commitment to the rules of the game. The complex six- and seven-party coalition governments of the early 1990s, with their "carousels" of incoming and outgoing ministers, gave way beginning in the later 1990s to two-party coalitions where ministerial shuffles were rarer. In great part the reason for greater government stability lay in the electoral law adopted in 1993. It rewarded parties winning the most votes with a disproportionate number of parliamentary seats. The Sejm became more powerful and autonomous and could now insist on the accountability of governments to it. It could force changes in prime ministers and other cabinet ministers, in this way ensuring a government more responsive to elected representatives.

In the end it is the grounds on which a government falls and another one is constituted that tells us about the health of a democratic system. Poland clearly has moved away from government crises triggered by destabilizing struggles for power between president and prime minister (as in the case of Wałęsa versus Prime Minister Jan Olszewski in 1992) to crises grounded in policy differences between coalition partners (as on taxation between the AWS and UW in 2000) and to seamless replacements of a tarnished prime minister by a new appointee from the same party (Marek Belka's takeover from Leszek Miller in 2004). The political rules of the game have taken root and political crises are now resolved using these rules.

The Judicial Branch

Chapter 8 of the 1997 constitution delineates the system of courts and tribunals as a separate branch of authority. The judicial system is made up of the Supreme Court, general courts, administrative courts (including the Supreme Administrative Court), and military courts. Supreme Court judges are appointed by the president on the advice of the National Judicial Council. They have life terms, can-

not be removed, are independent, and cannot belong to a political party or trade union.

Another judicial body is the *Constitutional Tribunal* which, as in France and Germany, rules on the constitutionality and offers binding interpretations of laws, delimits the jurisdiction of different branches of government, and undertakes other kinds of judicial review. The Constitutional Tribunal consists of 15 judges elected by the Sejm for one term lasting nine years. In its early years justices on the Tribunal saw its mission as laying the foundation for a democratic law-based state and were very proactive (some would say overly so) in shaping Polish legislation to reflect the principles and values found in Western countries.

A further important judicial body is the Tribunal of State to which leaders of national institutions—the president and the prime minister, individual ministers, heads of the National Bank, members of the National Radio and Television Council, the head of the Chief Inspectorate (which controls the work of the state administration and other state institutions), and the head of the armed forces—must answer for the constitutionality of their acts. During the 1990s both the Supreme Court and the Constitutional Tribunal issued rulings that upset both the executive branch of government and lawmakers. For example, in 1997 the Constitutional Tribunal concluded that the previous year's law easing restrictions on abortion did not fully comply with Poland's constitutional framework. The ruling could only be overridden by a two-thirds majority in the Sejm. The Catholic-influenced AWS government thought better than to try for a legislative override. In 2004 the Tribunal overturned a law on reform of the national health service which upset the government of Prime Minister Miller. The SLD had subsequently to revise the bill in order to have it take effect.

The Polish Third Republic also has a Civil Rights Ombudsperson. The official is chosen by the Sejm for a five-year term and is responsible for determining whether citizens' rights and freedoms are infringed upon by state bodies. The first three Ombudspersons (one was a woman) were legal scholars who won much praise for their work. About 50,000 letters from citizens per year were received by the office and the majority dealt with such routine issues as housing, pensions, taxes, and workers' rights. The 1997 constitution also established an Ombudsperson for Children's Rights. In these ways the new system has dramatized the break with the previous one by providing a panoply of institutional mechanisms for protecting civil rights.

The Advantages of Institutional Experimentation

There is something to be said for Poland's trial-and-error approach to institution-building after 1989. Nobel-Prize winning organizational theorist Douglass North offered an explanation for why some societies develop efficient, adaptive, growth-promoting institutions and others do not. The answer, he believed, lay in a society's openness to institutional innovation as well as its commitment to institutional elimination: "It is essential to have rules that eliminate not only failed economic organization but failed political organization as well. The effective structure of rules, therefore, not only rewards successes, but also vetoes the survival of maladapted parts of the organizational structure."[15] Given Poland's recent economic success and political stability, it appears that the country has skillfully carried out creative and flexible institutional adaptation.

Many political structures have been overhauled since the democratic breakthrough. Some were completely discarded and replaced by new ones. Functional ministries such as defense, foreign affairs, and internal affairs were remodeled and restaffed. The Supreme Court and the Constitutional Tribunal were invested with added responsibilities. A new State Security Agency (UOP) replaced the feared Communist security apparatus. However it still figured at the center of a controversy in 1995 and 1996 when several of its officials backed the internal affairs minister's claim that the then prime minister had worked for Soviet intelligence. The charges were not proved and the security apparatus again came under attack, as in the communist period, for playing dirty politics.

Other institutions inherited from the antecedent regime have, sometimes surprisingly, sur-

vived, if in an overhauled form. These include the Central Office of Planning, the Main Statistical Office, the National Bank, the Chief Inspectorate, the Ombudsperson, and the Office of the Council of Ministers. New institution-building was aimed at speeding up economic transformation and has included both the Economic and Social Committees of the Council of Ministers, for a time the Ministry of Property Transformation (or Privatization), the Ministry of Foreign Economic Cooperation, and the Anti-Monopolies Office. Institutional elimination has occurred when the changing context required it. Thus the privatization ministry was eliminated in 1996 to reflect the fact that the state should not be in the business of promoting market relations.

For the most part, then, the institutional design with which Poland entered the twenty-first century provided fertile soil for the growth of Polish democracy. But as we see later, many Poles believe that political failures, such as rampant corruption at the top, are attributable to poorly functioning institutions.

POLITICAL CULTURE

We need to be circumspect about the advances in democratic politics in Poland. As one specialist, Frances Millard, cautioned, "if the state institutions and political elites were quite successful in adapting themselves to the procedural requirements of liberal democracy, they were less successful in forging links with society."[16] The charge that political elites are out of touch with public opinion can be heard in many contemporary democracies and Poland is no exception. Can it be that the same Polish society that toppled communism finds itself estranged today from its elected representatives and embraces a value system different from that of its leaders? Examining a country's political culture can provide an answer to this important question.

Political culture is the notion that political values, attitudes, and behavior are deeply embedded in—not transient to—a particular nation. Political culture is rooted in the more enduring political orientations of a country. We have noted the rebellious streak cutting through Polish history, and the strong distrust of authoritarian government. If we focus on more recent data and trends, for example, electoral behavior after 1989, we may be able to identify emerging features of political culture.

On the basis of voting preferences we find that Poles' political preferences have been fickle since the democratic breakthrough. At the same time, surveys of citizen attitudes indicate that a value system is emerging that is significantly different from the one that supposedly existed under the Communist regime. On the basis of short-term trends, can we speak of a culture shift toward democratic values in Poland? Or is an irreversible cultural break with the past yet to occur?

Values and Identity

Norms about the community a citizen lives in are important in defining his or her place in a postmodern world characterized by fragmentation and transience. Have Poles been able to maintain a strong sense of national identity and continue to take pride in their nation and state? Or, with so much global culture shift generally, and the rapid shift from a political identity imposed by Russia to one shaped by the values of the West in Central Europe specifically, are Poles unclear and anxious about the community they live in?

In the World Values Survey of 43 nations conducted at a time when Poland was in its early transition years (1991–1993), the country ranked third overall in terms of identifying "the country as a whole" as "the geographical group you would say you belong to first of all."[17] In answer to the question "How proud are you to be Polish?" 69 percent answered "very proud"—putting it in fourth place.[18] Paradoxically, though, Poles ranked next-to-last when asked if they trusted their own nationality.[19] Both a sense of national identity and of patriotism seemed unproblematic in the early 1990s (also see Chapter 2).

Also noteworthy is the inclusive rather than exclusionary understanding of citizenship that Polish respondents have provided. Whereas sharply drawn ethnic boundaries would reflect a less open attitude to minorities, inclusiveness would suggest tolerance and liberalism. In a 1994 survey, respondents were asked who, in their view, was Polish. The most common answers were someone who speaks Polish (cited by 96 percent of respondents), whose citizenship is Polish (92 percent), whose parents were Polish (82 percent), or who lives in Poland (80 percent). Surprisingly, little more than one-half (57 percent) said that a Pole was someone who was Catholic.[20] These answers on national identity point to a considerably more liberal orientation than those warning us of Polish nationalism would lead us to believe. If political culture includes the types of relationships that exist between different groups, then we can say that tolerance, a core concept of Western liberalism, has grown since the 1990s.

Democratic Norms

A key aspect of political culture is citizen attitudes toward the system of government. For a democratic culture to take root in Poland, liberal values need to appear and authoritarian ones to fade. A more participant culture where citizens are informed about politics and make political demands is a further indication of a modern democratic system. Some scholars have highlighted the deferential, subject culture of many Slavic societies where citizens passively obey government officials, a tendency that may have been reinforced by Soviet-style authoritarianism.[21] Others have stressed the distinctiveness of national cultures—in the case of Poland, the experience of insurrectionism and antiauthoritarianism—and their general incompatibility with the communist normative system.[22] Others still point to the more recent experience of building a civil society—a private sphere of life for citizens free of governmental interference—that was undertaken in Poland in the mid-1970s, earlier than in other states in the region. Learning how to organize outside of the structures of power facilitated the transition to democratic processes, it is argued, and laid the groundwork for the spread of liberal values.

Early in the transition, Poles expressed comparatively little confidence in the emergent system. For example, in 1993, 52 percent of Poles surveyed claimed they were dissatisfied with the way Polish democracy functioned; 36 percent said they were satisfied. In 1998 satisfaction with Polish democracy reached an all-time high when those happy with it numbered only slightly fewer than those unhappy with it (41 and 46 percent respectively). Shortly after the election of the SLD government in 2001, dissatisfaction with the functioning of Polish democracy grew, and in mid-2004 only 21 percent were happy with it and 68 percent unhappy.[23] One of the factors explaining this trend was the growing popular perception that Poland was coming to resemble an undemocratic system more than a democratic one. The SLD was increasingly viewed as the "party of power" in the Third Republic, and the financial scandals that afflicted it after 2001 began to be seen by the public as symptoms of a rotten system rather than the foibles of a particular leader or party.

Another important reason for dissatisfaction was the sense that political institutions were not really representing citizen interests. A 1992 poll found that only 26 percent of respondents agreed "there are now organizations, associations, or unions in Poland that serve the interest of people like you"; 53 percent disagreed. This view has not changed much since then. Similarly, the 1999 survey research finding that the majority of Poles did not feel that politicians sufficiently represented their interests remained accurate five years later. Given that institutions and politicians are generally not seen as representing citizens' interests, it follows that the public has developed a sense of powerlessness. Thus, if in 1992 only 7 percent of respondents believed they had influence on the country in general, the proportion reached a high water mark of 19 percent in 1997 but fell to 15 percent in 2004. A remarkable (for a democracy) 83 percent in 2004 claimed that they had no influence on national affairs![24] It is an understatement to say, then, that the sense of political efficacy remains low in Poland.

Fifteen years after the democratic breakthrough, Poles still harbored conflicting feelings about the new and old systems. On the one hand, as we have observed, they were very critical—more so than others in Central Europe—about the functioning of their democracy. In their cost-benefit analyses a surprisingly high proportion of Poles concluded that the new democracy was not as advantageous as the previous communist system. In 2004 more Poles believed that the post-1989 changes had brought greater losses (37 percent) than gains (22 percent); 29 percent perceived an equal amount of gains and losses.[25] Poles' evaluation of various political institutions placed the Sejm—the core of the system of representative government—in last place (Figure 10.3).

On the other hand, Poles were more pleased than others that communism had been laid to rest. When asked in 1999 to reflect on whether the collapse of communism was a good thing, 80 percent of Poles (a figure similar to that of West Europeans) said yes and only 6 percent said no. The approval rate in other Central European countries was about 70 percent.[26] In 2004, in answer to the question whether the change of regime made 15 years earlier was worth it, 65 percent of Poles said yes and only 21 percent said no.[27] The conclusion drawn is that Poles are hardheaded in their evaluations of the old and new regimes. They are pleased that communism is gone, but they are highly critical of the "losses" that the new regime has inflicted on them. Desire for a more representative, effective democratic system that brings citizens real advantages—not a harkening back to communism—is the prevailing attitude of Poles today.

The early 1990s' World Values Survey highlighted an aspect of Polish exceptionalism: "almost all of the socialist or ex-socialist societies . . . are characterized by (1) survival values, and (2) a strong emphasis on state authority, rather than traditional authority. Poland is a striking exception, distinguished from the other socialist societies by her strong traditional-religious values."[28] It is a "hyper-Catholic society . . . manifesting relatively traditional cultural values across a wide range of areas. Not only in religion, but also in politics, gender roles, sexual norms, and family values, their values are far more traditional than those generally found in industrial societies."[29]

Religion was the single most important factor determining the outcome of the 1995 presidential and 1997 legislative elections. Catholic Poland strongly supported nationalist-oriented candidates while secular Poland backed the SLD. Catholicism played less of a role in the 2000 presidential, 2001 parliamentary, and 2004 European Parliament elec-

FIGURE 10.3 Public Opinion on Selected Institutions in Poland, June 2004 (in percent)

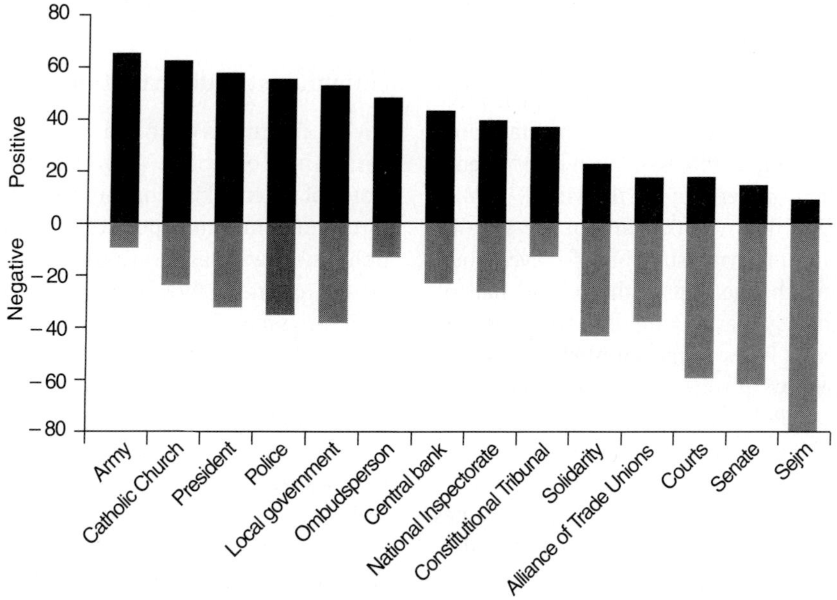

Source: Centrum Badama Opinii Spolecznej (CBOS), "Oceny dzialalnosci instytucji publicznych" (July 2004), www.cbos.pl. The answer "difficult to say" is excluded from the results.

tions, but it would be the 2005 round of elections that would make clear whether an emphatic break from the traditional religious value system had taken place.

Social and Economic Values

To what extent did a communist value system take hold in Poland? If we assume that the core values of this system were social justice and egalitarianism, then large sections of Polish society internalized such ideals during the communist period.[30] But communist values also prescribed deference to authority, the centrality of the common good, and, officially at least, a nonconsumerist way of life. In these areas, Polish political culture proved resilient to the Communist regime's indoctrination efforts.

At the outset of the 1990s, Poland ranked twenty-eighth out of 43 societies in terms of espousing post-materialist values. Let us review the meaning of this term and its opposite, materialism: "Materialist priorities are tapped by emphasis on such goals as economic growth, fighting rising prices, maintaining order and fighting crime; while postmaterialist values are reflected when top priority is given to such goals as giving people more say on the job or in government decisions, or protecting freedom of speech or moving toward a less impersonal, more humane society."[31] The economic *shock therapy* that Polish society experienced in the early 1990s forced citizens to shift to materialist priorities. This contrasted with the more idealistic project of building a civil society espoused by dissidents in the 1970s and 1980s.

Early in the 1990s the uncertain consequences of the transition to a market economy and democracy were reflected in public opinion that revealed considerable anxiety. Egalitarianism, the core value of the socialist normative order, carried over to the democratic system though with weaker societal commitment to it. One study carried out in the first years of the transition discovered that the issues considered important by the public were egalitarian in nature: unemployment, inflation, agriculture, poverty, crime, and housing.[32] Another study found that the policy of decommunizing public life was ranked last of 11 priorities identified by respondents (only 9 percent mentioned it). When asked what type of society was preferable—one in which individual interests dominated or where the state provided citizens with guarantees—Polish respondents displayed a slight preference for the latter.[33] Statist attitudes holding that it is the duty of the state to safeguard minimum living standards for everybody survived regime change. But in the second half of the decade the egalitarian mindset weakened as large numbers of Poles found employment in the more remunerative private sector. A 2000 report concluded that Poles now put freedom before equality in social life if faced with the choice.[34]

Today's political culture reflects the effects of 15 years of democratic experience. Some statist values remain but among young people in particular they have given way to individualist ones. Political behavior, a central aspect of political culture, is now channeled through the ballot box, though public demonstrations (against abortion and EU agricultural products, for health care reform and farm subsidies) also reflect the more liberalized culture. Some skeptics detected a lag between the precocious growth of democratic institutions and a more gradual transformation of societal values in Poland. But five years into the new century it seemed clear that Polish public opinion favored more democracy than the political institutions were delivering. If there was a democratic deficit in the country, it was now located not in its political culture but in the poorly functioning institutions of representative government.

POLITICAL SOCIALIZATION

The transition to democracy has led to a dramatic change in both the forms and content of political socialization work in the country—that is, the values that political authorities, using a variety of means, want their citizens to internalize. The very role in politics that was to be played by the school, the family, the newspaper, and the church service, was redefined. The meaning of patriotism, citizen-

ship, and personal success was altered. Political socialization tells us as much about the nature of a political system as the institutions it establishes.

Communist Indoctrination

The Communist regime had made political indoctrination into one of its priorities. An elaborate network of interlocking organizations was set up to carry out communist political teaching. The education system was based on a curriculum and incentive system rewarding those that internalized—or at least paid lip service to—socialist values. Socialization into the Marxist system of values extended from cheap state-run childcare facilities allowing both parents to work (and drawing their attention to the "magnanimous" communist welfare system), to universities and vocational colleges where students were trained to move smoothly into the labor market.

Parallel to the school system were youth organizations that prepared members for leadership roles in society and, for a select number, entry into the ruling Communist Party. On taking up employment, individuals were recruited into officially independent trade unions, workers' councils, and employees' committees. In fact, these organizations served as the schools of socialism, as Soviet founder Vladimir Lenin had referred to unions. When not at school or work, citizens were encouraged to take part in the self-management of publicly owned housing blocks where they lived. A hierarchical structure of residents' committees, from the floor one lived on to the neighborhood that one resided in, existed both to invite citizen participation and to control citizens' behavior. All these agents of socialization were supposed to ensure that social justice, order, and equality of condition were maintained.

The media, too, were in the hands of the party-state. For many decades Poles' sole source of political information was radio, television, and newspapers, all subject to the scrutiny of censors. The Communist "propaganda of success" permeated news content, reaching its peak in the 1970s by glorifying a mini-economic boom (the fact that it was produced by enormous Western loans was not mentioned). Political socialization now praised consumer culture, proclaiming that Communist economic planning had laid the foundation for a society of plenty. The virtue of austerity inculcated in the 1950s and 1960s was replaced by the call for people to enrich themselves and join the ranks of the "red bourgeoisie." Films and books supplemented the other media in portraying the value of *arrivisme,* going from humble origins to affluence by whatever means were necessary. A short-lived attempt was made in the early 1980s, under the martial law regime, to attack speculators and black marketers, but in the end there was no rolling back the emergence of a consumer society.

Patriotism was a central feature of Communist propaganda even if its meaning was distorted by the contradictory idea of proletarian internationalism, which prescribed a special relationship with the Soviet Union. Throughout the existence of the Polish People's Republic, there was an underlying tension discernible in propaganda between Polish patriotism and political russophilism. It even divided the Communist elite and in some measure contributed to the collapse of communism—a system identified by many as an alien, Russian-imposed ideological aberration.

Retooling Political Socialization

The new democratic system overhauled the content and methods of political socialization. The agents of socialization located in the public sphere—schools, mass organizations, the workplace, neighborhood groups, and the media—took a secondary role behind more traditional sources of values—peer group, family, church. The privatization of public life occurred in tandem with the privatization of the economy. There was now not one overarching value system propagated to all groups in society but several different ones. Children of working-class families were likely to be taught the value of solidarity, while those of the middle class were taught individualism. More than ever, peasant children were brought up to be good Catholics. Many children of the economic and social elite were now sent to schools in the West so as to internalize Western values (to be sure, part of the Communist elite had done likewise).

As in the West, young people rebelled against the values of their elders. In the early 1990s some of

the worst outbreaks of political violence involved young anarchists—many of them indistinguishable from street punks—attacking public buildings (the fact that these now housed Solidarity leaders was irrelevant). Initial enthusiasm about politics, triggered by regime change, was soon displaced by a waning interest among the young in the political concerns of their parents' generation. The number of drug users grew, and young victims of AIDS were often forced onto the streets to beg since there were no treatment centers for them. The pervasiveness of Western youth culture was seen in styles of dress (from preppy khakis to cargo pants), ways of speaking (creeping anglicisms), and tastes in music (rap). Indigenous popular musical forms emerged (for example discopolo, popular among rural youth), but in the cities it was American-style hip-hop that had greatest appeal.

Socialization within the family produced an ethnic revival as people discovered long-suppressed identities—Jewish, German, Silesian, Ukrainian, Lemko, Kashub. The religious and cultural institutions of minority peoples were revived and began to function as agents of socialization. For minority groups, the family, especially when it transmitted a maternal language and distinct cultural heritage, reemerged as a chief instrument of value dissemination.

Catholicism and Political Values

In the Communist era it was the Catholic Church that served as the alternative to socialist indoctrination. After the democratic breakthrough it attempted to inculcate Christian values even more aggressively. This created an unexpected backlash against the Church. Many Poles now regarded the Church as too influential in political life in the 1990s (discussed next). Outward signs of religiosity—attendance at mass, receiving first communion, making pilgrimages to the monastery at Czestochowa, turning out in enormous numbers for the Pope's visits—have remained pervasive. But, simultaneously, Polish society was quickly becoming more secular. Both Pope John Paul II and *Cardinal Józef Glemp,* Primate of the Polish Catholic Church since 1981, now cautioned Poles against submitting to the appeal of materialism. If Poles remained largely a devout, believing people, they began to differentiate faith in God from faith in the Church's role in politics.

Since the 1990s there has even been a rise in anticlericalism. Arguably, it was sparked by the Church's attempt to replace the state as the dominant form of political socialization. One Polish scholar described the negative impact that the Church was having in a capitalist society: "Catholicism has once again shown itself as a historical factor making pro-capitalist changes harder. Its communalism, pressure to subordinate the interests of the individual to those of the community, its dislike of the creation and use of wealth by the individual . . . were an important binding agent of dislike of the 'new.'"[35]

The Church's influence can be exaggerated. It sided with losing conservative parties in a series of elections (the exception was 1997). Its intervention in the abortion issue triggered a backlash. Large sections of society were disappointed in the leadership offered by Cardinal Glemp, who was viewed as too conservative and nationalistic. Many Poles were upset at his ineptness in dealing with controversies involving the Nazi death camp at Auschwitz. First a plan was announced to build a Carmelite convent close by, then ultranationalist Poles erected crosses on a nearby hillside to highlight the deaths of Catholics in Auschwitz, and finally a developer proposed to complete a shopping plaza in the area. Many Poles found Glemp's lack of resolve, ambivalence, and reticence to side with Jewish groups' protests unseemly.

Of course Catholicism still exerts considerable influence on the value system internalized by individual Poles and in the Polish family. Under tremendous stress due to economic hardships brought on by the transition, the Catholic family has, more than ever, performed the role of support group for its members. It may now be the most important agent of socialization professing collective, as opposed to individualistic, values. The notion of a common good is an important value in a time of upheaval and, in this respect, the Polish family may play a key role in safeguarding it.

The Church is sometimes accused of playing an insidious role in the socialization of women. Whereas officially the communist system treated the economic liberation of women as a high priority, Catholicism has stressed the unique role that women have to play as mothers and as the nucleus of the family. If the communist system effectively imposed a double burden on women—as indispensable participants in the labor market and as homemakers—the Church has taken a more one-sided view, seeing women as givers of life, raising children to be practicing Catholics, and forming the hearth of the family. The Communist regime, officially at least, sought to radicalize women and invited their participation in politics. In contrast the Church has encouraged women to perform traditional roles such as childrearing, cooking, and going to church—and if they are to vote it should be for Catholic candidates.[36] Clearly the church has failed in the first task: the fertility rate fell from 2.2 children per woman in 1987 to 1.4 in 1998. Higher living costs and child expenses, together with some women's deliberate choice to work rather than rear children, accounted for falling demographics (seen elsewhere in Central Europe as well).

In the 1990s women were the main victims of the transition to a market economy, accounting for nearly two-thirds of the nonmanual unemployed. Finding new employment was much more difficult, not helped by the dismantling of the state-run child care system. None of this has been the direct result of the Church resocializing females to take up their traditional roles, but many clerics have not concealed their satisfaction that economic imperatives have succeeded in changing women's roles in line with Catholic teachings.

Compulsory religious education in schools and an ultraconservative abortion law were the Church's doings, however. Because women account for a greater proportion of believers, they face more moral agonizing than men when deciding whether to conform to Catholic teaching. By internalizing Catholic values, Polish women may thus be tempted to reject some of the emancipatory ideas commonplace in Western countries. We should stress, nevertheless, that even when Catholic values lead to conservative attitudes among Polish women, it does not follow that they are less emancipated than their Western cohorts. Even without a strong women's movement in the country, there is a widespread awareness of the viable choices that women have in any modern society.

The Media Battles

Television, radio, and the press are major agents of socialization. Since 1989 the political knowledge of Polish citizens has expanded as government-controlled media have been democratized and other private media outlets established. If there is a problem with media content today, it is that few newspapers and newsmagazines are owned by Polish concerns; any bias that exists in reporting results from foreign ownership. Although French and Italian media conglomerates operate in Poland, the largest presence is on the part of the country's western neighbor; some have even spoken of Poland as a German media colony.

To be sure, the most widely read newspaper, *Gazeta Wyborcza* ("Electoral Gazette"), is largely Polish-owned and secular-oriented. It was established in 1989 by former dissident Michnik to break the state monopoly on the media and has since become a very successful commercial venture. A Polish edition of *Newsweek,* started up after 2000, has also become a success story and has edged out long-standing Polish newsmagazines (like *Polityka*) as the widest read weekly.

Sporadic attempts have been made to control publishing in democratic Poland. One, inspired by the Church, was the anti-pornography law passed by the Sejm which provided for jail sentences for newsagents who sold even soft porn like *Playboy*. The bill was vetoed in 2000 by President Kwaśniewski. Another alleged infringement of freedom of the press was the criminal charges brought by a public prosecutor against Polish publisher Jerzy Urban—a longtime maverick from the Communist era. Founder and editor of the weekly satirical *Nie,* he was accused of insulting Pope John Paul II by allowing publication in 2002 of an article entitled "Walking Sado-Masochism." In addition, in recent years several Polish journalists were sentenced to prison for slandering public officials. This has led to a protest against restrictions on press freedoms in Poland by the International Press Institute, a network of media executives, editors, and journalists representing over 120 countries.

Control over television has sparked many political battles in Poland. The most notorious of these has been so-called *Rywingate* in 2002 whose political repercussions are still being felt today. To understand why Rywingate happened it is important to know what the stakes have been in controlling television and radio. Between 1993 and 1997 the SLD government stacked the committee overseeing the media, the National Broadcasting Council, with its own supporters and filled the post of director of state television with a person from its own ranks. In turn between 1997 and 2001 the AWS-led Buzek government tried to do much the same. Governments of both the left and right were operating under the same assumptions as in the communist period—that control over television and radio broadcasting helps bring about public support for the government's position.

The tug-of-war over top positions in the Polish media had little effect on the free flow of information because the public had private channels (including many from Western Europe) to tune in to. Even if the state owned or controlled two television channels, a number of national radio stations, and a nationwide newspaper (*Rzeczpospolita*), these now faced stiff competition for an audience from the privately owned media. There could be as many different types of political socialization as there were channels. Thus, even a Catholic television station (TV Puls), headed by Franciscan monks launched family and religious television programming in 2001 in response to complaints of too much violence and sex on the main networks.

In 2002 the Sejm debated a new law on the media, and once again the rival political blocs jockeyed for the inside position. This time, however, the stakes were not about capturing the inside track to disseminate a political viewpoint but about making money. That summer an entrepreneur, Lew Rywin (who produced Roman Polanski's Oscar-winning movie *The Pianist*), visited *Gazeta Wyborcza* editor Michnik and offered to have changes made to the pending media bill that would allow the paper's parent company, Agora, to enter the television business. Rywin claimed to be acting on behalf of top people in the SLD including Prime Minister Miller. In exchange he requested a $17.5 million bribe from Michnik. Although he is a controversial figure, Michnik is generally viewed as a highly moralistic, incorruptible individual. The *Gazeta Wyborcza* editor taped his conversation with Rywin but, inexplicably, did not publicly reveal the story until his paper carried it in December (he later contended that he did not want to jeopardize Poland's ongoing, delicate accession negotiations with the EU). Apparently both Prime Minister Miller and President Kwaśniewski were told about the attempted bribe but also said nothing until the newspaper story was published.

The bribery scandal involving the media bill— together with charges of other SLD financial wrongdoings—led to a split within the party. The SLD's support among voters dropped to single digits. Rywingate also forced Miller to step down as prime minister the day after Poland officially joined the EU. In May 2004 the Sejm received a long-awaited report on the scandal from a Sejm investigation commission chaired by Deputy Zbigniew Ziobro. Approved by an absolute majority in the Sejm, the report claimed that Rywin served as go-between for Miller and several of his colleagues, as well as for a former TVP head and former secretary of the National Radio and Television Council. The Ziobro report recommended that Kwaśniewski, Miller, and a former SLD Justice Minister be brought before the Tribunal of State for having failed to notify authorities about the crime Rywin had committed. Whether and when this would happen would depend on the next parliamentary elections scheduled for 2005.

In sum, the political battles waged over television and radio have been fierce and have involved both control over a primary agent of political socialization and financial windfalls that can come from media ownership. In particular the rise and fall of the SLD are intricately connected to its efforts to have television on its side. Control over broadcasting is as divisive an issue as it was in the Communist era.

In recent years online sources of information have increased exponentially ensuring a freer flow of information to Polish citizens. Inevitably, the pressure to make profits has forced all media— whether Internet sites or television—to cater to the tastes of the wired, viewing, listening, and reading publics. This, in turn, has led to the widespread dissemination of fluff—a tried-and-true formula of the Western media. Increasingly, then, political news is overshadowed by infotainment in the commercially driven media industry. Political socialization has taken a back seat to product placement.

POLITICAL PARTICIPATION

The transition from communism to democracy involved a fundamental change in the nature of political participation. The communist system exhorted citizens to take part in politics through voting in elections, attendance at mass rallies and meetings, and membership in many different types of organizations that supposedly made inputs into the political system. Of course voting was purely a ceremonial function, attending rallies was of no more than symbolic importance, and joining various organizations was primarily a form of manipulated participation.

The introduction of electoral democracy meant that voting now had real significance. In the space of 12 years Poland had five parliamentary elections (1989, 1991, 1993, 1997, and 2001) and three direct presidential elections (1990, 1995, and 2000). Three referenda, in 1996, 1997, and 2003, were also held. In 2004 Poland's first election to the European Parliament took place. As meaningful participatory opportunities have expanded under democracy, the rate of participation has dropped off (Figure 10.4). Turnout for presidential contests has ranged from a low of 53 percent in the 1990 second round to a high of 68 percent in the 1995 runoff. Parliamentary elections have generally drawn about one-half of the electorate to the polling stations though, in the case of the European Parliament, only one-fifth voted. Turnout for referenda has increased gradually, from 32 percent in 1996 (on privatizing state assets), to 43 percent in 1997 (on the new constitution), to 59 percent in 2003 (on EU accession). In the latter case, Poles had two days to vote: a new referendum law required that for ratification of an international agreement more than one-half of voters had to cast ballots, and Polish authorities wanted to

FIGURE 10.4   Turnout in Elections and Referenda, 1989–2004

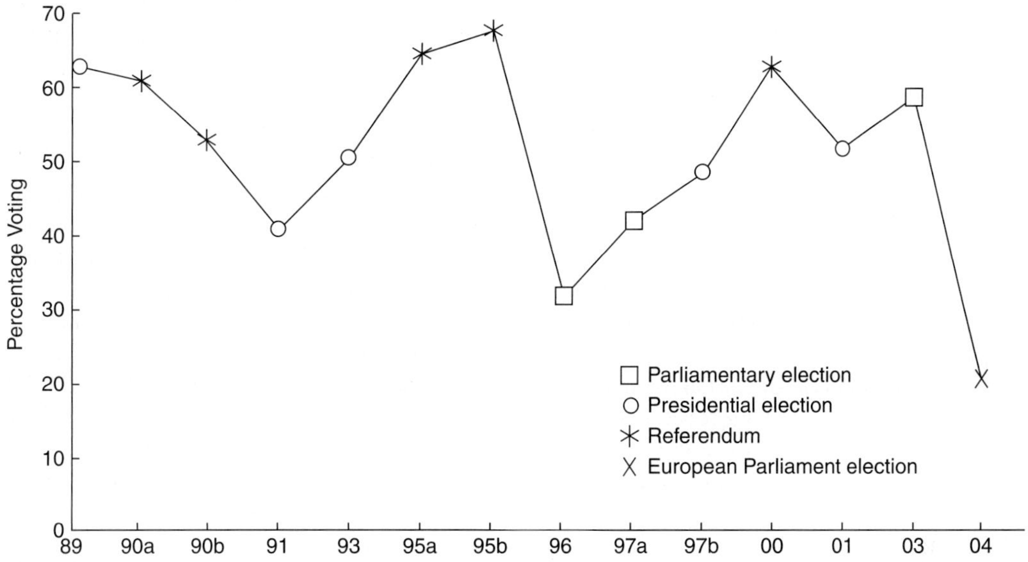

be sure Poles had every opportunity to vote on this historic issue. As elsewhere in electoral democracies, voting in local elections in Poland seldom exceeds the 10- to 25-percent range.

There are many explanations for citizen non-voting. Political parties have not offered clear and consistent programs making partisan identification difficult. Until recently there was near consensus among parties that market reform, less government, and NATO and EU membership were indispensable, blunting voters' interest. By and large, the new political leaders have lacked charisma. Exhaustion with politics after the struggles with the Communist regime in the 1980s led to greater citizen apathy. The opportunity to live a private life and ignore political involvement altogether is welcome after the constant mobilization and countermobilization of the 1980s. Many citizens are now enjoying the right to turn down opportunities for political participation, a right that did not exist under communism when not voting often led to harassment by the authorities. An optimistic view is that the political system simply is not overloaded with pressing citizen demands expressed through the ballot box. Finally,

as we have seen, it is possible that the creeping disillusionment with electoral democracy that we have noted is turning off a section of voters.

In what ways does the public take part in politics? The demise of the Communist Party in 1990 has left no mass-membership political parties in existence. Parties today are primarily electoral machines seeking to win over voters. Once they secure representation in the Sejm, they become parliamentary parties seeking to influence policymaking. Combined with a falloff in membership in mass organizations (trade unions, farmers' groups, student organizations) and a widespread reticence (or even apathy) about participating in civil society now that the struggle against communism is over, citizens have become less effective in aggregating their interests. Intermediary organizations between state and society are lacking (some that do exist are discussed later). To be sure, direct political action as through demonstrations is more frequent and does not involve the dangers it entailed under communism. But it often meets with a disdainful response on the part of the present political elite—a contrast with the overreaction to such action by Communist authorities.

Some Poles see the elite's reliance on the ballot box to settle disputes as devious. A general disaffection with politics—not just elections—is discernible in many established democracies and seems to be catching up with Poland. Whether this is a long-term trend or one that can undermine the legitimacy of the political system is difficult to foresee.

LEADERSHIP RECRUITMENT

Who are Poland's new political elites and where are they recruited from? If we focus on those individuals who have held executive power as either president or prime minister, we arrive at a very heterogeneous group in socio-occupational terms. One president was an electrician by profession (Wałęsa), the other an apparatchik in the former Communist bureaucracy specializing in youth and physical education (Kwaśniewski). Prime ministers have included a Catholic intellectual (Mazowiecki), a businessman (Bielecki), a Solidarity lawyer (Olszewski), a farmer (Pawlak), a law professor (Suchocka), a Marxist-trained economist (Oleksy), a Fulbright scholar with a doctorate in law (Cimoszewicz), a chemistry professor (Buzek), a Communist apparatchik (Miller), and an economics professor (Belka). Most of these very well-educated individuals (Bielecki the businessman had an economics degree, Pawlak the farmer held an engineering degree, though Kwaśniewski the president never completed his M.A.) finished their university studies when Poland was a communist system. Their different training symbolizes the pluralist nature of today's political elite.

Interesting patterns emerge if one looks at the social background of a wider political elite—those elected to parliament.[37] In terms of age, from 1991 to 2001 between 40 to 46 percent of deputies were between 40 and 49 years of age. In this period the proportion of those over 60 declined to under 5 percent. Men accounted for 87 percent of the Sejm, significantly higher than in Communist legislatures when the figure was about 75 percent. Approximately 80 percent of deputies had completed higher education and another 15 percent had finished high school. The best-represented occupations in 2001 were engineers (27 percent) followed by lawyers (16 percent), economists (10 percent), and farmers (7 percent). A study of 1993 deputies found that only 3 of 460 admitted to not knowing a foreign language. Of languages identified, Russian was known by 82 percent of deputies, English by 44 percent, and German by 40 percent.[38]

In short, Polish legislators seem to be exceptionally well educated compared with their Western counterparts, and they are an extraordinarily cosmopolitan group if we accept their self-described linguistic abilities at face value. The vast majority were first elected in 1991 or later, representing a new political elite. During the democratic transition, many leading members of the groups that opposed the Communist elite (like KOR and Solidarity) found that they had outlived their usefulness in politics. A few, like the legendary dissident Kuroń, remained highly respected politicians into the new century. As one typology of deputies pointed out, social activist was but one of eight categories of legislators in the 1990s. The others included politician, representative, specialist, negotiator, combatant, businessman, and parliamentarian.[39]

The disappearance of the old elite, along with the political inexperience of the many new party leaders and parliamentary deputies who appeared on the political scene in the early 1990s, allowed Wałęsa for a time to bully friends and foes alike. After 1995, however, the pluralistic elite emerging in parliament honed their skills, were prepared to challenge the established leaders, and became a force to be reckoned with. A consensus-building president like Kwaśniewski reflected the style of the new elite. But perhaps the most important question Poland will now ask about its political elite is the same one that has been debated for years in the United States and other older democracies. Do economic and political elites overlap, or have pluralism and circulation of elites become a regularity?

INTEREST GROUPS

Under the communist system interest groups did not really exist. Some mass organizations like trade unions, a women's league, and youth groups did nominally participate in the policy process but had no influence on issues outside of their respective jurisdictions. That was why the regime's begrudging recognition of the independent trade union Solidarity in 1980 was of such importance.

The democratic breakthrough in 1989 was accompanied by a surge of associational activity in Eastern Europe, conceptualized by one scholar as a "repluralization of politics."[40] One study found over 2,000 voluntary associations in existence in Poland in the early 1990s,[41] another estimated that there were up to 500 environmentalist groups alone,[42] and a third concluded that in 1995 "there were about 40 groups which could be sensibly called women's groups."[43] In the heady years following 1989, more powerful institutions like the Church and labor and business organizations believed that they could play a direct role in politics.

Most of the new, spontaneously created groups were short of the resources (membership numbers, finances) and skills (quality of leadership, negotiation skills) needed to engage in effective policy concertation. As with the initial proliferation of parties (370 were registered in 1997 when the law on political parties was finally changed), aggregate numbers were unreliable indicators of the place held in the political system by voluntary associations. Before we examine some of the most important socioeconomic organizations today, let us consider the part played by two long-powerful institutions in the country, the Catholic Church and the military.

The Catholic Church

The role assumed by the Church in Polish politics has a long history. Its importance in engaging the Communist regime in a battle for the minds of citizens from the 1940s to the 1980s—a battle that the Church won handily—is undeniable. (See Box 10.1.) Not surprisingly, more than any other institution the Church adopted a triumphalist attitude when the Communist regime collapsed. Indeed, some Church leaders unashamedly admitted that they had violated the terms of the roundtable agreement which required its neutrality. The Church used every means at its disposal—the

---

Box 10.1   Pope John Paul's 1979 Pilgrimage to Poland

In 1978 a Polish Cardinal, Karol Wojtyla, was elected Pope of the Roman Catholic Church. In 1979 he returned to Communist-ruled Poland on a Papal visit organized by the Polish Catholic Church. In 1980 the independent trade union Solidarity was formed, stripping the Communist Party of its monopoly on power. Nine years later Solidarity defeated the Communist Party in free elections. Does the end of communism, then, originate with the election of a Polish Pope?

"Certain American journalists have fostered a myth about John Paul II's role in the fall of communism. They depict him as a lonely hero in a Cold War thriller, a priest who from the start was slipping in and out of darkened doorways in the war against the Evil Empire. At the moment of perfect ripeness, Karol Wojtyla has himself elected Pope, flies home, and ignites the fuse he spent years fashioning. If the myth were pitched as a feature film, it would be John Wayne meets John Le Carre.

"The revolution launched by John Paul's return to Poland is one that conjures roads lined with weeping pilgrims, meadows of peaceful souls singing hymns, and most of all, of people swaying forward as one—reaching for the extraordinary man in white as he is borne through their midst. . . .

"John Paul II's 1979 trip was the fulcrum of revolution which led to the collapse of communism. Timothy Garton Ash put it this way, 'Without the Pope, no Solidarity. Without Solidarity, no Gorbachev. Without Gorbachev, no fall of communism.' (In fact, Gorbachev himself gave the Kremlin's long-term enemy this due, 'It would have been impossible without the Pope.')

"It took time; it took the Pope's support from Rome—some of it financial; it took several more trips in 1983 and 1987. But the flame was lit. It would smolder and flicker before it burned from one end of Poland to the other. Millions of people spread the revolution, but it began with the Pope's trip home in 1979. As General Jaruzelski said, 'That was the detonator.'"*

* From Jane Barnes and Helen Whitney, "John Paul II and the Fall of Communism" *Frontline*, PBS online (1999).

pulpit, its printing facilities, its meeting rooms, its many voluntary workers, above all its good name— to persuade citizens to vote against Communist candidates. Communist rulers who had so often tricked others into making deals that the rulers had no intention of keeping (such as registering Solidarity as a legal trade union in late 1980 and then banning it in late 1981) were now themselves taken in by the Church's pledge to act as an impartial mediator of the 1989 election.

We have described how the role of the Church in the politics of the Third Republic increasingly came under fire. The highly unpopular, restrictive abortion bill that had to be vetoed by the president, the requirement that public schools provide religious education (though pupils do not have to take it), the principle that Christian values should permeate public broadcasting, and the tough law on pornography that again required a presidential veto alienated many of the faithful, not to mention non-Catholics. Occasional anti-Semitic sentiments expressed by a few members of the Episcopate, lay Catholic groups, and individual priests have further tarnished the Church. The arrogance of the Episcopate and of some clerics has rankled many citizens. Radio Maryja, a nationalist Catholic radio network, has also polarized much of society.

Politicians were now able to capitalize on the Church's growing unpopularity. Kwaśniewski made known his indignation with the Church: "We are not going to have a theocratic state in the middle of Europe at the end of the twentieth century."[44] A 1994 survey found that 71 percent of respondents believed that the Church had too much influence in public life. From being the most trusted of all institutions in Poland throughout most of the 1970s and 1980s, by 1994 the Church had fallen behind the army and the police in trustworthiness: public confidence in the Church plummeted from 90 percent before communism's fall to only 50 percent by 1994. In 2004 63 percent of respondents gave the Church a positive assessment—an improvement on a decade earlier but not equal to its status under communism.

The Church's reduced political influence has been evident in its inability to have many of the principles it embraces made into law. When the Sejm debated writing a new constitution, the Church made the case for a preamble identifying Christian values as the set of principles underlying Polish society, recognition of its special role in the country, rejection of the notion of a secular state, and a constitutional ban on abortion. To be sure, the Church did not give up when these efforts failed at home: EU agreement in 2004 on a European constitution was delayed by the insistence of Poland— and Spain—that its preamble should refer to Europe's Christian heritage.

Another illustration of the Church's international role is the *Concordat* signed in 1993 between President Wałęsa and Pope John Paul II, approved by the Sejm only in 1998. The 1993 draft consisted of 29 articles beginning with the assertion that "The Catholic religion is practiced by the majority of the Polish population." A similar clause in the interwar constitution had become a source of controversy since, at the time, Poland had large ethnic and religious minorities. The 1993 Concordat institutionalized Catholic education in schools, while Church marriages were now to have the same legal status as civil ones (though the Church was prudent enough not to press for changes to existing divorce laws).

Probably the most contentious item in the agreement was Article 22, a cryptic clause dealing with restitution of Church property. A special church-state commission was to be set up to make changes in legislation. Moreover, "The new regulation will take into account the needs of the Church given its mission and the practice hitherto of church life in Poland." Opponents of the Concordat, largely on the left of the political spectrum, alleged that many of its provisions were in violation of the EU treaty. One Polish writer put it this way: "Anyone who naively believes today that church-state conflict was invented by the communists and, with their demise, this chapter is closed for all time is making a major and possibly costly mistake."[45]

SLD governments, often supported by the Polish Peasant Party, took care not to antagonize Pope John Paul and Cardinal Glemp and so did not bring up their objections to the Concordat. But it was the Catholic-oriented AWS government formed in 1997 that submitted the Concordat to the Sejm for ratification. It was approved and Kwaśniewski quickly signed it into law.

The Church has been aware that membership in the EU puts pressure on the country to become more secular. The Polish Pope, revered in Poland, warned of the threat to spiritual values posed by EU accession. There is something inexorable, however, about Poland accepting a stricter separation of church and state—a centuries-old arrangement found in many, though not all, Western European countries.

The Military

A central issue in the politics of new democracies is civil-military relations. A democracy requires civilian oversight over the military since civilian leaders are elected, military ones are not. In the case of Poland, fulfilling eligibility requirements for NATO entailed meeting its standards for democratic civilian control over the military establishment.

Complicating the problem in Poland of civil-military relations is the influence and visibility that the army had in politics in the last years of Communist rule. With the imposition of martial law in 1981 to crush the Solidarity movement, Polish generals violated a long-standing rule of communist systems—that the military remained subordinated to civilian, Communist Party leaders. The military-party distinction became blurred when General Jaruzelski went from being defense minister to prime minister, PUWP leader, and head of the Military Council for National Salvation—the body that ruled Poland for a year when martial law was imposed. As we have seen, Jaruzelski was also elected by the Sejm in 1989 as the first president of democratic Poland and held the office until direct elections were held in 1990. An earlier military figure, Pilsudski, became the role model for the new president, Walęsa, and so some Polish political currents believe that the military has a legitimate right to be involved in politics.

The first test of civilian control of the military in democratic Poland came with the so-called "Parys affair" in 1992. An upstart politician, Jan Parys, was named defense minister in a virulently anti-Communist government. He quickly an-nounced a purge of former Communist Party members from the military. Since the interim constitution gave the president powers in defense and security matters, however, Walęsa believed that he was the guarantor of civilian oversight of the military. He selected a general congenial to the military as candidate to become the new Chief of the General Staff. Defense Minister Parys objected and implied that Walęsa was planning a coup with the help of military leaders. For its part the military felt that it was caught in a power struggle between the executive and legislative branches of government. The struggle for power was resolved in dramatic fashion when the president got enough deputies in the Sejm to force the government's resignation in 1992.

Parys was not the only defense minister to fall victim to political intrigues. With the election of the ex-Communists to power in 1993, a Navy admiral was appointed defense minister. His personnel policy seemed to favor ex-Communists, leading to the accusation that he was reestablishing a "commissarocracy"—rule by Communist Party commissars. Walęsa was forced to fire the defense minister, in this way accepting the need for increased autonomy of the General Staff from the defense ministry. After Kwaśniewski became president civilian control over the military was tightened, allowing Poland to meet an important prerequisite for NATO membership.

To be sure, the General Staff has had reason to question the wisdom of strict civilian supervision of the military. A 50-percent cut in the size of the armed forces, budgetary cutbacks (until 1995), and clumsy civilian meddling in personnel matters has, in the words of one observer, led to "a siege mentality among the Polish senior officer corps."[46] This was exacerbated by the decision in 2003 by President Kwaśniewski and the Miller government to send Polish troops to Iraq to head the only non-American or British "stabilization sector." In addition to its own 2,500 soldiers, the Polish military was to command troops from some 20 other countries stationed in its sector.

The pro-Bush Iraq policy adopted by the SLD government but supported by other pro-Western parties in the Sejm quickly turned out to be a fiasco.[47] When Spain withdrew its troops from Iraq after the 2004 Madrid bombings, Poland became conspicuous by being the largest non-Anglo-American force involved in Iraq. Attacks on Polish troops by Iraqi insurgents increased, some 20 Polish soldiers had been killed by fall 2004, and the majority of Poles—usually pro-American—now expressed opposition to the military involvement in Iraq. Accordingly in September 2004 the Defense Minister announced that the Polish contingent was handing over troubled areas like Karbala and Najaf to the American military, was giving up its headquarters in Babylon to pro-American Iraqi forces, and was pulling a significant number of troops out of Iraq following elections in the country in early 2005. While the army remained the most valued institution in the country (Figure 10.3), political leaders who had taken the Iraq decision were more and more unpopular.

It is difficult, then, to criticize the Polish General Staff for its belief that civilian control of the military has produced greater political wrangling and bad decisions than it has respect for the military's professional interests. As loyal professional soldiers, military leaders have not publicly voiced criticism with politicians' bungling of the Iraq mission. But the General Staff's respect for the political establishment has undoubtedly diminished as a result of a series of questionable decisions taken in the name of civilian control.

Trade Unions

If the Catholic Church and the military are inextricable parts of Polish life, the same cannot be said of trade unions even though one, Solidarity, brought down the Communist regime. As with their counterparts in other countries, the overall membership and political influence of Polish labor unions has declined over the past two decades. In 2002 only about 6 percent of the adult population (or 18 percent of the workforce) belonged to a trade union. Fifty-two percent of all members were women, giving the lie to the popular stereotype of trade unionists as predominantly male. The two largest organizations, Solidarity and the All-Poland Alliance of Trade Unions (OPZZ) each had about 1.2 million members with another 1.5 million belonging to smaller union organizations.

Solidarity's decline is especially striking. (See Box 10.2.) From a peak of nearly 10 million in

1981, membership fell off throughout the 1980s when it was banned by the Communist authorities but also after the democratic breakthrough. Economic recession, a persistently high unemployment rate (approaching 20 percent), a widening private sector, major cuts in the size of state industry, unpopularity among young people entering the workforce, and a global decline in unionized labor slashed its membership. The 2001 legislative elections dealt Solidarity another blow. It failed to elect any Sejm deputies standing on its ticket, further eroding its influence at the center of Polish politics.

The much-disparaged former pro-Communist trade union OPZZ is today the equal of Solidarity even though its membership has fallen to one-third of what it was in 1994. Until recently the union enjoyed a privileged representational status as a distinct group within the parliamentary caucus of the SLD. In 1993 it accounted for 61 of the SLD's 171 deputies. A system of corporatism (discussed next) usually consists of the state determining how interest groups are to be represented. In Poland corporatism was stood on its head: it was the interest structure (the OPZZ) that helped determine state representation (in SLD governments). But after 2001 the SLD moved toward the British Labor Party's relationship with trade unions. The OPZZ was deprived of its privileged status within the party and no longer had its own bloc of deputies.

A Polish sociologist argued that "Systemic transformation disintegrates older interest structures and forms new ones."[48] Following a capitalist transformation, workers' interests have been "decomposed" into specific occupations—textile worker, coal miner, lathe operator—and, further, into particular firms.[49] Interest structures of the future are likely to reflect such differentiated socio-occupational categories of workers, so the future of centralized trade unions is not promising. Indeed wage bargaining sometimes takes place at the plant level: the case of employees at the former Lenin shipyard negotiating with new ownership is illustrative. Much bargaining is conducted industry-wide, for example, coal miners and school teachers.

Organized labor in Poland, once of legendary stature, has become fragmented. Successive Polish governments have succeeded in reducing union influence in politics—a strategy that paid off for lead-

Box 10.2   Goodbye to Solidarity

The rise and fall of Solidarity is a story about timeliness and obsolescence, about a romantic idea and political infighting, about historical agency and fate. In 2001, just before parliamentary elections were held, *The Economist* reflected: "Solidarity has had its ups and downs since the heroic days of 1980–81, when, at the Gdańsk shipyard and in the coal mines, trade-unionists like the young Lech Wałęsa, later President Wałęsa, raised the banner that in time swept away Soviet-imposed communism and helped to bring down that tyranny in Russia itself. But today's down may prove the end. That is a sad thought for all who remember the heroic past. But Poland's voters have to live in the world as it is."

In 2000, President Aleksander Kwaśniewski, a Politburo member in the former Communist Party and a founder of the post-Communist Alliance of the Democratic Left, was re-elected in a landslide. Solidarity-backed presidential candidates could not muster enough votes to force a runoff election. Another landslide victory for the post-Communists—and a further resounding defeat for Solidarity—was about to be recorded in the 2001 elections to the Sejm. Solidarity was not even going to reach the threshold needed to win seats in parliament. It would be relegated to the legislative sidelines, just like before the democratic breakthrough in 1989.

"Solidarity is already a husk of its former self. Its free-marketeers and pragmatists have defected in droves to new parties, or simply dropped out. Only trade-union diehards, old-guard Catholic nationalists and loyalists who see nowhere else to go remain within the movement, as it flounders to find a plausible electoral platform.

"Goodbye to Solidarity, then? Probably. And those heroic days, and the Gdańsk shipyard? Well, the shipyard, privatized in 1998, employs 3,800 people against 18,000 in 1980, and its workers were protesting this week against further layoffs. And Mr. Wałęsa? Voted out of the presidency in 1995, and his image fallen much lower since, in last year's presidential election he won just 1 percent of the vote."*

*From "The End of Solidarity," *The Economist* (August 16, 2001).

---

ers like Britain's Margaret Thatcher and U.S. President Ronald Reagan. To be sure, unions were allowed to influence policy on economic questions that concerned them, in particular through the Tripartite Commission discussed later. But the syndicalism that had brought down communism had in turn been destroyed by the new capitalist relations of production.

Business Groups

Many organizations have been established to represent the interests of Poland's new entrepreneurs. Owners and executives of private businesses have organized into a number of national organizations. The most important business lobby groups are the Business Center Club, the Polish Confederation of Private Employers, the Association of Polish Crafts, and the Polish Federation of Independent Entrepreneurs largely representing small and medium entrepreneurs. To this list we should add the Polish Confederation of Employers which is composed of many managers of state-owned enterprises. There is now an umbrella organization, the Polish Chamber of Commerce, to which over 500,000 Polish companies are affiliated. Sixty regional Chambers of Commerce have also been established.

The question that has faced Polish employers, as with their counterparts elsewhere, is whether they are better off in a unified, centralized organization that lobbies the government (as in France or Germany), or in an individualistic, highly decentralized business lobby (as in Britain or the United States). Whether business interests do become more confederated or remain decentralized may not be that important anyway in determining how much clout the lobby has. As in any democracy, the more important test is whether a pro-business or pro-labor party is in power.

Minority Groups

Some ethnic politics occurs in Poland. About one-half of all registered minority associations are German, most of them based in provinces bordering on the German Federal Republic where this minority is concentrated. The German minority has consistently been represented in the legislature. The 1993 electoral law exempted parties of national minorities from having to reach a 5 percent threshold for obtaining Sejm seats, allowing the German coalition to win four seats that year. After 2001 it was down to two deputies. While western Poland has generally voted for left-of-center candidates, districts with a large German population have supported more conservative candidates. The most influential German organization in the country is the Social-Cultural Association of the German Minority in Silesia. Supported by the German government, it has managed to carve out a measure of autonomy for itself.

Also functioning in democratic Poland are Ukrainian, Lithuanian, and Belarusan minority associations based in the eastern provinces. None currently has parliamentary representation. Numerous religious and secular Jewish associations exist, subsumed under the Coordinating Committee of Jewish Organizations. The Jewish Historical Institute is particularly active in trying to keep alive the centuries-old Jewish presence in Poland. Thanks to the efforts of Jewish organizations, in 1997 the Sejm enacted a law providing for restitution of Jewish communal property to remaining Jewish communities (fewer than 10,000 Jews live in Poland today). Efforts have been undertaken by both Polish and Jewish leaders to overcome negative stereotypes of each other. Stereotypes die hard, however. After the Catholic Church, it was Jews that in the mid-1990s Poles rated as having too much influence in the political system.

THE PARTY SYSTEM

Democracy is inextricably linked to political pluralism, a multiparty system, and free elections. In Poland the development of a competitive party system, where two or more parties seek electoral support to gain political influence, has taken many twists and turns from the 1990s on. Parties have come and gone, they have splintered, and they have entered into a variety of electoral pacts with changing names. Let us look at the example of a conservative Catholic political movement, which started its

political life as the Christian National Union. It ran in the 1991 Sejm election as Catholic Electoral Action, the 1993 one as Fatherland, and formed part of the Alliance for Poland supporting Wałęsa's presidential bid in 1995. For the 1997 legislative election it joined with Solidarity under the banner *Solidarity Electoral Action (AWS)* and for the 2001 one it was part of Solidarity Electoral Action of the Right.

In short, the fluidity of individual parties and party alliances has made keeping track of them very difficult. Changes to the *electoral law of 1993* were intended to reduce party fragmentation and consolidate a more stable party system. Parties that received less than 5 percent of the popular vote would not gain representation in the Sejm. Conversely, the larger vote-getting parties would get a disproportionately larger number of seats than their share of the vote entitled them to. It was the ex-Communists who best adapted to the new law by presenting a united coalition of the left in each election. Nevertheless, the 1993 electoral law did not produce a crystallized party system; indeed, it was possible that no party in the Sejm in that year would still be in the Sejm after the 2005 election.

Current Parties

Until recently all major parties in Poland have shared some common characteristics. They have accepted the rules of the game of the Third Republic and abide by the outcomes generated by these rules. There has been no threat, by former Communists or the right, to employ extraparliamentary means to obtain power. No major party has voiced a principled objection to a cornerstone of domestic policy—transition to a market economy—or to one of foreign policy—a pro-Western orientation that in security terms involves the country's membership in NATO.

The need to form broad-based coalitions that appeal to cross-sections of the electorate so as to win a large bloc of seats has explained the consensual politics of Polish parties. The AWS, for example, was a *catch-all party*, that is, an umbrella organization for numerous political groups, and it advanced a broad political program. Political expediency—to drive the ex-Communists from power in the 1997 parliamentary elections—united the disparate forces on the right. Once in power, however, the alliance proved so diverse that over the next four years it was plagued by internal disputes. From governing party it went after the 2001 election to an electoral bloc that failed to obtain the minimum number of votes to qualify for Sejm representation.

Another catch-all party that eventually became a victim of its diverse policy orientations was the *Freedom Union (UW)*. In 1991 it posted the strongest electoral showing of any party owing in large measure to its leaders' claim that it had no ideology or program. The UW has at various times included a left-of-center, welfare-state faction represented by former dissident Kuroń; a centrist Catholic section comprised of Mazowiecki supporters; and a neoliberal economic group headed by Balcerowicz. A series of poor electoral showings beginning in 1993 left the party out of the Sejm after 2001. UW has enough of a history, leaders with name recognition, and a core following among the better-educated, secular, urban public to continue to vie for seats in the Sejm. It represents a rare thread of continuity in the Third Republic party system.

Beginning with the 1993 election, the dominant party in terms of vote-getting and membership numbers became the SLD, the social-democratic successor to the former Communist Party. While in appearance the SLD originally resembled a catch-all organization, with various unions and parties in it, in practice it was dominated by the Social Democratic Party. In 1999 the post-Communist leadership dispensed with the fiction of the SLD being an alliance of many small parties and turned it into a single political party. Much of the electorate perceives the SLD as resembling a European social democratic party and only a minority still clings to the view that it is a successor party of the Communists. But the image of modernity that it projected was seriously tarnished by old-fashioned financial scandals (above all, Rywingate involving a bribe solicitation to ensure passage of a law favoring a media company) during Miller's prime ministership. A group of disaffected SLD deputies broke away in 2004 to form a new left-wing party, Social Democracy of Poland (SdP). It and the SLD combined seemed unlikely to gain more than a handful of seats in the 2005 Sejm election.

A regular coalition partner in SLD-led governments was the Polish Peasant Party (PSL), which for a time was the strongest political organization in rural Poland. Also a descendant of a Communist-era party, the PSL has defended private farmers whose economic interests have been undermined by the transition to a market economy and membership in the EU. The rural population accounts for over one-third of the electorate, giving the PSL a solid constituency to tap. But it has now fallen behind a radical agrarian movement, *Self-Defense* ("Samoobrona"), in electoral strength in the countryside.

The rise of Self-Defense is one of the most remarkable—and some would contend dangerous—phenomena in recent Third Republic politics. Unrepresented in the Sejm until 2001, at one point in spring 2004—just before Poland's formal accession into the EU—it had the declared support of one out of four Poles, making it the second most popular party in the country. Much of the party's success—and notoriety—is attributable to its populist leader, Andrzej Lepper, a frequent organizer of illegal and often violent agrarian protests beginning in the 1990s. Radically agrarian, anti-capitalist, anti-EU, antiestablishment and, to some extent pro-Russian, Self-Defense quickly became the consummate aggregator of the protest vote.

A second nationalist, anti-EU and antiestablishment party that has risen to prominence in recent years is the unusually named League of Polish Families (LPR). A conservative Catholic party, it made common cause with the secular Self-Defense movement to vehemently attack Polish policy on Iraq, demand the resignation of the corrupt SLD government, and insist on German war reparations even after Polish and German leaders had agreed in 2004 to waive reciprocal claims stemming from their countries' respective World War II human and territorial losses.

For the 2001 election a renewed effort—this time undertaken by the Civic Platform (PO)—was made to mobilize moderate, middle-class, largely urban voters who were deserting the Freedom Union. Even though trailing the SLD by a large margin in the election, it had come from nowhere to win the second-most number of votes and Sejm seats (Figure 10.5). The troubling vacuum found in the political

Figure 10.5 Party Representation in the 2001 Sejm and the 2004 European Parliament.

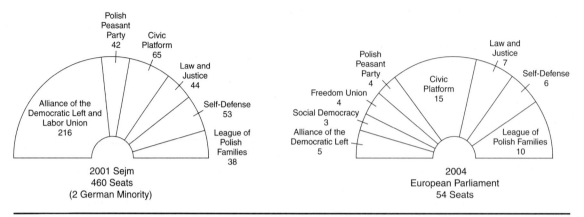

center was filled. The PO also attracted the new business class and played the role of responsible parliamentary opposition at a time of government when government financial scandals and radical antiestablishment movements plagued Polish politics. The performance of its leader, Jan Rokita, in the Sejm committee investigating Rywingate increased the PO's popularity, and the party was poised to head the new government elected in 2005.

One other party that did not exist before 2001 but that has become a political force is Law and Justice (PiS). Headed by Lech Kaczyński, a popular former Justice Minister and then mayor of Warsaw (officially called city president), the party was set up as a distinctly conservative alternative to the catch-all center-right AWS. It may be the most promising coalition partner that a PO-led government can find.

Table 10.2 depicts the nature of the left/right division within Polish politics. No one a decade ago could have predicted how the party system in existence today would reflect this left/right division since the actors have changed so much. It remains to be seen whether the current parties will be longer lived than their predecessors or whether some will disappear once the leaders around which they are built lose their appeal.

Election Results

One criterion by which democratic consolidation is measured is when a minimum of two free elections

Table 10.2 Main Political Orientations of the Polish Electorate

Left of Center	Right of Center
Western	Nationalist
Secular	Clerical
Urban	Rural
Business	Agrarian
Civil rights	Social order
Social liberalism	Christian values
Political liberalism	Authoritarian
Meta-communist	Anti-communist
Europhile	Anti-EU
Interdependence	National interest

are held. In Poland between 1990 and 2001, four parliamentary and three presidential elections were held. By this criterion, Poland's democratic system seems firmly rooted. Other political scientists believe that a smooth turnover of government, from incumbents to opposition, has to occur before we can speak of a consolidated democracy. This has also happened in Poland: four times in the case of the government and once in the case of the president. Indeed, since 1991 no government has been able to get reelected, with Solidarity-based blocs losing power in 1993 and 2001 and SLD-led coalitions being voted out in 1997 and 2005. As for the presidency, Walęsa suffered a narrow defeat in 1995

TABLE 10.3   Presidential Election Results, 1990–2000 (Top Five Vote-Getters)

	First Round (%)	Second Round (%)
1990 Candidate (Party)		
Lech Wałęsa (Solidarity KO)	40.0	74.3
Stanislaw Tymiński ("X")	23.1	25.7
Tadeusz Mazowiecki (ROAD)	18.1	
Wlodzimierz Cimoszewicz (SdRP)	9.2	
Roman Bartoszcze (PSL)	7.2	
1995 Candidate (Party)		
Aleksander Kwaśniewski (SLD)	35.1	51.7
Lech Wałęsa (nonparty)	33.1	48.3
Jacek Kuroń (UW)	9.2	
Jan Olszewski (RdR)	6.7	
Waldemar Pawlak (PSL)	4.3	
2000 Candidate (Party)		
Aleksander Kwaśniewski (SLD)	53.9	
Andrzej Olechowski (nonparty)	17.3	
Marian Krzaklewski (AWS)	15.6	
Jaroslaw Kalinowski (PSL)	6.0	
Andrzej Lepper (nonparty)	3.1	

at the hands of Kwaśniewski who was subsequently reelected in 2000.

Electoral outcomes have forced parties to form coalition governments around the party that has won the plurality of Sejm seats. In this way Poland resembles Germany rather than Britain or the United States, where winning parties capture the majority of seats. A political party must therefore do well both in elections and in coalition building to gain a share of power. Let us briefly review the Third Republic's electoral history.

PRESIDENTIAL ELECTIONS   In order to win the first direct presidential election held in 1990 (Table 10.3), a strong organizational basis was crucial, and former Solidarity union head Wałęsa had a distinct advantage over other candidates. He had secured the support of Solidarity groups and Catholic parties while his most serious rival, Prime Minister Mazowiecki, lacked any prior organization to base his campaign on. The SLD and PSL, which were well organized, were both tainted by their Communist pedigrees.

In the first round Wałęsa led the field but was well short of the 50 percent needed to avoid a

runoff (Table 10.3). The greatest shock was the elimination of Mazowiecki and the second-place showing of a political outsider Stan Tymiński, a Polish emigrant to Canada who claimed to have established successful businesses there and in Peru. The embarrassment produced by his performance, which was the result of a protest vote by citizens unhappy with the many problems caused by the transition, led nearly all political actors to rally around Wałęsa in the runoff. Three of four voters supported the Solidarity head in the second round.

In 1995, 13 candidates contested the first round of the presidential elections. The three-month campaign was notable for a surge in support for Wałęsa who closed in on longtime front-runner Kwaśniewski. The incumbent established himself as the only "electable" candidate of the center-right, and his campaign posters accurately depicted the choice in the election: "There are many other candidates. There is only one Wałęsa." The first round was indecisive with Kwaśniewski edging out Wałęsa by 35 to 33 percent.

Two television debates prior to the runoff were crucial in deciding the result. Kwaśniewski's youthfulness (he was 41), eloquence, and good manners stood in sharp contrast to a particularly ill-tempered and agitated Wałęsa. With a high turnout in the second round, Kwaśniewski won by a very slim margin: 51.7 percent to 48.3 percent. The decline in Wałęsa's fortunes was brought home in Popowie, the town in which he was born, where he lost by a margin of 13 percent. The election verdict was neither a repudiation of capitalism nor nostalgia for communism but a "retrospective" verdict—rejection of "five more years of this."

The 2000 election held none of the suspense of the previous one. The feeling was that the only person who was more popular than Kwaśniewski and could defeat him in an election was his wife. Twelve candidates contested the contest and Kwaśniewski won a handy majority in the first round, 37 percent ahead of the second-place finisher. Wałęsa got just 1 percent of the vote.

The reelection of Kwaśniewski was a milestone in recent Polish history. It showed that a party system based on the distinction drawn at the 1989 roundtable between a left-wing bloc and a Solidarity camp had become anachronistic. The top two vote-getters—Kwaśniewski and Andrzej Olechowski—were Communist-era officials. The winner received support from various social groups including modern, traditional, and Communist-era ones; his most serious weakness was scant support from farmers (Table 10.4). The right was in disarray but so were centrists as well as leftists with no associations to the former Communist Party. The election revealed the need for a reconfiguration of the Polish party system.

Since Kwaśniewski could not run for a third term, the 2005 presidential election was an open contest. Who would succeed him depended in part on how the new political parties we have described chose to fight the election, lining up their candidates and perhaps forming alliances. With the growing strength of the centrist PO and other new parties, it seemed likely that this election would not be a battle across the old lines of cleavage. In spite of the presence of radical candidates, the odds were that the new president would be as moderate as his predecessor.

PARLIAMENTARY ELECTIONS The first parliament to be elected freely was the product of a complicated electoral law. In 1991 anywhere from 7 to 17 members in each of 37 constituencies were elected, for a total of 391 seats. Sixty-nine other deputies were elected indirectly, from the "national lists" parties presented; seats were apportioned according to the share of the vote parties obtained in the constituencies (Table 10.5).

The effect of the electoral law was to provide just about any party gaining votes with Sejm representation; no minimum threshold for a share of the votes was set. The institutional designers of the new system wanted to make sure that no political force went unrepresented and that each could expect greater gains from participating in the electoral process than from carrying on political activity outside of it. At this time groups had more to lose from opting out of the electoral process than from staying in. If they faired poorly in one election they could always hope to do better the next time.

The 1991 elections were contested by parties having many different programs (the most frivolous was the Beer Lovers' Party). When this unmanageable legislature was dissolved by President Wałęsa in 1993, 29 parties were represented in the Sejm. Not surprisingly, the electoral law passed in 1993 was designed to limit party fragmentation: 391 seats were contested in multimember constituencies and 69 others were distributed to individual parties receiving at least 5 percent of the national vote; parties joining together to form electoral alliances had to clear an 8 percent threshold. The law produced the desired effect. Only one electoral alliance, the SLD, cleared the 8 percent threshold and just five individual parties crossed the 5 percent threshold.

Were it not for personal rivalries and internal disputes within the Solidarity camp, which led to a split in the popular vote, the election result would not have proved a stunning victory for the ex-Communists. Moreover economic shock therapy had created a political backlash, and the SLD got much mileage from its slogan: "It doesn't have to be like this."

Four years later it was the turn of the SLD to become victim of an anti-incumbent backlash. The breakdown in voting between left and right was not much different than in 1993, but running this time as a relatively united electoral coalition allowed the

TABLE 10.4 Support for 2000 Presidential Candidates by Demographic Category (in percent)

	Kwaśniewski SLD	Olechowski Ind.	Krzaklewski AWS	Kalinowski PSL	Lepper Self-Defense
Age					
18–24	16	19	10	11	14
25–39	27	31	23	31	28
40–59	41	39	39	43	41
60+	17	11	28	15	17
Sex					
Women	53	52	54	45	34
Men	47	48	46	56	66
Residence					
Cities (over 200,000)	23	35	27	5	9
Towns (50,000–200,000)	20	19	17	5	10
Towns (under 50,000)	26	24	24	13	17
Rural	30	22	32	78	65
Education					
Primary	13	7	16	23	25
Vocational	27	17	24	34	40
Secondary	45	47	40	34	30
University	15	30	20	9	4
Occupation					
Manager	11	20	12	6	3
Enterpreneur	8	13	8	4	5
Farmer	5	2	6	37	31
Blue-collar worker	17	11	13	13	19
Clerical	13	15	10	8	4
Housewife	4	3	4	4	3
Retired	26	16	35	18	22
Students	9	15	8	6	5
Unemployed	7	5	5	5	8

Source: Polish Television (TP SA). "Election Studio" program (October 8, 2000). http: 157.25.180.53 wybory2000.

center-right forces under the AWS banner to win. Within AWS the largest bloc of seats (52) went to representatives of the Solidarity trade union followed closely behind by Catholic groups (45). Ironically, an Evangelical Lutheran, Buzek, was chosen by AWS as prime minister. Its coalition partner was the underachieving but ambitious Freedom Union, which had won 60 seats. Since the UW held the balance of power in parliament, had both a prestigious past and leaders with name recognition, and was popular with Western politicians, it was able to obtain influential ministerial posts in the AWS-led government; for example, Balcerowicz returned to his posts of deputy prime minister and finance minister, his party colleague Bronislaw Geremek became foreign minister, and Poland's first woman prime minister, Hanna Suchocka, was appointed Justice Minister. The AWS-UW coalition furnished a conspicuous example of the tail wagging the dog. By 2000 long-standing differences between the AWS and UW came to a head leading to the latter's removal from the governing coalition.

The center-right was again divided, then, entering the 2001 parliamentary election. Both the AWS and UW went from being government parties to failing to gain any seats in the Sejm. The SLD

Table 10.5 Parliamentary Election Results 1991 to 2001 (Sejm only)

Party	1991 Election		1993 Election		1997 Election		2001 Election	
	Percent	Seats	Percent	Seats	Percent	Seats	Percent	Seats
Alliance of the Democratic Left (SLD)[a]	12.0	60	20.6	171	27.1	164	41.0	216
Polish Peasant Party (PSL)	8.7	48	15.3	132	7.3	27	9.0	42
Freedom Union (UW)[b]	12.3	62	10.7	74	13.4	60	3.1	0
Civic Platform (PO)	—	—	—	—	—	—	12.7	65
Self-Defense	—	—	2.8	0	—	—	10.2	53
Truth and Justice (PiS)	—	—	—	—	—	—	9.5	44
League of Polish Families (LPR)	—	—	—	—	—	—	7.9	38
Union of Labor (UP)[a]	—	—	7.2	41	4.7	0	—	—
Confederation for an Independent Poland (KPN)	7.5	46	5.6	22	—	—	—	—
Nonparty Bloc for Reform (BBWR)	—	—	5.4	16	—	—	—	—
German minority	—	—	0.6	4	0.6	2	0.4	2
Solidarity Electoral Action (AWS)[c]	5.1	27	4.6	0	33.8	201	5.6	0
Center Accord (PC)	8.7	44	4.5	0	—	—	—	—
Liberal Democratic Congress (KLD)	7.5	37	3.8	0	—	—	—	—
Catholic Election Action (WAK)	8.7	49	—	—	—	—	—	—
Peasant Accord (PL)	5.5	28	—	—	—	—	—	—
Other parties and Independents	24.0	59	18.9	0	13.2	6	0.6	0

[a] In 2003 the SLD and UP ran as one party.
[b] In 1991 and 1993 the UW ran as the Democratic Union (UD).
[c] In 1991 and 1993 the AWS electoral alliance ran as the Solidarity Party.

teamed up with a small leftist party to win 41 percent of the vote and close to a majority of Sejm seats. Indeed the SLD's share of the vote increased for the third election in a row, in a sense leaving it nowhere to go but down. A worrying development in 2001 was the rise of radical nationalist parties like Self-Defense and the League of Polish Families, which together gained close to 100 seats. By contrast a reassuring development was that two new moderate parties, Civic Forum and Law and Justice, won slightly over 100 seats. The 2005 parliamentary election shaped up to be a battle among these recent entrants on the political scene.

European Parliament Elections In June 2004 Poland held elections for 54 seats to the European Parliament. All the major political parties contested this first European election since Poland joined the EU but the turnout was a disappointing 21 percent. The result (Figure 10.5) confirmed the Civic Platform as the most important political force in the country: it garnered 24 percent of the vote and won 15 seats. The nationalist Eurosceptic League of Polish Families came next with 15 percent and 10 seats and the other anti-EU party, Self-Defense, did worse than expected with an 11 percent voting share and 6 seats. The center-right Law and Justice party placed just ahead of Self-Defense with 13 percent and 7 seats. The election proved a disaster for the ruling SLD: it obtained 9 percent of the vote and only 5 seats. Three other parties (the Freedom Union and Polish Peasant Party with 4 seats each, and Social Democracy with 3 seats) combined for 18 percent of the vote.

The results of elections to the European Parliament do not always provide an accurate barometer of voting intentions for the national legislature. The MEPs that are elected often reflect a voter backlash against an incumbent government. In the case of Poland, the 2004 European election result illustrated a backlash against the incumbent SLD government, but it further highlighted the extent to which the country's party system had changed since the late 1990s. Indeed, it presaged the party alignments that would follow the 2005 Sejm elections.

THE POLICYMAKING PROCESS

In a democratic system we can identify four distinct phases in the policymaking process: policy initiation, the legislative process, policy implementation, and judicial review. In the first phase, civic organizations and specialized interest groups generally play a central role. Political parties also serve as aggregators of interests that help shape policy formulation. The second phase, the legislative process, is where ideas about policy are turned into specific parliamentary bills, to be debated and voted upon (Figure 10.6). One study broke down the initiators of bills submitted to the Sejm between 1997 and 1999: 46 percent were from deputies, 43 percent came from the government, 3 percent were from Senators, and 2 percent came from the president (there was only one case of a civic legislative initiative).[50]

Bills with the highest probability of being enacted are those proposed by the governing coalition. Thus approximately two-thirds of government-sponsored bills between 1997 and 2001 became law compared to about 40 percent for both deputy- and presidentially sponsored bills. This is because all members of the ruling coalition that commands a majority of seats in the Sejm (the exception is a minority government which, by definition, does not) are exhorted to vote for bills. Successful bills go through three readings in the legislature though the first reading can be held in a Sejm committee—with the exception of bills concerned with the constitution, budget, state institutions, and civil rights. The fullest and most partisan debates take place during the second plenary reading when party discipline is crucial in determining a bill's fate. In general, Polish parties are not as disciplined as in Britain (with its system of three-line whips requiring MPs to vote as party leaders require) or as lax as in the United States (with crossover voting a regular feature).

After a bill has received a second reading, the third reading is usually a formality, though technical considerations may require that a committee carry out minor revisions. In the parliament that sat from 1993 to 1997, a total of 826 draft laws were introduced in the Sejm of which 473 (or 57 percent) successfully received a third reading. The Sejm that sat from 1997 to 2001 considered over 1,000 bills of which slightly less than 50 percent were enacted.[51]

After leaving the Sejm a bill must be considered by the Senate within 14 days. Any Senate objections can be overruled by an absolute majority in the Sejm so cases of Senate blockage are now rare. The president's signature is the final stage in how a bill becomes law. He has the right to veto a whole bill (not just one part of it) but he may be overridden by a 60 percent Sejm majority. Kwaśniewski vetoed six laws passed by the AWS government and only one veto was overridden (on establishing an Institute of National Memory). Instead of a veto, the president can also refer bills to the Constitutional Tribunal to test their constitutionality. Kwaśniewski did this to four AWS government bills, two of which were deemed constitutional and two of which were ruled unconstitutional by the Tribunal.

The legislative process offers interest groups three key occasions to influence policy: (1) when the government is drafting a bill for introduction in the Sejm; (2) between the first and second readings, when the bill is being studied by a Sejm committee; and (3) before the president signs it into law. In the first case lobbying is directed at the party of government as well as at the various advisory bodies connected to the cabinet (especially the Economic Committee of the Council of Ministers). In the second case, interest groups engage in lobbying Sejm

FIGURE 10.6   The Legislative Process

The Legislative Process

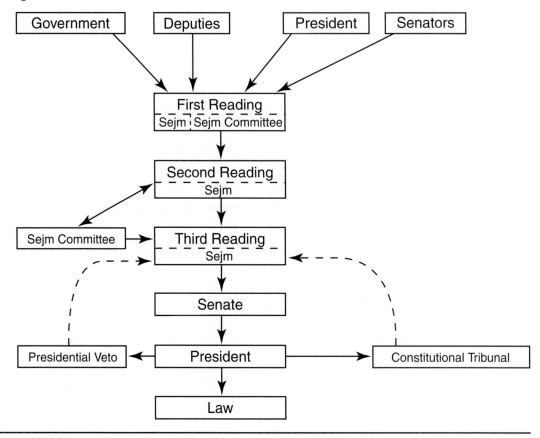

committee chairs, parliamentary caucus leaders, and backbench deputies. In the third case, the president's Chancellory is likely to be the target of intense lobbying. This is not to suggest that Polish interest groups have professionalized their lobbying techniques on the scale of their U.S. counterparts. As the policy cases we consider next indicate, ad hoc groups have often been involved in the policymaking process.

A third phase is carrying out policy. This is the role of the state and local bureaucracy with the Council of Ministers and individual ministers overseeing the process. Civil servants have generally had to be accountable to political leaders for administering policy but some of them have been political appointees of the government in power. The SLD in particular was repeatedly accused of appointing ex-Communists to high positions in the civil service.

The fourth phase occurs when policy comes under judicial review—for example, for infringing upon an individual's constitutional rights. This is the function of Poland's judicial system.

Policymaking involves many political actors. This apparent pluralism may mask the real distribution of power in the process, however. Corporatist structures—interest groups controlled by the state—have not disappeared altogether with the end of communism. This raises the question whether the state ultimately gets its way on issues it assigns priority to.

One way that the state can indirectly shape policy in a market economy is through *corporatism*. This is "a system of interest representation in which the constituent units are organized into a limited number of singular, compulsory, noncompetitive, hierarchically ordered and functionally differentiated categories, recognized or licensed, if not created, by the state and granted a deliberate representational monopoly within their respective categories in exchange for observing certain controls on their selection of leaders and articulation of demands and supports."[52] Corporatism is, then, a process of interest intermediation. *Concertation* is, in turn, a process whereby "affected interests . . . become incorporated within the policy process as recognized, indispensable negotiators and are made co-responsible (and occasionally completely responsible) for the implementation of policy decisions."[53] Concertation brings together peak labor and business organizations, as well as the state, to negotiate social pacts and formulate public policy. It is, then, an early stage of the policymaking process.

The best example in Poland of corporatist negotiation was the process leading up to the 1992 Pact on State Enterprises. Initiated by Labor Minister Kuroń and hammered out by trade unions, business groups, and ministry officials, it was designed to bring labor peace to the country. The Pact gave rise to the Polish Tripartite Commission for Social and Economic Issues whose task was to draft legislation following consultations and negotiations among representatives from business and labor organizations and the state. This consultative Commission employed concertation to develop policy on important issues.

The process of *tripartism*, as it was called, faced the problem of how influence was to be distributed among participating actors. By 1994 the Polish trade union movement had become so decentralized that labor's representatives to tripartite negotiations came from several different organizations—Solidarity, the OPZZ, and smaller unions. The business side was also not fully represented on the Tripartite Commission. The Confederation of Polish Employers (KPP) was the main business group on the Commission but it did not represent the rapidly expanding private sector that employed

nonunionized workers. Nevertheless the Commission played an influential role in shaping such policies as restructuring the mining industry, health care and pension reforms, employment, and indexation of salaries to inflation rates.

In 2001 a new act on the Tripartite Commission was passed. For a trade union or business group to gain representation, the act specified that it had to have 300,000 employees. The body's representative nature was enhanced and the partners involved in social dialogue were formalized. Even though the trade union movement was a shadow of its former self and the Commission's recommendations were not binding on lawmakers, the 2001 act highlighted the importance of concertation to the political process.

There are a dozen or so unions representing various groups in the agricultural sector though the most important are those affiliated to Rural Solidarity and Self-Defense. Agricultural unions do not have the equivalent of a Tripartite Commission in which to negotiate, and this has led to much direct action. The Ministry of Agriculture in Warsaw has been the target of repeated farmer protests—those organized by Self-Defense occasionally becoming violent. "Bargaining" in the agrarian sector is not unlike that in France, then. In 2002 the Polish government negotiated a generally favorable deal for farmers in its accession terms with the EU (see subsequent discussion), and protests have become less common.

POLICY OUTCOMES

Three major policy issues have dominated Polish politics since 1989: (1) establishing a free market economy; (2) framing a national security policy; and (3) integrating into European structures. All three areas are closely connected to consolidating a liberal democratic state.

Free Market Reform

Economic reform began in Poland even while the Communist Party was still in power. In 1987 the country was admitted to the World Bank, and the first steps were taken toward economic decentralization and price liberalization. A referendum held that year resulted in two-thirds of voters (though only

44 percent of eligible ones) expressing support for rapid economic change. In 1988 parliament adopted a law promoting private enterprise. In the first half of 1989, as the roundtable talks were being held, 1,300 private ventures were registered, many set up by members of the Communist nomenklature.

The Solidarity-based governments from 1989 to 1993 accelerated this economic transformation. Policies included restricting the money supply, controlling hyperinflation while freeing prices of nearly all products from state controls, limiting the budget deficit (5 percent of GDP was the target), promoting currency convertibility (helped by the creation by Western institutions of a *zloty* stabilization fund), and developing incentives for private enterprise.

Poland's economic policy was shaped by the IMF and overseen by Balcerowicz, appointed minister of finance and economic reform head in 1989. At the beginning of 1990 he introduced a crash stabilization package—popularly termed shock therapy. Its main features were a balanced government budget; strict fiscal, monetary, and income policies; and convertibility of the zloty. IMF aid was made contingent on keeping close to the 5-percent target.

The Balcerowicz plan also envisaged structural adjustment of the economy. Sweeping privatization would be the prerequisite for structural adjustment. In 1990 privatization laws were enacted that transformed 40 percent of state firms into public corporations while creating opportunities for the setting up of new private firms. One Polish economist believed that privatization of state-owned juggernauts was poorly conceived but was not critical to successful economic transformation. Instead, Poland's remarkable economic growth was owed mostly to "creating conditions for virtually unrestricted entry of private firms into all sectors of the economy and fields of activity."[54]

Jeffrey Sachs, a Harvard-based adviser to the Polish government, had recommended shock therapy, or the "big bang" approach to economic reform. He recognized the quandary of such reform: "Why should something 'so good' feel 'so bad.'"[55] Sachs was one of the first to draw the comparison between Poland's and Spain's economic development after 1950. Both countries had similar economic conditions then: comparable population size, large agricultural sectors, peripheral regions of Europe lagging behind in modernization, Catholicism. "Spain shot ahead of Poland in the next thirty-five years. Spain started to catch up with the rest of Western Europe, while Poland fell farther behind."[56] Economic integration with Europe was the major factor ensuring Spain's success.

On the other hand, a critic of the Balcerowicz plan questioned the assumptions and process of shock therapy. "The architects of reform were persuaded that their blueprint was sound—no, more: the only one possible."[57] Reform was unresponsive to public preferences: "Radical reform was a project initiated from above and launched by surprise, independently of public opinion and without the participation of organized political forces" and, accordingly, "had the effect of weakening democratic institutions."[58] A case in point was the passage of the Balcerowicz plan. The Sejm was "given sixteen pieces of legislation and told that it must approve the nine most important before the end of the month to meet the IMF conditions."[59]

The process of reform might have been contentious, but the success of the reforms was undeniable. According to the World Bank, annual GDP growth between 1993 and 2003 was 5.1 percent (the estimated GDP for 2003–2007 was 3.5 percent). Poland was the first country in Central Europe to register economic growth after 1989 and the first to have its GDP surpass the 1989 level. It quickly had the most privatized economy in the region (only privatization of the colossal, state-owned industrial enterprises proved laborious), a buoyant stock market, and robust consumer demand. The Polish state also cashed in on privatization: For example, in 1999 its revenues from sell-offs totaled over $8 billion. By the end of the 1990s Poland had become the biggest attractor of foreign direct investment in the region. The structure of the economy was increasingly modern and postindustrial: In 2003 two-thirds of GDP was accounted for by the service sector. In a 2000 survey of chief executives at the world's largest companies, Poland was ranked fifth as an attractive place for foreign direct investment. In 2004, the World Bank placed Poland eighth in its annual list of the top reforming countries that had improved their business climate only a year earlier.

Capitalism produces losers as well as winners. Unemployment remained at a very high level, hovering near 20 percent of the labor force, when Poland joined the EU in 2004. SLD governments proved as ineffective as center-right ones in addressing this persistent problem. Inflation was also not contained, thereby adversely affecting the millions in Poland (pensioners, the disabled, students) on fixed incomes. Whether these economic problems were a small price to pay for the country's generally successful adoption of a free market economy depended on where a citizen stood in the new economic structure.

Security Policy

The idea of *antemurale christianitatis,* discussed earlier in this chapter, has strong contemporary resonance in security matters. Since the democratic breakthrough, Polish politicians have debated what the most effective way of achieving long-term national security may be. Throughout the 1990s the consensus was that Poland should press for swift integration into European security structures. The continued fear of Russian revanchism—renewed after Vladimir Putin became president in 2000—convinced many political leaders that Poland's role should, once again, be that of a rampart defending Western civilization against the East. This role would be most effectively played within NATO, which Poland joined in 1998.

Significant changes having an impact on Poland's security occurred immediately after the collapse of the Soviet Union. The number of neighbors increased from three (the USSR, Czechoslovakia, and East Germany) to seven (Russia, Lithuania, Belarus, Ukraine, Slovakia, the Czech Republic, and Germany). Moreover, in the east, Poland's borders are shared with states (Belarus and Ukraine) suffering from varying degrees of political and economic instability. In the north, Poland's frontier with Russia—the Kaliningrad region—is a source of concern, because the region is separated from the rest of the Russian Federation. Negotiations on guaranteeing a corridor through Poland for Russians to use have proved difficult. They have become more complex since Poland joined the EU, given the EU's requirement that its external borders with non-EU member-states be made very secure.

In many ways, NATO membership was of little help in dealing with the security threats that arose after 9/11. The way that the Bush administration decided to respond to the terrorist attacks divided Europe. The calculus of Polish foreign policymakers was to lend support to the world's remaining superpower rather than to back the major EU states that opposed the U.S. invasion of Iraq. (See Box 10.3.) For its decision, Poland was given the cold shoulder by French and German diplomats. One German newspaper dubbed Poland the "Trojan ass" of Europe. Coupled with threats of terrorist attacks on Poland made by al-Qaeda leaders, it was difficult to see how Polish security was enhanced by its support for the Bush administration. On the other hand, it appeared by 2005 that Poland's foreign policy was coming more into line with the core EU member-states. Its defense minister announced that Polish troops in Iraq were to withdraw when the UN mandate for the stabilization mission expired at the end of 2005.

Poland's Iraq gamble appeared not to have paid off, whether measured in terms of successfully accomplishing its military mission, receiving lucrative contracts for Polish firms to rebuild Iraq, serving as an example to skeptical EU states about the country's newfound influence, or reflecting Poles' supposed pro-Americanism (Box 10.3).

Europeanness

Poland joined the EU six years after the start of accession negotiations in 1998. Of course Polish leaders had been talking of EU membership since 1989 but the process proved slower and more complex than the euphoria after the democratic breakthrough had suggested. It was only in 2000 that Poland submitted a detailed timetable to the EU Enlargement Commissioner on enacting 150 laws needed before accession could occur. By 2002 the EU had closed 27 chapters of the accession negotiations with only agriculture, fisheries, and the environment unresolved. Other outstanding issues included regulating the sale of Polish land to EU nationals and the movement of Polish workers into EU labor markets.

Box 10.3 Are Poles Becoming Anti-American?

Polls of Poles have repeatedly shown how pro-American this Central European nation is. Even as anti-American sentiments spread across the world following the 2003 U.S. invasion of Iraq, Poland seemed to be immune to the malaise. "Western visitors here have often been surprised by Poland's avid pro-Americanism. For some it's a pleasant surprise: They find none of the anti-American stereotypes common elsewhere in Europe. For others it's an unpleasant one: What about the victims of America's imperial power?

"Poles managed to find something deeply admirable in all American presidents: They appreciated Carter for his human rights agenda, Reagan for his gut anti-communism, Bush Senior for overseeing the end of the Cold War and Clinton for his commitment to an inclusive globalization.

"Until now. George W. Bush has managed to do what 45 years of Communist rule could not: puncture the image of essential American goodness that has always been the United States' key selling point." Poles are now asking whether it pays to be America's friend.

"The Iraq war has been the turning point. Poland was one of America's most zealous supporters, the leader of what Defense Secretary Rumsfeld dubbed the 'new Europe.' Unlike the situation in other supportive European countries, all major political parties supported the war. People elsewhere argued over whether Iraq really had weapons of mass destruction, but in Poland the calculus was more simple: America requested our help, so we gave it.

"Then came the torture at Abu Ghraib, showing irrefutable images of an America not to their liking. Bit by bit, the evidence grew that this was not the war the liberals had signed up for. Moreover, America seemed incapable of listening even to its allies."

This has led to an unprecedented anti-American backlash in Poland. In September 2004 President Kwasniewski, one of Bush's strongest supporters, urged the U.S. President to abandon his "neoconservative divide-and-rule policy."

"Adam Michnik once quipped that 'Poland is more pro-American than America is.' Bush has changed that."*

*From David Ost, "Letter from Poland," *The Nation* (October 4, 2004).

Poland's party politics were affected by the bid for EU membership. Pro-European opportunism, exemplified by the SLD, was matched by Euroskeptic opportunism, as in the case of Self-Defense and the LPR. Indeed, if the success of the SLD in the 1990s was the result of its pro-European orientation, the rise of the radical right after 2000 was the product of a nationalist backlash to the EU as enlargement became inevitable.

Poland's first years in the EU are shaped by a series of transitional arrangements. It has a 5-year period to reach a financial balance between contributions it pays into the EU general budget and funds it draws out of that budget. A 12-year moratorium (5 years longer than any other candidate country negotiated) has been placed on the purchase of Polish land by EU nationals—a highly emotional subject, especially with regard to Germans whose ancestors came from territories that Poland acquired after World War II. A 5-year tran-sition period was agreed upon for the purchase of vacation homes.

With regard to labor migration, a formula was adopted involving a maximum seven-year transitional period broken down into 2+3+2. That is, Polish citizens' right to work in EU countries is restricted for the first two years (through 2006) even though, during this period, Poles will enjoy priority over citizens from third, non-EU countries. If current EU members decide that their labor markets have been destabilized by immigration from the accession states, they can vote to extend the transition phase by three years (through 2009). A final two-year period limitation (through 2011) can be imposed.

The impact of the EU's Common Agricultural Policy on Poland's farmers was at the center of EU accession negotiations. Under the accession agreement the EU will phase in direct aid for Polish farmers over 10 years starting with 25 percent of the full EU rate in 2004, 30 percent in 2005, and so on.

Box 10.4   Are Poles Warming Up to the European Union?

One of the fiercest opponents of Poland's membership in the European Union has been a radical peasant leader who has inveighed that Polish farmers will be devastated by EU competition. But in October 2004 "fate played a joke on Andrzej Lepper. He became one of the first 5,000 Polish farmers to receive money from the European Union, which Poland, along with nine other countries, joined six months ago, on May 1.

"Lepper, 50, the populist farmer-leader of the anti-European Samoobrona Party, was given 8,000 zloty, or nearly $2,400, a sum he will receive regularly for the next several years as part of the EU's generous farm subsidy plan. The joke is that this tidy sum could be Lepper's political undoing. His support has come from the countryside, where he set up Samoobrona, or Self-Defense, in 1992 to campaign against Polish entry into the EU.

"As EU farm subsidies start trickling into the newly opened bank accounts of Poland's 1.4 million farmers, Lepper's support is crumbling. His vitriolic and sometimes violent campaigning among farmers to stop Poland from joining the EU is rapidly losing appeal. His doomsday predictions that farmers would be forgotten and left to starve have been proved wrong.

"The EU had never been popular in the depths of the Polish countryside, where populist politicians like Lepper often joined ranks with the local and still powerful Roman Catholic Church to oppose joining the Union. The Church, which played a big role in opposing the Communist regime, fears a democratic Poland will follow other European countries by becoming more secular." But the Church is losing influence in rural areas as young people leave for the more "secular" towns and cities in the hopes of finding jobs.

"Even mainstream Polish politicians tried to use Euroskepticism to extract concessions from Brussels during difficult accession talks. As the largest of the 10 new members, Poland had made so many demands that it exasperated its negotiating partners. Yet months after joining, the mood in Poland toward the EU is improving, with opinion polls showing 75 percent supporting Europe."*

*From Judy Dempsey, "Euroskepticism Fades in Polish Countryside," *International Herald Tribune* (November 2, 2004).

While the Polish government is required to contribute financial assistance to farmers for this period, the EU has established transitional topping up rates.

In sum, Poland is easing itself into the EU. It will be some time before it can become part of the Eurozone—depending on its economic stability and growth. Membership in the so-called Schengen zone, which facilitates the crossing of borders by EU nationals—and the enforcement of strict border controls on non-EU neighbors as, in Poland's case, Belarus and Ukraine—is also some years away. But the most difficult part of integrating into European structures is in Poland's past.

EU membership will accelerate Poland's acquisition of a European identity. (Box 10.4.) A crucial aspect in this process is the adoption of what we can term the *acquis communantaire cul-*

turel, the modal European culture that shapes political and economic practices in the EU. The question arises, then, how Poles think they differ today from the typical European. Generally Poles consider themselves more religious, patriotic, altruistic, and family-oriented than Europeans (Table 10.6). They also see themselves as poorer, more dishonest, and lacking in self-confidence, education, and culture. While these images have held constant over a decade, Poles now give themselves higher marks for being hardworking compared to 1994. Europeanness does mean something to Poles and on many measures it remains quite distinct from Polishness.

A Polish sociologist highlighted the problems caused by the uneven development between institutional and cultural growth: "To be already in

TABLE 10.6   Polish Respondents' Image of "The Typical Pole" and "The Typical European" (in percent)

	"Typical Pole"		"Typical "European"	
	1994	2004	1994	2004
Lives well	15	15	87	84
Lives poorly	75	72	3	4
Is religious	90	90	34	34
Is not religious	5	5	45	43
Is patriotic	78	72	51	51
Is not patriotic	17	20	32	28
Work is most important	18	25	59	52
Family is most important	66	61	18	25
Helps others	52	51	32	35
Only looks after his own interests	40	39	54	48
Is sure of himself	35	32	81	81
Is bewildered	56	57	10	7
Is educated	65	63	85	83
Is uneducated	25	25	6	5
Is cultured	55	57	76	69
Lacks culture	33	32	15	16
Works hard	56	76	85	78
Works badly	34	15	5	8
In a difficult situation works with others	72	64	61	55
Works on his own	21	26	20	21
Is honest	52	47	61	56
Is dishonest	31	34	16	18

Source: Centrum Badania Opinii Spolecznej (CBOS), "Typowy Polak i Europejczyk—Podobieństwa i różnice" (April 2004), www.cbos.pl.
The answer "difficult to say" is excluded from the results.

Europe, in a political and even an economic sense, is not yet the same as becoming a fully fledged European citizen. Joining the realm of European states and markets is not the same as entering European civil societies. Only the latter will signify a true and ultimate return to Europe."[60] The cultural divide between Western and Central Europe has been reduced, but Poland must do more to make what remains of the divide not politically salient.

Corruption

A dividing line that persists between Western and formerly communist Europe is transparent versus corrupt practices. Just before the enlargement decision the European Commission gave Poland a top grade for meeting its political criteria but singled it out for persisting corruption. In its 2000 report the international non-governmental organization monitoring corruption, *Transparency International* ranked Poland only forty-third of 80 states in its corruption perceptions index.[61] A 2000 World Bank report identified corruption "at the highest levels" as Poland's most serious problem. Based on interviews with government officials and the national audit office, the 1999 World Economic Forum survey ranked Poland fifty-second out of 59 countries in terms of governmental favoritism and forty-third in terms of insider trading. And a 2000 European Bank for Reconstruction and Development (EBRD) report on the legal systems of Central European states had found a largely negative perception of the effectiveness of Polish laws.

A history of democracy plus having wealth inhibit corrupt practices. Until recently Poland had neither. Credible political institutions also help prevent corruption, but Poland's are 15 years old. Still, how do we explain Poland being ranked sixty-fourth in Transparency International's 2003 corruption perceptions index—a drop of 20 places in 3 years—making the country suffer from one of the most corrupt images in all of Central and Eastern Europe?

A partisan explanation is to place the blame on the SLD, the former Communists, who governed Poland for 8 of 12 years ending in 2005. Rywingate, which involved the allegation that leaders in the governing SLD were willing to craft a law to favor a particular media group in exchange for a large bribe, seemed proof of this. A second major scandal which also involved the SLD was the "Orlen affair." President Kwaśniewski (former SLD leader) and his close friend Jan Kulczyk, the country's richest man, were implicated in a bribery attempt that involved Poland's largest oil company—and seventh-largest company of any kind in Eastern Europe (with a $9 billion profit in 2003)—PKN Orlen. According to documents of the Polish secret service Kulczyk, a shareholder in the 25 percent-state-owned Orlen, met in 2003 with Vladimir Alganov, a Russian working with a Russian energy company. The Polish billionaire promised to use his influence with President Kwaśniewski to secure the privatization of a major Polish oil refinery for the Russian company.

As if the influence-peddling charge was not enough, Alganov was an alleged KGB agent who had operated in Poland in the 1980s. He embarrassed the SLD by revealing that his company had paid a $5 million bribe in order to buy the refinery but nothing had come of it. The explanation for the lack of results from the bribe proved equally troubling. The parliamentary committee set up in 2004 to investigate Orlen's practices heard testimony that the bribe was indeed collected by the president of the company in 2002 but that he had refused to share the money with SLD government ministers, who then blocked the sale of the refinery. Kwaśniewski was implicated because his personal friend Kulczyk was the supposed intermediary, he had contacts with the SLD ministers waiting for their cut, and his wife's foundation had Orlen as one of its largest donors.

In Poland Rywingate and the Orlen affair are seen as part of a much broader SLD-organized system seeking to maximize kickbacks for party officials. Financial scandals linked to SLD regional leaders have also been exposed. The electoral backlash against the SLD is evidence that the public is unwilling to tolerate such "un-European" practices. But before we conclude that corruption is endemic to former Communists, we should recall that the four-year interlude in which a Solidarity coalition governed the country was also rife with corruption allegations.[62] The defense that "he did it first" has few takers today in Polish society.

CONCLUSION

Studying the democratic process is important in a country that was a precocious exponent of the idea but was also a victim of authoritarian rule. Zbigniew Brzezinski cautioned that "Though the notions of 'democracy' are fashionable, in much of the world the practice of democracy is still quite superficial and democratic institutions remain vulnerable."[63] To a great degree, new democratic regimes are judged by their current performance, thereby making them more vulnerable to collapse in the face of economic or social crisis.

This chapter has described the great strides that Poland has made to consolidate its democracy. In general, the country has recorded greater progress in institutional and economic development than in cultural transformation. The policy process is squarely based on political institutions that provide for fair, impartial outcomes. As in many established democracies, problems remain with institutional arrangements. An important one in Poland concerns what Bingham Powell has suggested is the need for a majoritarian vision. For it to exist, "a single cohesive party or at least an identifiable preelection coalition must gain unblocked control of the policymaking process to offer voters the forward-looking mandate conditions and retrospective accountability conditions necessary for the majoritarian vision."[64] Governments led by the SLD, a party whose origins lie in the communist period, came close to approximating majoritarian processes but governments of the center and right have not. To this extent Poland's political system remains handicapped. The Polish public seems to recognize this flaw: support is growing for replacing the proportional representation electoral system with a simple majority one.[65]

In economic terms, history as it has been played out in Poland has vindicated Adam Smith in his stress on the intimate relationship between commerce and liberty. As Barrington Moore put it, there can be no democracy without a bourgeoisie.[66] Sections of the Polish population remain opposed to the growth of a bourgeoisie but they have become a minority. To be sure, the resurgence of radical politics in recent years suggests that protest and discontent can grow in intensity even as democratic and free market values take hold. The existence of a middle class, however, should reassure us about the prospects for democratic stability in Poland.

Key Terms

Alliance of the
    Democratic Left
    (SLD)
antemurale
    christianitatis
Balcerowicz plan
catch-all party
Committee for Workers'
    Self-Defense (KOR)
concertation
Concordat
constitution of 1997
Constitutional Tribunal

contract Sejm
corporatism
Council of Ministers
electoral law of 1993
Cardinal Józef Glemp
General Wojciech
    Jaruzelski
Jacek Kuroń
Aleksander
    Kwaśniewski
liberum veto
martial law
May 1926 coup

Adam Michnik
Mieszko I
nomenklatura
pacted transition
partitioned
Józef Pilsudski
Polish October
Polish United Workers'
    Party (PUWP)
Ribbentrop-Molotov pact
romantic
    insurrectionism
roundtable talks

Rywingate
Second Republic
Sejm
shock therapy
Solidarity (Solidarność)
szlachta democracy
Third Republic
tripartism
Lech Wałęsa
Cardinal Stefan
    Wyszyński
Yalta agreement

List of Party Abbreviations

AWS Solidarity Electoral Action (Akcja Wyborcza
    Solidarność)
LPR League of Polish Families (Liga Polskich
    Rodzin)
OPZZ All-Poland Alliance of Trade Unions
    (Ogólnopolskie Porozumienie Zwiazków
    Zawodowych)
PiS Law and Justice (Prawo i Sprawiedliwość)

PO Civic Platform (Platforma Obywatelska)
PSL Polish Peasant Party (Polskie Stronnictwo
    Ludowe)
SdRP Social Democracy of the Polish Republic
    (Socjaldemokracja Rzeczypospolitej Polskiej)
SLD Alliance of the Democratic Left (Sojusz Lewicy
    Demokratycznej)
UW Freedom Union (Unia Wolności)

Suggested Readings

Castle, Marjorie. *Triggering Communism's Collapse: Perceptions and Power in Poland's Transition.* Lanham, MD: Rowman and Littlefield, 2003.

Castle, Marjorie, and Ray Taras. *Democracy in Poland.* Boulder, CO: Westview Press, 2002.

Davies, Norman. *God's Playground: A History of Poland,* Vols. 1–2. New York: Columbia University Press, 2004.

Dunn, Elizabeth C., Bruce Grant, and Nancy Ries, eds. *Privatizing Poland: Baby Food, Big Business, and the Remaking of Labor.* Ithaca, NY: Cornell University Press, 2004.

Ekiert, Grzegorz, and Jan Kubik. *Rebellious Civil Society: Popular Protest and Democratic Control in Poland, 1989–1993.* Ann Arbor, MI: University of Michigan Press, 1999.

Kaminski, Bartlomiej. *The Collapse of State Socialism: The Case of Poland.* Princeton, NJ: Princeton University Press, 1991.

Kurski, Jaroslaw. *Lech Wałęsa: Democrat or Dictator?* Boulder, CO: Westview, 1993.

Longhurst, Derry. *The New Atlanticist: Poland's Foreign and Security Priorities.* Oxford: Blackwell, 2005.

Michnik, Adam. *Letters from Freedom: Post-Cold War Realities and Perspectives.* Berkeley, CA: University of California Press, 1998.

Millard, Frances. *Polish Politics and Society.* London: Routledge, 1999.

Prazmowska, Anita J. *A History of Poland.* Harmondsworth, Middlesex: Palgrave Macmillan, 2004.

Sachs, Jeffrey. *Poland's Jump to the Market Economy.* Cambridge, MA: MIT Press, 1994.

Sanford, George. *Democratic Government in Poland.* Harmondsworth, Middlesex: Palgrave Macmillan, 2004.

Simon, Jeffrey. *Poland and NATO: A Study in Civil-Military Relations.* Lanham, MD: Rowman and Littlefield, 2003.

Slay, Ben. *The Polish Economy: Crisis, Reform, and Transformation.* Princeton, NJ: Princeton University Press, 1994.

Staar, Richard F., ed. *Transition to Democracy in Poland,* 2nd ed. New York: St. Martin's, 1998.

Internet Sources

The Polish-language site of the Polish edition of *Newsweek:* Newsweek.redakcja.pl

Official information from the various branches of government: Poland.gov.pl

Current political and social news: Poland.pl

General information for visitors, businesspeople, and people of Polish origin: Polandonline.com

Links to Polish-related websites: Polishworld.com

The Polish-language site of the weekly *Polityka:* Polityka.onet.pl

An English-language daily news site: Warsawvoice.com/pl

Endnotes

1. On the role of history in creating unique social characteristics in Poland, see Adam Podgorecki, *Polish Society* (New York: Praeger, 1994), Ch. 4.

2. This is the title of a history of Poland: Norman Davies, *Heart of Europe: A Short History of Poland* (New York: Oxford University Press, 1984).

3. Earl Vinecour, *Polish Jews: The Final Chapter* (New York: New York University Press, 1977), p. 1.

4. Jerzy Lukowski, *Liberty's Folly: The Polish-Lithuanian Commonwealth in the Eighteenth Century, 1697–1795* (London: Routledge, 1991), p. 25.

5. The romanticism versus pragmatism dichotomy is described by Adam Bromke, *Poland's Politics: Idealism vs. Realism* (Cambridge, MA: Harvard University Press, 1967).

6. Adam B. Seligman, *The Idea of Civil Society* (New York: Free Press, 1992), p. 8.

7. Data reported in Irving Kaplan, "The Society and Its Environment," in Harold D. Nelson, ed., *Poland: A Country Study* (Washington, DC: U.S. Government Printing Office, 1984), p. 107.

8. Główny Urząd Statystyczny, *Rocznik Statystyczny 1991* (Warsaw: GUS, 1991), pp. 24–26, 26–38.

9. See John Clark and Aaron Wildavsky, *The Moral Collapse of Communism: Poland as a Cautionary Tale* (San Francisco: Institute for Contemporary Studies Press, 1990).

10. This is my translation.

11. *Życie Warszawy* (August 27–28, 1988).

12. Jacek Zakowski, *Rok 1989: Geremek odpowiada, Zakowski pyta* (Warsaw: Plejada, 1990), p. 214.

13. Jadwiga Staniszkis, *The Dynamics of the Breakthrough in Eastern Europe: The Polish Experience* (Berkeley: University of California Press, 1991), p. 199.

14. Freedom House, *Freedom in the World 2004: The Annual Survey of Political Rights and Civil Liberties* (Washington: Freedom House, 2004).

15. Douglass C. North, *Institutions, Institutional Change, and Economic Performance* (Cambridge, England: Cambridge University Press, 1992), p. 81.

16. Frances Millard, *Polish Politics and Society* (London: Routledge, 1999), p. 177.

17. Ronald Inglehart, Miguel Basanez, and Alejandro Moreno, *Human Values and Beliefs: A Cross Cultural Sourcebook* (Ann Arbor, MI: University of Michigan Press, 1997), Table V320. See also Inglehart, *Modernization and Postmodernization: Cultural, Economic, and Political Change in 43 Societies* (Princeton, NJ: Princeton University Press, 1997).

18. Inglehart, Basanez, and Moreno, *Human Values and Beliefs,* Table V322. Ahead of Poland were Ireland, the United States, and India.

19. Inglehart, Basanez, and Moreno, *Human Values and Beliefs,* Table V340. With an 82-percent rate of trust in one's own nationality, Poles were approximately 15 percent below the mean, but still 27 percent ahead of the most trustless nation, the Russians, at 55 percent.

20. Centrum Badania Opinii Spolecznej (CBOS) (Fall 1994).

21. For a discussion of the congruence between a country's history of authoritarianism and communist totalitarianism, see Stephen White, John Gardner, and George

Schopflin, *Communist Political Systems: An Introduction* (New York: St. Martin's, 1987), Ch. 2.

22. See Janina Frentzel-Zagorska, "Civil Society in Poland and Hungary," *Soviet Studies* 42, No. 4 (October 1990): 759–77.

23. Centrum Badania Opinii Spolecznej (CBOS), "Postawy wobec demokracji" (June 2004), www.cbos.pl

24. Centrum Badania Opinii Spolecznej (CBOS), "Poczucie wplywu na sprawy publiczne" (June 2004), www.cbos.pl

25. Centrum Badania Opinii Spolecznej (CBOS), "Polacy o zmianach po 1989 roku" (June 2004), www.cbos.pl

26. Reported in *Business Central Europe* (December 1999/January 2000), p. 59.

27. Centrum Badania Opinii Spolecznej (CBOS), "Polacy o zmianach po 1989 roku" (June 2004), www.cbos.pl

28. Inglehart, Basanez, and Moreno, *Human Values and Beliefs*, p. 27.

29. Inglehart, Basanez, and Moreno, *Human Values and Beliefs*, pp. 30–31.

30. George Kolankiewicz and Ray Taras, "Poland: Socialism for Everyman?" in Archie Brown and Jack Gray, eds., *Political Culture and Political Change in Communist States* (New York: Holmes and Meier, 1979), pp. 101–30.

31. Inglehart, Basanez, and Moreno, *Human Values and Beliefs*, p. 19. See Table V405 for country rankings.

32. Ireneusz Bialecki and Bogdan W. Mach, "Orientacje spoleczno-ekonomiczne poslów na tle pogladów spoleczeństwa," in Jacek Wasilewski and Wlodzimierz Wesolowski, eds., *Poczatek parlamentarnej elity: poslowie kontraktowego Sejmu* (Warsaw: IFIS PAN, 1992), pp. 129–31.

33. Mary E. McIntosh and Martha Abele MacIver, "Coping with Freedom and Uncertainty: Public Opinion in Hungary, Poland, and Czechoslovakia 1989–1992," *International Journal of Public Opinion Research* 4, No. 4 (Winter 1992): 381–85.

34. Centrum Badania Opinii Spolecznej, "Freedom and Equality in Social Life" (February 2000). www.cbos.pl

35. Jan Winiecki, "The Reasons for Electoral Defeat Lie in Non-Economic Factors," in Jan Winiecki, ed., *Five Years After June: The Polish Transformation, 1989–1994* (London: Centre for Research into Communist Economies, 1996), p. 87.

36. For a detailed study, see Marilyn Rueschmeyer, ed., *Women in the Politics of Post-Communist Eastern Europe* (Armonk, NY: M. E. Sharpe, 1994).

37. Reported in George Sanford, *Democratic Government in Poland: Constitutional Politics Since 1989* (Basingstoke: Palgrave, 2002), pp. 110–114.

38. *Sejm Rzeczypospolitej Polskiej: II Kadencja-Przewodnik* (Warsaw: Wydawnictwo Sejmowe, 1994), pp. 240–46.

39. Irena Jackiewicz, *Nowe role w nowym Sejmie: poslowie Sejmu okresu transformacji, 1989–1993* (Warsaw: Wydawnictwo Sejmowe, 1996), pp. 113–118.

40. Sharon Wolchik, "The Repluralization of Politics in Czechoslovakia," *Communist and Post-Communist Studies* 26, No. 4 (December 1993): 412–31.

41. Grzegorz Ekiert and Jan Kubik, *Rebellious Civil Society: Popular Protests and Democratic Consolidation in Poland, 1989–1993* (Ann Arbor, MI: University of Michigan Press, 1999).

42. Piotr Glinski, "Environmentalism Among Polish Youth: A Maturing Social Movement," in *Communist and Post-Communist Studies*, Vol. 27, No. 2 (June 1994): 156–58. See also Barbara Hicks, *Environmental Politics: A Social Movement Between Regime and Politics* (New York: Columbia University Press, 1996).

43. Millard, *Polish Politics and Society*, p. 121.

44. Survey data and Kwaśniewski's statement are from Tom Hundley, "Catholic Church Losing Clout in Poland," *Chicago Tribune*, November 13, 1994.

45. Stanislaw Podemski, "Zadowoleni i niespokojni," *Polityka* 32 (August 7, 1993): 1.

46. Andrew A. Michta, "Civil-Military Relations in Poland After 1989: The Outer Limits of Change," *Problems of Post-Communism* 44, No. 2 (March–April 1997): 64.

47. For example, see Ray Taras, "Poland's Diplomatic Misadventure in Iraq," *Problems of Post-Communism* 51, No. 1 (January–February 2004).

48. Wlodzimierz Wesolowski, "Transformacja charakteru i struktury interesów: aktualne procesy, szanse i zagrozenia," in Andrzej Rychard and Michal Federowicz, eds., *Spoleczenstwo w transformacji: ekspertyzy i studia* (Warsaw: IFIS PAN, 1993), p. 138.

49. Wesolowski, "Transformacja charakteru i struktury interesów," p. 133.

50. Dariusz Chrzanowski, Piotr Radziewicz, and Wojciech Odrawaz-Sypniewski, *Analiza projektów ustaw wniesionych do Sejmu III kadencji* (Warsaw: Sejm Chancellery, 2000), p. 3.

51. *Sejm RP. Informacja o dzialalnosci Sejmu II i III kadencji.* See www.sejm.gov.pl

52. Philippe C. Schmitter, "Still the Century of Corporatism?" in Schmitter and Gerhard Lembruch, eds., *Trends Toward Corporatist Intermediation* (London: Sage, 1979), p. 13.

53. Philippe C. Schmitter, "Reflections on Where the Theory of Neo-Corporatism Has Gone and Where the Praxis of Neo-Corporatism May Be Going," in Gerhard Lehmbruch and Phillipe C. Schmitter, eds., *Patterns of Corporatist Policy-Making* (London: Sage, 1982), p. 263.

54. Jan Winiecki, "The Sources of Economic Success: Eliminating Barriers to Human Entrepreneurship—A Hayekian Lesson in Spontaneous Development," in Winiecki, *Five Years After June*, p. 41.

55. Jeffrey Sachs, "Western Financial Assistance and Russia's Reforms," in Shafiqul Islam and Michael Mandelbaum, eds., *Making Markets: Economic Transformation in Eastern Europe and the Post-Soviet States* (New York: Council on Foreign Relations Press, 1993), p. 146.

56. Jeffrey Sachs, *Poland's Jump to the Market Economy* (Cambridge, MA: MIT Press, 1994), p. 25.

57. Adam Przeworski, "Economic Reforms, Public Opinion, and Political Institutions: Poland in the Eastern European Perspective," in Luis Carlos Bresser Pereira, Jose Maria Maravall, and Adam Przeworski, eds., *Economic Reforms in*

New Democracies: A Social-Democratic Approach (Cambridge: Cambridge University Press, 1993), p. 183.

58. Przeworski, "Economic Reforms, Public Opinion, and Political Institutions," p. 180.

59. Przeworski, "Economic Reforms, Public Opinion, and Political Institutions," p. 176.

60. Piotr Sztompka, "The Intangibles and Imponderables of the Transition to Democracy," *Studies in Comparative Communism* 24, No. 3 (September 1991): 311.

61. See www.transparency.de.

62. The slogan attributed to the Solidarity government was "TKM" (*teraz kurwa my*)—an acronym for the loosely translated "F———, it's our turn now!" When Solidarity left government in 2001, 70 percent of Poles felt it had received kickbacks compared to 55 percent when the SLD left government in 1997.

63. Zbigniew Brzezinski, *Out of Control: Global Turmoil on the Eve of the 21st Century* (New York: Collier Books, 1993), p. 216.

64. G. Bingham Powell, Jr., *Elections as Instruments of Democracy: Majoritarian and Proportional Visions* (New Haven: Yale University Press, 2000) p. 234.

65. A September 2004 public opinion survey report found 43 percent of respondents in favor of a simple majority single-constituency system, 16 percent in favor of proportional representation, and 28 percent indifferent. Centrum Badania Opinii Spolecznej (CBOS), "Wybory większosciowe czy proporcjonalne?" (September 2004), www.cbos.pl

66. Barrington Moore, *Social Origins of Dictatorship and Democracy* (Boston: Beacon Press, 1966), Ch. 7.

Hungary

0   25   50 mi
0   40   80 km

SLOVAKIA

UKRAINE

AUSTRIA

Fertő Tó

Duna

BORSOD-ABAÚJ-ZEMPLÉN

Tisza

● Miskolc

SZABOLCS-SZATMÁR-BEREG

Salgótarján ●

NÓGRÁD

Eger ●

● Nyíregyháza

Győr ●

GYŐR-MOSON-SOPRON

KOMÁROM-ESZTERGOM

HEVES

Debrecen ●

Tatabánya ●

Budapest
★
BUDAPEST

HAJDÚ-BIHAR

Szombathely ●

VESZPRÉM

Székesfehérvár ●

PEST

JÁSZ-NAGYKUN-SZOLNOK

VAS

Veszprém ●

FEJÉR

Szolnok ●

N

Zalaegerszeg ●

Lake Balaton

ZALA

Kecskemét ●

BÉKÉS

SOMOGY

TOLNA

BÁCS-KISKUN

Duna

Tisza

CSONGRÁD

Békéscsaba ●

Kaposvár ●

Szekszárd ●

Szeged ●

Pécs ●

BARANYA

Dráva

ROMANIA

CROATIA

YUGOSLAVIA

Chapter 11

Politics in Hungary

KATHLEEN MONTGOMERY

Country Bio—Hungary

POPULATION: 10.1 Million

TERRITORY: Total Area: 93,030 kilometers (35,919 sq. mi)

YEAR OF INDEPENDENCE: 1001

YEAR OF CURRENT CONSTITUTION: 1949

CHIEF OF STATE: President Ferenc Madl

HEAD OF GOVERNMENT: Prime Minister Péter Medgyessy

LANGUAGES(S):   Hungarian 98.2%, other 1.8%

RELIGION: Roman Catholic 67.5%, Calvinist 20%, Lutheran 5%, atheist and other 7.4%

ETHNIC COMPOSITION: 90% Hungarian (Magyar); 4% Roma (Gypsy); 2.6% German; 2% Serb; 0.8% Slovak; 0.6% Romanian

---

The Hungarian democratic revolution of 1989–1990 took place without "breaking a single window pane."[1] There was no bloodshed; no dissident playwright emerged to lead the democratic forces, as in Czechoslovakia's velvet revolution; and no single group united society against Communist rule, as did Poland's Solidarity. Rather, reformist elements within the Communist leadership entered into negotiations with a relatively weak and fragmented opposition. Their compromises led to free, multiparty elections in which the Communists lost power for the first time in over 40 years.

This is not to say that the Hungarian transition was uneventful. There were moments of high drama—among them, when Foreign Minister Gyula Horn decided to allow East German citizens passage to the West via Hungarian borders. In little more than a month,

403

50,000 East Germans had voted with their feet, crossing Hungary to enter Austria. This triggered the fall of the Berlin Wall and provided a symbolic end to the Cold War. Hungary then had its place in Eastern Europe's year of miracles. But, change took place through what social scientists describe as a negotiated or "pacted" democratic transition.

This particular mode of transition raises interesting questions for social scientists. On the one hand, a high degree of elite bargaining might improve the chances of democratic consolidation and market transition by reducing conflict, managing social tensions, and providing national consensus behind difficult transition policies. On the other hand, it might allow the old elite to resurrect itself in the new democratic and capitalist landscape. If those in political and economic power under the former regime retain (or are thought to have retained) power, then citizens may question whether there has really been any change at all. What can we say about Hungary after more than a decade of democracy?

Scholars generally divide the post-Communist countries of Eastern Europe into two camps: a set of more or less consolidated and prosperous democracies, including Poland, Czech Republic, and Slovenia, and a group of semi-free and economically peripheral nations, such as Serbia, Albania, and Bulgaria. Hungary clearly belongs in the former category. It is the only East European country that has not seen a single post-Communist government fall prior to scheduled elections; and its party system increasingly appears to offer two rather broad ideological choices. Some observers have actually begun to describe Hungary as a two-party system.

Until recently, that stability seems to have paid dividends. The growth rate in the late 1990s averaged around 4 percent, and Hungary consistently received the highest level of foreign direct investment (FDI) in the region. The successor to the ruling Communist Party smoothly transformed itself into a European Social Democratic Party that, far from resisting democratization and marketization, moved Hungary through its most rapid period of transformation. The private sector in Hungary now accounts for well over 80 percent of GDP. Services have grown to 70 percent of GDP and roughly 65

percent of labor force employment; and foreign investment has helped to modernize Hungarian industry. Hungary is now a member of all the major Western economic and political institutions, including the IMF, OECD, UN, NATO, and, as of May 2004, the EU.

Some have attributed this success to a unique Hungarian brand of political pragmatism, blending elite level compromise and low levels of popular mobilization.[2] The Communist regime never imploded in Hungary, as it did in Czechoslovakia, and it was never overwhelmingly rejected at the ballot box. None of the top echelons of the Communist Party, the former *nomenklatura*, remain leaders in the reformed Socialist Party or the parliament. But, technocrats from the old regime continue to play a prominent role in the economy, social services, and education. This seemed like the best of both worlds to many observers in the 1990s. Hungary did not experience the dearth of capable elites seen in some post-Communist countries; and at the same time the integration of the Communist elite tied former authoritarians to the new rules of the democratic game.

The main story in Hungary since 1998, however, is the growing polarization between a left-liberal camp, led by the Communist successor *Hungarian Socialist Party (HSP)*, and a populist-nationalist and conservative camp, led by the *Alliance of Young Democrats-Civic Party* (commonly known by its acronym, *Fidesz*). Ordinarily, political scientists would cheer the movement toward a two-party system. Such systems are said to encourage ideological moderation, government efficiency, and system stability. But, those benefits may not materialize if the parties and electorate divide along cultural fault lines rather than clear social or policy-based cleavages.

This is the problem in Hungary today, where the dominant post-1990 cleavage is—surprisingly enough—the "national question." In multinational states such as the former Yugoslavia, we expect conflicts over who the state is "of and for." We are accustomed to elites in new states like Moldova and Kyrgyzstan "inventing" stories of peoplehood as a means of justifying statehood.[3] But, the Hungarian state was founded over a thousand years ago; and it was stripped of its national minorities in the settlements that ended the two world wars. Today, there is no real question about the historical legitimacy of a Hungarian state, nor is there any contest over issues like the state language. The national cleavage instead grows out of differing interpretations of Hungarian history and different understandings of the state's role vis-à-vis the nation. This focuses political debate on "culture wars" and personal rivalries. For the populist-nationalist camp, the HSP is merely a continuation of a Communist leadership that collaborated with a foreign power (the Soviet Union) to stifle Hungarian culture and national identity. They want to create a "more national" state, one that actively promotes and extends the historical and cultural nation. The socialist and liberal camp, in contrast, cannot get past the question of exactly who gets to define the nation. They look to the dark history of populism and nationalism in Hungary and see evidence of anti-Semitism, xenophobia, irrationality, romanticism, and arrogance.

These cultural clashes make it difficult to gain constructive cooperation across political allegiances. In a new democracy like Hungary, bifurcation and polarization could prove destabilizing. If politics becomes too deeply divided, governments may not be able to enact needed reforms. Weak government performance could adversely affect popular attitudes toward transition and democracy. In contrast, reforms pushed through in the absence of any national consensus are likely to be short lived, sporadic, and unevenly applied.

CURRENT POLICY CHALLENGES

Hungarian leaders in both camps insist that their country should no longer be viewed as an emerging democracy but rather as a political and economic system that is *converging* with the rest of Europe. Many of the issues that preoccupy Hungarians are the same issues that concern citizens in other European democracies. Hungarians worry about how to balance economic growth while preserving social welfare and how to have political freedom without sacrificing public order. Hungarian elites, however, have a habit of framing these issues in terms of different readings of Hungarian history, and that affects their ability to make policy on issues of substance. In 2001, for instance, parliament spent months wrangling over the precise contours of the millennial celebrations and where the crown of St. Stephen should be housed (see Box 11.1). Symbolic politics completely overshadowed the growing crises in health, pensions, and agriculture.

As in other European countries, policy challenges in Hungary derive from a combination of internal and external pressures. Internally, low birthrates and deteriorating age dependency ratios are rendering the pension system unsustainable (there will be nearly 80 pensioners for every 100 workers by the year 2016). High divorce and single motherhood rates, as well as inflation and unemployment, challenge the ability of the state to pay for social welfare. The health care system is particularly problematic, since government expenditures for health are higher than the OECD average, but health outcomes are generally worse. At the same time, the transition to a market economy has created new populations of need. There is a growing divide between rich and poor. Poverty is particularly widespread among children, women, the elderly, multichild households, and the Roma minority.

Hungary also faces very real external pressures associated with becoming a member of the EU and a competitor in the global marketplace. In order to enter the "European club" Hungary must bring its legal code into compliance with the EU *acquis communiautaire* (the large body of EU legislation described in Chapter 12). Many of the bills currently under review in parliament are designed to meet European standards—ranging from environmental protection to what kinds of food can be given to hogs. Popular support for EU membership remains over 50 percent, but Hungary's relationship to Europe is not without controversy. At times, policy challenges emanate from cross-pressures between internal constituencies and the exigencies of integration.

The Fidesz government's Status Law (later referred to as the Benefit Law) provides an interesting example. In 2000, the rightist coalition led by Fidesz backed a law to provide ethnic Hungarians living outside Hungary with the right to educational and social welfare benefits from the Hungarian state. To some extent, this was the government's nod to the radical right-wing *Hungarian Justice and Life*

Box 11.1 Crowngate

On January 1, 2000—one day after the official start of a new millennium—Hungary celebrated its own millennium. One thousand years earlier, Pope Sylvester II had presented a golden Sacred Crown to Saint Stephen (Szent István), Hungary's first Christian king. The millennial celebrations, planned by the Fidesz-led government and costing some 140 million dollars, included moving the crown of St. Stephen from the national museum to a display case in the parliament. That move touched off a Budapest within-the-beltway controversy that came to be known in the press as "Crowngate." Members of the Alliance of Free Democrats (AFD) and the Hungarian Socialist Party (HSP) accused the government of politicizing a national symbol and sending a dangerous message to Hungary's neighbors and nationalist elements within the country. Government representatives responded by saying that they only wanted to give the historic crown a place of honor and complained that the governing parties always oppose anything having to do with traditional values.

The importance of the crown itself has always resided more in what it represents than what it is. It is unlikely that the crown was ever actually worn by St. Stephen, since it contains gold bands of a more recent vintage, and two of its famous painted icons depict rulers who held the throne after Stephen's death. It nonetheless has become the most enduring symbol of the Hungarian nation and its legitimate, if beleaguered, claim to statehood. Over the centuries, the crown has been bent, lost on a roadside, stolen and then ransomed back, moved between Habsburg capitals, buried (in 1848), and kept in Fort Knox, Kentucky to prevent it from falling into Soviet hands. President Carter finally had it returned to Hungary's national museum in 1978.

Source: Donald G. McNeil, Jr., "Hungary's Millennium Fireworks," *The New York Times*, January 3, 2000.

Party (HJLP), an opposition party the government often relied upon to support its policies. The law also fulfilled the conservative parties' campaign promise to elevate the Hungarian culture and nation after years of neglect. The law, however, immediately raised alarms in Europe. The EU Venetian Commission determined that the law violated the national sovereignty of Hungary's neighbors. It did not help matters that the Hungarian prime minister publicly referred to Hungary as a nation of 15 million, when the modern state contains only about 10 million. Governments in Romania and Slovakia cited EU objections and demanded that Hungary either abandon the law or come to some agreement. In the end, for all the Fidesz government's rhetoric, it did not wish to stall negotiations to enter the EU in 2004. It passed legislation overriding the most controversial features of the law and reached bilateral agreements with Romania and Slovakia.

The economy is another area of contention. The economy suffered after the democratic transition. Between 1990 and 1993, real incomes continuously declined, and the GDP plummeted some 19 percent. Industrial and agricultural outputs fell by 40 and 50 percent respectively. Inflation rose to around 20 percent per year, and serious budget and current accounts deficits developed. Black market activity in the early 1990s accounted for 30 percent of Hungary's GDP. In March 1993, unemployment reached a peak of nearly 14 percent nationwide. Tax and welfare reforms carried out before the transition allowed Hungary to defer painful cuts in public expenditures and to privatize extensively without undercutting the old political-economic class.[4]

In 1995, a newly elected Socialist-led government found itself in the unlikely position of introducing an austerity economic reform program called the *Bokros csomag* (Bokros package), named after the finance minister who launched it. The reform plan called for university students to start paying tuition. It raised the retirement age to 62 (from 60 for men and 55 for women), eliminated the child welfare allowance that all families with children under the age of 3 had received, and introduced means-testing. It also devalued the forint by nearly 30 percent, reduced real wages, and privatized most of the country's heavily subsidized electricity and gas utilities.

While these economic reforms improved the economy, they were a continuing source of political conflict. In 1998, the Socialists and their liberal partners expected to be rewarded for the successes of their plan. Polls, however, showed that most Hungarians believed that their standard of living had deteriorated under the Bokros reforms. Income inequalities were rising, and services that had previously been regarded as social rights were now subject to fees and means-testing. The rightist parties skillfully painted the Socialists and their liberal allies as selling out the nation to foreigners at the expense of real Hungarians, an argument with particular appeal in those regions of the country least touched by the benefits of marketization. In the end, the Socialists lost the election to a rightist-national coalition.

The new Fidesz-led government maintained the broad macro-economic reforms of Bokros. But, under the slogan of "economic patriotism," the new prime minister, Viktor Orbán, gradually switched from an export-oriented economy to a domestic demand driven growth strategy and reinstated family benefits with new lifestyle tests that examined the mother's background, parenting techniques, and moral suitability.

After the 2002 election, the pendulum was again reversed. The new Socialist-led government of Péter Medgyessy immediately acknowledged the problems in the economy but blamed its predecessor for reckless and politically motivated overspending. The new government did inherit an enormous debt burden from its predecessor, but the Socialists also overpromised in the election and got themselves into trouble with wage hikes. In the context of extremely tight electoral competition, both of the major parties were keen to be viewed as "for the people." Unfortunately, they purchased that perception at the expense of sound fiscal policy.

As a result, the Hungarian economy has moderately declined in the past couple of years. The budget deficit in 2003 was equivalent to 5.6 percent of GDP, well over the 3 percent limit set for new EU members at Maastricht. External debt stood at 41.3 billion USD, over one-quarter of GDP and just slightly less than the country earned from exports. Rising wages have reduced Hungary's export competitiveness; and the Hungarian currency (the forint) is weak and overvalued. If Hungary is to join the Eurozone by 2008, external evaluators agree that the government will have to limit wage growth, cut public expenditures, and revise Hungary's tax code. But those changes will come at a domestic social and political cost.

Perhaps the biggest challenge today, then, is for government to overcome the divisions that undermine national consensus on consistent, long-term economic strategies. Péter Medgyessy recently sponsored several meetings with former prime ministers, but these were stiff affairs that did little to bring Fidesz into constructive partnership. Viktor Orbán continues to give his own state of the union address a few weeks before the official address, and he has established "civic cells" to continue mobilization against the current government. The Socialists, for their part, are internally divided and do not always agree with their coalition partner (the AFD). The two parties have openly split on issues like welfare reform and the hate speech law. Medgyessy keeps reshuffling his cabinet, and ministers continue to tender their resignations.

As long as the party landscape and the electorate are evenly split between the left-liberal and populist-right camps, this zigzag movement between alternating governments seems likely to continue. That is not necessarily a bad thing. Alternation of the party in power can be an indicator of democratization. Hungary's bifurcated party system with clear ideological options gives Hungary an advantage over many of its post-Communist neighbors. The Orbán government used its tenure (1998–2002) to consolidate power in the office of the prime minister. However, each successive government is likely to find itself in the position of having strong formal executive power undercut by slim majorities. The current Socialist-AFD government rules with a mere 10-vote cushion. That weakness—coupled with external pressure from EU integration as well as domestic economic difficulties—reduces government efficiency, which in turn undermines government support. The current camps could easily fragment, which would create new problems. Meanwhile, citizen trust in their democratic institutions has reached an all-time low.

How did a country that just a few years ago appeared the very poster child of successful transition find itself mired in such a growing sense of deadlock and division? The answer is complex and multicausal, involving, among other things, aspects of internal party politics and electoral rules. But, the roots of the contemporary cultural-ideological divide lie in contested interpretations of Hungary's past.

CONTESTED READINGS OF THE HUNGARIAN HISTORICAL STORY

No country is free from its history. According to political economist Douglass North, history *matters* because it shapes the context in which modern political actors make choices and behave.[5] In order to understand developments in Hungary today, we must first ask what Hungarian elites and citizens have learned from the past. What institutional choices were (and were not) available to Hungarian constitutional crafters during the fall of communism? And, which historical issues are continuing to shape Hungarian political prejudices and expectations?

At face value, Hungarian history follows the pattern found in much of Western Europe. Hungary took part in all of the European developmental experiences—feudalism, the Renaissance, the Reformation and counterreformation, and the Enlightenment—but it did so differently and less fully than most of the Western European states.[6]

The twin revolutions of urbanization and industrialization that helped modernize the rest of Europe came late to Hungary, which remained a semifeudal and comparatively backward society into the twentieth century. A late and unsatisfying nation-building experience led to a potent brand of frustrated nationalism; and protracted foreign rule interrupted the gradual development of democratic institutions (see Box 11.2).

Hungarians agree that their story is a story about survival against the odds,[7] but just how and why they have survived is open to interpretation. One camp focuses on Hungary's historical ability to adapt, compromise, and anchor itself to external models of progress. Novelist Tibor Dery once noted that "the spirit of Hungary has been marked, more than anything, by its historical destiny. Hungary was always the weakest, always came off second best in conflicts with other peoples, in historic struggles, and its revolutions. . . . That experience has imbued the Hungarian character with . . . sober realism."[8] Hungarian realism, however, vies with a more romantic impulse that interprets the Hungarian story as primarily one of revolution, rebellion, and martyrs who died in the cause of the nation. Today, the Socialists and Alliance of Free Democrats (AFD) interpret Hungarian history in realist terms. The populist-nationalist right, currently represented mainly by Fidesz, views the same history with various degrees of romanticism.

Box 11.2   The Hungarian Magna Carta

Unlike France and China, attempts in Hungary to centralize absolutist power invariably failed. In 1222 (just seven years after the British Magna Carta), King András (Andrew) II issued a Golden Bull which stated the limits of the monarch's powers. It contained 31 articles that reaffirmed rights previously granted to nobility and clergymen and set forth new privileges. The charter compelled the king to convoke the diet (predecessor to the modern parliament) regularly, forbade him to imprison a noble without a trial, and denied him the right to tax the estates of nobility or the Church. Foreigners were prohibited from owning landed estates, and (after 1231) Jews and Muslims were prohib-

ited from holding public office. Nobles no longer had to serve in the king's army abroad without pay. The king's county officials could be dismissed for misconduct, and their positions could no longer become hereditary. Finally, if the king or his successors violated the provisions of the Golden Bull, the nobles and bishops had the right to resist without being punished for treason. After 1222, all Hungarian kings were to swear to uphold the Golden Bull. With more auspicious geography, this might have led to the type of gradual democratic development that Britain experienced. Hungary was not so lucky.

Founding the State

The details of state founding are more or less agreed upon by both camps. Sometime around the end of the ninth century, approximately 250,000 Hungarians (*Magyar*) ended a long migration from the Ural Mountains region and came to rest in the Carpathian Basin, a large plain located at the crossroads of the European continent. Other nomadic groups, such as the Huns and Avars, had also swept into the unprotected region, but only the Magyars established a permanent presence. After a crushing defeat in 955 at the hands of German forces, King István (Stephen) unified the Magyar tribes and began a process of sedentarization, forcing the roaming bands of horsemen to engage in agriculture. He adopted Christianity and showed that he was willing to spread it by means of force. In 1001, his efforts were rewarded with a crown from the Pope. Hungary officially became a Christian nation, and Latin replaced Hungary's unique native language (*magyarul*) as the language of administration.

The crowning of St. Stephen is central to the Hungarian founding myth, but it can be interpreted in several ways. It can be: the moment when "Hungarians reject a backward east and are included in a progressive west . . ."; the cultural and political arrival of Hungarians in Europe; or the first "narrative of change and renewal . . . of state (re-) construction after a historical rupture."[9] For the socialist-liberal camp, post-Communist politics ought to draw upon the Western and modernizing elements of the story. The lesson is that Hungarians have survived because their leaders embraced Western models of progress and used the state to achieve that transformation. The emphasis is on adaptation. Populist-nationalists, in contrast, see the coronation as a story of national success and power and proof that Hungary's national identity is intrinsically Christian. Like the socialists and liberals, they look to Stephen as the prototype for post-Communist leadership, but not because he chose progress (i.e., Westernization). They look to St. Stephen because he was not shy about asserting Hungarian power. He made Hungary into an actor that did not have to walk on its knees to join some progressive club. The coronation was recognition of Hungary's rightful place in European Christendom.

The founding of the state is not, of course, the only aspect of history that divides contemporary Hungarian politics. What happened to Hungary as a nation and a state after St. Stephen is equally contested. The post-founding narrative revolves around a series of historical "tragedies" that the Hungarian state survived. The reader should examine the historical summary that follows with an eye to how each camp might interpret the same events and actors as evidence for their particular worldviews.

Surviving the Tragedies

For the first 500 years after the coronation of St. Stephen, the leadership of Hungary passed through a variety of different families—some native, some foreign—as the boundaries of the state shifted. Then, in 1526, Ottoman Turks defeated Hungarian troops in the battle at Mohács in what many regard as the first great tragedy of Hungarian history. The Hungarian state was partitioned three ways. Muslim Turks ruled the central portion of Hungary for the next 150 years. Western lands came under the control of Catholic and counterreformationist Habsburgs. Transylvania became a relatively autonomous Turkish vassal state.

Hungarian lands were finally reunited in 1699 but not under the banner of a sovereign Hungarian state. Hungary became part of the Austrian Habsburg Empire. The Habsburgs encouraged the spread of German speakers into Hungarian territory as a means of unifying its vast multinational Empire. That policy inadvertently helped to mobilize Hungarian national leaders around the issue of cultural preservation. The nationalist sentiment that swept Europe in the Napoleonic wars touched Hungary as well. In 1848, Hungarian leaders demanded the right of self-determination. Less than a year later, Lajos Kossuth proclaimed Hungary an independent republic. The Austrian Emperor responded by enlisting the support of some 200,000 Russian troops to crush the incipient revolution. This was the second great tragedy.

Eventually, a combination of internal and external pressures forced the Habsburgs to negotiate with Hungarian leaders. The product of these negotiations was the Great Compromise (*Kiegyezés*) of 1867. Hungary would become part of a dual monarchy ruled by the "Emperor of Austria and Apostolic King of Hungary." To some Hungarians, acceptance of this compromise seemed like treason; they wanted nothing short of full independence. Dualism, however, was a time of extraordinary creativity and advancement for Hungary. Budapest became one of the great capitals of Europe, and Hungary modernized in the areas of industry, commerce, communication, and education.

Hungarian national leaders, who had gained administrative control over lands that included large national minority populations, launched intense programs of *Magyarization*. The key to social and economic mobility was a willingness to adopt Hungarian culture, including the language. Large numbers of Germans and Jews assimilated (often voluntarily). In less than 120 years, the Hungarian population tripled to roughly 10 million. But, Hungary still lacked independent statehood and congruence between state and national boundaries. Large Romanian, Slovak, Croatian, Ruthenian, and Roma populations resisted assimilation. At the outbreak of World War I, Magyars comprised less than half the population in their territory.

Independent statehood was regained with the collapse of the Habsburg Empire at the end of World War I. Hungary became a Republic with Count Mihály Károlyi as its minister-president. Weakened by inflation, territorial losses, and refugee pressures, however, the fledgling democracy fell in 1919 to a Hungarian Soviet Republic headed by Béla Kun. The Kun regime, which lasted only 133 days, launched a radical nationalization program and violently repressed its perceived enemies. The Red Terror was followed by a White Terror, during which reactionary forces executed and imprisoned anyone suspected of involvement with Bolshevism, particularly Jews.

On November 14, 1919, Admiral Miklós Horthy—a representative of the old semifeudal ruling class—stepped in to fill the political void. He was elected as regent of a nominal Hungarian Monarchy and remained so throughout the interwar period, even as prime ministers and governments changed. Horthy promised an era of stability, but external decisions made by more powerful countries would render that impossible. At the Trianon palace

at Versailles, Hungarian representatives were forced to sign the *Trianon Treaty*, a peace agreement in which Hungary retained only a third of its original territory. Seven out of every twenty Hungarians—a total of 3.3 million people—fell under foreign rule, and Hungary was left to nurse irredentist claims against its neighbors. Trianon, which in the minds of many Hungarians amounted to a second partition, marks the third great tragedy of Hungarian history. Perhaps more than any other single event, Trianon shaped Hungary's interwar politics.

Two main ideological tendencies emerged during the interwar period, linked by little more than their desire for territorial revision following Trianon. These two camps were *urbanism* and *populism*. Urbanists—mostly members of the Budapest-based intelligentsia and middle classes—were strongly inspired by the liberal traditions of the nineteenth century and the development of democracy in the West. Populism grew out of a movement of radical writers who railed against the economic and social influences of "cosmopolitan forces" (particularly the Jews) and valorized a rural way of life. Suspicious of foreign influences, they called for a "Third Way," between the liberal and capitalist traditions of the West and the statist authoritarian (and particularly Bolshevik) influences of the East.

Interwar conditions proved more propitious for populism. From 1921 to 1931, a Christian national movement ruled the country with the support of rural landowners and the Catholic Church, whose members constituted two-thirds of the post-Trianon population. This government passed anti-Semitic legislation to appease populists and the rural peasantry but rarely enforced these laws.

The global depression at the end of the decade undermined the agrarian base of the moderate-conservative regime. That paved the way for the radical right-wing government of Gyula Gömbös, an anti-Semite and populist, whom critics referred to as "Gömbölini," after the Italian dictator Mussolini.[10] Gömbös moved Hungary closer to the German Third Reich and allowed a fascist group, the Arrow Cross, to gain strength. In 1939, the Arrow Cross became the second largest party in parliament.

Hungary entered World War II on the side of the Axis Powers in order to revise its borders and reunite the lost populations of Magyars. The strategy paid dividends at first. Hungary assisted in the dismemberment of Czechoslovakia and Yugoslavia and received as compensation prized territory in Northern Transylvania and Serbia. By the summer of 1941, Hungary had regained half the territory it had lost at Trianon and was allied with the Axis forces. In the final year of the war, Horthy attempted to withdraw Hungary from the Axis, but Hitler would not allow it. In March of 1944, German forces occupied Hungary.[11]

Hungary remained occupied territory until it was "liberated" by Soviets later that year. In 1945, the Soviet authorities allowed the first free election in Hungarian history. The sizable peasant and small landholder interests gave the Independent Smallholders' Party an outright majority of seats in the National Assembly. This new rightist government took power in the shadow of Soviet tanks. It was soon forced to sign a peace accord that reasserted the deeply unpopular Trianon borders. Meanwhile the Communist Party, which held only 76 out of 415 Assembly seats, secured changes in the electoral rules that helped it to win a plurality (22 percent) in 1947. The Communists, with Soviet support, used this position to purge political enemies and take control of the state.

By 1949, Hungary was a political and economic satellite of the Soviet Union (see Figure 11.1). Its political system reflected the Soviet requirement of Communist Party monopoly on power, a ban on "factions," and democratic centralism. Its economy was transformed along the Stalinist model of central planning and agriculture was largely collectivized. Hungary joined the Council for Mutual Economic Assistance (CMEA) where trade relations heavily favored the Soviet Union. Foreign policy was tied to Soviet interests through the Warsaw Pact. Mátyás Rákosi, the Moscow-trained Party First Secretary, imposed the Soviet system through coercion, widespread terror, and massive political "reeducation" programs.

The death of Stalin and the process of de-Stalinization in the region led Hungary to test the boundaries of Soviet tolerance for "independent roads." The challenge emanated from the top of the Hungarian political system and was led by the

FIGURE 11.1   Major Hungarian Events/Leaders Since World War II

1945	First free elections Smallholders' coalition
1948–49	Rakosi imposes Soviet system
1953	Imre Nagy
1956	Uprising crushed Janos Kadar new 1st Secretary
1957–67	"Soft dictatorship" develops
1968	New Economic Mechanism
Early 1970s	Universal welfare system expands
Late 1970s	Economic crisis
1982	Hungary joins IMF
1985	40 independents elected
1987	HDF forms
1988	Kadar ousted
1989	AFD and Fidesz form Roundtable Talks
1990	Multiparty elections HDF-led coalition
1994	HSP-led coalition
1995	Bokros package
1998	Fidesz-led coalition
2002	Socialist-led coalition
2004	Join European Union

reformist prime minister, Imre Nagy. It began as a fairly conservative effort to tailor Communism to better fit the unique Hungarian circumstances, but soon thousands of students became involved, and their demands became increasingly radical. In 1956 they called for multiparty elections and the immediate withdrawal of Soviet troops from Hungarian soil. Eventually, Hungary crossed the tripwire for Soviet intervention by saying that it would withdraw from the Warsaw Pact.

The Soviet response was swift and brutal. On November 3, 1956—for the second time in little more than a century—Russian forces invaded Hungary to crush a revolution. The Soviets installed János Kádár as general secretary of the Hungarian Socialist Workers' Party. Under their orders, he lured Imre Nagy from safety in the Yugoslav Embassy with promises of immunity. They had Nagy summarily tried, executed, and buried in an unmarked grave. The internal police force rounded up insurgents and suspected sympathizers. An estimated 25,000 were imprisoned, nearly 230 were executed, and some 200,000 fled the country.

1956 was the last great tragedy for the Hungarian nation, but out of it came a unique Hungarian adaptation. At first it seemed that Kádár would use traditional methods of coercion to reassert Soviet hegemony. Over time, however, he proved far more pragmatic. He realized that the way to maintain control in Hungary was to provide stability and prosperity. He did this by essentially negotiating a dual pact between the Hungarian Communist Party—officially known as the *Hungarian Socialist Workers' Party (HSWP)*—and the Soviets, on the one hand, and the Party and Hungarian society, on the other. Kádár offered Moscow a Hungary that would not openly challenge Soviet domination. In return he sought limited freedom to introduce nationally tailored economic and social reforms.

The cornerstone of this unique Hungarian form of communism, which came to be known as *Kádárism* or *goulash communism*, was an economic reform package launched in 1968 called the *New Economic Mechanism (NEM)*. The NEM introduced various market elements to an otherwise centrally planned economy. The NEM significantly liberalized the price structure; deregulated private, state,

and cooperative enterprises; introduced private forms of property[12] and a personal income tax, commercialized the banking system; and introduced a securities market and unemployment compensation. Like the earlier Kiegyezés, the Kádárist compromise did not fulfill Hungary's dreams of full independence, but it did allow Hungarians to develop a better standard of living than most of their Communist neighbors. With goulash communism Hungary became jokingly known as the "happiest barracks" in Eastern Europe.

The NEM, however, was never fully implemented. It lurched forward and back in measures primarily designed to meet the party's political needs. In the end, the promise of better material conditions was purchased through foreign borrowing rather than economic growth.[13] Hungary became a member of the International Monetary Fund (IMF) in 1982. By the mid-1980s, the country had some $20 billion in external debt, growth had stagnated, and social spending as a percent of GDP exceeded the OECD average. As goulash communism began to fall noticeably short of its promises, the legitimacy of Kádár's rule increasingly relied on the perception that he was the best guarantor of protection against arbitrary Soviet intervention.

The rise to power of Mikhail Gorbachev in the Soviet Union—and his calls for perestroika and glasnost at home—revealed the bankruptcy of the Kádárist pact. When it became clear that the Soviet Union would no longer enforce the Brezhnev Doctrine of military intervention, Kádár went from being Hungary's liberator to the primary obstacle to freer politics.[14] This loss of legitimacy provided space in which fledgling opposition groups and reformist elements within the party could begin a process of negotiation.[15]

Negotiated Revolution

There were several turning points in the democratization process. In 1985, various strands of the anti-Communist opposition met together for the first time. During that same year, some 40 independent candidates were elected to the parliament. These deputies fought for reforms to transform the legislature into more than a mere rubber-stamp for Communist Party decisions. In 1987, unofficial publications (*samizdat*) boldly called for political pluralism, freedom of the press, and radical economic reforms. That same year, the populist wing of the democratic opposition defied the official ban on factions and formed the *Hungarian Democratic Forum* (*HDF*). This group did not initially see itself as a political party or a direct challenge to the HSWP. In fact, reformist members of the Communist Party attended the gathering.

The HSWP was initially divided over the appropriate response to this burgeoning pluralism. In April of 1988, four prominent reformist intellectuals were expelled from the party. Hardliners called for a Special Party Conference in May to regain control over events in the nation. At the end of that conference, however, it was Kádár who got ousted from power. He was replaced by the apparently more reform-minded Károly Grósz. With this, the party hoped to manage the crisis by making reform concessions. This process of top-down reform continued throughout the transition, pressed forward by growing social pluralism.

In the autumn of 1988, the "Network of Free Initiatives," a coordinating center for a number of dissident opposition movements, established a party called the *Alliance of Free Democrats (AFD)*. Discussion clubs in the Budapest law and economics faculties formed a party of Young Democrats

(Fidesz). Several parties with roots in the pre-Communist period—notably the *Independent Smallholders' Party (ISP)* and the *Christian Democratic People's Party (CDPP)*—also reestablished themselves.

Reform elements of the party responded by trying to remain out in front of the growing popular demands. In January of 1989, they called for the exhumation and identification of the remains of Imre Nagy and launched an official reevaluation of the previous 40 years of history. The events of 1956 would no longer be referred to as a "counter-revolution" but an "uprising" against oligarchic rule. Members of the Committee for Historical Justice were allowed to organize a ceremonial reburial of Imre Nagy (see Box 11.3).

Less than one month later, the HSWP backed its symbolism with a formal acknowledgment that Hungary would become a multiparty democracy. It also agreed to enter power-sharing negotiations with representatives from the main social organizations (for example, official Trade Unions) and the eight most important opposition groups. These negotiations were called *Roundtable Talks*, following the Polish example. They began on June 13, 1989, and ended in mid-September with an agreement to hold free multiparty elections, revise the constitution, and establish a new electoral law.

As talks moved toward the announcement of free elections, the reform wing of the party

---

Box 11.3   1848, 1956, and 1989

Timothy Garton Ash, a Western journalist on hand at the ceremony to rebury Imre Nagy, described the following scene: "Heroes' Square, 16 June, 1989. The great neo-classical columns are wrapped in black cloth. From the colonnades hang huge red, white, and green national flags, but each with a hole in the middle, a reminder of how the insurgents of 1956 cut out the hammer and sickle from their flags. Ceremonial flames burn beside the six coffins arrayed on the steps of the temple-like Gallery of Art: five named coffins for Imre Nagy and his closest associates, the sixth, a symbolic coffin of the Unknown Insurgent . . . the crowd, perhaps some 200,000 strong, is still quiet, subdued, when the raven-haired Viktor Orbán of the

Young Democrats [takes the stand shouting]: "Citizens! Forty years ago, although starting from Russian occupation and communist dictatorship, the Hungarian nation just once had a chance, and the strength and courage, to realize the aims of 1848 . . . we can put an end to the communist dictatorship; if we are determined enough we can force the Party to submit itself to free elections; and if we do not lose sight of the ideals of 1956, then we will be able to elect a government that will start immediate negotiations for the swift withdrawal of Russian Troops."

Source: Timothy Garton Ash, *The Magic Lantern* (New York: Random House, 1990).

dissolved the HSWP and founded the new Hungarian Socialist Party (HSP). The party tried to distance itself from the mistakes of the past, while retaining the positive reformist legacy. That strategy failed, and the 1990 elections made the Hungarian Democratic Forum the largest party in the new democratic parliament. The HDF formed a center-right coalition and set about the enormous task of transforming Hungary into a working democracy and market economy.

By 1993, however, the party-political landscape was already beginning to shake out into a left liberal (urbanist) camp and a Christian-conservative (populist) right. The populist wing of the HDF was expelled from the party's parliamentary benches and formed its own group, the Hungarian Justice and Life Party (HJLP). A minor coalition partner, the Independent Smallholders, split in two, with most members and resources following the populist-nationalist leadership of József Torgyán.

After the 1994 election of a socialist-liberal government, the political camps further consolidated with the movement of the former youth party, Fidesz, from a European-liberal party to a populist party of the right. Fidesz gained success in 1998 by framing the national question in explicitly anti-Communist terms.[16] It established itself as *the* party to oppose the former Communists. Over the course of the past two elections, the smaller parties on the right have collapsed. Fidesz has largely absorbed their support.

The 2002 elections were much more closely contested and conflictual than prior elections. For the first time, the competition narrowed to two main parties, the HSP and Fidesz. To date, that bifurcation remains, with recent evidence of a popular shift toward Fidesz.

History Lessons

The free multiparty elections of 1990 marked the end of one period of political development in Hungary and inaugurated a new era of independence and democracy. But interpretations of key historical actors and events—state founding, partitions, failed revolutions, Trianon, Communist takeover, the 1956 uprising, and negotiated revolution—continue to shape the post-Communist political debate. These debates followed a historical division between urbanists and populists, but we should be careful not to overstretch the comparison. There are important differences between post-Communist politics and the politics of the interwar period. Not least, Hungary is now a member of the European Union, participating in a globalized and Europeanized economy and culture. One reason that the current polarization looks and sounds so much like the urbanist-populist rift of the 1930s is that Hungarian elites draw upon history as a template for dealing with the problems of post-Communism.

The populist-conservative right actually represents a wide array of ideologies linked primarily by a desire to elevate Hungarian culture and national identity after a long history of foreign domination. They call upon the memory of Kossuth and Nagy and all the other martyrs of the past who rebelled against foreign domination to preserve the Hungarian nation. Socialists and liberals also hold diverse policy approaches, but they are united in viewing Hungary's historical experience as evidence of survival through compromise, adaptation, and modernizing leadership—from King Stephen to the Dualists, Nagy to Kadar, and all the reformists within the HSWP who negotiated the transition from Communism.

Unfortunately, Hungarian history is filled with examples of excess on both sides. Socialists and liberals today need only look to the interwar era to see how populism can deteriorate into its ugliest forms, and how state action based on a national identity of blood and Christianity can come to disastrous end. The populist right need only remind its supporters of how many urban intellectuals embraced Bolshevism, how local Communists collaborated in crushing the heroic uprising of 1956, or how Communists rigged elections to seize power in the first place.

It remains to be seen whether pragmatism or romanticism will prevail in post-Communist Hungary. Perhaps the two instincts will continue to pull against one another, institutionalized into party competition between two broad worldview camps. Alternatively, the party system could fragment, or one side might manage to capture the lion's share of support. Much depends on the behavior and rhetoric of Hungarian elites and the willingness of average Hungarians to tolerate the social and economic pain of transition and integration.

SOCIAL FORCES IN TRANSITION

The system change of 1989–1990 was not intended to be a social revolution, like the Communist takeover of 1949 that forced Hungary through a rapid process of industrialization and modernization. Post-Communist Hungary continues to reflect many of its prior demographic features. Hungary has an aging population, caused primarily by declining birthrates. Since the 1960s, the number of professional and skilled workers has been increasing and the number of agricultural workers declining. Today, only about 7 percent of Hungarians are employed in agriculture, and only about 3 percent can be categorized as self-employed peasants. Hungary also has a highly educated population with a high level of female workforce participation and extensive social welfare commitments. These features have not changed in any substantial way since the fall of Communism.

More dramatic social change has come in the area of the economy. The collapse of the centrally planned economy led to a rapid expansion in private employment, with all that entails. There have been winners and losers in this transition. Traditionally marginalized groups, such as gypsies (or *Roma*), are falling further behind, and integration in Western markets helps some regions of the country while pushing others to the periphery.

Social Structure and Income Inequality

The state-socialist regime was dedicated to the creation of an egalitarian society. Under the surface, however, social class divisions were a potent source of resentment. The top members of the party-state apparatus—the nomenklatura—had access to greater privileges than ordinary citizens had.[17] Goulash communism partially offset this by making social welfare benefits universal and offering a wide array of citizens the opportunity to improve their living conditions through participation in the unofficial or "second" economy. That promoted the development of a middle class.

Since the transition, the middle stratum has expanded and moved into the private sector. There

has been dramatic growth in the number of individuals who claim to be entrepreneurs, and the largest growth in employment has come from small- to middle-sized private enterprises. The percent of the population categorized as self-employed merchants and artisans, a category almost eliminated (at least officially) during the Communist era, has returned to 1949 levels. All of this is encouraging, given the importance of a relatively autonomous middle class for the development of stable democracy.

On the downside, class differences hidden during the Communist regime have come into the open and grown wider.[18] The GINI coefficients presented in Figure 11.2 show that, while income disparities decreased from the early 1970s through the last years of Kádárism, they have expanded since the transition. According to one study, net household income has declined among the poorest groups all the way up through the middle class; only the top 20 percent have gained since transition.[19]

Regional Disparities

The capital city, Budapest, shows more evidence of the benefits of marketization than the provincial cities and towns. That helps to explain the strong support for the HSP and AFD in Budapest. With nearly 20 percent of the nation's inhabitants, Budapest forms an administrative, economic, and cultural center. Approximately half of all foreign trade comes to Budapest, and the city is Hungary's largest employer. The simple visual difference between Budapest and the provinces is striking. When you leave the capital, Western billboards disappear and the trendy pubs and American-style restaurants are replaced by traditional *sörözők* (beer bars).

The country as a whole is increasingly divided according to region. The western region has prospered after the transition due to its proximity to natural resources and Western markets. The agricultural region in the central plains has suffered from a loss of government subsidies and a decline in agricultural production. Without question, the most economically depressed areas are the industrial rustbelt cities in the northeastern part of the country. The counties of Nógrád, Szabolcs, and Borsod (see the map at the beginning of the chapter) have

FIGURE 11.2   Distribution of Household Income

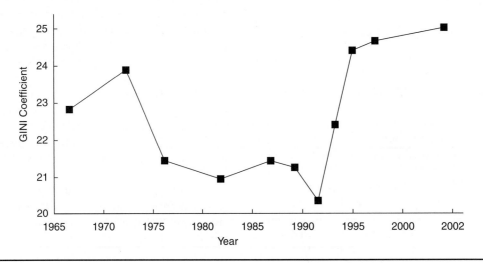

*GINI coefficient measures social inequality on a scale of 0–100, where 0 = perfect equality and 100 = perfect inequality.

Source: UN/WIDER-UNDP World Income Inequality Database.

the lowest per capita GDP in the country. Steel cities, such as Ózd near the Slovakian border, were built by the Communist regime to produce a single major industrial product. The loss of state subsidies has forced the inefficient and bloated industries in these cities to shut down. Unemployment in some cases has risen to 40 and 50 percent. The northeastern cities also face the worst pollution and crime problems in the country and have the largest concentration of gypsies, many of whom are illiterate and poor.

Ethnic Minorities

The Communist regime officially prohibited expressions of nationalism and anti-Semitism. This should have been easy to enforce, since Magyars form the overwhelming majority of the population. Less than 1 percent of the current population is Jewish, while Germans, Slovaks, Ruthenians, Serbs, Croats, Roma (gypsies), and others account for approximately 3.5 percent. Hungary lost its minority nations in the Treaty of Trianon, and the postwar Jewish and Roma populations are very small due to the genocide committed against them during World

War II.[20] Approximately 200,000 Hungarian Jews and 30 percent of the prewar Roma population were murdered in the Holocaust (what the Roma refer to as the *Devouring*).[21]

The roots of anti-Semitic and anti-Roma sentiments run very deep, however. Roma have always existed outside the dominant culture. Historically, they were nomadic and worked in nonagrarian trades (blacksmiths, musicians, palm readers, and contract miners). The Communist regime forced them to settle in housing projects built by the state. Populists saw this as special treatment and claimed that the Roma were becoming affluent through crime, misuse of state resources, and "Jew work" (work that makes money without manual labor). Jews, for their part, were largely assimilated by the outbreak of World War II. Originally recruited to Hungarian cities to carry out the work of modernization, Jews eventually formed the core of an affluent, urban middle class. This made them ready targets for frustration in the twentieth century.

Populist parties have resurrected those resentments in the post-Communist period to paint their liberal and Socialist opponents as somehow less Hungarian. They have accused the liberal parties, which are primarily based in Budapest, of being "too Jewish." Anti-Semitism is sometimes couched in attacks on intellectuals, "Bolsheviks" (a direct historical reference with no real equivalent in Hungary today), or urbanites.

At the same time, violence against Roma and dark-skinned foreigners has increased. Racist violence takes place on the fringes of society, but its ideological partner, radical populism, has found some mainstream expressions. The so-called "mother" of the skinhead movement, Izabella Király, was a member of parliament from 1990 to 1994. The Hungarian Justice and Life Party, which sat in parliament from 1998 to 2002 contains members with open ties to skinhead organizations (what they euphemistically refer to as "short-haired young men with strong national feelings"). The HJLP failed to cross the 5 percent threshold for parliamentary representation in the last election, which must be seen as a positive sign. HJLP voters, however, have not disappeared. They have shifted their support, instead, to the main rightist party, Fidesz. They continue to express themselves through movement politics and organizing.

Growing income inequalities may exacerbate resentments toward the small Jewish and Roma minorities. Less-educated groups who are marginalized by the market transition look for someone to blame. Jews have historically filled that role. Poverty and unemployment among Roma help to account for higher crime rates within that population. That, in turn, heightens the perception among the majority population that Roma are dangerous and alien.

Surveys, however, show that open anti-Semitism and openly negative attitudes toward Roma have become less accepted in Hungarian society over the past decade. In 1993, 14–15 percent of the adult population openly professed to "not like the Jews." That figure decreased to 6 percent by 2002–2003. Approximately 40 percent of adults claimed to be "averse" toward Roma in the early 1990s. That proportion had decreased to around 37 percent by 2002–2003. This is still a significant portion of the population, but the decline in overt racism and anti-Semitism must be considered a positive development, particularly when combined with the collapse of voter support for the radical right-wing Hungarian Justice and Life Party.[22]

Women in Transition

Women were supposed to be emancipated under Communism through their mass participation in the paid labor force. This feat was made possible by state subsidized day care, liberal abortion laws, free education, paid leaves to care for sick children, and the guarantee of a job after maternity leave. The reality of women's lives stood in stark contrast to the promise, however. Men remained the primary breadwinners in most two-parent households. Women were concentrated in lower-pay, lower-prestige jobs and continued to do much of the cooking, shopping, cleaning, and childcare often without the benefit of household conveniences.[23] This dual burden became triple with the additional responsibility of all socialist citizens to engage in political activity.

Since the transition, there has been a retraditionalization of social values, including attitudes regarding the proper social role of women.[24] This pattern, found throughout post-Communist Eastern Europe, reflects both a resurgent nationalism and a backlash against Communist policies of directive emancipation, which reduced women's equality to mandatory participation in the paid labor force. Implementation of the Bokros program reinforced the burden of family responsibilities for women and, for many, heightened the appeal of a retreat to domesticity. Few families can afford to lose female wages, so women continue to participate in paid labor at very high rates, but they now have even less support for this.

The intensity of women's dual burdens helps to explain the low levels of female representation in the Hungarian parliament. The current level of female representation stands at nearly 10 percent, but it has gone as low as 7 percent. Many factors account for this, but "time" and "family obligations" top the list of obstacles cited by female politicians.[25]

THE NEW DEMOCRATIC STRUCTURES

New democratic institutions now exist to ensure popular representation. It is the task of these institutions to accommodate the interests of all groups in Hungarian society. These institutions must be structured in such a way that democratic procedures will be viewed as fair and legitimate. They must be representative but at the same time they must be able to efficiently resolve conflicts through public policy. After a little more than a decade, what can we say about the design and performance of Hungary's democratic institutions?

As earlier sections of this chapter have already suggested, the institutions of Hungary's post-Communist democracy developed through a process of negotiation epitomized by (but not limited to) Roundtable Talks. This process reflected both the efforts of transitional actors to secure for themselves an advantageous place in the new democracy and a widespread commitment to reach agreement. Often this resulted in compromises that maintained the balance of power among actors.

Because the strength of regime and opposition actors was closely matched, neither side could unilaterally impose its preferences on new democratic rules and institutions. They designed protections against either side getting too much control. Chiefly, they set aside a certain number of "laws of constitutional force" that would require a special majority (two-thirds of the full chamber) for passage. These laws include everything from the media and state budget to new parliamentary rules (Standing Orders) and adoption of a revised constitution. The Socialists and the democratic opposition further agreed to establish a strong and independent Constitutional Court as a counterbalance to a powerful cabinet in a unicameral parliamentary system.

These institutions—the strong court, two-thirds laws, and cabinet government (as opposed to a presidential or semi-presidential system)—created further incentives for negotiation after the 1990 election. That election failed to produce a majority cabinet. The Hungarian Democratic Forum (HDF) chose to form a coalition with two minor parties, leaving the second largest party, the Alliance of Free Democrats (AFD), in opposition. In order to govern under these circumstances, the HDF and the AFD-led opposition negotiated a *Little Pact*. The AFD agreed to accept a *constructive vote of non-confidence*, after the German model. This meant that a government would only fall if a majority of the Assembly could agree on a replacement. In re-

turn, the HDF agreed that the new president would be AFD member, Árpád Göncz.[26]

Since the HDF-led coalition barely held 50 percent of the seats in the Assembly, it did not attempt to ratify a new constitution. The two-thirds problem should have become moot in 1994 when the victorious Socialist Party invited the Alliance of Free Democrats to form an oversized coalition. Together, the two governing parties had enough votes to clear the two-thirds hurdle for achieving a new constitution. The Socialist government, however, did not press its advantage. It granted the opposition *overrepresentation* on key constitutional and parliamentary rules drafting committees. The government even went so far as to make a written offer to the opposition, which stated: "Although we are entitled to amend the constitution with our two-thirds majority, we believe that the opposition should be fully involved in the drafting of the new constitution. Therefore we will only amend the constitution if we can achieve either a four-fifths majority or the support of all parties minus one."[27]

In the end, this high threshold could never be achieved. The Socialists wanted language that would strengthen the institutional representation of trade unions; the right wanted to include references to Hungarian minorities in neighboring states. Both parties withdrew their support from the draft constitution when it became clear that a final document would not include their preferred wording. Today, Hungary continues to operate under the 1949 Soviet-inspired constitution that was modified by the last Communist parliament in preparation for the transition to multi-party democracy.[28] For populist-nationalists, the fact that Hungary is still operating under a Communist constitution that does not make a single reference to the Magyar nation remains powerful evidence that the Socialists and urbanist liberals are antinational.

The amended constitution does set forth the framework for a working parliamentary democracy. It identifies parliament as the leading decision-making body in the country and endows it with the power to elect both the prime minister *and* the president of the republic. It also outlines a powerful and independent court, a system of regional governance, and an Ombudsman's Office. Those features have become firmly entrenched in the post-Communist system.

The Legislature

A National Assembly existed under Communist rule but, in keeping with the basic Soviet party-state model, it was not a genuine working legislature. Its deputies were elected directly and did not give up their original occupations. At an ideological level, this was a way of ensuring the representation of workers and those with direct knowledge about local matters. At a practical level, it was made possible by short and infrequent legislative sessions (assembling every three to four years for no more than a few days). Plenary sessions did little more than ratify policy decisions made in the executive bodies of the party and state, the Politburo and Presidential Council.

Since the transition, the Hungarian National Assembly (*Országgyülés*) has become a full-time legislature and the central institution of government (see Figure 11.3). It passes legislation, debates policy issues, and elects the prime minister and the presi-

dent. The ornate parliament building sits on the left bank of the Danube River in Budapest. It seats 386 members of parliament (MPs), who serve a four-year term unless the parliament is dissolved early.

The need for sweeping legislative changes during the transition elevated the significance of the Assembly's legislative function. Legislators spend more time working on legislation than any other area of parliamentary work, including government oversight and constituency service. In the first parliament alone, over 300 laws were enacted.[29] Many of these were hastily prepared and required significant modification, leading observers to criticize the parliament as a "law factory." Still, the ability of this fledgling democratic legislature to so quickly establish a legal framework for the political and economic transition stands as an impressive accomplishment.

In addition to passing legislation, the National Assembly also serves as a forum for public debate. The Standing Orders stipulate that parties may

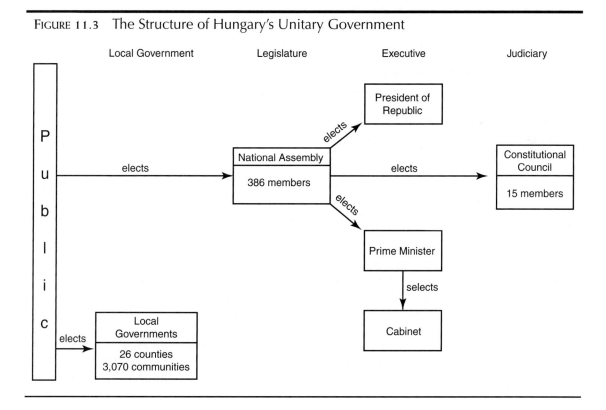

FIGURE 11.3 The Structure of Hungary's Unitary Government

comment on a given piece of legislation (within a strict time frame) and MPs may offer speeches before the session's work begins. These speeches rarely pertain to any item on the agenda, but because they are televised, they have become one of the most lively—if least productive—activities in parliament.

During Roundtable Negotiations, the Assembly's role in overseeing and scrutinizing the activities of the government was one of the most important institutional features for a new democratic legislature. As a result, there are several formal oversight instruments in the National Assembly, including three types of parliamentary questions, political debate, and investigative committees. Though MPs (particularly those in opposition benches) make wide use of these tools, the oversight function of the Hungarian legislature has been relatively weak. Votes of confidence cannot be readily used as tools of oversight, due to the "constructive" requirement.

The oversight function of the parliament has also been reduced through institutional changes introduced by the Fidesz-led coalition (1998–2002). The Orbán administration argued that Hungary needed more clearly articulated differences between the major parties and between government and opposition. This challenged the spirit of cooperation and institutional neutrality that prevailed in the early years of transition. Fidesz saw its electoral success in 1998 as a popular mandate to overturn what had increasingly come to be seen as collusion among elites—across party lines and the parliamentary floor. His centralizing policies, however, resulted in a shift in the balance of power between the legislative and executive branches of government.[30]

Prime Minister

The Orbán administration strengthened the prime minister by creating the Office of the Prime Minister along the German model. The head of this office holds ministerial rank and enjoys substantial powers. The Fidesz government placed the majority of policymaking control in the hands of the prime minister. The prime minister is elected by the National Assembly and thus represents a majority of parliament while directing the executive branch of government.

The constructive vote of non-confidence also strengthens the preeminence of the prime minister. As in Germany, the prime minister does not depend on maintaining a majority on all of his legislative proposals to remain in power. The constructive vote is one reason why Hungary has not had any government turnover between elections, despite at times having weak cabinets. When József Antall died in December of 1993, his replacement, Péter Boross, inherited a mere two-vote majority in the Assembly. On one occasion Boross was actually booed from the podium from which he was addressing the chamber. The current government of Péter Medgyessy is similarly weak and crisis-prone. Without the constructive vote of confidence the current Socialist-AFD government might well have fallen.

Stability is certainly good for a new democracy, but it has a down side. The constructive vote reduces the government's ability to push through its policy agenda. Members of the governing majority may withdraw their support for government policies without the threat that the government will fall. Hence, party leaders complain about the difficulty of getting members to show up for important votes, and the government cannot always ensure a majority for its proposals.

The Cabinet

According to the constitution, the prime minister selects his cabinet, which is formally called the Council of Ministers (see Figure 11.3). The Prime Minister also decides the number of ministers to include. (There is also an informal cabinet that refers to a smaller working body of ministers.) The prime minister has formal discretion to choose individuals to serve in the Council of Ministers. Motions of no confidence may only be raised against the government as a whole and not against individual ministers.

Practically speaking, cabinet formation often involves a strong element of interparty negotiation, since each post-Communist cabinet has been formed by coalition. In order to get the AFD to agree to enter the coalition in 1994, the Socialist Party was forced to accept AFD members in key ministries. Fidesz was forced in 1998 to make the controversial leader of its minor coalition partner, the Independent Smallholders' Party, Minister of Agriculture. Currently, the AFD controls 4 of 17 ministries with only 4 percent of the seats in the Assembly.

Partly as a consequence of this, prime ministers often propose legislation and issue decrees without the consultation or approval of the cabinet. Socialist Prime Minister Gyula Horn was accused of excluding his coalition partners from policymaking when he issued a response to the Constitutional Court on a major economic ruling without even showing it to AFD ministers. Viktor Orbán formed desks in the Office of the Prime Minister that mirror each ministry's jursidiction. This strengthened the power of the prime minister vis-à-vis the cabinet to such an extent that observers now compare the Hungarian system to German "chancellor democracy."

President

According to the constitution, "The head of state of Hungary shall be the President of the Republic, who shall represent the unity of the nation and safeguard the democratic functioning of the state organization."[31] The president, who is elected by parliament to serve a five-year term, must relinquish any other state, social, or political office. Many presidential powers are strictly ceremonial: the president confers titles and medals, appoints the rectors of universities, promotes generals, receives ambassadors, and enters into international agreements on behalf of Hungary. These appointments and signatures are made on the advice of ministers and with the consent of the Assembly.

The president also possesses several potentially substantive powers, including the right to sit in on parliamentary sessions, initiate legislative proposals and plebiscites, and refer laws to the Constitutional Court. The first President Árpád Göncz, elected in 1990 and reelected in 1995, used his right to introduce legislation and to refer legislation to the Constitutional Court. Most of the legislation adopted in the Assembly emanates from the government, so the president has little real policy influence in that regard. The precise role of the president, however, is somewhat ambiguous in the constitution. Much depends on the personality of the individual who

holds the office and whether that person will adopt a maximalist interpretation of the role.

The current president, Ferenc Madl, was elected in 2000 with Fidesz-ISP-HDF backing. He has been accused of partisanship and of using his position to undermine the socialist-liberal coalition. The president, for example, referred the government's hate speech law to the Constitutional Court on the grounds that it violated free speech and was too broadly defined (a concern of the populist-right). Critics complain that Madl tries to make the government look weak and thereby help the right back into power. Whether or not this claim is fair with regard to Madl, the ambiguity of the amended constitution does leave room for conflict when prime minister and president represent different camps.

Local Governments

Hungary has never been a federal system, but it does have a history of regional representation that dates back to medieval times. The traditional structure of local governments continued to operate during the Communist era but largely as an instrument of applying central government guidelines to the localities. Under strong popular pressure, the new democratic parliament passed a law in 1990 that granted greater autonomy to towns and villages. Under the new system, local governments are popularly elected in 19 counties and 8 cities with county status, including the capital city, Budapest, which is further subdivided into 22 districts. The county units are broken down into some 3,070 communities, each of which has a directly elected local council. All of these governments form a single layer. County governments do not have any greater autonomy or authority than the smallest community council.

On paper, these local governments are granted a degree of autonomy unusual even in Western Europe. In practice, they have fallen short of citizen expectations for local representation. Many of the local governments represent very small communities—over 50 percent cover populations of no more than a thousand. These small entities rely heavily on the central government for funding. The larger towns also receive a large percentage of their operating budgets from the central government. This allows local leaders to eschew the politically painful option of raising taxes and, at the same time, reduces the practical autonomy of the governments.

Citizens who find that they cannot get the help they need at the local level are forced to press their grievances at the national level, through MPs and letters to ministers and the Ombudsman. This increases the demand load of the central government. At the same time, the activities of the national and the local governments have not been well coordinated. Local governments are often controlled by different parties than the national legislature and, despite the creation of regional oversight boards, there still is no clear-cut legal framework to guide intergovernmental relations. As a consequence, disparities in health and social welfare are widening across the regions.[32]

The Judicial System

A law-governed state has been one of the chief aims of the democratic transition. During Roundtable Negotiations, the HSWP argued for a relatively weak Constitutional Court, half of which would be drawn from the existing Socialist parliament and half to be determined by the majority in a newly elected democratic parliament (a majority which the Socialists still believed they could control).[33] Representatives of the fledgling opposition groups, however, pressed for a strong court, based on the German model, which would limit the legislative authority of the National Assembly and ensure that the decisions of lower-court judges conform to the law of the land. In the end, all sides agreed that a powerful court would act as a check against whatever party might control the cabinet.

The 15-member Court contains justices who may serve a 9-year term, with one opportunity for reelection. These members are selected through a two-thirds vote in the National Assembly. These justices, in turn, select a president and vice-president from within their own ranks to serve a 3-year term. A candidate may not have served as a leading member of government, been a paid employee of a political party, or held a top position in the state administration during the 4 years prior to the first democratic election. This exclusion rule eliminated the possibility that the Communists would control the new court and use it as a means of stifling opposition.

The Constitutional Court has been operational since January 1990 and has acted as a significant brake on executive power. In the 1990–1994 parliamentary cycle, the Court received 260 decisions to investigate (including 21 parliamentary acts and 12 governmental decrees); it declared 31 percent of these unconstitutional. Seven laws were sent to the Court by the president of the republic and six of these were overturned.[34] Given this record, the Hungarian Court is considered by some analysts to be one of the boldest and most authoritative in the world.

The rest of the judicial system (consisting of county, municipal, and district courts) is monitored by the Justice Ministry and the Supreme Court. The president of the Supreme Court and the chief public prosecutor are elected by the National Assembly. Judges are appointed by the president of the republic.

Hungary has a strong tradition of legal scholarship and vests a great deal of authority in the hands of judges.[35] There is no jury system and no exclusionary rule for evidence admission. Judges must therefore be trusted to have the wisdom and training to make prudent decisions based on legal statutes.

A DEMOCRATIC POLITICAL CULTURE IN THE MAKING?

Political culture studies are particularly interesting in the context of new democracies because they can help us to predict both the viability and the style of democracy that will develop (see Chapter 2). Hungary, like most of its neighbors, has had only limited experience with democratic governance—in the immediate aftermath of World War I and just prior to the Communist takeover. One of the causes for the breakdown of interwar democracy was the absence of a democratic political culture. Fascist authoritarianism was palatable for a majority of Hungarians, because it promised to further Hungary's national goals and restore prosperity. Populist-nationalists favored discriminatory solutions that made Jews and foreigners the scapegoats for Hungary's problems. In addition, many citizens craved a strong father figure who would lead Hungary out of chaos.

The German electorate displayed many of the same cultural characteristics prior to the establishment of democracy (see Chapter 7). However, the postwar West German culture was remade and now displays strong and stable support for democratic values and institutions. In Hungary today, does the culture support democracy? Has the culture been transformed in ways that aid in democratization, marketization, and European integration? In order to address these questions, it is first necessary to examine the contours of the political culture Hungarians brought with them into the new democratic era.

The Cultural Legacy of Soft Dictatorship

The success of center-right parties in 1990—and particularly the historical Smallholders' Party—created a popular impression that Hungary had returned to pre-Communist social alignments. The underlying assumption was that Communist rule had acted as a sort of lid that covered up earlier cultural patterns without fundamentally altering them. Modern Hungarian political culture naturally has antecedents in the pre-Communist past, but this observation underplays the impact of Kádárism on Hungarian expectations and patterns of political involvement.

During the Rákosi era, citizens were forced to participate. There were massive reeducation efforts designed to purge adult citizens of their prior political affiliation. Children were indoctrinated through Communist pioneer organizations and the schools. Seminar attendance was mandatory and citizens could expect to be visited by agitation and propaganda teams. Martial music and Soviet songs were played over loudspeakers in the public squares.

Kádár shifted the focus away from coercion. He summed up the difference in his approach to political socialization in the now famous statement, "whereas the Rákosiites used to say, those who are not with us, are against us, we say that those who are not against us are with us."[36] Hungarian citizens, exhausted from forced political participation and demoralized by the failure of the 1956 revolution, willingly withdrew from public life and into the private sphere of family and friends. They traded participation and political

voice for the promise of a more comfortable material life for themselves and their families.

The Kádár regime still used various propaganda techniques to inculcate the basic Communist values of building socialism, anti-Westernism, antinationalism, and antiindividualism.[37] But, the official ideological message was contradicted by the promise of goulash communism to repay political apathy with material rewards. The end result was that, rather than creating a new socialist morality of collective discipline, altruism, and revolutionary consciousness, the post-1956 Communist regime developed an introverted and materially oriented brand of individualism.

A *European Value Systems Study* conducted in 1982 asked respondents in more than 20 countries about their attitudes regarding individualism versus altruism and sociability. Over 80 percent of Hungarian respondents answered "no" to the question "Is there anything that you would sacrifice yourself for, outside your family?" No other European country came close to being as individualistic and apolitical as the Hungarians. This legacy of goulash communism affects the way that citizens view the post-Communist system and how they relate to the institutions of democracy.

Citizen Attitudes Toward the New System

At the broadest level, analyses of political culture are concerned with citizen values regarding the political system as a whole. Due to the dual nature of transition, the question of support for democracy is intimately tied with support for market reforms. Hence we must ask about both the degree to which Hungarians trust and support their governments and the degree to which they support the transition to a market economy. Do they wish for a return to Communist rule or the emergence of a strong leader who can "get things done"? Do they see democracy as able to perform efficiently and fairly? The answers to these questions are not entirely straightforward in the Hungarian case.

Surveys indicate that the concrete situation of many Hungarians has improved since 1991. More and more people are beginning to claim that they make enough money from their regular job to make a living. That is, fewer rely on income from the black economy or moonlighting. There has also been a continued increase in consumption of consumer durables (televisions, cars, and household appliances) that began with goulash communism. Hungarians widely believe that since the system change they have better opportunities to travel and more say in the decisions that affect their lives.

In spite of all this, popular evaluations of the present economic and political systems are rather low. When asked to compare the situation today with the old regime, less than half of Hungarian respondents (46 percent) say that "the fall of communism was worthwhile."[38] Much of this pessimism appears to be related to negative evaluations of the economy. Less than 10 percent of the respondents in the same survey claim that life is better today than under Communism in the areas of material living standard, job security, and free time. Hungarians seem equally pessimistic about the future. Only 20 percent of Hungarian respondents in a 2003 *Eurobarometer* survey said they thought their nation's economy (or their personal financial situation) would improve in the coming year.[39]

Taken together these data should be read as nostalgia for the personal security of the past more than a rejection of democracy. Goulash communism provided a guarantee of employment and universal social welfare benefits. Hungarians, unlike their neighbors, did not have to wait in long lines for food and shoddy consumer goods. The regime was also less repressive than Communist leaderships in other satellite states. Because of that, it is easy for Hungarians today to look back at the years of *soft dictatorship* and say "that wasn't so bad" and "at least back then you were safe from crime, you had a job and a pension."

Hungarian voters have repeatedly made clear that what they want from government, what they value most, is a high degree of personal security with a steady improvement of living standards. That's at least partly why they keep switching the party in power. No government has managed to achieve economic growth without retrenching social benefits and exacerbating social inequality. The high (and at times contradictory) expectations Hungarians have of their leaders may also help to explain why they trust their institutions so little. Survey data presented in Figure 11.4 show that Hungarians actually trust European institutions far more than homegrown ones. Hungarians have never been much impressed by partisan fighting, and that may

Figure 11.4   Trust in Institutions (% answering "tend to trust")

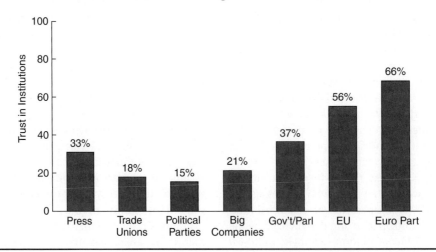

Source: Gallup Organization, Hungary, "Eurobarometer 2003:4: Public Opinion in the Candidate Countries." Brussels: European Commission, February, 2004.

explain the dismal trust in political parties. However, trade unions, big corporations, and the government/parliament do not fare much better in the eyes of average citizens.

The combination of economic pessimism, nostalgia for goulash communism, and low institutional trust would seem to bode ill for democracy in Hungary. But, thus far, there is no evidence that Hungarians would embrace change outside of the democratic framework. Since the transition, Hungarians have consistently rejected the notion of suspending parliament and the multiparty system (with less than 30 percent ever claiming to support such a proposition).[40] The 2002 Comparative Study of Electoral Systems survey in Hungary included several items regarding the democratic system. Notably, over 80 percent of respondents agree that democracy is better than any other form of government. Hungarians do not long for authoritarianism. They seem to long for better government performance. Slightly less than half of respondents claimed to be satisfied with the *way* democracy is working in their country; 83 percent thought corruption is widespread; and nearly a quarter said that the party they voted for in the last election performed badly. Hungarians want democracy, but they want a democracy that is transparent and performs well in the areas that matter to them.

POLITICAL SOCIALIZATION

The system change of 1989–1990 has, in many respects, allowed the political culture inadvertently produced by Kádárism—individualism, consumerism, and de-politicization—to come into the open. Schools and formal institutions of propaganda no longer stress the inculcation of Socialist values. The press and news media are now largely in private hands, responding to content cues determined by market shares rather than ideology. Families have continued the trends of atomization witnessed in the latter years of Communism. A generation gap also has emerged between young people with the skills and flexibility to navigate a more competitive economic system and the older generation, often seen as depleting state coffers. Social scientists generally depict political socialization

as the handing down of values from one generation to the next. But, if the older generation is seen as the product of a failed system, where do new generations receive their civic education? How are the new values of liberal democracy and market capitalism being taught?

The Family

In traditional Hungary, the family served as the primary source of political socialization. It provided security and identity to individuals and reinforced social and political values. In rural areas, it also formed the basic economic unit. During the interwar years, however, family cohesion began to break down. Modernization and industrialization increased mobility. This process accelerated during and after Communist takeover. The state-socialist drive for rapid, heavy industrialization and forced agricultural collectivization profoundly uprooted traditional family structures. Whole towns were built to service new factory complexes. Young peasants left the farm for new urban opportunities. Meanwhile, the state-socialist ideology of productive labor made it mandatory for able-bodied women to work for pay outside the home. Patterns of family life changed dramatically. Families spent less time together, and outside institutions took up the role of socializing the young.

Traditionally, the Hungarian household was highly patriarchal. The father's values and political beliefs were the values and political beliefs of the family. By 1987, however, over 75 percent of women who could work did. This diminished the dominance of the male head of the family, sometimes causing men to become "the big baby at home," acting out with violence or drinking.[41] Women took on the role of superwoman martyrs, spending little time on leisure activities, sports, or reading newspapers. Men no longer dictated the family position on all things; but women lacked the information, time, or inclination to confidently persuade others of their views.

In the final years of Communist rule, there was widespread concern over a crisis in the family evidenced by rising rates of divorce, common law marriage, and out-of-wedlock births. Populists decried working women as undermining the nation by choosing not to have children (most Hungarian families have only one or two children) or raising their children indifferently. The Communist regime was also concerned over the declining birthrate and the lack of proper socialization within the home. It tried to amend these problems by granting three-year maternity leaves and other incentives for marriage and childbearing. These policies did little to change the basic trends: Hungary was following the path of secularization and family transformation seen in all of the postindustrial nations.

But, the Hungarian family was far from dead. It remained an important source of solidarity and identity. Family members helped one another secure housing, find employment, locate goods in the black and gray markets, and get into good schools. Workers also used sick leaves and work absences to spend time with family. Post-Communist elites valorized the family as the center of all genuine social interaction. The family in Communist Hungary, however, was not a place to discuss politics. It was to be an apolitical sphere where people could retreat from the excessive interferences of the party-state. Though Kádárism relieved Hungary of the worst excesses of Communist propaganda and censorship, the HSWP maintained an internal police force and workers' militias (stationed in each workplace) to monitor "heterodox thinking" and "counterrevolutionary activities." Family members could be enlisted to inform on one another, so it was best for all concerned to keep politics separate from family life.

Even today, most Hungarians continue to prefer to "keep their noses out of politics" and to keep family and politics separate. Moreover, the socializing power of the family seems to be continuing the pattern of breakdown that so worried Communist leaders and their populist critics. Between 1989 and 1999, the divorce rate in Hungary rose by 19 percent (to 56 divorces out of every 100 marriages). Increasing numbers of young people are choosing to cohabitate (the marriage rate went down by 2 percent). The percentage of children living in single-mother households rose to 7 percent. Families are also becoming more time-starved than ever. In a competitive job market it is no longer possible to be absent from work without consequences. Leaves are less generous

than they were under Communism, and commuting to work is now the norm. Over a million villagers commute to the cities for work each day. Many Hungarians perform some kind of small farming to supplement their incomes; and it remains common to work more than one job to make ends meet.

Surveys show that Hungarian men and women idealize a traditional family model and a strong male breadwinner ideology.[42] But in reality, the Hungarian family has changed and probably for good. Institutions like the schools and the media have a more direct role in political and cultural socialization.

Schools

Despite years of depoliticization, it turns out that young Hungarians hold strong political opinions. A study conducted by the University Entrance Information Service in 2001 asked 34,000 final-year secondary school students which twentieth-century figures from Hungary and the rest of the world they most admired or disliked. In the international category, U.S. President George Bush was the second most widely condemned individual, liked less than Osama bin Laden and Saddam Hussein, and liked better than only Adolf Hitler. On the domestic front, Viktor Orbán was the most widely admired political leader. The fact that young people are forming strong and independent political opinions testifies to the enormous transformation of the education system in Hungary.

Before the Communist assumption of power in 1947, religion was the primary influence on education. The Roman Catholic Church sponsored and controlled most schools, and the social and material status of students strongly influenced the type and extent of schooling they received. In secondary and higher-level schools only 5 percent of enrollment came from worker or peasant backgrounds. In 1948, the Communists changed all that. They secularized almost all schools, placed them under government control, and made education universal (setting quotas for workers, peasants, and women in higher education). The schools were to act as a primary source of political socialization molding citizens to work for the benefit of the entire society. Technical and vocational training replaced traditional humanities, and Marxism-Leninism became the basis for the curriculum. Russian language instruction was mandatory, and many textbooks were translations of Soviet texts.[43]

After the failed uprising of 1956, Hungarian leaders softened the Sovietization of the curriculum in favor of a more nationally based instruction. By the 1960s, socioeconomic class criteria for school admission were formally abandoned. Tuition was free for all students from age 6 up to the university level. By 1986, 92 percent of 6-year-olds attended one of the country's 4,804 kindergartens. Parents paid a fee for preschool based on income, but such institutions were heavily subsidized by local councils or the enterprises that sponsored them.

At first the near universal access to education was a large enough accomplishment to satisfy the postwar generation. By the mid-1980s, however, Hungarians began to see their educational system as inferior to other European countries. Critics noted, among other things, that Hungary spent only about 6 percent of its national budget on education, less than half the proportion spent by many European countries. Political considerations were often used as a criterion for student placement. The educational system began to experience shortages of both classrooms and teachers. Some primary school classes had up to 40 students.

During the system change of 1989–1990, the national schools curriculum ceased to revolve around Marxism-Leninism. The government took a much less direct role in education as a means of civic education and propaganda. At the same time, educational influences became much more pluralistic and market driven. Following the trend that began under Communism, the family has become a less direct source of political socialization than schools. But, parents now have far more input over curricular matters than ever before. This means that a lot of different interests are being articulated and a lot of players have a stake in the operation of the system.

Teachers, schools, and parents have a growing variety of curricular programs, teaching aids, and textbooks from which to choose. Economic constraints remain a limitation on reform. One of the main dilemmas of the Hungarian education system today is that it inherited an employment structure

in which job security was considered a basic value and pay rates were suppressed. In market conditions, it is difficult for schools to attract top quality teachers when pay is low. Parents with private resources can compensate by going into private schools or moving to areas with better schools. The state is no longer the only provider. The Catholic Church and other religious institutions are beginning to open (or reopen) private schools. This has added to the diversity of opportunity and the "multicolored" nature of the educational supply.[44] There is, however, growing concern that the Hungarian public school system is underfunded and increasingly unequal.

It is well understood that the market economy places a premium on education. Those with education are able to thrive and secure their own welfare in a competitive environment. In rural and economically depressed regions, however, Hungarian schools struggle to provide students with the most basic services—textbooks, hot meals, and classroom conditions conducive to learning. As a result, children in those communities are far less likely to go on to higher education. They are also less likely to develop civic and participatory values or a level of political knowledge that would allow them to make informed choices and influence decision makers.

Only 40 percent of Roma children even complete elementary school. In fact, educational attainment is so low among the Roma minority that some educational reformers are now calling for the creation of separate Roma schools. Advocates argue that the mainstream schools are so clearly failing that separate schools—tailored directly to the needs of Romany children and removed from the often hostile climate in Magyar majority schools—will allow state funds to be concentrated where need is greatest. Critics charge that this amounts to little more than a "separate but equal" policy. Hungarians often complain that the Roma population lacks interpersonal trust, confidence in institutions, and civic values necessary to assimilate into a modern European market democracy. If that is the case, there is little question that something must be done to expand the educational opportunities among Roma youth. Without education, the Roma threaten to become a permanent underclass.

Media

The print and broadcast media during Communist rule were highly censored and controlled by the party-state. Freedom of the press was guaranteed in the constitution, and in 1986 a separate press law was passed by the parliament, but the law was largely window dressing. It required citizens to obtain a license before they were allowed to establish a publishing company. The radio and television sectors remained a de facto party monopoly administered by a state appointed committee.

Since the abolition of the licensing system in 1989 and the eventual passage of a new broadcasting law in 1995, the Hungarian media scene has become thoroughly marketized. The main characteristics include strong foreign ownership (foreign companies have a controlling interest in the top three dailies, the top three radio broadcasts, and the top two commercial television stations); a declining political press and growing numbers of tabloids and commercial radio and television channels; a weak public service broadcasting sector; and a deeply divided journalistic community.[45]

The major political dailies, in spite of foreign ownership, are viewed by elites and the public as party newspapers. The widest circulation daily, *Népszabadság*, is the Socialist paper. *Magyar Nemzet* is the largest newspaper of the right. Journalists in each paper tend to report along party lines, and readers subscribe to the paper whose ideological orientation they most support. "The deep political divide between the 'two worlds' in Hungary is mirrored in the political press."[46] Not only mirrored, the two worlds are actually structured and reinforced through the print media. Party newspapers act as the transmission belt between a bifurcated elite and the masses.

Tabloids, consumer magazines, and commercial television are, on the other hand, mostly uninterested in politics. They work on a cultural level, socializing commercial values and global consumer culture. The Hungarian media market is now flooded with "comparatively cheap global entertainment—quiz shows, game shows, B-movies,

and infotainment—interrupted by lengthy commercial breaks."[47] Some critics depict this as voracious global media monopolies gobbling up a defenseless small nation market. The suppliers of commercial programming are indeed mostly foreign. The United States is a major supplier, but so is Latin America. Mexican and Brazilian soap operas are hugely popular, as are some of the French, British, and German entertainment programs. It should be noted, however, that foreign media conglomerates are selling the programs that Hungarian viewers have signaled that they like to watch. Ratings for the intellectual and cultural programming provided by public radio and television are abysmally low.

So, the market is working. But, is it working well for a newly democratized society? When the Communist party-state controlled the content of print and broadcast media, the news always reflected the needs of the ruling HSWP. That same control allowed the state to offer programming aimed at cultural enrichment and education. There was little variety and the quality of production was often low, but children were not exposed to pornographic, violent, or generally inane content. Everyone—from workers and peasants to nomenklatura—hypothetically had access to the same educational and artistic content. Today, the commercial media respond to consumer demand identified through extensive global market research. In this way, the media, perhaps more than any other institution, is teaching Hungarians—right in their living rooms—to integrate with a broader European and global consumer culture.

The prominent political scientist and social commentator, Robert Putnam, has raised concern about media supply and consumption patterns in America, blaming television, among other factors, for the breakdown of civicness and sociability that once seemed to support American democracy.[48] In Hungary, it does seem that the Kádárist legacies of individualism, consumerism, and weakened civic attachments are being reinforced and given new expression in the marketized media. Populists see the spread of globalized mass consumer culture as something that is being foisted on Hungary from the outside—a new kind of foreign domination. The media moguls of today clearly are not members of the old nomenklatura, and they are not acting as a mouthpiece for post-Communist governments either. Every government since 1990 has tried to intervene in the media market, but none has ultimately been very successful, because the owners of the media are interested primarily in market shares and profits. Ironically, it may turn out that freedom from party propaganda is also the freedom to watch bad commercial TV alone in one's apartment.

Citizen Participation

Participation forms a key element of democracy. Through it, citizens express their preferences, choose their representatives, and shape public policies. In Hungary, however, citizens have been reluctant to engage in either the activities associated with representative democracy (voting) or participatory democracy (signing petitions, protesting, and other forms of direct citizen action). The Kádár government encouraged Hungarians to value material well-being over political freedom and participation. Those priorities, as the discussion of media demonstrates, are being reinforced in the post-Communist era.

Immediately after the transition, when citizen interest in politics seemed to be high, Hungarians ranked participation and having a say in political matters far below the values of "having a life without worries" and being "well-off."[49] More recent survey data suggest that this trend is continuing. Hungarians consistently value social order and price stability over participation and freedom of speech.[50]

It follows that Hungary would post the lowest voter turnout in Eastern Europe in 1990 (63 percent in the first round and 46 percent in the second). In 1991–1992, several by-elections had to be declared invalid due to less than 10 percent participation. The situation was slightly better in the 1994 parliamentary elections, with 68 percent turnout in the first round and 55 percent in the second. In 1998 the situation deteriorated again. Only around 56 percent turned out for the first and second rounds, despite the fact that there was a very tight race to control the next parliament. More voters mobilized in the close elections of 2002—73.5 percent in the second round of voting in the districts. But, participation seems to stop at the polling place. Figure 11.5 shows the types of

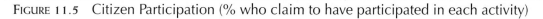

FIGURE 11.5   Citizen Participation (% who claim to have participated in each activity)

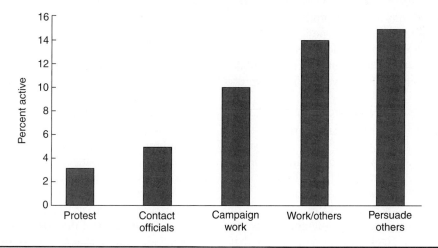

Source: Comparative Study of Electoral Systems, Hungary 2002.

conventional and unconventional participation citizens engaged in during 2002. Only 15 percent claimed to try to persuade others of their opinions. Few Hungarians get involved in political campaigns, grassroots politics, or even try to contact politicians and officials.

The development of a bifurcated and polarized political landscape has raised the stakes of participation. But much of the polarization is at the elite level. Hungarians typically have viewed party infighting unfavorably, and some voters choose not to turn out at all to express their disgust with parties in general. Recall that only 15 percent of Hungarians say they trust their political parties.

This does not mean that we should expect to see disgruntled Hungarians taking it to the streets. In the post-Communist period voter apathy has usually been matched by a reluctance to participate in unconventional activities such as demonstrations or signing petitions. Less than 3 percent of survey respondents in Figure 11.5 had participated in a protest or demonstration at any time in the past five years. Since 1990, a few small protests have been staged around the new issues such as gay rights, minority rights, and environmental protection. Agricultural workers picketed outside the Assembly during the debate on land privatization. Nationalist groups have demonstrated during traditional Hungarian celebrations. A major spontaneous outburst—the taxi drivers' strike—nearly brought the first government to a standstill. Large protests, several of which had to be dispersed by police, forced the Constitutional Court to consider a recount of the vote after the 2002 election. But strikes and public protests are not normal means of political expression in Hungary.

Most of the time, conflicts are managed preemptively through elite negotiation. When strikes occur, they tend to emanate from major state-controlled sectors, such as transportation, energy, and education. They are quickly resolved through compromise with the government, and often give the impression of "scripted theater." Members of parliament, in fact, expect that interests will be articulated in this manner, indicating on surveys that they view direct lobbying as an illegitimate source of pressure.[51] Major interest groups, for their part, do very little direct lobbying, preferring to send leaders to negotiate new laws with party leaders and bureaucratic officials.[52]

Hungary has emerged as such a stable political system partly because its citizens are willing to accept elite bargaining and negotiation without becoming directly involved. Too much popular involvement could easily overwhelm a political system that is trying to make a major system change. Hungary's elite-dominated interest articulation and aggregation functions can also mean that many smaller voices get marginalized. One could list here the problems of the Roma minority, pensioners, the poor, the unemployed and homeless, large families, and women. Their issues are not readily picked up by any of the major parties or peak organizations.[53]

Citizen Expectations of Government

Governments exist to serve specific needs but what those tasks should be is a matter for debate. What is the proper scope of government activity? How much should the state become involved in the regulation of the economy and in the provision of social welfare? Citizen expectations in these areas vary from country to country. Interestingly, though, the dilemmas faced by Western and Eastern European governments have converged since the fall of communism. Extensive tax and welfare states developed on both sides of the Iron Curtain. New and established democracies alike must find ways to balance citizen expectations for social welfare with the need to balance budgets and compete in global markets.

In Hungary, universal welfare benefits were first extended under Kádár as a part of the social pact. By 1972, approximately 99 percent of the population had social insurance. By 1975, every Hungarian citizen was entitled to free health care. The percentage of preschool-aged children getting placed in the day care system rose to nearly 90 percent, and the number of doctors and hospital beds surpassed the levels found in most Western industrial states. It is clear in retrospect that much of this was made possible by foreign loans and substandard provision of services. The guarantee of social welfare has nevertheless become a deeply ingrained expectation for Hungarian citizens who otherwise favor free markets.

In 1991 László Bruszt and János Simon found that fully 71 percent of Hungarians agreed with the statement "The capitalist economy based on free private initiative is the best for our country."[54] However, a majority of citizens still expected a strong government role in providing universal employment, regulating prices, and reducing inequalities between the rich and poor.

Nearly a decade after the transition, Hungarians continued to believe in a liberal market economy *and* a strong role for the state in equalizing social conditions. Fully 65 percent of respondents in a 1998 *New Democracies Barometer* survey said that "the State should be responsible for everyone's economic security." The percent agreeing with that statement in Poland and the Czech Republic was only 52 and 45 respectively.

There are two particularly relevant trends in public attitudes toward the welfare state: (1) the overwhelming majority of Hungarians favor programs such as family allowances, three-year paid maternity leaves, sickness pay, and free medical care; and (2) Hungarians prefer universal, comprehensive benefits to means-testing.[55] Citizens expect the government to pay for benefits regardless of work status or income. The only exception to this trend is in the area of pensions, which were converted to a contributory system almost 30 years ago. Citizens accept the idea of contribution leading to entitlement in this area. In every other respect, Hungarians favor a Scandinavian-style social democratic welfare system.

The problem, of course, is that Hungarians expect many of the same things from their government as citizens in the most affluent Western European nations. To put the problem in concrete terms: Hungarians want Norway's welfare system, but Norway's GDP per capita is roughly three times greater than Hungary's. Norway's budget revenue was 71.7 billion dollars in 2003. Hungary's budget revenue was a mere 13 billion, and 37 percent of that went to servicing the country's external debt.

Hungarians consistently say that they want lower taxes, and international observers concur that the personal tax rate is too high and too regressive.

But, the state has trouble collecting the taxes it already levies. Hungarian tax morality is notoriously low. In a 2003 survey, 91 percent of Hungarian respondents claimed to have seen, read, or heard about tax evasion in their country.[56]

Hungarians want lower taxes, better and more extensive services; and they want their leaders to focus on domestic issues. The main parties have tried to respond to this blend of introverted materialism and welfarism by trying to outbid each other on spending promises. The result: Fidesz left the country deeper in debt on its way out of office, and the new Socialist government raised the wages of some workers as much as 50 percent within months of taking office (much to the alarm of Hungary's creditors).

ELITE LEVEL POLITICS

The standard characterization of Hungarian politics is "elite-dominated." Who comprises the post-Communist elite? The "people's revolution" of 1989–1990 did not represent a complete overthrow of the old elite. Neither, however, is the post-Communist elite merely old wine in new bottles. The post–1990 Hungarian elite represent a true break with the Communist-era power structure, though the process of change has been gradual. In the economic realm it started in the 1980s, when turnover in key positions doubled the rate it had been in previous decades. From that point on the "old elite" ceased to exist.

It is no longer necessary to be a member of any particular party to be part of the economic elite. Nomenklatura lists ended with the fall of Communist rule. In 1990, half the economic elite had working-class fathers, reflecting Communist quotas; by 1993 that figure had dropped to 35 percent. Post–1990 economic elites are also younger than their Communist-era predecessors. Young people are more likely to have the kinds of training, travel experience, and language skills that make them valuable in the global economy. They are also less risk averse and therefore more entrepreneurial than their elders.

While many of the new entrepreneurs and expanding middle class are of genuinely post-Communist vintage, much of the technocratic economic community come from the late Communist period. There has been little rupture with the past in that regard, except in 1998–2002, when Fidesz cleaned house as part of its core strategy to replace the cultural, political, and economic elites of the "former Communists." About half of the post-Communist members of the economic ministries, banking, and State Enterprise boards held similar positions prior to 1989.

The transformation of the political elite has been more thoroughgoing. One indication of this is the decline in representation of women, workers, and peasants. Under Communist rule, the National Assembly was to act as a symbolic mirror of society, and quotas were used to achieve a descriptive balance of various social groups. Affirmative action became less pronounced after the introduction of a new electoral law in 1983, but the last Communist legislature still consisted of nearly 35 percent blue-collar workers and over 20 percent women. When citizens were finally given the opportunity to freely express their preferences, they returned Hungary to Western norms of recruitment. That is, they chose a less representative institution in terms of social groups, favoring highly educated male candidates of the dominant ethnicity.

Hungarian voters initially preferred young, inexperienced candidates as well—political outsiders who were not tainted by participation in the old regime. Over 95 percent of the political class recruited in the 1990 elections had never served in a national legislature. The median age was only 45 and several members from the Young Democrats Party (Fidesz) were in their early twenties. Few had any sort of direct political experience and most held degrees in the humanities, theology, and the social sciences. Candidates with strong local bona fides—doctors, teachers, and veterinarians—also fared well in the first elections.

Subsequent elections have continued the pattern of rewarding highly educated male candidates, but there has been a backlash against inexperience. By the second democratic election over one-third of the deputies elected were incumbents, and as many as 80 members of the Socialist Party's parliamentary group had been members of the apparatus of the Communist Youth League or of the HSWP before 1989.[57] Many others gained their political experience as representatives of local government or mayors.

The disappearance of political amateurs is also reflected in the occupational and educational backgrounds of the MPs. The number of members trained in the humanities and social sciences has gone down, while the number of lawyers and economists has increased. Party affiliation has also become far more important than it was in the 1990 election, when the party labels still meant very little.[58] In 1990, ten MPs were elected either without a party affiliation or with multiple party sponsors. In 1994 and again in 1998, only one member was elected in this manner. In 2002 not a single member elected to parliament ran as an independent.

In little more than a decade Hungary has not only ousted the former Communist nomenklatura, it has established a new political class based on criteria very similar to those of most Western democracies. When given an opportunity to genuinely choose their representatives, Hungarian voters prefer politicians who they believe will have the time and training to be full-time representatives. This trend may be disturbing from the point of view of minority and female representation, but it also stands testament to the change from a largely ceremonial legislature to genuine parliamentary democracy.

INTEREST GROUPS IN TRANSITION

Democracy requires mechanisms for articulating the interests of citizens and groups. This area of political life—often described by political scientists as "civil society"—had only a limited chance to develop in Hungary prior to the transition. Under the state-socialist regime, official interest groups, from trade unions to women's and youth organizations, were thoroughly coopted and controlled by the Communist Party. When communism fell, they lost their official position in society. Today, some are struggling to establish themselves as legitimate representatives of their constituents in an open political environment. Others, like the Communist Youth League (KISZ), have disappeared entirely and been replaced by a myriad of new organizations formed on the basis of shared interests (for example, sports, music, hobbies).

Most observers of contemporary Hungarian politics decry the underdevelopment of civil society. For some, the failure to strengthen and develop civic initiatives and deepen popular participation is the result of a "betrayal of the intellectuals." They argue that the intellectual elite appropriated the concept of civil society to legitimate its own behavior rather than foster the growth of real grassroots. Others blame the political parties in Hungary for exercising excessive control over the civil sector. Still others emphasize the loss of public interest after the euphoric period of 1989, the cultural inheritance of passivity from the Kádárism, and the time burden imposed by economic hardships.[59]

There has been a rapid and substantive proliferation of independent associational activity, from a low of 6,570 in 1982 to nearly 50,000 groups in 1997. But, many of these voluntary associations are organized on common interests (sport, leisure, education) and do not actively try to influence decision makers. Coming out of a reform Communist experience we might expect large, concentrated interests—trade unions, business associations, churches, and so forth—to play a more active role in decision making. Are they better placed to articulate the interests of their constituents within the democratic political system?

During the Roundtable period, the liberal opposition argued fiercely on behalf of rules that would encourage pluralism; they believed this was the surest means of undermining single-party control. The Socialists, the HDF, and the historical parties, on the other hand, favored a corporatist model involving government consultation with peak associations. Ultimately, it was agreed that corporate interests would be represented through a series of chambers (*kamarák*) that would meet with government representatives in an Interest Reconciliation Council (IRC). The operation of this institution for several years, however, did not actually lead to the consolidation of groups into a few peak associations. The old official associations have splintered, and new groups have proliferated and fragmented. If the Socialist government had been successful in achieving its preferred draft constitution, the role of the IRC would have been guaranteed, and we might have seen a gradual consolidation of interest groups into chambers. Since the draft constitution was never adopted, the IRC went on the chopping block when the Orbán government came to power.

In order to understand the current state of interest representation in Hungary, the following discussion will focus on the chief successors of the traditional interest groups—labor and employers' associations, the churches, women, and youth. It will also discuss a few of the more important groups that existed outside the Communist system of interests, such as minority interests and new politics groups. The military, which was a powerful entrenched interest in many communist countries, never played much of a role in Hungary and thus will not be discussed here.

Labor and Employers

Trade unions held a place of pride in the former communist system. They existed as an arm of the party-state bureaucracy and could provide benefits for their members.

Since the regime change, the trade union structure has splintered and some six national trade union associations have come into being. The largest of these is the National Federation of Hungarian Trade Unions (MSZOSZ), the lineal descendant of the counterfeit labor movement in the old regime. The two largest new labor associations are the League of Independent Trade Unions (LIGA) and the National Federation of Workers' Councils (MOSZ).

The older unions have come under sharp political attack for their cooperation with the former regime, but membership is declining. Barely a quarter of Hungarian workers belong to a trade union. This is hardly surprising since the unions spent the early 1990s struggling over the redistribution of union property and did almost nothing to fight massive layoffs and plant closures. The Socialist government of 1994–1998 hardly worried about trade union pressure against its tough neoliberal economic reforms. The railway strike in 1999 was the country's longest strike since World War II; it lasted only five days and involved only one of the nation's main rail unions. In the end, the strike was declared illegal, the strikers went back to work, and the government did not give in to demands for higher wages.

The unions, for their part, have been disengaged from the political process in part due to their complicated relationship to the party-political scene. They do not want to be too closely associated with the HSP, their natural ally, for fear of being tainted by the Stalinist past or by the free-market policies of the modern party. On the other side of the political spectrum, the Fidesz government was no friend to the unions. The rightist government increased the authority of work councils to strike bargains with management without union involvement and dissolved the health insurance and pension boards on which unions (particularly MSzoSz) had a dominant position. Those moves further weakened the already marginalized unions in terms of their capacity to influence decision making on social security issues affecting their members.

As weak as the trade unions seem to be, employers' associations enjoy even fewer historical precedents and social roots. A Chamber of Commerce existed during the Communist regime, but in practice there was no genuine institutional representation for entrepreneurs, particularly those working in the unofficial second economy. With the fall of communism and the move to marketize, a revamped Chamber of Commerce emerged to represent state-owned companies. Privatization created a constituency for other employers associations, as well. The larger private firms have organized under the National Association of Manufacturers (GYOSZ). The National Association of Entrepreneurs (VOSZ) has emerged to represent small and medium-sized private enterprises.

As with the trade unions, there is a problem of fragmentation. There are currently some nine business associations divided according to different areas of economic activity. It is difficult for these organizations to act in concert or to identify what exactly constitutes "business or employer interest" when employers now vary so widely—from new enterprises to joint stock ventures to large conglomerates. Foreign-owned companies are also common in Hungary, and those companies have remained outside the interest articulation structures for Hungarian businesses.

The Churches

Though religion remains a salient social cleavage in Hungary, churches play a less significant role in politics than elsewhere in the region. One reason is that Hungary has a majority church (over 60 percent Roman Catholic), but not a dominant one. Protestants (mostly Calvinists and Lutherans) account for nearly 30 percent of the religious population. Another reason is that much of the population is secularized. Only about 11 to 15 percent of adults go to church regularly. Finally, Hungarian churches under Kádár never really played an oppositional role. Unlike the Catholic Church in Poland, Hungarian churches did not challenge the regime for the loyalties of the population or actively create space for civil society formation.

Despite all this, churches were nonetheless eager to flex their muscles in the new political space created by democracy. Local churches seized school buildings to compensate for property confiscated by the Communists. Churches vocally sought a more restrictive abortion law, and they won the restoration of some former church assets while a rightist government held power between 1990 and 1994.

In an era of pluralism, the historical churches cannot claim the exclusive franchise to represent people of faith. New churches—Mormons, evangelical Protestant groups, Hare Krishna, and Christian Scientists—are all gaining a foothold in Hungary. The Protestant churches (particularly the Calvinists) are losing members most quickly, both to the new religious groups and to atheism. The Catholic population has been holding its own.[60]

The Hungarian population is becoming more secular overall, but at a higher rate among Protestants. If Protestants (especially the Calvinists) are associated with a liberal worldview, then the denominational shift has implications for political affiliation among people of faith. The religious cleavage in Hungary is increasingly a divide between traditional-minded Catholics and irreligious voters. The former group finds representation in the nationalist-Christian and populist parties.

Women

Women were officially represented in Communist Hungary through a Party organization and a womens' political caucus in the legislature. The purpose of these institutions was to subsume women's interests to the interests of the party as articulated by the topmost, almost exclusively male, leaders.

Since the fall of the Communist regime, the official women's organization has been replaced by a variety of groups expressing heterogeneous policy preferences. A few small feminist organizations formed to fight planned legislative restrictions on abortion, and female members of the Alliance of Free Democrats formed an organization called MONA.

Until the collapse of smaller rightist parties, it was possible to say that conservative women were somewhat better organized. The Christian Democrats and the Independent Smallholders' Party maintained women's auxiliary organizations. These groups emphasized the traditional role of women as the bearers of Magyar language and culture and, in a very literal sense, the reproducers of the Hungarian nation. In 1993, a tiny National Party of Hungarian Mothers formed to advocate the father-headed household and encourage women to stay in the home. The HDF actually has a very popular female president, Ibolya Dávid, but the HDF has been all but absorbed into Fidesz. That does not bode well for women's participation, since Fidesz is so masculinist in its leadership composition and style that it is sometimes jokingly referred to as a "frat party."

The main way that women can exert a voice in the Hungarian system is through the ballot box. All of the major parties make rhetorical commitments to women, but so far they have been far less willing to promote female politicians.[61] At the high point of Kádárism, women held around 30 percent of the seats in the legislature. That figure dropped to 7 percent in the 1990 election. The success of the Socialist Party and its liberal ally in 1994 increased female representation to 11 percent, but the figure declined again in 1998 to 8 percent. The return of the HSP-AFD coalition in 2002, however, did not improve women's access to power. Only 9 percent of the parliament is currently female, a figure which places Hungary below the average for European Union countries and below several of its post-Communist neighbors.

This has important ramifications for the post-Communist policy agenda. With a divorce rate higher than the European Union average, Hungary has many single-parent (usually female-headed) households. Studies have shown that these households are at highest risk for poverty. It is estimated that nearly 50 percent of children and teenagers now fall into the lowest two deciles of household income.[62] Women might be expected to emphasize this issue if they were represented in larger numbers. Another issue of particular concern to women is pension reform. Already the age of retirement for women has been raised. Debates over health care reform will also be of interest to women, since women are disproportionately employed in the state health care sector and make widest use of leaves to care for sick children and relatives.

The left-liberal camp has tended to reduce "women's issues" to a set of consumer demands, promising that a successful transition to the market will bring prosperity and thereby make household conveniences more widely available. This, they say, will reduce the dual burden and improve women's lives. In the meantime, women, who are most heavily dependent on the welfare state (as both clients and employees), are bearing a disproportionate amount of the cost associated with marketization.

These circumstances would seem ripe for the formation of a pro-equality women's movement, but to date nothing of substance has emerged. Post-Communist citizens are suspicious of Western-style feminism, because the Communist regime used feminist rhetoric to reduce equality to mandatory employment. Many women say that they have had enough of that kind of equality. At the same time, the parties on the right of the ideological spectrum—parties that are not apt to promote gender equity—are promising the continuation of social safety nets for vulnerable groups. Thus far, women have had little opportunity to affect policy or the culture of decision making.

Minorities

Ethnic minorities have never had political representation in Hungary. At best, they were restricted to the right of privately preserving their cultural heritage. This has changed under the democratic system. In 1993, the Assembly passed an Act on National and Ethnic Minority Rights that is considered one of the most liberal in Europe. The drafters of the law hoped that it would set an example for neighboring states with Magyar minorities. They also hoped that the law would help to curb violence against minorities, which reached a peak in 1993 when 48 skinheads went on a rampage and beat a man they mistook for a Roma, seriously injured three blacks, and attacked a Roma pub.

As the largest minority group in Hungary, the Roma stand to gain the most from the law. Coordinated political activity, however, has proved elusive. Literally dozens of rival interest groups and proto-parties have emerged to represent the Roma minority. These groups fight bitterly among themselves (often along clan lines) and the majority of the Roma community resists political organization entirely. Several minority groups entered the 1998 elections together under the umbrella "Minority Forum," but they failed to gain any representation.

The major political parties usually deal with the "Gypsy problem" when they are discussing the "crime problem." Little has been done to address the fact that hundreds of thousands of Roma are living on the periphery of Hungarian society in concentrated pockets of poverty, illiteracy, and unemployment. These disenfranchised people have yet to find their place in the new democratic system. But with much higher birthrates than the population at large, their plight is one of the issues that the democratic system will have to face in coming years.

NEW POLITICS GROUPS

As in Western Europe, groups representing the so-called new values issues have emerged in Hungary.[63] The most substantial of these is the Green movement, which has its roots in the late-Communist era. In the 1980s, groups such as the Danube-Circle managed to block the planned construction of the GabČikovo-Nagymaros hydraulic power dam on the Danube River. This marked a major milestone in the emergence of pluralism in Hungary.

In many ways, the Green movement was part of a broader backlash against the Communist regime. Many citizens associated environmental degradation with insensitive regime policies that failed to take into consideration the health and lifestyle concerns of the population. Central planners were will-

ing to manipulate the natural environment in order to meet plan targets set forth arbitrarily by central authorities. The Green movement unified against these actions. Since the transition, the policy issues are more diverse and the movement has become less unified. Numerous environmental parties and groups now exist but the "Green Force" in Hungarian politics has largely failed to materialize.[64]

DEMOCRATIC ELECTIONS AND THE EMERGING PARTY SYSTEM

Genuinely independent interest groups serve democracy by articulating citizen demands and interests. Parties, in turn, ought to aggregate those interests and represent them in the political process by recruiting and nominating candidates and structuring voter choices. In Hungary, the electoral rules have conspired with a historically based cultural cleavage to produce what is starting to look, at least on the surface, like a two-party system. The top-down nature of Hungary's transition allowed the ideological and cultural differences within the elite to structure the emerging party system far more than what we see in most of the other post-Communist countries. As a result, Hungary has not had a single government fall prior to scheduled elections. The same four parties that currently sit in parliament have done so since the founding election. Only three other parties have ever won parliamentary representation. In 2002, not a single independent deputy entered parliament. The number of candidates winning in the first round of district contests jumped to 45 (from a previous maximum of 5). In addition, the proportion of the county list vote taken by the two largest parties reached a new high of 83 percent—up from 65 percent in 1998. Such rapid consolidation is a stunning achievement in such a young party system.

The Electoral System and Its Consequences

Much of this owes to the electoral system Hungary "chose" during Roundtable Talks. The complicated system, which observers have aptly noted is worthy of the country that gave us the Rubik's Cube, emerged, like so many other aspects of the Hungarian system, from a process of elite bargaining and compromise. At the Roundtable Talks, the Hungarian Socialist Party (HSP) called for plurality elections in single-member districts, arguing that a pure proportional representation (PR) system would be "impersonal, inimical to voters in the provinces . . . it would be enough for 'listed' candidates to send their photos to the voting district."[65] The HSP also believed that it might be able to use its reformist credentials to win in a majoritarian system. Smaller parties resurrected from the pre-Communist period wanted PR with county-based party lists—the same system that helped them succeed in 1945 and 1947. No group was strong enough to impose its will, so they compromised and came up with an electoral law that combines elements of several different models.

There are three paths through which a candidate may enter the Hungarian National Assembly:

1. 176 seats are filled through two-round elections in single-member electoral districts. As in France, a majority (50 percent plus 1) is required to take the seat in the first round of voting. Seats that cannot be filled through this method (and most cannot) go to a second round in which the top three candidates compete for a plurality of the vote.

2. 152 seats are allocated through PR ballots in the 19 historical counties (*megyek*) and Budapest. Lists are closed, so voters cannot change the rank ordering of candidates on a given party list.

3. The remaining seats are allocated on a national list according to a proportional distribution of *scrap votes* (*töredék szavazatok*). Scrap votes are the votes cast for a particular party in territorial contests that were insufficient to elect the party's candidate.[66] Ordinarily such votes would be "wasted." Hungary recycles these lost votes for parties that clear the 5 percent threshold and then allocates national list seats based on the proportion of scrap votes each party received.

The combination of PR and local constituency representation provided a familiar model for Hungarians. Many elites admired the German hybrid system, so often praised for its role in the success of democracy in that country. Hybrid electoral rules were also familiar to voters, because they had been used seven times in Hungary's electoral history, including the last Communist election in 1985 when a number of members were elected from a national list.

As in the German system, only those parties that gain 5 percent of the total vote cast in the territorial contests can participate in the PR element. The threshold was intended to discourage potentially dangerous party fragmentation and to reduce the likelihood that an extremist party would enter the Assembly. To take this a step further, the Hungarian hybrid system (unlike the German) is non-compensatory. If a party were to win all of the district seats, it would still be allowed to participate in the proportional allocation of seats on either the county or national lists. As a result, the outcome is less proportional than outcomes in the German system (see Chapter 7).

In fact, the Hungarian system behaves in a more majoritarian fashion—is more punishing to small parties—than even the classic British first-past-the-post system. In addition to the electoral threshold and the non-compensatory nature of the hybrid formula, the dual-ballot district races tend to act as a primary that winnows competition into two broad families. This is very similar to the way the system works in France (see Chapter 6). Most district candidates do not win on the first round. In the second round, smaller parties usually step down to support the most popular party from their ideological camp. In the 2002 election, for example, the HDF candidate in a district would step down to support the more popular Fidesz candidate. Similarly, the AFD or the leftist Workers' Party candidate would withdraw to help the Socialist candidate defeat a rightist opponent.

The use of scrap votes on the national lists also tends to overreward larger parties. The smallest parties cannot participate in the proportional allocation of seats, but even those parties that manage to cross the 5 percent threshold may not get much additional help from the national list. The AFD's experience in 2002 is illustrative. Fidesz-HDF won

95 district seats and county seats. It also took away 26 national list seats. The HSP won fewer district seats (78), but it managed to pick up 69 county list seats and the largest number of national list seats with 31. The AFD won only 2 district seats and 4 county lists. It was compensated somewhat with 13 national list seats, but that was nothing when compared with the HSP. The HSP won just 15 fewer direct seats than Fidesz, so it had a very large pool of scrap votes. Since it had the largest proportion of scrap votes, it received the largest proportion of the national list seats.

These complicated features of the Hungarian system have helped to whittle down the number of parties in the system, discourage new parties from entry, and reinforce the two historic camps that divide the political culture. Table 11.1 summarizes these developments. Nearly 50 parties registered to contest the founding democratic elections, including a Winnie-the-Pooh Party and a Beer Lover's Union. Only 6 of these ultimately achieved parliamentary representation: the HDF, CDPP, and ISP (which together formed a moderate right coalition), the AFD, the HSP, and Fidesz.

TABLE 11.1   Party System Consolidation

	Left/Liberal		Right	
	Left	Center Liberal	Moderate	Populist/Extreme
After 1990 elections	HSP	AFD Fidesz	HDF CDPP ISP	
1991–94	HSP ⟶	⟵ AFD Fidesz ⟶	HDF expels (HJLP) ⟶ CDPP ISP ⟶	
	HDF tries to unify disparate right; HSP and AFD develop common ground in opposition; HJLP forms as extreme right alternative; Fidesz rejects cooperation with Socialists.			
After 1994 elections	HSP AFD		HDF CDPP Fidesz	ISP
	Fidesz sets out to unite moderate right under its banner.			
1996–98	HSP AFD		HDF (split) CDPP (split)	⟵ ISP
	Moderates split from more radical populists in HDF and CDPP. The moderates join Fidesz. Right finds common ground in opposition to Bokros package.			
After 1998 election	HSP AFD		HDF Fidesz ISP	HJLP
2001–2002	ISP collapses and key figures join Fidesz; HDF merges with Fidesz for electoral purposes.			
After 2002 elections	HSP AFD		Fidesz-MDF	

Source: Adapted from Brigid Fowler, "Hungary's 2002 Parliamentary Elections," ESRC Briefing Note 2/02 May 2002, p. 3.

The same six parties returned to parliament in 1994, but with an almost complete reversal of fortunes. The HSP and AFD left the opposition benches and went into government. The founding democratic government wound up in opposition with Fidesz, the only party that did not change its position. Fidesz was beginning to look like a party of permanent opposition, like the Liberal Democrats in the UK. To change that, Viktor Orbán led Fidesz into the rightist camp.

The 1998 election was much more hotly contested than prior elections. The results of that competition, in turn, deepened the bifurcation and polarization of the system. The historical Christian Democratic Party failed to clear the 5 percent threshold and ceased to exist as a competitive party. Fidesz picked up most of its supporters and moderate members. Fidesz further consolidated its position on the right with splits in the HDF and the collapse of its chief rival, the Independent Smallholders' Party (ISP).

By 2002, the HDF had weakened to the point that it practically merged with Fidesz for electoral purposes. The radical right wing HJLP, the only new entry to the parliament in the post-Communist period, failed to clear the electoral threshold. Fidesz was the only major force still standing on the right. Some critics charged that Fidesz used "salami tactics" to divide and conquer its competitors, and

particularly that Fidesz had secretly launched the corruption scandals that destroyed the ISP. Whether that is the case or not, Fidesz certainly emerged as *the* force to lead the anti-Communist and populist camp.

The HSP was rocked by its defeat in 1998, and dropped its top leadership. The liberal AFD, widely blamed for the social pain of the Bokros package, had its worst showing ever in 2002, with only 4 percent of the seats in the parliament. With the withering away of the HDF and the AFD, party competition looks more or less like a two-party contest. Figure 11.6 shows how closely matched support for the two camps is in Hungary today. The chart showing the party composition of parliament in 2002 is divided almost equally between the two camps. This has had the tendency to "hollow out" the ideological center and force the remaining mainstream parties into ever more dramatic attempts to differentiate themselves and appeal to voters.

Before discussing the ideological and cleavage bases of the parties in detail, it makes sense to look a bit more closely at the four parties that remain players in the parliament.

The Main Parties

ALLIANCE OF FREE DEMOCRATS The AFD began its life as a small organization comprised mostly of

---

FIGURE 11.6   Political Representation in the Hungarian National Assembly, 1998 and 2002

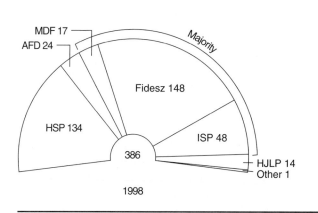

1998

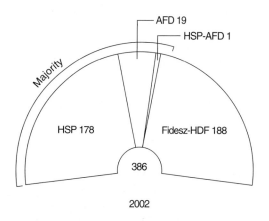

2002

intellectuals (economists, sociologists, and lawyers) who had produced *samizdat* materials throughout the 1970s and early 1980s. The party developed a nationwide following virtually overnight, drawing a number of supporters when it exposed the "Danube-gate" scandal (the continued tapping of opposition party leaders' telephones by the security services). The resulting cleavage between the core of intellectual founders and the mass membership erupted into open conflict in 1991 when the party president János Kis resigned, and the membership chose a less intellectual pragmatist to replace him instead of one of the dissident old guard. Several of the AFD's founders responded by leaving the party's executive.

Another leadership change in 1992 ended most of the internal fights. The intellectuals receded from decision making, and several chose not to seek reelection in 1994. Gábor Kuncze, a relatively unknown politician with a teddy-bear charm and a large mustache, was the AFD candidate for prime minister in the 1994 elections. This was an effort to demonstrate the movement away from the party's Budapest intellectual roots.

In the early stages of party formation, the AFD's dissident core favored a classical liberal ideology, including a rapid transition to market economics. Yet, there were always differences of opinion between those who preferred a Thatcherite approach to the economy and those who took a more social-liberal (even social democratic) view.[67] The 1994 platform elevated the latter position with references to increased state intervention in the economy to create jobs, calls for transforming maternity and pension benefits into "citizens' rights," and proposals to create an "adequate social minimum" through universal health care and special subsidies for families of school-aged children. The party has recently returned to a tougher stance on economic reform and fiscal restraint, however, clashing with the Socialists over the proper approach to key areas of welfare reform and budgeting.

The AFD is sharply differentiated from the nationalist-conservative parties in terms of worldview. It is generally pro-Western. It favors open trade, foreign investment, religious freedom, and low taxes. Some of its MPs are leaders in the effort to protect the rights of groups who have suffered from discrimination, such as Roma, homosexuals, and Jews.

The AFD has little competition for the liberal or the truly urbanist vote, but its electoral fortunes have none the less been in steady decline. In 1998 voters primarily blamed the AFD for the painful aspects of the Bokros package, giving the party only 7.5 percent of the vote and 24 seats. In response, the AFD tried to shed its image as insensitive and overly intellectual, even adopting a regional quota for its party lists to better represent provincial interests. But, the AFD is dogged by the perception on the populist right that it is a cosmopolitan party. It is not a great stretch for some politicians to move from "cosmopolitan" to "Jewish" and to label the AFD as un-Hungarian or somehow opposed to or out of step with the core values of the nation. Liberalism has never enjoyed much popular support in Hungary (or anywhere else in East-Central Europe for that matter). In a climate of increasingly divisive rhetoric, the two main parties are moving away from the center on cultural issues and trying to outflank one another on welfare populism. The AFD cannot credibly move too far right on cultural issues or move too far toward economic populism without fundamentally altering the party's approach to the economy. It remains to be seen if the AFD will be able to cross the threshold for parliamentary representation in future elections.

ALLIANCE OF YOUNG DEMOCRATS—HUNGARIAN CIVIC PARTY (FIDESZ)   Fidesz, more than any of the other major parties, has searched for an ideological and social cleavage to represent. It was initially formed as an alternative to the Communist Party youth organization, with its membership restricted to those 35 years of age or younger. This stipulation has been dropped but the party's electoral support is still strong among voters in the 19 to 35 age bracket.

From its inception, Fidesz had an advantage over the other parties; it had perhaps the only truly charismatic leader in the Hungarian transition, Viktor Orbán. During the first parliament, Fidesz became a tight-knit parliamentary group, holding a lead in public opinion polls from 1991 through the end of 1993. The party's electoral base and organization, however, never seemed to fully take root.

Fidesz failed to win any of the five by-elections held in the 1990–1994 parliament, and there were serious divisions within the leadership. One branch of the party, led by Orbán, wanted to retool the anti-Communist youth organization into a party that could be elected to government. In order to do this, he thought that the party should move toward the ideological right. The other wing of Fidesz sought to maintain the cafe-intellectual roots of the party and to pursue a social-liberal program.

The Orbán wing ultimately prevailed. In 1993, Fidesz rejected its previous ties with liberal parties like the AFD and began to talk to the HDF's populist leader, Sándor Lezsak. In 1995 it added "Civic Party" to its title. In 2000 Fidesz formally decided to leave the Liberal International, of which it had been a member since 1993, and join the center-right European People's Party. It now describes itself as a "bourgeois" or "citizen's" party. What that means precisely is not always clear. After taking power in 1998, Fidesz seemed to define "citizen" or "bourgeois" in anti-Communist terms. It became imperative for the party to expand its social base. It did so by concentrating power in the chancellory and working to wipe away all remnants of the socialist-liberal elite. All of the disparate strands of nationalism, Christianity, and right-radicalism are now compressed into the notion of "citizens' bourgeois society" and treated as the positive contrast to the "evil past"—the negative socialist-liberal forces which prevent the evolution of bourgeois values in society.[68] To popularize the new approach, Fidesz increased relations with and financial support for the "historical churches" and ignored the fact that in the 1980s millions of citizens were directly or indirectly involved in the HSWP.

After taking power in 1998, the party's popularity dropped. That is not at all unusual for a governing party, but most scholars and pundits agree that Fidesz hurt itself in several ways. The Fidesz administration had problems with its more radical junior coalition partner, the ISP, and with the HJLP, which sat in opposition but exerted influence over the government. Critics also leveled charges of corruption and cronyism against the government, and often depicted Orbán as arrogant and unsympathetic. He angered many people by overturning the ideologi-cally neutral state and rejecting the trend of compromise and negotiation that had become the norm in transition and posttransition politics. He upset the formal balance of powers in the constitution by, among other things, concentrating power in the office of the prime minister. The Fidesz government also tried to exert control over the media, which Orbán complained was dominated by his opponents. His government also took a direct role in funding cultural projects, such as the House of Terror Museum built in the headquarters of the formerly notorious secret police. The museum, not coincidentally, opened just weeks before the start of the 2002 campaign in which Fidesz labeled the HSP as a "party of the past."

In the end, Orbán apparently scared some voters away and scared others into supporting the left-liberal camp in 2002. Many uncommitted voters found Fidesz's style high handed and divisive. Those voters nudged the HSP into a victorious position, though Fidesz won the largest number of seats of any party and won in the national vote. Four years of a weak HSP coalition may be enough to return Viktor Orbán and his party to the top, however. Public opinion polls show Orbán as the most popular politician in the country at present.

THE HUNGARIAN DEMOCRATIC FORUM (HDF)   Perhaps more than any other party in Hungary, the HDF fit the definition of an "umbrella party." This term—coined to describe broad movements of Communist opposition, such as Poland's Solidarity or the Czech Civic Forum—captured a phenomenon of the transition period. Political tendencies and social groups that under normal political conditions would have been rivals were joined together in a common cause. The HDF brought together populist writers, reformist elements in the Communist Party, moderate Christian Democrats, and extreme nationalists. Initially, the Forum was reluctant to describe itself as a political party, seeing itself instead as a broad grassroots movement. When free elections were scheduled, the HDF finally registered as a party. It sought to differentiate itself from others in the field by claiming to be the "calm force" in Hungarian politics, a break from the Communist past but an advocate of more gradual change than the radical opposition.

József Antall took leadership of the party in 1990, and many believed that he was the one person who could cement the party's disparate elements. At times, he seemed to rely on the populist rhetoric of nationalism and anti-Semitism, but after the 1990 elections it became clear that he would pursue a moderate conservative path. As prime minister, he expelled the populist wing led by extreme nationalist István Csurka. That group went on to form the Hungarian Justice and Life Party, which crossed the threshold for parliamentary representation in 1998 but has since ceased to be a parliamentary party.

The HDF's internal problems were not over after the expulsion of the Csurka wing, however. The devastating defeat of 1994 split the party again along populist-moderate lines. The party that emerged from these divisions is led by the only female party president, Ibolya Dávid, and cleaves more closely to a populist line. The more moderate members of the HDF split off to form a new party, which never managed to cross the electoral threshold. The rump HDF chose to cooperate with Fidesz rather than challenge it as the moderate-conservative alternative to the Socialists, Liberals, and Ultranationalists. The party got back into power under Fidesz's wing in 1998 but only as a very junior coalition party.

In 2002 all of the HDF candidates were jointly sponsored with Fidesz, and HDF candidates withdrew from district races to support Fidesz. After the election, when Fidesz was barely edged back into opposition, the HDF candidates split from Fidesz and sat as HDF members in order to effectively double the group's representation in committees and chamber leadership positions. Most observers today, however, regard the HDF as little more than a satellite of Fidesz.

HUNGARIAN SOCIALIST PARTY (HSP) The HSP is the direct descendant of the Hungarian Communist Party (HSWP after 1956). Its history is virtually synonymous with post-1949 Hungarian history until the Fourteenth Party Congress in October 1989, when it accepted that it would no longer serve a "leading role" in society. Gyula Horn took over the post of party president in May 1990 and became the

prime minister when the HSP won the parliamentary majority in 1994.

The party's platform changed when it dropped the word "Workers'" from its name in October 1989. It now espouses a European-style social democratic approach that includes mixed forms of property within a market economy. It differs very little from the other mainstream parties in its support for market reforms and its willingness to join Western economic and security organizations. With acceptance into the Socialist International, the HSP effectively eclipsed the Social Democratic Party of Hungary as the main leftist alternative. Old party functionaries still play a role in the party, particularly in the middle ranks, but most of the orthodox Communists abandoned the HSP in 1989–1990 to join the reconstituted HSWP (now called the Workers' Party).

Today the HSP claims about 35,000 members. It has maintained a fairly unified fraction in parliament, but there are occasional differences between the national and local party leaderships and among platforms represented within the party. The left-wing platform is a neo-Marxist group with little support outside a small circle of Budapest intellectuals. The "Social Democratic Community" has a great deal of influence within the party but few members are actually involved in it. The pragmatic "Socialist Group" has larger support among the party cadres. It is led by the former head of Hungary's largest Trade Union (MSZOSZ), Sándor Nagy.

The HSP's electoral fortunes seemed bleak after the 1990 elections, but (other than the defection of Imre Pozsgay in 1993) the parliamentary fraction remained intact and performed well in its opposition role. The party's image began to improve in 1993 and it ultimately overtook Fidesz as the leading party in the polls. Early in 1994, the HSP began to forge ties with key social groups, promising leaders of these groups (including MSZOSZ) a place on the party lists in exchange for their electoral support.

By the May 1994 election, the HSP clearly emerged as the strongest political force, the only party with sufficient nominations to contest every seat in the country. It won almost 33 percent of the votes cast. Its support spread across the social spectrum (though it was less popular among the very old and the very young) and it won a plurality in every county throughout Hungary. In declining industrial areas, like the steel town of Dunaújváros, it was even more successful, securing nearly 50 percent of the vote.

Four years later, the strong economic recovery seemed to suggest another Socialist victory. The HSP therefore aimed at winning an outright majority in the Assembly. The Socialist campaign openly criticized the party's minor coalition partner, the AFD, laying the blame for the painful aspects of transition at that party's feet. The rightist parties, led by Fidesz, had meanwhile established themselves as a credible alternative and entered agreements of mutual support for one another. The election turned into a major defeat for the governing parties. The HSP lost only slightly in terms of the popular vote, but it ended up with only 134 seats—compared to 148 for Fidesz and 48 for the Smallholders.

The defeat, though it hardly represented a popular backlash, placed the HSP in the opposition benches and caused concern within the party leadership. At a September 1998 Party Congress, former Prime Minister Gyula Horn stepped down as party leader. The party went through a leadership crisis that lasted almost until the 2002 election. The party eventually asked Péter Medgyessy, a non-partisan and rather bland former banking executive, to serve as the party's candidate for prime minister. He proved an uncontroversial and steady foil to Viktor Orbán's sometimes frightening passions. But, as prime minister he was immediately embroiled in a scandal (see Box 11.4) that some say has caused permanent damage to the left. Medgyessy has managed—no small thanks to the constructive vote of non-confidence—to keep the Socialist government from falling. He and the Socialist Party have been slipping dramatically in public opinion polls. If the HSP loses in the upcoming election, the HSP will certainly go looking for a new leader.

Ideological and Cleavage Bases of the Emerging Party System

On many broad issues the Hungarian parties differ very little. All agree that Hungary should operate as some form of market economy and integrate with Europe. All wish to increase the prominence of Hungary's cultural heritage after years of Soviet domination. The two biggest parties both claim to support entrepreneurs, but Fidesz's economic policy involves an expanded family policy intended to bolster the birthrate, increase the minimum wage, abolish university tuition fees, and protect Hungarian farmland from foreign ownership. HSP economic policy calls for means-testing of welfare benefits and reform of the ailing health, pension, and agricultural sectors, all prescriptions urged by Hungary's creditors. But, fearing that the economic populism of Fidesz might outflank it on the left, the Socialists promised voters immediate payoffs in the 2002 campaign.

Outsiders are often baffled when they try to match the names of Hungary's parties with their expected ideological and policy positions. The international markets, for example, responded positively when the successor to the Communist Party defeated Fidesz in 2002, because the HSP is generally regarded as the pro-business and free market party. Journalists made much of this, claiming that in Hungary "everything is backwards" and there has been a role reversal between left and right.

The reason everything appears to be backwards is that the Hungarian party system primarily divides along the cultural faultlines outlined earlier—between national, populist, or right-wing forces, and urbanist, cosmopolitan, and left-liberal ones (see Table 11.2 for a summary). This division effectively absorbs the standard left-right economic cleavage as well as the post-Communist/anti-Communist divide. The AFD was once the Communist regime's greatest enemy. Today the AFD and HSP, despite that adversarial history and some major differences over economic policy, are linked together by a common urbanist, secular, and rational style. The opinion streams on the right are equally diverse, including a variety of approaches to the market, EU, and Hungarian minorities living abroad. In 2002 Fidesz drew support from across those many strands, because all the groupings in the populist-nationalist camp oppose the post-Communist status quo, albeit for different reasons.

Partly due to the tough electoral competition in 2002, the populist-urbanist cleavage has shaped the

Box 11.4   The Puffy Jacket and D-209

The Hungarian Socialist Party (HSP) is the direct lineal descendent of the Hungarian Socialist Workers' Party (HSWP). Because the negotiated revolution did not involve purging Communists from public life, scandals periodically emerge about the past activities of top HSP politicians, including two post-Communist prime ministers, Gyula Horn and Péter Medgyessy. Gyula Horn had been foreign minister in the last Communist government and was widely respected for opening Hungary's borders and signing the document that would withdraw Soviet troops from Hungarian soil. During the 1994 campaign, charges emerged that Horn, as a member of the Puffy Jackets (pufajkás)—the volunteer police that rounded up insurgents and sympathizers in the 1956 Uprising—had carried out his duties with particular brutality. He allegedly kicked a young boy's teeth out. Horn, who did not directly deny the charge, was elected prime minister in 1998.

In the case of Péter Medgyessy, the current prime minister, charges implicating him in high-level secret police work did not surface until after the election, when his party formed a bare majority government with the help of the AFD. Fidesz, the party that won the largest number of seats, contested the elections all the way to the Constitutional Court and alluded to Communist-style electoral alchemy. Within a month, the Fidesz-friendly news daily *Magyar Nemzet* broke a story claiming that Medgyessy worked as a KGB coun-

terintelligence agent in the Finance Ministry between 1977 and 1982. Medgyessy initially denied the charge in parliament. *Magyar Nemzet* responded with allegations that Medgyessy informed on his friends and wrote reports on "counterrevolutionary activities." They quoted from a document in which "Comrade D-209" (allegedly Medgyessy's code name) was given a promotion to the rank of lieutenant. Medgyessy claimed that the document was a forgery. Some days later he admitted that he had been an operative during the time period in question, but claimed that he was primarily responsible for catching spies from other Warsaw Pact nations seeking to undermine Hungary's bid to enter the IMF. Medgyessy made a public apology and asked the Hungarian people for forgiveness. Meanwhile his government launched 21 inquiries into alleged corruption in the predecessor (Fidesz-led) government; and the leftist press leapt to his defense, reminding readers that the popular former HDF prime minister (now deceased) always claimed that he had damning evidence about Viktor Orbán's past, and that a former Fidesz president had been forced to resign his position after it came out that his father had also been a secret agent in the Communist regime. Ultimately, Medgyessy was able to weather the storm of calls for his resignation. But, in the eyes of the opposition he will always be Comrade D-209.

main parties' positions on everything from EU membership to foreign policy and social welfare. A common European outlook is one of the integrating forces in the HSP-AFD relationship. They have taken a pragmatic, technocratic stance, committing their parties to modernization and treating Europe as practically synonymous with progress. The AFD, in particular, describes EU membership as the key to guaranteeing the democratic order, the rule of law, deepening the market economy, and improving living standards. In contrast, Fidesz and its various partners started out calling for the fastest possible integration of Hungary with EU as part of a "natural claim to harmonize . . . the [country's] position on the cultural map of Europe with . . . [its] position in the European economy."[69] This was consistent

with the right's unwillingness to see Hungary as a relatively poor and backward nation and its insistence that the Hungarian historical legacy is one of successful participation in European Christendom. Fidesz rhetoric in the late 1990s emphasized hard bargaining with Brussels, making it clear that Hungary would dictate the conditions and timing of its membership, and that there is "life outside the Union." Negotiations during the Fidesz coalition's tenure generally continued apace. For the domestic audience, however, the party's rhetoric emphasized its image as a staunch defender of national interests. In particular, Fidesz (and to an even greater extent the more radical members of the right) insisted that Hungary would not blindly accept the EU requirement that it begin to allow foreign acquisition of farmland.

TABLE 11.2   Two Worlds of Hungarian Politics

Orientation:	cosmopolitan urbanist left liberal	national populist right wing
Main Party:	HSP	Fidesz
Others:	AFD	HDF, ISP, CDPP, HJLP

Values/views:	internationalism
	secular
	rational style
	individualist (but with social
	   solidarity)
	approve post-Communist
	   status quo
	Hungary is small, backward
	   state with a dubious past
	accommodate/catch up with West
	pro-EU; EU super-state federalism
		nationalism
		organized Christianity
		emotional style
		collectivist (culture tradition)
		
		dissatisfied with status quo
		   (root out/replace Communists)
		success, survival rebellion
		   against foreign threats
		Third way/Hungarian model
		Euro-skeptical; EU of nations

During and after the 2002 election campaign Fidesz rhetoric has become even more Euro-skeptical, tying this with a broader critique of big business and globalization. During the campaign, Orbán accused the Socialists of shifting their allegiance from Moscow to Brussels. One of his favorite lines was, "The same people who used to lecture us about Socialist internationalism now tell us how to be true Europeans." He also claimed that unless Fidesz won the elections, the Socialists and liberals would enter the EU and allow the motherland to be sold off to foreigners, a move that would push most of Hungary's small farmers off the land. Orbán sharply criticized the Socialist government's support of the U.S. war in Iraq, claiming that the socialist-liberal camp was once again showing its willingness to toady-up to foreign interests. In response to the government's planned health care reforms, a health care expert from Fidesz claimed "Banks and the financial world will gain control over health care modernization." A Fidesz MP and former health minister called the law "anti-life."[70]

For elites, then, this "two worlds" motif has proved a powerful framework for interpreting and acting on post-1990 developments and generating party "brand identification." Only one significant

party, Fidesz, has switched camps. All post-Communist governments have been drawn exclusively from one "world" or the other. Since no government has yet secured reelection, the system has alternated between the two worlds in each election. Journalists associated with the differing camps' newspapers rarely try to hide their biases. In some public professions, affiliation with one camp or the other can be a key to career advancement. Differences between the two worlds also are clearly evident in the way elites speak and behave. The populist-nationalist camp is often depicted in popular discourse as confident (even cocky), arrogant, and aggressive. Fidesz leaders, for example, have suggested that only Fidesz can speak about and for the nation and only Fidesz has earned a right to govern. In the 2002 campaign, one Fidesz deputy called political rivals "traitors" and urged them to set a good example by hanging themselves. Those in the left-liberal camp are alternately painted by their critics as dreamy café-intellectuals (typically stereotyped as urban Jews) or bland, passionless apparatchik-type throwbacks to the Communist era.

What is less clear is how well the two worlds are rooted in Hungarian society. Hungarian voters have looked to a succession of parties to improve their living standards, and some general patterns of party support have emerged over time. It would be an exaggeration to conclude that the two worlds of Hungarian culture represent a reinforcing cleavage structure involving the usual cleavages (class, urban-rural, religious). We cannot say that working class or low income voters overwhelmingly prefer the left-liberal world or that religious voters always choose the populist right.

Voter preferences are still relatively fluid. Across the first two rounds of elections, it is estimated that less than one-fifth of the voting age population was attached to any single party.[71] In a 2002 survey, over a quarter of Hungarian respondents (27 percent) said that there was no party that represents their views.[72] Such voters are not firmly attached to any of the existing parties, and their behavior can be unpredictable, shifting between electoral rounds and between national and local elections. Noncommitted voters look for promises of economic and social security. Arguably it was to those voters that the HDF's 1990 "calm force" slogan was intended to appeal. In 1994, the HSP was able to lure some 43 percent of the weakly attached voters with an appeal to nostalgia for the security of "goulash communism." In 2002, it appears that some of the weakly attached voters were scared off by the Fidesz style and rhetoric and voted Socialist to block another Fidesz-led government.

Data presented in Table 11.3 clearly show that the two main parties draw upon heterogeneous and broadly similar bases of support. There is almost no difference among Fidesz and HSP voters along the lines of gender, education, occupation, and socioeconomic status. Fidesz, as we might expect given the party's rhetoric, is slightly less likely to have irreligious supporters and slightly more likely to be supported by the very religious—but only marginally so. Both Fidesz and the HSP have solid support from those who claim to be moderately religious; and there is no discernible difference in party preference between those who belong to one of the historical churches (Roman Catholic, Lutheran, Calvinist) and those who do not (either because they are attached to a nontraditional church or have no religious affiliation). Fidesz and HSP supporters cross the spectrum of household incomes. Fidesz

TABLE 11.3   Demographic Bases of Party Preference, 2002

Demographic Characteristics	Fidesz	HSP
Gender		
Female	62.5	62.9
Male	37.5	37.1
Educational level		
<Complete secondary education	56.4	53.8
Completed secondary (or vocational)	31.7	33.7
University (some or completed)	11.9	12.5
Urban/rural residence		
Rural	42.4	35.1
Small-mid town	34.8	34.8
Large town/city	22.9	30.0
Region		
Center (Budapest and Pest)	21.6	31.2
Plainland (East)	23.8	17.3
Transdanubia (West)	33.8	25.2
North	7.6	16.4
Northeast	6.7	13.1
Religious feeling		
Irreligious	22.2	35.9
Moderately religious	56.0	53.6
Very religious	21.8	10.5
Religious attachment		
Member of historical church	35.6	35.4
Not a member	64.4	64.6
Occupation		
White collar	35.2	41.6
Worker	51.0	46.0
Farmer	2.8	2.9
Self-employed	11.0	9.5
Household income by quintile		
Lowest	15.8	18.0
Second lowest	21.0	20.3
Middle	22.7	17.6
Second highest	22.3	23.4
Highest	18.2	20.7
Age		
<40 years	40.1	24.6
40–59 years	33.3	38.2
60+ years	26.6	37.1

Source: Comparative Study of Electoral Systems, Hungary 2002.
Note: Respondents named the party that "best represents" their views after the 2002 election. Categories totals may be slightly different from 100% because of rounding error.

actually appears more strongly supported by workers, the traditional cleavage base of leftist parties, than the HSP. Union membership is generally weak in Hungary, and less than 10 percent of HSP or Fidesz supporters in the 2002 survey reported in Table 11.3 claimed to be union members.

The main differences in party support between the two biggest parties are age and region. Fidesz is much more strongly supported among younger voters. The HSP is slightly more preferred among the oldest age cohort. There is also a long-standing regional pattern of voting behavior that is underlined by an urban-rural divide, both of which stack up more neatly with the current cultural divide than either class or religion. The left-liberal camp clearly does better in the center (Budapest and Pest) and in the economically depressed north and northeastern regions. In 2002, Fidesz won only 4 of Budapest's 32 districts, all in the wealthy parts of Buda (the portion of the capital in the hills above the Danube River). The HSP and AFD held onto most of Budapest and the ex-industrial regions in the north and rustbelt cities in the northeast. Fidesz-HDF swept the relatively rich western part of the country, Pest county, and the poorer agricultural regions, winning over half of the provincial constituencies. This pattern has roots dating back as far as 1985.[73] The country is typically seen as dividing in economic and cultural terms along a south-west/north-east (east-west) axis. Culturally, rightist and Christian-national votes have tended to emanate from the west and north of the country, dating all the way back to the 1930s. These regions also see themselves as "winners" in the economic transition. The left vote has historically emanated from the less developed areas in the country and, more recently, from the old industrial areas. This territorial axis holds up still, but it also has an urban-provincial dimension. The AFD draws its support almost exclusively from Budapest. The HSP has also been able to maintain strong support in Budapest. Fidesz performs much better in the provinces, in 2002 picking up much of the ISP's provincial support.

The smaller, less successful parties have more clearly defined cleavage bases. The HJLP draws much of its base from the un- and underemployed and male voters. The extreme left Workers' Party draws much more heavily on workers and the lowest educated strata of society. The AFD's support is drawn almost exclusively from Budapest intellectuals, white-collar workers, and the self-employed, while the HDF and the now defunct CDPP have little support among the irreligious. They rely heavily on the religious and moderately religious. These niche parties have struggled under Hungary's current electoral rules. As we have seen, the parties that have managed to style themselves as broad catch-all people's parties (the HSP and Fidesz) have been far more successful.

That success, in turn, creates incentives for the big parties to expand their social bases even more. Unfortunately, that drive has not led to increasingly moderate or centrist politics. In political systems where the bulk of the electorate is located in the ideological center, majoritarian electoral rules may encourage parties to compete for the middle ground, in some cases making their platforms so ideologically bland that the choice for voters appears to be between "tweedle-dee and tweedle-dum." In Hungary, the electoral rules encourage parties to seek support from the extremes within their "world camp." Figure 11.7 clearly shows that Hungarian voters are not clustered around the middle in terms of their ideological self-placement. The terms left and right may not mean quite the same thing to Hungarians that they do in countries where party competition is structured more clearly around a socioeconomic divide. What is important here is that only slightly more than a quarter of Hungarians place themselves in the center of the spectrum. Thirty-eight percent cluster in the middle three positions on the continuum. Fully 23 percent place themselves in the most extreme left; and 20 percent place themselves in the three positions furthest to the right. The main parties' desire to consolidate their respective camps is seen in the increasingly sharp nationalist rhetoric of Fidesz, even between voting rounds in 2002, and in the HSP's electoral promises to raise wages and negotiate farm protections with the EU.

A two-party system in an ideologically diverse electorate and a landscape dominated by a cultural cleavage does not necessarily produce ideological

FIGURE 11.7   Left-Right Self-Placement of Hungarian Voters, 2002

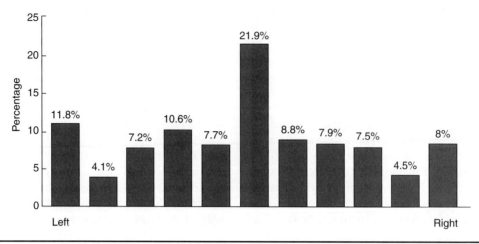

Source: *Comparative Study of Electoral Systems, Hungary* 2002.

moderation or good governance. It is difficult for either major party to win an outright majority, and the potential coalition partners are becoming fewer and weaker. Only strong, sizable coalitions are likely to produce the majorities necessary to enact some of Hungary's most pressing reforms. But, the currently bifurcated party system may not last. The two biggest parties mask a real diversity of opinions. New parties may emerge to better represent voters, or large parties may fragment. Polling data from 2003 onwards show a sharp decline in support for the Socialist government among some of its core constituency, including voters over 50 and Budapest dwellers.[74] Fidesz appears well placed to prevail in the next election. Whether this will give Hungarian voters what they want remains to be seen.

POLICY PROCESS AND PERFORMANCE

One of the keys to the success of multiparty parliamentary democracy in Hungary is the government's ability to create public policies that resolve social conflicts and achieve economic prosperity. Despite the problems with polarization and party bickering in recent years, institutions and processes for making public policy have developed rather quickly.

The idea for a new policy may emerge from a variety of sources—a university study, an MP who sees a problem in his constituency, or an individual citizen. In practice, however, the Hungarian policy process (as in most countries) is dominated by government proposals and those of the prime minister in particular. Legislation can be initiated by MPs, committees, the president of the Republic, and the government. Private initiatives are placed on the agenda only if they have the approval of a committee appointed by the speaker.

Once a bill has been initiated, it must go through three readings (see Figure 11.8 for details of the process). In the first reading, the bill is placed on the legislative calendar and assigned to the relevant committee(s). Any committee or MP can submit amendments to the bill at this time. The committee of jurisdiction takes an especially active role at this stage of the process. It can call on interest groups and ministerial representatives to testify on the proposal and initiate investigative hearings.

There are Twelve Standing Committees in the National Assembly and approximately six special committees. There is also a "supercommittee" which must review all legislation to ensure that it adheres to legal and constitutional norms. The standing committees more or less follow the minis-

FIGURE 11.8   The Legislative Process

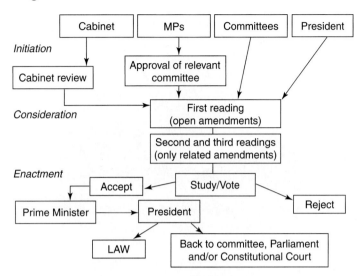

terial divisions and adhere to the Western norm of specialization. Members of the Budget Committee tend to be economists and so forth.

Committee seats are divided in proportion to party strength in the parliament. We might therefore expect voting within the committees to reflect the will of the government. However, since committee chairs and vice chairs are divided between the government and opposition parties, policymaking in committees tends to follow a model of interparty consensus. Fractions maintain a high degree of authority in this process. They bring their own experts and specialists to committee hearings and caucus before the vote in order to establish the party's position.

Once a bill has reached second and third readings, members may submit only amendments related to those made in the first reading. This rule has reduced the overburden of legislative amendments that created logjams in the first parliament. MPs have made wide use of amendments in the past to raise issues of local concern, but rules now require that MP-sponsored amendments receive the support of at least one-third of the relevant committees in order to be voted upon.

When a bill has been through the committee hearings, it is studied and voted upon in a plenary session of the Assembly. If it is approved, it then goes to the prime minister for approval into law. The president must also review the law and has the right to challenge it by sending it back to the committee or to parliament for further discussion, or in some cases referring it to the Constitutional Court. On certain occasions the president has used this power to stall and obstruct legislation that he did not favor. In most cases, however, proposals emanating from the executive pass the Assembly (often in highly modified form) and are enacted into law.

Policy Outputs

Prior to the fall of the Communist empire in the early 1990s, no political system had ever attempted a wholesale shift from central planning to market economics. Privatization of state-owned enterprises was a feature of Thatcherism in Britain, but that project took place on a small scale *within* a stable democracy and a market economy. The task in Hungary has been to build stable democracy while moving from a primarily state-owned economy (with

FIGURE 11.9   Distribution of Total Public Expenditures, 2002

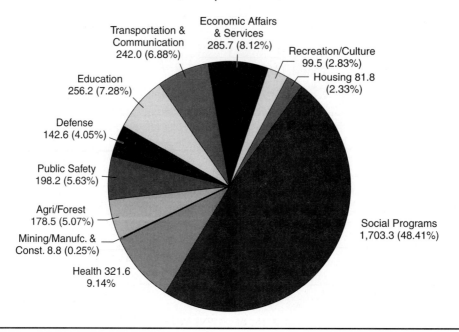

Source: Government Finance Statistics Yearbook (International Monetary Fund, 2002).

Note: In Forint-Billions (total 3,905 billion excluding 1,375 Ft/billion for "other" expenditures)

some market elements) to a fully developed capitalist system.

To date, the deepest and most thorough-going economic reform remains the Bokros package. Despite the promise of Bokros to revamp the nation's public sector, the most prominent area of government activity remains the provision of social welfare (see Figure 11.9). Nearly half of all public spending is devoted to social programs (48.4 percent), with additional spending on health policies.

Each successive government has brought a shift in worldview, and that has resulted in a kind of ping-pong match over the details of social welfare, particularly family policy. The Socialists and their liberal allies have sought to reduce public spending by reducing benefit levels and restricting access—in short, moving Hungary away from a universal access model to a means-testing model. The right-national camp sees family policy as central to its notion of national renewal. It introduced policies that promise very generous leave and child benefit

policies and replaced means-testing with lifestyle tests (appealing to the Christian-traditionalist streams of the populist-right).

Throughout this process, critics have noted that Hungary continues to underinvest in education, spending only a slightly higher percentage of the budget than under the Communist governments (see Figure 11.9). Medgyessy and the Socialists promised to remedy this in the 2002 campaign, but their only real measures were to immediately hike the wages of some teachers as much as 50 percent. Teachers in Hungary are woefully underpaid, but the way in which the wage increase was handled smacked more of politics than real policy change. Reforms of health care, pensions, and agriculture, areas notably absent from the Fidesz coalition's agenda, have been raised by the HSP-AFD government. Infighting, scandals, and cabinet reshuffles have sidetracked the ability of the fragile coalition to accomplish much in those areas. Rural interests, doctors, and pensioners form unusually proactive

Box 11.5 How Much Should I Tip the Doctor?

In Hungary, the healthcare system is supposedly free, but a recent survey of corruption in Budapest found that 71 percent of respondents think that doctors and nurses have to be offered gifts in return for their services, 59 percent believe that bribery is necessary to get things done in the private sector, and 46 percent believe that police must be bribed. Most consider gratuities paid to public employees unethical, but fewer than one in three believe it is corrupt to give a gratuity to a doctor. The practice of tipping started before WWII, when uninsured rural residents traditionally paid for medical services with small amounts of cash or gifts—fresh eggs, sausage, or homemade brandy. Peasants continued this practice after the communists created universal medical coverage in 1952, but amounts remained modest until the arrival of the free market. As some Hungarians became wealthier, they changed tipping from a small token of gratitude to a means of attaining better and faster service. Today, there are no official rates, but as an example of scale: the average monthly after tax salary is 89,000 forints; the gratuity for a baby delivery is typically between 50,000–100,000 forints. Senior doctors benefit most

from the system. Hungarians pay an estimated 50 to 100 billion forints annually in tips to doctors, but fewer than 20 percent of the doctors collect over 80 percent of the gratuities. This distorts investment as well. For example, many hospitals have ultrasound and CT scanners—with access jealously guarded by senior doctors because their use usually garners a tip—but hygiene is not properly maintained in bathrooms and cafeterias. The tipping system, say critics, shows that doctors are not accountable and patients are not given the choice or level of service the system promises. Reforms have been resisted by the Hungarian Doctor's Chamber, which maintains that tipping is simply a traditional practice and that legal limitations would threaten the authority and autonomy of physicians.

Data: Gallup-UNICRI (United Nations Interregional Crime Research Institute), March 2000, N=1513.

Christopher Condon, "Hungary's Patience Running Out on Doctors' Insistence on Right to Tips," *The Financial Times, Limited*, March 9, 2004, Tuesday, London, Edition 3.

and critical constituencies, making reform delicate and politically risky (see Box 11.5). In order to fulfill the desire of Hungarians for steady improvement of living conditions and strong social rights, government will eventually have to tackle those tough problems.

PAYING THE PRICE OF NEGOTIATED REVOLUTION?

In May of 2004, Hungary entered the European Union. That moment marked the culmination of a remarkable journey away from the political and economic system that kept Hungary from participating in European prosperity and democracy for 40 years. The question today is not whether Hungary will become a part of Europe. It already is, and the focus has shifted to debates over how quickly Hungary can enter the Eurozone. Even the great policy challenge of post-communism—transition to a market economy—is now converging with the

Europe-wide concern about how to balance citizen demands for extensive social welfare with economic growth and tough financial constraints. Despite some bumpy relations in the late nineties, Hungary has also forged peaceful relations with all of its neighbors.

Students born in the 1980s may find it difficult to imagine that things could have turned out differently. The Hungarian revolution of 1989 may not have broken a single window pane, but earlier uprisings and revolutions in Hungarian history were tragically violent. Some hardliners in the HSWP believed (and believe to this day) that the Communist regime could have been maintained with a sufficient application of force. The peaceful transfer of power in 1989–1990 was not inevitable. It was the product of choices made by political actors. Those choices have helped Hungary to swiftly develop working democratic and market institutions and integrate with European and global economic, security, and political frameworks.

The smoothness of the transition, however, is not entirely without costs. The contemporary polarization into "two worlds" may be one legacy. Communists were never purposively purged from public life until the Fidesz government came to power in 1998. That fact has allowed Fidesz to mobilize and unify the right by folding those associated with the former Communists into a broader category that they juxtapose to "bourgeois citizens' society." More than a decade after the fall of communism, this framework still has resonance, because many Hungarians believe that there has been little change in the economic and power elite of the country. It does not matter that millions of Hungarians were involved, either directly or indirectly, with the former ruling HSWP. There is still deep popular hostility to the nomenklatura and to the idea of people getting ahead through connections. For elites that mobilize that hostility, the nomenklatura is always "them" and not "us."

The hybrid electoral rules negotiated by softline Communists and a relatively weak and fragmented opposition have helped transform this cultural cleavage into a bifurcated party system. The almost-two-party system obscures wide variation in opinion and groupings and encourages a hollowing out of the center. Between the first and second round of district voting in 2002, for example, Fidesz sought to overturn the first-round success of the HSP by becoming more radical, not by heading to the center to capture noncommitted voters as we might expect in a two-party system. In this way, Fidesz sought to secure the support of HJLP and ISP supporters whose parties had collapsed. If Hungarian voters were concentrated in the center of the spectrum on the cultural or socioeconomic cleavage, an electoral system that creates competition between large parties might lead to moderate politics. All of the incentives would be in place to compete for the center ground. That is not the case in Hungary.

For some of Hungary's neighbors, this complaint must seem a bit like crying for the "poor little rich kid." In Poland and Ukraine, the thought of bifurcation and consolidation of their volatile and fragmented party systems might seem like very nice work indeed. That feature of Hungarian politics has afforded a high level of political stability. But, it is also contributing to political infighting, deadlock, and sporadically implemented policies. Voters are disgusted by the endless round of scandals, as data on trust in parties amply demonstrate.

The Socialists are not quite sure who they are, at least in the sense that they clearly are no longer the party of the working class. They can't even come to agreement on a party member as their prime minister. They have come to be known as a party of big business and the free market, but they also tend to pick up support from the regional "losers" of the transition. Viktor Orbán and Fidesz, on the other hand, seem to be whatever they think will unify the disparate strands on the right. They act like a party of power with remarkably transformist aspirations. This is not a very comfortable image given the historical record of populism in Hungary. Both of the main parties can be accused of working primarily to discredit their opponents, and they are helped in this endeavor by partisan newspapers. Meanwhile, it seems Hungarian citizens mostly want to be boring and prosperous. They are getting fed up with party politics and often seem motivated from election to election by a desire to throw out the bums. The majority, however, do not seek extra-constitutional remedies for their grievances. Democracy is well accepted, and conflicts center on different views of Hungary's historical and national identity and how best to move the nation forward.

 Key Terms

| Alliance of Free Democrats (AFD) | Bokros csomag (Bokros package) | constructive vote of non-confidence | Hungarian Justice and Life Party (HJLP) |
| Alliance of Young Democrats-Civic Party (Fidesz) | Christian Democratic People's Party (CDPP) | goulash communism Hungarian Democratic Forum (HDF) | Hungarian Socialist Party (HSP); the main successor to the HSWP |

| Hungarian Socialist Workers' Party (HSWP); the former Communist Party | Independent Smallholders' Party (ISP) Kádárism Kiegyezés Magyar | Magyarization New Economic Mechanism (NEM) nomenklatura populism | Roma Roundtable Talks scrap votes soft dictatorship Trianon Treaty urbanism |

Internet Source

Hungarian Parliament: http://www.parlament.hu/parl_en.htm
Portal to government agencies: http://www.magyarorszag.hu/angol/orszaginfo
Hungarian Embassy in the United States: http://www.huembwas.org/

Hungarian resources online: http://www.hungaria.org
Budapest Sun Newspaper: http://www.budapestsun.com/
Gallup Opinion Data for Hungary: http://www.gallup.hu/english.htm

Suggested Readings

Andorka, Rudolf, Tamás Kolosi, Richard Rose, and György Vukovich, eds. *A Society Transformed: Hungary in Time-Space Perspective.* Budapest: Central European University Press, 1999.

Bozoki, Andras, and John T. Ishiyama. *The Communist Successor Parties of Central and Eastern Europe.* Armonk, NY: M. E. Sharpe, Inc., 2002.

Fowler, Brigid. "Nation, State, Europe, and National Revival in Hungarian Party Politics: The Case of the Millennial Celebrations," in *Europe-Asia Studies,* Vol. 56, No. 1, January 2004, 57–83.

Haney, Lynne. *Inventing the Needy: Gender and the Politics of Welfare in Hungary.* Berkeley, University of California Press, 2002.

Janos, Andrew C. *The Politics of Backwardness in Hungary, 1825–1945.* Princeton: Princeton University Press, 1982.

Korosenyi, Andras. *Government and Politics in Hungary.* Budapest: CEU Press, 1999.

Lendvai, Paul. *Hungary: The Art of Survival.* London: I. B. Tauris, 1988.

O'Neil, Patrick. *Revolution from Within: the Hungarian Socialist Workers' Party and the Collapse of Communism.* Northampton, MA: E. Elgar, 1998.

Sugar, Peter, et al., eds. *A History of Hungary.* Bloomington, Indiana: Indiana University Press, 1994.

Tökés, Rudolf L. *Hungary's Negotiated Revolution: Economic Reforms, Social Change, and Political Succession: 1957–1990.* Cambridge: Cambridge University Press, 1996.

Endnotes

1. János Simon, "Post-Paternalist Political Culture in Hungary: Relationship Between Citizens and Politics During and After the 'Melancholic Revolution' (1989–1991)," *Communist and Post-Communist Studies* 26, No. 2 (1993): 226–38.

2. Anna Seleny, "Old Political Rationalities and New Democracies: Compromise and Confrontation in Hungary and Poland" *World Politics,* Vol. 51, No. 4, 1999, p. 488. Seleny sets forth the notion that Hungary represents a corporatist bargaining model of consolidation and outlines the ways in which both the formal and informal manifestations of this model emanate from pre-transition political rationalities and discourses.

3. For an interesting discussion see: Rogers Smith, *Stories of Peoplehood* (Cambridge University Press, 2003).

4. David Stark, "Path Dependence and Privatization Strategies in East Central Europe," *East European Politics and Society* 6 (1992): 17–54; and Aaslund, "Old Political Rationalities and New Democracies."

5. A number of political scientists now draw upon the notion of "path dependency" to explain institutional choices, arguing that political actors may choose their institutions but they do not do so under conditions of their own design. This idea has its origins in the work of Douglass North; see, for example,

his *Institutions, Institutional Change, and Economic Performance* (Cambridge, England: Cambridge University Press, 1992).

6. George Schöpflin, "The Political Traditions of Eastern Europe," *Daedalus* 119, No. 1 (Winter 1990).

7. For background on Hungarian history, see Peter F. Sugar, Péter Hanák, and Tibor Frank, eds., *A History of Hungary* (Bloomington: Indiana University Press, 1990); Nigel Swain, *The Rise and Fall of Feasible Socialism* (London: Verso, 1992); Ivan Volgyes, *Hungary: A Nation of Contradictions* (Boulder: Westview Press, 1982); William Shawcross, *Crime and Compromise: Janos Kadar and the Politics of Hungary Since the Revolution* (New York: E. P. Dutton & Company, 1974); William F. Robinson, *The Pattern of Reform in Hungary: A Political, Economic, and Cultural Analysis* (New York: Praeger, 1973); Hans-Georg Heinrich, *Hungary: Politics, Economics, Society* (Boulder: Lynne Reinner, 1986); and Elemer Hankiss, *East European Alternatives* (Oxford: Clarendon Press, 1990).

8. Quoted in Paul Lendvai, *Hungary: The Art of Survival* (London: I. B. Tauris, 1988), p. 12.

9. From Brigid Fowler's analysis of the Hungarian Millennial Celebrations, "Nation, State, Europe and National Revival in Hungarian Party Politics: The Case of the Millennial Commemorations," *Europe-Asia Studies*, Vol. 56, No. 1, January 2004, 57–83.

10. For this reference and a useful summary of Hungarian political history, see Tamás Kolosi and Richard Rose, "Introduction: Scaling Change in Hungary" in Rudolf Andorka, et al., eds., *A Society Transformed: Hungary in Time-Space Perspective* (Budapest: Central European University Press, 1999).

11. For a detailed discussion of this point, see Joseph Rothschild, *Return to Diversity* (Oxford: Oxford University Press, 1993), pp. 3–24.

12. For example, before the Antall government came to power, taxis, restaurants, hotels, and small shops were allowed to operate under private ownership or rental bases. Small-scale industrial enterprises with 20 (and later as many as 40) were also allowed, but the large, heavy industries (the nation's major employers) remained in state hands. In the 1980s, however, even these were broken down into smaller units. For example, the shoe and meat industrial conglomerates or trusts were broken into member companies that were granted independence. This organizational decentralization was expected to aid in the process of privatization and was seen as a leg-up over countries like Russia and Czechoslovakia.

13. János Kornai, *The Road to a Free Economy: Shifting from a Socialist System: The Example of Hungary* (New York: Norton, 1990).

14. András Bozóki, András Körösényi, and George Schöpflin, eds., *Post-Communist Transition: Emerging Pluralism in Hungary* (London: Pinter, 1992).

15. Béla Király and András Bozóki, eds., *Lawful Revolution in Hungary* (New York: Columbia University Press, 1995); Patrick O'Neil, "Revolution from Within: Institutional Analysis, Transitions from Authoritarianism and the Case of Hungary," *World Politics* 48, No. 4 (1996).

16. Fowler, 58.

17. Ákos Róna-Tas, "The First Shall Be Last? Entrepreneurship and Communist Cadres in the Transition from Socialism," *American Journal of Sociology* 100, No. 1 (July 1994): 40–69.

18. T. Kolosi, "Gazdagabbak lettünk?" [Are we richer?], *Népszabadság* (September 25, 1993), p. 14.

19. Éva Ehrlich and Gábor Révész, *Hungary and Its Prospects: 1985–2005* (Budapest: Akadémia Kiadó, 1995).

20. Paul Lendvai, *Anti-Semitism Without Jews: Communist Eastern Europe* (Garden City, NY: Doubleday, 1971).

21. Martin Gilbert, *Atlas of the Holocaust* (New York: MacMillan, 1982), p. 44; Martin Gilbert, *The Holocaust: A Record of the Destruction of Jewish Life in Europe During the Dark Years of Nazi Rule* (New York: Noonday Press, 1975), p. 22.

22. Hungarian Gallup Institute data and Szonda-Ipsos party support data in this section reported in: "Batthany Report: Public Opinion Surveys in the Press," prepared by the InnoRural Research Group for the Lajos Batthany Foundation, September 2003.

23. Barbara Einhorn, *Cinderella Goes to Market: Citizenship, Gender and Women's Movements in East Central Europe* (London: Verso, 1993); Chris Corrin, ed., *Superwomen and the Double Burden: Women's Experience of Change in Central and Eastern Europe and the Former Soviet Union* (London: Scarlet Press, 1992); Marilyn Rueschemeyer, *Women in the Politics of Post-Communist Eastern Europe* (Armonk NY: M. E. Sharpe, 1994).

24. Beth Stark, Sue Thomas, and Clyde Wilcox, "Popular Support for Electing Women in Eastern Europe," in Richard Matland and Kathleen Montgomery, eds., *Women's Access to Political Power in Post-Communist Europe* (Oxford: Oxford University Press, 2003).

25. Richard Matland and Kathleen Montgomery, eds., *Women's Access to Political Power in Post-Communist Europe* (Oxford: Oxford University Press, 2003).

26. On this point, see Patrick O'Neil, "Presidential Power in Post-Communist Europe: The Hungarian Case in Comparative Perspective," *The Journal of Communist Studies* 9, No. 3 (1993).

27. MP interview quoted in Seleny, 1999, p. 496.

28. Attila Ágh, "The Permanent 'Constitutional Crisis' in the Democratic Transition: The Case of Hungary," in Joachim Jens Hesse and Vincent Wright, *Constitutional Policy and Change in Europe* (Oxford: Oxford University Press, 1995), pp. 296–326.

29. Records of parliamentary activities are available to the public in Hungarian through the *Országgyülési Napló* (Parliamentary Diary) and the *Országgyülési Almanach* (Parliamentary Almanac).

30. Racz, 749.

31. The Constitution of the Republic of Hungary, Chapter III, Section 29.

32. *Statistical Yearbook on CECs 1998—A Statistical View of Central Europe* (Luxembourg: Eurostat Press Office).

33. Schiemann, John, Myopic Bargains, Transitions to Democracy, and Democratic Consolidation: The Negotiated Ori-

gins of Hungary's Constitutional Court (Paper prepared for the Midwest Political Science Association Meeting, Chicago, April 23–25, 1998).

34. Ágh, "Democratic Parliamentarism," p. 19.

35. Csaba Varga, *Transition to the Rule of Law: On the Democratic Transformation in Hungary* (Budapest: Project on Comparative Legal Cultures of the Faculty of Law of Loránd Eötvös University and the Institute for Legal Studies of the Hungarian Academy of Sciences, 1995).

36. Cited in Bennett Kovrig, *Communism in Hungary, from Kun to Kádár* (Stanford, CA: Hoover Institution Press, 1979), p. 350.

37. On Communist-era political socialization, see Iván Völgyes, *Political Socialization in Eastern Europe: A Comparative Framework* (New York: Praeger, 1975).

38. This according to a 2000 poll conducted by the Czech opinion poll agency IVVM and its colleague agencies in Poland (CBOS) and Hungary (TARKI). The sample questioned in each country was between 1,000–1,500.

39. Candidate Countries Eurobarometer 2003.4 published online by *The Gallup Organization, Hungary*, 2003.

40. Rose and Haerpfer, "Change and Stability," p. 35.

41. Susan Gal and Gail Kligman, *The Politics of Gender After Socialism* (Princeton, NJ: Princeton University Press, 2000), p. 54.

42. The retraditionalization of gender roles in Hungary and other East European countries has been written about at length. Good sources include: Matland and Montogmery, *Women's Access to Political Power in Post-Communist Europe*; Gal and Kligman, *The Politics of Gender After Socialism*. See also: Ronald Inglehart and Pippa Norris, *Rising Tide: Gender Equality and Cultural Change Around the World* (Cambridge: Cambridge University Press, 2003).

43. For historical background see: Helen Ridley, et al., "Civic Education for Democracy in Hungary," *International Journal of Social Education*, Vol. 12, No. 2, Spring–Summer, 1997: pp. 62–72.

44. Report of the Országos Közoktatási Intézet (National Public Education Institute) "The Strengths and Weaknesses of the System" and "The Socio-Economic Environment of Education" (1998) available from the Hungarian Ministry of Education website. http://www.oki.hu/.

45. Mihály Gálik, "Hungary" in Media Ownership and Its Impact on Media Independence and Pluralism" proceedings of the Regional Conference, Bled, Slovenia 11–12 June 2004.

46. Gálik, p. 215.

47. Ildiko Kaposi, "Voices from the Hungarian Edge," Global Media Ownership Discussion, Open Democracy Institute, 5/12/2001.

48. Robert Putnam, *Bowling Alone: The Collapse and Revival of American Community* (Simon and Schuster, New York, 2001).

49. According to the 1991 Times-Mirror "Pulse of Europe" Survey, Hungarians displayed the lowest interest in politics of any of the Eastern or Western European countries in the survey.

50. Andorka, "Dissatisfaction and Alienation" in Andorka, et al., p. 149.

51. See David Judge and Gabriella Ilonszki, "Member-Constituency Linkages in the Hungarian Parliament," *Legislative Studies Quarterly* 20, No. 2 (1995); Kathleen Montgomery, "Interest Group Representation in the Hungarian Parliament," in Attila Ágh and Gabriella Ilonszki, eds., *Parliaments and Organized Interests: The Second Steps* (Budapest: Hungarian Centre for Democracy Studies, 1996).

52. Terry Cox and Laszlo Vass, "Government-Interest Group Relations in Hungarian Politics Since 1989," *Europe-Asia Studies*, Vol. 52, No. 6 (2000): 1095–1114.

53. Zsofia Szilagyi, "Communication Breakdown Between the Government and the Public," in *Transition: Events and Issues in the Former Soviet Union and East-Central and Southeastern Europe* 2, 6 (March 1996), pp. 41–43.

54. László Bruszt and János Simon, "The Change in Citizens' Political Orientations During the Transition to Democracy in Hungary" (Budapest: Institute of Political Science of Hungarian Academy of Sciences, 1990–1991); Hankiss, *East European Alternatives*, p. 204.

55. Péter Róbert, "A szociálpolitikával kapcsolatos attitüdök alakulása" [Changing Attitudes on Social Welfare] in *Magyarország politikai évkönyve* [Political Yearbook of Hungary] (Budapest: Hungarian Center for Democracy Studies, 1996).

56. From Candidate Countries Eurobarometer, "Attitudes Related to Defrauding the European Union and Its Budget." European Commission: European Office in the Fight Against Fraud. January 2004.

57. Edith Oltay, "The Former Communists' Election Victory in Hungary," *RFE/RL* 3, 25 (June 24, 1994).

58. Barnabas Racz and István Kukorelli, "The 'Second Generation' Post-Communist Elections in Hungary in 1994," *Europe-Asia Studies*, 47, No. 2 (1995): 251–79.

59. Summary of arguments in Terry Cox and Laszlo Vass, "Government-Interest Group Relations in Hungarian Politics Since 1989," *Europe-Asia Studies*, Vol. 52, No. 6 (2000): 1095–1114.

60. Miklós Tomka and István Harcsa, "Religious Denomination and Practice," in Andorka, et al., eds., *A Society Transformed: Hungary in Time-Space Perspective* (Budapest: CEU, 1999), pp. 61–72.

61. Kathleen Montgomery and Gabriella Ilonszki, "Weak Mobilization, Hidden Majoritarianism, and Resurgence of the Right: A Recipe for Female Under-Representation in Hungary" in Matland and Montgomery, eds., *Women's Access to Political Power in Post-Communist Europe*.

62. Ehrlich and Révész, *Hungary and Its Prospects*, p. 88.

63. Ronald Inglehart, *Modernization and Postmodernization* (Princeton: Princeton University Press, 1997).

64. Éva Hajba, "The Rise and Fall of the Hungarian Greens," in Terry Cox and Andy Furlong, eds., *Hungary: The Politics of Transition* (London: Frank Cass, 1995).

65. István Kukorelli, "The Birth, Testing, and Results of the 1989 Hungarian Electoral Law," *Soviet Studies* 43, No. 1 (1991): 143.

66. By now the details of the Hungarian electoral system and its consequences have been summarized in numerous articles. For example, see John R. Hibbing and Samuel C. Patterson, "A Democratic Legislature in the Making: The Historic Hungarian Elections of 1990," *Comparative Political Studies* 24, No. 4 (January 1992); Kukorelli, "The Birth, Testing, and Results of the 1989 Hungarian Electoral Law"; András Körösényi, "Hungary," *Electoral Studies* 9, No. 4 (December 1990); John T. Ishiyama, "Electoral System Experimentation in the New Eastern Europe: The Single Transferable Vote and the Additional Members System in Estonia and Hungary," *East European Quarterly* 29, No. 4 (Winter 1995).

67. The AFD was finally granted membership in the Liberal International in September 1993 after three years of confusion over whether the party should be considered liberal or social democratic.

68. Barnabas Racz, "The Left in Hungary and the 2002 Parliamentary Elections," *Europe Asia Studies*, Vol. 55, No. 5 (2003): 747–69.

69. Quoted in Agnes Batory, "The Political Context of EU Ascension in Hungary," The Royal Institute of European Affairs: European Programme Briefing Paper, November 2002.

70. Quoted in Financial Times Information, Hungarian News Agency, MTI (May 5, 2004), "Opposition Critical of Government's Healthcare Reform Plans."

71. Ferenc Gaszó and István Stumpf, "Parties and Voters After Two Elections," in *Hungarian Parliamentary Election 1994*, a report of the Institute for Political Science of the Hungarian Academy of Sciences, 1994.

72. Comparative Study of Electoral Systems, 2001–2006. Data available through the University of Michigan's Inter-University Consortium for Political and Social Research (ICPSR), 2004.

73. Racz, Barnabas, "Regional Voting Trends in Hungarian National Elections 1985–2002." *East European Quarterly* XXXVII, No. 4 (2004).

74. Bathyanyi Report, 2003.

Chapter 12

Politics in the European Union

ALBERTA SBRAGIA

European Union Bio

POPULATION: 453.7 Million

TERRITORY: 2,372 sq. mi

YEAR OF LEGAL CREATION: 1958

PRESIDENT: Rotates among member-states

LANGUAGES: German 19.8%, French 14.2%, English 13.7%, Italian 12.7%, Spanish 8.7%, Polish 8.5%, Other 22.4%

RELIGION: Roman Catholic 58%, Protestant 20%, Jewish 0.2%, Muslim 2%, Orthodox 3%, Other & unaffiliated 16.8%

The *European Union (EU)* represents a remarkable attempt by the nation-states of Europe to construct a framework of governance in which together they make collective decisions about a broad range of issues. As an organization, the EU is far more legally authoritative and institutionally sophisticated than any other international body. The 25 member nations have not, however, renounced the vigorous pursuit of their "national interest" in any policy area. Yet, by agreeing to pursue that interest within an organization as constraining as the European Union, the member-states have recognized the ultimate superiority of multilateral, as opposed to unilateral, decision making and action in a variety of policy arenas.

The term European Union is often used interchangeably with the term European Community. The original European Economic Community (EEC) established with the Treaty of Rome in 1958 gradually came to be known as the European Community (EC). The Treaty of Maastricht changed the name of the EC to the European Union. In certain legal contexts, however, the term European Community is still used. In this chapter, we determine usage by what seems most appropriate given the historical period being discussed.

Although the European Union resembles an international organization in certain ways, it is in fact very different. To begin with, it includes institutions that are not directly controlled by the member-states and that exercise real policymaking power. Although the EU has similarities to a traditional national political system, it is clearly distinct from the other political systems discussed in this book. For example, it does not have its own military or its own police force, and it does not belong to the United Nations. It is not a sovereign entity in the way that traditional nation-states are sovereign in international affairs. Furthermore, it is governed without a prime minister and a cabinet as found in traditional parliamentary democracies. Rather than being governed by an elected government, a group of institutions collectively makes EU policy. Although the EU produces binding laws, the fact that it does so without having a traditional "government" is perhaps the EU's most confusing feature.

National governments believe that by becoming members of the Union, they can achieve both peace and prosperity for themselves and for Europe. The Union is an experiment in "pooling sovereignty." National governments have over time agreed to restrict their own ability to make decisions unilaterally; they have agreed to make decisions in concert with other member governments and with institutions that are not under their control. In many policy areas, a national government, when outvoted by other governments, is legally required to comply with the decision it opposed. This process does not cover all policy areas, but it does cover many. Unilateral decision making by national governments has become less frequent as the EU's policy agenda has gradually expanded.

The consequences of belonging to the European Union are serious for member-states. In fact, some analysts have calculated that "today only 20 to 25 percent of the legal texts applicable in France are produced by the [French] parliament or the government in complete autonomy, that is, without any previous consultation in Brussels."[1] Membership in the Union is not to be taken lightly, for it changes the policy processes and the policy outcomes of national political systems. Membership carries with it serious and binding economic and political commitments. Individual nations belonging to the Union can be increasingly thought of as member-states of a larger collectivity that shapes their policy options. However, membership does not change the culture of a country—the same language is spoken before and after accession, for example, and its "way of life" goes on after accession as it did before. A country makes a serious political and economic commitment when it joins the European Union but it does not commit to changing its culture.

WHY "EUROPE"?

Why have the individual nation-states of Europe—among the oldest in the world—decided to "pool their sovereignty"? Why have they accepted the sharing of power with institutions not directly controlled by the member-states? After all, political scientists tend to argue that the protection and maintenance of sovereignty is the top priority of governments throughout the world. Why did the process of European integration begin in the first place?

National leaders initiated the drive for European integration out of fear—fear that the history of European warfare would repeat itself unless they found a new way in which to live together. At its core, the Union is rooted in the desire to transcend European history, a history filled with "rivers of blood" to use Winston Churchill's famous phrase. European integration is an attempt to change the geopolitics of Europe. By entangling the domestic institutions of individual nation-states within the institutions of the European Union, integration has changed (hopefully forever) the relations between European states. Such a change in international relations, however, has "fed back" into national political systems. Domestic policies, institutions, and modes of governance have been changed by virtue of belonging to the Union.[2]

The integration effort was initially anchored in the belief that it represents the best answer to what is known as "the German Question." That is, integration (rather than confrontation) was the best way to keep Germany firmly in the company of peaceful democratic nations and to keep it from playing a destructive role in European geopolitics. The attempt to ensure that Germany was a cooperative rather than a threatening neighbor led to a historic restructuring of relations among European states. This has also had a significant impact on domestic politics and policy.

Although the fear of potential German aggression was an initial motive for European integration, other important spurs to integration have more recently come into play. European business firms' fear of losing competitiveness relative to American and Japanese firms is one such spur. A growing acceptance that international problems such as environmental pollution, illegal immigration, and organized crime require transnational solutions is another. The less than stellar European role in dealing with the various Balkan crises, including Kosovo, has pushed governments to increase their coordination in the defense area.

The enlargement of the Union from 15 to 25 members in May 2004 led national leaders to agree on a constitutional treaty (commonly referred to as a "constitution for Europe") that will be either ratified or rejected by national parliaments or referenda in the next few years.

Government leaders have acknowledged, sometimes reluctantly, that together they can have a much greater impact on problems than through individual action. Essentially, they have had to decide whether they wanted to exercise "a share of more effective power or [have] exclusive control over a less effective or wholly ineffective power."[3] Old-fashioned sovereignty—that is exclusive control over policymaking—is associated with "naive sovereignty."[4] The result is that Brussels, the city that symbolizes the European Union, has gradually come to supplement, constrain, lead, and at times supplant national capitals.

The international (European) relations and the domestic politics of the members of the European Union are increasingly intertwined. While the Union is not a traditional state and cannot be viewed as the "United States of Europe," it is an extremely important form of governance. A complete analysis of politics, policymaking, and economics in any member-state must consider the impact of the Union.

National governments have sometimes led this effort at integration. At other times, they have acquiesced in accepting it, or they have resisted it. Whatever their stance toward European integration, however, national governments play a key role in shaping and directing it. The institutions of the Community not controlled by the member-states, including the European Court of Justice, also play a role in keeping the process of integration moving, especially when the member-states do not exercise leadership.

The European Union is now so important that much of what happens in national capitals cannot be understood without considering Brussels. However, neither can one understand what happens in Brussels without taking national capitals into account.[5] Brussels is not nearly as divorced from national politics as is Washington from the politics of state capitals in the United States.[6]

The European Union's political system is entangled with the politics of its constituent member-states while simultaneously having its own separate institutional identity and political dynamics. That balance between entanglement and autonomy makes it both complex and fascinating. The "separateness" of the Union's political dynamics is rooted in the role of the various institutions involved in the policymaking process at the Union level, institutions that form a highly sophisticated and complex policymaking machinery. Most of those institutions do not strictly represent the interests of national governments. This means that national governments operating within the Union need to accommodate, respond to, and compromise with institutions representing the "supranational" interest.

HISTORICAL ORIGINS

Precisely because of the linkage between national systems and the European Union discussed earlier, the Union is considered to be *sui generis*. Although it is recognizable to students of federal systems such as the United States, Canada, and the Federal Republic of Germany, it is also recognizable to students of international organizations such as the United Nations. In fact, the Union as a political system stands somewhere between a federal system and an international organization. To understand why—and why it is still moving along that continuum—it is important to understand its historical origins.

Those origins have shaped subsequent developments much as the historical underpinnings of the American Constitution have shaped American politics. Its historical origins help explain why the Union does not look more like a traditional state, why the electorate often plays an indirect role, and why the national governments play such an important role in a framework that does have strong supranational elements to it.

The European Union is the most important institutional manifestation of the process of European integration. It has succeeded in moving toward an integrated Europe, whereas other European institutions (such as the completely separate Council of Europe) have not. The desire for integration is rooted in European history, much of it the result of the numerous and bloody centuries-old conflicts between France and Germany (see Chapters 6 and 7).

Recent history makes it clear why so many in postwar Europe were afraid that the past would continue to haunt Europe's future. Between 1870 (the Franco-Prussian War) and 1945, France and Germany had fought three times, twice in conflicts so vast that they were known as "world" wars. Only 21 years separated the end of World War I (1918) from the beginning of World War II (1939). Both France and Germany had also been involved in the traumatic Spanish Civil War (1933–1936), which foreshadowed the world war to come.

European integration is linked to the creation of institutions that have some autonomy apart from the member governments. While member governments continue to be pivotal, they are not the only important actors. Institutions that have some independence from the member governments are also important. The existence of such independent institutions—cohabiting with institutions that are more tightly controlled by member governments—is known as "supranationality." Intergovernmentalism, by contrast, refers to institutional arrangements in which only national governments matter in the making of policy. European integration therefore is symbolized by a supranational component existing alongside an intergovernmental one. The symbiotic relationship between the two makes the politics of European integration so intriguing.

Supranational Integration: Schuman, Monnet, and the European Coal and Steel Community

The effort toward European integration—understood as having a supranational component—dates from May 9, 1950 and the *Schuman Plan* (see Figure 12.1). On that day, French Foreign Minister Robert Schuman proposed the creation of an international organization to coordinate activity in the coal and steel industries. Designed to ensure Franco-German reconciliation and representing "a first step in the federation of Europe," Schuman's proposal represented a reversal of French foreign policy toward Germany. France changed from a policy of unremitting hostility to one of reconciliation. Rather than viewing Russia/USSR as the key to constraining German power (the view historically taken by France), Schuman envisioned a Germany embedded in an integrated framework as the way to constrain German might. That view was a radical break with the past and helps explain why today's European Union represents such an extraordinary development. At its core, the Union has attempted to break the underlying dynamics of European geopolitical history.

Above all, the Schuman Plan was, in Schuman's own words, "a leap into the unknown."[7] France declared its willingness to restrict its own sovereignty in the fields of coal and steel in order to ensure that German sovereignty would be equally limited. Reconciliation was tried as an alternative to the "balance of power" international game that had brought so much death and destruction to Europe. Schuman hoped that war would become "politically unthinkable and economically impossible."[8]

That "leap into the unknown" had been designed by Jean Monnet, then general commissary for the French Plan of Modernization and Equipment. Monnet developed the plan in an atmosphere of tremendous secrecy. Monnet was to play a critical role in the process of European integration throughout the following decade and beyond, so much so that he is sometimes referred to as "Mr. Europe." Monnet underscored the strategic impor-

FIGURE 12.1 The Timetable for European Integration

May 1950	Schuman Plan
1952	Treaty of Paris (European Coal and Steel Community) (ECSC)
1954	European Defense Community defeated
1958	Treaty of Rome—European Economic Community (EEC)
1966	Luxembourg Compromise (Legitimated use of national veto)
1973	Britain, Denmark, and Ireland join the EC
1979	Direct election of European Parliament
1981	Greece joins the EC
1986	Spain and Portugal join the EC
1987	Single European Act (SEA)
1993	Maastricht Treaty
1995	Austria, Sweden, and Finland join the EU
1999	Introduction of euro as a "virtual" currency, Treaty of Amsterdam
2002	The euro is introduced into daily use
2003	Treaty of Nice
2004	The EU enlarges to 10 new countries: Cyprus, Czech Republic, Estonia, Hungary, Latvia, Lithuania, Malta, Poland, Slovakia, Slovenia
2004	Member-states agree on the European constitution

tance of having a "supranational" component in any initiative designed to achieve integration. In his view, supranationality was necessary to prevent the old interstate balance of power dynamics from becoming preeminent. His role in articulating the importance of supranationality in European integration was so important that many consider Monnet to be "the most important single architect of the European Community."[9]

The Franco-German relationship lay at the core of the Schuman Plan, and that relationship remains the central one within the process of European integration. France is Germany's key interlocutor in Europe, and Germany is France's key referent. When they agree on the need for further integration, France and Germany provide the political energy, the driving force, and the momentum for achieving further integration.

In addition to reversing French foreign policy toward Germany, the Schuman Plan invited democratic nations in Europe to join in forming an organization that would implement the vision outlined in the plan. Germany, Italy, Belgium, Luxembourg, and the Netherlands (the latter three known as the Benelux countries) responded. Negotiations began a month later, and these nations signed the Treaty of Paris, which established the European Coal and Steel Community (ECSC), on April 18, 1951. Although the ECSC was overshadowed by future developments in integration, it represented the first key step in overcoming the ancient divisions of continental Europe.

Negotiating Europe

The European Coal and Steel Community focused on economics as the most appropriate arena for integration. In particular, interstate trade and the prosperity that was thought to flow from such trade was to be fostered by integration. In turn, integration would be fostered by the results of such trade. This view has shaped the evolution of European integration and its substantive policy core: economics, economic policy, and trade in the pursuit of economic prosperity.

Underlying this concern with prosperity was the notion that prosperity facilitates peace. Because

the interwar years (1918–1939) had seen economic tumult throughout much of Europe and the simultaneous rise of fascism and Nazism, economic prosperity was considered necessary for both democracy and peace.

The negotiations over the Schuman Plan did not involve only economic issues, however. Both domestic and foreign policy were major considerations. Foreign affairs—closely intertwined with domestic politics—emerged as a critical concern for all heads of state after World War II.

Why Join Europe?

It is useful to consider why these other countries accepted Schuman's invitation to discuss integration. We find an often entangled combination of political/economic and geopolitical reasons—the Siamese twins of Europe. Economics played an important role in the first attempt at integration and has remained as a critical factor. It might be argued that integration proceeds fastest when the political/economic and geopolitical reasons reinforce one another.

European integration was not inevitable. It represented a political choice. If different leaders had been in power, it might well not have occurred. While integration addressed the needs of the political leaders who accepted Schuman's invitation, these leaders were also predisposed to the idea. All of the leaders who decided to accept Schuman's invitation were from the Christian Democratic Party. (Schuman was a Christian Democrat as well.) Their party affiliation gave them a common bond and a set of ideological referents and beliefs that provided a basis for similar views of the world. Their ideology was a cognitive lens through which leaders and followers could define problems and choose solutions. The leaders who agreed had a great deal in common.

Schuman's own life experience encouraged him to shape "French foreign policy to his vision of a Europe in which France and Germany were reconciled and the suffering of the border provinces ended."[10] (See Box 12.1). For Konrad Adenauer, who became German Chancellor in 1949, the proposed community represented a way for Germany to become an accepted and respectable member of

Box 12.1   Robert Schuman: A True "European" (1886–1963)

Born in Luxembourg and raised in German-speaking part of Lorraine

Attended German universities

Drafted into German Army in World War I

Became French citizen in 1919 when Alsace-Lorraine was restored to France under Treaty of Versailles

Elected to French Parliament

Refused to serve under Vichy Regime

Imprisoned by Gestapo for condemning expulsions of French population of Lorraine

Escaped in 1942 and became active in French Resistance

Helped to found Christian Democratic Party (MRP) in 1944

November 1947–December 1952–Served as either premier or foreign minister of France

November 1950–Proposed the Schuman Plan, the catalyst for European integration

1958–1963–Served as a member of the European Assembly, the forerunner of the European Parliament

---

both Europe and the international system. Personally, he anxiously sought closer ties with France. He was also confident that the German coal and steel producers were in a strong enough position that their interests would be safeguarded. In both strategic and personal terms, therefore, Schuman's proposal was attractive. By contrast, Kurt Schumacher, the leader of the German Social Democratic Party, opposed integration with France. Although other key members of the Social Democrats supported European integration and the European Coal and Steel Community, he strongly opposed both. He saw the ECSC as both too capitalist and too dominated by the Christian Democratic Party.[11] The fact that Adenauer rather than Schumacher was chancellor when Schuman made his proposal was undoubtedly significant in shaping the history of European integration.

For the Benelux countries, dependent on trade with their neighbors, Schuman's proposal represented an attractive way of solving the German Question. The Dutch Foreign Ministry saw the Schuman Plan as creating "the capability for Europe to profit by Germany's strength without being threatened by it."[12] Once Belgium was able to obtain special treatment of its coal mines, the Benelux countries were on board.

The Italian Christian Democratic premier Alcide de Gasperi made a different calculus.[13] He viewed integration as a way both to escape Italy's fascist past and to keep the strong Soviet-linked Ital-

ian Communist Party from coming to power. (The Communist Party opposed the Schuman Plan, viewing it as increasing American domination in Europe.) Eventually, European integration also represented a way to modernize the country, partially by ensuring export markets and partially by ensuring that millions of Italians could emigrate and work in the rest of Europe.

Although in 2004 most of Europe was in the European Union, in 1950 the governments of only six countries saw European integration as being in their interest.

Why Stay Out of Europe?

The countries that did not join in 1951 made their decisions on a variety of grounds. Spain and Portugal were under dictatorships and thus did not qualify for membership, while Greece was experiencing a civil war. The Scandinavians were uninterested in "supranational" schemes: the Nordic Union was based on intergovernmental cooperation rather than integration through supranationality. The Eastern European countries were in the Soviet sphere of influence and were simply unable even to consider answering Schuman's invitation. All of these countries were to join the drive toward European integration much later. The United Kingdom, the most important country to absent itself from the ECSC, did not join for a variety of reasons. Perhaps the most important, Britain saw itself as a world power, the leader of an empire, rather than as a state that needed to be concerned with its "European" role. The British rejection of the French government's invitation to participate in the ECSC negotiations was to be a defining moment for the future relationship of Britain with an integrated Europe.[14]

The Cold War, the United States, and European Integration

American influence on European integration in the 1950s was expressed in a number of ways. The United States, the "maker" of the international system, decisively shaped global institutions so as to break down trade barriers, protectionism, and imperial preferences and thereby create a liberal international economic system.[15]

The United States also influenced Europe more directly. The postwar period, especially between 1947 and 1950, was a crucial one for institutionally linking the United States to Europe. On June 5, 1947, the United States announced the outlines for the *Marshall Plan* (1948–1951). By insisting that Europe coordinate requests for Marshall Plan aid rather than allow each recipient country to deal bilaterally with the United States, the plan helped set the stage for European integration, "not least in the fostering of new modes of thinking."[16] Later, the United States provided strong support for both the Schuman Plan and the European Economic Community.[17]

While the Marshall Plan linked the United States and Europe economically, the Americans also became involved militarily. In April 1949, the Atlantic Pact was signed and the *North Atlantic Treaty Organization (NATO)* was born. Through NATO, the United States and Canada committed themselves militarily to European defense.

Six weeks after Schuman made his historic announcement on May 9, 1950, war broke out when North Korea invaded South Korea. The Korean War was a pivotal event in the American relationship to Europe and thereby for the future of European integration. The American government feared that the Soviet Union would invade Western Europe via Germany. The United States therefore backed German rearmament, announced (in

September 1950) that American troops would be incorporated into the NATO defense force, and that German divisions would be put under NATO command.

The European Defense Community (EDC) emerged as a counterproposal, which called for a European army incorporating all German forces. However, the French parliament definitively rejected the proposal on August 30, 1954. Although the EDC was dead, German rearmament was still on the agenda. In May 1955 Germany was recognized as a sovereign state and accepted as a member of NATO. The dream of a European army was stillborn. In a similar vein, the possibility of an independent European role in international politics was remote. "The European state system was, for the first time since the seventeenth century, firmly embedded in an international order dominated by others."[18]

The incorporation of both American troops and Germany in NATO within the context of the Cold War set the framework within which security and defense issues would be considered even after the end of the Cold War. Those issues were essentially taken off the agenda of European integration.[19] The Bretton Woods system had taken international monetary policy off the agenda. The path of integration was profoundly shaped by the fact that European integration took place within the "NATO-Bretton Woods system" in which the United States exercised hegemony in the West.[20]

It was not until the 1980s (in response to the breakdown of the Bretton Woods system) that the Community seriously addressed the issue of international finance (in the form of exchange rates) from an integrationist perspective. And the issue of security and defense policy remained within a transatlantic arena of discussion.[21]

It was not until 1999 that Europe began seriously discussing the creation of a separate European military force to be used for crisis management and even that would be linked to NATO. The process of European integration, therefore, has until very recently incorporated only selected issues rather than concerning itself with all those issues traditionally considered "high politics." The exclusion of such issues ensured that European integration would not lead to the establishment of a European state in the traditional sense.

The European Economic Community

In May 1955, the Assembly of the ECSC asked the foreign ministers of the Six to draft new treaties to further European integration. The *Treaty of Rome* established the *European Economic Community (EEC)* and came into force on January 1, 1958. One of the French negotiators, Robert Marjolin, articulated the hopes and symbolism attached to the signing of the Treaty of Rome:

> I do not believe it is an exaggeration to say that this date [March 25, 1957] represents one of the greatest moments of Europe's history. Who would have thought during the 1930s, and even during the ten years that followed the war, that European states which had been tearing one another apart for so many centuries and some of which, like France and Italy, still had very closed economies, would form a common market intended eventually to become an economic area that could be linked to one great dynamic market?[22]

The Treaty of Rome included a much wider range of economic arenas and modified the institutional structure of the ECSC in important ways. Unlike the superseded ECSC, the European Economic Community has remained at the core of the integration process. The close working relationship that gradually developed among the six countries operating within the ECSC transferred over into the EEC. The Treaty of Rome called for the creation of a common market—the free movement of people, goods, services, and labor—among the six signatories. It called for a common agricultural policy (the latter provision had been included in order to convince the French parliament to ratify the treaty). It also called for measures to move the EEC beyond a mere common market. It embodied both economic and political objectives: "Whilst the Treaty of Rome is virtually exclusively concerned with economic cooperation, there was (and remains) an underlying

political agenda. There is no doubt that its architects saw it . . . as another step on the road to political union."[23]

The Expansion of Europe

Two models of "Europe" developed during the 1960s. The EEC, with its supranational dimension, symbolized the first. The *European Free Trade Association (EFTA)* symbolized the second. EFTA was established in 1960 with Britain playing a leading role in its birth and Norway, Sweden, Denmark, Switzerland, Austria, and Portugal joining the British-led initiative. It was entirely intergovernmental, lacked any supranational element, and was concerned only with free trade. Whereas EFTA did not compromise sovereignty, the ECC created an entanglement and a fusion between national and community powers.[24]

Over time, the supranational model eclipsed the intergovernmental. Only Iceland, Norway, and Switzerland remain in EFTA. The decline of EFTA was presaged by the UK's decision to apply for membership in the EEC. After two vetoes by President De Gaulle of France, the British, along with Ireland and Denmark (for whom the UK was a key trading partner), finally joined in 1973 when Georges Pompidou replaced De Gaulle as President of France. Norway had also applied and been accepted, but its electorate rejected membership in a referendum in 1972.

In 1981 Greece joined and in 1986 Spain and Portugal did the same. The accession of all three was viewed as consolidating their transition to democracy and as widening European integration to the Mediterranean. In 1995, Austria, Sweden, and Finland joined; Norway's electorate again refused accession in a referendum. On May 1, 2004, ten new countries joined the Union, in what is referred to as the "big bang enlargement": Czech Republic, Cyprus, Estonia, Hungary, Latvia, Lithuania, Malta, Poland, Slovakia, and Slovenia. Bulgaria and Romania have been promised accession for 2007, and it is likely that Croatia will join in 2007 as well. In addition, the EU has made it clear that the map of the EU would not be completed without all the Balkan countries. More controversially, Turkey was

Box 12.2   Candidate Countries for Membership in the European Union as of 2004

Countries seeking to enter the EU must first be officially accepted as candidate countries by the current 25 member-states. The second stage in the process of accession involves entering into complex negotiations during which the candidate countries must demonstrate that they satisfy criteria laid down by the EU. Once negotiations are completed both the European Parliament and all 25 national parliaments must approve the accession of the candidate countries.

Bulgaria and Romania—Negotiations began 2000—set to join in 2007.
Croatia—Negotiations will start in early 2005.
Turkey—It was recognized as a candidate country at the Helsinki Summit in December 1999—member-states decided in December 2004 that negotiations will start in October 2005

---

also recognized as a candidate country at the Helsinki Summit of December 1999, but accession negotiations have not yet begun (see Box 12.2). Of the four poorest countries included in the enlargements before 2004, Ireland, Spain, and Portugal are typically viewed as "success" stories. Greece, in contrast, has been far more problematic for the Union. Its internal politics have been such that the fit between Brussels and Athens has been far from an easy one.[25]

Most of the countries included in the 2004 enlargement are much less prosperous than are the 15 "old" member-states. Many believe that with EU membership, the kind of assistance which the EU has provided Italy, Spain, Ireland, Portugal, and Greece will help the new entrants progress economically. Many in the "old" EU hope that the "newcomers" will do as well as Portugal, Spain, and Ireland, all of whom have become prosperous and active supporters of European integration.

Beyond the Treaty of Rome

The dismantling of tariffs within the Community did indeed increase trade among the six signatories of the Treaty of Rome. However, the increased volatility of financial markets, rooted in the breakdown of the Bretton Woods economic system, threatened the expansion of trade. In 1979 the Six supported a Franco-German initiative designed to minimize the fluctuations in exchange rates. They established the European Monetary System (EMS), which served as the foundation for a common currency and Economic and Monetary Union (EMU). Britain, however, declined to join the EMS's key mechanism, the exchange rate mechanism. Again, the Six had taken the process of European integration one step further, but without British participation. Britain remained outside until October 1990, just before Margaret Thatcher was forced out of office by her own political party.

While the British government did not want to tie the British pound to the currencies of the Six, it was concerned with the declining competitiveness of European industry with its American and Japanese counterparts. Beginning with the election of Margaret Thatcher as prime minister in 1979, political elites in Europe gradually became more sympathetic to the idea that the opening of markets was necessary both to spur economic growth and to improve the competitiveness of European firms in the emerging global economy. The election of Christian Democratic Chancellor Kohl in Germany in 1982 and the ill-fated fortunes of the French Socialist government's policies from 1981 to 1983 led to an emerging consensus that Europe needed to establish a true common market, one in which so-called nontariff barriers were dismantled. Experts increasingly saw markets as promoters of economic growth rather than simply as a mechanism from which workers needed extensive protection.

The new president of the European Commission, Jacques Delors, crystallized the emerging consensus. Delors' own father was left for dead by German troops in World War I, but he played a key role in the movement toward European integration. Appointed in 1985, Delors seized on the idea for an internal market (the new name given to the "common market" with the connotation of removing nontariff barriers). The internal market project revitalized the Community, ensured Delors' place in the history of European integration, and gave the Community a much higher profile than it had previously had.

The process led to the Single European Act, a major amendment to the Treaty of Rome. For Delors, the single-market project was a way to use economics to pursue a political agenda. As he explained in a radio interview in 1993, "If this job was about making a single market I wouldn't have come here in 1985. We're not here just to make a single market—that doesn't interest me—but to make a political union."[26]

The Single European Act

The decision to amend the Treaty of Rome was made in 1985, and the *Single European Act (SEA)* came into force in 1987. The SEA changed the decision rules for legislation designed to create the internal market in that qualified majority voting rather than unanimity was to apply to such legislation. (A qualified majority requires more votes for approval than does a simple majority.) A national government could not veto legislation introduced for the explicit purpose of creating the market (the veto had been legitimated in January 1966 in the Luxembourg Compromise). Furthermore, the SEA increased the powers of the European Parliament and increased the Community's powers in the area of environmental protection.

The drive for the single market came to be known as the "1992" Project—1992 was the deadline for the adoption of Community legislation needed to remove nontariff barriers. The adoption of a single market represented a milestone in the history of European integration. It was analogous in importance to the "interstate commerce clause" in the American constitution. Just as that clause undergirded the growth of federal power in nineteenth-century America, the single market represented a

major step in the integration of Europe and the power of the Community institutions.

A single market minimizes nontariff barriers. Such barriers accumulate over time and are often closely tied to cultural traditions, which means that overriding them can be politically sensitive. For that very reason, the single market has been so important. By examining barriers from the perspective of whether they inhibit the possibilities open to an exporter to a certain country, the single market opens to scrutiny many institutional arrangements in both the public and private sectors which have been accepted over time. Germany could not exclude beer made in an "unGerman" way, Italy could not exclude pasta made with "foreign" wheat, and so forth.

The 1992 Project was above all a project of regulatory reform—national deregulation combined with re-regulation at the Community level. Market forces were strengthened in order to improve the ability of European firms to compete globally. Regulation was implemented in Brussels rather than the national level. The European Community began setting up regulatory agencies—such as the European Agency for the Evaluation of Medicinal Products to regulate pharmaceuticals—that have complemented national regulatory frameworks. Although national economic systems were deregulated, re-regulation occurred in Brussels. Furthermore, environmental regulation was increasingly concentrated at the Community level. Finally, the Commission began exercising its powers in the area of competition policy (which covers antitrust and state aids) much more aggressively.[27] Protected markets, such as those in the telecommunications and air transport sectors, were gradually liberalized (so that phone calls and intra-European air travel became far cheaper than they had been). The protectionist policies which economic integration was meant to overturn were gradually eroded or eliminated. By the late 1990s, the Community's regulatory reach was so important that some analysts considered it a "regulatory state."[28]

The Maastricht Treaty

The single market of the late 1980s was largely viewed as a success. Business investment climbed, and Europe enjoyed a new sense of economic optimism. Under these circumstances, an initiative to move to a European central bank and a common currency as an extension of the single market began to attract support. Central bank governors, under the chairmanship of Jacques Delors, began to lay out a framework for achieving a common currency.

While that effort was underway, the Berlin Wall fell in November 1989. German unification, once barely considered, now became a reality (see Chapter 7). A new Germany was on the scene. Would it continue to face westward—to Brussels—or would it face toward the East? What role would the new Germany play in a Europe fundamentally changed by the end of the Cold War? How could Europe "contain" this economic powerhouse that had just added more than 16 million inhabitants? These questions were especially pressing, as the problems—and especially the huge costs—associated with German unification were still unacknowledged by most observers.

One response to a new version of the old "German Question" was to move toward a new treaty that would bind Germany even more firmly to the West by further tying German institutions to those of the Community. The purpose was to ensure that a "European Germany" would not be supplanted by a "German Europe." Helmut Kohl, the chancellor of Germany, for whom memories of World War II were still keen, strongly supported embedding Germany in a more deeply integrated European Community. The result was the *Treaty of European Union (TEU)*, usually referred to as the *Maastricht Treaty* after the small Dutch town in which the final negotiations took place in December 1991.

The Maastricht Treaty came into effect in November 1993. It represented another milestone in the history of European integration, moving the process of European integration into two critical new arenas as well as entrenching the Community's jurisdiction over the pivotal area of monetary policy. The treaty is complex. It changed the name of the European Community to that of the European Union (EU). Most importantly, it changed the structure of the Community by establishing three "pillars" in which the Community institutions played different roles. That same structure was retained in

the subsequent Treaty of Amsterdam and the Treaty of Nice which that came into effect in 1999 and in 2003 respectively.

In the Maastricht, Amsterdam, and Nice treaties, the European Council and the Council of Ministers were important in all three pillars, whereas the other Community institutions were central only in pillar one. The more federally inclined members of the Union saw the pillar structure as a transition phase, one that would ultimately lead to all three areas of policy being brought under the Community's institutions. The more intergovernmentalist members viewed the pillar structure as a safeguard against precisely that kind of evolutionary development.

Pillar One: The Extension of the Treaty of Rome

Pillar one as defined by Maastricht encompassed the creation of the *Economic and Monetary Union (EMU)*—including a new European Central Bank and a common currency (the euro) as well as incorporation of all the policy areas previously falling under the Community's jurisdiction. The *acquis communautaire*—all the accumulated laws and judicial decisions adopted since the signing of Treaty of Rome—belonged to the first pillar. For example, the single market, agriculture, environmental policy, regional policy, research and technological development, consumer protection, trade policy, fisheries policy, competition policy, and transportation policy all fell under pillar one.

Decision-making procedures within pillar one were firmly rooted within the traditional European Community institutions while expanding the Parliament's decision-making power. Policy areas that were designated as falling under the jurisdiction of pillar one were dealt with within the institutional machinery of the Commission, the Parliament, the Council of Ministers, the presidency, the European Court of Justice, the European Council, and the new European Central Bank. Under Maastricht, however, the UK and Denmark were allowed to "opt out" of the common currency as well as several other provisions if they so wished. In September 2000, the Danish public voted against joining the euro and in 2003 Swedish voters also rejected the euro in a referendum. In general, pillar one under Maastricht includes everything that the "old" European Community included plus the new European Central Bank and the euro for those countries that joined the Eurozone.

Pillars Two and Three: An Intergovernmental Compromise

Pillars two and three expanded the scope of what became renamed the European Union by encompassing policy areas that had been outside the scope of European integration. The institutional structures that governed pillars two and three differed from those found in pillar one. Pillar two referred to the area of the *Common Foreign and Security Policy (CFSP)* and pillar three referred to what is known as *Justice and Home Affairs (JHA)* (internal security). In both pillars, the Council of Ministers rather than the Commission was primarily responsible for action, unanimous voting was required, the Parliament was largely excluded, and the European Court of Justice did not exercise jurisdiction.

The fact that the Council of Ministers rather than the European Commission was established as the key institution represented a compromise. On one side were those countries that favored a more "federal" model of integration and therefore supported giving the Commission its traditional powers in these areas. On the other side were those governments (Britain and France) that were worried about sovereignty. Pillars two and three therefore were brought within the process of integration but were governed by the European Council and the Council of Ministers, the most intergovernmental institutions within the Community's institutional framework.

Treaty of Amsterdam

The *Treaty of Amsterdam* came into effect in 1999 and significantly changed the policy and institutional landscape established by the Maastricht Treaty. First of all, most issues of pillar three under Maastricht were now placed within pillar one, significantly strengthening the policy reach of the Commission and the influence of the European Court of

Justice. Along with that expansion, the treaty enhanced the power of the Commission president vis à vis the other commissioners. Second, the treaty increased the power of the European Parliament by both simplifying and expanding the use of co-decision in a wide range of issue areas. Third, the powers of the EU in several policy areas, including public health (critical to the European welfare state) and CFSP, both of which are very sensitive for national sovereignty, were enhanced. Public health is firmly under the Union's institutions in pillar one, while CFSP is firmly in the intergovernmental pillar two.

The transfer of most policy areas within the "old" pillar three to pillar one represented a very significant step in the process of European integration. Internal security is traditionally viewed as absolutely central to national sovereignty. In the post-Amsterdam period, issues such as asylum, immigration, and judicial cooperation in civil matters came within the policy remit of the Commission and, with some restrictions, the jurisdiction of the European Court of Justice. In Maastricht, the member-states had given up their sovereignty in the area of monetary policy by accepting the euro, but they had been very reluctant to "Europeanize" internal security. The Treaty of Amsterdam represented their new willingness to "pool" their sovereignty in the area of Justice and Home Affairs. (In the United States, the Department of Justice is concerned with most of the same issue areas.) The intergovernmental pillar three of the Maastricht Treaty was widely viewed as having been a failure so that the Treaty of Amsterdam signaled the new willingness of the member-states to try to make it more effective by bringing it under the Commission's umbrella.

In a similar vein, in October 1999 the member-states met at a special summit in Tampere, Finland, and agreed to numerous initiatives that mark a major turning point in the member-states' willingness to accept further integration in this extremely sensitive area (see Box 12.3). Only two policy areas remain within the "new" pillar three after Amsterdam—police cooperation (including the European Police Office known as EUROPOL which under Amsterdam was given stronger powers and a more operational role) and judicial cooperation in criminal matters. Even here, the member-states were

Box 12.3   Justice and Home Affairs (JHA) Pillars 1 and 3

The Treaty of Amsterdam, the 1999 European Council Summit in Tampere, Finland, and responses to terrorist attacks in the United States and Spain resulted in much deeper integration in the sensitive area of internal security. The EU increased the level of intergovernmental cooperation and the powers of the Commission and the European Court of Justice were broadened so that Justice and Home Affairs is now viewed as a key component of an integrating Europe. Included among the important new initiatives in this area were:

EUROPOL given significant new powers to initiate criminal investigations

Police and immigration officials given cross-national legal powers in all EU member-states

Network of Union public prosecutors (Eurojust)

European Police College to train law enforcement officials

European Arrest Warrant (EAW) created to make process of arrest and extradition of fugitives within the EU more efficient

Antiterrorism czar appointed to coordinate counterterrorism efforts among the member states

Joint investigative teams to combat terrorism and drug trafficking

Task force of senior police officers

Development of
- Common EU asylum and immigration policy
- Harmonized approach to dealing with refugees (including a European refugee fund)
- Standardized methods of combating illegal immigration
- Tougher laws against money-laundering
- Policies to ensure that court judgments issued in one country are enforceable throughout the Union

willing to be less intergovernmental. The European Court of Justice was completely excluded in the old pillar three, but it was given a limited role in the post-Amsterdam pillar three. Furthermore, the Commission as well as the member-states have the right of initiative in all matters falling under pillar three. This is an expansion of the role of the Commission. Some convergence of criminal legislation is now possible, so that Amsterdam is viewed by some as contributing "towards creating a common European criminal law."[29]

Finally, the EU's reaction to the September 11, 2001 terrorist attack on the United States and the March 11, 2004 terrorist attack on a Madrid train station further strengthened the EU's role in the area of Justice and Home Affairs. The member-states accepted the creation of a "European arrest warrant" and the appointment of an EU antiterrrorism "czar." However, the EU has not created a European version of the Central Intelligence Agency (CIA). Intelligence gathering remains a strictly national function; however, with much greater cooperation and coordination among national intelligence agencies than had been the case before 2001.

With regard to pillar two of the Maastricht Treaty, Amsterdam enhanced the powers of the Union in the area of a common foreign and security policy. Institutionally, the Secretary-General of the Council of Ministers was also appointed as the High Representative for the EU Common Foreign and Security Policy ("Mr. CFSP"). Javier Solana, widely respected in his previous posts as NATO Secretary-General and Spanish Foreign Affairs Minister was appointed to that position when the Treaty of Amsterdam came into effect in 1999.

The Treaty of Nice

The *Treaty of Nice*, the fourth revision of the Rome Treaties entered into force on February 1, 2003. The treaty attempted to prepare the EU for its enlargement to Central and Eastern Europe. In particular, the treaty sought to streamline decision making in the EU's institutions. Making decisions with 25 countries would be much more difficult than with 15 countries. Streamlining decision making, however, necessarily changes the distribution of power within the institutions concerned. In particular, the small states, which had historically been overrepresented in the EU's institutions, fought to keep their privileged position. The large member-states argued that since enlargement would add so many small states to the Union, maintaining the privileges of small states would lead to an unbalanced Union in which the populous member-states would be deprived of their appropriate role. The final deal was reached in the early morning of the last day of the Nice European Council in December 2000.

In addition to finding a compromise between the demands of the small and large member-states (in which the small states did relatively well), the Treaty of Nice also introduced some important changes. Institutionally, it allowed each member-state to appoint only one commissioner (previously, the larger member-states had appointed two commissioners). Second, the Treaty of Nice introduced qualified majority voting to choose the president of the Commission and increased his power vis à vis other commissioners. Third, a new weighting of votes was accepted in the Council of Ministers (that weighting represented the concrete results of the compromise between the large and small states). Fourth, qualified majority voting (as opposed to unanimity) was extended to roughly 30 new policy areas. It strengthened the EU's role in the area of security and defense, and created a new *Political and Security Committee (PSC)*.

The Nice Treaty was rejected by Irish voters in a referendum held in 2001, but it was subsequently accepted in a referendum in 2002. Many interpreted the initial defeat as an indication that European publics were uneasy about the changes to the Union that the enlargement to the East would inevitably bring.

THE INSTITUTIONS

The institutional structure of the European Union is based on the complex divisions represented by different institutions in different policy areas (see Figure 12.2). The sophisticated policymaking process normally associated with the Community resides in pillar one—including key policymaking institutions such as the European Commission, the Council of Ministers, the European Parliament, the European Council, European Court of Justice, and the European Central Bank.

Whereas the other institutions all interact with one another, the European Central Bank (located in Frankfurt, Germany) is very independent from all the other institutions. However, Justice and Home Affairs within pillar one still excludes the Parliament. The Commission and the Council are the central policymaking actors in areas such as immigration, visa policy, and asylum policy. In pillars two and three, the European Council and the Council of Ministers are the key institutional actors.

The European Commission

The *European Commission*, located in Brussels, is the Community's most visible institution in day-to-day policymaking. Its institutional mission within the Community is to promote integration. Toward that end, the Commission is made up of the College of Commissioners, the decision-making body within the Commission, and civil servants that do the important technocratic work typical of all bureaucracies. The College of Commissioners is the political (although not in a partisan sense) component of the Commission while the civil servants are the administrative sector. The term "Commission" is used in the press to refer either to the civil servants, the College, or both.

The Commission is composed of 25 commissioners who collectively make up the College of Commissioners. Each commissioner is appointed by the head of a member-state, but once appointed the commissioner is able to act independently of his country's national government. A commissioner does not take instructions from the national government and can operate quite autonomously. That independence gives the Commission as a whole its "supranational" authority and power.

Each commissioner serves for a five-year term, and can be reappointed if the national government so wishes. Each has one vote. And each is in charge of certain policy areas (environment, trade, external relations, agriculture, research and technology, transport, or telecommunications, for example). When they meet collectively every Wednesday, they are known as the College of Commissioners.

FIGURE 12.2   The Structure of the European Union

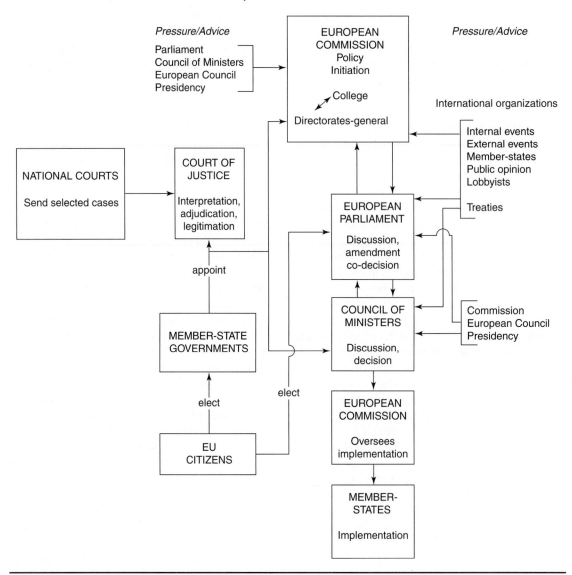

Source: Taken from John McCormick, *European Union: Politics and Policies* (Boulder, CO: Westview Press, 1996), p. 207.

The president of the Commission is the most important commissioner; the Treaty of Amsterdam and the Treaty of Nice enhanced his influence within the Commission. In the post-Nice era, the European Council nominally chose the president by qualified majority voting. However, the current Commission president, the Portuguese Jose Manuel Barroso, was selected by the European Council in June 2004 by consensus. The reliance on consensus rather than qualified majority voting acknowledged the political reality that a Commission president would be ineffective if one of the large member-states opposed his appointment. (In fact, Barroso was selected after other proposed candidates were in effect vetoed by one or more of the large member-states.) The European Council's nomination then must be approved by the European Parliament. Typically a president from a large country is succeeded by a president from a small country. (Barroso is from Portugal, a small country, while his predecessor Romano Prodi was from Italy, a large country.) Strong Commission presidents leave an imprint: Walter Hallstein, the first president, and Jacques Delors (1985–1995) both led the Commission in ways that increased its profile and prestige. Commission presidents, however, are constrained by the fact that they do not appoint their fellow commissioners and have relatively little formal control over them. Even Jacques Delors at the height of his power and prestige was unable to convince some governments to reappoint commissioners he would have liked to have returned to the Commission.

The Treaty of Nice, however, did strengthen the president's hand to some extent. For example, the president may now request a member of the Commission to resign after obtaining the approval of the College. Jose Barroso, the first Commission president in the post-Nice era, took advantage of his newly strengthened position to allocate desirable portfolios to small countries. The fact that France, traditionally a very influential country in the EU, was given responsibility for transport rather than a more presitigious assignment was taken as a sign that President Barroso would not be shy about using the new powers of the Commission president.

Nonetheless, the role of the president of the Commission is not similar to that of a prime minister. The president is not accountable to Parliament in the way that a national prime minister is and does not become president of the Commission through an election. He is appointed by the national governments rather than being elected, as are prime ministers. In a similar vein, the Commission is not a "government" in that it is not selected by either the voters (as is the president of France) or the legislature (as are prime ministers).

The Commission has a number of important powers, but its most pivotal power is contained in pillar one: it is the only institution that can propose legislation in pillar one. Neither the Council of Ministers nor the European Parliament can initiate legislation. The monopoly exercised by the Commission over policy initiation is one of its most important formal powers. Although the initiation power is limited by the Parliament's power to ask for a legislative proposal, the fact that it must be the Commission which drafts the proposal gives the Commission important leverage in the legislative process. This power thus enables the Commission to shape the policy agenda. The Commission also manages the Community's budget, is involved in external relations, monitors the application of Community law in the member-states, and generally is expected to make the arguments and proposals necessary to promote further integration.

The College of Commissioners decides by majority vote which proposals for legislation to send to the Council of Ministers and the European Parliament. The College can also decide to take antitrust action (without the approval of the Council of Ministers) and can argue cases before the European Court of Justice.

The Commission's bureaucracy, although very small in comparison to national bureaucracies, is the most important administrative component of the entire Community and is key to the Commission's ability to promote the process of integration. Sometimes known as Eurocrats, officials who work for the Commission are multilingual and highly educated. They typically receive their position after passing a competitive examination. They do the initial drafting of the legislation (which is then approved by the College) and are present at the negotiations within the Council of Ministers on all proposals from the College of Commissioners. Commission officials are emphatically not the functional equivalents of international civil servants, such as officials who work for global international organizations such as the United Nations. Commission officials are viewed as having much more authority when dealing with national officials than are traditional international civil servants.[30]

The operations of its civil servants allow the Commission to play a complex role. Commission officials often operate very effectively behind the scenes. They consult with a wide variety of interest groups and often receive complaints about non-compliance with Community laws from citizens in the member-states.

Fundamentally, the Commission promotes European integration and provides the administrative resources absolutely essential for policymaking in a system as complex as the European Union. Without the Commission, the European Union would not have an administrative apparatus.

Because of its centrality in the definition of problems and the formulation of policy, its access to significant administrative resources, and its links to a variety of groups throughout the Community, the Commission plays a key role in policymaking. It is at the heart of the European Union.[31] The fact that the European Union has a policymaking body not directly controlled by the member-states and able to wield important influence clearly distinguishes the organization as different from all other international bodies. The Commission as an institution symbolizes that supranational dimension within European integration that was so vigorously promoted by Jean Monnet.

The Council of the European Union (Council of Ministers)

The Council of the EU is usually referred to as the *Council of Ministers*. It adopts Community legislation and develops the budget along with the Commission and the Parliament. It is the top decision-making body. Its decisions, often taken in conjunction with the European Parliament in pillar one, become Community law. Its members are ministers from national governments. If a national government loses an election, the ministers from the new government immediately participate in the Council's decision-making process.

The Council of Ministers, as the Union's main legislature, is a more powerful decision maker than either the Commission or the Parliament. It, rather than the Parliament, formulates the EU's trade policy and is the dominant actor in the area of Justice and Home Affairs. Above all, it adopts Community legislation that is then incorporated into national legal codes. It does not, however, participate in the formation of the Commission and cannot dismiss it.

Technically speaking, there are nine Councils of Ministers and the term "Council of Ministers" is applied to each sectoral council (see Box 12.4). Each Council is composed of the relevant ministers from each of the member-state governments (or someone delegated to represent them).

Hierarchically, the most important configuration is the General Affairs and External Relations Council (GAERC), which brings together the foreign affairs ministers. The GAERC deals with external relations, but also with horizontal matters, such as the coordination of decisions, the preparation and follow-up of the European Council, as well as institutional and administrative questions. The GAERC meets at least once a month. Other councils also meet frequently reflecting the fact that the Community is more active in certain policy areas. For example, the Council of Agriculture and Fisheries meets at least once a month, whereas the Council of Environment Ministers meets once formally and once informally within every three-month period.

All ministers operating within a Council do not carry the same weight as they have unequal voting power (see Table 12.1). In a similar vein, not all Councils are equal in significance. Although the most important is the GAERC, finance ministers are constantly competing with foreign ministers for influence, and in pillar one the Council of Economic and Finance Ministers (especially the Euro-Group) comes next in the hierarchy of influence.[32] The Justice and Home Affairs Council became important after the Maastricht Treaty came into effect and is now a key council in both pillar one and pillar three.

The Council of Ministers is the EU institution in which national interests are represented, defended, and ultimately compromised in the interests of reaching agreement. It is a "club" in the sense that the participants understand that ultimately compromises will have to be made by everyone and because its participants acknowledge that the Council is not a traditional international organization. Although the Council zealously guards its prerogatives and keeps a close eye on activities to ensure that the Commission does not encroach on the Council's territory, it must be emphasized that the

Box 12.4   The Nine Councils of Ministers

There are nine sectoral Councils, each of which is referred to as the "Council of Ministers." The nine sectoral Council configurations are:

GAERC (General Affairs and External Relations
   Council)
Economy and Finances
Justice and Home Affairs
Employment, Social Policy, Health, and Consumer
   Affairs

Competitiveness
Transport, Telecommunications, and Energy
Agriculture and Fisheries
Environment
Education, Youth, and Culture

Each Council is composed of the relevant ministers from each of the member-state governments (or someone delegated to represent them).

TABLE 12.1   Distribution of Power Before and After the Treaty of Nice

Member-State	Number of Commissioners		Number of Votes in Council of Ministers Under QMV		Number of Members of European Parliament (MEPs)	
	Before Nice Treaty	After Nice Treaty (2004)	Before Nice Treaty	After Nice Treaty (2004)	Before Nice Treaty	After Nice Treaty (2004)
Germany	2	1	10	29	99	99
UK	2	1	10	29	87	78
France	2	1	10	29	87	78
Italy	2	1	10	29	87	78
Spain	2	1	8	27	64	54
Poland	—	1	—	27	—	54
Netherlands	1	1	5	12	31	27
Greece	1	1	5	12	25	24
Czech Republic	—	1	—	12	—	24
Belgium	1	1	5	12	25	24
Hungary	—	1	—	12	—	24
Portugal	1	1	5	12	25	24
Sweden	1	1	4	10	22	19
Austria	1	1	4	10	21	18
Slovakia	—	1	—	7	—	14
Denmark	1	1	3	7	16	14
Finland	1	1	3	7	16	14
Ireland	1	1	3	7	15	13
Lithuania	—	1	—	7	—	13
Latvia	—	1	—	4	—	9
Slovenia	—	1	—	4	—	7
Estonia	—	1	—	4	—	6
Cyprus	—	1	—	4	—	6
Luxembourg	1	1	2	4	6	6
Malta	—	1	—	3	—	5

Source: Population figures from *Eurostat Yearbook 2004*, published October 1, 2004.

Council is very much an EU institution. While it represents national interests, it does so within the framework of European integration.[33] Member-states, by operating within the framework of the Council, accept an institutional framework that leads to a collective—rather than a unilateral—decision. By participating in the Council, national governments give up the maneuverability and autonomy that is implicit in national (unilateral) decision making. It is for that reason that "Euroskeptics" argue that participation in the Union means giving up sovereignty—defined as the ability to make unilateral decisions.

In contrast, the power of the Council of Ministers ensures that the Union always adopts legislation that meets with the approval of most or all of the member-state governments. The Community does not impose legislation on national governments—they adopt the legislation themselves in the Council of Ministers (and in many areas in partnership with the European Parliament). Opposition parties in national parliaments, however, do not have access to Council of Ministers meetings. So the EU does in fact enhance the power of those political parties that are in government at the national level.

The Council of Ministers plays a stronger role in pillars two and three than it does in pillar one. In pillar one, the policymaking process gives an important role to both the Commission and the Parliament (the latter, however, is excluded from Justice and Home Affairs even in pillar one), and the European Court of Justice can be central. The Commission plays a smaller role, and the Parliament no role, in the policymaking process within pillars two and three.

The culture of the Council is based on negotiation and is predisposed toward finding agreement:

> The whole system depends on a crucial assumption that there is give and take between the positions of the member-states and that, whatever the starting positions of the members, there is *both* scope for those positions to evolve *and* a predisposition to find agreement. Thus atmospherics, mutual confidence and trust are important ingredients.[34]

The member governments, acting within the Council of Ministers, are engaged in an institutional process that is unlike that of any other legislative body in the world. Multinational, bound by Community rather than international law, and (in pillar one) engaged in important relationships with the Commission and the European Parliament, the Council of Ministers "locks" national ministers into an ongoing cooperative venture that includes a shared and enlarging policy agenda. It is that "locking" effect that helps ensure that national officials do not decide to act unilaterally rather than multilaterally.

Although some analysts view the Council as blocking further integration, comparison with other attempts at regional integration throughout the world highlights the importance of having national ministers involved in the nitty-gritty of policymaking at the European level. The Council of Ministers, in essence, is the guarantor of European integration in that national governments must participate in it and cannot ignore it. Without the Council, the actions of the Commission and the Parliament could conceivably be ignored by national governments, but their membership in the Council helps ensure that national governments address the issues proposed by the Commission.

The European Council

The key strategic institution within the Union is clearly the *European Council*. Strictly speaking, it does not form part of the Council of Ministers hierarchy, but it is closely linked to it. The European Council does not adopt legislation, leaving that to the Council of Ministers. It does, however, set out the key guidelines for action and future development. The European Council is attended by prime ministers (the president in the case of Cyprus, France, and Finland), foreign ministers, the Commission president and another designated commissioner. The foreign ministers provide the institutional continuity between the Council of Ministers and the European Council.

The Council meets formally four times a year in "summits" held in Brussels since the 2004 enlargement. (If a presidency decides to organize an informal summit, it can organize it wherever it wants.) These meetings receive far more publicity than do meetings of the various sectoral Councils and may well symbolize the European Union for the average citizen.

The European Council usually operates through unanimity even when it is not required to do so. The European Council now "occupies a position at the apex of the EU's institutional system, overseeing the work of each of the three pillars, and the specialized sectoral Councils which operate therein. It monitors their work, sets framework principles to guide their future deliberations, takes or clears major political decisions, and frequently engages in trouble-shooting."[35] It is the European Council, for example, that has decided key issues such as whether enlargement to Eastern Europe would occur, when it would occur, and whether Turkey could begin accession negotiations.

The European Council, as well as the Council of Ministers, is chaired by representatives of the member-state government holding the *Presidency of the European Council and the Council of Ministers*. Every six months the presidency of the European Union rotates, so that each member government exercises the powers of the presidency in both the European Council and the Council of Ministers. The head of state or government of the country holding the presidency, along with the Commission president and the High Representative for Foreign and Security Policy of the Council of Ministers (Javier Solana), represents the Union at summit meetings with non-EU leaders. For example, in June 2004 Irish Prime Minister Ahern represented the presidency at a U.S.-EU summit. Most burdensome perhaps is the fact that officials representing the member-state government holding the presidency chair all of the hundreds of meetings that go on in the Council of Ministers.

Finally, the European Council controls the agenda and negotiations of the *Intergovernmental Conference (IGC)* which is called to revise treaties. The most difficult compromises made at the IGC—the Single European Act, the Maastricht Treaty, the Treaty of Amsterdam, the Treaty of Nice, and the proposed constitutional treaty which is currently being debated across Europe—were all made at the end of the negotiations by the European Council. Only prime ministers (accompanied by their for-

eign ministers) or heads of state have the political power necessary to make concessions that are very difficult for national governments to accept but which are critical for the success of negotiations.

The European Parliament

The *European Parliament* is the only supranational assembly in the world whose members are chosen by voters rather than by governments. Its 732 members serve five-year terms congruent with the commissioners' five-year terms. *Members of the European Parliament (MEPs)* are elected at the same time across the Community, but each country uses its own electoral system. (A uniform European Community electoral system does not yet exist.) Because of the disproportionate influence of small countries (discussed later) in the Community, members represent constituencies vastly different in size (see Table 12.1).

Turnover is very high after each parliamentary election. After the 1999 parliamentary election, over half of all the MEPS were new rather than returning incumbents. Some MEPs continue on to distinguished careers in national politics, especially in France (where 10 of the 16 prime ministers and 4 of the 6 presidents in the Fifth Republic were MEPs). In reverse, six former prime ministers were elected as MEPs in the 1999 elections, and over 10 percent of MEPs have been ministers in national governments. Roughly 30 percent of the MEPs in the 1999–2004 Parliament were women, with the highest proportion in the Finnish delegation and the lowest in the Italian.[36] In the 2004—2009 Parliament, 222 MEPS were women.

The Parliament argues that it is the only directly elected European institution (it became directly elected in 1979) and is therefore closer to the citizens of Europe than either the Commission or the Council. Thus, the Parliament has pressured, coaxed, threatened, and in general become an important presence on the political scene. It is not yet an equal partner with the other institutions across the board. For example, it cannot decide the total size of the EU's budget nor formulate the EU's trade policy; it is excluded from spending on agriculture, foreign policy issues other than enlargement, and is largely excluded from the area of Justice and Home Affairs.

Nonetheless, since the Treaty of Amsterdam went into effect in 1999, its influence is very strong on most legislation falling under pillar one. The Treaty of Nice further reinforced the Parliament's power of being a co-legislator with the Council of Ministers. The Parliament can only ask the Commission to draft proposals rather than initiating its own draft proposals. However, the Parliament, in those areas in which it has jurisdiction, is able to offer amendments which can substantially change the proposal offered by both the Commission and the Council of Ministers. In the year after Amsterdam went into effect, the Parliament had 81 percent of its amendments accepted by the Council of Ministers. This indicates that it is effective in shaping legislation.[37]

The Parliament has control (within limits) of so-called "noncompulsory" spending. This includes spending not directed toward agricultural support (the largest single portion of the budget) or based on international agreements with third countries. Over time, the proportion of noncompulsory spending as a percentage of the total budget has increased. Currently, it is over 50 percent and in 1999, the Parliament and the Council of Ministers agreed that 10 percent of spending in agriculture traditionally classified as compulsory would be reclassified as noncompulsory.[38] In fact, the granting of budgetary authority to the Parliament in 1975 could be seen as a key step that has undergirded the subsequent increases in the parliamentary power.

The Parliament's formal powers were strengthened by the Treaty of Maastricht and strengthened still further by Amsterdam and Nice which extended the use of the co-decision procedure in the adoption of legislation. The Parliament's power of co-decision allows it to stop legislation which it does not want, even if the Council of Ministers unanimously supports it. In cases in which the Parliament and Council approve different versions of a piece of legislation, conciliation talks are held to try to agree on a compromise. If such talks fail, the legislation dies. Now that co-decision is so frequently used within pillar one, the Council and the Parliament contact each other early in the legislative process so that conciliation talks will not be necessary. Between November 1993 and April 1999, 165 directives requiring co-decision were dealt with and

40 percent required conciliation talks (three of the proposed directives considered were killed as no agreement could be reached). However, in the year after Amsterdam, 65 pieces of legislation were addressed and only 25 percent required conciliation talks.[39]

Parliament also exercises the right to approve the president of the Commission as well as giving a formal vote of approval of the College of Commissioners as a whole. Finally, it also approves the president of the European Central Bank. The Parliament must also assent to certain international agreements, including accession treaties and association agreements.

Most of the Parliament's work is done in committee. Each committee can decide whether its work will be done in public view or in closed session. Whereas committees in most national parliaments work in closed session, most European parliamentary committees now work in public. Each MEP is a full member of at least one committee. Final parliamentary approval however has to be granted in plenary sessions, and at times committee recommendations are overridden in the plenary.

The European Court of Justice

The *European Court of Justice*, located in Luxembourg, is a powerful "supranational" institution making what is in effect judicial law. The Court is composed of one judge from each member-state (chosen by the national government). Judges serve a six-year term of office that can be renewed. They elect one of the sitting judges as president. The ECJ established the Court of First Instance, which began operating in November 1989. That court has a more limited jurisdiction and cannot hear what might be termed constitutionally important cases.

The European Court of Justice is often the arbiter in disputes between an individual member-state and the Commission. It also handles interinstitutional disputes—for example, between the Commission and the Council of Ministers. Individual citizens can bring cases before the Courts only if a Community action has directly harmed them. It is typically easier for a firm to argue such harm than a noneconomic actor. Non-governmental groups such as environmental organizations do not have easy access to the Court. Since the Nice Treaty, the European Parliament can also bring a case to court. The Court has jurisdiction over issue areas falling within pillar one as well as very limited jurisdiction in pillar three.

Most of the Court's cases come from national courts asking for a preliminary ruling. The national court then takes the ECJ's preliminary ruling and delivers it as its own opinion. National judges therefore are an important factor in developing the effectiveness of the Community's legal order.

Initially established as an international court operating under the constraints of international law, the Court rather quickly began to represent the "European interest" in its own right. After the Treaty of Rome went into effect, the Court "constitutionalized" that international law under which it had been operating. Rather than simply becoming an international court with limited impact, it gradually evolved into a powerful body resembling, in some striking albeit limited ways, the U.S. Supreme Court. Its influence in the policymaking process is such that one scholar has concluded that "for many areas of European and national policy, knowing the position of the ECJ is as important as knowing the position of the member-states and national interest groups."[40] The Court performs an important role in the policymaking process as we discuss later.

The Single Currency and the European Central Bank

Although Economic and Monetary Union (EMU) had been discussed since the late 1960s, it was not until the Maastricht Treaty that a timetable was established and a serious commitment made to move ahead to that milestone of integration. A *single currency* and a *European Central Bank* were established in 1999, and citizens began using the common currency (the euro) in January 2002.

The political dynamics behind EMU were clear to political elites but difficult to explain to the general public. Under the previous European Monetary System (EMS) established in 1979, currencies were allowed to fluctuate only within an agreed-upon range. The German Bundesbank was the dominant decision maker. The German currency, the Deutsche mark, became the "anchor currency." That is, when the Bundesbank raised interest rates, the other EMS members were forced to follow in order to keep their currencies within the range to which they had agreed. When such a need arose during a recession, this had a harmful impact on national economies. The high interest rates in a recession exacerbated high unemployment and therefore were very painful.

The high cost of German unification led the German Bundesbank to raise interest rates while many other EMS members were in a recession. The French and the Italians in particular realized that they needed to gain a voice in European monetary policy. To do so, they had to give up their own monetary sovereignty (largely illusory in any case because of the dynamics of the EMS) and convince the Germans to give up their own monetary sovereignty. This would occur within the framework of a European Central Bank in which each central bank would have equal representation.

Although the Bundesbank was reluctant to embrace EMU, Chancellor Kohl, anxious to show that unification was not leading Germany away from the European Community, agreed to economic and monetary union. The decision over EMU fell within the "Chancellor's prerogative."[41] That is, the ultimate decision about EMU was the Chancellor's. The Maastricht Treaty embodied that agreement. The German government, however, insisted on certain conditions in order to ensure that the new *euro-currency* would be as "strong" a currency as the deutsche mark that the Germans were to give up. In particular, the European Central Bank was to have price stability (rather than, for example, low unemployment or high rates of economic growth) as its primary objective. Countries were not allowed to join EMU unless their deficits were at 3 percent of GDP or lower.

Years of brutal budget cutting were required for many countries (such as Italy) to qualify. In 1999, 11 countries joined what became known as the Eurozone; Britain, Sweden, and Denmark stayed out. Greece was allowed to join in 2001.

The European Central Bank, established in Frankfurt, is composed of the governors of the national central banks. It is extremely independent of all the other EU institutions as well as of the member-state governments. It is arguably the most independent central bank in the world. In fact, that independence has been criticized, but the ECB believes it is necessary to convince the financial markets that it will not pursue a monetary policy that would allow inflation. Price stability is its policy mantra.

NATIONAL GOVERNMENTS AS ACTORS

As already indicated in our discussion of the Community's institutions, national governments play a key role in the Community's policymaking process. Their influence is felt directly in the Council of Ministers and through the power of appointment in the Commission and the European Court of Justice. Typically, the focus on understanding how and why national governments operate as they do within the European Union highlights the role of ruling parties and bureaucracies. National governments are able to defend their national interest in all the Union's institutions in one fashion or another. The opportunity to defend one's national interest has lubricated the path of integration for the member-states.

The need to prepare the Union's institutions for enlargement, however, highlighted the disproportionate power of the small member-states. This feature of the Union had not been the subject of controversy since the Treaty of Rome. As the negotiations proceeded for the Treaty of Nice, the disproportionality of size became the object of intense political conflict among the current member-states. Simply put, the negotiations for the Treaty of Nice forced the question of *which* governments could adequately defend their national interests in the future. In addition to wielding disproportionate power within the EU as indicated by Table 12.1, small countries have a status largely equal to that of the large countries in the European Court of Justice, the European Council, and the governing council of the European Central Bank. Given that many new small countries would join the EU once enlargement occurred,

the large member-states in 2000 sought to redress the balance in the negotiations leading to the Treaty of Nice.

The small states, however, feared being "pushed around" by the large states and rejected many of the demands made by the four large states (France, Germany, Italy, and the UK). The last half of 2000 was filled with acrimony as the small states accused the large of trying to weaken the Commission (which the small states view as an ally) in the name of efficient decision making, of trying to make the EU more intergovernmental so that the large states would have more influence, and of being insensitive to the national interests of the small states. The large states, for their part, were adamant that they needed more power within the Council of Ministers (through a reallocation of voting weights) and were likely to want more representation in the European Parliament. Furthermore, they viewed their proposals for the Commission as strengthening it by making it more effective. In brief, the large states wanted to ensure that the next enlargement did not privilege small countries even further. The small member-states worried that if the large member-states were allowed to gain too much power, the EU was going to become more like an international organization (in which small countries fare very badly) and less like a federation (in which small subfederal units exercise disproportionate power as they do in the United States). The small countries wanted the policymaking process to respect their wishes as it has since the Treaty of Rome. The final compromise gave the large states less power than they had desired, but nonetheless gave them more than they had in the pre-Nice period. Poland and Spain (through exploiting their position as "medium-size" countries as well as through very tough bargaining) gained an especially privileged position.

The issue of the appropriate balance between large and small states reemerged during the negotiations over what is known as the Constitution for Europe (but is actually a constitutional treaty). The final compromise, obtained in June 2004 after months of bitter negotiations, gave the big member-states more power than they had had under the Treaty of Nice but less than they had desired. It is not clear whether that compromise will satisfy the parliaments and electorates that need to accept it.

POLITICAL PARTIES

Political parties do not play the same role in European Union politics as they do in the national politics of the European countries described in this book. On the one hand, political parties in Europe generally do not offer alternative policies and analyses at the European level. In almost every member-state the focus of party competition throughout the development of the EU has continued to be domestic politics.[42] Thus, while national elections may determine which party controls the government that chooses representatives to the Commission and the Council of Ministers, the electoral debate has seldom focused on the policies of those representatives. Even direct elections to the European Parliament have tended to operate primarily as referenda on the domestic achievements and promises of the competing parties.

On the other hand, this inattention is encouraged by the fact that election outcomes do not directly determine the control of the EU's governing institutions.

Politics in the European Union revolves around broad territorial (national) divisions rather than the socioeconomic divisions that characterize politics at the national level. The "left-right" division so pivotal in structuring political party positions at the national level manifests itself less often and in different ways in Brussels. Political conflict at the European Union level is characterized by "the dominance of national, cultural, and territorial differences over socio-economic divisions."[43] Whereas differences related to class have shaped political conflict in Europe throughout the postwar period, those differences have been muted in Brussels where national differences are more significant. "It is, therefore, essentially via governments that political parties influence European affairs."[44]

The histories of national political parties are not rooted in conflicts over European integration. Until voters in some member-states became concerned with the impact of integration, parties had not addressed policy issues dealt with in Brussels.

Even when integration became more politicized, major parties did not take clear positions on the issues they would face in the Council of Ministers. On the contrary, they cloaked their actions in the garb of national interest:

> Instead of defending their participation in European regulatory decision-making on the grounds of fulfilling an electoral mandate, ruling parties have consistently defended such actions on the grounds that they have done their best to protect national interests, thus casting European politics as a zero-sum game between the member-states.[45]

In spite of not offering European-level policy alternatives, parties have nonetheless begun to organize a bit more extensively on the European level than they have in the past. In 1992 and 1993, all the major transnational party federations began institutionalizing themselves to a greater degree. Furthermore, the transnational federations have begun meeting right before the European Council meetings, so that prime ministers and other leading politicians as well as members of the European Parliament and commissioners from each of the leading political families gather to discuss EU issues.[46] Whether and how quickly transnational parties will evolve, however, is still an open question.

The issues with which the Community deals typically have a strong economic component that often manifests itself in technical issues not usually the subject of political discourse. That economic component is shaped by the Treaty of Rome and the Single European Act, both of which embodied a certain model of economics. Expanding cross-border trade and competition, as well as opening economies and markets, are the Union's key economic objectives. That model does not easily address political problems in the way that parties have traditionally done so in national contexts. Finally, much national party competition revolves around issues related to the welfare state. The Community does not directly legislate on welfare state issues, which means that a central element of national political party conflict is not even on the Community agenda.[47]

Parliamentary Elections

Elections to the European Parliament differ from national parliamentary elections in a variety of ways. Most centrally, they do not set in motion a process of government formation in the same way as do national elections in the member-states. Turnout is higher in national (and sometimes even in subnational) elections. The big parties typically do better in national elections, while small parties do better in elections to the European Parliament. Worrisome for those concerned about the "democratic deficit" (discussed later in this chapter), in most countries the turnout for parliamentary elections has declined since the elections of 1979 (see Table 12.2). The lowest turnout was in the 2004 elections.

European elections are described as "pale reflections of national elections."[48] The electoral campaign does not highlight choices to be made at the European level, but rather emphasizes the kinds of issues typically debated within the voters' "habitual national party context."[49]

National elections are often viewed as "first-order" elections. Elections to the European Parliament are "second-order" elections because no actual

TABLE 12.2   Turnout in the European Parliament Elections, 1979–2004

	1979	1981	1984	1987	1989	1994	1995	1996	1999	2004
EU	63.0	—	61.0	—	58.5	56.8	—	—	49.4	45.7
Belgium	91.6	—	92.2	—	90.7	90.7	—	—	90.0	90.8
Luxembourg	88.9	—	87.0	—	87.4	88.5	—	—	85.8	89.0
Malta	—	—	—	—	—	—	—	—	—	82.4
Italy	85.5	—	83.9	—	81.5	74.8	—	—	70.8	73.1
Cyprus	—	—	—	—	—	—	—	—	—	71.2
Greece	—	78.6	77.2	—	79.9	71.2	—	—	70.2	63.4
Ireland	63.6	—	47.6	—	68.3	44.0	—	—	50.5	58.8
Lithuania	—	—	—	—	—	—	—	—	—	48.4
Denmark	47.1	—	52.3	—	46.1	52.9	—	—	50.4	47.9
Spain	—	—	—	68.9	54.8	59.1	—	—	64.4	45.1
Germany	65.7	—	56.8	—	62.4	60.0	—	—	45.2	43.0
France	60.7	—	56.7	—	48.7	52.7	—	—	47.0	42.8
Austria	—	—	—	—	—	—	—	67.7	49.0	42.4
Latvia	—	—	—	—	—	—	—	—	—	41.3
Finland	—	—	—	—	—	—	—	60.3	30.1	39.4
Netherlands	57.8	—	50.5	—	47.2	35.7	—	—	29.9	39.3
Portugal	—	—	—	72.2	51.1	35.5	—	—	40.4	38.6
Hungary	—	—	—	—	—	—	—	—	—	38.5
United Kingdom	31.6	—	32.6	—	36.2	36.4	—	—	24.0	38.3
Sweden	—	—	—	—	—	—	41.6	—	38.3	37.8
Czech Republic	—	—	—	—	—	—	—	—	—	28.3
Slovenia	—	—	—	—	—	—	—	—	—	28.3
Estonia	—	—	—	—	—	—	—	—	—	26.8
Poland	—	—	—	—	—	—	—	—	—	20.9
Slovakia	—	—	—	—	—	—	—	—	—	17.0

Source: Francis Jacobs, Richard Corbett, and Michael Shackleton, *The European Parliament*, 4th ed. (London: John Harper, 2000), p. 25. Information regarding 2004 elections from European Parliament website: http://1www.elections2004.eu.int/ep-election/sites/en/results1306/turnout_ep/turnout_table.html

executive power is at stake. Rather than focusing on European issues, elections to the Parliament provide a forum for voters to express their support of, or discontent with, national parties. National cues, rather than the specific policies of the European Union, are paramount in shaping how voters cast their ballots.[50]

Parties in the European Parliament

Within the Community's institutions, political parties are most visible in the European Parliament. Europe's extraordinary cultural and political diversity is demonstrated by the fact that over 164 parties are represented in the European Parliament. These in turn are combined in Political Groups which are the centers of power within the Parliament (see Table 12.3). After the 2004 parliamentary elections, seven Political Groups emerged. Each party group includes MEPs with a political affinity and from at least two member-states. The groups set the parliamentary agenda and de facto choose the president and 14 vice-presidents of the Parliament as well as the chairs, vice-chairs, and rapporteurs of the various parliamentary committees. The groups each have staffs.

Political Groups in the European Parliament do not perform the same role as do parties in national parliaments. The appointment of the executive—that is the Commission—is not formally determined by the Parliament. However, in 2004, Commission President Barroso was chosen from the political family (center-right) that had the largest number of seats in the European Parliament. Neither do the groups influence the portfolios that the individual commissioners receive. The groups do not have any influence on the partisan coloring of the ministers in the Council of Ministers. National governments choose both the commissioners and the ministers in the Council of Ministers. To understand the difference between a party in a national parliament and a Political Group in the European Parliament, it is important to remember that

TABLE 12.3   Political Groups in the European Parliament (2004–2009)

Group	Number of Political Parties in Group	Number of Member-States Represented	Number of Seats (732 Total)
European People's Party (Christian Democrats) and European Democrats (EPP-ED)	44	25	268
Party of European Socialists (PES)	27	23	200
Alliance for Liberals and Democrats for Europe (ALDE)	30	19	88
Greens/European Free Alliance (Greens/EFA)	19	13	42
European United Left/Nordic Green Left (EUL/NGL)	18	14	41
Union for a Europe of Nations (UEN)	7	6	27
Independence/Democracy (IND/DEM)	8	10	37
Nonattached	11	8	29

Source: "Chronique Élections 2004, Édition Spéciale: Composition du Parlement Européen au 20/07/04," Parlement Européen, Direction Générale de l'Information et des Relations Publiques, July 20, 2004.

"European elections do not initiate a process of government formation, as they do in most parliamentary democracies."[51]

The Political Groups provide an important channel of information for national parties. They are also important in organizing meetings, typically held before European Council meetings. At these sessions, heads of government and commissioners from that particular party, party leaders, and the chair of the Political Group meet to try to achieve a consensus on certain key issues affecting European integration.

The two largest Political Groups are the center-right European People's Party (previously named the Christian Democrats) and the center-left Socialist Group. Until the parliamentary elections of 1999, the Socialists had the most seats and were the dominant party within the Parliament. However, in 1999, much to the shock of the Socialists, the European People's Party (EPP) won 233 seats while the Socialists won only 180. The trend was repeated in 2004 when the EPP won 278 seats and the Socialists won 199 seats. Whereas previously the Socialists and the EPP had engaged in a kind of "grand coalition" and shared the committee chairmanships and the presidency of the Parliament amongst themselves, the EPP decided to pursue a different strategy. It concluded an informal alliance with the third largest party, the Liberals (with 51 seats) and agreed to share the presidency of the Parliament with the Liberals rather than with the Socialists. Most importantly, however, it began to stress the left-right division within the Parliament and the Commission. The Parliament became more "politicized." Rather than subordinating partisan conflict to the desire to increase the Parliament's power vis à vis the Commission and the Council of Ministers, the EPP highlighted the policy differences between the Socialists and the center-right parties. The EPP views government intervention in the market less favorably than do the Socialists. In fact, the Parliament voted in ways that were more pro-business and less environmentally friendly than had been the case in the past. After the 2004 elections, the EPP and the Socialist Group again decided to share the committees chairmanship and the presidency of the EP among themselves so that the "grand coalition" has reemerged.

It is important to note, however, that the party families (especially the EPP and the Socialists) have traditionally cooperated with one another. The EPP, the Socialists, and the Liberals still need to cooperate because neither one alone can mobilize the majorities needed under parliamentary procedures. Given the necessity to cooperate, the Parliament is not the forum for the kinds of partisan clashes found in the British House of Commons (see Chapter 5).[52] Nonetheless, adversarialism is now present in the Parliament to a greater degree, especially since the 1999 elections. Partisanship which divides tends to dilute the Parliament's power when dealing with the other institutions. For example, when the partisan divisions between right and left are highlighted on an issue, the Parliament is in a weaker position when entering conciliation talks with the Council than when there is a unitary parliamentary position. In general, politics within the Parliament is now less predictable and more fluid than had been the case in the past. The EPP is itself divided between members from the Christian Democrats who have traditionally been very strongly in favor of European integration and Euroskeptics. This means that the political dynamics of the Parliament are very complex. They are less structured than in the past. At times partisanship is subordinated so that the Parliament can act in a unified manner vis à vis the other institutions. At other times, however, partisanship is so strong that the Parliament is internally divided and therefore weakened when dealing with the Council or the Commission.[53]

The 2004 elections were marked by a low turnout (in the 10 new countries, overall participation was only at 26 percent, with notable exception in Malta and Cyprus). The elections also showed a clear gain for smaller, Euroskeptic, or populist parties compared to more traditional parties. In the UK, for instance, the UK Independence Party (UKIP), whose agenda calls for complete withdrawal of the UK from the EU, placed third after the Conservatives and the Labor Party with 17 percent of the votes. In Sweden, Poland, and Denmark, Euroskeptic parties also gained ground. Voters punished their government either because of their support to the Iraq war (in the UK), or because of poor economic performances (in France and Germany).

INTEREST GROUPS

As the Community has expanded the range of policies about which it can legislate, a "seemingly endless increase in interest group mobilization at the European level" has occurred.[54] Their number has grown so rapidly that scholars better understand the role of interest groups in national systems than in the Community. Research is still trying to catch up with the growth and activity of groups. What is clear is that the system of policymaking within the Union is so open that interest groups can participate at some point in the process of making public policy.

Interest groups interact with the Community's institutions in relatively unpredictable ways and at different points in the policy process. They lobby the Parliament for favorable amendments to Commission and Council of Ministers proposals as well as the relevant Commission officials. They are an integral part of the policy process in Brussels much as they are in Britain, Germany, The Netherlands, Denmark, and Sweden. Although groups representing a variety of interests are ever more numerous in Brussels, the structure of interest group interaction is not "corporatist," as it is in several European nations (see Chapter 3). That is, business and labor groups do not work with government officials in a structured way to make policy.

Interest groups are so numerous (in 2000, there were about 900 interest groups operating at the EU level in the Commission directory) that both the Commission and the Parliament feel the need to regularize their activities. The Parliament in 1996 decided to establish a register of interest groups. Once registered, each interest group receives a one-year pass for access to the Parliament after they have accepted a code of conduct. The Commission also developed some guidelines to help guide Commission officials in their dealings with representatives of interest groups and to improve transparency.[55] The Commission, which is the object of most of the lobbying, found it particularly difficult to maintain access to its relatively small staff while not being overwhelmed by the demands on its time and attention. Although regulation exists, there are no uniform rules across EU institutions on the participation of interest groups in the EU decision-making process.

Since political parties are not the key actors in Brussels that they are in national political systems and due to the absence of a "government" in the traditional sense, the Commission is the key target of interest groups because of its role in initiating legislation. The Commission encourages European-level groups, which it sees as a way to support further integration. Such groups are transnational actors—that is, they bring together national associations to form a European group. Transnational groups are not, however, as important as many had assumed, at least partially because national associations often find it difficult to agree on a common position. Many groups are much weaker than their national counterparts. National organizations, rather than the European federations of such organizations, often possess the information that is the interest group's chief asset and the resource most valuable to the Commission as it attempts to formulate policy. Thus the Commission "unwittingly undermine[s] the development of effective European-level groups by frequently consulting directly with national groups and individual firms."[56]

Although it is difficult to gauge the relative power and influence of diverse groups, many analysts argue that business interests have the most access and are the most influential.[57] Trade unions, although members of the European Trade Union Conference, have been unable to organize as effectively. In general, labor representatives are less visible in policy debates. Environmental and consumer groups, although nurtured and supported by the Commission, are still much weaker in general than are business groups.

In spite of the number of interest groups operating in Brussels and their varied activities, it is important not to overestimate their influence. As indicated earlier, the Economic and Monetary Union represents a historic milestone for European integration. The new European Central Bank and the euro are key changes in the economic landscape of the Union. Yet interest groups were not involved at key decision-making points. Business groups, labor representatives, and associations representing banks were all excluded. Heads of state and government and finance ministers along with their advisers and civil servants were the key actors in negotiations about EMU, not interest groups. The same general argument can be made about the decision in the Treaty of Amsterdam to Europeanize pillar three—interest groups were not relevant.

Although interest groups are not necessarily included in the "historic" decisions, they are typically woven into the Community's policy process. In particular, sophisticated groups lobby at both the national and European level. They lobby the Commission when it is drafting the legislation, the Parliament for favorable amendments, and national officials who will be involved when the issue reaches the Council of Ministers. The European Union has many access points for groups or individual actors, and they are increasingly taking advantage of all of them. A large business firm's lobbying effort may therefore use its national association—which has an office in the national capital as well as an office in Brussels, a Euro-association that brings together national associations, and the firm's own office in Brussels. It can thus lobby a variety of officials using a variety of venues and strategies. To be effective, lobby groups also need to coordinate across European, subnational, and national levels, as EU laws need to be transposed into national laws.

PUBLIC OPINION—DOES IT MATTER?

The European Community is different from the national systems which constitute it in that mass politics plays a different role. It is also an ambiguous role, and scholars are still in the process of delineating how public opinion intersects with the Community's policymaking process. In the Community, the wishes of voters are transmitted primarily through national governments. In national systems, the voters directly choose those in power. Because the Community involves negotiations among governments, similar in that sense to international relations, governments can pursue policies somewhat independently from the wishes of voters.

Governments, once in power, have more discretion on issues related to integration than they do on national issues centrally identified with their political party. The question of "Europe" is not clearly positioned within national political systems. It tends to divide political parties internally rather

than to distinguish one party from another. A prime minister therefore tends to exercise considerable discretion when deciding broad issues of European integration. In countries where referenda are common (Denmark and Sweden, for example), voters can express their views more directly and have them be more binding than can voters in countries without referenda (such as Germany). In some cases, where referenda are possible but infrequent (France), the results can be surprising. This was evident when President Mitterrand, assuming that the French would support the Maastricht Treaty, called for a referendum—only to see the treaty supported by the thinnest of margins. Even when referenda are used, the substantive results can be somewhat surprising. Norwegian voters rejected membership in the Community (having rejected it already once before) in a 1995 referendum. Still, Norwegian governments have tried to pass legislation and pursue economic policies compatible with those being adopted by the European Union. If one examines selected aspects of Norwegian public policy, it would not be immediately obvious that Norway is not a member of the Union. In addition, the initial rejection of the Nice Treaty in a 2001 Irish referendum left many in the EU astonished, considering how much Ireland benefited economically from the process of integration.

That discretion has implications for the role of public opinion, which emerges as a factor that does not constrain political leaders as directly as it does in national, strictly domestic, politics. That is not to say that it does not constrain them at all. However, the type of constraint exercised is more subtle and diffuse. Public opinion as expressed in the elections to the European Parliament is again diluted as the Parliament does not form the government.

Although compromise is a normal part of the democratic process, especially in systems with coalition governments, national politicians do not feel comfortable explaining the policy positions they take in Brussels to their mass electorate. While political elites understand the necessity for compromise, the Community's decision-making process is often presented to mass publics as one in which countries lose or win. Depending on the circumstances, ministers either claim to have "won" (when carrying out popular policies) or to have been "forced" by the Community to take an (unpopular) action.

When taking unpopular actions, it is quite likely that the national government voted in favor of the unpopular action, but the government conveniently does not mention that fact. The process of "scapegoating" Brussels is made easier because the legislation approved by the Council of Ministers often does not actually take effect until several years later. Only the most sophisticated newspaper reporter is likely to track the legislative history of an EU law which, when it goes into effect, is criticized by national politicians.

The lack of a direct transmission belt between public opinion and voting and the EU executive has led many to argue that a "democratic deficit" exists. Some argue that a much stronger European Parliament is necessary for the deficit to be remedied. Others argue that national parliaments need to be given a stronger role in the Community policy process. Yet neither of these two positions confronts the fact that the Union is not a state. As long as the policy process involves bargaining among legally constituted national governments, the influence of public opinion will face many of the same constraints they have faced in the making of foreign policy. Multilateral decision making that requires bargaining with foreigners is not the same as decision making within national systems in which foreigners do not play a role. That difference raises difficult issues in trying to remedy the democratic deficit.

The Council of Ministers operates in a great deal of secrecy, and that secrecy helps political leaders operate in Brussels with less scrutiny than they receive in their national capitals. Minutes of Council meetings, even when accessible to the public, are often not very revealing of the political dynamics which led to the decision being reported in the minutes.[58] The deals made between ministers are often not revealed to the press. Each minister may well claim "victory" for his or her position, but what is typically not revealed is what concessions were made by that same minister. Even though the Council could not reach a decision without each national government being willing to compromise, ministers do not publicize their role in reaching a compromise.

The secrecy accompanying Council of Ministers decision making has led many critics to identify such secrecy as a contributor to the democratic deficit. The fact that citizens do not know what kinds of concessions their national government made or even how their government voted on a particular piece of legislation leads to a lack of "transparency" in the Community's operations, which is seen by many as intrinsically undemocratic.

Again, secrecy in decision making is more characteristic of international relations than of domestic politics. Many international "deals" are made away from public scrutiny. The making of foreign policy is one of the least transparent policy arenas within national systems. International diplomacy has historically been rooted in secrecy, partially so that negotiators can protect their negotiating flexibility and thereby arrive at a compromise. Negotiations with foreign states differ in important ways from negotiations carried on by domestic actors within a national system. Although the European Union exhibits a great deal of integration, and negotiations within the Council of Ministers differ in significant ways from those in other international forums, such negotiations are nonetheless different from their domestic counterparts.[59] The Union is composed of states that still regard each other as foreign. That basic fact affects the dynamics of negotiation and raises difficult questions about whether such a system can be democratized without paralyzing its decision-making capacity.

However, as Brussels has come to penetrate more and more deeply into domestic political systems and as it has come to wield greater power in policy areas traditionally seen as domestic, the lack of openness in its decision making has become increasingly problematic. Given the lack of strong European transnational parties that could claim some legitimacy in the tradition of "party government" and the lack of oversight by national parliaments over the EU's executive levels, the Council of Ministers is open to the charge that it is "undemocratic." But can multilateral decision making involving foreign governments be democratic in the same way in which national systems are? Can public opinion be as influential?

The current policy process does not allow public opinion, defined either ideologically or nationally, to be directly transmitted into decision making. The relative absence of transnational political parties and the discretion exercised by national ministers both dilute the impact of public opinion. It is therefore difficult to predict the position a national government will take by looking at the state of public opinion. Chancellor Helmut Kohl, for example, strongly supported the drive for a single currency even though at times a majority of Germans opposed it. While elections that bring in new political parties can certainly change a government's position on integration, such change is not automatic.

In spite of the relative insulation policymaking has enjoyed, public opinion became far more important during the ratification of the Maastricht Treaty.[60] That ratification process politicized the issue of European integration, so much so that elites negotiating the Treaty of Amsterdam in 1997 had to keep public opinion in the forefront of their calculations. (That is particularly true for political leaders in countries that use referenda for ratification.) Such politicization did not, however, lead to a political debate in any country about the desirability of the common currency in the campaign for the 1994 European Parliament elections. Most probably the issue would have divided political parties internally and therefore was kept off the agenda by those same parties.[61]

Although it can be argued that adverse public opinion has mainly slowed down the progress of integration rather than changed its orientation in any fundamental way, there is no doubt that political leaders now take it into account tactically if not strategically. However, outside of a referendum, public opinion becomes most influential when it is mobilized by political parties. European political parties are divided by religion, the proper role of government in the economy, and the limits of social welfare rather than by issues linked to European integration. Thus they have not capitalized on different opinions about integration within the mass electorate. In addition, they have not engaged in a sustained debate about the policy choices presented by integration. Consequently, public opinion has less impact on the European arena than it does on

the national, except when referenda are involved. As we will see in the conclusions, several member-states will hold a referendum on the new constitutional treaty. One of the challenges for national governments is thus now to sell the new treaty to their population.

Cross-National Differences

Support for European integration typically varies cross-nationally. It is important to remember that there is no "European" public opinion; there is instead only public opinion within 25 different national political discourses. Such segmentation is reinforced by the lack of a "European" media; nationally based newspapers and television reporting strengthen the notion of national opinion, national electorates, and national victories and losses within the Community. In a similar vein, the notion of a "European identity" gains more support in some member-states than others, but is secondary to national identity. Public support for "Europe" generally rose until 1989, went into decline subsequently, and in late 1994 began to stabilize at a lower level of support than had been found in the pre-1989 period.[62]

In general, the citizens of the founding six members are more supportive of European integration than are the citizens of Britain and Denmark. The latter show far more ambivalence than do others. The citizens of Sweden, Finland, and Austria seem to share such ambivalence. In mid-2004, only 8 percent of the Irish and 7 percent of the Luxembourghese and Greeks thought EU membership was a bad thing while 20 percent of the Danes, 33 percent of the Swedes, 29 percent of the Austrians, and 29 percent of the British judged membership negatively. If we examine only the original big member-states, we find that in early 2004 only 13 percent of the Italians, 18 percent of the French, and 14 percent of the Germans thought EU membership was a "bad thing."[63] (See Figure 12.3.)

In the countries that joined in 2004, Estonian citizens were the most skeptical of integration with only 38 percent seeing EU membership as a good thing (although only 16 percent saw it as a bad thing and 37 percent were neutral). Support for membership was greatest in Cyprus with 59 percent

FIGURE 12.3   Public Support for European Integration

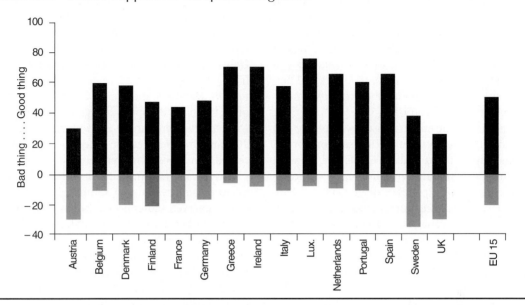

Source: *Eurobarometer* 61, Spring 2004. The figure plots the percent of the public in each nation that say member in the European Union is a "bad thing" or a "good thing."

FIGURE 12.4   Who is Pro-European?

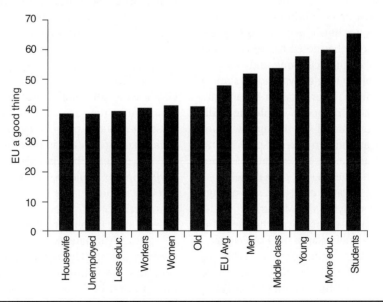

Source: *Eurobarometer* 61, Spring 2004. Figure presents the percentage in EU 15 who say membership is a good thing.

of Cypriots saying EU membership was a good thing. Support for the euro was generally high, with Estonia (46 percent) and Malta (48 percent) showing the least support. The common security and defense policy was the policy that received the highest rate of approval among the 10 new countries (76 percent).[64] In the 10 new member countries, 62 percent of the citizens supported their country's membership in the fall of 2003.[65]

Support for the euro has also been volatile and has generally been lower than has support for EU membership. Support peaked (64 percent in favor) in autumn 1998, and then fell after it was introduced as a "virtual" currency on January 1, 1999. Support varies cross-nationally, however. In mid-2000, only 14 percent of Italians opposed the euro while 29 percent of the French and 39 percent of Germans did so and 61 percent of the British. In September 2000, 53 percent of Danes voting in a referendum on the euro voted against Danish membership. Three years later, 56 percent of Swedes also rejected the adoption of the euro. By contrast, most Europeans favor a common foreign and security policy.

The citizens of states that joined in 1981 and 1986 (Greece, Spain, and Portugal) have consistently been favorable, far more favorable than the attitudes of the Danes and the British. For members such as the Irish, the Spanish, and the Portuguese, favorable attitudes may be rooted in the view that the modernization of the economic and political system is inextricably entangled with admission to the Union. Modern Spain or modern Ireland are viewed as intrinsically "European" while the traditional Spain was outside of the European mainstream. In general, attitudes in Greece, Spain, Portugal, and Ireland are now as favorable toward integration as are attitudes in the original Six.[66]

Public opinion became especially salient during the process of ratifying the Maastricht Treaty. Given the broad consensus among all the key political parties in the member-states, the leaders meeting in Maastricht in December 1991 expected no trouble during ratification of the treaty. Much to the surprise of political elites, however, the Danish electorate voted "no" on Maastricht on June 1992. The Danes only voted "yes" in May 1993 after the Danish government had obtained key "opt-outs" from central provisions of Maastricht. Even more troubling was the French reaction to Maastricht. In October 1992, the French barely approved the ratification of Maastricht. The shock waves from the Danish and French results obscured the fact that the Irish electorate approved the treaty by a substantial margin. Denmark and France became the symbols of a troubled European integration whereas the Irish results were largely discounted. However in 2001, the Irish rejected the Nice Treaty and only accepted it in a second referendum.

Most analysts interpreted the results of the Maastricht referenda as a warning light that mass electorates were either hostile to or deeply skeptical about further European integration. Within the Commission itself, a new sense of caution and circumspection emerged. National politicians clearly interpreted the referenda as a vote on integration, and the importance of public opinion in setting the parameters for elite action increased.

In sum, the role of public opinion concerning integration is still ambiguous. How to mobilize public opinion in a system of multilateral decision making involving foreigners is still an open question. The issues linked to European integration, although nearly 50 years old, have not yet found their place on the national political agenda as shaped by national political parties.

THE POLICYMAKING PROCESS

Given the institutional complexity of the European Union—its unusual institutions, its differing decision-making procedures across pillars—the policymaking process is more varied, segmented, and less uniform than in nation-states. The system itself is in flux while the cast of political characters is often unpredictable. Nonetheless, certain key characteristics of the Community make that process more understandable.

First, small states wield a surprising amount of power within the Union (see Table 12.1). The large countries have more administrative resources to bring to bear in the Union's policymaking process, but small member-states typically focus on issues of particular concern to them and do extraordinarily well in defending their national interests in those areas. Especially in pillar one, where the small member-states tend to view the Commission as an ally that can help protect them from overly aggressive big country pressure, officials representing small member-state governments can be quite important in the policymaking process.

Second, Germany has made disproportionate net financial contributions to the Union, as Table 12.4 indicates. If Germany refuses to support a new initiative that would require new expenditure, its opposition is particularly important because of Germany's role as paymaster.

As it stands, the Union's budget is very small compared to the member-states. In 1997 the Community spent under 1.2 percent of the Community's gross national product. In 2003, it only spent 1.02 percent, while the ceiling is at 1.27 percent. The lack of money encourages the Union to use reg-

ulation rather than expenditure as an instrument of policy. Expenditures are comparatively small; however, they are very important for the smaller, poorer countries. Between 1994 and 1999, Community funds (known as structural funds) accounted for 3.67 percent of Greek GDP, 2.8 percent of Irish GDP, 4 percent of Portuguese GDP, and 1.7 percent of Spanish GDP.[67]

Third, questions about expenditure and financial resources invariably run up into the compulsory expenditure for the Common Agricultural Policy (CAP), which has dominated the Community's budget. Although CAP spending has declined significantly—from roughly 70 percent of the budget in 1984 to under 45 percent—it still represents the single largest expenditure. Designed as a key element of the European postwar welfare state, it maintains the incomes of farmers by keeping food prices high and cheaper agricultural products out of the European Community's market. International actors (the United States especially) as well as some member-states, the United Kingdom in particular, have consistently criticized CAP. The GATT Agreement on Agriculture and reforms which the Commission successfully promoted in 1992 reduced the budgetary burden of agriculture. However, a great deal more change is needed if the accession of the post-Communist applicant countries with their large agricultural sectors are not to intolerably strain the Union's finances. Although the Commission had hoped for more reform, the Berlin European Council meeting of 1999 agreed on only relatively modest changes. In essence, Germany, facing very strong French resistance to major changes in the financing of the CAP, agreed to continue its role as paymaster of the Union. Even though Germany is the largest contributor because it pays (in 1997 figures) 28.2 percent of the total EU budget, it agreed to receive only 14.2 percent of CAP monies, while France receives 22.5 percent of the CAP while only contributing 17.5 percent of the EU's budget.[68] (See Table 12.4.)

Fourth, the policy process is rooted in a culture in which consensus building is highly valued. Even when qualified majority voting is permissible, the Commission as well as member-states try to agree on legislation that is acceptable to all 25 member-states.

TABLE 12.4 Member-States' Shares in EU Financing and in EU₁₅ GNP (percent of total, data for 1997), including UK

Country	Share in EU GNP	Share in Financing of EU Budget
Austria	2.6	2.8
Belgium	3.1	3.9
Denmark	1.9	2.0
Finland	1.4	1.4
France	17.2	17.5
Germany	26.0	28.2
Greece	1.5	1.6
Ireland	0.8	0.9
Italy	14.2	11.5
Luxembourg	0.2	0.2
Netherlands	4.5	6.4
Portugal	1.2	1.4
Spain	6.6	7.1
Sweden	2.7	3.1
UK	16.1	11.9

Source: European Commission, *Agenda 2000: Financing the European Union* (1998).
In Bridge Laffan and Michael Shackleton, "The Budget," *Policy-Making in the European Union,* Helen Wallace and William Wallace, eds. (Oxford, England: Oxford University Press, 2000), Ch. 8, p. 234.

The consensual style of decision making reflects the style in many of the member-states, but is clearly different from the more adversarial political cultures found in Britain and France.

Finally, the Community is characterized by such diversity of interests, administrative and political cultures, and regulatory arrangements that the policy outcomes tend to show the influence of several models. No national government can impose its own framework on others, and no national government consistently accepts models alien to its own traditions. In the field of regulation, analysts describe the outcome as a "patchwork" that incorporates aspects of varied traditions.[69] In a similar vein, no national government consistently loses in terms of policy outcomes.

Policy Initiation

The European Commission formally initiates all policy in pillar one. In the process of following its proposals through the policy process it interacts closely with both the Council of Ministers and the European Parliament. The Commission can be viewed as the spoke in the wheel, with constant and routine contacts with both the Parliament and the Council. The Commission is the focal point of attention in the policymaking system because it is instrumental in shaping the agenda of the other institutions. The Commission's "work in progress" is an excellent predictor of the issues that the Council and the Parliament will be debating in the future.

The Commission is represented at all meetings within the Council of Ministers and the Parliament but neither the Council nor the Parliament is represented at Commission meetings. The role of the Commission in the Council is so visible that it is sometimes referred to as the "twenty-sixth member state." The Commission plays such a powerful role in various stages of the policymaking process that it can be described as a "co-player" with the Council of Ministers: "neither institution can act without the other."[70] In many policy areas now, however, the European Parliament has become a "third co-player."

THE COMMISSION PRESIDENT The *President of the Commission* plays a critical role in the policy process (in pillar one) because of the visibility and the in-tensely political nature of the position. He is appointed as a commissioner by his home country, but he is chosen (in practice) as president by consensus by the 25 heads of state and government and has to be approved by the European Parliament. Jacques Delors, the president from 1985 to 1995, was a commissioner from France (having served as the French Minister of Finance) and the longest-serving Commission president in the Community's history. He was followed by Jacques Santer, appointed in 1995, the former prime minister of Luxembourg, who was forced to resign along with the entire Commission in March 1999. Romano Prodi, the former prime minister of Italy, was his successor. In June 2004, Jose Manuel Barroso, the prime minister of Portugal, was designated as the next president and took office in November 2004.

Choosing a president of the Commission is a delicate, intensely political task carried out by the chief executives of the member governments when meeting in the European Council. Delors was chosen because another Frenchman, Claude Cheysson, was opposed by British Prime Minister Margaret Thatcher and German Chancellor Helmut Kohl. His successor, Jacques Santer, was chosen because the choice of the French and Germans was vetoed by John Major (the British prime minister). Santer then became the candidate who could receive unanimous support. Barroso was chosen because the Franco-German choice was considered too federalist by the UK. Jean-Claude Juncker, the popular prime minister of Luxembourg refused to be a candidate, and Chris Patten, the British choice, did not speak good French and did not come from a country that participates in the Eurozone (those being France's requirements for the new president).

Jacques Delors was especially important in increasing the prestige and political weight of the Commission, both within the Community and in the international arena. Described by his admirers as strategic, brilliant, intellectual, and visionary, he was, critics argued, arrogant and too much of a centralizer, and did not give enough consideration to the wishes of national governments or the other commissioners. Both his critics and admirers would agree, however, that under his leadership the Community made some of its most important steps toward further integration. His advocacy and implementation of the *1992 Project*, the initiative to create a single market, will undoubtedly give him a firm place in the history of European integration. It is possible that future histories of the Community will identify Monnet and Delors as the two most important individuals associated with the project of European integration in the twentieth century.

CIVIL SERVICE The Commission's civil service is organized by Directorate-General (DG) rather than by ministry, as in national executives. The Commission's Secretary-General plays an important albeit discreet role in coordinating the work of the various directorate-generals. He is responsible for the relations between the Commission and the Parliament and the Council of Ministers and is the only non-commissioner who sits with the commissioners when the College meets.

NATIONAL GOVERNMENTS The relationship between the Commission and the national governments is critical. Delors' success in Brussels made him a potential candidate for the French presidency, which in fact strengthened his political power in BrusselS.[71] His close friendship with German Chancellor Kohl throughout Delors' tenure was also an important political resource. When Romano Prodi faced problems, the fact that he did not receive support from the Italian government (whose prime minister was Prodi's arch-rival in Italian domestic politics) added to his travails. Thus are the politics of Brussels and the politics of key national capitals entangled. Power in a national political system, especially within the French or German system, is a tremendous asset when operating within the Community's policymaking system.

The Commission is in constant contact with national executives during the routine of policy initiation. The commissioners have political contacts at the highest national level while Commission officials have frequent contact with their national counterparts. In fact, the Commission often introduces proposals at the behest of a national government.

The national governments must be dealt with by the Commission president as soon as the appointments process begins in national capitals. Prodi was in a stronger position to bargain with the national governments because of the increased

powers given to the president by the Treaty of Amsterdam and Barroso was in an even stronger position. However, there were definitely limits to their ability to persuade the national governments to appoint the people they preferred. Barroso was pleased that more women were appointed to his Commission than had been the case previously (there are 8 out of 25), but he could not himself appoint any female commissioners. After negotiations between the Commission president and national governments, each commissioner is given a portfolio—a specific policy area for which he or she is primarily responsible. For example, one commissioner is in charge of environmental policy while another is responsible for the internal market and still another for transportation programs. As in a national cabinet, some portfolios are more attractive and prestigious than others. Those dealing with external relations are always desirable, as are those dealing with economic matters. At the beginning of each new term, the president assigns portfolios with an eye to seniority, national government pressure, expertise, and political clout back home. In assigning a policy area to each commissioner, President Barroso has seemingly acted more independently from the member-states than many had expected. Even though the big states now have only one commissioner, he has not given the big member-states the posts they sought for their commissioners. For instance, France was pushing for the competition post, but was given the transport post.

The policy initiation process, broadly defined, is complex because commissioners must deal with their national governments, other national governments in the areas of their policy responsibilities, and with the institutions of the Community. Given that the Commission is involved in nearly all phases of the policy process in pillar one, officials contact an innumerable range of actors as a proposal is drafted, refined, accepted by the College of Commissioners, and then shepherded through the Community's institutional process.

Although commissioners are required formally to represent the European interest, they need to keep their prime ministers at home happy if they want to be reappointed. In general, commissioners try to represent both the European and the national interest within certain boundaries. While they do not accept instructions from their government, they typically do put forth policy positions (especially in areas such as industrial, competition [antitrust], and environmental policy) that are recognizable as "national" positions.

Keeping a political master minimally satisfied without sacrificing one's European credentials can be a difficult tightrope to walk. Typically, an effective commissioner informs his colleagues in Brussels when a proposed piece of legislation will run into severe political trouble with his national government. Conversely, he will keep his capital well informed about developments within the Commission so that the national capital is not surprised. Finally, he will mobilize his colleagues in the College of Commissioners to support the positions he advocates, positions that his national government is likely to support.

Legislating Policy

Once the College of Commissioners approves draft legislation by majority vote, it goes to the Council of Ministers and often the Parliament. In both cases, the Commission's proposal will undergo amendments although usually the main lines of the Commission's proposal are accepted. Depending on the subject matter, the Council can legislate by itself or more often needs to approve a draft of the legislation which then will be amended by the Parliament under what is known as the "co-decision" procedure. In the latter case, both the Council and the Parliament need to agree in order for a bill to become a law. If the Council agrees on a piece of legislation but the Parliament and the Council cannot jointly come to an agreement, the legislation dies and is not enacted.

The Commission does not have the political clout in relation to the Council of Ministers that, say, the German chancellor or the U.S. president has in relation to the Bundesrat or the Senate. The Commission's leverage over the collectivity of national governments comes more from the power that accompanies the setting of the policy agenda and the definition of problems than from the formal powers typically associated with a cabinet or executive branch.

COREPER   When ministers fly into Brussels for Council of Ministers meetings, they consider only the most difficult issues, those that need compromise at the high political level of a minister. The *Committee of Permanent Representatives* (known as *COREPER*, its French acronym) has already negotiated most of the other issues.

COREPER is critical to the successful functioning of the Council of Ministers as an institution. Some analysts view it as "the contemporary battlefield on which the nations of Europe settle their differences."[72] This group, made up of the ambassadors to the European Union from each of the member-states, resolves all but the most politically sensitive issues embedded in the legislation passed by the Council of Ministers. The group meets every Thursday morning, with the Commission and the Secretariat of the Council of Ministers both represented. At least once a month, they have a very private lunch at which time no interpreters and no note takers are present; English and French are the only languages spoken. That kind of privacy allows the real deals to be made, as both the Commission representatives and the ambassadors can select what they report back to their superiors. In the words of one participant, "It's very simple, there are no spies."[73]

COREPER represents the views of national capitals in Brussels and gives officials in those same capitals a sense of which arguments are likely to be accepted by the other national governments within the Council of Ministers. COREPER officials play a key role in the entanglement of the "European" and the "national." They are taken seriously by both national and Community officials.[74] COREPER operates in pillar one while the Political and Security Committee (PSC) plays a similar function in security-related issues of pillar two. According to the Nice Treaty, the PSC monitors the international situation covered by the areas of the second pillar. It also contributes to the definition of the CFSP by giving opinions to the Council. The PSC is composed of senior ambassadors from the national permanent representations to the EU.

The Parliament has become a much more important legislative actor in many policy arenas. The triangular relationship between the Commission, the Council, and the Parliament is one in which the Commission and the Parliament have typically been allies. Increasingly, the Council and the Parliament are participating in direct relations as the co-decision procedure forces the Council to take the Parliament seriously. Given the Parliament's significant budgetary powers, the three institutions are inextricably linked when fashioning budgetary policy.[75]

Policy Implementation

The Commission is the "motor" of European integration, but it is not the implementor of Community legislation. That function falls to the member-states. The Commission's civil service is too small to carry out the duties of monitoring that a national bureaucracy naturally assumes. Furthermore, the Commission does not have all the enforcement powers of a national bureaucracy.

The Commission is largely restricted to the use of legal instruments in its efforts to oversee implementation. In particular, it can bring a member-state government before the European Court of Justice if a directive passed by the Council of Ministers has not been appropriately "transposed" into national law. It can also bring a member-state before the Court if the implementation of a Community directive is not properly pursued. Such an action is difficult, however, because the Commission does not have the power physically to enter a member-state to gather the kind of evidence it would need to persuade the European Court of Justice. Non-governmental groups (NGOs) and private citizens do, however, write to the Commission with complaints of infringements of Community law. The Commission often uses informal pressure on a national government to improve the execution of directives on the ground.

Judicial Review

The European Court of Justice has evolved in a way that the member-states did not expect. Established to ensure that the Commission did not overstep its authority, the Court, however, expanded the scope of Community authority in several ways. Most importantly, it declared that Community law was supreme—that is, superior to member-state law.[76] It also ruled that the Community gained powers in external relations in those areas in which it approved intra-Community legislation, thereby giving the Community a much greater international profile than had been anticipated.

The sweep and direction of the Court's decisions have been so important that the Court has been viewed by some as the "motor" of European integration at times when national governments were reluctant to move integration forward. Although its power is limited by the constraints that affect all courts, it has also gradually obtained the unique legitimacy enjoyed by courts. The process of integration would have proceeded much more slowly, and in some areas might not have proceeded at all, without the Court's activism. Martin Shapiro offers this explanation:

> The European Court of Justice has played a crucial role in shaping the European Community. In a sense, the Court created the present-day Community; it declared the Treaty of Rome to be not just a treaty but a constitutional instrument that obliged individual citizens and national government officials to abide by those provisions that were enforceable through their normal judicial processes.[77]

Several factors have helped the Court in its integrationist project. First, the use of legal reasoning and argument seems apolitical. In that sense, the very language and procedures of the judiciary and the legal profession help "mask" the political consequences of legal decisions.[78] Second, it is very difficult for the member-states to agree among themselves to pass legislation overriding Court decisions. In fact, the supranational institutions in general benefit from the fact that each one typically has allies on any issue among at least several states. Dissenting states therefore find it difficult to reverse "integrationist" decisions or processes once they are established.[79]

Third, the Court has benefited from the use of national courts (through what is known as the preliminary ruling system) in implementing Community law. Once national judges accepted the legitimacy of the rulings of the European Court of Justice, the maneuverability available to national governments that disagreed with the Court's decisions narrowed considerably. It is difficult for national governments to ignore the decisions of their own national courts so the Court's use of national judges has given the Court powerful allies within the member-states themselves.

The Court has been a powerful instrument of integration. Until very recently, it typically promoted further integration through its decisions and has been viewed as a powerful ally of the Commission as well as of the Parliament. In policy terms, it set the stage for the single market with groundbreaking decisions, granted the Commission external power in those areas in which the Community was allowed to legislate internally, decided the boundaries within which environmental protection could act as a nontariff barrier, and promoted gender equality in the workplace.

In general, the Court has "constitutionalized" the treaties that underpin the Community and has evolved into "a vertically integrated legal regime conferring judicially enforceable rights and obligations on all legal persons and entities, public and private, within EC territory."[80] The Court therefore provides the Community with a legal order in which EC law is supreme to national law, a supremacy accepted by national judges. The Court, in the words of one of its distinguished judges, has sought "to fashion a constitutional framework for a quasi-federal structure in Europe."[81]

EXTERNAL RELATIONS

The powers of the Commission in the field of external relations have been growing. The Treaty of Rome specifically identified the Commission as representing the Community in organizations such as the Organization for Economic Cooperation and Development (OECD) and the United Nations Economic Commission for Europe (UNECE): the Commission was thus granted an external role very early. Furthermore, the fact that the Commission was the sole negotiator for the Community in the various rounds of the General Agreement on Tariffs and Trade (GATT) enhanced the Community's presence in the field of international economic relations. It, along with the member-states, became a contracting party to the World Trade Organization (WTO).

The EU (whether represented by the Commission or the Commission and the Presidency of the Council of Ministers) has struggled to be granted recognition in the United Nations. While it has the status of an observer, it has pressed very hard to be treated as an equal partner in, for example, international environmental negotiations. In the case of global agreements (such as the Montreal Protocol limiting CFCs), for example, the Commission bargained hard and long to be recognized as a signatory.[82] Generally, outside of the trade area, the member-states regard treaties as "mixed" agreements in which the Commission signs on behalf of the Community and the member-states sign as well.

ENTANGLEMENT OF THE "NATIONAL" AND THE "EUROPEAN"

The coexistence of "intergovernmental" and "supranational" elements within the Community makes the Community clearly distinct from any of the nation-states that belong to the Community. The institutions are in a delicate balance. Some (the Council of Ministers) are intended to ensure that the views of national governments are respected and that integration does not proceed further than that permitted by the "permissive consensus" within which national governments have operated. The functions of other institutions (the Commission, the European Court of Justice, and the Parliament) are to push the goal of integration, to set the agenda, raise issues, and keep the pressure on to further integrate. These institutions might test the boundaries of the "permissive consensus." They project a broad strategic "European" perspective that does not match the views of any of the national governments per se but represents the interest of the collectivity rather than that of any specific member government. They are the "supranational" component of the Community. Proponents of a more "federal" Europe see the Court, the Parliament, and the Commission as the institutions that should be given more power, while the proponents of an "intergovernmental" Europe wish to increase the power of the Council of Ministers and the European Council.

Because political parties have much less power than they do at the national level and because the key institutions are not directly elected, the Community's institutions qua institutions are more important than at the national level. The Union is above all its institutions. There is not a European Union political culture, media, party system, electoral system, welfare state, or society. National diversity in all those areas is so great that the Union is identified more by its institutions than by those societal and cultural factors so important in shaping national polities.[83] In brief, there is no European Union "public" or "culture" as such.

Given the delicate balance between institutions and the still evolving nature of the European Union, it is not surprising that much of the "politics" observed in Brussels involves the various institutions jockeying for institutional power. The Council of Ministers, the Commission, and the Parliament are constantly trying to maximize their institutional reach and influence as they collectively struggle to construct a consensus on proposed legislation. The Commission tries to protect itself from encroachments from both the Parliament and the Council of Ministers, and the Council and the Parliament eye each other warily. Rather than being based on some kind of balance of power between the executive and the legislative branches as in the United States, the Community's political system is based on a balance between the representation of national interests and of "European" interests. The (national) governmental interest and the supranational interest coexist, but are in constant tension. In that sense, the Community is more recognizable to students of federal systems than of unitary systems, for in federal systems the states and the federal government are typically struggling to maximize their own power.

In a parallel vein, those institutions representing national governments are "Europeanized" so that national governments when operating within them are enmeshed in a decision-making machinery that is significantly different from that of a traditional international organization and from decision making at the national level. A national government operating within the Council of Ministers is a "co-decision maker," rather than a "decision maker," as it is when operating unilaterally at the national level.[84]

The member governments of the Community collectively work together so that each individual national government has submitted to the "European" collectivity in the foregoing of unilateral decision making. A national government operates within the boundaries of the Community's institutional structure in a qualitatively different manner from the way it operates unilaterally in other international forums or at home. In brief, France in the European Union acts differently from France in the rest of the world, as does Paris acting as the sole decision maker in French national politics.

The *supranational* and the *intergovernmental* institutions are both integral to the project of European integration. The Council of Ministers, the main intergovernmental body, is there to bring the member-states to a collective view in contrast to the unilateral national decision making that would take place if the European Union did not exist. A national government participating in the Council of Ministers is not acting unilaterally. The Union's institutions, whether representing national governments or the "European" interest, all implicitly reject the exercise of unilateral national power.

The rejection of unilateral national power across a broad range of issues makes the European Union so distinctive when viewed from the outside. Even when the member-states decide to cooperate within the Council of Ministers, downgrade the Commission's role, and exclude the European Court of Justice, the degree of integration that they accept is far greater than that found in other parts of the world. Even when an arrangement is considered to be "intergovernmental" by Europeans, it would be considered far too integrationist for a country such as the United States to accept. The debate between the "intergovernmental" states (such as the United Kingdom and Denmark) and the "federalist" states (such as the Benelux states, Germany, and Italy) takes place within a context in which the rejection of the exercise of unilateral national decision making is much more commonly accepted than it is anywhere else in the world. In brief, an "intergovernmental" posture within the European Union would typically be considered as radically "integrationist" or "federalist" in Asia, North America, or Latin America.[85]

POLICY PERFORMANCE

National governments provide social services; the European Union makes laws, but it does not engage, with a few exceptions (such as agriculture and regional policy) in activities that involve large public expenditure. The Union's comparatively small budget keeps it from engaging in the kinds of activities traditionally the province of national governments.

The Union does engage in regulation, for the costs of regulation are borne by the objects of regulation rather than the regulators.[86] The creation of the single market led to the Union's emergence as an important regulator of economic activity. Its role consisted of removing national regulations that impeded cross-border trade and re-regulating at the EU level to ensure that safety standards, for example, were instituted. The processs of regulatory reform therefore empowered the EU while eliminating many national nontariff barriers to trade.

The Single-Market Program

As already mentioned, the Single European Act allowed the member-states to create a true single market. The single-market program involved the removal of nontariff barriers from the Community's economy. Regulatory barriers that protected national markets from competition, as well as from goods and services produced in other EU countries, have been largely dismantled. The 1992 Project (the goal was to approve nearly 300 pieces of single-market legislation in Brussels by 1992, a goal largely achieved) was the foundation stone of the more integrated European economy with which Europe entered the twenty-first century. Its effects in both the economic and the political spheres were huge. Once firms no longer benefited from protected national markets, they realized they had to become global rather than simply European players to survive the competition from American firms. These same American firms were attracted to the single market, invested huge sums in building production facilities in Europe, and bought promising European firms. European firms therefore entered the American market in a sustained fashion, set up production facilities in the United States, and bought promising American firms. Interestingly, the relationship be-

came quite symmetrical—the number of Americans working for European firms roughly equaled the number of Europeans working for American firms.[87]

There are still a few areas in which agreement has not been reached, but the Community's legislative program for the single market is largely finished. Whereas in 1980, a citizen from one EU country was stopped when crossing the border into another EU state, by 2004 the frontiers within the EU were usually crossed without any interruption. Capital can now move freely without national governments imposing capital controls. Firms based in one country can acquire firms in other member-states, and banks can set up offices outside their home country. Airlines, previously protected from each other, now compete with one another, and low-cost carriers have emerged (symbolized by Ryanair). The telecommunications sector is now open to fierce competition; previously it had been a monopoly run by the state. As a result of the competitive forces unleashed by the single market, nationalized industries have increasingly been privatized throughout the member-states thereby transforming the European economy. The single-market program was such a pivotal program for the process of European integration that the proponents of the single currency argued that a single market required a single currency—"one market, one currency."

External Relations

Since the implementation of the single-market program, the EU has become far more active in the area of external relations. The EU has been involved in external relations since the Rome Treaties, through the role of the Commission in trade negotiations, as well as through the EU role in development policy. The EU is the world's biggest donor of humanitarian aid. The EU's development policy dates from the special relationship (primarily in the area of trade) which France insisted should exist between the EU and France's colonies and overseas territories. The special relationship was strengthened when Britain joined the Community as its former colonies also benefited from that relationship. The first Lome Convention of 1975 established the cooperative framework within which the then Community and the developing world with links to Europe developed. The EU also strengthened its relations with countries of the Maghreb and the Masreq.

Today, the European Union is the world's leading development partner, in terms of aid, trade, and direct investment. Together, the EU and its member-states provide 55 percent of all official international development aid.

In foreign policy, the EU has been slower in acquiring a role, first because foreign policy and international security touch the core of national sovereignty, and second because the defense of Europe was left to the North Atlantic Treaty Organization (NATO). Since the 1970s however, member-states have coordinated their positions on foreign policy issues through the European Political Cooperation (EPC). EPC, however, represented a nonbinding commitment and thus did not yield substantive policy outcomes. The end of the Cold War and the uncertainty of a continued U.S. military involvement in Europe, along with the poor military performance of member-states (particularly France) during the first Gulf war led to the creation of the second pillar of the EU during the Maastricht negotiations. Known as the Common Foreign and Security Policy of the EU (CFSP), the second pillar is mainly intergovernmental in that the Commission has only a shared right of initiative (rather than the monopoly of initiative which it enjoys in pillar one) with the member-states. The EP and the ECJ have no role at all. As defined in the Maastricht Treaty, the CFSP also entails the eventual creation of a genuine EU defense policy, not however in competition with NATO. The first test of the EU's new CFSP was the Yugoslav wars of the early 1990s, in which the EU did not fare well, except in the area of humanitarian aid. The wars only ended when the United States and NATO became involved. The Treaty of Amsterdam strengthened the commitment of the member-states to CFSP, but it did not become a major area of Union policy until the British and French, the two major actors in European defense, came to an agreement at a Franco-British summit at St. Malo, France, in December 1998.

Essentially, the UK, a traditional supporter of NATO and concerned that a European defense policy would weaken NATO, agreed to cooperate with European efforts to develop a European capability in security and defense policy. The French, who had traditionally supported a European defense posture independent of NATO, agreed that such efforts should not weaken NATO. The EU would develop a common defense policy within the framework of the CFSP through summit meetings among the fifteen's foreign ministers and defense ministers. For the first time, defense ministers, who previously had operated solely within NATO, would be brought under the EU's umbrella, although still meeting informally.

Once the Franco-British bargain had been struck—the UK willing to become more European in its defense policy in return for the French accepting NATO's crucial role in Europe's collective defense—movement came quickly. The Helsinki European Council in December 1999 agreed to develop by 2003 a collective European capability to deploy a rapid-reaction force of 60,000 troops for crisis management operations. These troops would be capable of deployment at 60 days' notice and remain operational for 1 year. They would intervene in humanitarian and rescue tasks as well as in peacekeeping and crisis management (what is referred to in the EU jargon as the Petersberg tasks). Since March 2000 a Political and Security Committee meets weekly at the ambassadorial level and a military committee (MC) and a military staff within the Council's structures provide the Council of Ministers with military expertise. The year 2001 also saw the inclusion of the Western European Union (WEU) in the EU—the WEU only keeping its collective defense role through its Article V.

The major challenge to the European Security and Defense Policy (ESDP) is in the area of military capabilities. The Europeans, with the exception of France and the United Kingdom, are extremely weak in what is called C3I (control, command, communication, and intelligence).

Since the goal of the ESDP is not to create a European army, EU-NATO relations are critical. Yet these two organizations have had no relationship with each other throughout the entire postwar period (see Box 12.5). Although France initially wanted to keep NATO at arm's length from the ESDP, it reversed its position in April 2000 and at

Box 12.5 European Integration and Transatlantic Security Meet at Last

Since 1949 responsibility for European defense policy has been in the hands of individual governments and the North Atlantic Treaty Organization, an intergovernmental body involving (and relying heavily upon) the United States. In 1999 the member-states of the

European Union finally agreed to take important steps in the direction of more integrated defense and security policies, by cooperating with NATO, rather than replacing it.

	EU	NATO
Membership:	European member-states only	Transatlantic membership (most EU states, Norway, Turkey, U.S., and Canada)
Main Objective:	Political & economic integration	Collective defense and peace-keeping (out-of-area) operations
Key Officials:	Foreign Ministers and, after 1999, Defense Ministers and the High Representative for Common Foreign and Security Policy	Foreign and Defense Ministers
Headquarters:	Headquartered in Brussels	Headquartered in Brussels
Type of Organization:	Supranational organization	Intergovernmental organization
Role of U.S.:	U.S. does not have a "seat at the table"	U.S. has the most important "seat at the table"
EU-NATO Relationship:	No relationship with NATO until 2000— relationship formalized in the Copenhagen Agreement of December 2002	No relationship with EU until 2000

the Feira European Council Summit in June 2000 agreed to the establishment of four ad-hoc EU/NATO working groups. In September 2000, for the first time, the Interim Political and Security Committee and NATO's Permanent Council met— the first formal high-level contact between the EU and NATO. In December 2002 at the Copenhagen Summit, the EU and NATO reached an agreement about the EU's use of NATO military assets in operations in which NATO as a whole is not involved. Assurances were given that the ESDP would not affect any vital interest of a non-EU NATO member.

The agreement allowed the EU to launch its first military operation April 1, 2003, when it took over from NATO in Macedonia. A second military operation, without the use of NATO assets, was launched in June 2003 in the Republic of Congo. At

the end of 2004, the EU was also poised to take over the bigger NATO peacekeeping operation in Bosnia.

Does the European Union Make a Difference?

The European Union now affects a great many people, some of them more directly than others. It makes the most difference for the farmer whose prices and subsidies are largely dependent on the decisions made by the Council of Agricultural Ministers and the Commission. Fishermen's catches and allotments are significantly influenced by Brussels. Businesspeople are affected by the provisions of the single market (especially the mobility of capital and the liberalization of numerous once-protected markets), the move to the euro, the robust antitrust policy implemented by the Commission (and coordinated with the antitrust policy of the United States in relevant cases), and the Union's environmental policy. Bankers and investors are affected by the policies of the European Central Bank and the move to a common currency. Environmentalists want to increase environmental protection. Consumers are worried about the safety of the food they eat; soccer players now enjoy "free agency" because of the EU. Women seek equal pay for equal work. Airline passengers benefit from airline deregulation. Retirees can decide to live in another member-state. Regional government officials receive funds from Brussels to help their region develop roads and jobs. Patients benefit from more rapid approval of new medicinal drugs now that they fall under the jurisdiction of the EU. Telephone users have benefited enormously in terms of both price and level of service from the deregulation of the telecommunications sector pushed through by the Commission. In 2002, everyone living in the 12 member-states that have accepted the euro became accustomed to paying their bills by using a new currency and relinquishing their old familiar national currency.

By contrast, in areas such as the provision of health care, education, urban policies, social security, and unemployment compensation, national governments have retained the right to unilaterally make policy. These policy areas are only indirectly affected by the European Union. The "welfare state" is largely still under the unilateral control of national policymakers (although its financing is affected by the policies of the European Central Bank). In areas related to economic activity and social regulation (consumer and environmental protection, for example), rather than social services, the European Union is particularly relevant. Thus, the European Union does not legislate the health benefits that any citizen of any member-state is entitled to enjoy. However, the fact that the doctor chosen by a patient may be of a different nationality from the patient occurs because EU regulations recognize medical degrees across borders. The drugs that the doctor prescribes are under EU regulations if they are new to the market, and the competition among firms selling that drug is shaped by EU rules.

Countries outside of the EU are also particularly aware of the European Union. The United States must bargain with the Union in important global forums such as the World Trade Organization; poor developing world countries are given preferential access to EU markets as institutionalized in the Cotonou Agreement. Countries such as Turkey and Israel and in the Mediterranean have negotiated special trade agreements with the Union.[88] Although at this point in time the EU is not yet a true "military" power, its economic reach and power make it an important international actor.

From the beginning, the external economic role that "Europe" would play if organized into a relatively integrated unit has been an important consideration for European policymakers. In the field of agriculture, for example, the Common Agricultural Policy allowed the Community to ward off strong American pressure to open up the European agricultural market.[89] This external role was particularly important given that the states initially involved in European integration were not "self-confident" states. Their capacities were not in any way similar to those enjoyed by the United States, a superpower with enormous resources and global power.[90] European integration allowed these states to have much greater influence in the international environment than if they had exercised traditional sovereignty. Public opinion attitudes among mass electorates, in fact, show high degrees of support for Union activity regarding the international environment in all policy arenas, not simply those having to do with economics. "European elites may emphasize the difficulties of coordinating foreign and defense policies among the European states, but European publics see this as a natural area of joint action."[91] In fact, as we have seen, the leaders of the EU member-states are following the lead of public opinion in cooperating more extensively in the field of foreign and security policy.

POLICY CHALLENGES

The European Union faces three key challenges in the years ahead—all extremely difficult. How to digest the May 2004 enlargement to Eastern and

Central Europe without undermining the process of integration is one. The second involves having the recently agreed upon European Constitutional Treaty accepted by the 25 member-states, some of them through a referendum. The third requires creating a balance between integration and the protection of cultural diversity so that ordinary citizens of very diverse member-states do not feel they are being culturally "homogenized" and blame European integration for that threat to their identity.

The Challenge of Enlargement

How can the European Union digest the enlargement to 10 new member countries? Having recently regained their independence, support for EU membership in the 10 candidate countries was at a steady level of 52 percent in 2003. The highest level of support was in Cyprus (59 percent), Slovakia (58 percent), and Hungary (56 percent). The lowest level was in Estonia (38 percent) and Latvia (46 percent). In addition, the 2004 enlargement (plus the prospective 2007 enlargement to Bulgaria, Romania, and Croatia and the commitment to eventually accept all the Balkan countries) has left the question as to where the borders of the EU will finally come to rest.

The new entrants from the East and the South are primarily small states (with the exception of Poland) with large agricultural populations. These nations will all be net gainers under present distributive policies within the Union. Funds that previously helped the poorer member-states—Spain, Portugal, Ireland, and Greece—will either need to be expanded, eliminated, or redirected toward the new entrants. In 2002, for example, even Slovenia, the wealthiest of the 10, had a per capita GDP that was only 70 percent of the EU average; the Czech Republic and Hungary had 57 percent and 50 percent respectively. Latvia had a per capita GDP that was only 35 percent of the EU's GDP per capita.

Perhaps the key question, however, is how to restructure the policymaking institutions of the European Union. Should each member-state be allowed one commissioner or should there be a rotation of countries with a commissioner? If the latter

option were chosen, would the Commission have the legitimacy required to offend the big member-states? How should votes in the Council of Ministers be allocated? Small countries are by far the majority of the 10 states, with only Poland (with a population of 39 million) having a population of more than 10 million. Enlargement will change the dynamics of coalitions within the Council, especially if the use of qualified majority voting expands so as to avoid decision-making paralysis. The big member-states have opposed maintaining the disproportionate power of small countries, but the small member-states have been determined to protect their role in the decision-making process. In December 2000, some of these issues were addressed in the negotiations for the Treaty of Nice, which incorporated very difficult compromises. The Nice Treaty decided to adopt a system of re-weighting of votes within the Council (a total of 237 votes were allocated to the 15 member-states, with a qualified majority threshold set at 169 votes). As from November 1, 2004 and taking into consideration the 2004 enlargement, a Council decision is adopted when it receives at least 232 votes out of 321, reflecting the majority of the members of the Council (subject to the demographic clause), combined with a double or even triple majority. While the re-weighting of votes favors the large member-states, the qualified majority must also be a majority of the member-states. This is combined with a system known as the "demographic safety net," which means that each member-state can request verification of whether the qualified majority represents at least 62 percent of the population of the Union. If this condition is not fulfilled, the decision cannot be adopted.

The Central and Eastern European countries viewed admission to the Union as a necessary component of their road toward democratization, a market economy, and a "return to Europe" (that Europe of which they were a part before the Cold War). From the point of view of the previous EU member-states, admitting the countries of Central and Eastern Europe involved a whole series of decisions with profound implications for the future governance of the Union. Whereas Germany favored enlargement, that federalist perspective was countered by the United Kingdom, which favored enlargement but thought it would lead toward a more "intergovernmental" Community with fewer inroads on national sovereignty. Countries that have benefited from the EU's special programs for poorer countries—Greece, Spain, Portugal, and Ireland—view the "newcomers" as competitors for funds that have accelerated their own economic modernization.[92]

As the Union faces eastward, therefore, it has to answer questions about where its final external frontier will be. Will it be the eastern border of Poland? Or beyond? It has to answer questions about whether it will become more integrated or less integrated, as the current stage of integration is likely to lead to paralysis if extended to a Union with many more countries. It will have to consider whether it must become more integrated in the area of foreign and security policy. Or does NATO enlargement to admit Central European countries imply that those countries will not favor the further development of a European (rather than transatlantic) defense identity even if the "old" EU members desire it? As Europe enters the next century, it is striking that an organization rooted in the geopolitics of the past is the arbiter of "the challenge of continental order."[93] The European Union has succeeded to such an extent that it now has the responsibility of drawing the political and economic map of Europe. Yet the average man in the street is not certain that he wants to accept that responsibility.

The EU Constitution

The questions raised earlier about decision making, the avoidance of paralysis, and a more coherent European Union in international affairs have occupied both EU and national politicians since the Treaty of Nice was signed in 2000. The answers to many of those questions were finally given in June 2004. The 25 heads of state and of government meeting in Brussels agreed on a new constitutional treaty. It is hoped that this treaty will bring stability to the decision-making procedures and institutional design of the Union and end the cycle of treaty-making which began with the 1986 Single European Act.

A constitutional convention that met for one and a half years under the chairmanship of former French President Valery Giscard d'Estaing prepared the reforms. The constitutional convention was as an alternative to the Intergovernmental Conferences (IGC) that had traditionally revised treaties. In an IGC, representatives of member-states met and negotiated often hard-fought bargains among themselves. The European Union resembled a traditional international organization when it was engaged in negotiating an IGC. The constitutional convention was convened in order to make the process of treaty revision more transparent, democratic, and open to more actors than just national representatives. The convention, besides including national government representatives from the 25, included representatives from the European Commission, the European Parliament, and national parliaments. The convention also met with representatives from civil society.

The members of the convention agreed on a draft constitution in July 2003. It presented the draft to the member-states who started renegotiating various points of contention. It took another year for the national representatives to agree on the new treaty.

The provisions that led to the bitter negotiations were the ones that already proved contentious during the Amsterdam and Nice negotiations: the size of the Commission, the number of seats in the European Parliament, and the weighting of votes in the Council of Ministers. These key questions pitted big member-states against small member-states and emphasized the dual nature of the EU: a supranational organization where member-states still are key power-holders.

If the new constitutional treaty passes the test of ratification and referendum (it is not expected to enter into force until 2007), the key changes to the EU decision-making process would be the following:

- A president of the EU: chosen by the EU heads of state and of government for 2.5 years (renewable once) to chair the European Council and represent the EU abroad.
- An EU foreign affairs minister (who will become vice-president of the European Commission): chosen by the member-states to chair

meetings of EU foreign affairs ministers; formulate policies on issues from terrorism to peace-keeping; and represent the EU abroad with the EU president.

- The definition of a new Qualified Majority Vote (QMV): 55 percent of member-states (representing at least 15 countries) and 65 percent of the EU population. The voting minority must comprise at least 4 states.
- The size of the Commission: starting in 2014, the Commission's size will be equal to two-thirds of the member-states.

Cultural Diversity

As of 2004, the European Union was composed of 25 member-states, including most of Scandinavia, key Mediterranean countries, and former Soviet satellites. The Union's gross national product and population are larger than that of the United States, and today it is the largest market in the industrialized world. As the Union has expanded, what has become more striking is its cultural diversity. As the economies of the 25 are more intertwined and as more policy areas are included in an integrated Europe's policy portfolio, questions of national identity are more salient. Diverse European cultures have emerged out of many centuries of disparate historical experiences, and the current economic convergence is proceeding far more quickly than is any type of cultural (or linguistic) convergence. Although the EU is firmly committed to protecting cultural diversity, the tension between culture, economics, policy, and identity are more pronounced now that the Euro-

pean Union includes nearly all of Western Europe and a big part of Eastern Europe. How far will the average person accept being made into a "European" in political and economic terms without feeling that his or her identity is being fundamentally threatened? That question has not yet been answered.

The question of a "European" identity is further complicated by whether Turkey actually belongs in the European Union. The need to decide whether accession negotiations should begin with Turkey (which had been officially accepted as a candidate country in 1999) divides mass electorates (which generally opposed Turkish membership) from their elected leaders (many of which supported it) as well as the political class itself. The very difficult history that has shaped the relationship between Christian Europe and Muslim Turkey (and its predecessor the Ottoman Empire) has brought issues of identity, previously of secondary importance, to the fore as the debate over Turkish accession has developed. The consequence of such a debate over "European" identity is unpredictable. Ironically, the debate over Turkey may make "the 25" feel more European than they did before the issue of Turkey came onto the political agenda. The history that binds the 25 together and separates them from Turkey is much discussed and debated. Yet the question of Turkish accession also presents an opportunity for the EU. Given the capabilities of the Turkish military, an EU with Turkey as a member could play a major role in geopolitics. The Turkish question may well force the EU to choose between cultural affinity and a major geopolitical role.

 Key Terms

Council of Ministers (Council of the European Union)	Economic and Monetary Union (EMU)	European Economic Community (EEC)	Intergovernmental Conference (IGC)
Committee of Permanent Representatives (COREPER)	European Central Bank European Commission European Council European Court of Justice	European Free Trade Association (EFTA) European Parliament European Union (EU) intergovernmental	Justice and Home Affairs (JHA) Maastricht Treaty (Treaty of European Union)

Marshall Plan
Members of the
European
Parliament (MEPs)
North Atlantic Treaty
Organization
(NATO)

Political and Security
Committee (PSC)
Presidency of the
European Council
and the Council of
Ministers

President of the
Commission
Schuman Plan
single currency (euro)
Single European Act
(SEA)
supranational

Treaty of Amsterdam
Treaty of Nice
Treaty of Rome
1992 Project

Internet Resources

The European Commission:
The European Parliament:
The Council of the EU:

Commission Delegation in Washington, DC:
EU-Related News:
EU-RELATED NEWS: www.eupolitix.com

Suggested Readings

Bomberg, Elizabeth, and Alexander Stubb, eds. *The European Union: How Does It Work?* New York: Oxford University Press, 2003.

Cini, Michelle, ed. *European Union Politics.* Oxford: Oxford University Press, 2002.

Corbett, Richard, Francis Jacobs, and Michael Shackleton. *The European Parliament,* 4th ed. London: John Harper, 2000.

Cowles, Maria, Thomas Risse, and James Caporaso, eds. *Transforming Europe.* Ithaca, NY: Cornell University Press, 2001.

Dinan, Desmond. *Europe Recast: A History of European Union.* New York: Palgrave Macmillan, 2004.

Dinan, Desmond, ed. *Encyclopedia of the European Union.* Boulder, CO: Lynne Rienner, 2000.

Gillingham, John. *European Integration 1950–2003: Superstate or New Market Economy?* New York: Cambridge University Press, 2003.

Hayes-Renshaw, Fiona, and Helen Wallace. *The Council of Ministers.* London: Macmillan, 1997.

Gilbert, Mark. *Surpassing Realism—The Politics of European Integration Since 1945.* Lanham, MD: Rowman and Littlefield, 2003.

Keohane, Robert O., and Stanley Hoffmann, eds. *The New European Community: Decisionmaking and Institutional Change.* Boulder, CO: Westview, 1991.

Moravcsik, Andrew. *The Choice for Europe: Social Purpose & State Power from Messina to Maastricht.* Ithaca, NY: Cornell University Press, 1998.

Parsons, Craig. *A Certain Idea of Europe.* Ithaca: Cornell University Press, 2003.

Peterson, John, and Michael Shackleton, eds. *The Institutions of the European Union.* New York: Oxford University Press, 2002.

Rosamond, Ben. *Theories of European Integration.* New York: St Martin's, 2000.

Ross, George. *Jacques Delors and European Integration.* Oxford, England: Oxford University Press, 1995.

Sbragia, Alberta M. *Euro-Politics: Institutions and Policy-Making in the "New" European Community.* Washington: Brookings Institution, 1992.

Sbragia, Alberta M. "The Treaty of Nice, Institutional Balance, and Uncertainty." *Governance: An International Journal of Policy, Administration and Institutions,* Vol. 15, No. 3, July 2002, pp. 393–410.

Smith, Michael E. *Europe's Foreign and Security Policy: The Institutionalization of Cooperation.* New York: Cambridge University Press, 2004.

Trachtenberg, Marc. *A Constructed Peace: The Making of the European Settlement 1945–63.* Princeton: Princeton University Press, 1999.

Wallace, Helen, and William Wallace, eds. *Policy-Making in the European Union,* 4th ed. Oxford, England: Oxford University Press, 2000.

Winand, Pascaline. *Eisenhower, Kennedy, and the United States of Europe.* New York: St. Martin's, 1993.

Endnotes

1. Giandomenico Majone, "The Rise of Statutory Regulation in Europe," in Giandomenico Majone, ed., *Regulating Europe* (New York: Routledge, 1996), p. 57.
2. Beate Kohler-Koch, "Catching Up with Change: The Transformation of Governance in the European Union," *Journal of European Public Policy* 3, No. 3 (September 1996): 359–80.
3. Jack Hayward, "Populist Challenge to Elitist Democracy in Europe," in Jack Hayward, ed., *Elitism, Populism, and European Politics* (Oxford, England: Clarendon, 1996), p. 29.
4. Wolfgang Wessels, "The EC Council: The Community's Decisionmaking Center," in Robert O. Keohane and Stanley Hoffman, eds. *The New European Community: Decisionmaking and Institutional Change,* (Boulder, CO: Westview, 1991), p. 136.
5. Many scholars have debated whether national governments are the only real decision makers in the Union, with the Community institutions which do not represent state interests being in fact agents of the national governments, or whether national governments share their decision-making power with those other "non-state-centric" institutions. For example, see Andrew Moravcsik, *The Choice for Europe* (Ithaca, NY: Cornell University Press, 1998); Gary Marks, Liesbet Hooghe, and Kermit Blank, "European Integration from the 1980s: State-Centric v. Multi-Level Governance," *Journal of Common Market Studies* 34, No. 3 (September 1996): 341–78; James A. Caporaso and John T. S. Keeler, "The European Union and Regional Integration Theory," in Carolyn Rhodes and Sonia Mazey, ed., *Building a European Polity?* (Boulder, CO: Lynne Rienner, 1995), pp. 29–62.
6. Alberta M. Sbragia, "Introduction," in Alberta M. Sbragia, ed., *Euro-Politics: Institutions and Policymaking in the "New" European Community* (Washington: Brookings Institution, 1992), pp. 1–22.
7. Cited in Edmund Dell, *The Schuman Plan and the British Abdication of Leadership in Europe* (New York: Oxford University Press, 1995), p. 22.
8. John Gillingham, *Coal, Steel, and the Rebirth of Europe, 1945–1955: The Germans and French from Ruhr Conflict to Economic Community* (Cambridge, England: Cambridge University Press, 1991), p. xi.
9. George Ross, *Jacques Delors and European Integration* (New York: Oxford University Press, 1995), p. 1.
10. F. Roy Willis, "Schuman Breaks the Deadlock," in F. Roy Willis, ed., *European Integration* (New York: New Viewpoints, 1975), p. 27.
11. For a sophisticated study of Kurt Schumacher and his attitude toward France and European integration, see Lewis J. Edinger, *Kurt Schumacher: A Study in Personality and Political Behavior* (Stanford, CA: Stanford University Press, 1965), pp. 144–89.
12. Albert Kersten, "A Welcome Surprise? The Netherlands and the Schuman Plan Negotiations," in Klaus Schwabe, ed., *Die Anfange des Schuman-Plans 1950/51; The Beginnings of the Schuman Plan,* contributions to the Symposium in Aachen, May 28–30, 1986 (Baden-Baden, Germany: Nomosverlag, 1988), p. 287.
13. See F. Roy Willis, *Italy Chooses Europe* (New York: Oxford University Press, 1971), pp. 1–52.
14. Dell, *The Schuman Plan and the British Abdication of Leadership in Europe*, p. 4.
15. Stephen D. Krasner, "United States Commercial and Monetary Policy: Unraveling the Paradox of External Strength and Internal Weakness," in Peter Katzenstein, ed., *Between Power and Plenty: Foreign Economic Policies of Advanced Industrial States* (Madison: University of Wisconsin Press, 1978), p. 52.
16. Derek W. Urwin, The Community of Europe: A History of European Integration since 1945, 2nd ed. (New York: Longman, 1995), p. 21.
17. Pascaline Winand, *Eisenhower, Kennedy, and the United States of Europe* (New York: St. Martin's, 1993).
18. Miles Kahler, "The Survival of the State in European International Relations," in Charles Maier, ed., *Changing Boundaries of the Political* (Cambridge, England: Cambridge University Press, 1987), p. 289.
19. William Wallace, *Regional Integration: The West European Experience* (Washington: Brookings Institution, 1994), p. 11. See also David Armstrong, Lorna Lloyd, and John Redmond, *From Versailles to Maastricht: International Organization in the Twentieth Century* (New York: St. Martin's, 1996), p. 148.
20. Peter Ludlow, "The European Commission," in Keohane and Hoffman, eds., *The New European Community*, p. 111.
21. I have drawn heavily from Winand, *Eisenhower, Kennedy, and the United States of Europe*, pp. 24–73.
22. Cited in Desmond Dinan, *Ever Closer Union? An Introduction to the European Community* (Boulder, CO: Lynne Rienner, 1994), p. 34.
23. David Armstrong, Lorna Lloyd, and John Redmond, *From Versailles to Maastricht: International Organization in the Twentieth Century* (New York: St. Martin's, 1996), p. 159.
24. Wolfgang Wessels, "Institutions of the EU System: Models of Explanation," in Dietrich Rometsch and Wolfgang Wessels, eds., *The European Union and Member States: Towards Institutional Fusion?* (New York: Manchester University Press, 1996), pp. 20–36.
25. Graham T. Allison and Kalypso Nicolaidis, eds., *The Greek Paradox: Promise vs. Performance* (Cambridge, MA: MIT Press, 1997).
26. Cited in Charles Grant, *Delors: Inside the House That Jacques Built* (London: Nicholas Brealey, 1994), p. 70.
27. David Allen, "Competition Policy: Policing the Single Market," in Helen Wallace and William Wallace, eds., *Policy-Making in the European Union*, 3rd ed. (Oxford, England: Oxford University Press, 1996), pp. 157–84.

28. Giandomenico Majone, "The Rise of the Regulatory State in Europe," *West European Politics* 17, No. 3 (July 1994): 77–101; see also Majone, *Regulating Europe.*

29. Damian Chalmers and Erika Szysczak, *European Union Law: Towards a European Polity?* Volume II, Brookfield, VT: Ashgate, 1998, 146–47.

30. Wallace, *Regional Integration: The West European Experience,* p. 34.

31. Neill Nugent, ed., *At the Heart of the Union: Studies of the European Commission,* 2nd ed. (New York: St. Martin's Press, 2000); Alberta Sbragia, "The European Union as Coxswain: Governance by Steering," in Jon Pierre, ed., *Debating Governance: Authority, Steering, and Democracy* (Oxford: Oxford University Press, 2000), pp. 219–40.

32. Dinan, *Ever Closer Union,* pp. 247–49; Hayes-Renshaw and Wallace, *The Council of Ministers,* pp. 7, 29–32.

33. Alberta Sbragia, "The Community: A Balancing Act," *Publius* 23 (Summer 1993): 23–38; Wolfgang Wessels, "The EC Council: The Community's Decisionmaking Center," in Keohane and Hoffmann, eds., *The New European Community* (Boulder, CO: Westview, 1991), pp. 133–54.

34. Hayes-Renshaw and Wallace, *The Council of Ministers,* p. 18.

35. Hayes-Renshaw and Wallace, *The Council of Ministers,* p. 163.

36. Richard Corbett, Francis Jacobs, and Michael Shackleton, *The European Parliament,* 4th ed. (London: John Harper, 2000), pp. 49–54.

37. Rory Watson, "MEPs win 81% of tussles over new EU laws," *European Voice* 19–25 (October 2000): p. 5.

38. Richard Corbett, Francis Jacobs, and Michael Shackleton, *The European Parliament,* 4th ed. (London: John Harper, 2000), p. 226.

39. Rory Watson, "MEPs win 81% of tussles over new EU laws," *European Voice* 19–25 (October 2000), p. 5; Michael Shackleton, "The Politics of Codecision," *Journal of Common Market Studies* 38 (June 2000): 327.

40. Karen J. Alter, "The European Court's Political Power," *West European Politics* 19, No. 3 (July 1996): 458.

41. Beate Kohler-Koch, "Germany: Fragmented but Strong Lobbying," in M.P.C.M. van Schendelen, ed., *National Public and Private EC Lobbying* (Brookfield, England: Dartmouth, 1993), p. 32.

42. Denmark is an exception: the People's Movement against the European Community competes in European parliamentary elections—but not in domestic elections—on an anti-integration platform. Vernon Bogdanor, "The European Union, the Political Class, and the People," in Jack Hayward, ed., *Elitism, Populism, and European Politics* (Oxford, England: Clarendon, 1996), p. 110.

43. Simon Hix, "Parties at the European Level and the Legitimacy of EU Socio-Economic Policy," *Journal of Common Market Studies* 33, No. 4 (December 1995): 534.

44. John Gaffney, "Introduction: Political Parties and the European Union," in John Gaffney, ed., *Political Parties and the European Union* (London: Routledge, 1996), p. 13.

45. Mark Franklin and Cees van der Eijk, "The Problem: Representation and Democracy in the European Union," in Cees

van der Eijk and Mark N. Franklin, eds., *Choosing Europe? The European Electorate and National Politics in the Face of Union* (Ann Arbor: University of Michigan Press, 1996), p. 8.

46. Simon Hix, "Parties at the European Level and the Legitimacy of EU Socio-Economic Policy," *Journal of Common Market Studies* 33, No. 4 (December 1995): 545; Robert Ladrech, "Partisanship and Party Formation in European Union Politics," *Comparative Politics* (January 1997): 176.

47. For an analysis of how the Community's policies indirectly affect various aspects of welfare state provision, see Stephen Leibried and Paul Pierson, eds., *European Social Policy: Between Fragmentation and Integration* (Washington: Brookings Institution, 1995).

48. Mark Franklin, "European Elections and the European Voter," in Jeremy J. Richardson, ed., *European Union: Power and Policymaking* (London: Routledge, 1996), p. 187.

49. Michael Marsh and Mark Franklin, "The Foundations: Unanswered Questions from the Study of European Elections, 1979–1994," in Cees van der Eijk and Mark N. Franklin, ed., *Choosing Europe? The European Electorate and National Politics in the Face of Union* (Ann Arbor: University of Michigan Press, 1996), p. 11.

50. Cees van der Eijk and Mark Franklin, "The Research: Studying the Elections of 1989 and 1994," in van der Eijk and Franklin, *Choosing Europe,* p. 42.

51. Mark Franklin and Cees van der Eijk, "The Problem: Representation and Democracy in the European Union," in van der Eijk and Franklin, *Choosing Europe,* p. 5.

52. For a good description of the differences between the British House of Commons and the European Parliament, see Bogdanor, "Britain," pp. 211–15.

53. Gareth Harding, "Winds of Change Blow Through Parliament," *European Voice* 8–14 (June 2000): p. 18; "Breaking New Ground in Euro-politics," *European Voice* 10–17 (November 1999): 22.

54. Sonia Mazey and Jeremy Richardson, "The Logic of Organization," in Jeremy J. Richardson, ed., *European Union: Power and Policy-Making* (London: Routledge, 1996), p. 204.

55. Sonia Mazey and Jeremy Richardson, "Promiscuous Policymaking: The European Policy Style?" in Carolyn Rhodes and Sonia Mazey, eds., *Building a European Polity? The State of the European Union,* Vol. 3 (Boulder, CO: Lynne Rienner, 1995), p. 342; Andrew M. McLaughlin and Justin Greenwood, "The Management of Interest Representation in the European Union," *Journal of Common Market Studies* 33, No. 1 (March 1995): 143–56.

56. Mazey and Richardson, "Promiscuous Policymaking," p. 350.

57. For a discussion of a powerful business group, see Maria Green Cowles, "Setting the Agenda for a New Europe: The ERT and EC 1992," *Journal of Common Market Studies* 33 (December 1995): 501–26.

58. See EC regulation no. 1049/2001 of the European Parliament and of the Council of 30 May 2001 regarding public access to European Parliament, Council, and Commission documents; Council decision of 29 November 2001

amending the Council's Rules of procedure (2001/840/EC); Council Decision of 22 March 2004 adopting the Council's Rules of procedure (2004/338/EC).

59. For a sophisticated discussion of how bargaining and negotiations proceed within the Council of Ministers, see Hayes-Renshaw and Wallace, *The Council of Ministers*, pp. 244–73.

60. Russell J. Dalton and Richard Eichenberg, "Citizen Support for Policy Integration," in Wayne Sandholtz and Alec Stone Sweet, eds., *European Integration and Supranational Governance* (Oxford: Oxford University Press, 1998), pp. 250–82.

61. Mark Franklin, Cees van der Eijk, and Michael Marsh, "Conclusions: The Electoral Connection and the Democratic Deficit," in van der Eijk and Franklin, *Choosing Europe*, p. 370.

62. European Commission, *Eurobarometer* 43 (Autumn 1995): xi.

63. European Commission, Eurobarometer: Public Opinion in the European Union 61 (Spring 2004): p. 8.

64. European Commission, Eurobarometer 2003.4: Public Opinion in the Candidate Countries (February 2004): 78, 130, 136.

65. European Commission, Eurobarometer 2003.4: Public Opinion in the Candidate Countries (February 2003): 78.

66. Oskar Niedermayer, "Trends and Contrasts," in Oskar Niedermayer and Richard Sinnott, eds., *Public Opinion and Internationalized Governance* (Oxford: Oxford University Press, 1995), pp. 59–62; Christopher Anderson, "Economic Uncertainty and European Solidarity Revisited: Trends in Public Support for European Integration," in Rhodes and Mazey, eds., *Building a European Polity*, pp. 111–33.

67. Brigid Laffan and Michael Shackleton, "The Budget: Who Gets What, When, and How," in *Policy-Making in the European Union*, 4th ed. (Oxford, England: Oxford University Press, 2000), pp. 213–14.

68. Elmar Rieger, "The Common Agricultural Policy: Politics Against Markets," in Helen Wallace and William Wallace, eds., *Policy-Making in the European Union*, 4th ed. (Oxford: Oxford University Press, 2000), pp. 202–203.

69. A. Heritier, "The Accommodation of Diversity in European Policy-Making and Its Outcomes: Regulatory Policy as a Patchwork," *Journal of European Public Policy* 3, 2 (1996): 149–67.

70. Dietrich Rometsch and Wolfgang Wessels, "The Commission and the Council of Ministers," in Geoffrey Edwards and David Spence, eds., *The European Commission* (Essex: Longman, 1994), p. 221.

71. He was widely considered a major presidential contender, and in November 1994 the Socialist Party Conference announced that it would support Delors if he decided to run for the French presidency. However, on December 11, 1994, Delors announced that he would not be a candidate after all. Colete Ysmal, "France," *European Journal of Political Research* 28, No. 3, 4 (December 1995): 337.

72. Lionel Barber, "The Men Who Run Europe," *Financial Times*, March 11–12, 1995, sect. 2, p. I.

73. Barber, "The Men Who Run Europe," p. II.

74. Hayes-Renshaw and Wallace, *The Council of Ministers*, p. 76.

75. Martin Westlake, *The Commission and the Parliament: Partners and Rivals in the European Policy-Making Process* (London: Butterworths, 1994), p. 10; Brigid Laffan, *The Finances of the European Union* (New York: St. Martin's, 1997).

76. See Joseph Weiler, "The Transformation of Europe," *Yale Law Journal* 100 (1991): 2403–83 and "A Quiet Revolution: The European Court of Justice and Its Interlocutors," *Comparative Political Studies* 26, No. 4 (January 1994): 510–34; Eric Stein, "Lawyers, Judges and the Making of a Transnational Constitution," *American Journal of International Law* 75/1 (1981); Anne-Marie Slaughter Burley and Walter Mattli, "Europe Before the Court: A Political Theory of Legal Integration," *International Organization* 47 (1993): 41–76; Martin Shapiro, "The European Court of Justice," in Sbragia, *Euro-Politics*, pp. 123–56; Alter, "The European Court's Political Power," pp. 458–87.

77. Shapiro, "The European Court of Justice," p. 123.

78. Burley and Mattli, "Europe Before the Court," pp. 72–73.

79. Karen Alter, "Who Are the 'Masters of the Treaty'? European Governments and the European Court of Justice," *International Organization* 52, No. 1 (Winter 1998): 121–48; Alec Stone Sweet and Thomas L. Brunell, "Constructing a Supranational Constitution: Dispute Resolution and Governance in the European Community," *American Political Science Review* 92, No. 1 (March 1998): 63–81.

80. Alec Stone Sweet and Thomas L. Brunell, "Constructing a Supranational Constitution: Dispute, Resolution and Governance in the European Community," *American Political Science Review* 92, No. 1 (March 1998): 63–82.

81. C. Federico Mancini, "The Making of a Constitution for Europe," in Keohand and Hoffmann, *The New European Community*, p. 178.

82. Alberta Sbragia, "Institution-Building from Above and from Below: The European Community in Global Environmental Politics," in Wayne Sandholtz and Alec Stone, eds., *European Integration and Supranational Governance.*

83. For instance, even the imported titles on best-seller book lists differ in the various member-states. In a similar vein, even though the inhabitants of Freiburg, Germany, and of Strasbourg, France, are close geographically, they do not buy each other's newspapers. Ralf Dahrendorf, "Mediocre Elites Elected by Mediocre Peoples," in Jack Hayward, ed., *Elitism, Populism, and European Politics* (Oxford, England: Clarendon, 1996), p. 7.

84. Wolfgang Wessels, "The EC Council," p. 136.

85. For example, see Miles Kahler, *Regional Futures and Transatlantic Economic Relations* (New York: Council on Foreign Relations Press, 1995).

86. Majone, *Regulating Europe.*

87. Alberta Sbragia, "The Transatlantic Relationship: A Case of Deepening and Broadening," in Carolyn Rhodes, ed., *The European Union in the World Community* (Boulder, CO: Lynne Rienner, 1998), pp. 147–64.

88. To get a sense of the policy areas in which the Union is most important, see Wallace and Wallace, *Policy-Making in the European Union*, 4th ed; Calingaert, *European Integration Revisited*; Dinan, *Ever Closer Union*, 2nd ed. Part III.

89. Elmar Rieger, "The Common Agricultural Policy: External and Internal Dimensions," in Wallace and Wallace, *Policy-Making in the European Union*, 3rd ed. pp. 102–106.

90. William Wallace, "Government Without Statehood: The Unstable Equilibrium," in Wallace and Wallace, *Policy-Making in the European Union*, 3rd ed., p. 453.

91. Dalton and Eichenberg, "Citizen Support for Policy Integration," p. 260.

92. Anna Michalski and Helen Wallace, *The European Community: The Challenge of Enlargement* (London: Royal Institute of International Affairs, 1992), p. 55.

93. Brigid Laffan, "The Intergovernmental Conference and the Challenge of Governance in the European Union," European Community Studies Association Conference, Brock University, Ontario Canada, May 31–June 2, 1996, p. 29.

APPENDIX

A GUIDE TO COMPARING NATIONS

Topics	Ch. 1–4	England	France	Germany	Spain	Russia	Poland	Hungary	EU
History	3–7	87–90	137	194–199	248–252	304–308	353–360	408–415	457–468
Social Conditions	7–19,	90–95	137–139, 144–146	199–202	252–253	319	353–357	415–417	466–467
Executive	63–71	96–102	172–174	204–205	253–255, 258–260	308–310	362–363	420–422	471–477
Parliament	63–71	102–103	174–178	203–204	255–258	310–312	363–364	419–420	477–478
Judiciary	71–72	—	142	205–207	260–263	313	365–366	422	478–479
Provincial Government	71–72	90–93	178–181	201–202	263–264	313–318	—	421–422	—
Political Culture	24–35	108	143–146	207–211	264–266	318–321	366–369	422–425	486–490
Political Socialization	—	108–111	147–151	211–214	266–268	321–322	370–374	425–429	—
Recruitment/ Participation	35–42	111–118	151–153	214–216	—	322–325	374–376	429–431	—
Interest Groups	38–41	115–116	153–157	217–221	268–273	325–330	376–382	432–436	485–486
Parties and Elections	72–75	118–122	158–172	221–229	273–281	330–336	382–389	436–448	481–484
Policy Process	76–78	122–129	172–178	230–234	257–258	310–312	389–391	448–449	490–497
Outputs and Outcomes	78–81	129–131	181–184	234–241	285–294	336–340	391–397	449–450	498–504
International Relations	7–8	94–95	184–195	240–241	294–296	344–345	393–395	451–452	498–500

Index